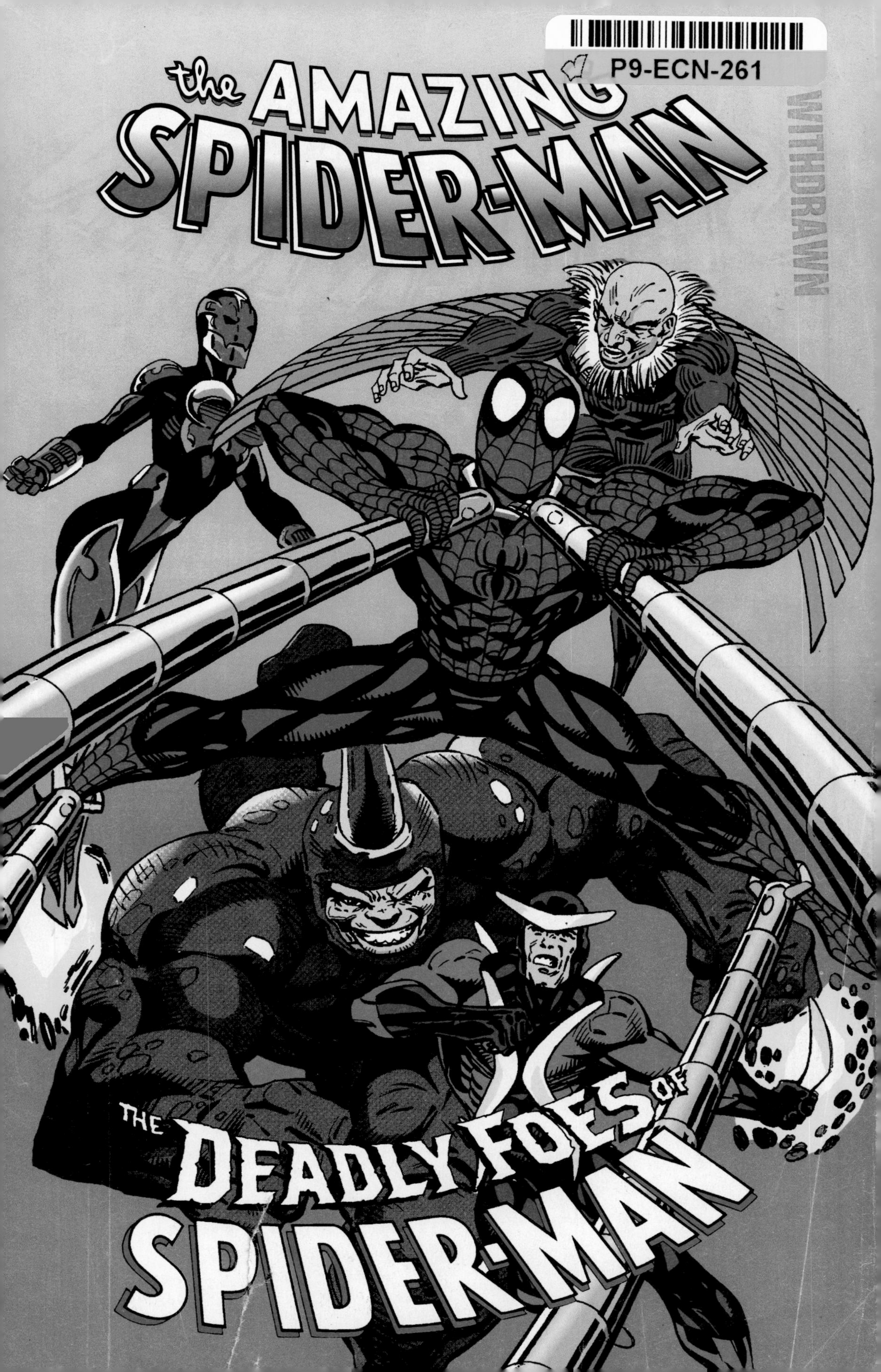
the AMAZING SPIDER-MAN
THE DEADLY FOES OF SPIDER-MAN

the AMAZING SPIDER-MAN

WRITER
Danny Fingeroth

PENCILERS
Al Milgrom
Kerry Gammill
Scott McDaniel
David Boller
Keith Pollard

INKERS
Mike Machlan
Al Milgrom
Brad Vancata
Ian Akin
Keith Aiken
Jim Amash
Harry Candelario
Frank Turner
Mike DeCarlo

COLORISTS
Paty Cockrum
Mike Thomas
Dave Sampson
William Hodge

LETTERERS
Joe Rosen
Diana Albers
with Dave Sharpe
Sergio Cariello
Susan Crespi

EDITORS
Terry Kavanagh
Rob Tokar

SPIDER-MAN: DEADLY FOES OF SPIDER-MAN. Contains material originally published in magazine form as DEADLY FOES OF SPIDER-MAN #1-4 and LETHAL FOES OF SPIDER-MAN #1-4. First printing 2011. ISBN# 978-0-7851-5855-4. Published by MARVEL WORLDWIDE, INC., a subsidiary of MARVEL ENTERTAINMENT, LLC. OFFICE OF PUBLICATION: 135 West 50th Street, New York, NY 10020. Copyright © 1991, 1993 and 2011 Marvel Characters, Inc. All rights reserved. $24.99 per copy in the U.S. and $27.99 in Canada (GST #R127032852); Canadian Agreement #40668537. All characters featured in this issue and the distinctive names and likenesses thereof, and all related indicia are trademarks of Marvel Characters, Inc. No similarity between any of the names, characters, persons, and/or institutions in this magazine with those of any living or dead person or institution is intended, and any such similarity which may exist is purely coincidental. **Printed in the U.S.A.** ALAN FINE, EVP - Office of the President, Marvel Worldwide, Inc. and EVP & CMO Marvel Characters B.V.; DAN BUCKLEY, Publisher & President - Print, Animation & Digital Divisions; JOE QUESADA, Chief Creative Officer; JIM SOKOLOWSKI, Chief Operating Officer; DAVID BOGART, SVP of Business Affairs & Talent Management; TOM BREVOORT, SVP of Publishing; C.B. CEBULSKI, SVP of Creator & Content Development; DAVID GABRIEL, SVP of Publishing Sales & Circulation; MICHAEL PASCIULLO, SVP of Brand Planning & Communications; JIM O'KEEFE, VP of Operations & Logistics; DAN CARR, Executive Director of Publishing Technology; SUSAN CRESPI, Editorial Operations Manager; ALEX MORALES, Publishing Operations Manager; STAN LEE, Chairman Emeritus. For information regarding advertising in Marvel Comics or on Marvel.com, please contact John Dokes, SVP Integrated Sales and Marketing, at jdokes@marvel.com. For Marvel subscription inquiries, please call 800-217-9158. **Manufactured between 9/21/2011 and 10/10/2011 by R.R. DONNELLEY, INC., SALEM, VA, USA.**

10 9 8 7 6 5 4 3 2 1

THE DEADLY FOES OF SPIDER-MAN

FRONT COVER ARTISTS
David Boller & Brad Vancata

BACK COVER ARTIST
Al Milgrom

COVER COLORIST
John Kalisz

COLLECTION EDITOR
Mark D. Beazley

EDITORIAL ASSISTANTS
James Emmett & Joe Hochstein

ASSISTANT EDITORS
Nelson Ribeiro & Alex Starbuck

EDITOR, SPECIAL PROJECTS
Jennifer Grünwald

SENIOR EDITOR, SPECIAL PROJECTS
Jeff Youngquist

RESEARCH
Chris Buchner

LAYOUT
Jeph York

PRODUCTION
ColorTek

SENIOR VICE PRESIDENT OF SALES
David Gabriel

SVP OF BRAND PLANNING & COMMUNICATIONS
Michael Pasciullo

EDITOR IN CHIEF
Axel Alonso

CHIEF CREATIVE OFFICER
Joe Quesada

PUBLISHER
Dan Buckley

EXECUTIVE PRODUCER
Alan Fine

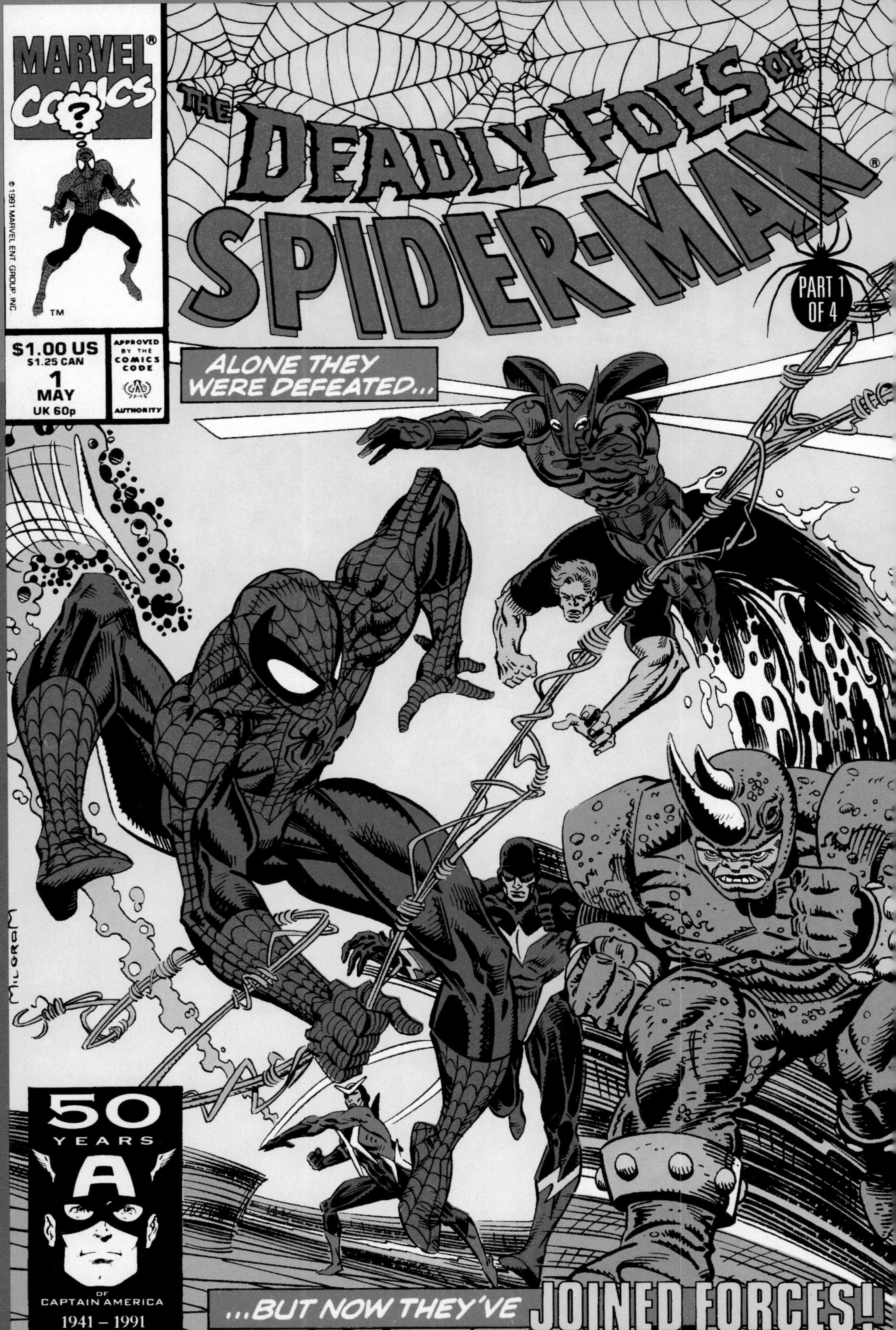
MARVEL COMICS
THE DEADLY FOES OF SPIDER-MAN
PART 1 OF 4
© 1991 MARVEL ENT. GROUP, INC.
$1.00 US
$1.25 CAN
1
MAY
UK 60p
APPROVED BY THE COMICS CODE AUTHORITY
ALONE THEY WERE DEFEATED...
MILGROM
50 YEARS OF CAPTAIN AMERICA
1941 – 1991
...BUT NOW THEY'VE JOINED FORCES!

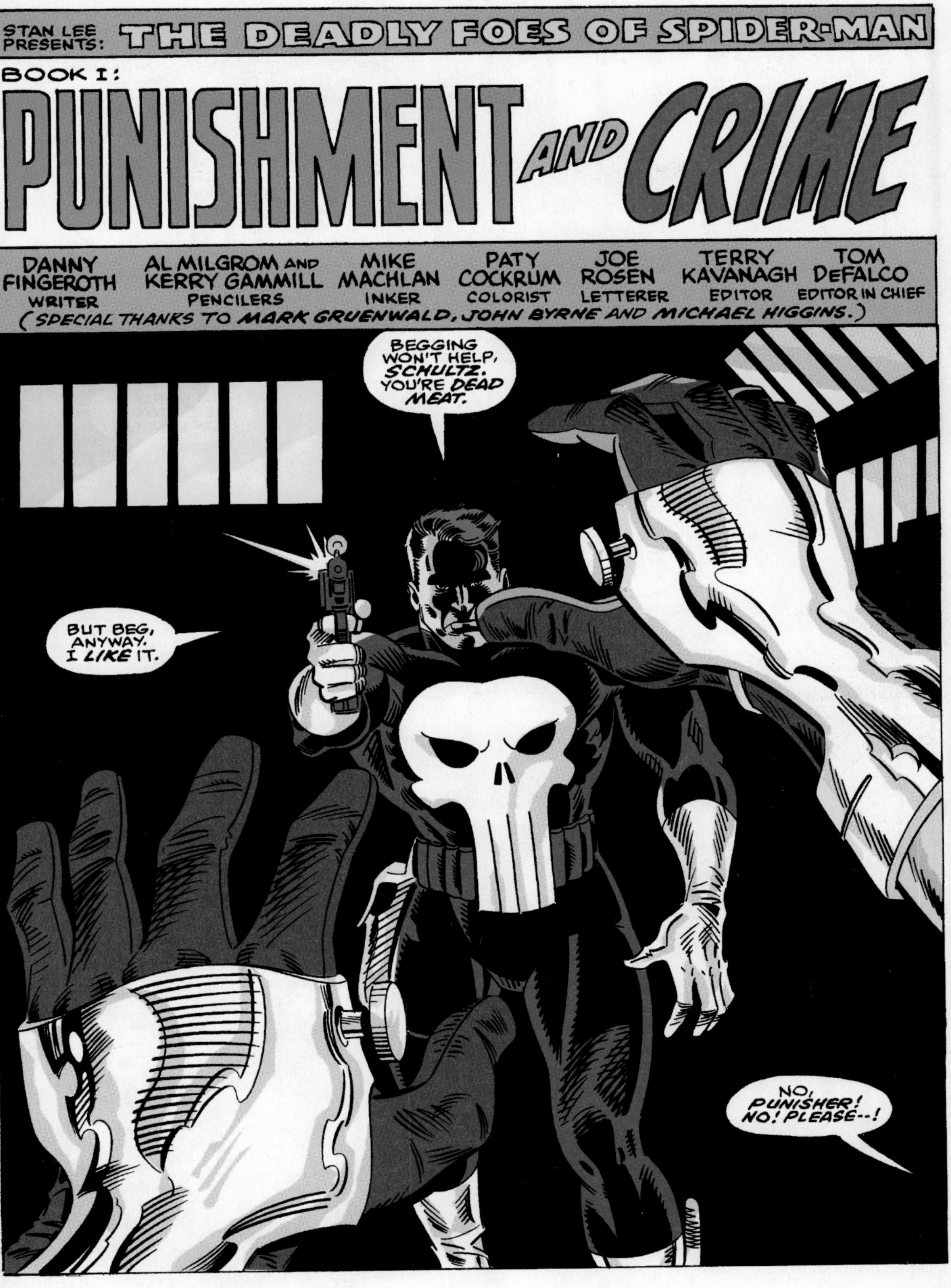
STAN LEE PRESENTS: THE DEADLY FOES OF SPIDER-MAN
BOOK I:
PUNISHMENT AND CRIME
DANNY FINGEROTH WRITER
AL MILGROM AND KERRY GAMMILL PENCILERS
MIKE MACHLAN INKER
PATY COCKRUM COLORIST
JOE ROSEN LETTERER
TERRY KAVANAGH EDITOR
TOM DeFALCO EDITOR IN CHIEF
(SPECIAL THANKS TO MARK GRUENWALD, JOHN BYRNE AND MICHAEL HIGGINS.)
BEGGING WON'T HELP, SCHULTZ. YOU'RE DEAD MEAT.
BUT BEG, ANYWAY. I LIKE IT.
NO, PUNISHER! NO! PLEASE--!

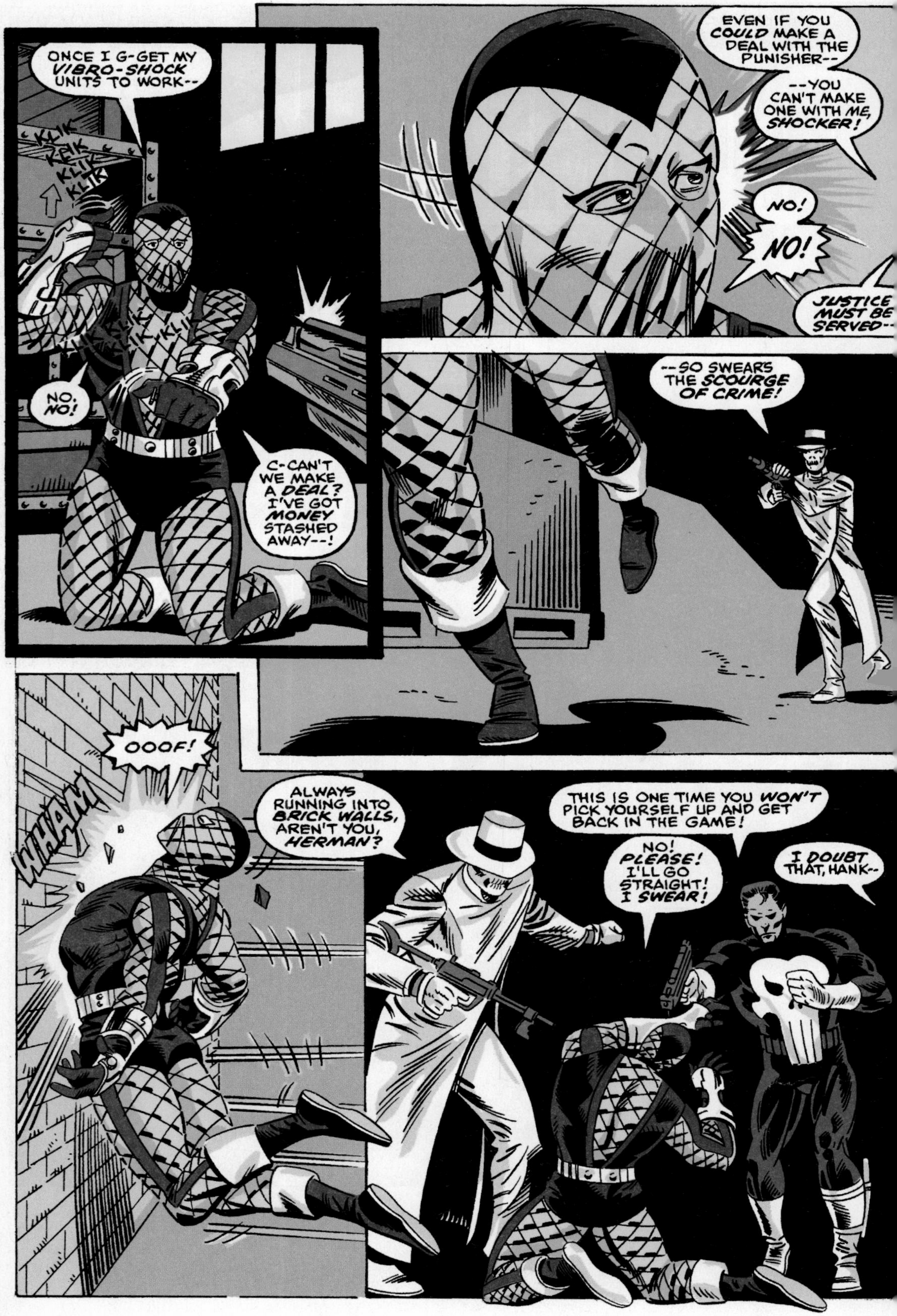
ONCE I G-GET MY VIBRO-SHOCK UNITS TO WORK--
KLIK KLIK KLIK KLIK
NO, NO!
C-CAN'T WE MAKE A DEAL? I'VE GOT MONEY STASHED AWAY--!
EVEN IF YOU COULD MAKE A DEAL WITH THE PUNISHER--
--YOU CAN'T MAKE ONE WITH ME, SHOCKER!
NO!
NO!
JUSTICE MUST BE SERVED--
--SO SWEARS THE SCOURGE OF CRIME!
OOOF!
WHAM
ALWAYS RUNNING INTO BRICK WALLS, AREN'T YOU, HERMAN?
THIS IS ONE TIME YOU WON'T PICK YOURSELF UP AND GET BACK IN THE GAME!
NO! PLEASE! I'LL GO STRAIGHT! I SWEAR!
I DOUBT THAT, HANK--

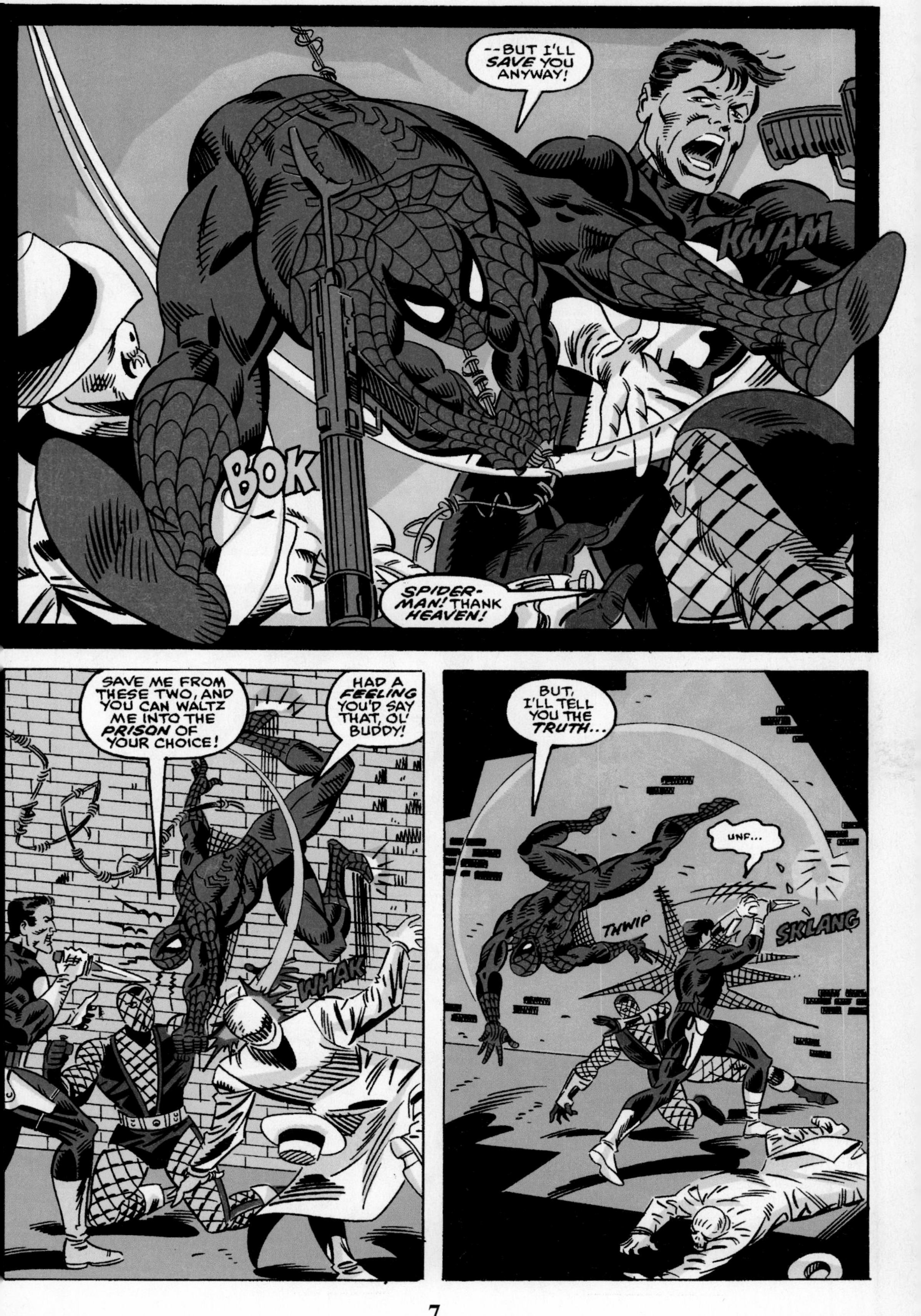
--BUT I'LL SAVE YOU ANYWAY!
KWAM
BOK
SPIDER-MAN! THANK HEAVEN!
SAVE ME FROM THESE TWO, AND YOU CAN WALTZ ME INTO THE PRISON OF YOUR CHOICE!
HAD A FEELING YOU'D SAY THAT, OL' BUDDY!
WHAK
BUT, I'LL TELL YOU THE TRUTH...
UNF...
THWIP
SKLANG

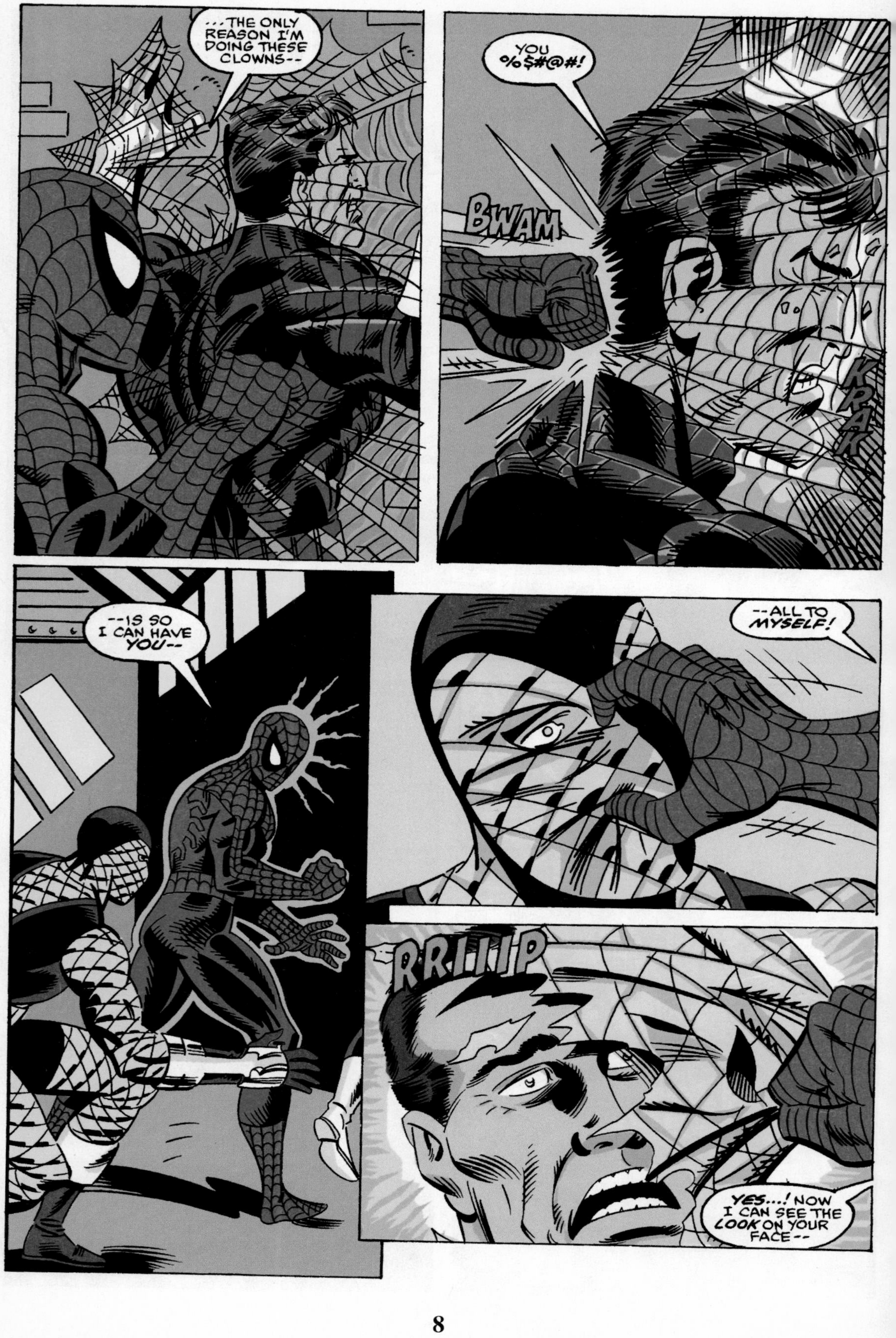
...THE ONLY REASON I'M DOING THESE CLOWNS--
YOU %$#@#!
BWAM
KRAK
--IS SO I CAN HAVE YOU--
--ALL TO MYSELF!
RRIIIP
YES...! NOW I CAN SEE THE LOOK ON YOUR FACE--

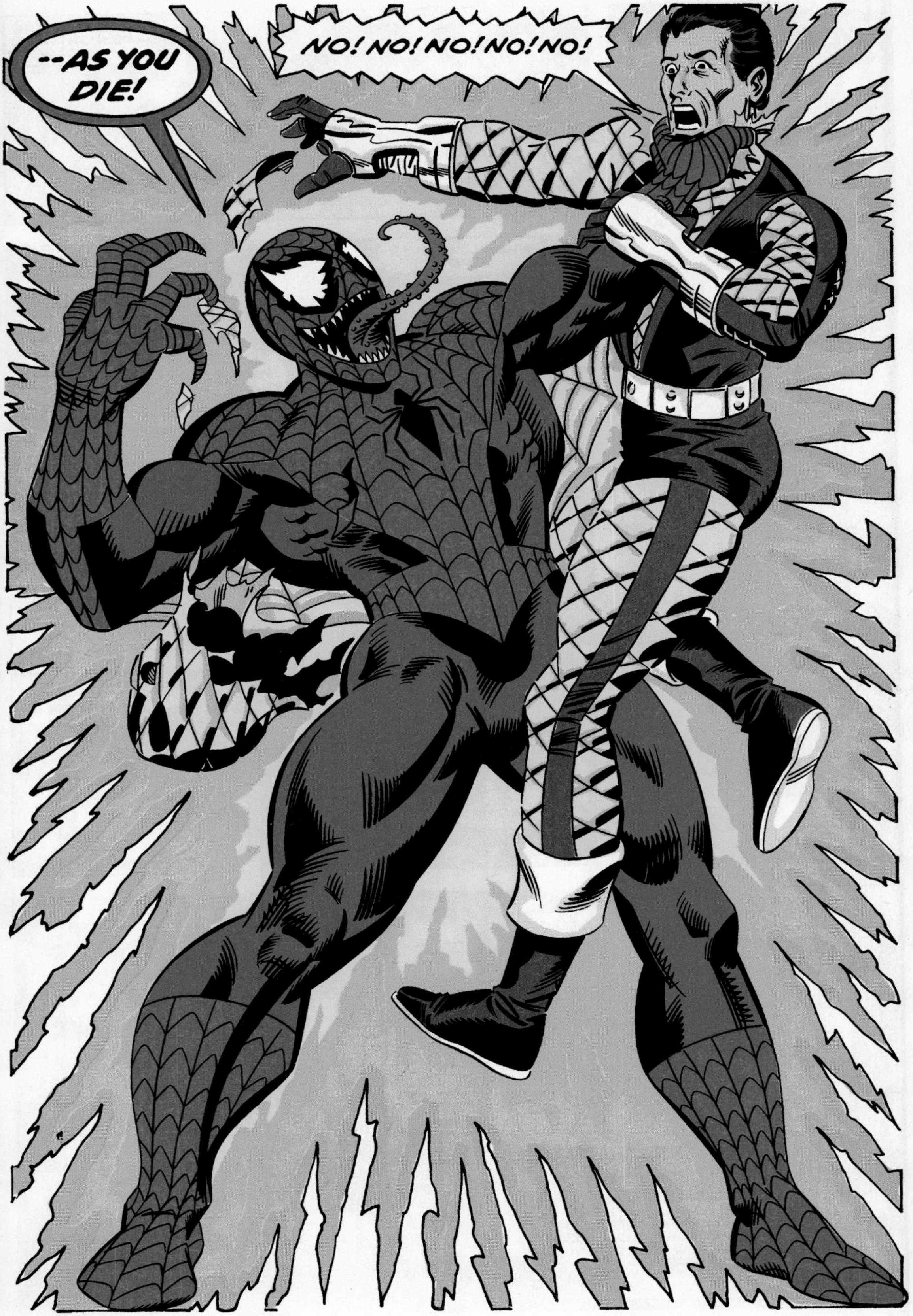
--AS YOU DIE!
NO! NO! NO! NO! NO!

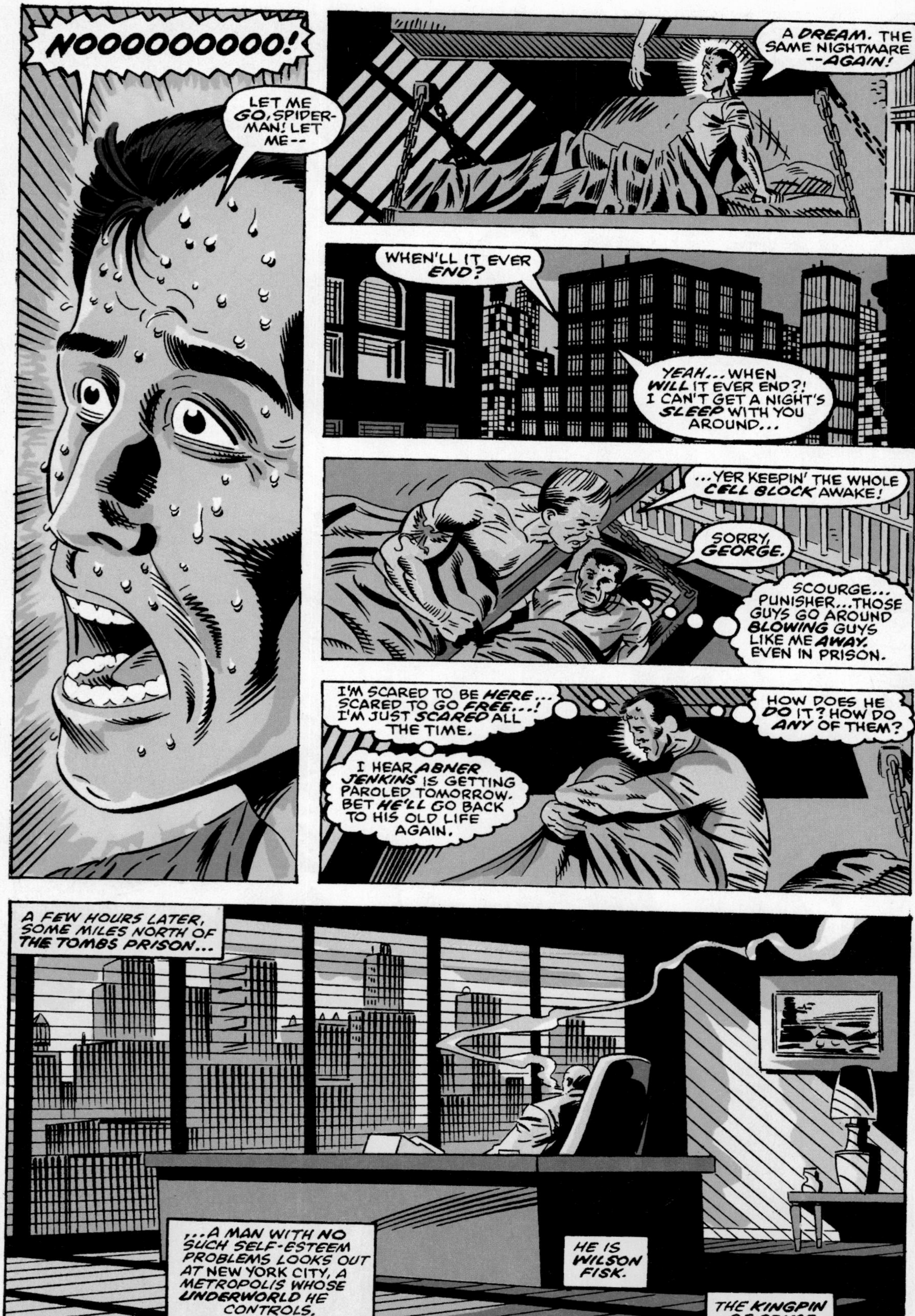

NOOOOOOOOO!
LET ME GO, SPIDER-MAN! LET ME--
A DREAM. THE SAME NIGHTMARE --AGAIN!
WHEN'LL IT EVER END?
YEAH... WHEN WILL IT EVER END?! I CAN'T GET A NIGHT'S SLEEP WITH YOU AROUND...
...YER KEEPIN' THE WHOLE CELL BLOCK AWAKE!
SORRY, GEORGE.
SCOURGE... PUNISHER... THOSE GUYS GO AROUND BLOWING GUYS LIKE ME AWAY. EVEN IN PRISON.
I'M SCARED TO BE HERE... SCARED TO GO FREE...! I'M JUST SCARED ALL THE TIME.
HOW DOES HE DO IT? HOW DO ANY OF THEM?
I HEAR ABNER JENKINS IS GETTING PAROLED TOMORROW. BET HE'LL GO BACK TO HIS OLD LIFE AGAIN.
A FEW HOURS LATER, SOME MILES NORTH OF THE TOMBS PRISON...
...A MAN WITH NO SUCH SELF-ESTEEM PROBLEMS LOOKS OUT AT NEW YORK CITY, A METROPOLIS WHOSE UNDERWORLD HE CONTROLS.
HE IS WILSON FISK.
THE KINGPIN OF CRIME.

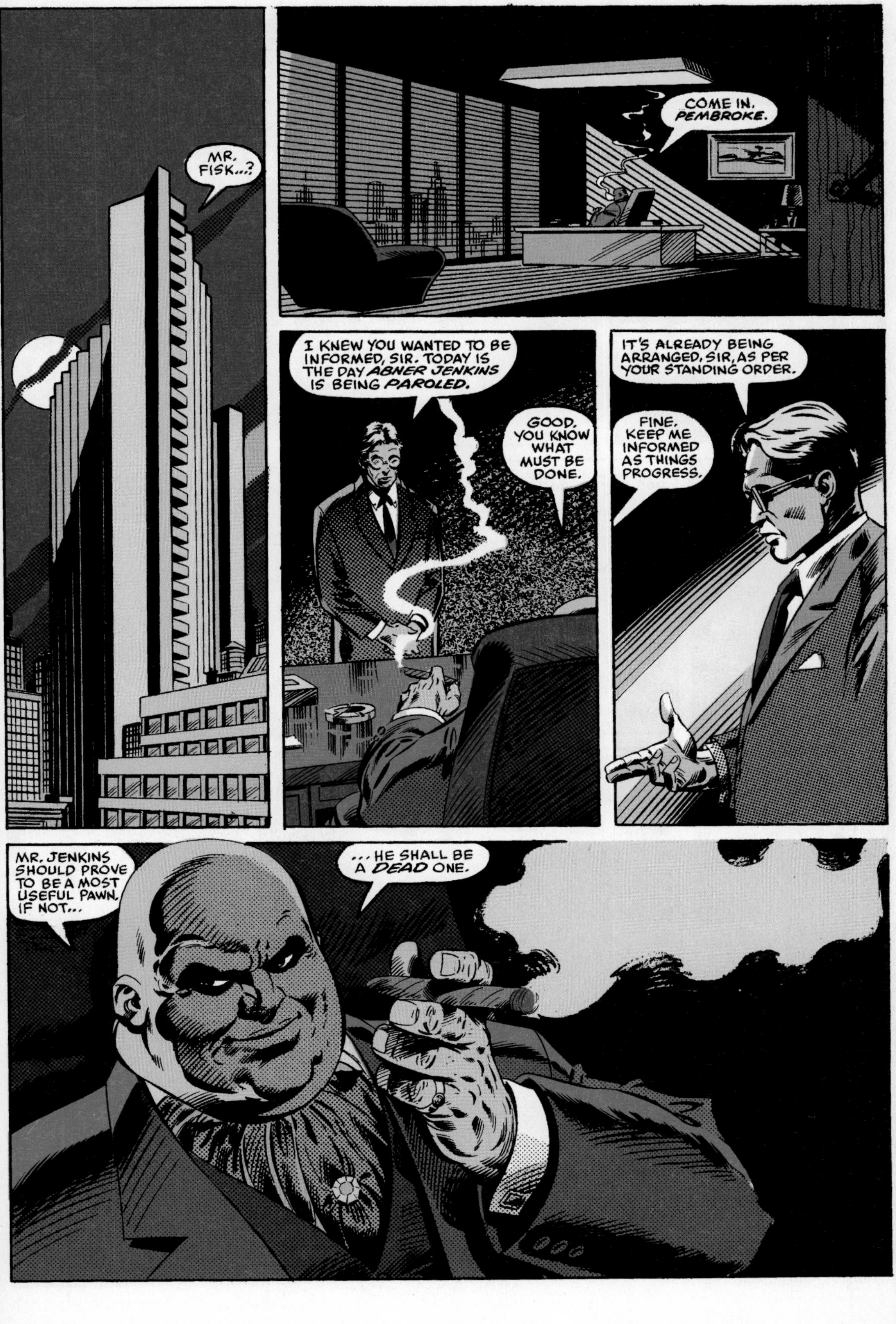
MR. FISK...?
COME IN, PEMBROKE.
I KNEW YOU WANTED TO BE INFORMED, SIR. TODAY IS THE DAY ABNER JENKINS IS BEING PAROLED.
GOOD. YOU KNOW WHAT MUST BE DONE.
IT'S ALREADY BEING ARRANGED, SIR, AS PER YOUR STANDING ORDER.
FINE. KEEP ME INFORMED AS THINGS PROGRESS.
MR. JENKINS SHOULD PROVE TO BE A MOST USEFUL PAWN, IF NOT...
...HE SHALL BE A DEAD ONE.

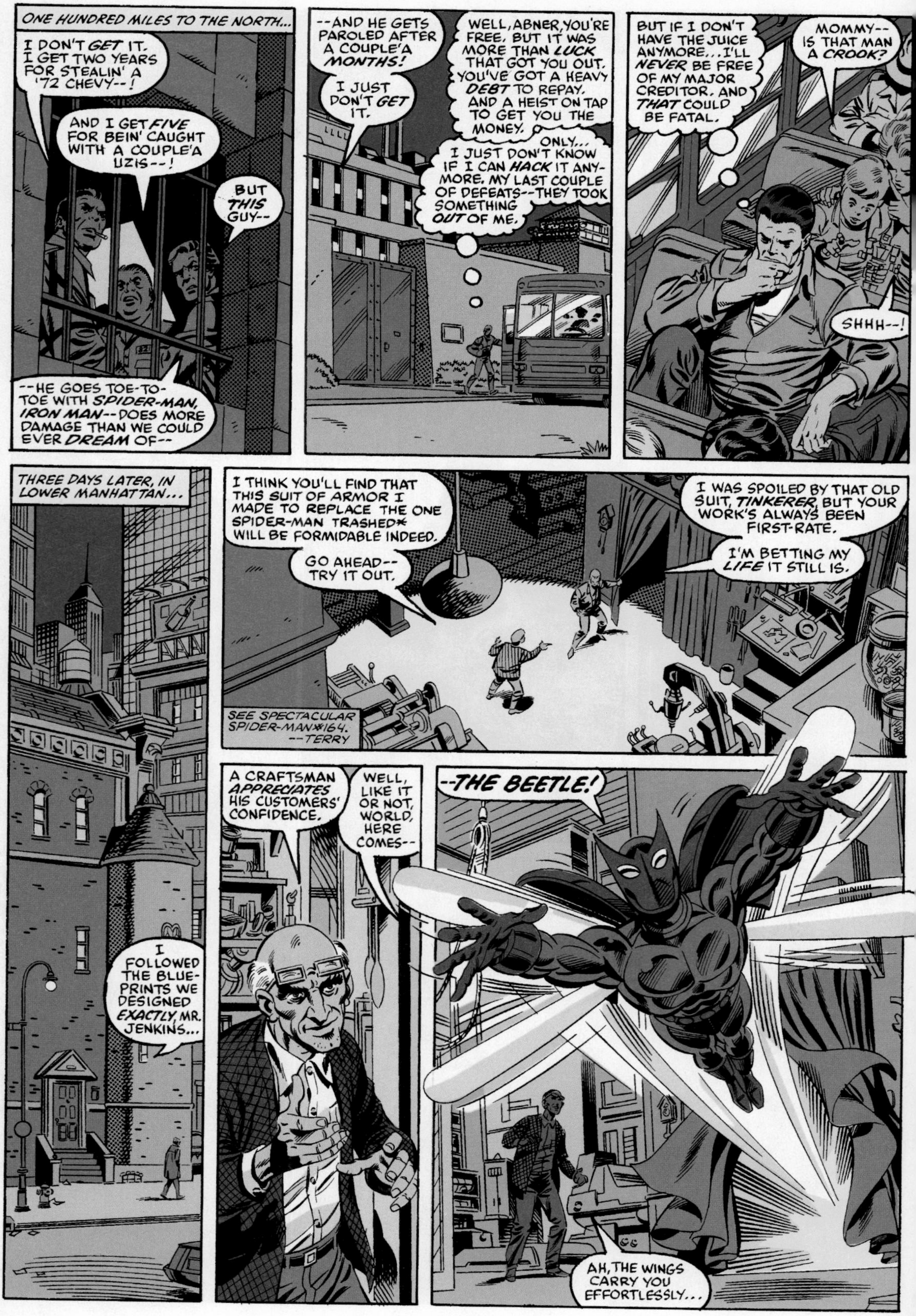
ONE HUNDRED MILES TO THE NORTH...
I DON'T GET IT. I GET TWO YEARS FOR STEALIN' A '72 CHEVY--!
AND I GET FIVE FOR BEIN' CAUGHT WITH A COUPLE'A UZIS--!
BUT THIS GUY--
--HE GOES TOE-TO-TOE WITH SPIDER-MAN, IRON MAN--DOES MORE DAMAGE THAN WE COULD EVER DREAM OF--
--AND HE GETS PAROLED AFTER A COUPLE'A MONTHS!
I JUST DON'T GET IT.
WELL, ABNER, YOU'RE FREE. BUT IT WAS MORE THAN LUCK THAT GOT YOU OUT. YOU'VE GOT A HEAVY DEBT TO REPAY. AND A HEIST ON TAP TO GET YOU THE MONEY.
ONLY... I JUST DON'T KNOW IF I CAN HACK IT ANYMORE. MY LAST COUPLE OF DEFEATS--THEY TOOK SOMETHING OUT OF ME.
BUT IF I DON'T HAVE THE JUICE ANYMORE... I'LL NEVER BE FREE OF MY MAJOR CREDITOR. AND THAT COULD BE FATAL.
MOMMY--IS THAT MAN A CROOK?
SHHH--!
THREE DAYS LATER, IN LOWER MANHATTAN...
I THINK YOU'LL FIND THAT THIS SUIT OF ARMOR I MADE TO REPLACE THE ONE SPIDER-MAN TRASHED* WILL BE FORMIDABLE INDEED.
GO AHEAD--TRY IT OUT.
I WAS SPOILED BY THAT OLD SUIT, TINKERER, BUT YOUR WORK'S ALWAYS BEEN FIRST-RATE.
I'M BETTING MY LIFE IT STILL IS.
*SEE SPECTACULAR SPIDER-MAN #164. --TERRY
I FOLLOWED THE BLUE-PRINTS WE DESIGNED EXACTLY, MR. JENKINS...
A CRAFTSMAN APPRECIATES HIS CUSTOMERS' CONFIDENCE.
WELL, LIKE IT OR NOT, WORLD, HERE COMES--
--THE BEETLE!
AH, THE WINGS CARRY YOU EFFORTLESSLY...

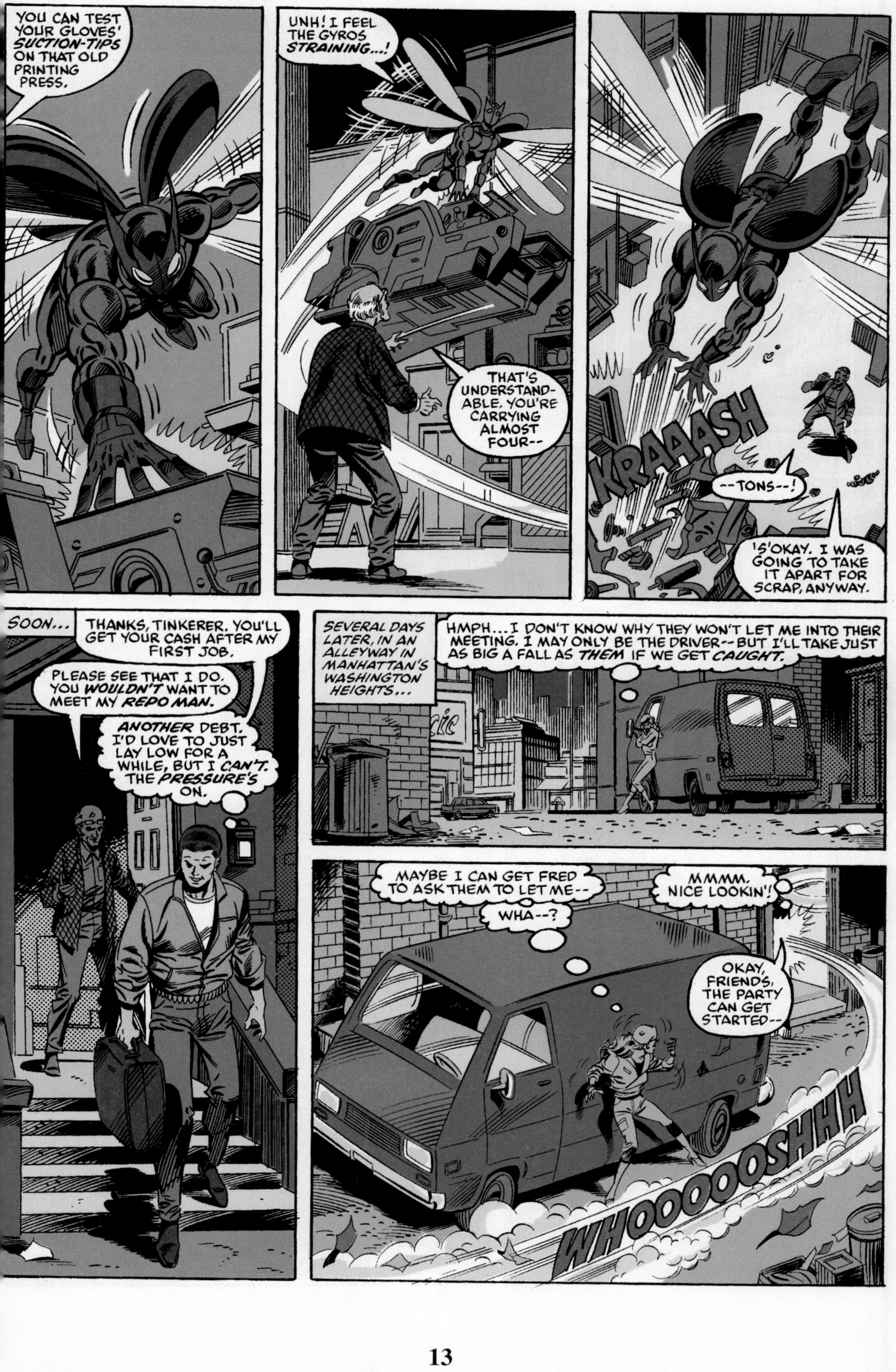
YOU CAN TEST YOUR GLOVES' SUCTION-TIPS ON THAT OLD PRINTING PRESS.
UNH! I FEEL THE GYROS STRAINING...!
THAT'S UNDERSTAND-ABLE. YOU'RE CARRYING ALMOST FOUR--
KRAAASH
--TONS--!
'S'OKAY. I WAS GOING TO TAKE IT APART FOR SCRAP, ANYWAY.
SOON...
THANKS, TINKERER. YOU'LL GET YOUR CASH AFTER MY FIRST JOB.
PLEASE SEE THAT I DO. YOU WOULDN'T WANT TO MEET MY REPO MAN.
ANOTHER DEBT. I'D LOVE TO JUST LAY LOW FOR A WHILE, BUT I CAN'T. THE PRESSURE'S ON.
SEVERAL DAYS LATER, IN AN ALLEYWAY IN MANHATTAN'S WASHINGTON HEIGHTS...
HMPH... I DON'T KNOW WHY THEY WON'T LET ME INTO THEIR MEETING. I MAY ONLY BE THE DRIVER-- BUT I'LL TAKE JUST AS BIG A FALL AS THEM IF WE GET CAUGHT.
MAYBE I CAN GET FRED TO ASK THEM TO LET ME--
WHA--?
MMMM. NICE LOOKIN'!
OKAY, FRIENDS, THE PARTY CAN GET STARTED--
WHOOOOOOSHHH

--NOW THAT *SPEED DEMON'S* HERE!

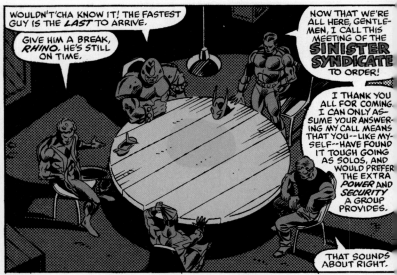

WOULDN'T'CHA KNOW IT! THE FASTEST GUY IS THE *LAST* TO ARRIVE.

GIVE HIM A BREAK, *RHINO.* HE'S STILL ON TIME.

NOW THAT WE'RE ALL HERE, GENTLEMEN, I CALL THIS MEETING OF THE **SINISTER SYNDICATE** TO ORDER!

I THANK YOU ALL FOR COMING. I CAN ONLY ASSUME YOUR ANSWERING MY CALL MEANS THAT YOU--LIKE MYSELF--HAVE FOUND IT TOUGH GOING AS SOLOS, AND WOULD PREFER THE EXTRA *POWER* AND *SECURITY* A GROUP PROVIDES.

THAT SOUNDS ABOUT RIGHT.

GOOD, I CAN PROMISE YOU, *HYDRO MAN*--AND THE REST OF YOU--THAT UNDER MY LEADERSHIP, WE WILL ALL GATHER *ENORMOUS* WEALTH.

AS A MATTER OF FACT, I HAVE A JOB PLANNED THIS VERY *NIGH*--

WAIT A SECOND!

BOOMERANG...?

LAST TIME OUT, WE NEARLY GOT OUR *HEADS* HANDED TO US!

MAYBE IT'S TIME FOR SOMEONE *ELSE* TO LEAD THE TEAM. LIKE *ME*.

LISTEN, FRIEND, *I* ORGANIZED THIS TEAM-- *I* DEVISED THE PLAN--

--AND *I* HAVE THE POWER TO LEAD US TO SUCCESS!

SKAZZZAK

UNDERSTAND?!

YOU THINK YOUR LOUSY *ELECTRO-BITES* ARE ANY MATCH FOR MY *BOOMERANGS?*

WHY, THIS *SHOCK-RANG* ALONE CAN--

WHA--?!

SHUT UP AND SIT DOWN, FRED.

ABNER'S SMART. I GOT FAITH IN HIM, HE'LL MAKE US LOTS OF *MONEY.*

AND *MONEY'S* WHAT I NEED TO PAY FOR THE OPERATIONS SO I CAN GET THIS BLAMED *RHINO-SKIN* REMOVED AND GO STRAIGHT.*

NO FIGHTIN'! NO ARGUIN'! JUST FOLLOW THE BEETLE-- OR *SPLIT.*

S-SURE... IF THAT'S HOW EVERY-BODY *ELSE* FEELS...

RUUNNCH!

THIS SERIES TAKES PLACE BEFORE AMAZING SPIDER-MAN #344. --T.

14

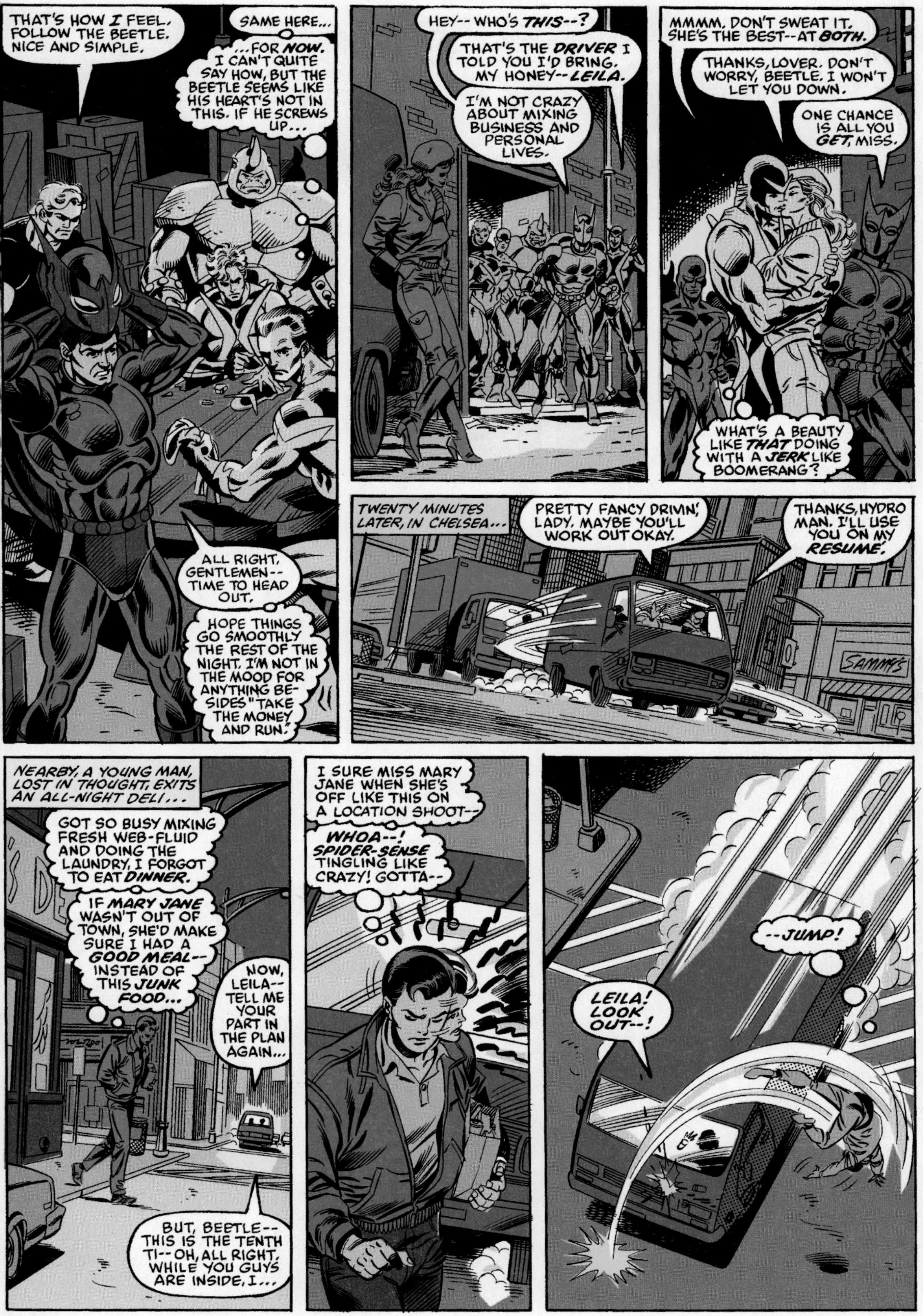
THAT'S HOW I FEEL. FOLLOW THE BEETLE. NICE AND SIMPLE.
SAME HERE...
...FOR NOW. I CAN'T QUITE SAY HOW, BUT THE BEETLE SEEMS LIKE HIS HEART'S NOT IN THIS. IF HE SCREWS UP...
ALL RIGHT, GENTLEMEN-- TIME TO HEAD OUT.
HOPE THINGS GO SMOOTHLY THE REST OF THE NIGHT. I'M NOT IN THE MOOD FOR ANYTHING BESIDES "TAKE THE MONEY AND RUN."
HEY-- WHO'S THIS--?
THAT'S THE DRIVER I TOLD YOU I'D BRING. MY HONEY--LEILA.
I'M NOT CRAZY ABOUT MIXING BUSINESS AND PERSONAL LIVES.
MMMM. DON'T SWEAT IT. SHE'S THE BEST--AT BOTH.
THANKS, LOVER. DON'T WORRY, BEETLE. I WON'T LET YOU DOWN.
ONE CHANCE IS ALL YOU GET, MISS.
WHAT'S A BEAUTY LIKE THAT DOING WITH A JERK LIKE BOOMERANG?
TWENTY MINUTES LATER, IN CHELSEA...
PRETTY FANCY DRIVIN', LADY. MAYBE YOU'LL WORK OUT OKAY.
THANKS, HYDRO MAN. I'LL USE YOU ON MY RESUME.
SAMMY'S
NEARBY, A YOUNG MAN, LOST IN THOUGHT, EXITS AN ALL-NIGHT DELI...
GOT SO BUSY MIXING FRESH WEB-FLUID AND DOING THE LAUNDRY, I FORGOT TO EAT DINNER.
IF MARY JANE WASN'T OUT OF TOWN, SHE'D MAKE SURE I HAD A GOOD MEAL-- INSTEAD OF THIS JUNK FOOD...
NOW, LEILA-- TELL ME YOUR PART IN THE PLAN AGAIN...
BUT, BEETLE-- THIS IS THE TENTH TI-- OH, ALL RIGHT. WHILE YOU GUYS ARE INSIDE, I...
I SURE MISS MARY JANE WHEN SHE'S OFF LIKE THIS ON A LOCATION SHOOT--
WHOA--! SPIDER-SENSE TINGLING LIKE CRAZY! GOTTA--
--JUMP!
LEILA! LOOK OUT--!

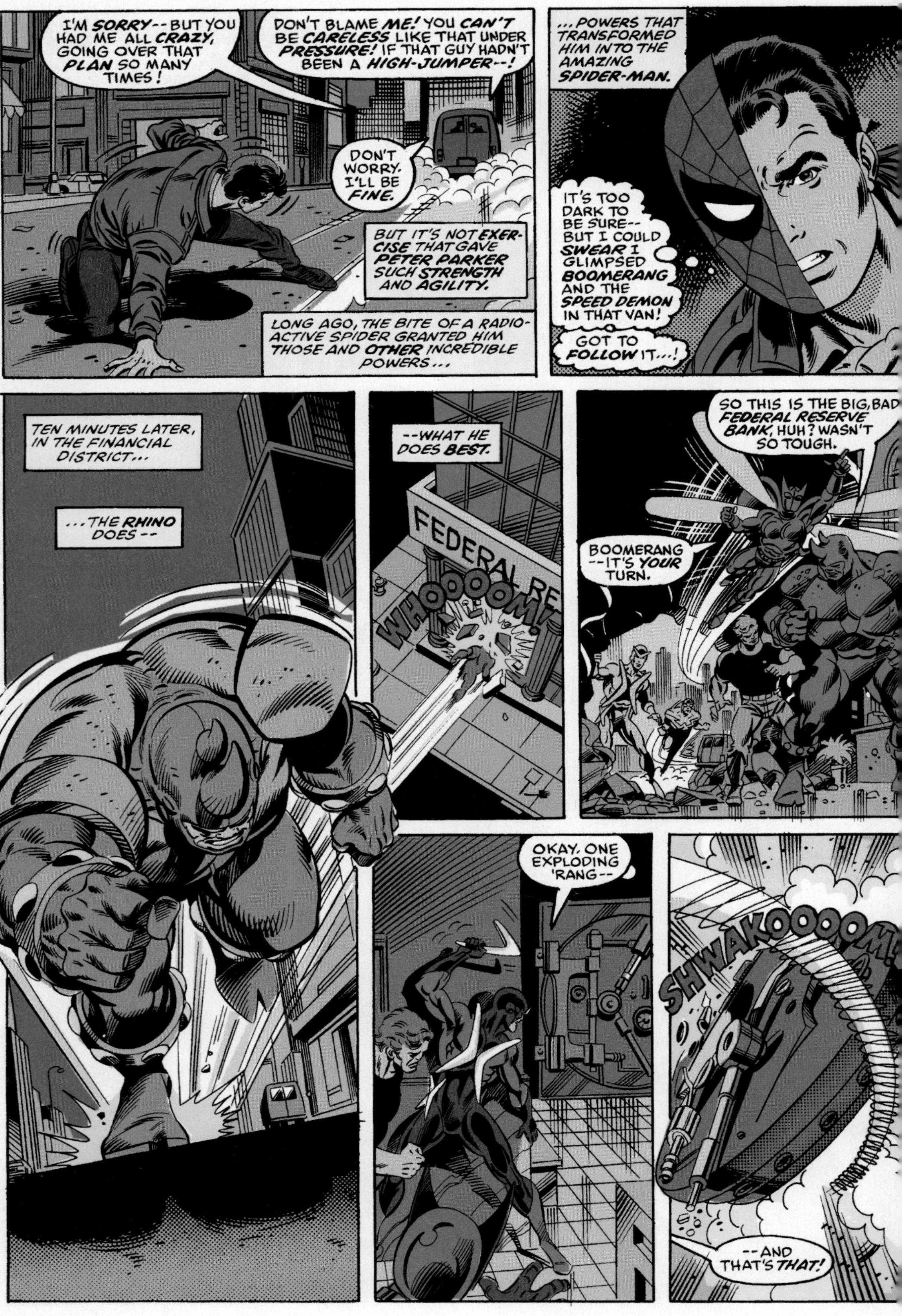
I'M SORRY--BUT YOU HAD ME ALL CRAZY, GOING OVER THAT PLAN SO MANY TIMES!
DON'T BLAME ME! YOU CAN'T BE CARELESS LIKE THAT UNDER PRESSURE! IF THAT GUY HADN'T BEEN A HIGH-JUMPER--!
DON'T WORRY. I'LL BE FINE.
BUT IT'S NOT EXERCISE THAT GAVE PETER PARKER SUCH STRENGTH AND AGILITY.
LONG AGO, THE BITE OF A RADIOACTIVE SPIDER GRANTED HIM THOSE AND OTHER INCREDIBLE POWERS...
...POWERS THAT TRANSFORMED HIM INTO THE AMAZING SPIDER-MAN.
IT'S TOO DARK TO BE SURE--BUT I COULD SWEAR I GLIMPSED BOOMERANG AND THE SPEED DEMON IN THAT VAN!
GOT TO FOLLOW IT...!
TEN MINUTES LATER, IN THE FINANCIAL DISTRICT...
...THE RHINO DOES--
--WHAT HE DOES BEST.
FEDERAL RE
WHOOOOOM!
SO THIS IS THE BIG, BAD FEDERAL RESERVE BANK, HUH? WASN'T SO TOUGH.
BOOMERANG--IT'S YOUR TURN.
OKAY. ONE EXPLODING 'RANG--
SHWAKOOOOOM!
--AND THAT'S THAT!

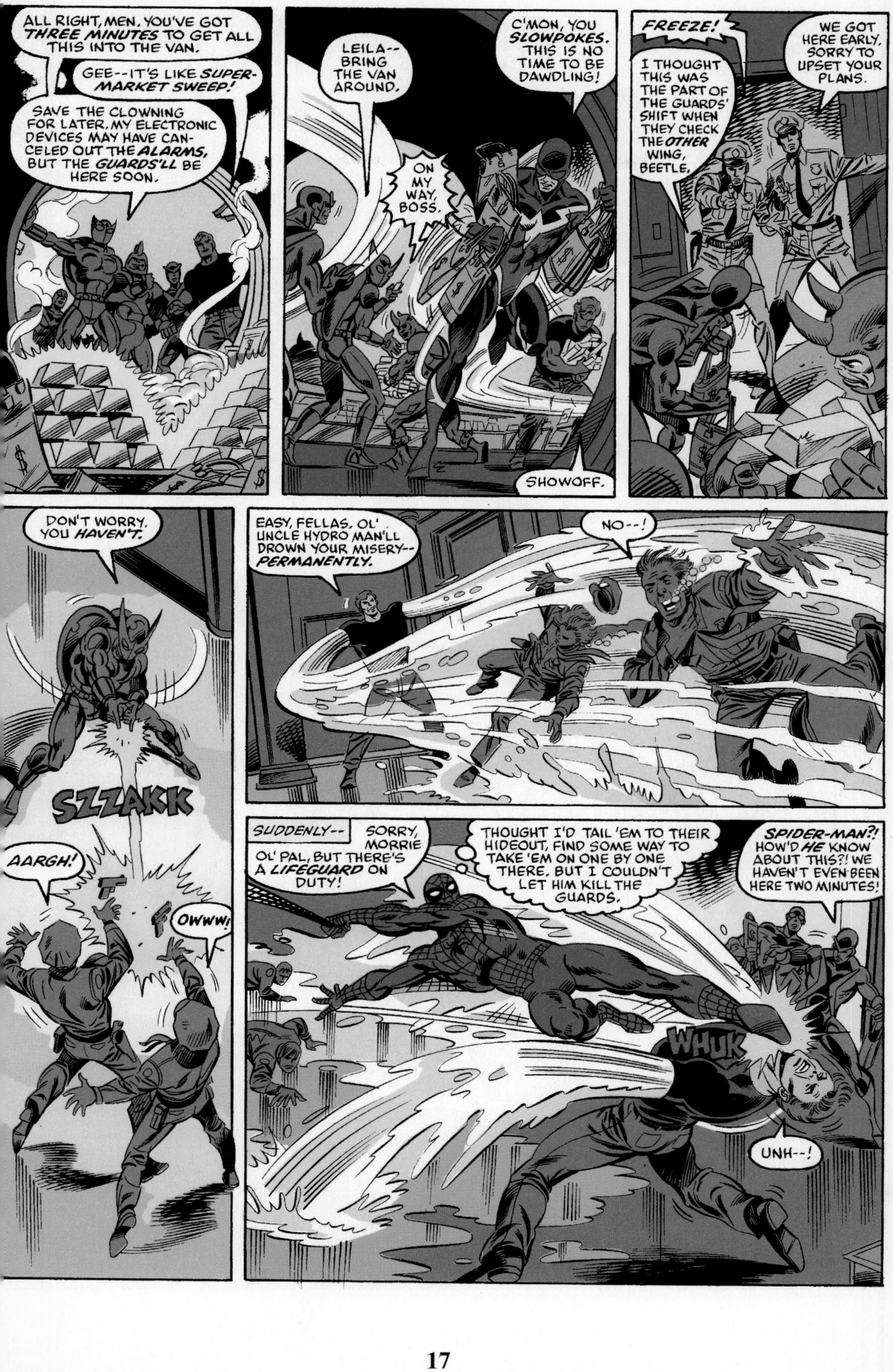

ALL RIGHT, MEN. YOU'VE GOT THREE MINUTES TO GET ALL THIS INTO THE VAN.
GEE--IT'S LIKE SUPERMARKET SWEEP!
SAVE THE CLOWNING FOR LATER. MY ELECTRONIC DEVICES MAY HAVE CANCELED OUT THE ALARMS, BUT THE GUARDS'LL BE HERE SOON.
LEILA--BRING THE VAN AROUND.
ON MY WAY, BOSS.
C'MON, YOU SLOWPOKES. THIS IS NO TIME TO BE DAWDLING!
SHOWOFF.
FREEZE!
I THOUGHT THIS WAS THE PART OF THE GUARDS' SHIFT WHEN THEY CHECK THE OTHER WING, BEETLE.
WE GOT HERE EARLY. SORRY TO UPSET YOUR PLANS.
DON'T WORRY. YOU HAVEN'T.
SZZAKK
AARGH!
OWWW!
EASY, FELLAS. OL' UNCLE HYDRO MAN'LL DROWN YOUR MISERY--PERMANENTLY.
NO--!
SUDDENLY--
SORRY, MORRIE OL' PAL, BUT THERE'S A LIFEGUARD ON DUTY!
THOUGHT I'D TAIL 'EM TO THEIR HIDEOUT, FIND SOME WAY TO TAKE 'EM ON ONE BY ONE THERE. BUT I COULDN'T LET HIM KILL THE GUARDS.
SPIDER-MAN?! HOW'D HE KNOW ABOUT THIS?! WE HAVEN'T EVEN BEEN HERE TWO MINUTES!
WHUK
UNH--!

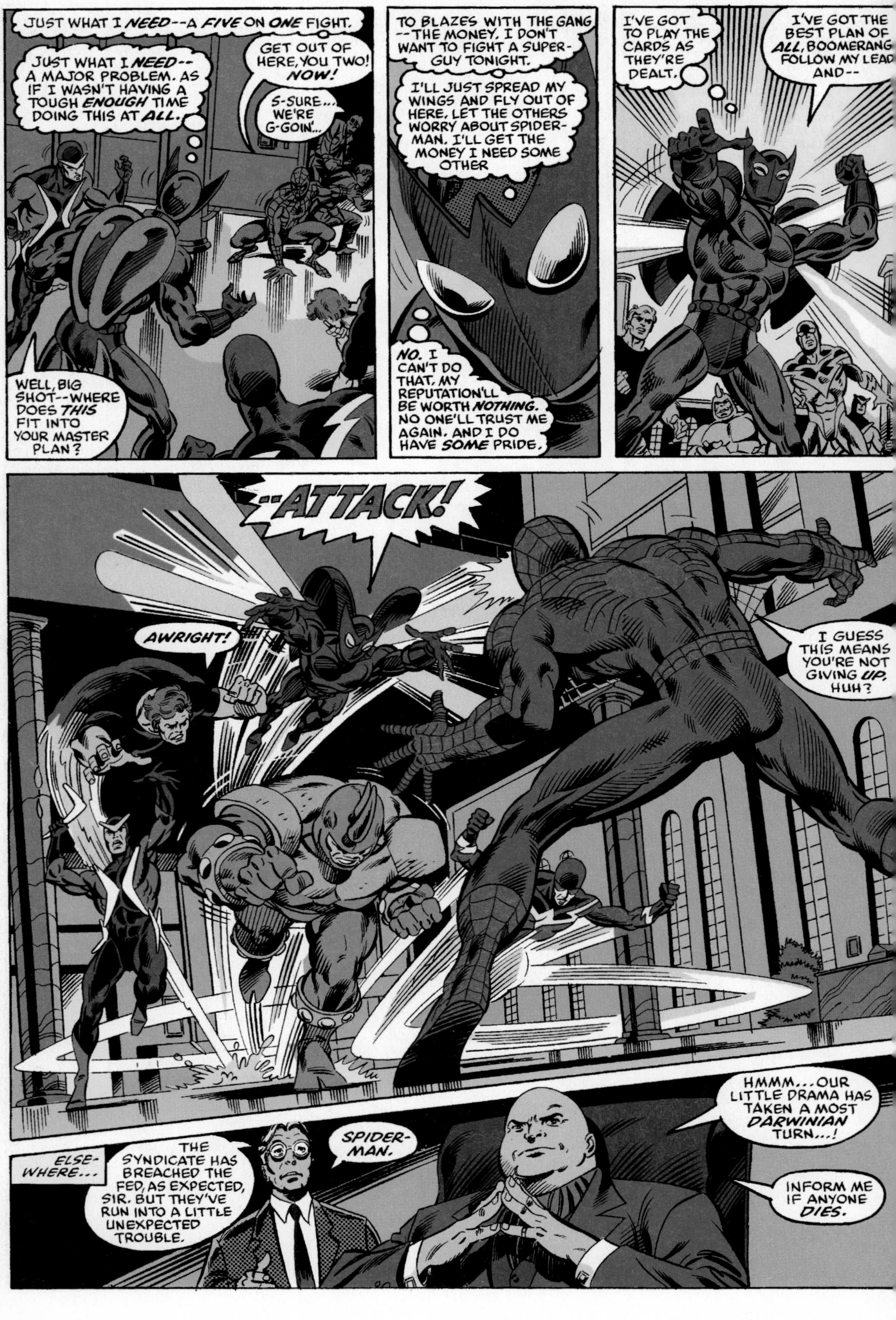
JUST WHAT I NEED--A FIVE ON ONE FIGHT.
JUST WHAT I NEED--A MAJOR PROBLEM. AS IF I WASN'T HAVING A TOUGH ENOUGH TIME DOING THIS AT ALL.
GET OUT OF HERE, YOU TWO! NOW!
S-SURE... WE'RE G-GOIN'...
WELL, BIG SHOT--WHERE DOES THIS FIT INTO YOUR MASTER PLAN?
TO BLAZES WITH THE GANG--THE MONEY. I DON'T WANT TO FIGHT A SUPER-GUY TONIGHT.
I'LL JUST SPREAD MY WINGS AND FLY OUT OF HERE. LET THE OTHERS WORRY ABOUT SPIDER-MAN. I'LL GET THE MONEY I NEED SOME OTHER
NO. I CAN'T DO THAT. MY REPUTATION'LL BE WORTH NOTHING. NO ONE'LL TRUST ME AGAIN. AND I DO HAVE SOME PRIDE.
I'VE GOT TO PLAY THE CARDS AS THEY'RE DEALT.
I'VE GOT THE BEST PLAN OF ALL, BOOMERANG FOLLOW MY LEAD AND--
--ATTACK!
AWRIGHT!
I GUESS THIS MEANS YOU'RE NOT GIVING UP, HUH?
ELSEWHERE...
THE SYNDICATE HAS BREACHED THE FED, AS EXPECTED, SIR. BUT THEY'VE RUN INTO A LITTLE UNEXPECTED TROUBLE.
SPIDER-MAN.
HMMM...OUR LITTLE DRAMA HAS TAKEN A MOST DARWINIAN TURN...!
INFORM ME IF ANYONE DIES.

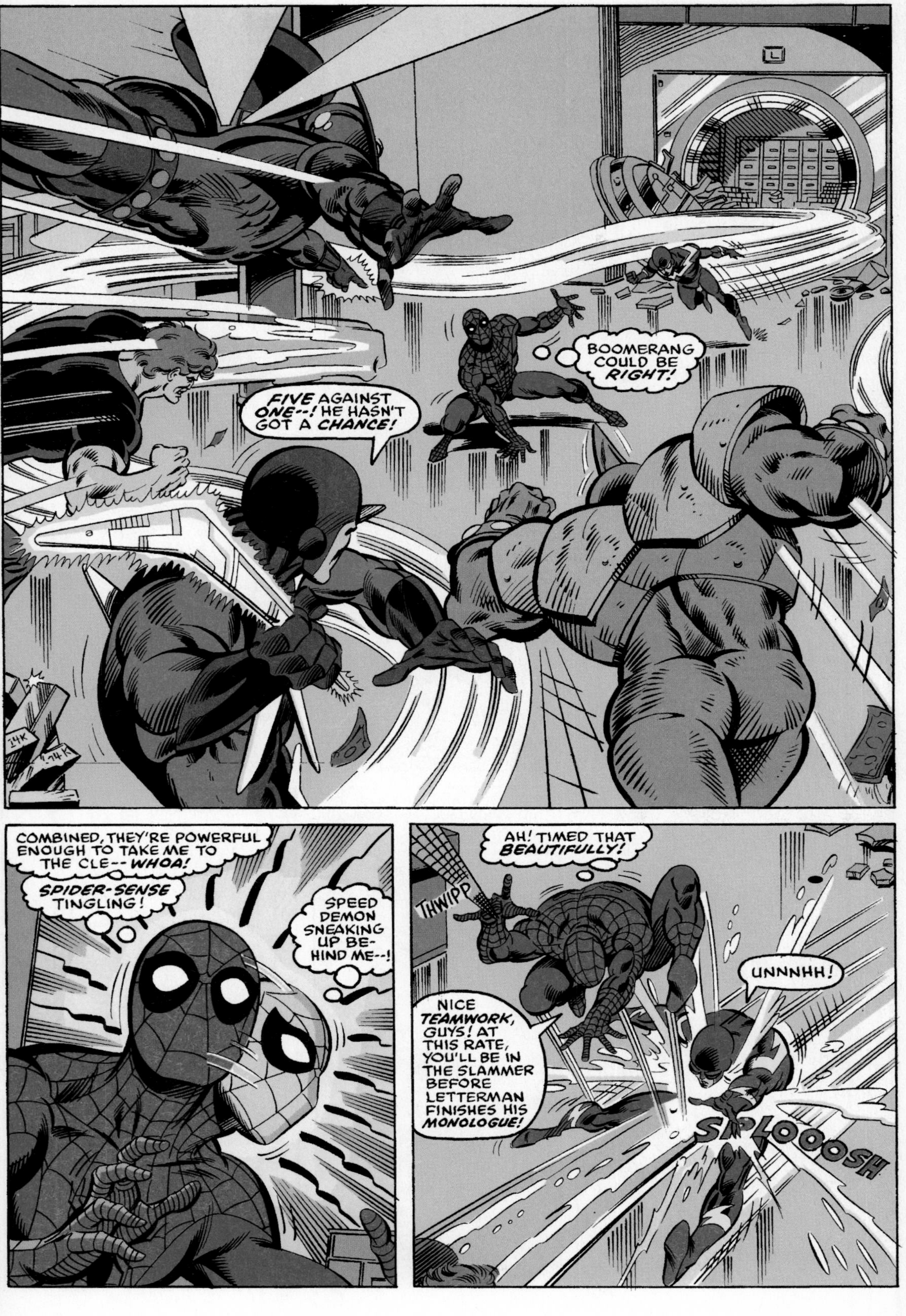
BOOMERANG COULD BE RIGHT!
FIVE AGAINST ONE--! HE HASN'T GOT A CHANCE!
COMBINED, THEY'RE POWERFUL ENOUGH TO TAKE ME TO THE CLE-- WHOA!
SPIDER-SENSE TINGLING!
SPEED DEMON SNEAKING UP BE-HIND ME--!
AH! TIMED THAT BEAUTIFULLY!
THWIPP
UNNNHH!
NICE TEAMWORK, GUYS! AT THIS RATE, YOU'LL BE IN THE SLAMMER BEFORE LETTERMAN FINISHES HIS MONOLOGUE!
SPLOOOSH

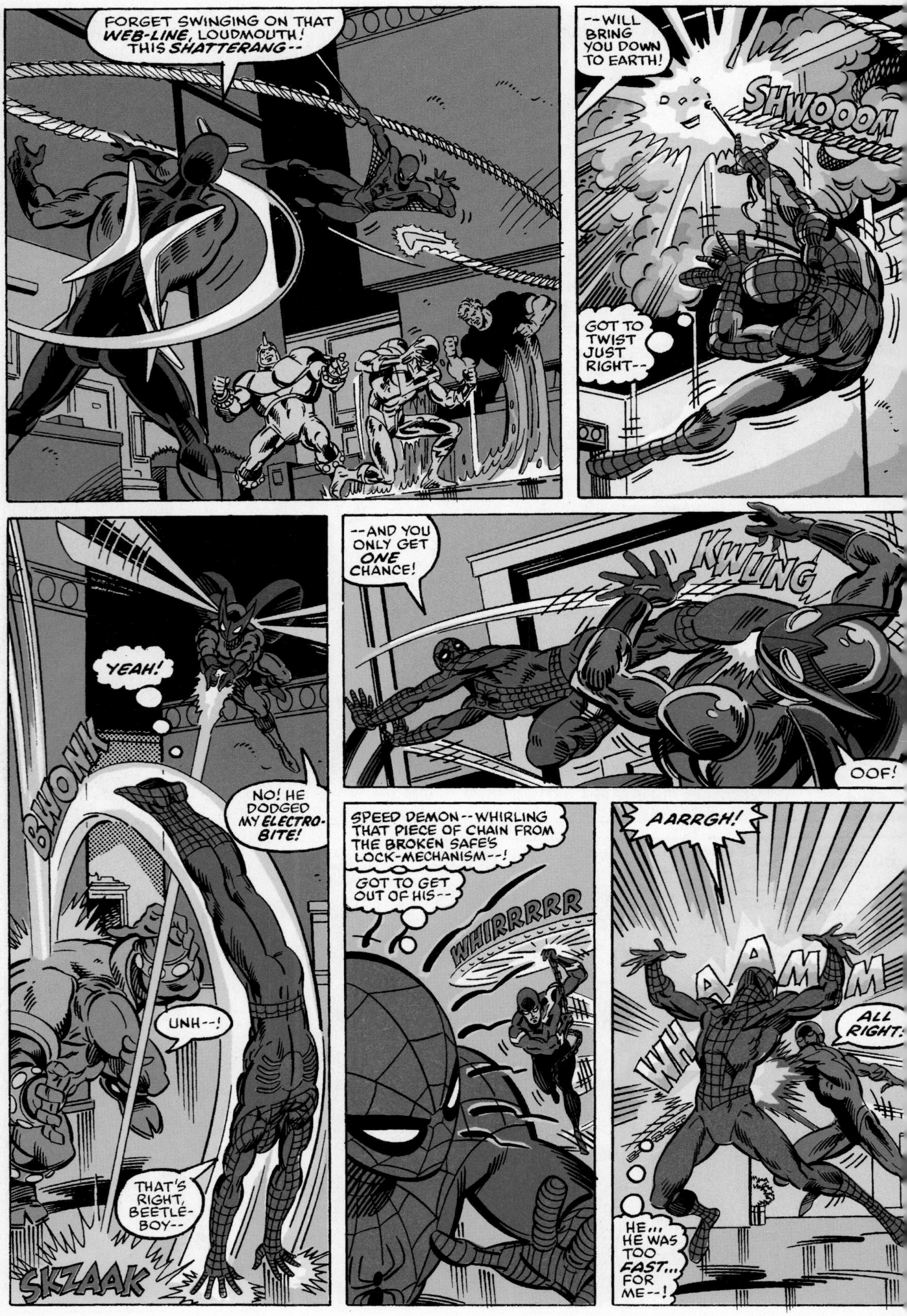
FORGET SWINGING ON THAT WEB-LINE, LOUDMOUTH! THIS SHATTERANG--
--WILL BRING YOU DOWN TO EARTH!
SHWOOOM
GOT TO TWIST JUST RIGHT--
YEAH!
BWONK
NO! HE DODGED MY ELECTRO-BITE!
UNH--!
THAT'S RIGHT, BEETLE-BOY--
SKZAAK
--AND YOU ONLY GET ONE CHANCE!
KWUNG
OOF!
SPEED DEMON--WHIRLING THAT PIECE OF CHAIN FROM THE BROKEN SAFE'S LOCK-MECHANISM--!
GOT TO GET OUT OF HIS--
WHIRRRRR
AARRGH!
WHAAMM
ALL RIGHT.
HE... HE WAS TOO FAST... FOR ME--!

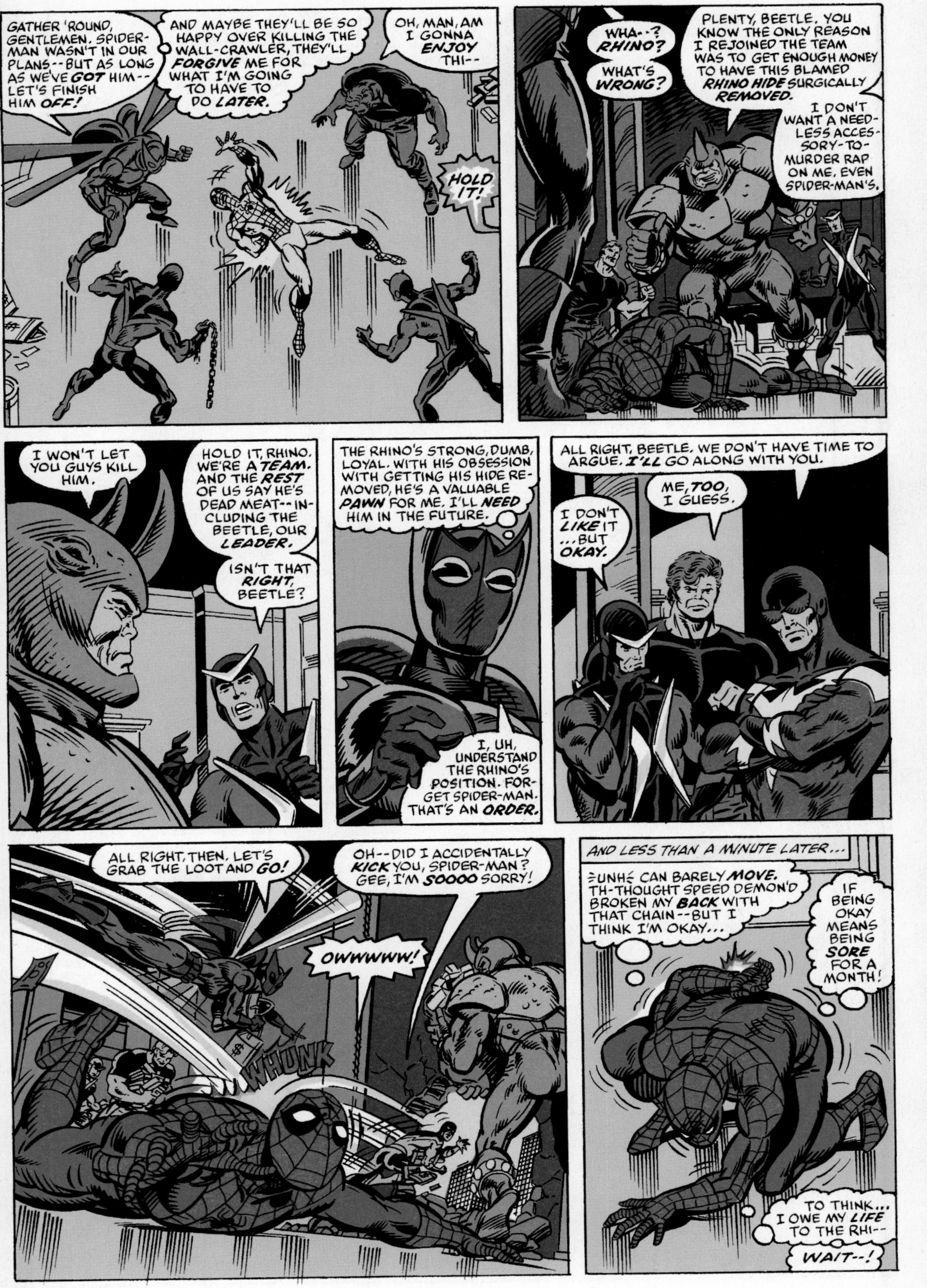
GATHER 'ROUND, GENTLEMEN. SPIDER-MAN WASN'T IN OUR PLANS--BUT AS LONG AS WE'VE GOT HIM--LET'S FINISH HIM OFF!
AND MAYBE THEY'LL BE SO HAPPY OVER KILLING THE WALL-CRAWLER, THEY'LL FORGIVE ME FOR WHAT I'M GOING TO HAVE TO DO LATER.
OH, MAN, AM I GONNA ENJOY THI--
HOLD IT!
WHA--? RHINO?
WHAT'S WRONG?
PLENTY, BEETLE. YOU KNOW THE ONLY REASON I REJOINED THE TEAM WAS TO GET ENOUGH MONEY TO HAVE THIS BLAMED RHINO HIDE SURGICALLY REMOVED.
I DON'T WANT A NEEDLESS ACCESSORY-TO-MURDER RAP ON ME. EVEN SPIDER-MAN'S.
I WON'T LET YOU GUYS KILL HIM.
HOLD IT, RHINO. WE'RE A TEAM. AND THE REST OF US SAY HE'S DEAD MEAT--INCLUDING THE BEETLE, OUR LEADER.
ISN'T THAT RIGHT, BEETLE?
THE RHINO'S STRONG, DUMB, LOYAL. WITH HIS OBSESSION WITH GETTING HIS HIDE REMOVED, HE'S A VALUABLE PAWN FOR ME. I'LL NEED HIM IN THE FUTURE.
I, UH, UNDERSTAND THE RHINO'S POSITION. FORGET SPIDER-MAN. THAT'S AN ORDER.
ALL RIGHT, BEETLE. WE DON'T HAVE TIME TO ARGUE. I'LL GO ALONG WITH YOU.
ME, TOO, I GUESS.
I DON'T LIKE IT ...BUT OKAY.
ALL RIGHT, THEN. LET'S GRAB THE LOOT AND GO!
OH--DID I ACCIDENTALLY KICK YOU, SPIDER-MAN? GEE, I'M SOOOO SORRY!
OWWWWW!
WHUNK
AND LESS THAN A MINUTE LATER...
UNH! CAN BARELY MOVE. TH-THOUGHT SPEED DEMON'D BROKEN MY BACK WITH THAT CHAIN--BUT I THINK I'M OKAY...
IF BEING OKAY MEANS BEING SORE FOR A MONTH!
TO THINK... I OWE MY LIFE TO THE RHI--
WAIT--!

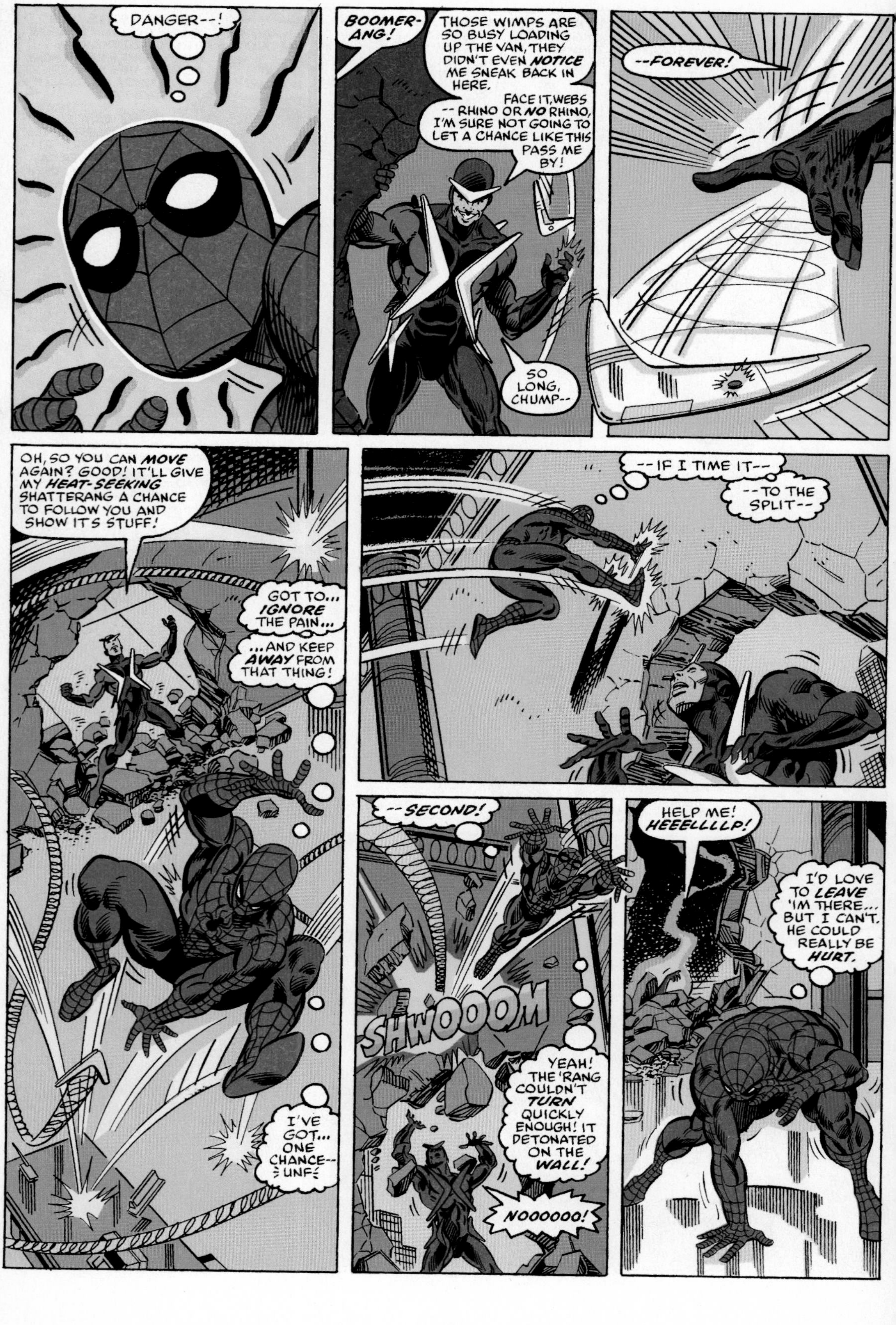
DANGER--!
BOOMER-ANG!
THOSE WIMPS ARE SO BUSY LOADING UP THE VAN, THEY DIDN'T EVEN NOTICE ME SNEAK BACK IN HERE.
FACE IT, WEBS -- RHINO OR NO RHINO, I'M SURE NOT GOING TO LET A CHANCE LIKE THIS PASS ME BY!
SO LONG, CHUMP--
--FOREVER!
OH, SO YOU CAN MOVE AGAIN? GOOD! IT'LL GIVE MY HEAT-SEEKING SHATTERANG A CHANCE TO FOLLOW YOU AND SHOW ITS STUFF!
GOT TO... IGNORE THE PAIN...
...AND KEEP AWAY FROM THAT THING!
I'VE GOT... ONE CHANCE-- UNF!
--IF I TIME IT--
--TO THE SPLIT--
--SECOND!
SHWOOOM
YEAH! THE 'RANG COULDN'T TURN QUICKLY ENOUGH! IT DETONATED ON THE WALL!
NOOOOOO!
HELP ME! HEEELLLLLP!
I'D LOVE TO LEAVE 'IM THERE... BUT I CAN'T. HE COULD REALLY BE HURT.

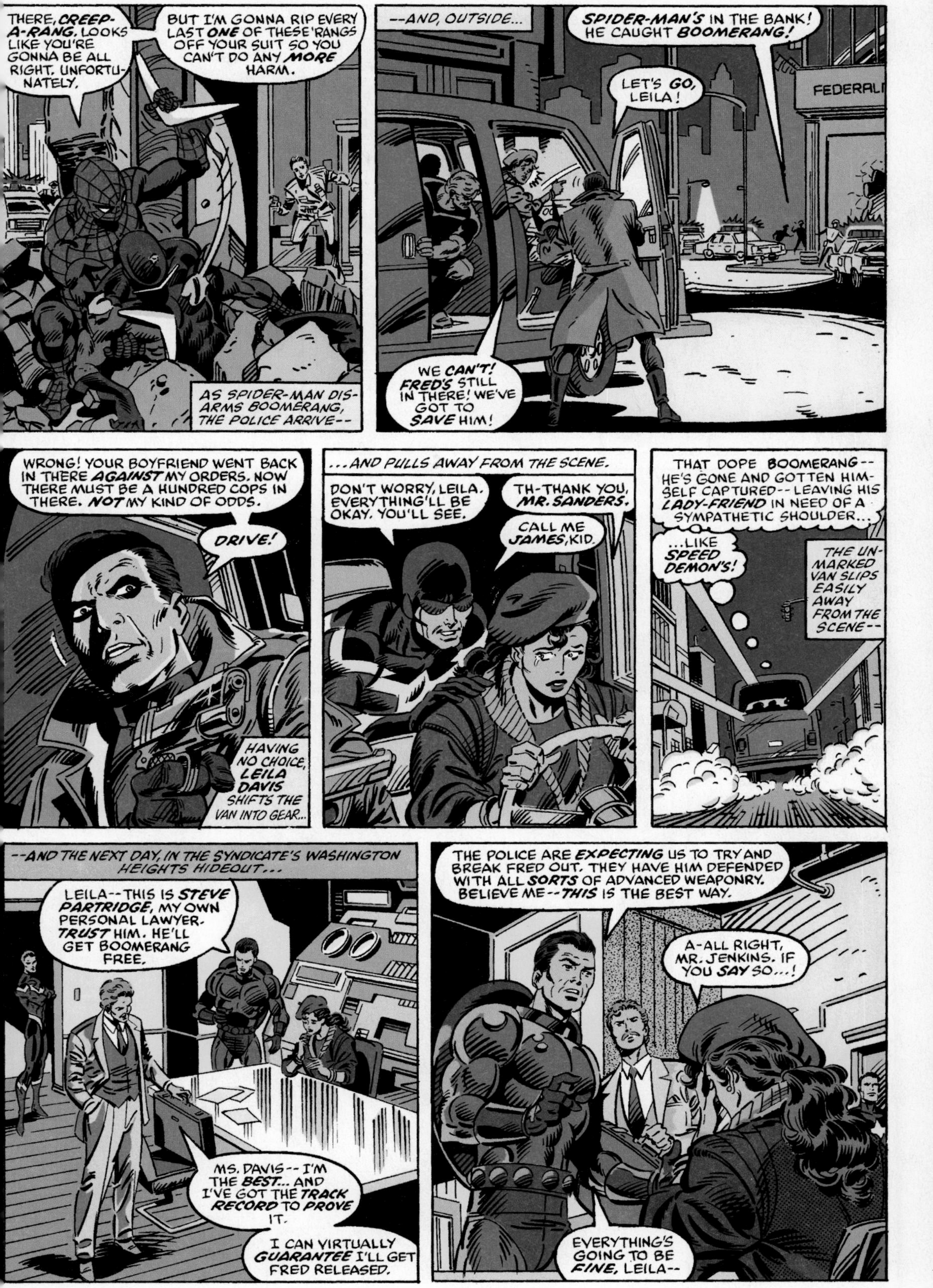
THERE, CREEP-A-RANG. LOOKS LIKE YOU'RE GONNA BE ALL RIGHT. UNFORTU-NATELY.
BUT I'M GONNA RIP EVERY LAST ONE OF THESE 'RANGS OFF YOUR SUIT SO YOU CAN'T DO ANY MORE HARM.
AS SPIDER-MAN DIS-ARMS BOOMERANG, THE POLICE ARRIVE--
--AND, OUTSIDE...
SPIDER-MAN'S IN THE BANK! HE CAUGHT BOOMERANG!
LET'S GO, LEILA!
FEDERAL
WE CAN'T! FRED'S STILL IN THERE! WE'VE GOT TO SAVE HIM!
WRONG! YOUR BOYFRIEND WENT BACK IN THERE AGAINST MY ORDERS. NOW THERE MUST BE A HUNDRED COPS IN THERE. NOT MY KIND OF ODDS.
DRIVE!
HAVING NO CHOICE, LEILA DAVIS SHIFTS THE VAN INTO GEAR...
...AND PULLS AWAY FROM THE SCENE.
DON'T WORRY, LEILA. EVERYTHING'LL BE OKAY. YOU'LL SEE.
TH-THANK YOU, MR. SANDERS.
CALL ME JAMES, KID.
THAT DOPE BOOMERANG-- HE'S GONE AND GOTTEN HIM-SELF CAPTURED--LEAVING HIS LADY-FRIEND IN NEED OF A SYMPATHETIC SHOULDER...
...LIKE SPEED DEMON'S!
THE UN-MARKED VAN SLIPS EASILY AWAY FROM THE SCENE--
--AND THE NEXT DAY, IN THE SYNDICATE'S WASHINGTON HEIGHTS HIDEOUT...
LEILA--THIS IS STEVE PARTRIDGE, MY OWN PERSONAL LAWYER. TRUST HIM. HE'LL GET BOOMERANG FREE.
MS. DAVIS--I'M THE BEST... AND I'VE GOT THE TRACK RECORD TO PROVE IT.
I CAN VIRTUALLY GUARANTEE I'LL GET FRED RELEASED.
THE POLICE ARE EXPECTING US TO TRY AND BREAK FRED OUT. THEY HAVE HIM DEFENDED WITH ALL SORTS OF ADVANCED WEAPONRY. BELIEVE ME--THIS IS THE BEST WAY.
A-ALL RIGHT, MR. JENKINS. IF YOU SAY SO...!
EVERYTHING'S GOING TO BE FINE, LEILA--

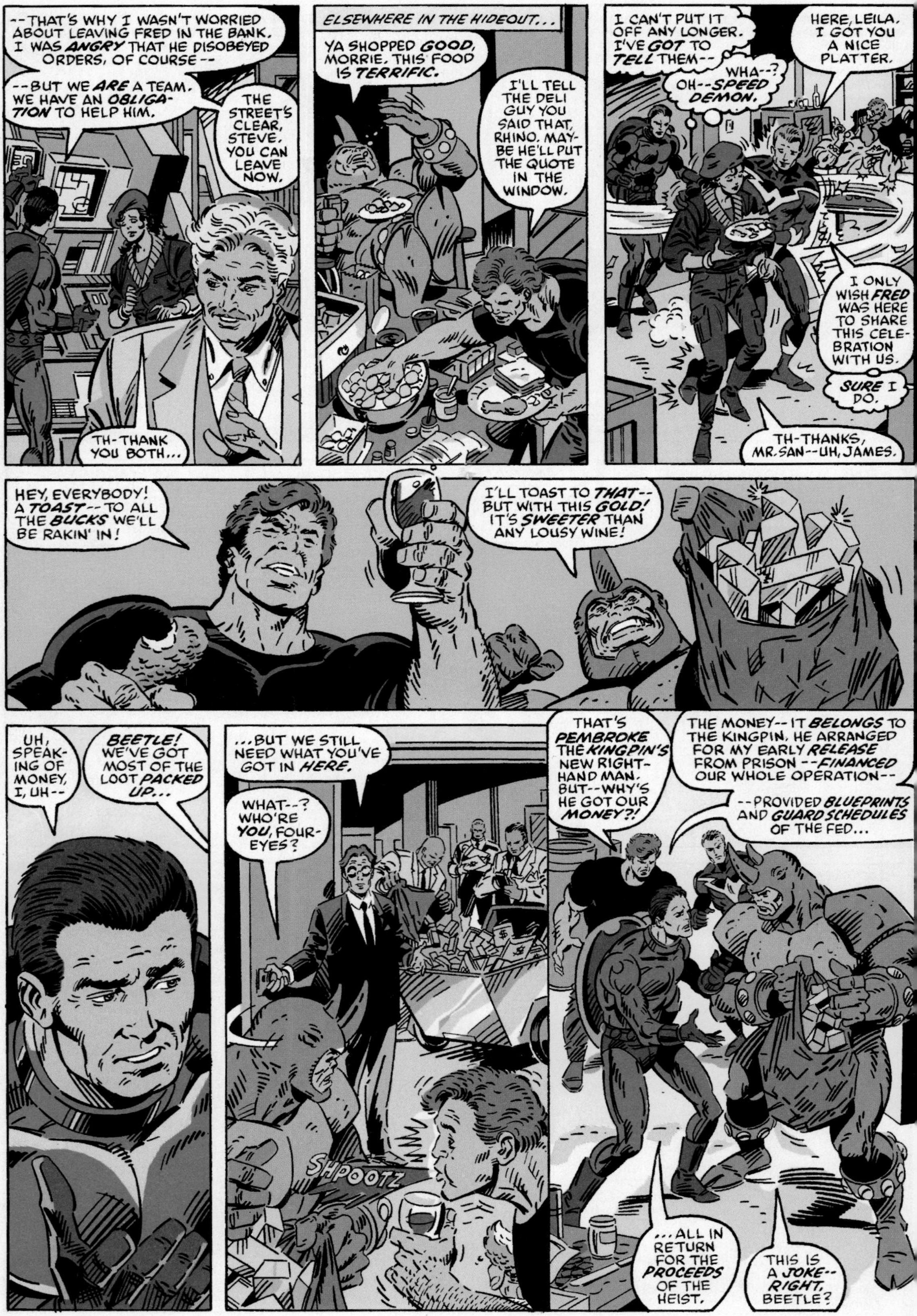
--THAT'S WHY I WASN'T WORRIED ABOUT LEAVING FRED IN THE BANK. I WAS ANGRY THAT HE DISOBEYED ORDERS, OF COURSE--
--BUT WE ARE A TEAM. WE HAVE AN OBLIGATION TO HELP HIM.
THE STREET'S CLEAR, STEVE. YOU CAN LEAVE NOW.
TH-THANK YOU BOTH...
ELSEWHERE IN THE HIDEOUT...
YA SHOPPED GOOD, MORRIE. THIS FOOD IS TERRIFIC.
I'LL TELL THE DELI GUY YOU SAID THAT, RHINO. MAYBE HE'LL PUT THE QUOTE IN THE WINDOW.
I CAN'T PUT IT OFF ANY LONGER. I'VE GOT TO TELL THEM--
WHA--? OH--SPEED DEMON.
HERE, LEILA. I GOT YOU A NICE PLATTER.
I ONLY WISH FRED WAS HERE TO SHARE THIS CELEBRATION WITH US.
SURE I DO.
TH-THANKS, MR. SAN--UH, JAMES.
HEY, EVERYBODY! A TOAST--TO ALL THE BUCKS WE'LL BE RAKIN' IN!
I'LL TOAST TO THAT--BUT WITH THIS GOLD! IT'S SWEETER THAN ANY LOUSY WINE!
UH, SPEAKING OF MONEY, I, UH--
BEETLE! WE'VE GOT MOST OF THE LOOT PACKED UP...
...BUT WE STILL NEED WHAT YOU'VE GOT IN HERE.
WHAT--? WHO'RE YOU, FOUR-EYES?
SHPOOTZ
THAT'S PEMBROKE, THE KINGPIN'S NEW RIGHT-HAND MAN. BUT--WHY'S HE GOT OUR MONEY?!
THE MONEY--IT BELONGS TO THE KINGPIN. HE ARRANGED FOR MY EARLY RELEASE FROM PRISON--FINANCED OUR WHOLE OPERATION--
--PROVIDED BLUEPRINTS AND GUARD SCHEDULES OF THE FED...
...ALL IN RETURN FOR THE PROCEEDS OF THE HEIST.
THIS IS A JOKE--RIGHT, BEETLE?

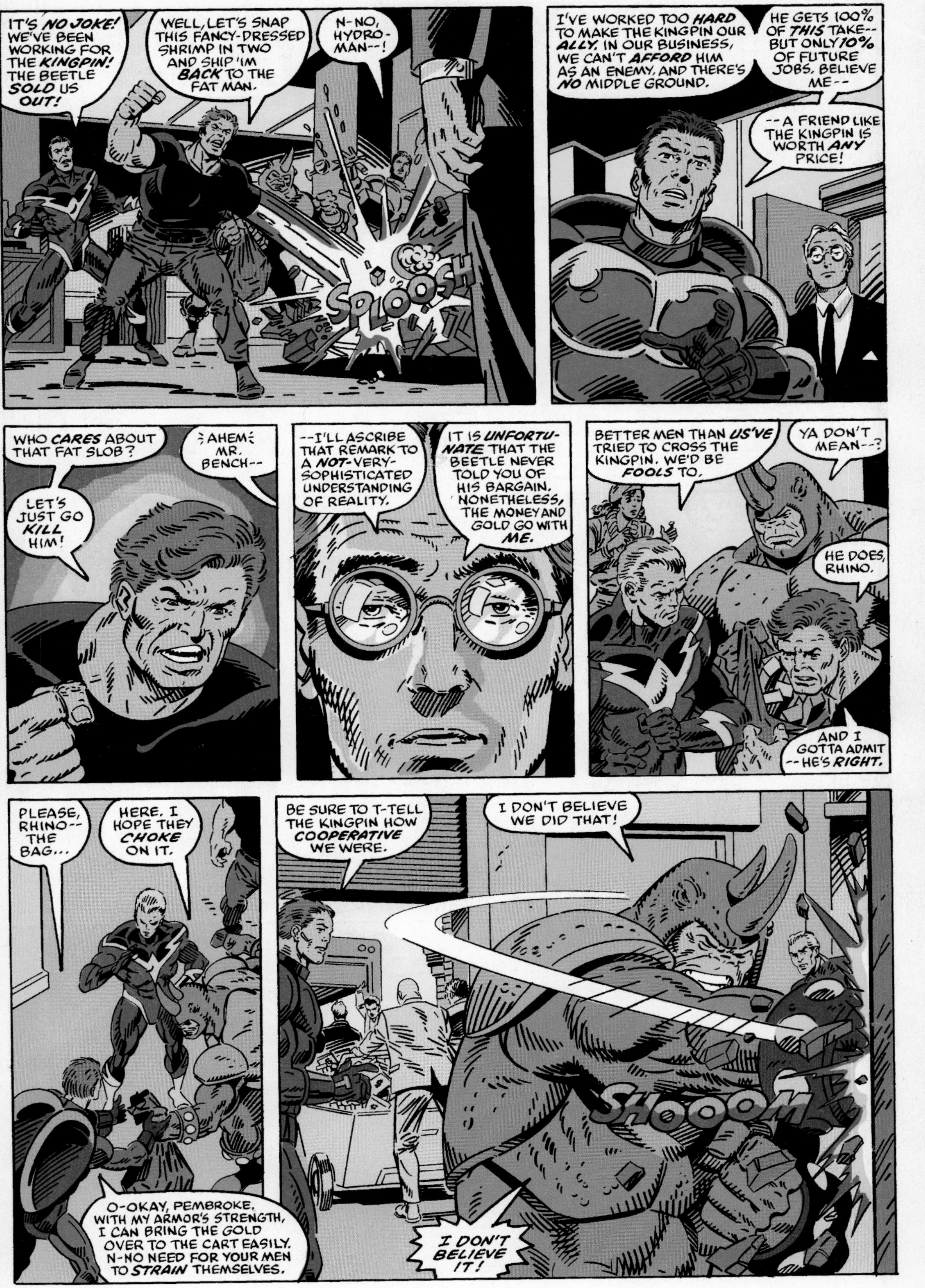

IT'S NO JOKE! WE'VE BEEN WORKING FOR THE KINGPIN! THE BEETLE SOLD US OUT!
WELL, LET'S SNAP THIS FANCY-DRESSED SHRIMP IN TWO AND SHIP 'IM BACK TO THE FAT MAN.
N-NO, HYDRO-MAN--!
SPLOOSH
I'VE WORKED TOO HARD TO MAKE THE KINGPIN OUR ALLY. IN OUR BUSINESS, WE CAN'T AFFORD HIM AS AN ENEMY, AND THERE'S NO MIDDLE GROUND.
HE GETS 100% OF THIS TAKE-- BUT ONLY 10% OF FUTURE JOBS. BELIEVE ME--
--A FRIEND LIKE THE KINGPIN IS WORTH ANY PRICE!
WHO CARES ABOUT THAT FAT SLOB?
LET'S JUST GO KILL HIM!
AHEM MR. BENCH--
--I'LL ASCRIBE THAT REMARK TO A NOT-VERY-SOPHISTICATED UNDERSTANDING OF REALITY.
IT IS UNFORTUNATE THAT THE BEETLE NEVER TOLD YOU OF HIS BARGAIN. NONETHELESS, THE MONEY AND GOLD GO WITH ME.
BETTER MEN THAN US'VE TRIED TO CROSS THE KINGPIN. WE'D BE FOOLS TO.
YA DON'T MEAN--?
HE DOES, RHINO.
AND I GOTTA ADMIT --HE'S RIGHT.
PLEASE, RHINO-- THE BAG...
HERE. I HOPE THEY CHOKE ON IT.
O-OKAY, PEMBROKE. WITH MY ARMOR'S STRENGTH, I CAN BRING THE GOLD OVER TO THE CART EASILY. N-NO NEED FOR YOUR MEN TO STRAIN THEMSELVES.
BE SURE TO T-TELL THE KINGPIN HOW COOPERATIVE WE WERE.
I DON'T BELIEVE WE DID THAT!
SHOOOM
I DON'T BELIEVE IT!

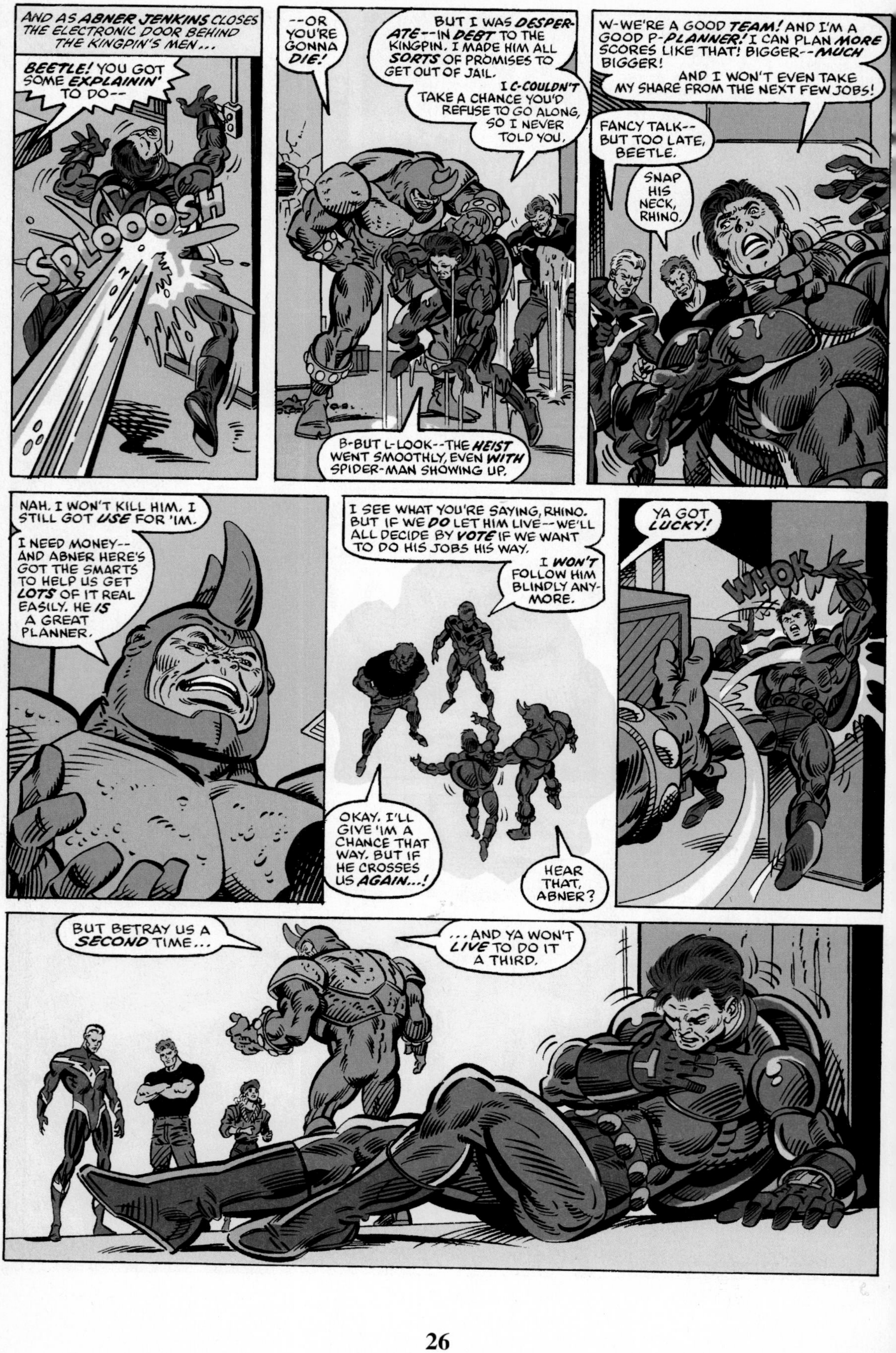
AND AS ABNER JENKINS CLOSES THE ELECTRONIC DOOR BEHIND THE KINGPIN'S MEN...
BEETLE! YOU GOT SOME EXPLAININ' TO DO--
SPLOOOSH
--OR YOU'RE GONNA DIE!
B-BUT L-LOOK--THE HEIST WENT SMOOTHLY, EVEN WITH SPIDER-MAN SHOWING UP.
BUT I WAS DESPERATE--IN DEBT TO THE KINGPIN. I MADE HIM ALL SORTS OF PROMISES TO GET OUT OF JAIL.
I C-COULDN'T TAKE A CHANCE YOU'D REFUSE TO GO ALONG, SO I NEVER TOLD YOU.
W-WE'RE A GOOD TEAM! AND I'M A GOOD P-PLANNER! I CAN PLAN MORE SCORES LIKE THAT! BIGGER--MUCH BIGGER!
AND I WON'T EVEN TAKE MY SHARE FROM THE NEXT FEW JOBS!
FANCY TALK--BUT TOO LATE, BEETLE.
SNAP HIS NECK, RHINO.
NAH. I WON'T KILL HIM. I STILL GOT USE FOR 'IM.
I NEED MONEY--AND ABNER HERE'S GOT THE SMARTS TO HELP US GET LOTS OF IT REAL EASILY. HE IS A GREAT PLANNER.
I SEE WHAT YOU'RE SAYING, RHINO. BUT IF WE DO LET HIM LIVE--WE'LL ALL DECIDE BY VOTE IF WE WANT TO DO HIS JOBS HIS WAY.
I WON'T FOLLOW HIM BLINDLY ANYMORE.
OKAY. I'LL GIVE 'IM A CHANCE THAT WAY. BUT IF HE CROSSES US AGAIN...!
HEAR THAT, ABNER?
YA GOT LUCKY!
WHOK
BUT BETRAY US A SECOND TIME...
...AND YA WON'T LIVE TO DO IT A THIRD.

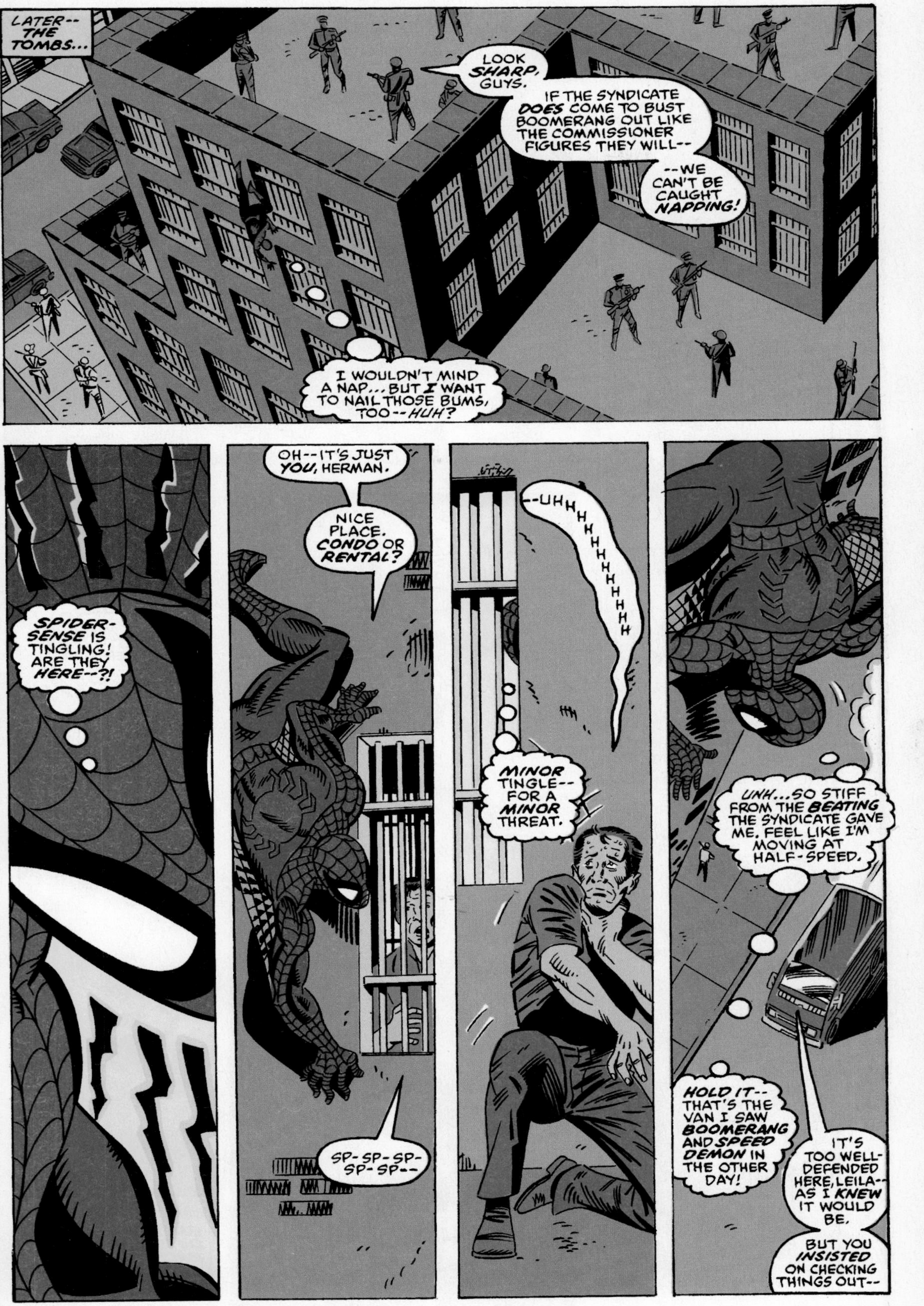
LATER-- THE TOMBS...
LOOK SHARP, GUYS.
IF THE SYNDICATE DOES COME TO BUST BOOMERANG OUT LIKE THE COMMISSIONER FIGURES THEY WILL--
--WE CAN'T BE CAUGHT NAPPING!
I WOULDN'T MIND A NAP... BUT I WANT TO NAIL THOSE BUMS, TOO--HUH?
SPIDER-SENSE IS TINGLING! ARE THEY HERE--?!
OH--IT'S JUST YOU, HERMAN.
NICE PLACE. CONDO OR RENTAL?
SP-SP-SP-SP-SP--
--UHHHHHHHHHHHH
MINOR TINGLE-- FOR A MINOR THREAT.
UNH...SO STIFF FROM THE BEATING THE SYNDICATE GAVE ME. FEEL LIKE I'M MOVING AT HALF-SPEED.
HOLD IT-- THAT'S THE VAN I SAW BOOMERANG AND SPEED DEMON IN THE OTHER DAY!
IT'S TOO WELL-DEFENDED HERE, LEILA-- AS I KNEW IT WOULD BE.
BUT YOU INSISTED ON CHECKING THINGS OUT--

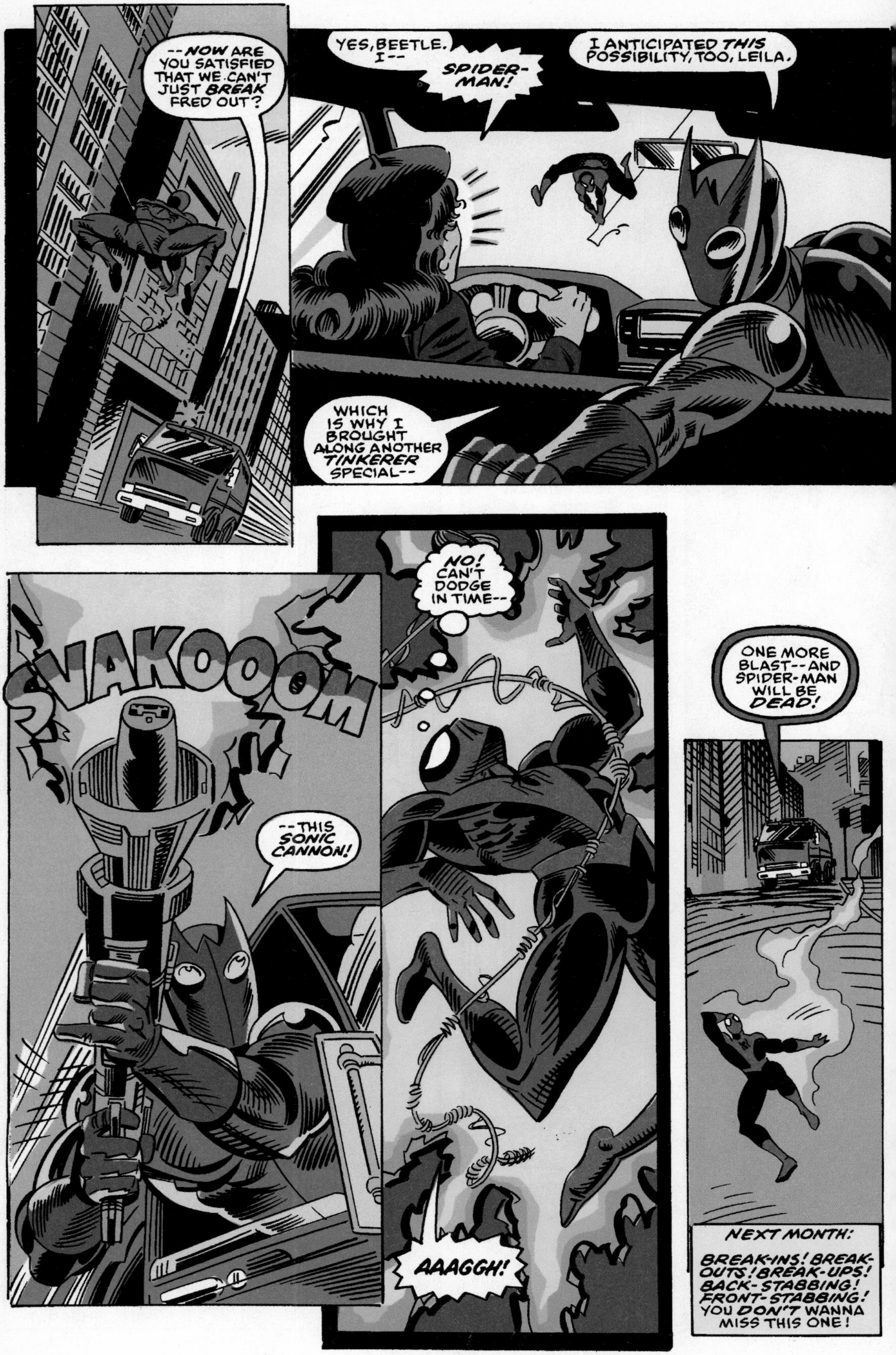
--NOW ARE YOU SATISFIED THAT WE CAN'T JUST BREAK FRED OUT?
YES, BEETLE. I--
SPIDER-MAN!
I ANTICIPATED THIS POSSIBILITY, TOO, LEILA.
WHICH IS WHY I BROUGHT ALONG ANOTHER TINKERER SPECIAL--
SVAKOOOM
--THIS SONIC CANNON!
NO! CAN'T DODGE IN TIME--
AAAGGH!
ONE MORE BLAST--AND SPIDER-MAN WILL BE DEAD!
NEXT MONTH:
BREAK-INS! BREAK-OUTS! BREAK-UPS! BACK-STABBING! FRONT-STABBING! YOU DON'T WANNA MISS THIS ONE!

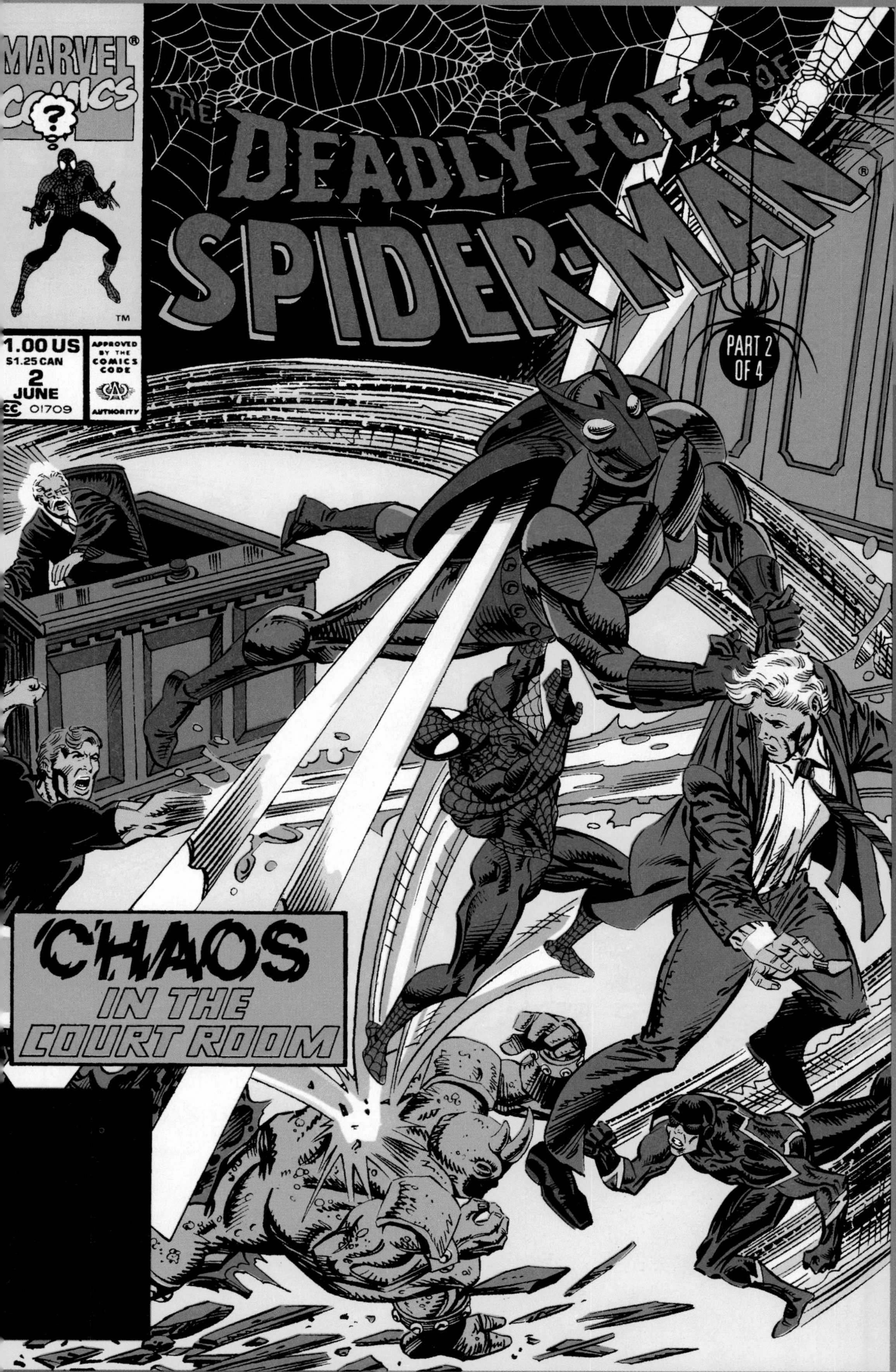

MARVEL® COMICS
?
TM
THE DEADLY FOES OF SPIDER-MAN®
PART 2 OF 4
1.00 US
$1.25 CAN
2
JUNE
01709
APPROVED BY THE COMICS CODE AUTHORITY
CHAOS IN THE COURT ROOM

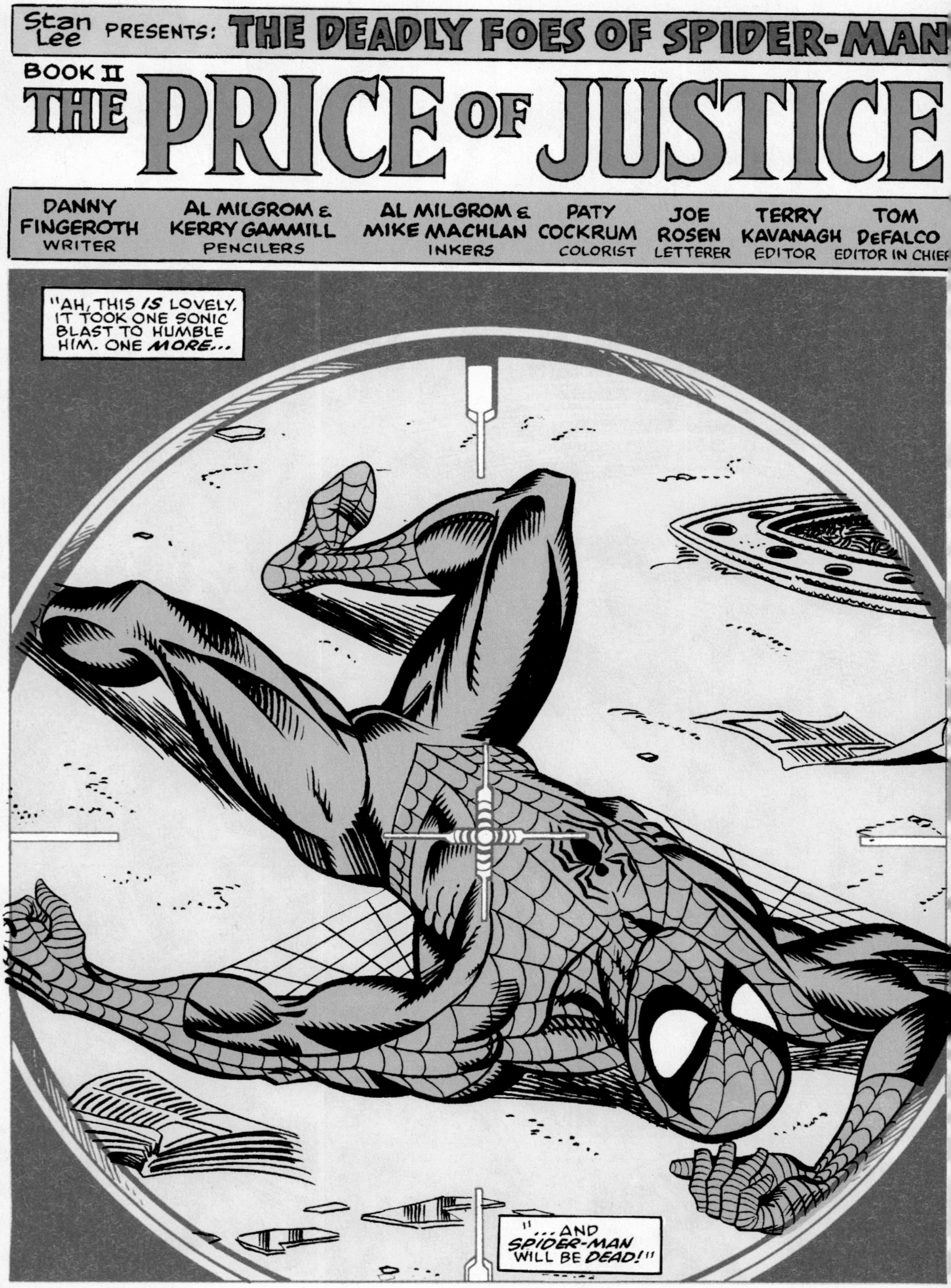
Stan Lee PRESENTS: THE DEADLY FOES OF SPIDER-MAN
BOOK II
THE PRICE OF JUSTICE
DANNY FINGEROTH WRITER
AL MILGROM & KERRY GAMMILL PENCILERS
AL MILGROM & MIKE MACHLAN INKERS
PATY COCKRUM COLORIST
JOE ROSEN LETTERER
TERRY KAVANAGH EDITOR
TOM DeFALCO EDITOR IN CHIEF
"AH, THIS IS LOVELY. IT TOOK ONE SONIC BLAST TO HUMBLE HIM. ONE MORE...
"...AND SPIDER-MAN WILL BE DEAD!"

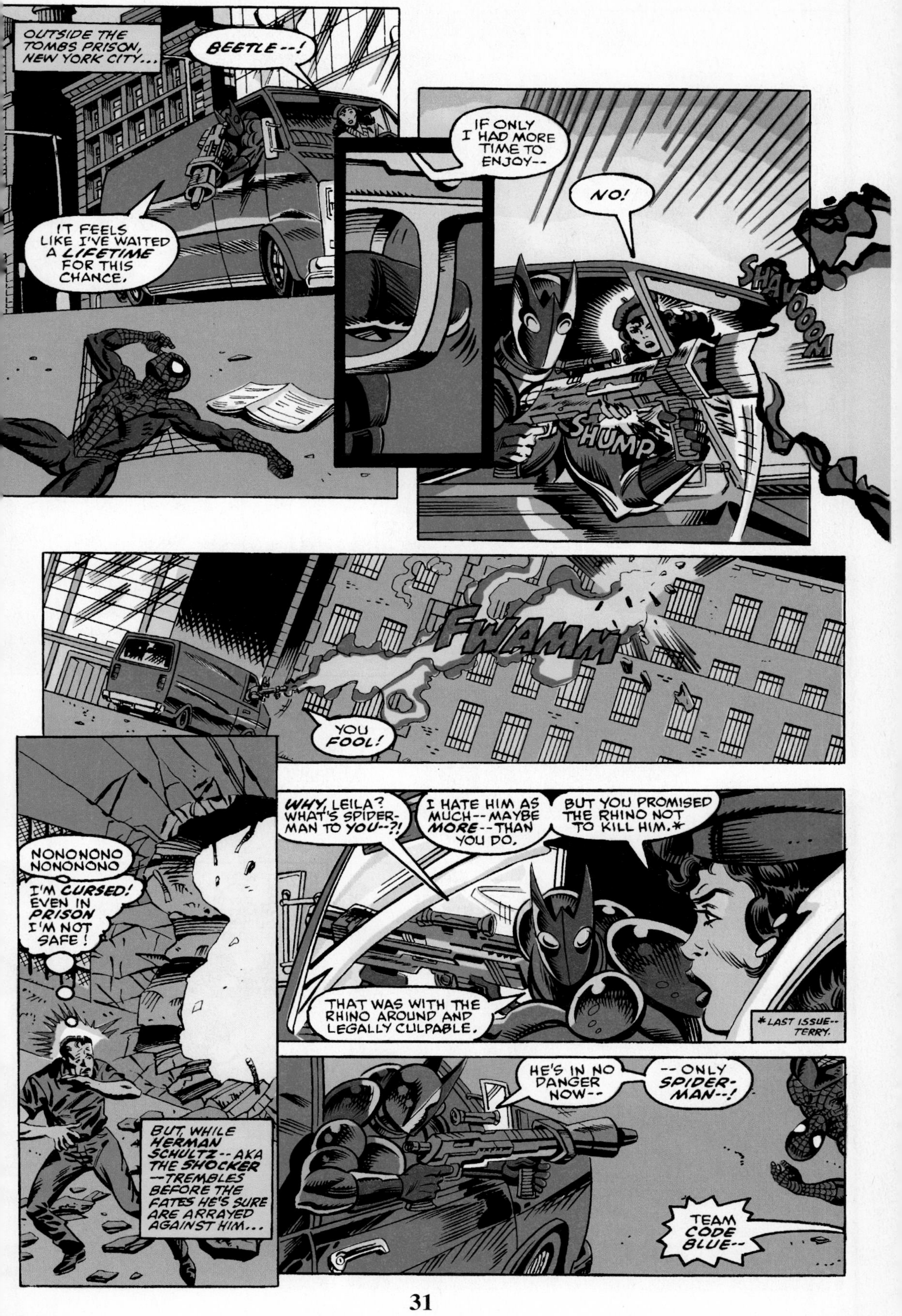
OUTSIDE THE TOMBS PRISON, NEW YORK CITY...
BEETLE--!
IT FEELS LIKE I'VE WAITED A LIFETIME FOR THIS CHANCE.
IF ONLY I HAD MORE TIME TO ENJOY--
NO!
SHAVOOOM
SHUMP
FWAMM
YOU FOOL!
NONONONO NONONONO
I'M CURSED! EVEN IN PRISON I'M NOT SAFE!
BUT, WHILE HERMAN SCHULTZ--AKA THE SHOCKER--TREMBLES BEFORE THE FATES HE'S SURE ARE ARRAYED AGAINST HIM...
WHY, LEILA? WHAT'S SPIDER-MAN TO YOU--?!
I HATE HIM AS MUCH--MAYBE MORE--THAN YOU DO.
BUT YOU PROMISED THE RHINO NOT TO KILL HIM.*
THAT WAS WITH THE RHINO AROUND AND LEGALLY CULPABLE.
*LAST ISSUE--TERRY.
HE'S IN NO DANGER NOW--
--ONLY SPIDER-MAN--!
TEAM CODE BLUE--

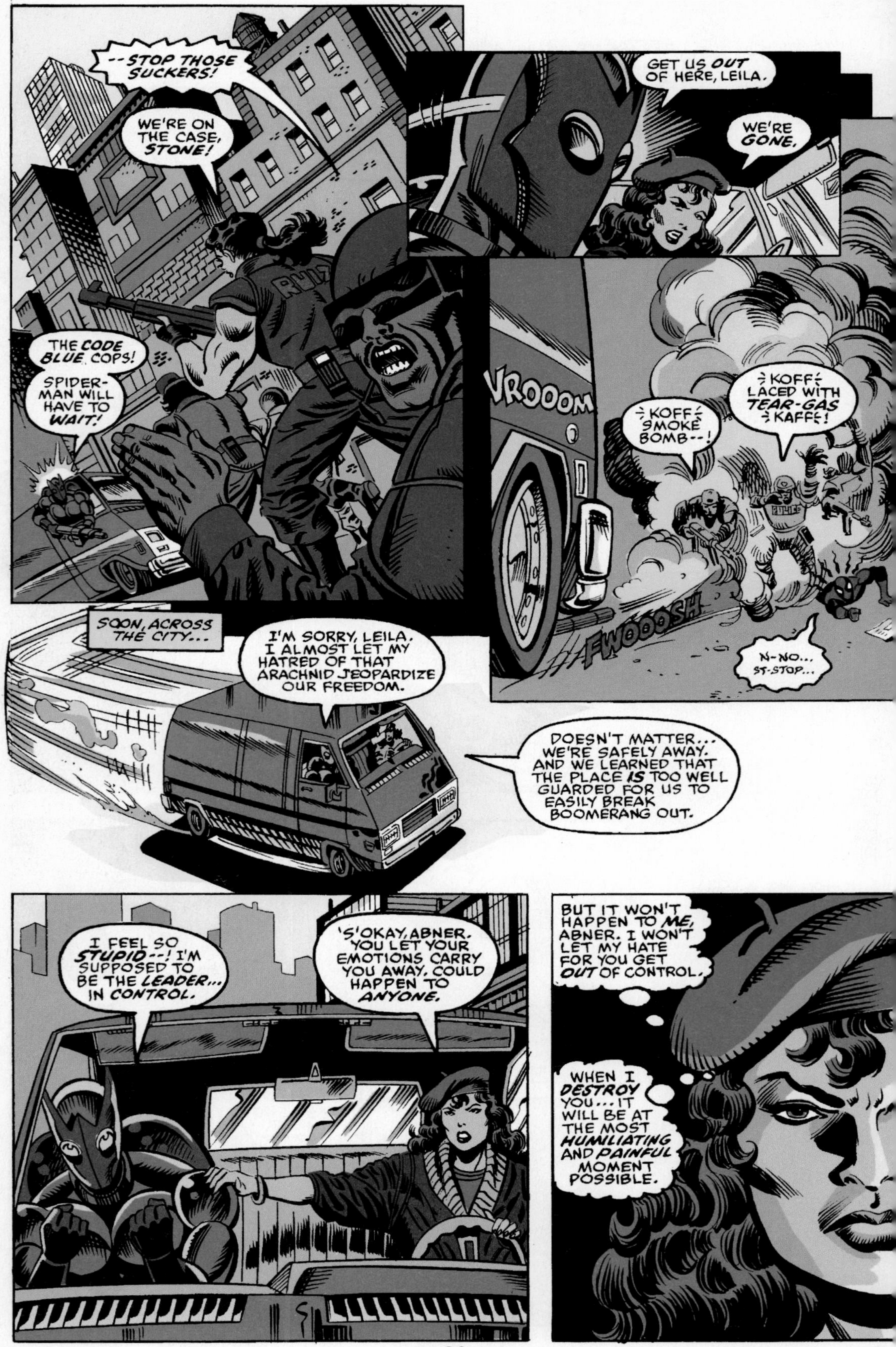
--STOP THOSE SUCKERS!
WE'RE ON THE CASE, STONE!
THE CODE BLUE COPS!
SPIDER-MAN WILL HAVE TO WAIT!
GET US OUT OF HERE, LEILA.
WE'RE GONE.
VROOOM
KOFF SMOKE BOMB--!
KOFF LACED WITH TEAR-GAS KAFF!
FWOOOSH
N-NO... ST-STOP...
SOON, ACROSS THE CITY...
I'M SORRY, LEILA. I ALMOST LET MY HATRED OF THAT ARACHNID JEOPARDIZE OUR FREEDOM.
DOESN'T MATTER... WE'RE SAFELY AWAY. AND WE LEARNED THAT THE PLACE IS TOO WELL GUARDED FOR US TO EASILY BREAK BOOMERANG OUT.
I FEEL SO STUPID--! I'M SUPPOSED TO BE THE LEADER... IN CONTROL.
'S'OKAY, ABNER. YOU LET YOUR EMOTIONS CARRY YOU AWAY. COULD HAPPEN TO ANYONE.
BUT IT WON'T HAPPEN TO ME, ABNER. I WON'T LET MY HATE FOR YOU GET OUT OF CONTROL.
WHEN I DESTROY YOU... IT WILL BE AT THE MOST HUMILIATING AND PAINFUL MOMENT POSSIBLE.

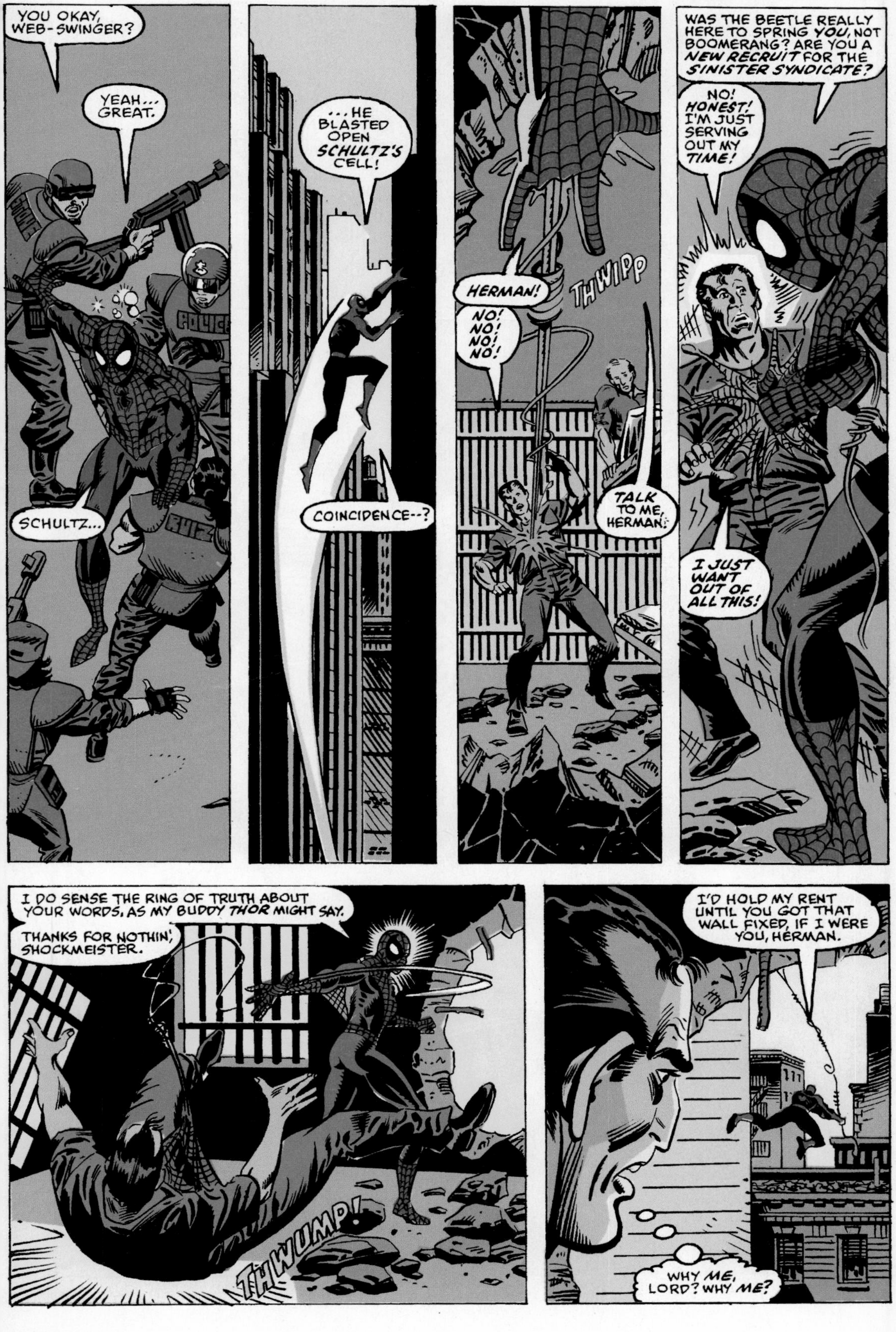
YOU OKAY, WEB-SWINGER?
YEAH... GREAT.
SCHULTZ...
...HE BLASTED OPEN SCHULTZ'S CELL!
COINCIDENCE--?
HERMAN!
NO! NO! NO! NO!
THWIPP
TALK TO ME, HERMAN!
WAS THE BEETLE REALLY HERE TO SPRING YOU, NOT BOOMERANG? ARE YOU A NEW RECRUIT FOR THE SINISTER SYNDICATE?
NO! HONEST! I'M JUST SERVING OUT MY TIME!
I JUST WANT OUT OF ALL THIS!
I DO SENSE THE RING OF TRUTH ABOUT YOUR WORDS, AS MY BUDDY THOR MIGHT SAY.
THANKS FOR NOTHIN', SHOCKMEISTER.
THWUMP!
I'D HOLD MY RENT UNTIL YOU GOT THAT WALL FIXED, IF I WERE YOU, HERMAN.
WHY ME, LORD? WHY ME?

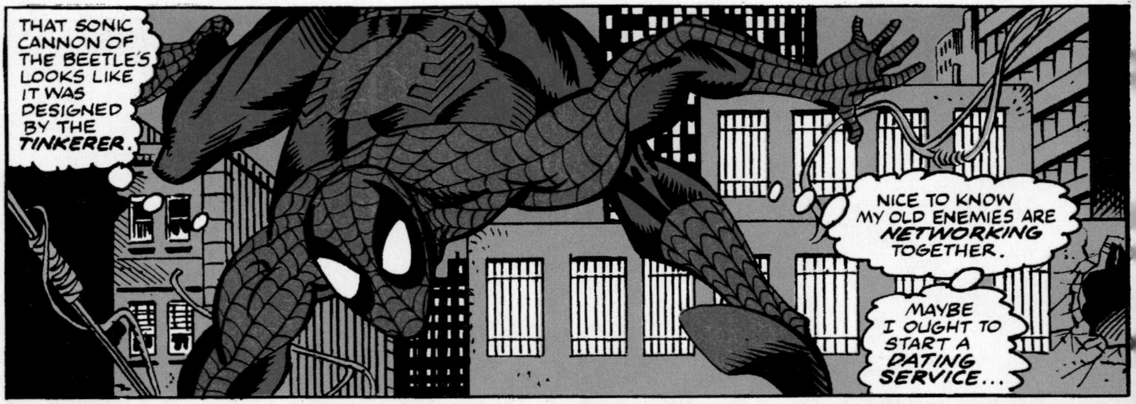
THAT SONIC CANNON OF THE BEETLE'S LOOKS LIKE IT WAS DESIGNED BY THE TINKERER.
NICE TO KNOW MY OLD ENEMIES ARE NETWORKING TOGETHER.
MAYBE I OUGHT TO START A DATING SERVICE...

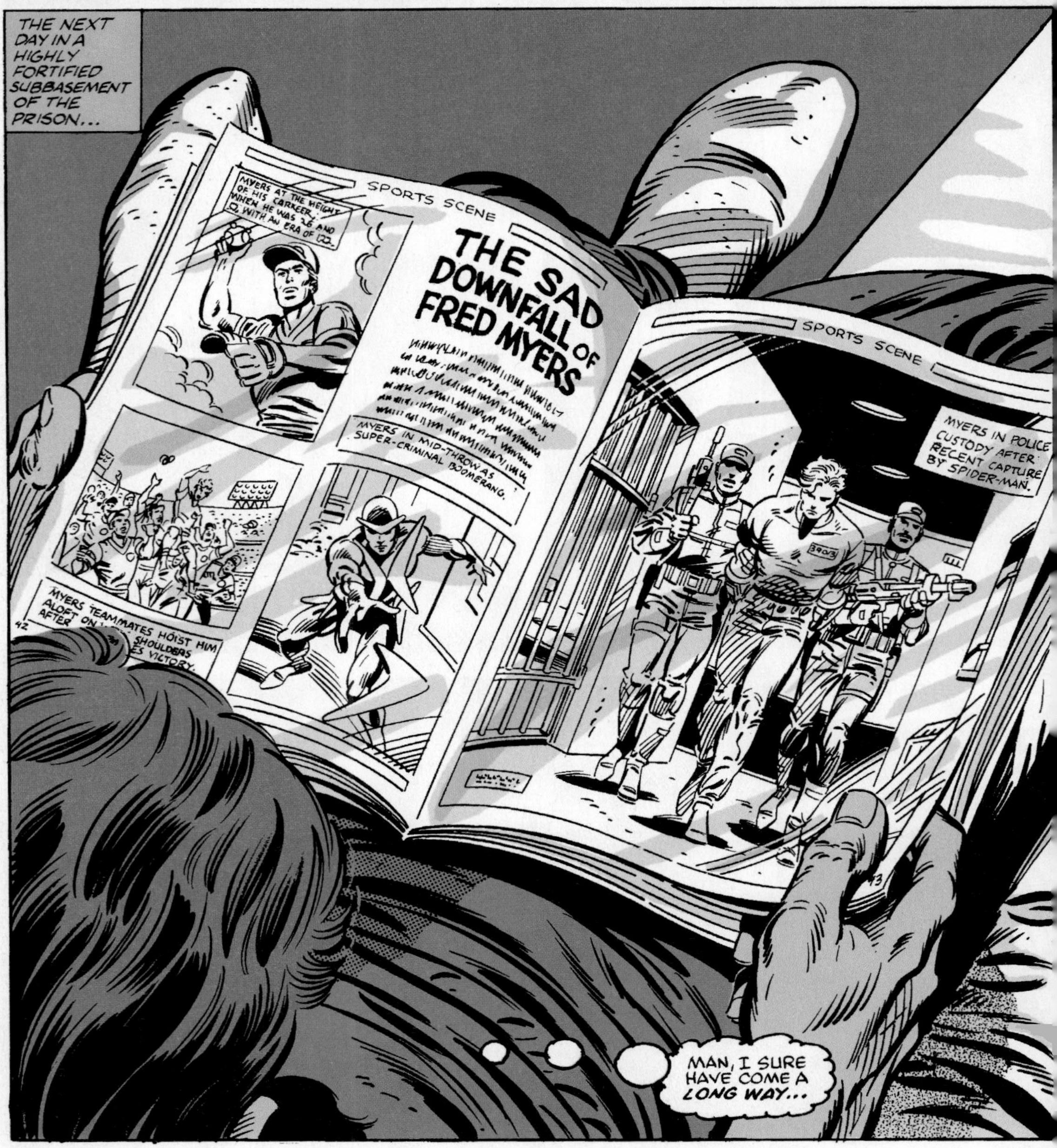
THE NEXT DAY IN A HIGHLY FORTIFIED SUBBASEMENT OF THE PRISON...
SPORTS SCENE
MYERS AT THE HEIGHT OF HIS CARREER, WHEN HE WAS 26 AND
THE SAD DOWNFALL OF FRED MYERS
MYERS IN MID-THROW AS SUPER-CRIMINAL BOOMERANG.
SPORTS SCENE
MYERS IN POLICE CUSTODY AFTER RECENT CAPTURE BY SPIDER-MAN.
MAN, I SURE HAVE COME A LONG WAY...

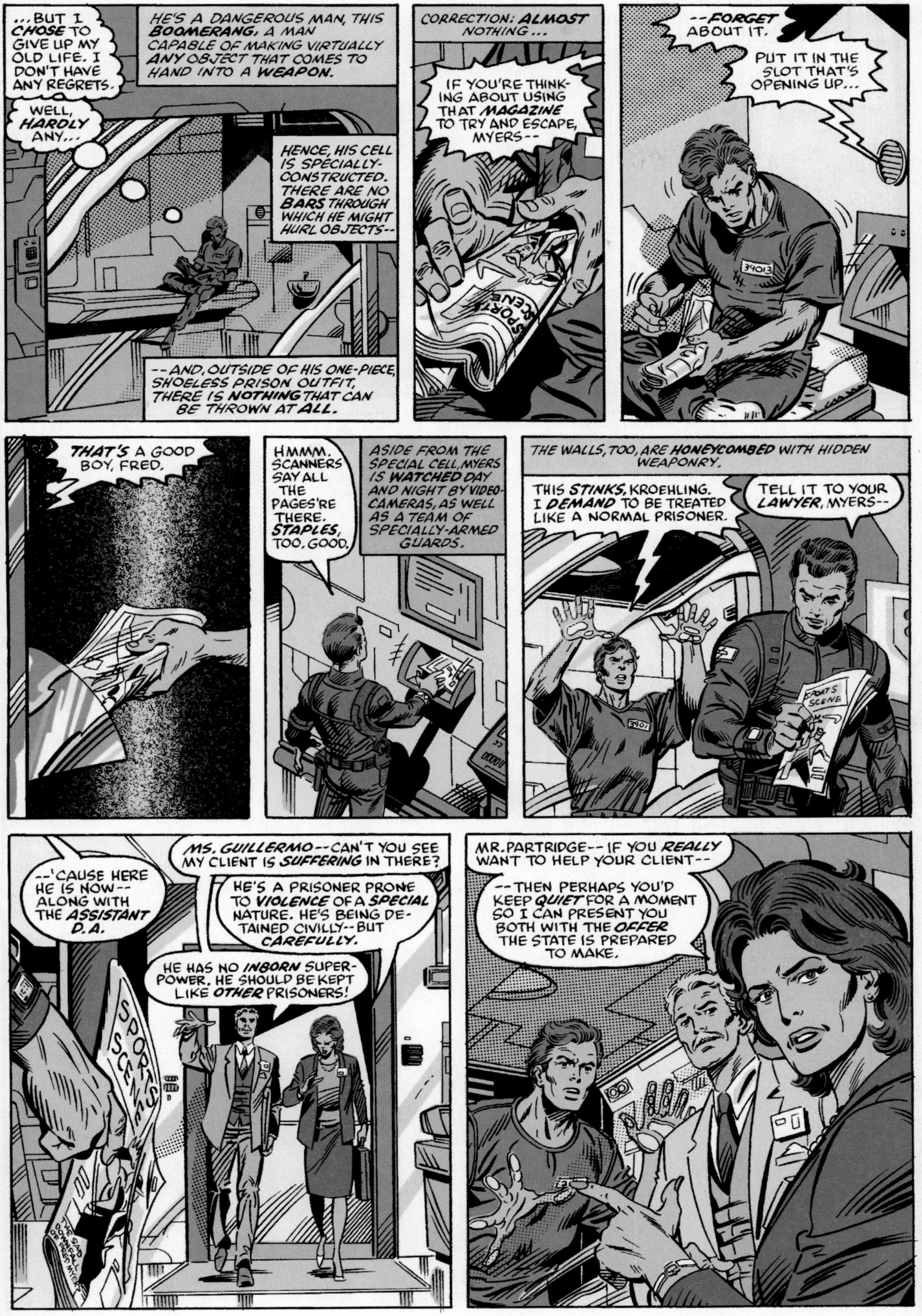

...BUT I CHOSE TO GIVE UP MY OLD LIFE. I DON'T HAVE ANY REGRETS.
HE'S A DANGEROUS MAN, THIS BOOMERANG, A MAN CAPABLE OF MAKING VIRTUALLY ANY OBJECT THAT COMES TO HAND INTO A WEAPON.
WELL, HARDLY ANY...
HENCE, HIS CELL IS SPECIALLY-CONSTRUCTED. THERE ARE NO BARS THROUGH WHICH HE MIGHT HURL OBJECTS--
--AND, OUTSIDE OF HIS ONE-PIECE, SHOELESS PRISON OUTFIT, THERE IS NOTHING THAT CAN BE THROWN AT ALL.
CORRECTION: ALMOST NOTHING...
IF YOU'RE THINKING ABOUT USING THAT MAGAZINE TO TRY AND ESCAPE, MYERS--
SPORTS SCENE
--FORGET ABOUT IT.
PUT IT IN THE SLOT THAT'S OPENING UP...
39013
THAT'S A GOOD BOY, FRED.
HMMM. SCANNERS SAY ALL THE PAGES'RE THERE. STAPLES, TOO. GOOD.
ASIDE FROM THE SPECIAL CELL, MYERS IS WATCHED DAY AND NIGHT BY VIDEO-CAMERAS, AS WELL AS A TEAM OF SPECIALLY-ARMED GUARDS.
THE WALLS, TOO, ARE HONEYCOMBED WITH HIDDEN WEAPONRY.
THIS STINKS, KROEHLING. I DEMAND TO BE TREATED LIKE A NORMAL PRISONER.
TELL IT TO YOUR LAWYER, MYERS--
SPORTS SCENE
--'CAUSE HERE HE IS NOW--ALONG WITH THE ASSISTANT D.A.
MS. GUILLERMO--CAN'T YOU SEE MY CLIENT IS SUFFERING IN THERE?
HE'S A PRISONER PRONE TO VIOLENCE OF A SPECIAL NATURE. HE'S BEING DETAINED CIVILLY--BUT CAREFULLY.
HE HAS NO INBORN SUPER-POWER. HE SHOULD BE KEPT LIKE OTHER PRISONERS!
SPORTS SCENE
MR. PARTRIDGE--IF YOU REALLY WANT TO HELP YOUR CLIENT--
--THEN PERHAPS YOU'D KEEP QUIET FOR A MOMENT SO I CAN PRESENT YOU BOTH WITH THE OFFER THE STATE IS PREPARED TO MAKE.

SIMULTANEOUSLY, IN UPPER MANHATTAN...

NOOOOO!

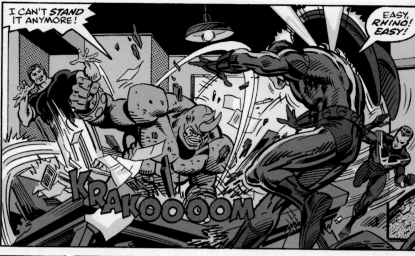

I CAN'T *STAND* IT ANYMORE!

EASY, *RHINO!* EASY!

KRAKOOOOOM

WHY DOES IT HAVE TO BE SO *COMPLI-CATED* TO PLAN A *SIMPLE* HEIST?!

IF YOU THREE WOULD LEAVE THE PLANNING TO *ME*--INSTEAD OF *DOUBLE-CHECKING* EVERY STEP I SUGGEST-- I COULD PLAN OUR JOBS IN A *TENTH* OF THE TIME.

IF YOU HADN'T *BETRAYED* US ON OUR LAST JOB, BEETLE, WE WOULDN'T *HAVE* TA KEEP CHECKIN' UP ON YA.

BUT YA *DID!*

I SCREWED UP. I *ADMIT* IT. I USED OUR TAKE TO PAY OFF A PERSONAL DEBT TO THE *KINGPIN.* BUT THAT PAY-OFF *ALSO* ASSURES THAT WE CAN NOW OPERATE IN THE KINGPIN'S TERRITORY FREE OF INTERFERENCE.

HAH! HE *STILL* GETS 10% OF OUR TAKES!

THAT'S GETTING AWAY *CHEAP* TO HAVE THE FAT MAN ON OUR SIDE, *HYDRO-MAN.*

YOU GUYS ARGUE, I'M GOING INSIDE.

PENNY FOR YOUR THOUGHTS, LEILA...

I MISS FRED *SO,* JAMES. I WISH HE WAS *OUT* ALREADY.

WE'RE TAKING CARE OF IT. YOUR BOY-FRIEND'LL BE FREE SOON.

BUT BY THEN, IF I HAVE MY WAY, YOU'LL BE IN LOVE WITH *ME.*

I DON'T EXPECT YOU TO BE IN *LOVE* WITH THE OFFER, BUT IT'S THE BEST YOU'LL GET: *TELL* US WHERE TO FIND YOUR SYNDICATE TEAMMATES, *TESTIFY* AGAINST THEM--

--AND WE'LL GO EASY ON YOU... GIVE YOU A *NEW NAME* AND *RE-SETTLE* YOU IN ANOTHER STATE.

I.... I DON'T *KNOW,* STEVE...

...WHAT DO *YOU* THINK?

FRED, I'M THE *BEST.* I'LL GET YOU OFF, NO PROBLEM. I'M BET-TING I CAN EVEN GET YOUR *WHOLE RECORD* WIPED *CLEAN.*

DON'T TAKE THE DEAL.

36

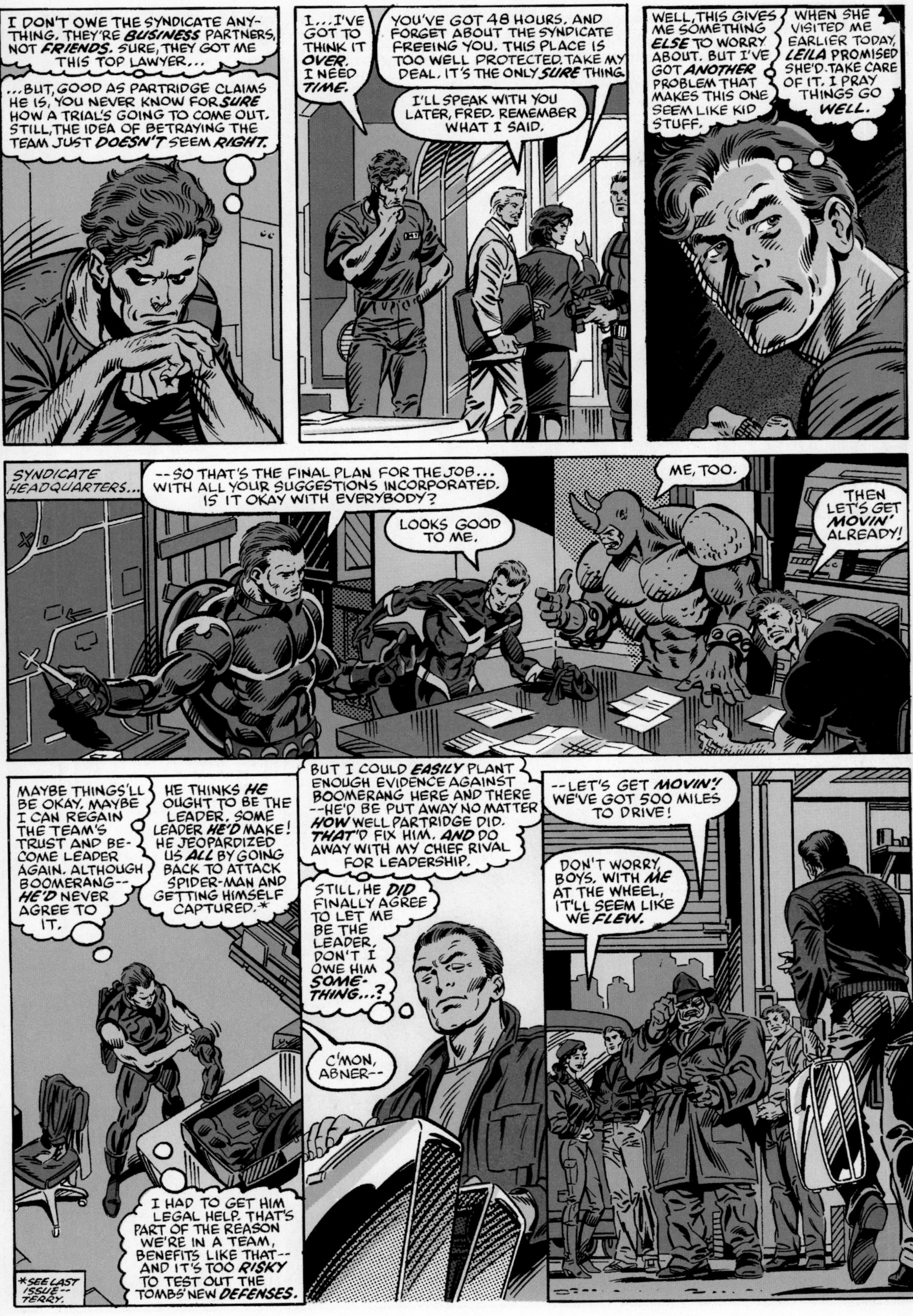
I DON'T OWE THE SYNDICATE ANYTHING. THEY'RE BUSINESS PARTNERS, NOT FRIENDS. SURE, THEY GOT ME THIS TOP LAWYER...
...BUT, GOOD AS PARTRIDGE CLAIMS HE IS, YOU NEVER KNOW FOR SURE HOW A TRIAL'S GOING TO COME OUT. STILL, THE IDEA OF BETRAYING THE TEAM JUST DOESN'T SEEM RIGHT.
I...I'VE GOT TO THINK IT OVER. I NEED TIME.
YOU'VE GOT 48 HOURS, AND FORGET ABOUT THE SYNDICATE FREEING YOU. THIS PLACE IS TOO WELL PROTECTED. TAKE MY DEAL. IT'S THE ONLY SURE THING.
I'LL SPEAK WITH YOU LATER, FRED. REMEMBER WHAT I SAID.
WELL, THIS GIVES ME SOMETHING ELSE TO WORRY ABOUT. BUT I'VE GOT ANOTHER PROBLEM THAT MAKES THIS ONE SEEM LIKE KID STUFF.
WHEN SHE VISITED ME EARLIER TODAY, LEILA PROMISED SHE'D TAKE CARE OF IT. I PRAY THINGS GO WELL.
SYNDICATE HEADQUARTERS...
--SO THAT'S THE FINAL PLAN FOR THE JOB... WITH ALL YOUR SUGGESTIONS INCORPORATED. IS IT OKAY WITH EVERYBODY?
LOOKS GOOD TO ME.
ME, TOO.
THEN LET'S GET MOVIN' ALREADY!
MAYBE THINGS'LL BE OKAY. MAYBE I CAN REGAIN THE TEAM'S TRUST AND BECOME LEADER AGAIN. ALTHOUGH BOOMERANG--HE'D NEVER AGREE TO IT.
HE THINKS HE OUGHT TO BE THE LEADER. SOME LEADER HE'D MAKE! HE JEOPARDIZED US ALL BY GOING BACK TO ATTACK SPIDER-MAN AND GETTING HIMSELF CAPTURED.*
I HAD TO GET HIM LEGAL HELP. THAT'S PART OF THE REASON WE'RE IN A TEAM, BENEFITS LIKE THAT--AND IT'S TOO RISKY TO TEST OUT THE TOMBS' NEW DEFENSES.
*SEE LAST ISSUE--TERRY.
BUT I COULD EASILY PLANT ENOUGH EVIDENCE AGAINST BOOMERANG HERE AND THERE--HE'D BE PUT AWAY NO MATTER HOW WELL PARTRIDGE DID. THAT'D FIX HIM. AND DO AWAY WITH MY CHIEF RIVAL FOR LEADERSHIP.
STILL, HE DID FINALLY AGREE TO LET ME BE THE LEADER. DON'T I OWE HIM SOMETHING...?
C'MON, ABNER--
--LET'S GET MOVIN'! WE'VE GOT 500 MILES TO DRIVE!
DON'T WORRY, BOYS. WITH ME AT THE WHEEL, IT'LL SEEM LIKE WE FLEW.

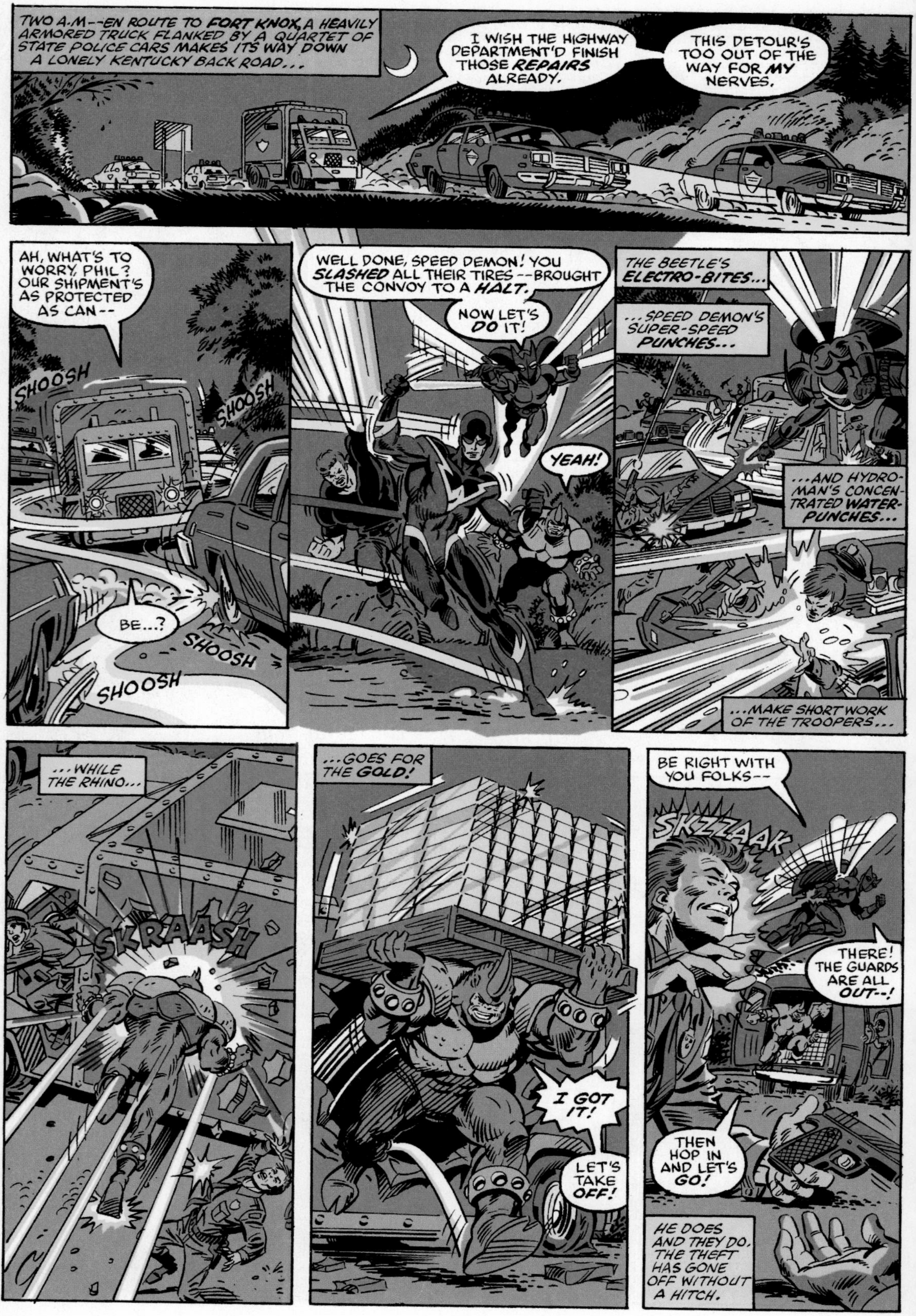
TWO A.M.--EN ROUTE TO FORT KNOX, A HEAVILY ARMORED TRUCK FLANKED BY A QUARTET OF STATE POLICE CARS MAKES ITS WAY DOWN A LONELY KENTUCKY BACK ROAD...
I WISH THE HIGHWAY DEPARTMENT'D FINISH THOSE REPAIRS ALREADY.
THIS DETOUR'S TOO OUT OF THE WAY FOR MY NERVES.
AH, WHAT'S TO WORRY, PHIL? OUR SHIPMENT'S AS PROTECTED AS CAN--
SHOOSH
SHOOSH
BE...?
SHOOSH
SHOOSH
WELL DONE, SPEED DEMON! YOU SLASHED ALL THEIR TIRES--BROUGHT THE CONVOY TO A HALT.
NOW LET'S DO IT!
YEAH!
THE BEETLE'S ELECTRO-BITES...
...SPEED DEMON'S SUPER-SPEED PUNCHES...
...AND HYDRO-MAN'S CONCENTRATED WATER-PUNCHES...
...MAKE SHORT WORK OF THE TROOPERS...
...WHILE THE RHINO...
SKRAASH
...GOES FOR THE GOLD!
I GOT IT!
LET'S TAKE OFF!
BE RIGHT WITH YOU FOLKS--
SKZZAAK
THERE! THE GUARDS ARE ALL OUT--!
THEN HOP IN AND LET'S GO!
HE DOES AND THEY DO. THE THEFT HAS GONE OFF WITHOUT A HITCH.

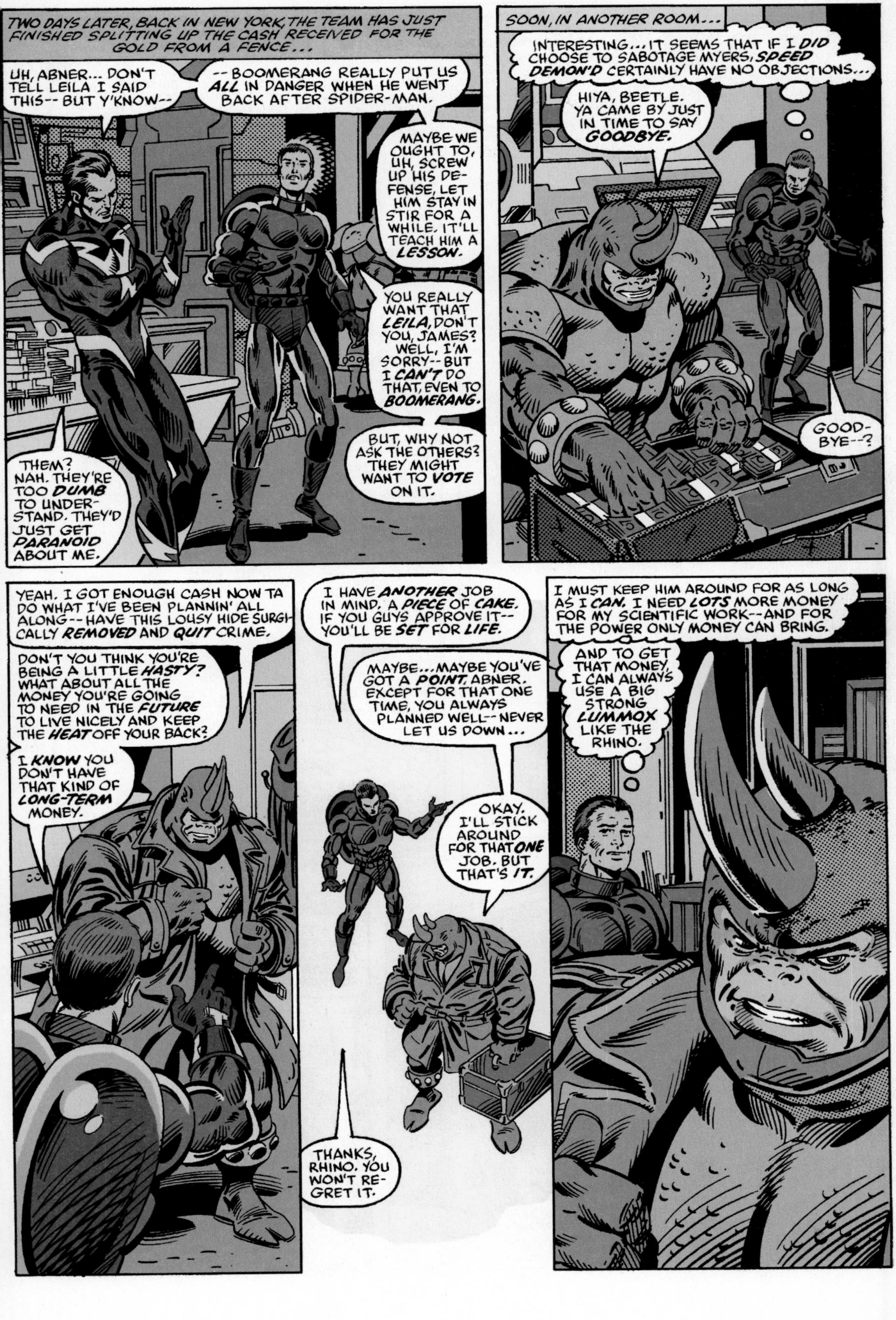
TWO DAYS LATER, BACK IN NEW YORK, THE TEAM HAS JUST FINISHED SPLITTING UP THE CASH RECEIVED FOR THE GOLD FROM A FENCE...
UH, ABNER... DON'T TELL LEILA I SAID THIS-- BUT Y'KNOW--
--BOOMERANG REALLY PUT US ALL IN DANGER WHEN HE WENT BACK AFTER SPIDER-MAN.
MAYBE WE OUGHT TO, UH, SCREW UP HIS DEFENSE, LET HIM STAY IN STIR FOR A WHILE. IT'LL TEACH HIM A LESSON.
YOU REALLY WANT THAT LEILA, DON'T YOU, JAMES? WELL, I'M SORRY-- BUT I CAN'T DO THAT, EVEN TO BOOMERANG.
BUT, WHY NOT ASK THE OTHERS? THEY MIGHT WANT TO VOTE ON IT.
THEM? NAH. THEY'RE TOO DUMB TO UNDERSTAND. THEY'D JUST GET PARANOID ABOUT ME.
SOON, IN ANOTHER ROOM...
INTERESTING... IT SEEMS THAT IF I DID CHOOSE TO SABOTAGE MYERS, SPEED DEMON'D CERTAINLY HAVE NO OBJECTIONS...
HIYA, BEETLE. YA CAME BY JUST IN TIME TO SAY GOODBYE.
GOOD-BYE--?
YEAH. I GOT ENOUGH CASH NOW TA DO WHAT I'VE BEEN PLANNIN' ALL ALONG-- HAVE THIS LOUSY HIDE SURGICALLY REMOVED AND QUIT CRIME.
DON'T YOU THINK YOU'RE BEING A LITTLE HASTY? WHAT ABOUT ALL THE MONEY YOU'RE GOING TO NEED IN THE FUTURE TO LIVE NICELY AND KEEP THE HEAT OFF YOUR BACK?
I KNOW YOU DON'T HAVE THAT KIND OF LONG-TERM MONEY.
I HAVE ANOTHER JOB IN MIND. A PIECE OF CAKE. IF YOU GUYS APPROVE IT-- YOU'LL BE SET FOR LIFE.
MAYBE... MAYBE YOU'VE GOT A POINT, ABNER. EXCEPT FOR THAT ONE TIME, YOU ALWAYS PLANNED WELL-- NEVER LET US DOWN...
OKAY. I'LL STICK AROUND FOR THAT ONE JOB. BUT THAT'S IT.
THANKS, RHINO. YOU WON'T REGRET IT.
I MUST KEEP HIM AROUND FOR AS LONG AS I CAN. I NEED LOTS MORE MONEY FOR MY SCIENTIFIC WORK--AND FOR THE POWER ONLY MONEY CAN BRING.
AND TO GET THAT MONEY, I CAN ALWAYS USE A BIG STRONG LUMMOX LIKE THE RHINO.

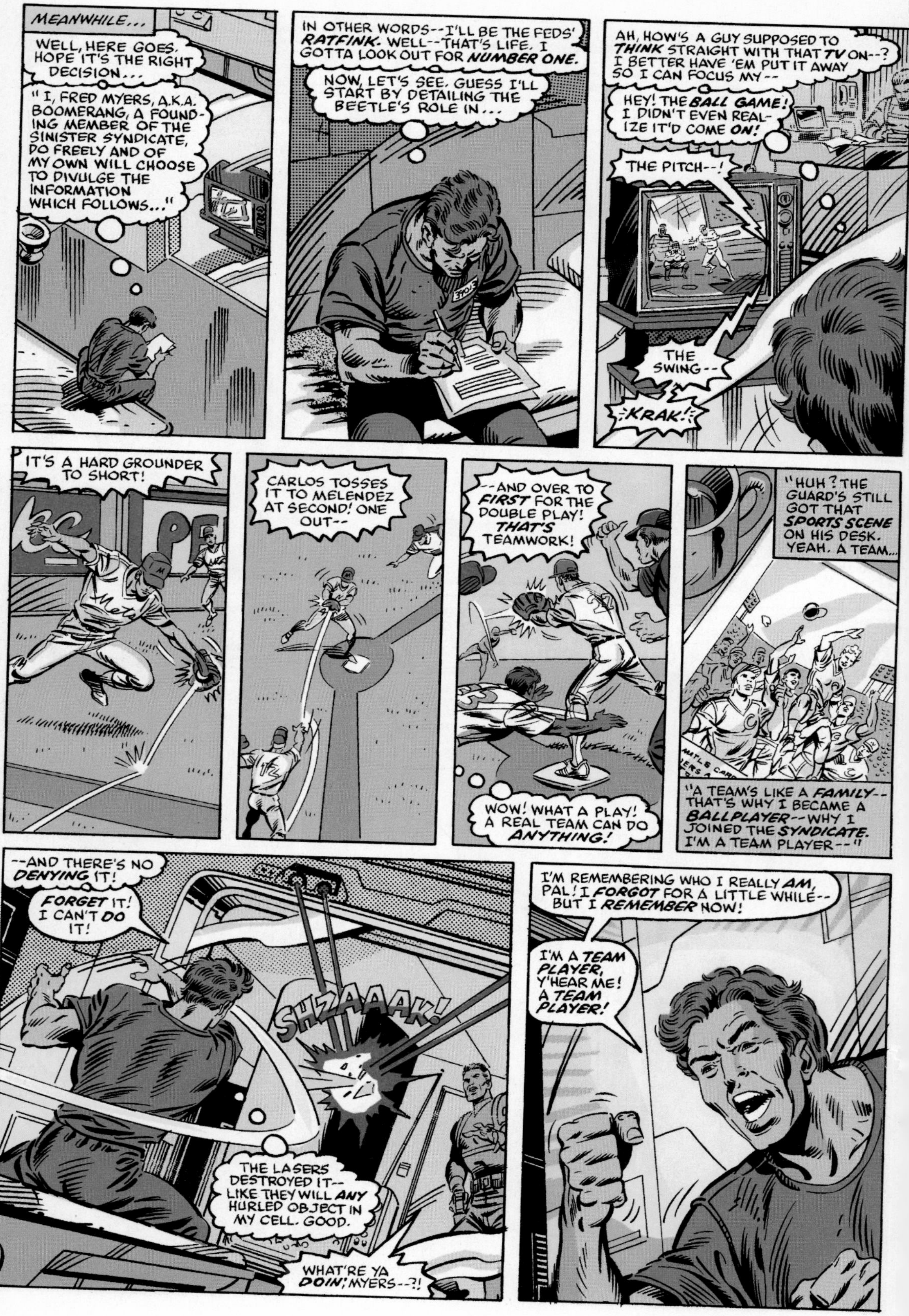
MEANWHILE...
WELL, HERE GOES. HOPE IT'S THE RIGHT DECISION...
"I, FRED MYERS, A.K.A. BOOMERANG, A FOUNDING MEMBER OF THE SINISTER SYNDICATE, DO FREELY AND OF MY OWN WILL CHOOSE TO DIVULGE THE INFORMATION WHICH FOLLOWS..."
IN OTHER WORDS--I'LL BE THE FEDS' RATFINK. WELL--THAT'S LIFE. I GOTTA LOOK OUT FOR NUMBER ONE.
NOW, LET'S SEE. GUESS I'LL START BY DETAILING THE BEETLE'S ROLE IN...
AH, HOW'S A GUY SUPPOSED TO THINK STRAIGHT WITH THAT TV ON--? I BETTER HAVE 'EM PUT IT AWAY SO I CAN FOCUS MY--
HEY! THE BALL GAME! I DIDN'T EVEN REALIZE IT'D COME ON!
THE PITCH--!
THE SWING--
KRAK!
IT'S A HARD GROUNDER TO SHORT!
CARLOS TOSSES IT TO MELENDEZ AT SECOND! ONE OUT--
--AND OVER TO FIRST FOR THE DOUBLE PLAY! THAT'S TEAMWORK!
WOW! WHAT A PLAY! A REAL TEAM CAN DO ANYTHING!
"HUH? THE GUARD'S STILL GOT THAT SPORTS SCENE ON HIS DESK. YEAH. A TEAM...
"A TEAM'S LIKE A FAMILY--THAT'S WHY I BECAME A BALLPLAYER--WHY I JOINED THE SYNDICATE. I'M A TEAM PLAYER--"
--AND THERE'S NO DENYING IT!
FORGET IT! I CAN'T DO IT!
SHZAAAAK!
THE LASERS DESTROYED IT--LIKE THEY WILL ANY HURLED OBJECT IN MY CELL. GOOD.
WHAT'RE YA DOIN', MYERS--?!
I'M REMEMBERING WHO I REALLY AM, PAL! I FORGOT FOR A LITTLE WHILE--BUT I REMEMBER NOW!
I'M A TEAM PLAYER, Y'HEAR ME! A TEAM PLAYER!

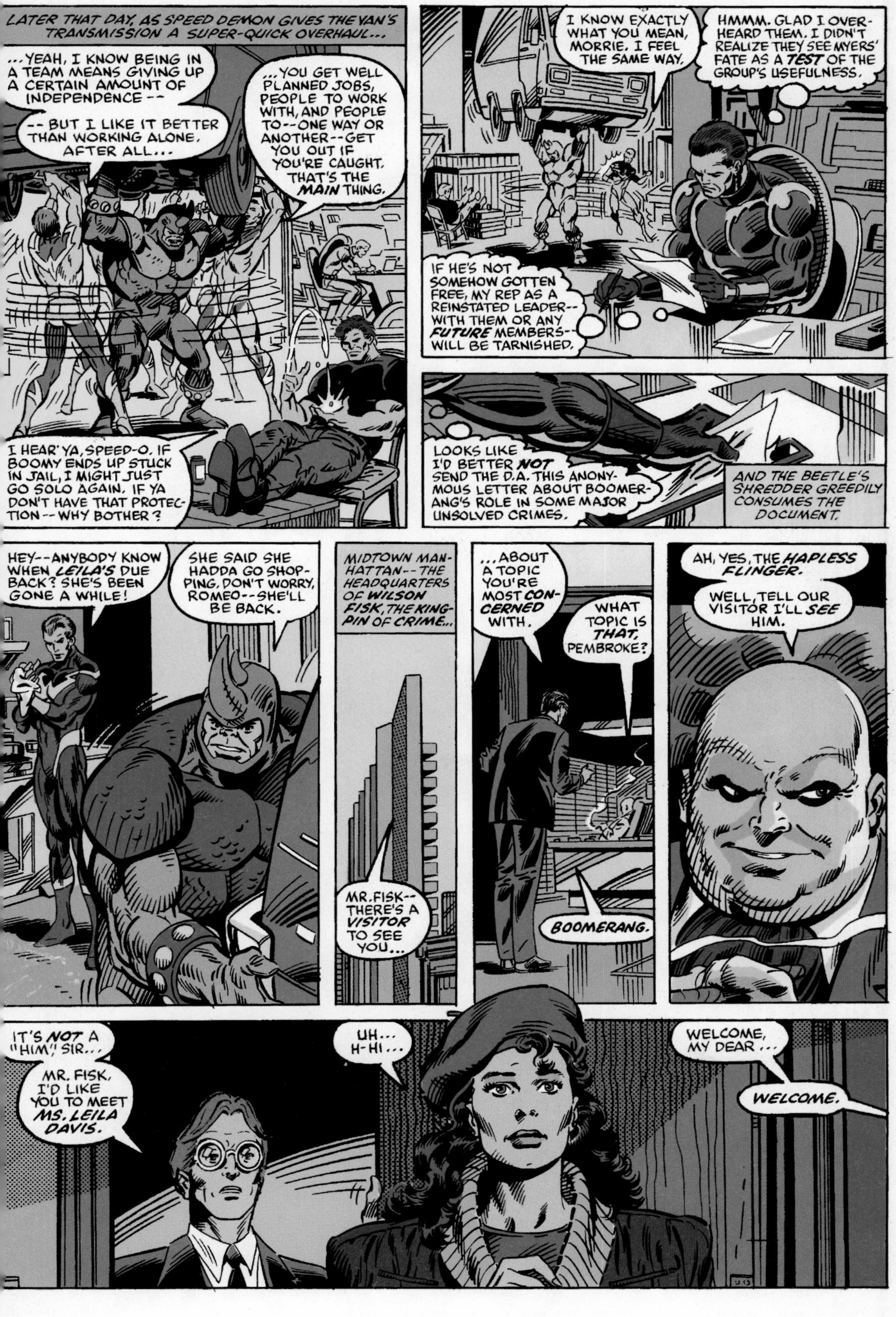
LATER THAT DAY, AS SPEED DEMON GIVES THE VAN'S TRANSMISSION A SUPER-QUICK OVERHAUL...
...YEAH, I KNOW BEING IN A TEAM MEANS GIVING UP A CERTAIN AMOUNT OF INDEPENDENCE --
-- BUT I LIKE IT BETTER THAN WORKING ALONE, AFTER ALL...
...YOU GET WELL PLANNED JOBS, PEOPLE TO WORK WITH, AND PEOPLE TO--ONE WAY OR ANOTHER--GET YOU OUT IF YOU'RE CAUGHT. THAT'S THE MAIN THING.
I HEAR' YA, SPEED-O. IF BOOMY ENDS UP STUCK IN JAIL, I MIGHT JUST GO SOLO AGAIN. IF YA DON'T HAVE THAT PROTECTION -- WHY BOTHER?
I KNOW EXACTLY WHAT YOU MEAN, MORRIE. I FEEL THE SAME WAY.
HMMM. GLAD I OVERHEARD THEM. I DIDN'T REALIZE THEY SEE MYERS' FATE AS A TEST OF THE GROUP'S USEFULNESS.
IF HE'S NOT SOMEHOW GOTTEN FREE, MY REP AS A REINSTATED LEADER--WITH THEM OR ANY FUTURE MEMBERS--WILL BE TARNISHED.
LOOKS LIKE I'D BETTER NOT SEND THE D.A. THIS ANONYMOUS LETTER ABOUT BOOMERANG'S ROLE IN SOME MAJOR UNSOLVED CRIMES.
AND THE BEETLE'S SHREDDER GREEDILY CONSUMES THE DOCUMENT.
HEY--ANYBODY KNOW WHEN LEILA'S DUE BACK? SHE'S BEEN GONE A WHILE!
SHE SAID SHE HADDA GO SHOPPING. DON'T WORRY, ROMEO--SHE'LL BE BACK.
MIDTOWN MANHATTAN--THE HEADQUARTERS OF WILSON FISK, THE KINGPIN OF CRIME...
MR. FISK--THERE'S A VISITOR TO SEE YOU...
...ABOUT A TOPIC YOU'RE MOST CONCERNED WITH.
WHAT TOPIC IS THAT, PEMBROKE?
BOOMERANG.
AH, YES, THE HAPLESS FLINGER.
WELL, TELL OUR VISITOR I'LL SEE HIM.
IT'S NOT A "HIM," SIR...
MR. FISK, I'D LIKE YOU TO MEET MS. LEILA DAVIS.
UH... H-HI...
WELCOME, MY DEAR...
WELCOME.

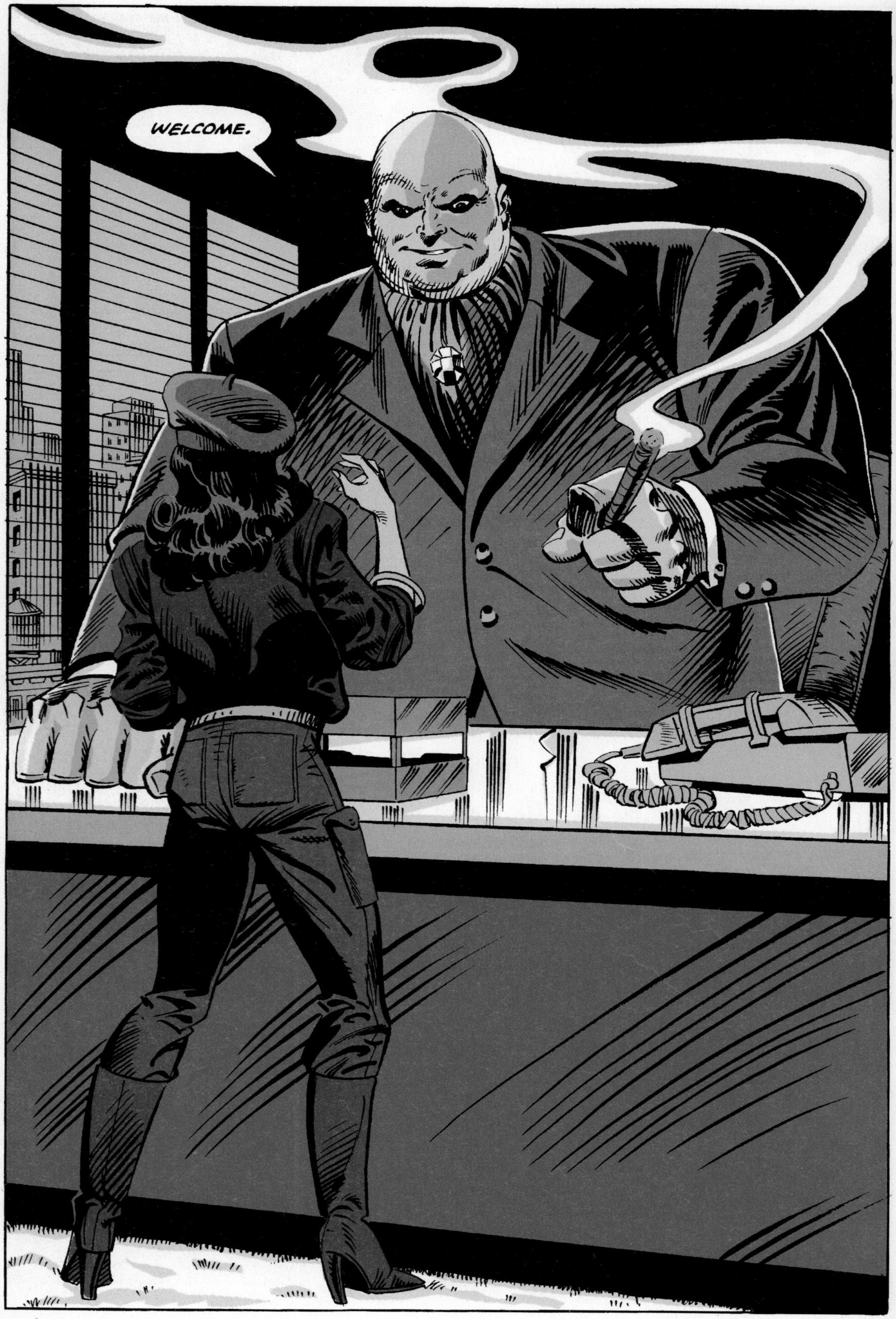
WELCOME.

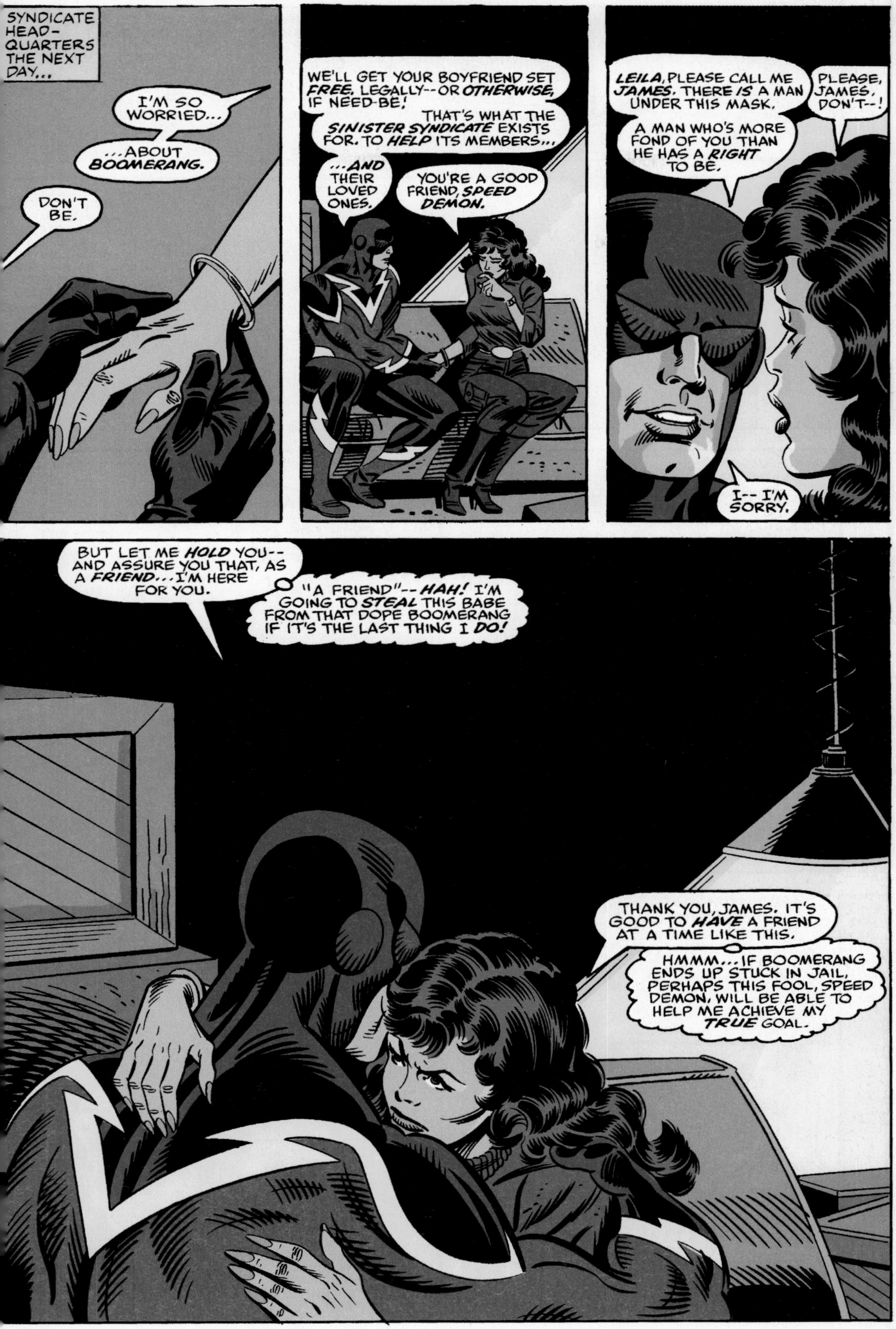
SYNDICATE HEAD-QUARTERS THE NEXT DAY...
I'M SO WORRIED...
...ABOUT BOOMERANG.
DON'T BE.
WE'LL GET YOUR BOYFRIEND SET FREE. LEGALLY--OR OTHERWISE, IF NEED-BE!
THAT'S WHAT THE SINISTER SYNDICATE EXISTS FOR. TO HELP ITS MEMBERS...
...AND THEIR LOVED ONES.
YOU'RE A GOOD FRIEND, SPEED DEMON.
LEILA, PLEASE CALL ME JAMES. THERE IS A MAN UNDER THIS MASK.
A MAN WHO'S MORE FOND OF YOU THAN HE HAS A RIGHT TO BE.
PLEASE, JAMES, DON'T--!
I-- I'M SORRY.
BUT LET ME HOLD YOU--AND ASSURE YOU THAT, AS A FRIEND... I'M HERE FOR YOU.
"A FRIEND"--HAH! I'M GOING TO STEAL THIS BABE FROM THAT DOPE BOOMERANG IF IT'S THE LAST THING I DO!
THANK YOU, JAMES. IT'S GOOD TO HAVE A FRIEND AT A TIME LIKE THIS.
HMMM... IF BOOMERANG ENDS UP STUCK IN JAIL, PERHAPS THIS FOOL, SPEED DEMON, WILL BE ABLE TO HELP ME ACHIEVE MY TRUE GOAL.

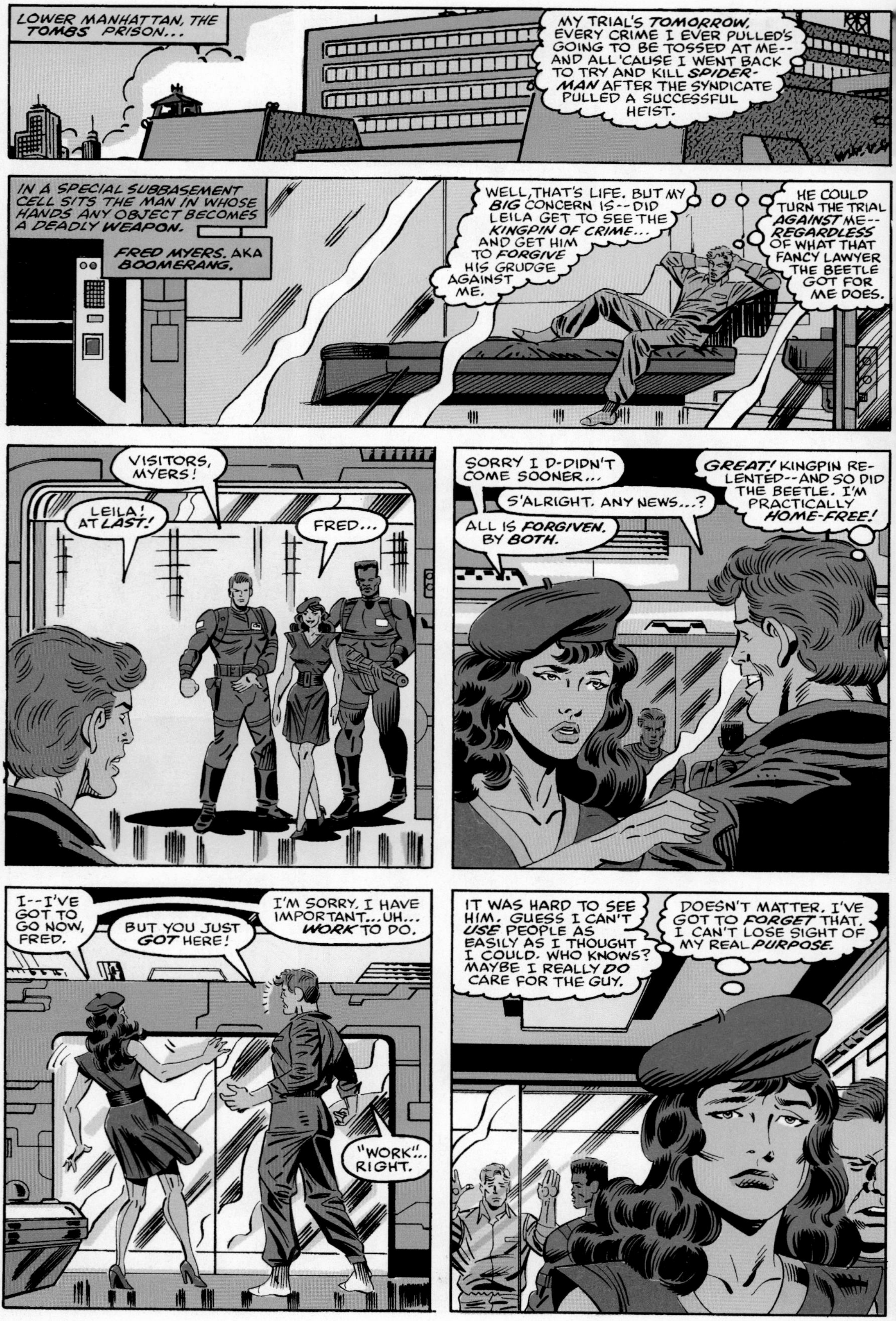
LOWER MANHATTAN, THE TOMBS PRISON...
MY TRIAL'S TOMORROW. EVERY CRIME I EVER PULLED'S GOING TO BE TOSSED AT ME-- AND ALL 'CAUSE I WENT BACK TO TRY AND KILL SPIDER-MAN AFTER THE SYNDICATE PULLED A SUCCESSFUL HEIST.
IN A SPECIAL SUBBASEMENT CELL SITS THE MAN IN WHOSE HANDS ANY OBJECT BECOMES A DEADLY WEAPON.
FRED MYERS, AKA BOOMERANG.
WELL, THAT'S LIFE. BUT MY BIG CONCERN IS--DID LEILA GET TO SEE THE KINGPIN OF CRIME... AND GET HIM TO FORGIVE HIS GRUDGE AGAINST ME.
HE COULD TURN THE TRIAL AGAINST ME-- REGARDLESS OF WHAT THAT FANCY LAWYER THE BEETLE GOT FOR ME DOES.
VISITORS, MYERS!
LEILA! AT LAST!
FRED...
SORRY I D-DIDN'T COME SOONER...
S'ALRIGHT. ANY NEWS...?
ALL IS FORGIVEN. BY BOTH.
GREAT! KINGPIN RE-LENTED--AND SO DID THE BEETLE. I'M PRACTICALLY HOME-FREE!
I--I'VE GOT TO GO NOW, FRED.
BUT YOU JUST GOT HERE!
I'M SORRY. I HAVE IMPORTANT...UH... WORK TO DO.
"WORK"... RIGHT.
IT WAS HARD TO SEE HIM. GUESS I CAN'T USE PEOPLE AS EASILY AS I THOUGHT I COULD. WHO KNOWS? MAYBE I REALLY DO CARE FOR THE GUY.
DOESN'T MATTER. I'VE GOT TO FORGET THAT. I CAN'T LOSE SIGHT OF MY REAL PURPOSE.

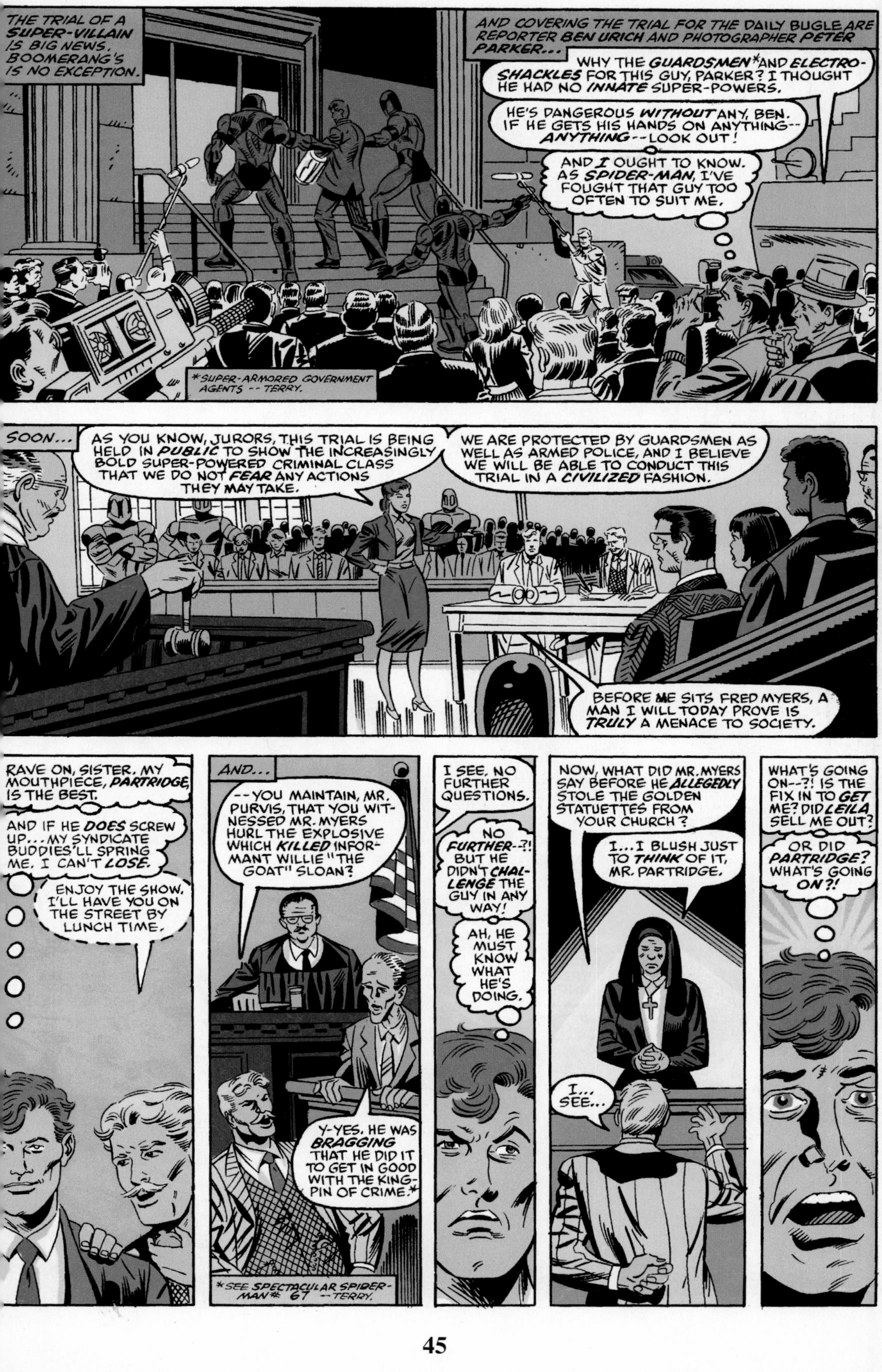
THE TRIAL OF A SUPER-VILLAIN IS BIG NEWS. BOOMERANG'S IS NO EXCEPTION.
AND COVERING THE TRIAL FOR THE DAILY BUGLE ARE REPORTER BEN URICH AND PHOTOGRAPHER PETER PARKER...
WHY THE GUARDSMEN* AND ELECTRO-SHACKLES FOR THIS GUY, PARKER? I THOUGHT HE HAD NO INNATE SUPER-POWERS.
HE'S DANGEROUS WITHOUT ANY, BEN. IF HE GETS HIS HANDS ON ANYTHING-- ANYTHING--LOOK OUT!
AND I OUGHT TO KNOW. AS SPIDER-MAN, I'VE FOUGHT THAT GUY TOO OFTEN TO SUIT ME.
*SUPER-ARMORED GOVERNMENT AGENTS --TERRY.
SOON...
AS YOU KNOW, JURORS, THIS TRIAL IS BEING HELD IN PUBLIC TO SHOW THE INCREASINGLY BOLD SUPER-POWERED CRIMINAL CLASS THAT WE DO NOT FEAR ANY ACTIONS THEY MAY TAKE.
WE ARE PROTECTED BY GUARDSMEN AS WELL AS ARMED POLICE, AND I BELIEVE WE WILL BE ABLE TO CONDUCT THIS TRIAL IN A CIVILIZED FASHION.
BEFORE ME SITS FRED MYERS, A MAN I WILL TODAY PROVE IS TRULY A MENACE TO SOCIETY.
RAVE ON, SISTER. MY MOUTHPIECE, PARTRIDGE, IS THE BEST.
AND IF HE DOES SCREW UP... MY SYNDICATE BUDDIES'LL SPRING ME. I CAN'T LOSE.
ENJOY THE SHOW. I'LL HAVE YOU ON THE STREET BY LUNCH TIME.
AND...
--YOU MAINTAIN, MR. PURVIS, THAT YOU WITNESSED MR. MYERS HURL THE EXPLOSIVE WHICH KILLED INFORMANT WILLIE "THE GOAT" SLOAN?
Y-YES. HE WAS BRAGGING THAT HE DID IT TO GET IN GOOD WITH THE KINGPIN OF CRIME.*
*SEE SPECTACULAR SPIDER-MAN #67 --TERRY.
I SEE. NO FURTHER QUESTIONS.
NO FURTHER--?! BUT HE DIDN'T CHALLENGE THE GUY IN ANY WAY!
AH, HE MUST KNOW WHAT HE'S DOING.
NOW, WHAT DID MR. MYERS SAY BEFORE HE ALLEGEDLY STOLE THE GOLDEN STATUETTES FROM YOUR CHURCH?
I... I BLUSH JUST TO THINK OF IT, MR. PARTRIDGE.
I... SEE...
WHAT'S GOING ON--?! IS THE FIX IN TO GET ME? DID LEILA SELL ME OUT?
OR DID PARTRIDGE? WHAT'S GOING ON?!

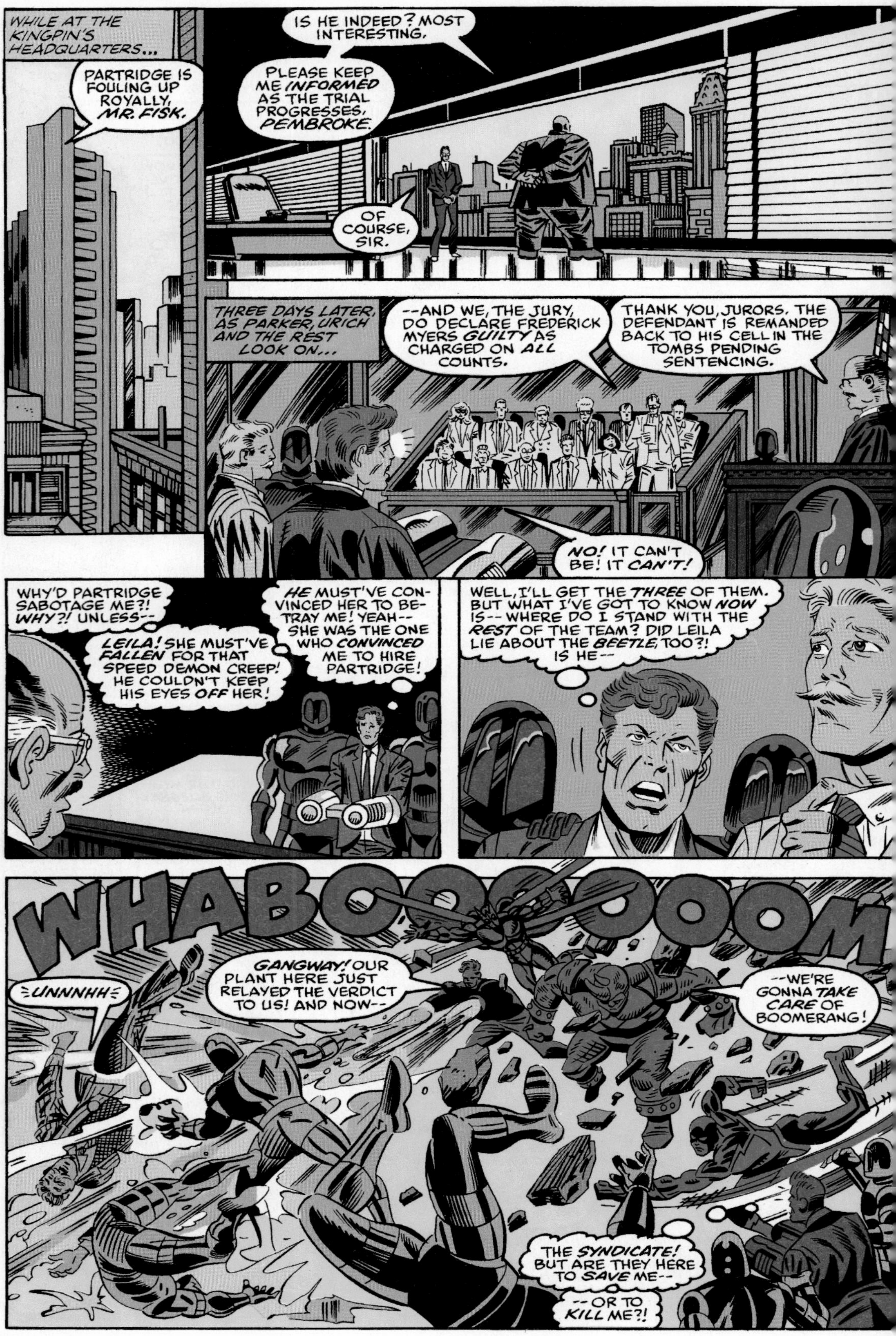

WHILE AT THE KINGPIN'S HEADQUARTERS...
PARTRIDGE IS FOULING UP ROYALLY, MR. FISK.
IS HE INDEED? MOST INTERESTING.
PLEASE KEEP ME INFORMED AS THE TRIAL PROGRESSES, PEMBROKE.
OF COURSE, SIR.
THREE DAYS LATER, AS PARKER, URICH AND THE REST LOOK ON...
--AND WE, THE JURY, DO DECLARE FREDERICK MYERS GUILTY AS CHARGED ON ALL COUNTS.
THANK YOU, JURORS. THE DEFENDANT IS REMANDED BACK TO HIS CELL IN THE TOMBS PENDING SENTENCING.
NO! IT CAN'T BE! IT CAN'T!
WHY'D PARTRIDGE SABOTAGE ME?! WHY?! UNLESS--
LEILA! SHE MUST'VE FALLEN FOR THAT SPEED DEMON CREEP! HE COULDN'T KEEP HIS EYES OFF HER!
HE MUST'VE CONVINCED HER TO BETRAY ME! YEAH-- SHE WAS THE ONE WHO CONVINCED ME TO HIRE PARTRIDGE!
WELL, I'LL GET THE THREE OF THEM. BUT WHAT I'VE GOT TO KNOW NOW IS-- WHERE DO I STAND WITH THE REST OF THE TEAM? DID LEILA LIE ABOUT THE BEETLE, TOO?! IS HE--
WHABOOOOOOM
UNNNHH
GANGWAY! OUR PLANT HERE JUST RELAYED THE VERDICT TO US! AND NOW--
--WE'RE GONNA TAKE CARE OF BOOMERANG!
THE SYNDICATE! BUT ARE THEY HERE TO SAVE ME--
--OR TO KILL ME?!

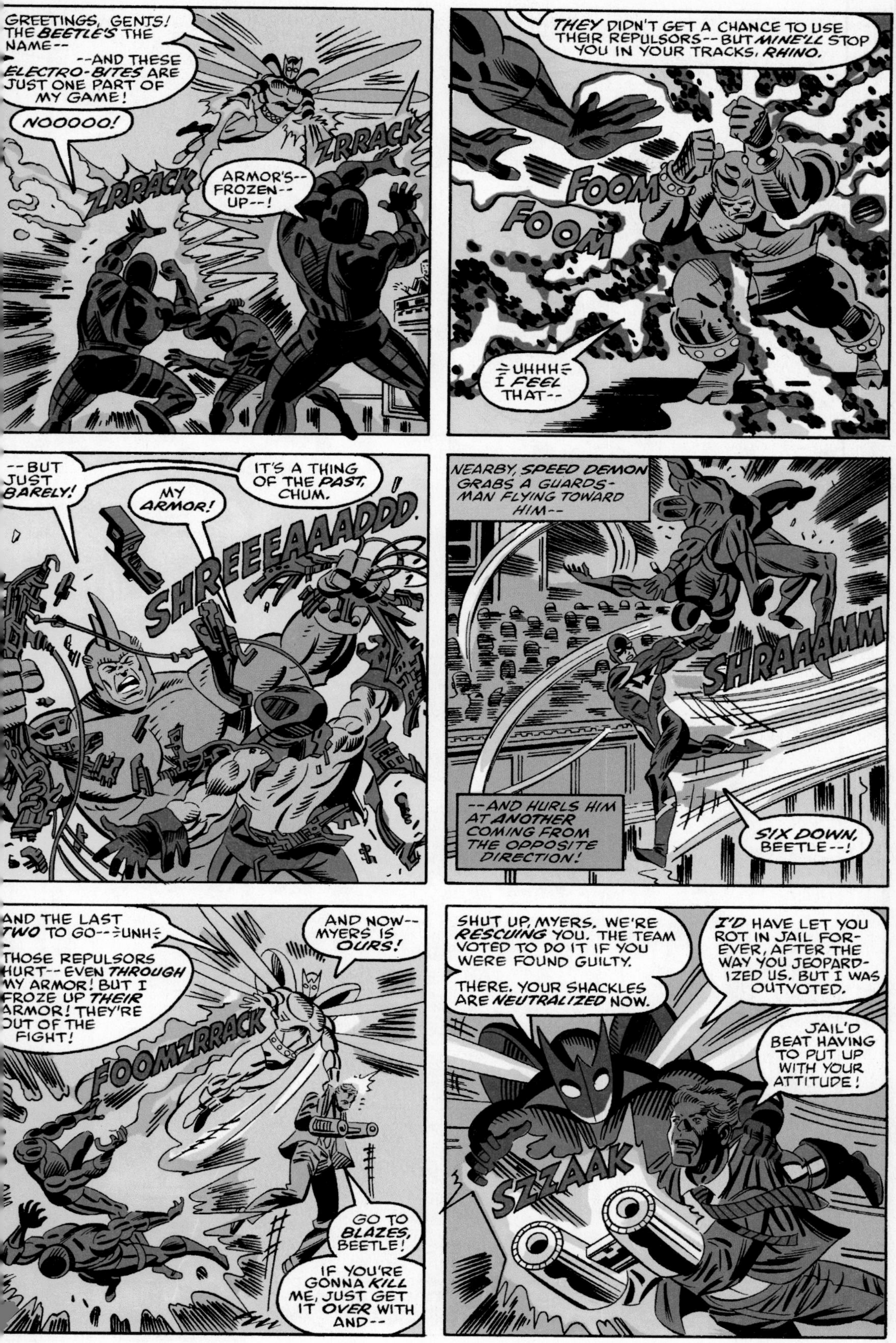
GREETINGS, GENTS! THE BEETLE'S THE NAME--
--AND THESE ELECTRO-BITES ARE JUST ONE PART OF MY GAME!
NOOOOO!
ZRRACK
ZRRACK
ARMOR'S-- FROZEN-- UP--!
THEY DIDN'T GET A CHANCE TO USE THEIR REPULSORS--BUT MINE'LL STOP YOU IN YOUR TRACKS, RHINO.
FOOM
FOOM
UHHH I FEEL THAT--
--BUT JUST BARELY!
IT'S A THING OF THE PAST, CHUM.
MY ARMOR!
SHREEEAAADDD
NEARBY, SPEED DEMON GRABS A GUARDSMAN FLYING TOWARD HIM--
SHRAAAMM
--AND HURLS HIM AT ANOTHER COMING FROM THE OPPOSITE DIRECTION!
SIX DOWN, BEETLE--!
AND THE LAST TWO TO GO-- UNH
THOSE REPULSORS HURT--EVEN THROUGH MY ARMOR! BUT I FROZE UP THEIR ARMOR! THEY'RE OUT OF THE FIGHT!
AND NOW-- MYERS IS OURS!
FOOMZRRACK
GO TO BLAZES, BEETLE!
IF YOU'RE GONNA KILL ME, JUST GET IT OVER WITH AND--
SHUT UP, MYERS. WE'RE RESCUING YOU. THE TEAM VOTED TO DO IT IF YOU WERE FOUND GUILTY.
THERE. YOUR SHACKLES ARE NEUTRALIZED NOW.
I'D HAVE LET YOU ROT IN JAIL FOREVER, AFTER THE WAY YOU JEOPARDIZED US. BUT I WAS OUTVOTED.
JAIL'D BEAT HAVING TO PUT UP WITH YOUR ATTITUDE!
SZZAAK

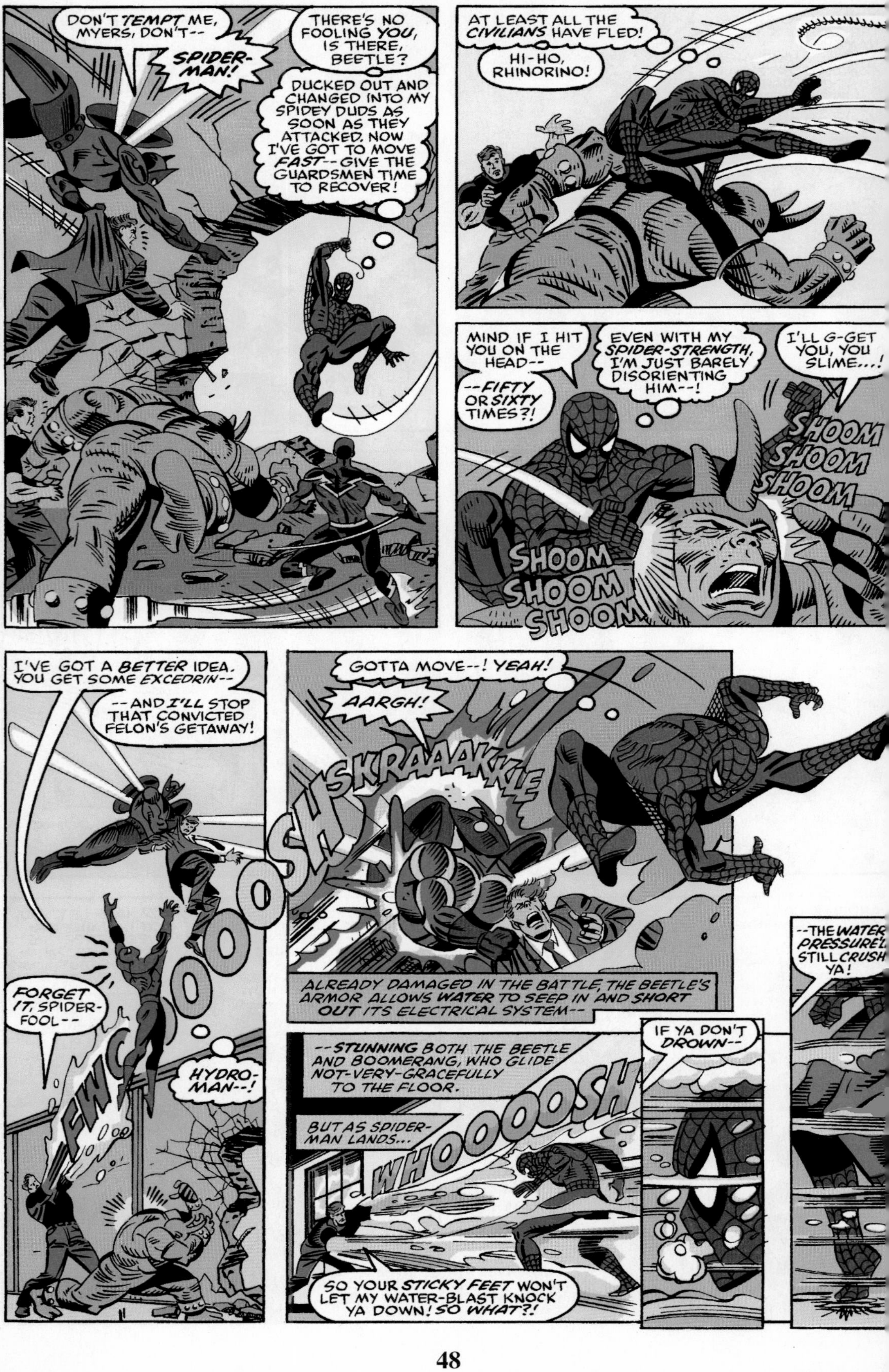
DON'T TEMPT ME, MYERS, DON'T--
SPIDER-MAN!
THERE'S NO FOOLING YOU, IS THERE, BEETLE?
DUCKED OUT AND CHANGED INTO MY SPIDEY DUDS AS SOON AS THEY ATTACKED. NOW I'VE GOT TO MOVE FAST--GIVE THE GUARDSMEN TIME TO RECOVER!
AT LEAST ALL THE CIVILIANS HAVE FLED!
HI-HO, RHINORINO!
MIND IF I HIT YOU ON THE HEAD--
--FIFTY OR SIXTY TIMES?!
EVEN WITH MY SPIDER-STRENGTH, I'M JUST BARELY DISORIENTING HIM--!
I'LL G-GET YOU, YOU SLIME...!
SHOOM SHOOM SHOOM
SHOOM SHOOM SHOOM
I'VE GOT A BETTER IDEA. YOU GET SOME EXCEDRIN--
--AND I'LL STOP THAT CONVICTED FELON'S GETAWAY!
FORGET IT, SPIDER-FOOL--
HYDRO-MAN--!
FWOOOOOOSH
GOTTA MOVE--! YEAH!
AARGH!
SKRAAAKKLE
ALREADY DAMAGED IN THE BATTLE, THE BEETLE'S ARMOR ALLOWS WATER TO SEEP IN AND SHORT OUT ITS ELECTRICAL SYSTEM--
--STUNNING BOTH THE BEETLE AND BOOMERANG, WHO GLIDE NOT-VERY-GRACEFULLY TO THE FLOOR.
BUT AS SPIDER-MAN LANDS...
WHOOOOOSH
SO YOUR STICKY FEET WON'T LET MY WATER-BLAST KNOCK YA DOWN! SO WHAT?!
IF YA DON'T DROWN--
--THE WATER PRESSURE'LL STILL CRUSH YA!

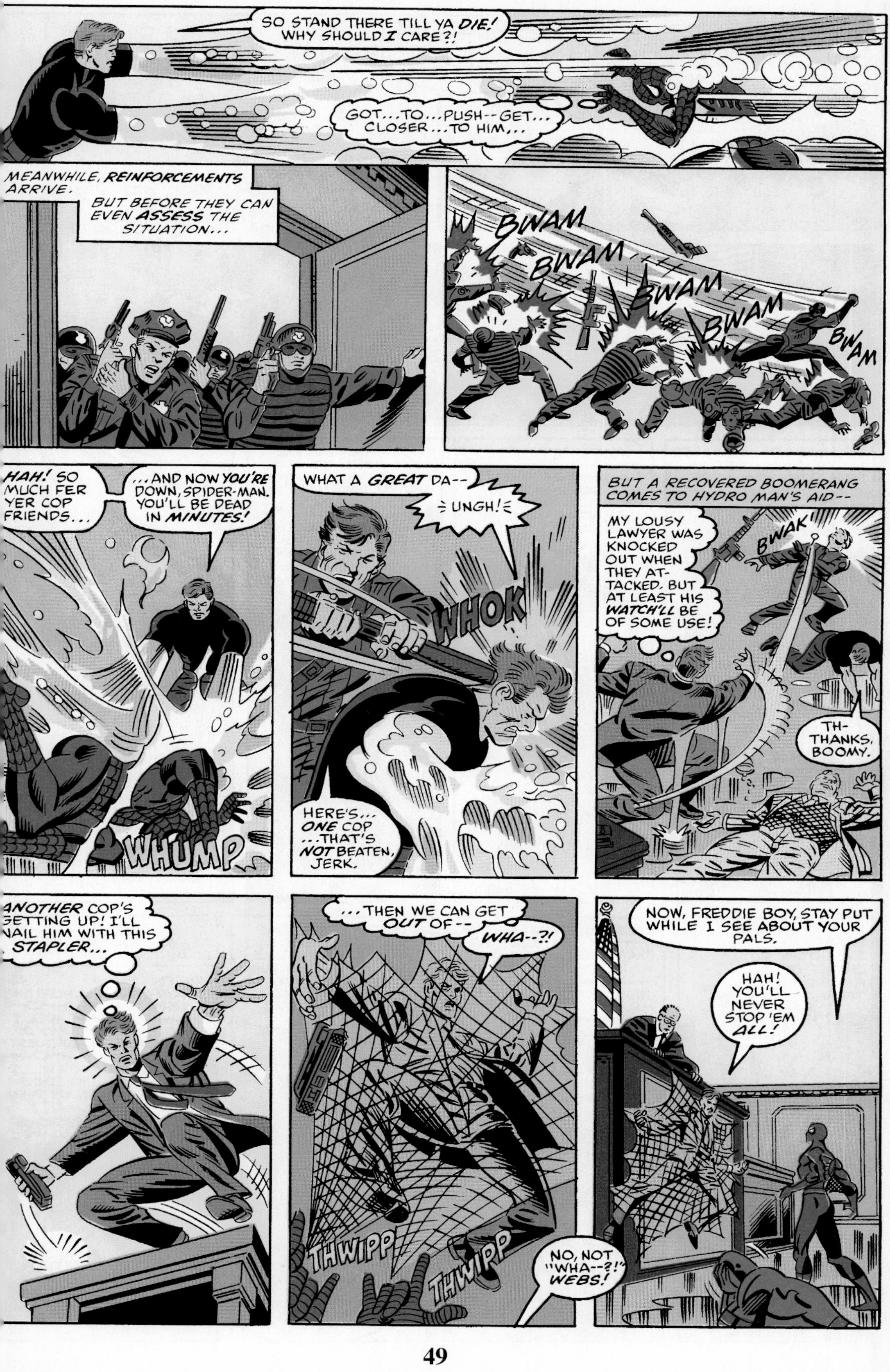
SO STAND THERE TILL YA DIE! WHY SHOULD I CARE?!
GOT...TO...PUSH--GET... CLOSER...TO HIM,...
MEANWHILE, REINFORCEMENTS ARRIVE.
BUT BEFORE THEY CAN EVEN ASSESS THE SITUATION...
BWAM
BWAM
BWAM
BWAM
BWAM
HAH! SO MUCH FER YER COP FRIENDS...
...AND NOW YOU'RE DOWN, SPIDER-MAN. YOU'LL BE DEAD IN MINUTES!
WHUMP
WHAT A GREAT DA--
UNGH!
WHOK
HERE'S... ONE COP ...THAT'S NOT BEATEN, JERK.
BUT A RECOVERED BOOMERANG COMES TO HYDRO MAN'S AID--
MY LOUSY LAWYER WAS KNOCKED OUT WHEN THEY ATTACKED. BUT AT LEAST HIS WATCH'LL BE OF SOME USE!
BWAK
TH- THANKS, BOOMY.
ANOTHER COP'S GETTING UP! I'LL NAIL HIM WITH THIS STAPLER...
...THEN WE CAN GET OUT OF--
WHA--?!
THWIPP
THWIPP
NO, NOT "WHA--?!" WEBS!
NOW, FREDDIE BOY, STAY PUT WHILE I SEE ABOUT YOUR PALS.
HAH! YOU'LL NEVER STOP 'EM ALL!

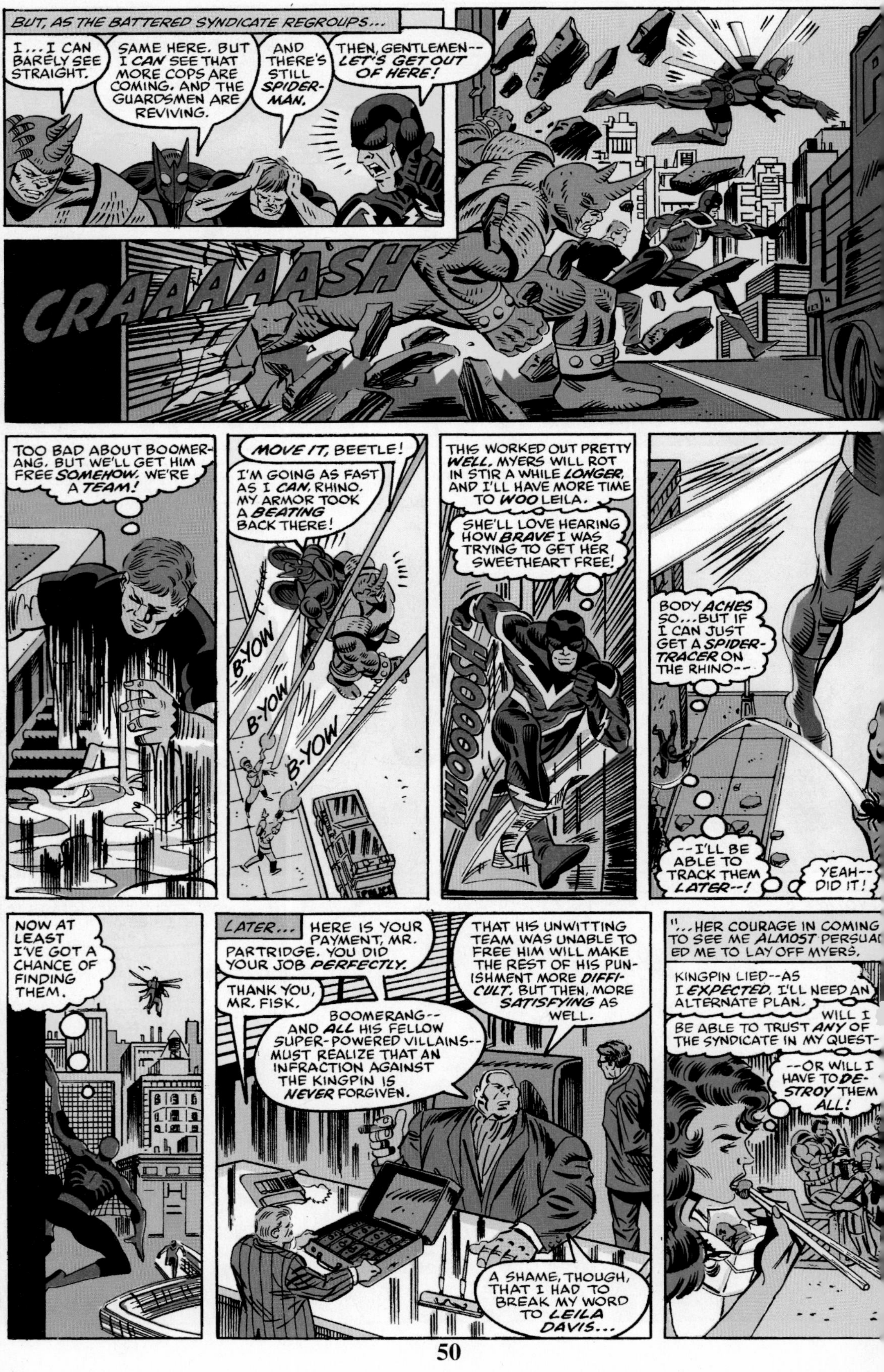

BUT, AS THE BATTERED SYNDICATE REGROUPS...
I...I CAN BARELY SEE STRAIGHT.
SAME HERE. BUT I CAN SEE THAT MORE COPS ARE COMING. AND THE GUARDSMEN ARE REVIVING.
AND THERE'S STILL SPIDER-MAN.
THEN, GENTLEMEN-- LET'S GET OUT OF HERE!
CRAAAAASH
TOO BAD ABOUT BOOMERANG. BUT WE'LL GET HIM FREE SOMEHOW. WE'RE A TEAM!
MOVE IT, BEETLE!
I'M GOING AS FAST AS I CAN, RHINO. MY ARMOR TOOK A BEATING BACK THERE!
B-YOW
B-YOW
B-YOW
THIS WORKED OUT PRETTY WELL. MYERS WILL ROT IN STIR A WHILE LONGER, AND I'LL HAVE MORE TIME TO WOO LEILA.
SHE'LL LOVE HEARING HOW BRAVE I WAS TRYING TO GET HER SWEETHEART FREE!
WHOOOOSH
BODY ACHES SO...BUT IF I CAN JUST GET A SPIDER-TRACER ON THE RHINO--
--I'LL BE ABLE TO TRACK THEM LATER--!
YEAH-- DID IT!
NOW AT LEAST I'VE GOT A CHANCE OF FINDING THEM.
LATER...
HERE IS YOUR PAYMENT, MR. PARTRIDGE. YOU DID YOUR JOB PERFECTLY.
THANK YOU, MR. FISK.
BOOMERANG-- AND ALL HIS FELLOW SUPER-POWERED VILLAINS-- MUST REALIZE THAT AN INFRACTION AGAINST THE KINGPIN IS NEVER FORGIVEN.
THAT HIS UNWITTING TEAM WAS UNABLE TO FREE HIM WILL MAKE THE REST OF HIS PUNISHMENT MORE DIFFICULT. BUT THEN, MORE SATISFYING AS WELL.
A SHAME, THOUGH, THAT I HAD TO BREAK MY WORD TO LEILA DAVIS...
"...HER COURAGE IN COMING TO SEE ME ALMOST PERSUADED ME TO LAY OFF MYERS."
KINGPIN LIED--AS I EXPECTED. I'LL NEED AN ALTERNATE PLAN.
WILL I BE ABLE TO TRUST ANY OF THE SYNDICATE IN MY QUEST--
--OR WILL I HAVE TO DESTROY THEM ALL!

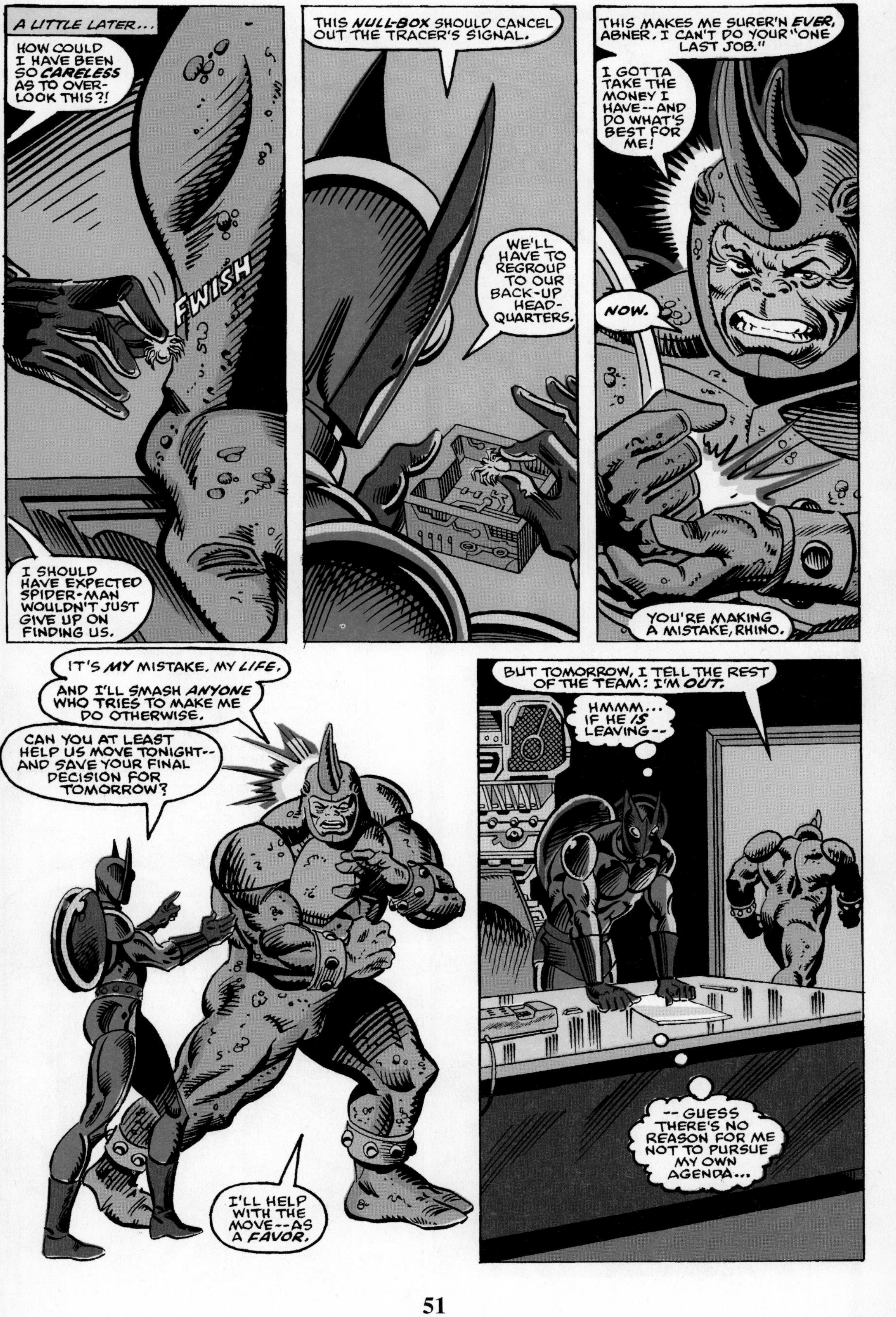
A LITTLE LATER...
HOW COULD I HAVE BEEN SO CARELESS AS TO OVER-LOOK THIS?!
FWISH
I SHOULD HAVE EXPECTED SPIDER-MAN WOULDN'T JUST GIVE UP ON FINDING US.
THIS NULL-BOX SHOULD CANCEL OUT THE TRACER'S SIGNAL.
WE'LL HAVE TO REGROUP TO OUR BACK-UP HEAD-QUARTERS.
THIS MAKES ME SURER'N EVER, ABNER. I CAN'T DO YOUR "ONE LAST JOB."
I GOTTA TAKE THE MONEY I HAVE--AND DO WHAT'S BEST FOR ME!
NOW.
YOU'RE MAKING A MISTAKE, RHINO.
IT'S MY MISTAKE. MY LIFE.
AND I'LL SMASH ANYONE WHO TRIES TO MAKE ME DO OTHERWISE.
CAN YOU AT LEAST HELP US MOVE TONIGHT--AND SAVE YOUR FINAL DECISION FOR TOMORROW?
I'LL HELP WITH THE MOVE--AS A FAVOR.
BUT TOMORROW, I TELL THE REST OF THE TEAM: I'M OUT.
HMMM... IF HE IS LEAVING--
--GUESS THERE'S NO REASON FOR ME NOT TO PURSUE MY OWN AGENDA...

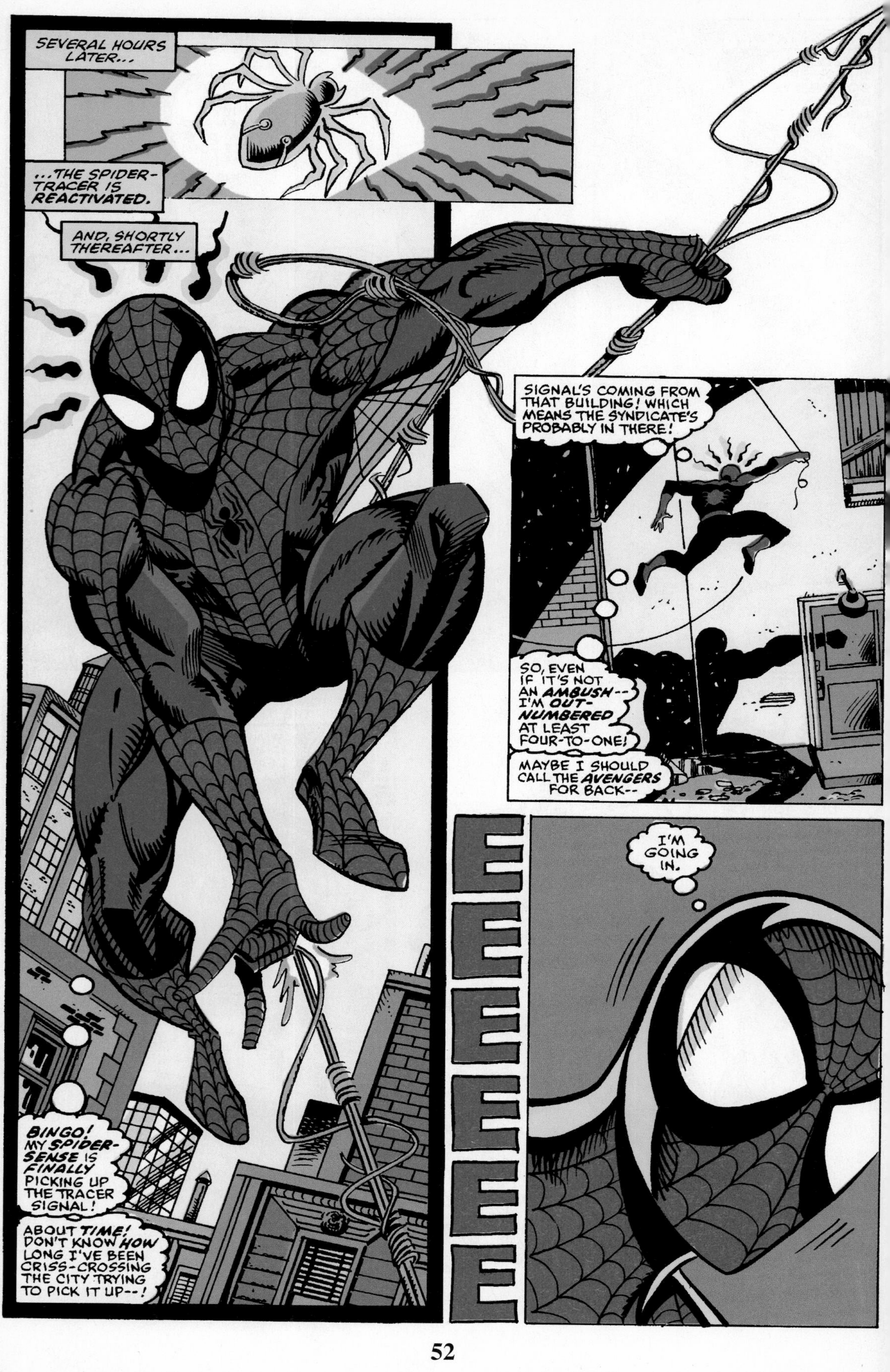
SEVERAL HOURS LATER...
...THE SPIDER-TRACER IS REACTIVATED.
AND, SHORTLY THEREAFTER...
BINGO! MY SPIDER-SENSE IS FINALLY PICKING UP THE TRACER SIGNAL!
ABOUT TIME! DON'T KNOW HOW LONG I'VE BEEN CRISS-CROSSING THE CITY TRYING TO PICK IT UP--!
SIGNAL'S COMING FROM THAT BUILDING! WHICH MEANS THE SYNDICATE'S PROBABLY IN THERE!
SO, EVEN IF IT'S NOT AN AMBUSH-- I'M OUT-NUMBERED AT LEAST FOUR-TO-ONE!
MAYBE I SHOULD CALL THE AVENGERS FOR BACK--
EEEEEEEE
I'M GOING IN.

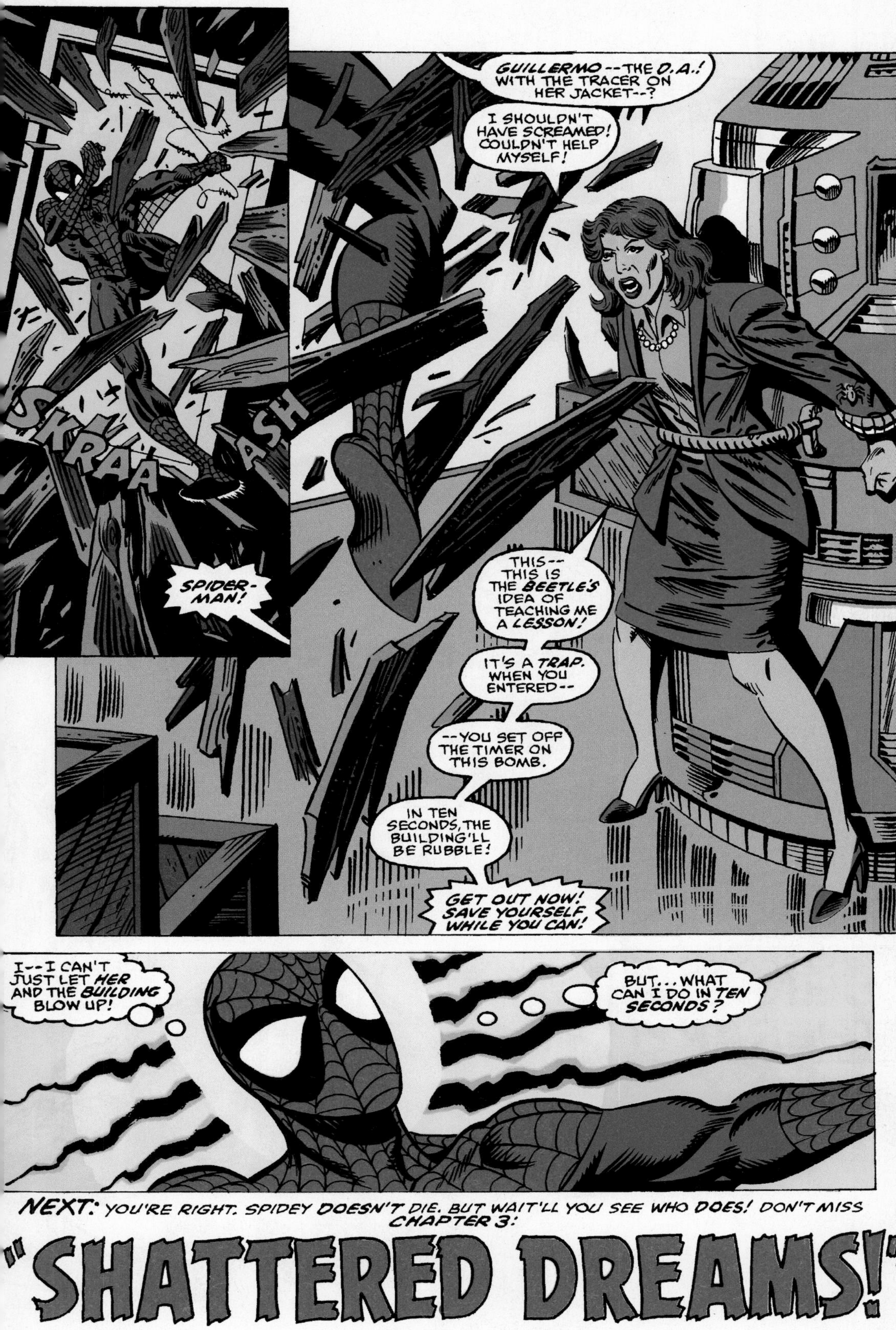
SKRAAAASH
SPIDER-MAN!
GUILLERMO--THE D.A.! WITH THE TRACER ON HER JACKET--?
I SHOULDN'T HAVE SCREAMED! COULDN'T HELP MYSELF!
THIS-- THIS IS THE BEETLE'S IDEA OF TEACHING ME A LESSON!
IT'S A TRAP. WHEN YOU ENTERED--
--YOU SET OFF THE TIMER ON THIS BOMB.
IN TEN SECONDS, THE BUILDING'LL BE RUBBLE!
GET OUT NOW! SAVE YOURSELF WHILE YOU CAN!
I--I CAN'T JUST LET HER AND THE BUILDING BLOW UP!
BUT... WHAT CAN I DO IN TEN SECONDS?

NEXT: YOU'RE RIGHT. SPIDEY *DOESN'T* DIE. BUT WAIT'LL YOU SEE WHO *DOES!* DON'T MISS *CHAPTER 3:*

"SHATTERED DREAMS!"

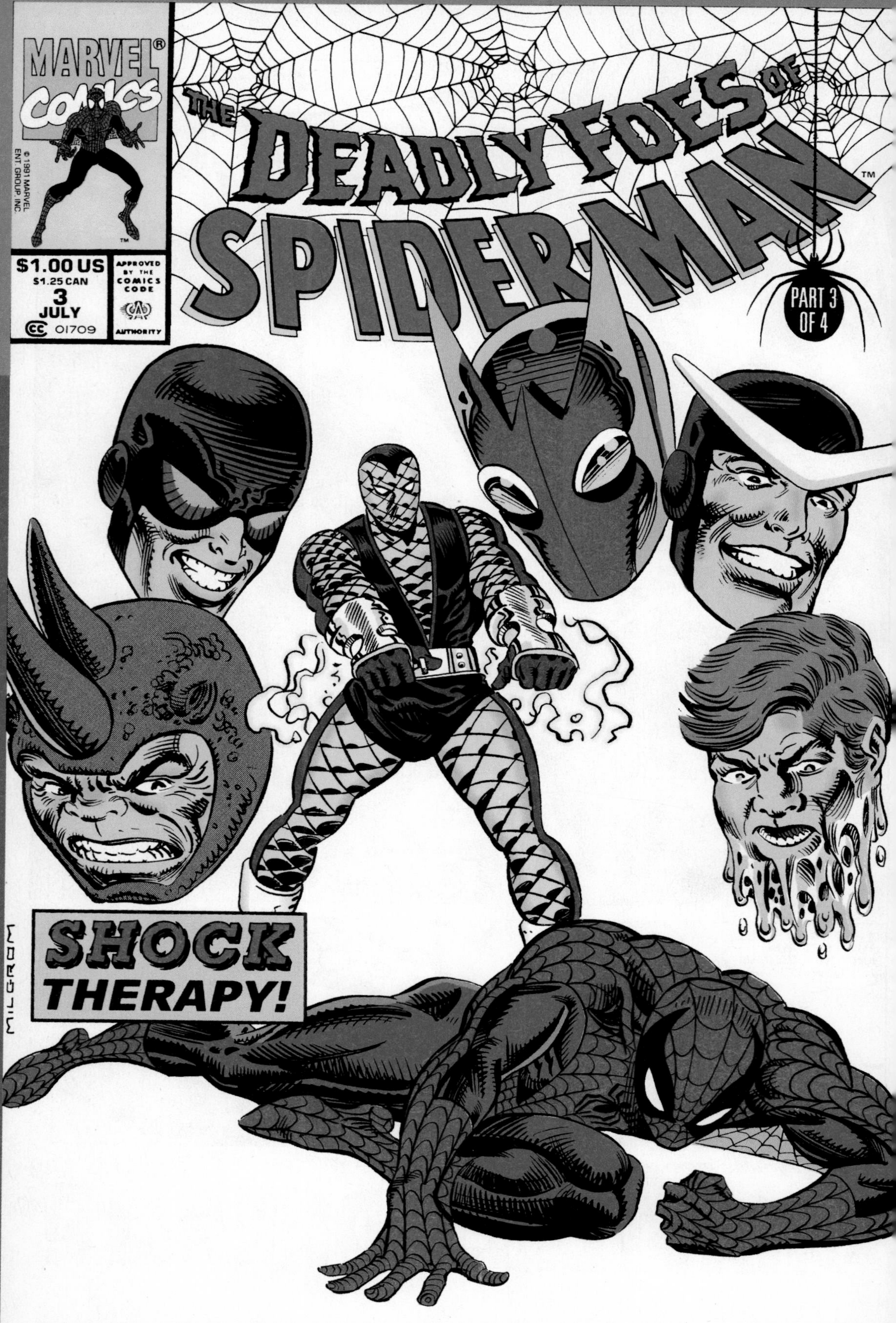
MARVEL®
COMICS
© 1991 MARVEL ENT. GROUP, INC.
THE DEADLY FOES OF SPIDER-MAN™
$1.00 US
$1.25 CAN
3
JULY
01709
APPROVED BY THE COMICS CODE AUTHORITY
PART 3 OF 4
SHOCK THERAPY!
MILGROM

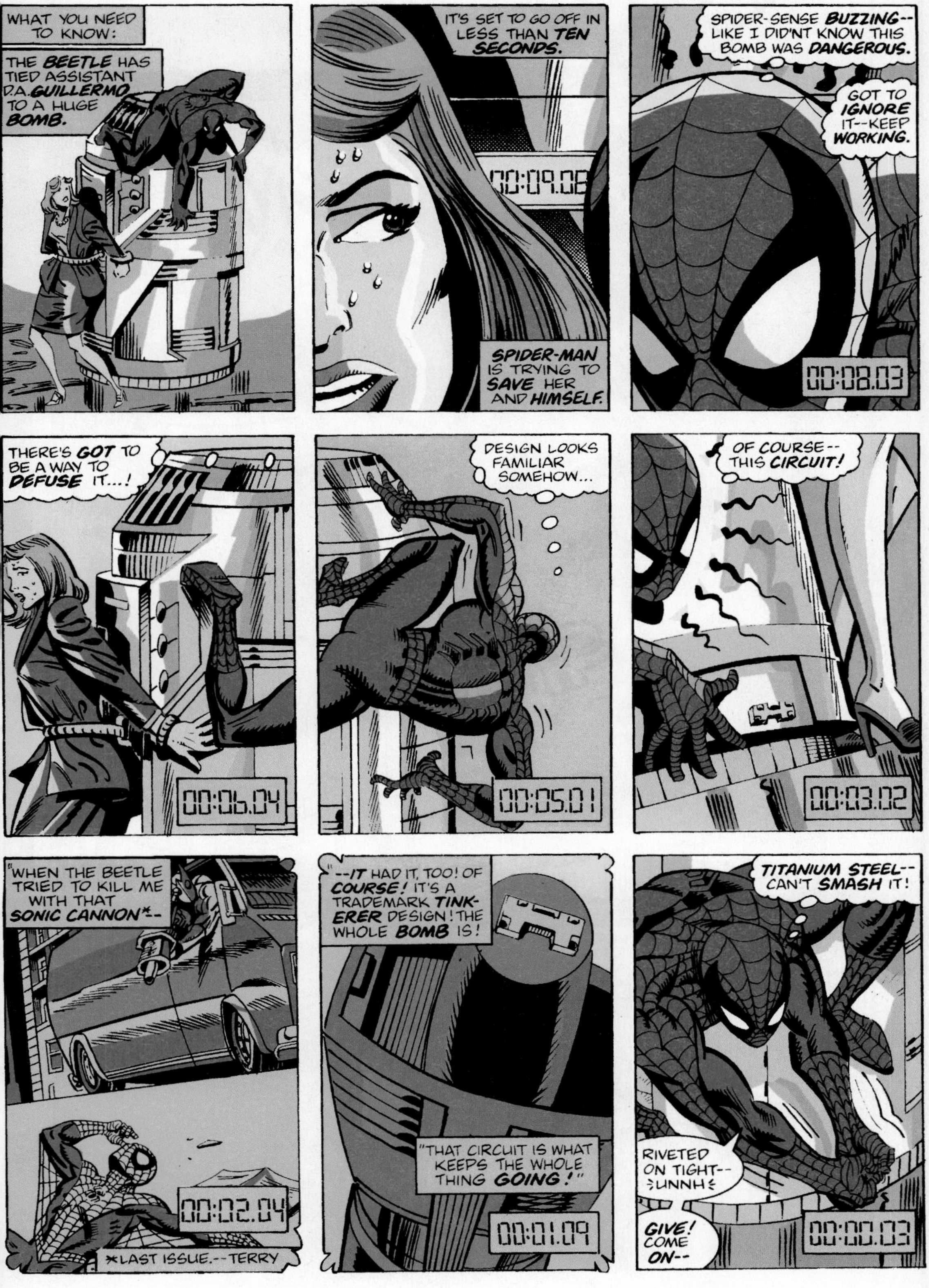
WHAT YOU NEED TO KNOW:
THE BEETLE HAS TIED ASSISTANT D.A. GUILLERMO TO A HUGE BOMB.
IT'S SET TO GO OFF IN LESS THAN TEN SECONDS.
00:09.06
SPIDER-MAN IS TRYING TO SAVE HER AND HIMSELF.
SPIDER-SENSE BUZZING-- LIKE I DIDN'T KNOW THIS BOMB WAS DANGEROUS.
GOT TO IGNORE IT--KEEP WORKING.
00:08.03
THERE'S GOT TO BE A WAY TO DEFUSE IT...!
00:06.04
DESIGN LOOKS FAMILIAR SOMEHOW...
00:05.01
OF COURSE-- THIS CIRCUIT!
00:03.02
"WHEN THE BEETLE TRIED TO KILL ME WITH THAT SONIC CANNON*--
00:02.04
*LAST ISSUE.--TERRY
"--IT HAD IT, TOO! OF COURSE! IT'S A TRADEMARK TINKERER DESIGN! THE WHOLE BOMB IS!
"THAT CIRCUIT IS WHAT KEEPS THE WHOLE THING GOING!"
00:01.09
TITANIUM STEEL-- CAN'T SMASH IT!
RIVETED ON TIGHT-- UNNH
GIVE! COME ON--
00:00.03

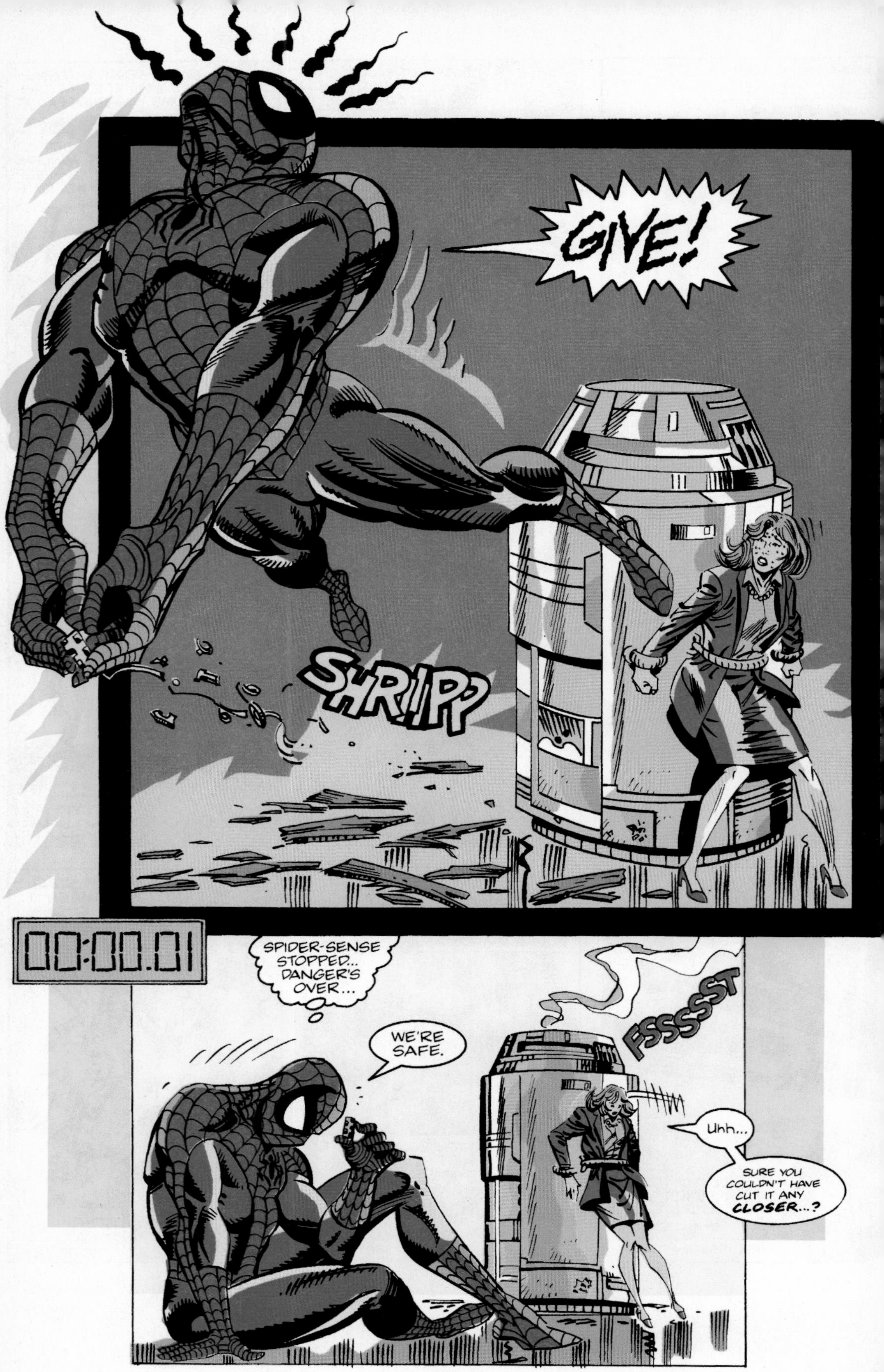
GIVE!
SHRIPP
00:00.01
SPIDER-SENSE STOPPED... DANGER'S OVER...
WE'RE SAFE.
FSSSSST
Uhh...
SURE YOU COULDN'T HAVE CUT IT ANY CLOSER...?

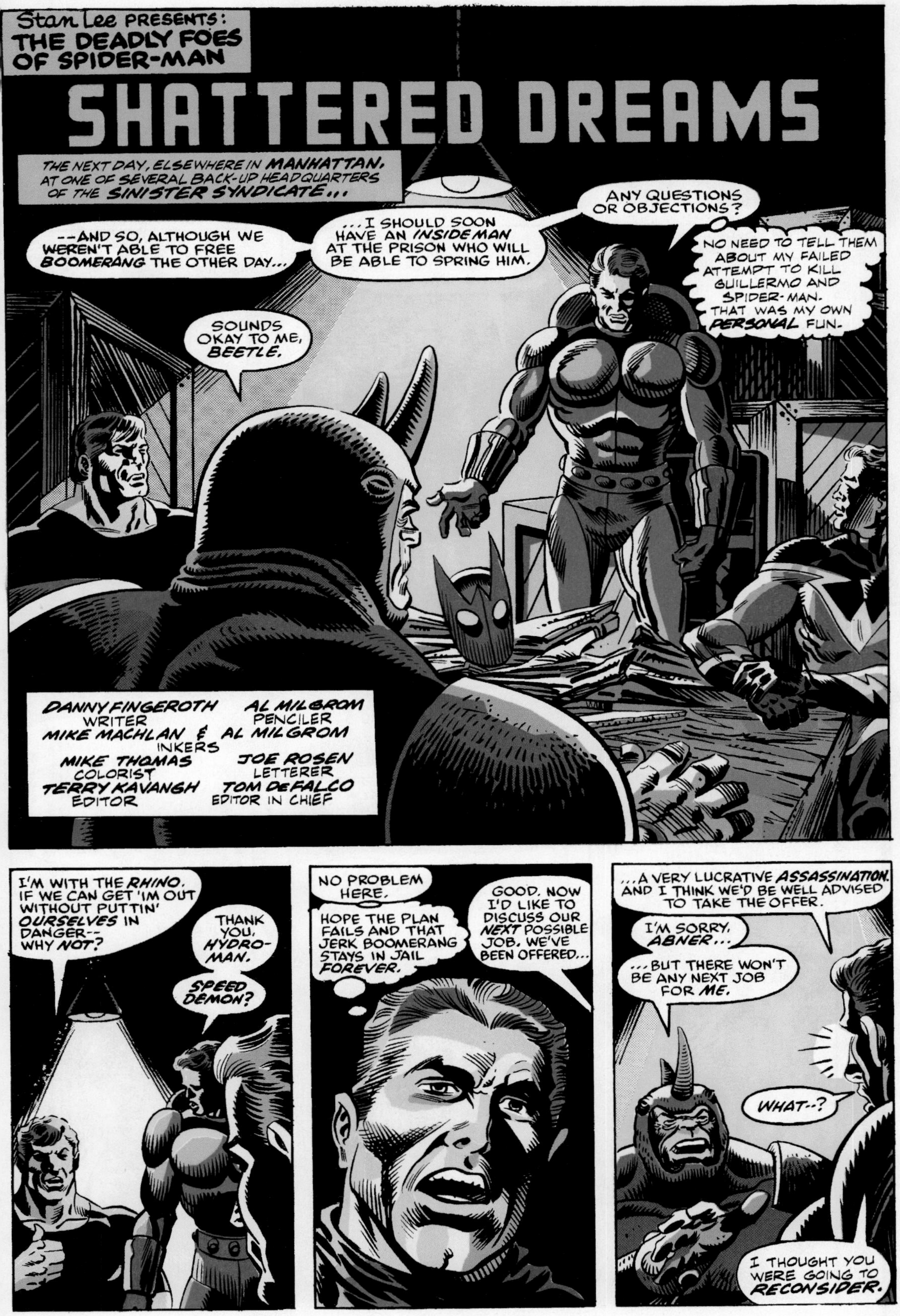

Stan Lee PRESENTS:
THE DEADLY FOES OF SPIDER-MAN
SHATTERED DREAMS
THE NEXT DAY, ELSEWHERE IN MANHATTAN, AT ONE OF SEVERAL BACK-UP HEADQUARTERS OF THE SINISTER SYNDICATE...
--AND SO, ALTHOUGH WE WEREN'T ABLE TO FREE BOOMERANG THE OTHER DAY...
...I SHOULD SOON HAVE AN INSIDE MAN AT THE PRISON WHO WILL BE ABLE TO SPRING HIM.
ANY QUESTIONS OR OBJECTIONS?
NO NEED TO TELL THEM ABOUT MY FAILED ATTEMPT TO KILL GUILLERMO AND SPIDER-MAN. THAT WAS MY OWN PERSONAL FUN.
SOUNDS OKAY TO ME, BEETLE.
DANNY FINGEROTH WRITER
AL MILGROM PENCILER
MIKE MACHLAN & AL MILGROM INKERS
MIKE THOMAS COLORIST
JOE ROSEN LETTERER
TERRY KAVANGH EDITOR
TOM DEFALCO EDITOR IN CHIEF
I'M WITH THE RHINO. IF WE CAN GET 'IM OUT WITHOUT PUTTIN' OURSELVES IN DANGER-- WHY NOT?
THANK YOU, HYDRO-MAN.
SPEED DEMON?
NO PROBLEM HERE.
HOPE THE PLAN FAILS AND THAT JERK BOOMERANG STAYS IN JAIL FOREVER.
GOOD. NOW I'D LIKE TO DISCUSS OUR NEXT POSSIBLE JOB. WE'VE BEEN OFFERED...
...A VERY LUCRATIVE ASSASSINATION. AND I THINK WE'D BE WELL ADVISED TO TAKE THE OFFER.
I'M SORRY, ABNER...
...BUT THERE WON'T BE ANY NEXT JOB FOR ME.
WHAT--?
I THOUGHT YOU WERE GOING TO RECONSIDER.

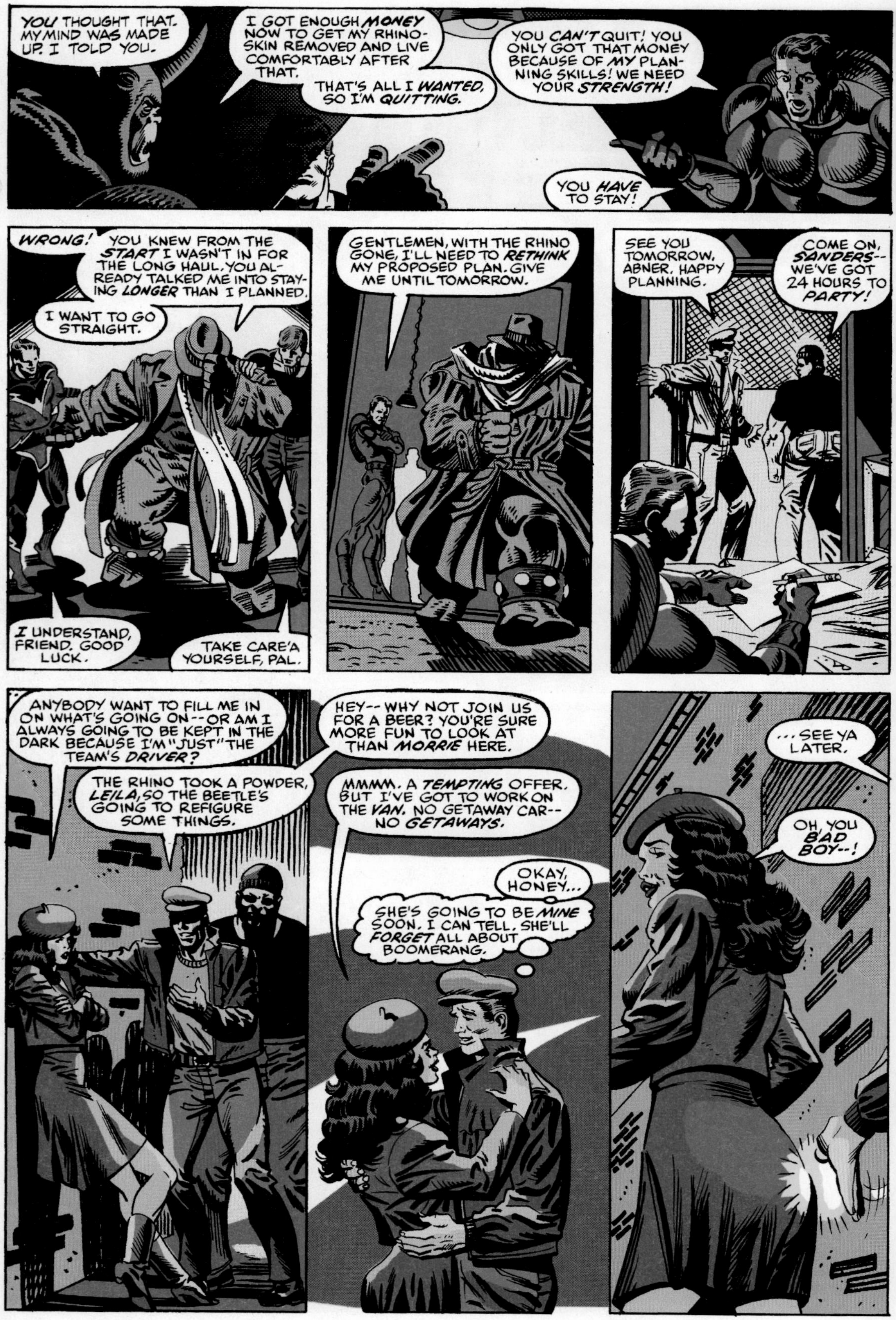
YOU THOUGHT THAT. MY MIND WAS MADE UP. I TOLD YOU.
I GOT ENOUGH MONEY NOW TO GET MY RHINO-SKIN REMOVED AND LIVE COMFORTABLY AFTER THAT.
THAT'S ALL I WANTED, SO I'M QUITTING.
YOU CAN'T QUIT! YOU ONLY GOT THAT MONEY BECAUSE OF MY PLANNING SKILLS! WE NEED YOUR STRENGTH!
YOU HAVE TO STAY!
WRONG!
YOU KNEW FROM THE START I WASN'T IN FOR THE LONG HAUL. YOU ALREADY TALKED ME INTO STAYING LONGER THAN I PLANNED.
I WANT TO GO STRAIGHT.
I UNDERSTAND, FRIEND. GOOD LUCK.
TAKE CARE'A YOURSELF, PAL.
GENTLEMEN, WITH THE RHINO GONE, I'LL NEED TO RETHINK MY PROPOSED PLAN. GIVE ME UNTIL TOMORROW.
SEE YOU TOMORROW, ABNER. HAPPY PLANNING.
COME ON, SANDERS-- WE'VE GOT 24 HOURS TO PARTY!
ANYBODY WANT TO FILL ME IN ON WHAT'S GOING ON--OR AM I ALWAYS GOING TO BE KEPT IN THE DARK BECAUSE I'M "JUST" THE TEAM'S DRIVER?
THE RHINO TOOK A POWDER, LEILA, SO THE BEETLE'S GOING TO REFIGURE SOME THINGS.
HEY-- WHY NOT JOIN US FOR A BEER? YOU'RE SURE MORE FUN TO LOOK AT THAN MORRIE HERE.
MMMM. A TEMPTING OFFER. BUT I'VE GOT TO WORK ON THE VAN. NO GETAWAY CAR-- NO GETAWAYS.
OKAY, HONEY...
SHE'S GOING TO BE MINE SOON. I CAN TELL. SHE'LL FORGET ALL ABOUT BOOMERANG.
...SEE YA LATER.
OH, YOU BAD BOY--!

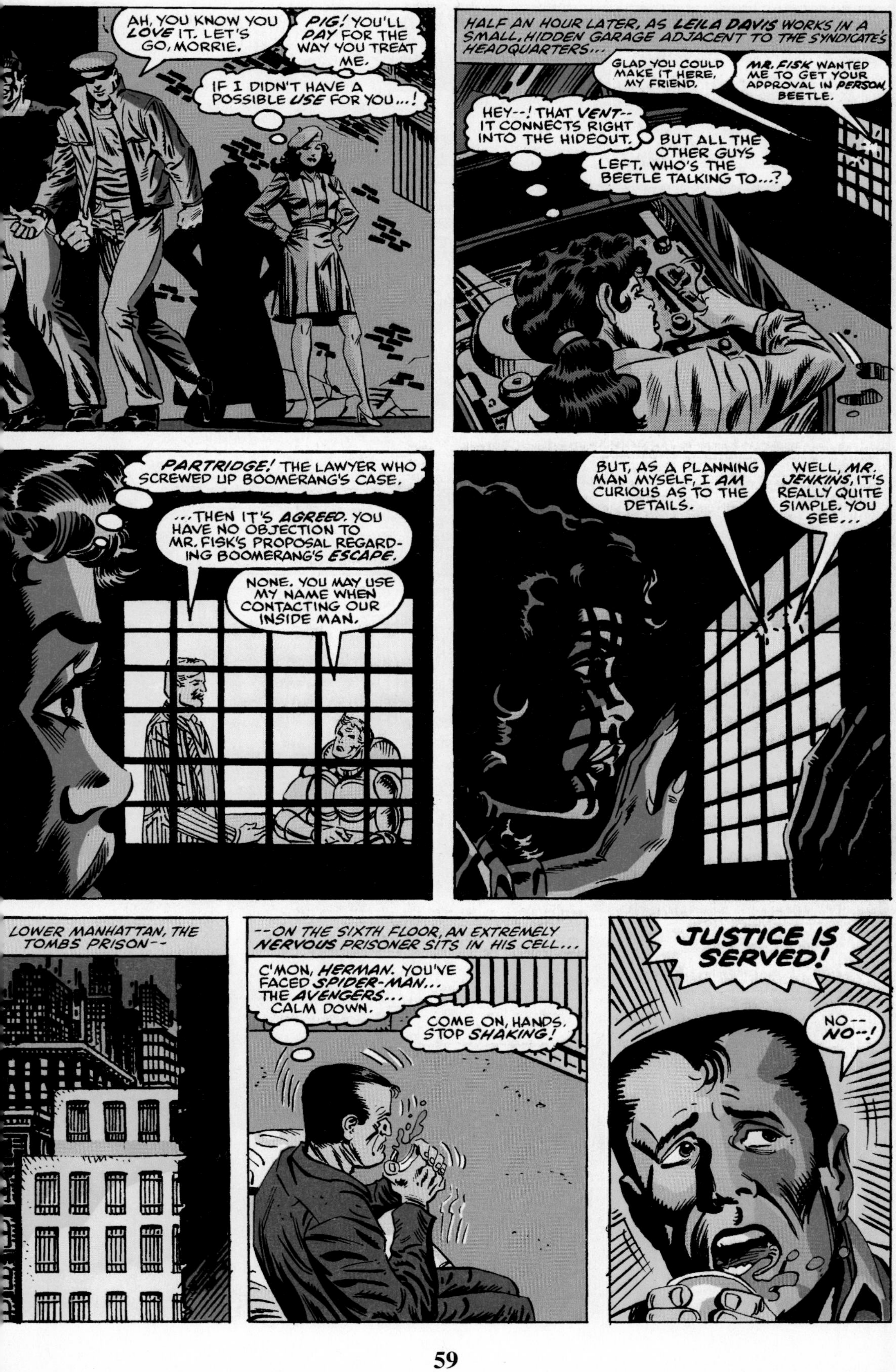

AH, YOU KNOW YOU LOVE IT. LET'S GO, MORRIE.
PIG! YOU'LL PAY FOR THE WAY YOU TREAT ME.
IF I DIDN'T HAVE A POSSIBLE USE FOR YOU...!
HALF AN HOUR LATER, AS LEILA DAVIS WORKS IN A SMALL, HIDDEN GARAGE ADJACENT TO THE SYNDICATE'S HEADQUARTERS...
GLAD YOU COULD MAKE IT HERE, MY FRIEND.
MR. FISK WANTED ME TO GET YOUR APPROVAL IN PERSON, BEETLE.
HEY--! THAT VENT-- IT CONNECTS RIGHT INTO THE HIDEOUT.
BUT ALL THE OTHER GUYS LEFT. WHO'S THE BEETLE TALKING TO...?
PARTRIDGE! THE LAWYER WHO SCREWED UP BOOMERANG'S CASE.
...THEN IT'S AGREED. YOU HAVE NO OBJECTION TO MR. FISK'S PROPOSAL REGARDING BOOMERANG'S ESCAPE.
NONE. YOU MAY USE MY NAME WHEN CONTACTING OUR INSIDE MAN.
BUT, AS A PLANNING MAN MYSELF, I AM CURIOUS AS TO THE DETAILS.
WELL, MR. JENKINS, IT'S REALLY QUITE SIMPLE. YOU SEE...
LOWER MANHATTAN, THE TOMBS PRISON--
--ON THE SIXTH FLOOR, AN EXTREMELY NERVOUS PRISONER SITS IN HIS CELL...
C'MON, HERMAN. YOU'VE FACED SPIDER-MAN... THE AVENGERS... CALM DOWN.
COME ON, HANDS. STOP SHAKING!
JUSTICE IS SERVED!
NO-- NO--!

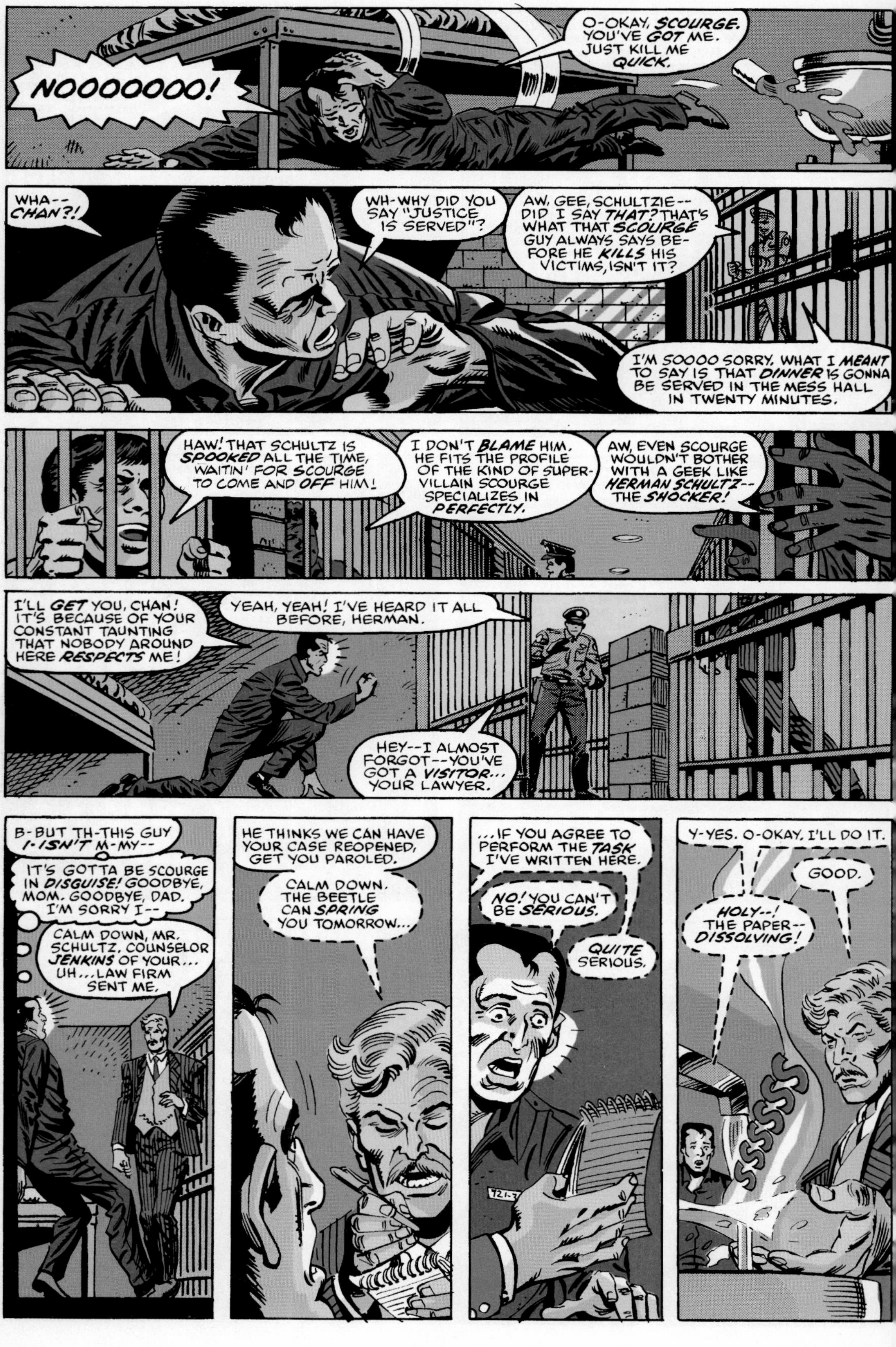
O-OKAY, SCOURGE. YOU'VE GOT ME. JUST KILL ME QUICK.
NOOOOOOO!
WHA-- CHAN?!
WH-WHY DID YOU SAY "JUSTICE IS SERVED"?
AW, GEE, SCHULTZIE-- DID I SAY THAT? THAT'S WHAT THAT SCOURGE GUY ALWAYS SAYS BEFORE HE KILLS HIS VICTIMS, ISN'T IT?
I'M SOOOO SORRY. WHAT I MEANT TO SAY IS THAT DINNER IS GONNA BE SERVED IN THE MESS HALL IN TWENTY MINUTES.
HAW! THAT SCHULTZ IS SPOOKED ALL THE TIME, WAITIN' FOR SCOURGE TO COME AND OFF HIM!
I DON'T BLAME HIM. HE FITS THE PROFILE OF THE KIND OF SUPER-VILLAIN SCOURGE SPECIALIZES IN PERFECTLY.
AW, EVEN SCOURGE WOULDN'T BOTHER WITH A GEEK LIKE HERMAN SCHULTZ-- THE SHOCKER!
I'LL GET YOU, CHAN! IT'S BECAUSE OF YOUR CONSTANT TAUNTING THAT NOBODY AROUND HERE RESPECTS ME!
YEAH, YEAH! I'VE HEARD IT ALL BEFORE, HERMAN.
HEY--I ALMOST FORGOT--YOU'VE GOT A VISITOR... YOUR LAWYER.
B-BUT TH-THIS GUY I-ISN'T M-MY--
IT'S GOTTA BE SCOURGE IN DISGUISE! GOODBYE, MOM. GOODBYE, DAD. I'M SORRY I--
CALM DOWN, MR. SCHULTZ. COUNSELOR JENKINS OF YOUR... UH...LAW FIRM SENT ME.
HE THINKS WE CAN HAVE YOUR CASE REOPENED, GET YOU PAROLED.
CALM DOWN. THE BEETLE CAN SPRING YOU TOMORROW...
...IF YOU AGREE TO PERFORM THE TASK I'VE WRITTEN HERE.
NO! YOU CAN'T BE SERIOUS.
QUITE SERIOUS.
Y-YES. O-OKAY. I'LL DO IT.
GOOD.
HOLY--! THE PAPER-- DISSOLVING!

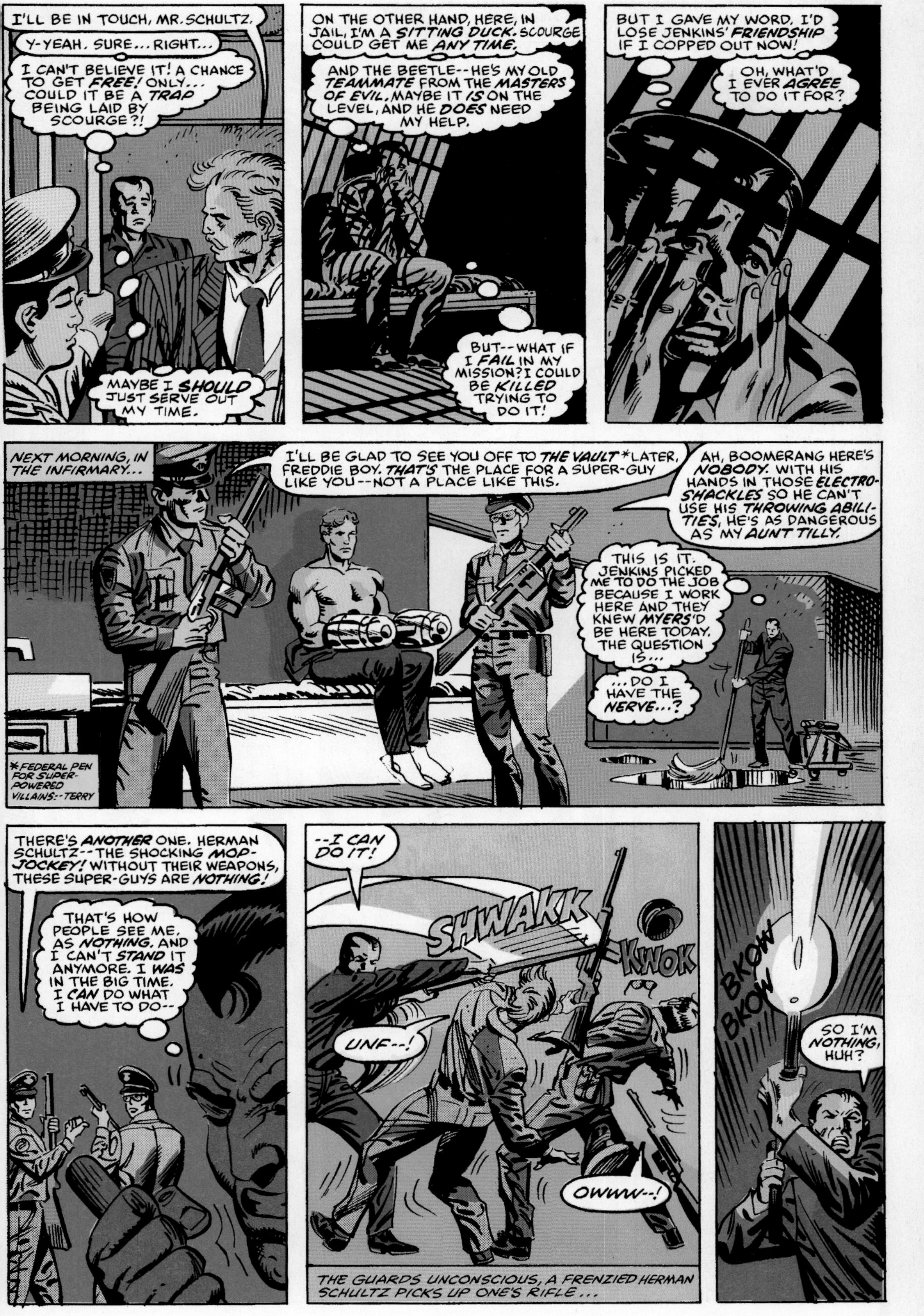
I'LL BE IN TOUCH, MR. SCHULTZ.
Y-YEAH. SURE... RIGHT...
I CAN'T BELIEVE IT! A CHANCE TO GET FREE! ONLY... COULD IT BE A TRAP BEING LAID BY SCOURGE?!
MAYBE I SHOULD JUST SERVE OUT MY TIME.
ON THE OTHER HAND, HERE, IN JAIL, I'M A SITTING DUCK. SCOURGE COULD GET ME ANY TIME.
AND THE BEETLE--HE'S MY OLD TEAMMATE FROM THE MASTERS OF EVIL, MAYBE IT IS ON THE LEVEL, AND HE DOES NEED MY HELP.
BUT--WHAT IF I FAIL IN MY MISSION? I COULD BE KILLED TRYING TO DO IT!
BUT I GAVE MY WORD. I'D LOSE JENKINS' FRIENDSHIP IF I COPPED OUT NOW!
OH, WHAT'D I EVER AGREE TO DO IT FOR?
NEXT MORNING, IN THE INFIRMARY...
I'LL BE GLAD TO SEE YOU OFF TO THE VAULT* LATER, FREDDIE BOY. THAT'S THE PLACE FOR A SUPER-GUY LIKE YOU--NOT A PLACE LIKE THIS.
AH, BOOMERANG HERE'S NOBODY. WITH HIS HANDS IN THOSE ELECTRO-SHACKLES SO HE CAN'T USE HIS THROWING ABILITIES, HE'S AS DANGEROUS AS MY AUNT TILLY.
THIS IS IT. JENKINS PICKED ME TO DO THE JOB BECAUSE I WORK HERE AND THEY KNEW MYERS'D BE HERE TODAY. THE QUESTION IS...
...DO I HAVE THE NERVE...?
*FEDERAL PEN FOR SUPER-POWERED VILLAINS.--TERRY
THERE'S ANOTHER ONE. HERMAN SCHULTZ--THE SHOCKING MOP-JOCKEY! WITHOUT THEIR WEAPONS, THESE SUPER-GUYS ARE NOTHING!
THAT'S HOW PEOPLE SEE ME, AS NOTHING. AND I CAN'T STAND IT ANYMORE. I WAS IN THE BIG TIME. I CAN DO WHAT I HAVE TO DO--
--I CAN DO IT!
SHWAKK
KWOK
UNF--!
OWWW--!
THE GUARDS UNCONSCIOUS, A FRENZIED HERMAN SCHULTZ PICKS UP ONE'S RIFLE...
BKOW
BKOW
SO I'M NOTHING, HUH?

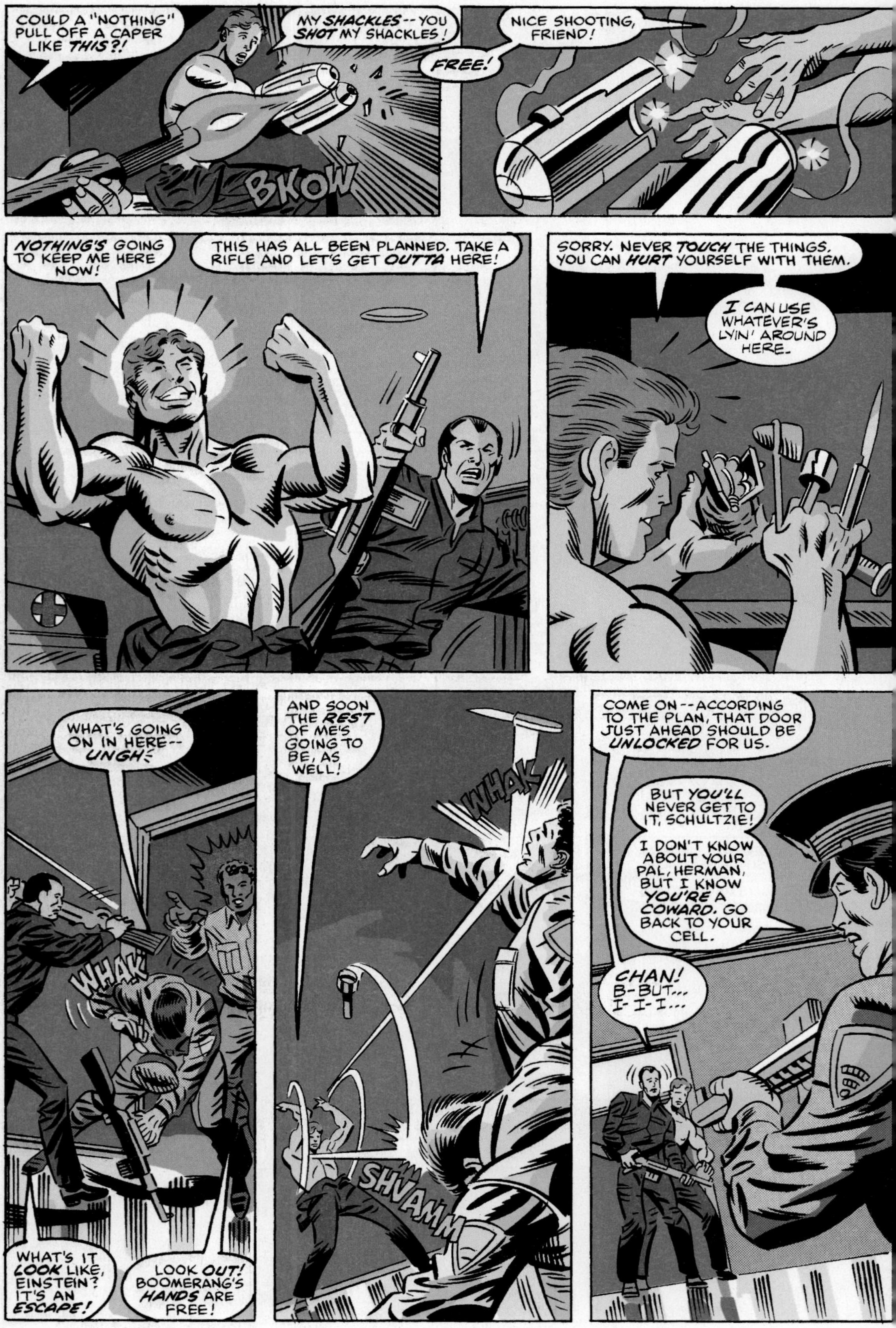
COULD A "NOTHING" PULL OFF A CAPER LIKE THIS?!
MY SHACKLES--YOU SHOT MY SHACKLES!
BKOW
NICE SHOOTING, FRIEND!
FREE!
NOTHING'S GOING TO KEEP ME HERE NOW!
THIS HAS ALL BEEN PLANNED. TAKE A RIFLE AND LET'S GET OUTTA HERE!
SORRY. NEVER TOUCH THE THINGS. YOU CAN HURT YOURSELF WITH THEM.
I CAN USE WHATEVER'S LYIN' AROUND HERE.
WHAT'S GOING ON IN HERE-- UNGH!
WHAK
WHAT'S IT LOOK LIKE, EINSTEIN? IT'S AN ESCAPE!
LOOK OUT! BOOMERANG'S HANDS ARE FREE!
AND SOON THE REST OF ME'S GOING TO BE, AS WELL!
WHAK
SHVAMM
COME ON--ACCORDING TO THE PLAN, THAT DOOR JUST AHEAD SHOULD BE UNLOCKED FOR US.
BUT YOU'LL NEVER GET TO IT, SCHULTZIE!
I DON'T KNOW ABOUT YOUR PAL, HERMAN, BUT I KNOW YOU'RE A COWARD. GO BACK TO YOUR CELL.
CHAN! B-BUT... I- I- I...

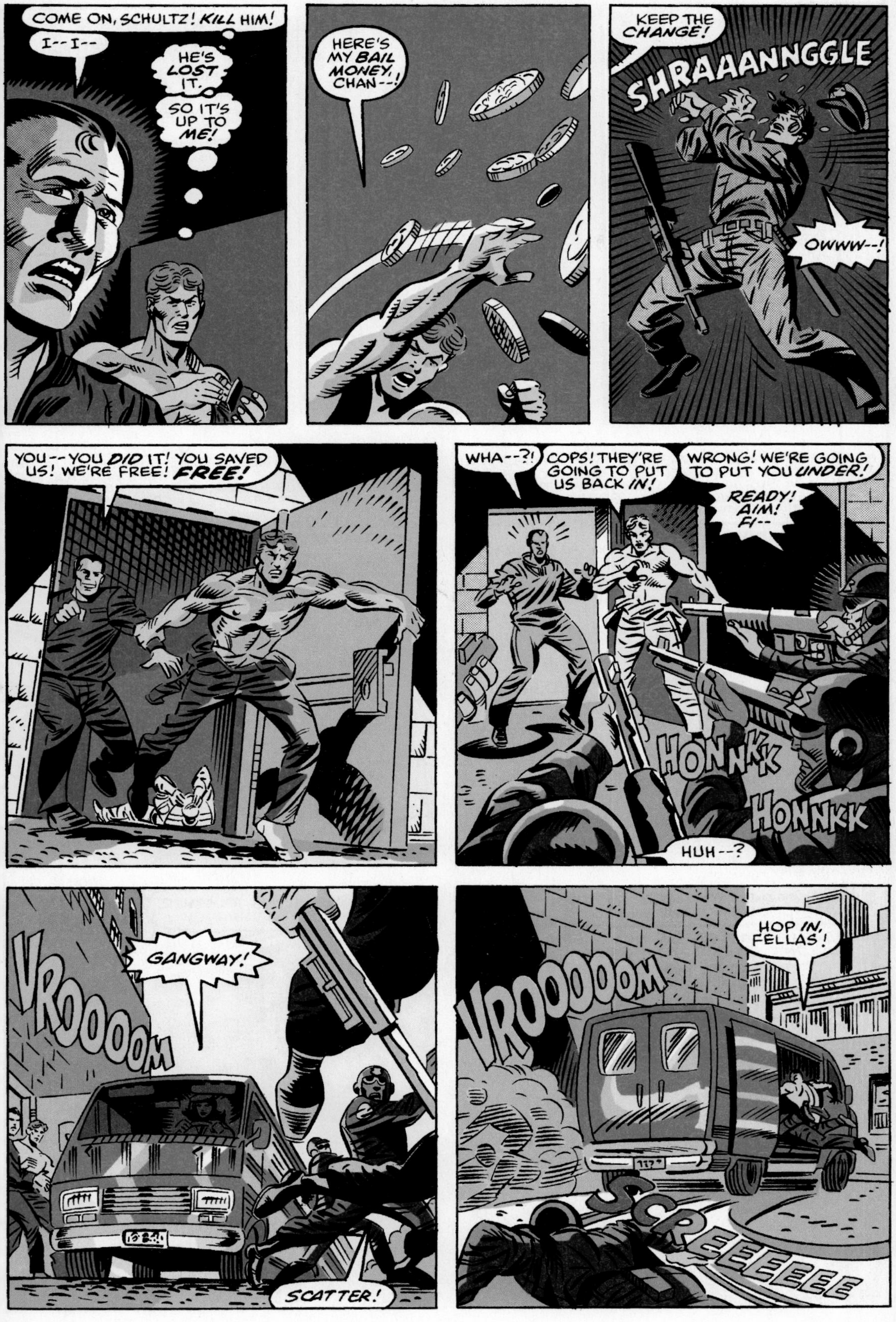
COME ON, SCHULTZ! KILL HIM!
I-- I--
HE'S LOST IT.
SO IT'S UP TO ME!
HERE'S MY BAIL MONEY, CHAN--!
KEEP THE CHANGE!
SHRAAANNGGLE
OWWW--!
YOU--YOU DID IT! YOU SAVED US! WE'RE FREE! FREE!
WHA--?!
COPS! THEY'RE GOING TO PUT US BACK IN!
WRONG! WE'RE GOING TO PUT YOU UNDER!
READY! AIM! FI--
HONNKK
HONNKK
HUH--?
VROOOOOM
GANGWAY!
SCATTER!
VROOOOOM
HOP IN, FELLAS!
SCREEEEEEE

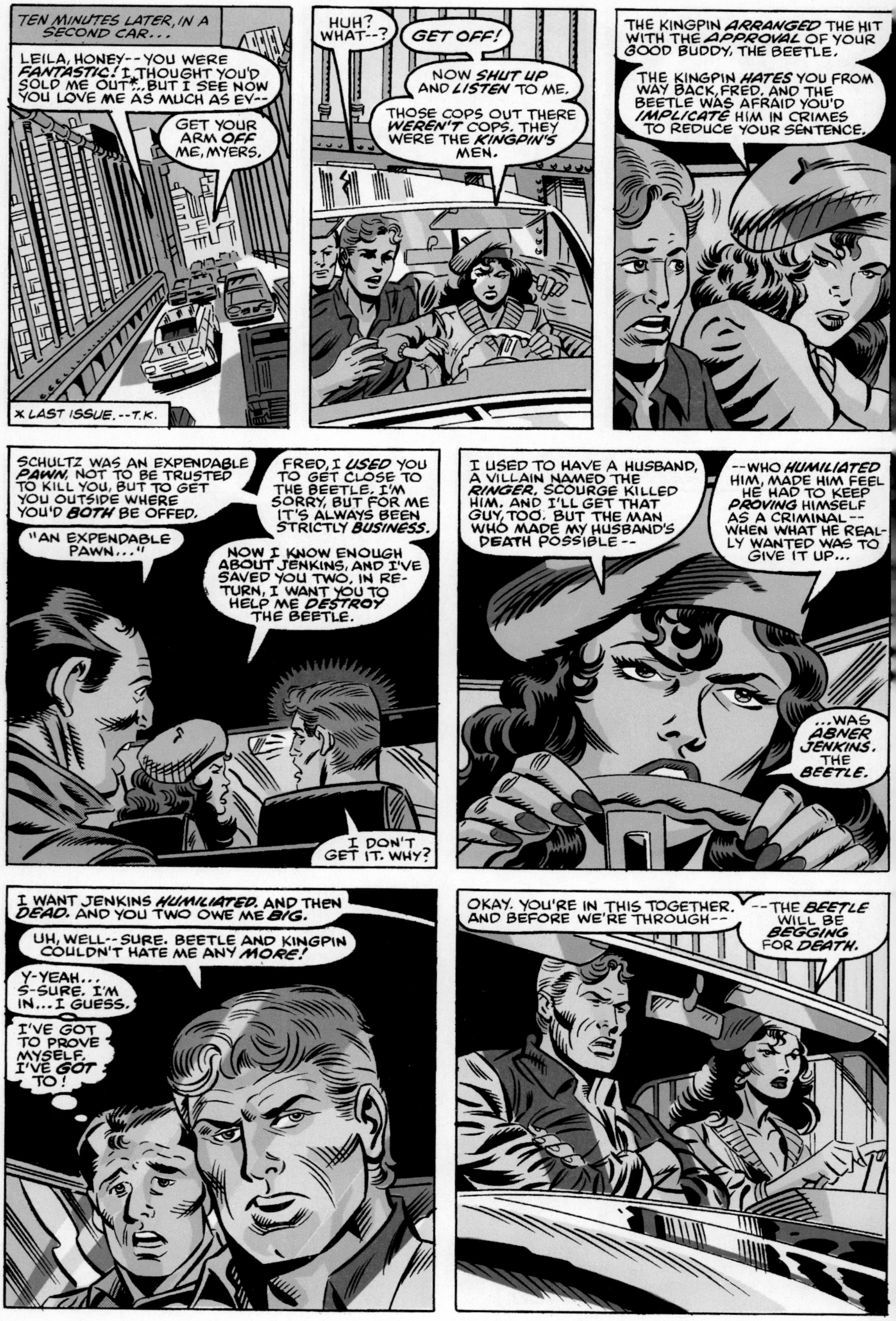
TEN MINUTES LATER, IN A SECOND CAR...
LEILA, HONEY--YOU WERE FANTASTIC! I THOUGHT YOU'D SOLD ME OUT*...BUT I SEE NOW YOU LOVE ME AS MUCH AS EV--
GET YOUR ARM OFF ME, MYERS.
* LAST ISSUE. --T.K.
HUH? WHAT--?
GET OFF!
NOW SHUT UP AND LISTEN TO ME.
THOSE COPS OUT THERE WEREN'T COPS. THEY WERE THE KINGPIN'S MEN.
THE KINGPIN ARRANGED THE HIT WITH THE APPROVAL OF YOUR GOOD BUDDY, THE BEETLE.
THE KINGPIN HATES YOU FROM WAY BACK, FRED. AND THE BEETLE WAS AFRAID YOU'D IMPLICATE HIM IN CRIMES TO REDUCE YOUR SENTENCE.
SCHULTZ WAS AN EXPENDABLE PAWN, NOT TO BE TRUSTED TO KILL YOU, BUT TO GET YOU OUTSIDE WHERE YOU'D BOTH BE OFFED.
FRED, I USED YOU TO GET CLOSE TO THE BEETLE. I'M SORRY, BUT FOR ME IT'S ALWAYS BEEN STRICTLY BUSINESS.
"AN EXPENDABLE PAWN..."
NOW I KNOW ENOUGH ABOUT JENKINS, AND I'VE SAVED YOU TWO. IN RETURN, I WANT YOU TO HELP ME DESTROY THE BEETLE.
I DON'T GET IT. WHY?
I USED TO HAVE A HUSBAND, A VILLAIN NAMED THE RINGER. SCOURGE KILLED HIM. AND I'LL GET THAT GUY, TOO. BUT THE MAN WHO MADE MY HUSBAND'S DEATH POSSIBLE--
--WHO HUMILIATED HIM, MADE HIM FEEL HE HAD TO KEEP PROVING HIMSELF AS A CRIMINAL--WHEN WHAT HE REALLY WANTED WAS TO GIVE IT UP...
...WAS ABNER JENKINS. THE BEETLE.
I WANT JENKINS HUMILIATED. AND THEN DEAD. AND YOU TWO OWE ME BIG.
UH, WELL--SURE. BEETLE AND KINGPIN COULDN'T HATE ME ANY MORE!
Y-YEAH... S-SURE. I'M IN... I GUESS.
I'VE GOT TO PROVE MYSELF. I'VE GOT TO!
OKAY. YOU'RE IN THIS TOGETHER. AND BEFORE WE'RE THROUGH--
--THE BEETLE WILL BE BEGGING FOR DEATH.

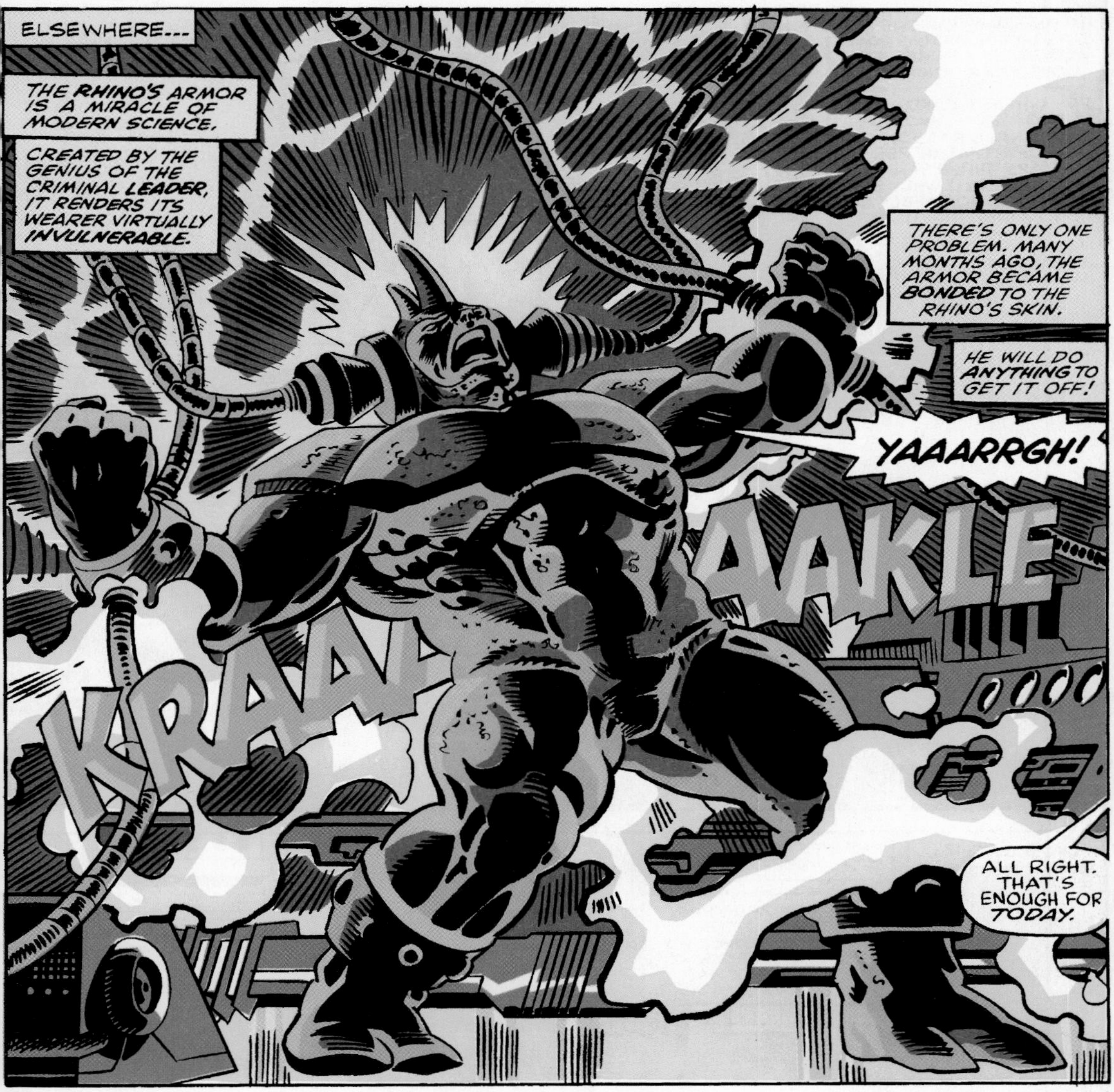
ELSEWHERE...
THE RHINO'S ARMOR IS A MIRACLE OF MODERN SCIENCE.
CREATED BY THE GENIUS OF THE CRIMINAL LEADER, IT RENDERS ITS WEARER VIRTUALLY INVULNERABLE.
THERE'S ONLY ONE PROBLEM. MANY MONTHS AGO, THE ARMOR BECAME BONDED TO THE RHINO'S SKIN.
HE WILL DO ANYTHING TO GET IT OFF!
YAAARRGH!
KRAAAAKLE
ALL RIGHT. THAT'S ENOUGH FOR TODAY.

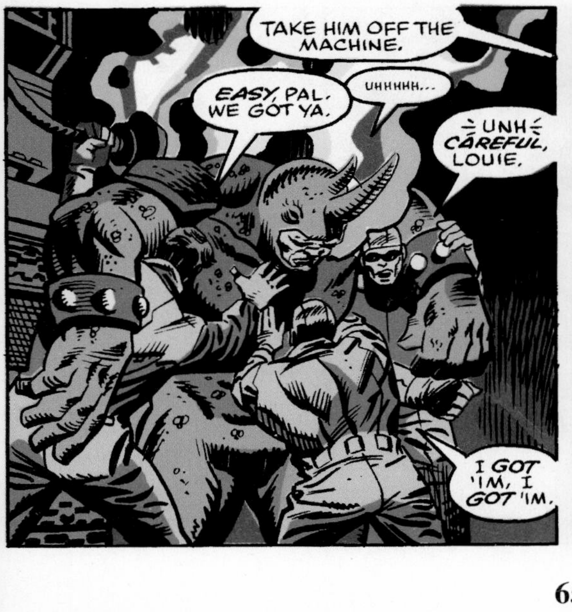
TAKE HIM OFF THE MACHINE.
EASY, PAL. WE GOT YA.
UHHHHH...
UNH CAREFUL, LOUIE.
I GOT 'IM, I GOT 'IM.

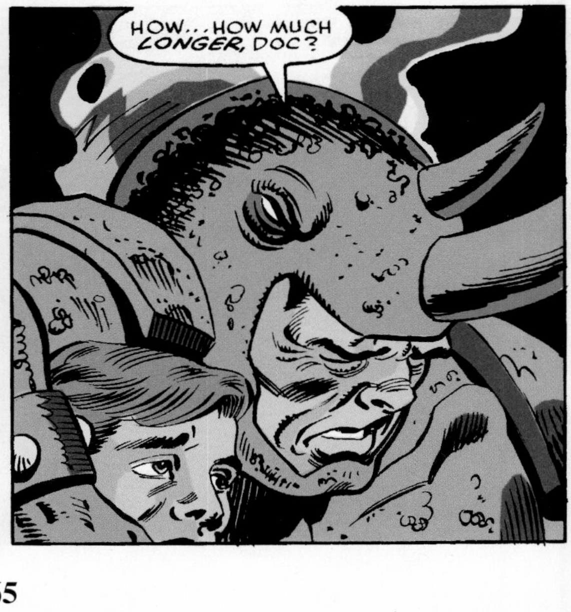
HOW... HOW MUCH LONGER, DOC?

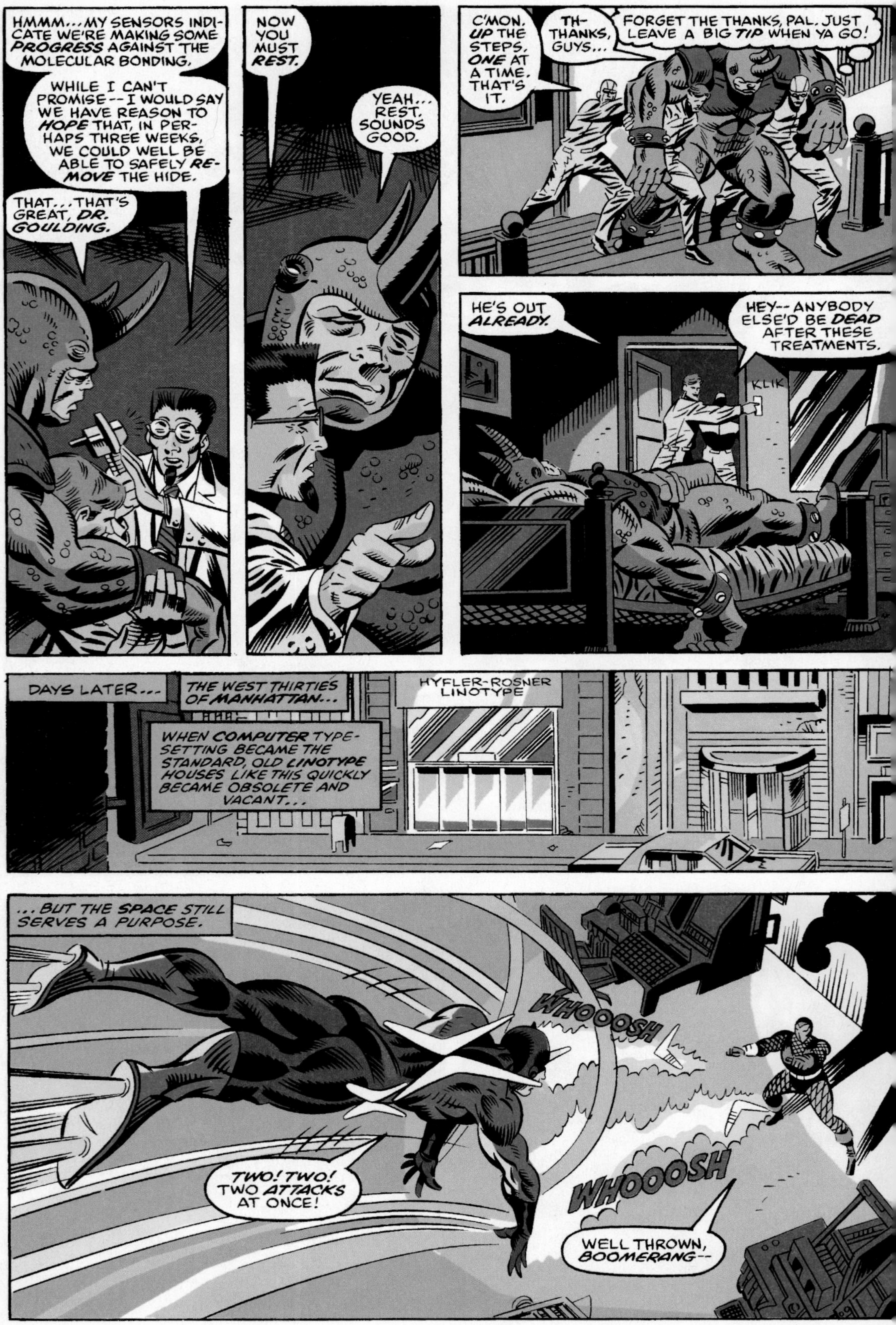

HMMM... MY SENSORS INDICATE WE'RE MAKING SOME PROGRESS AGAINST THE MOLECULAR BONDING.
WHILE I CAN'T PROMISE -- I WOULD SAY WE HAVE REASON TO HOPE THAT, IN PERHAPS THREE WEEKS, WE COULD WELL BE ABLE TO SAFELY REMOVE THE HIDE.
THAT... THAT'S GREAT, DR. GOULDING.
NOW YOU MUST REST.
YEAH... REST. SOUNDS GOOD.
C'MON. UP THE STEPS. ONE AT A TIME. THAT'S IT.
TH-THANKS, GUYS...
FORGET THE THANKS, PAL. JUST LEAVE A BIG TIP WHEN YA GO!
HE'S OUT ALREADY.
HEY-- ANYBODY ELSE'D BE DEAD AFTER THESE TREATMENTS.
KLIK
DAYS LATER...
THE WEST THIRTIES OF MANHATTAN...
HYFLER-ROSNER LINOTYPE
WHEN COMPUTER TYPESETTING BECAME THE STANDARD, OLD LINOTYPE HOUSES LIKE THIS QUICKLY BECAME OBSOLETE AND VACANT...
...BUT THE SPACE STILL SERVES A PURPOSE.
WHOOOSH
TWO! TWO! TWO ATTACKS AT ONCE!
WHOOOSH
WELL THROWN, BOOMERANG--

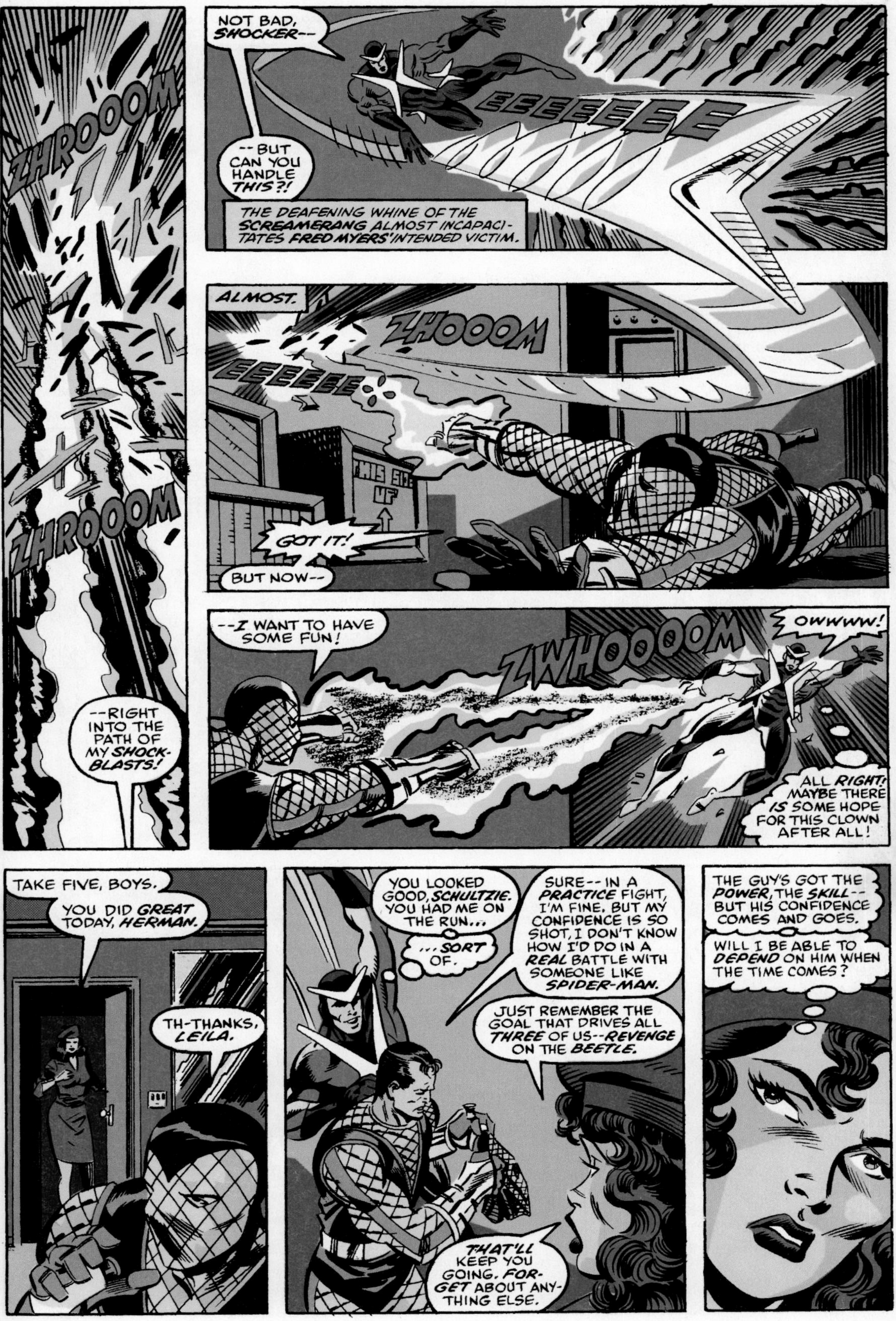
ZHROOOM
ZHROOOM
--RIGHT INTO THE PATH OF MY SHOCK-BLASTS!
NOT BAD, SHOCKER--
EEEEEEE
--BUT CAN YOU HANDLE THIS?!
THE DEAFENING WHINE OF THE SCREAMERANG ALMOST INCAPACITATES FRED MYERS' INTENDED VICTIM.
ALMOST.
ZHOOOM
EEEEEE
GOT IT!
BUT NOW--
--I WANT TO HAVE SOME FUN!
ZWHOOOOOM
OWWWW!
ALL RIGHT! MAYBE THERE IS SOME HOPE FOR THIS CLOWN AFTER ALL!
TAKE FIVE, BOYS.
YOU DID GREAT TODAY, HERMAN.
TH-THANKS, LEILA.
YOU LOOKED GOOD, SCHULTZIE. YOU HAD ME ON THE RUN...
...SORT OF.
SURE-- IN A PRACTICE FIGHT, I'M FINE. BUT MY CONFIDENCE IS SO SHOT, I DON'T KNOW HOW I'D DO IN A REAL BATTLE WITH SOMEONE LIKE SPIDER-MAN.
JUST REMEMBER THE GOAL THAT DRIVES ALL THREE OF US--REVENGE ON THE BEETLE.
THAT'LL KEEP YOU GOING. FORGET ABOUT ANYTHING ELSE.
THE GUY'S GOT THE POWER, THE SKILL-- BUT HIS CONFIDENCE COMES AND GOES.
WILL I BE ABLE TO DEPEND ON HIM WHEN THE TIME COMES?

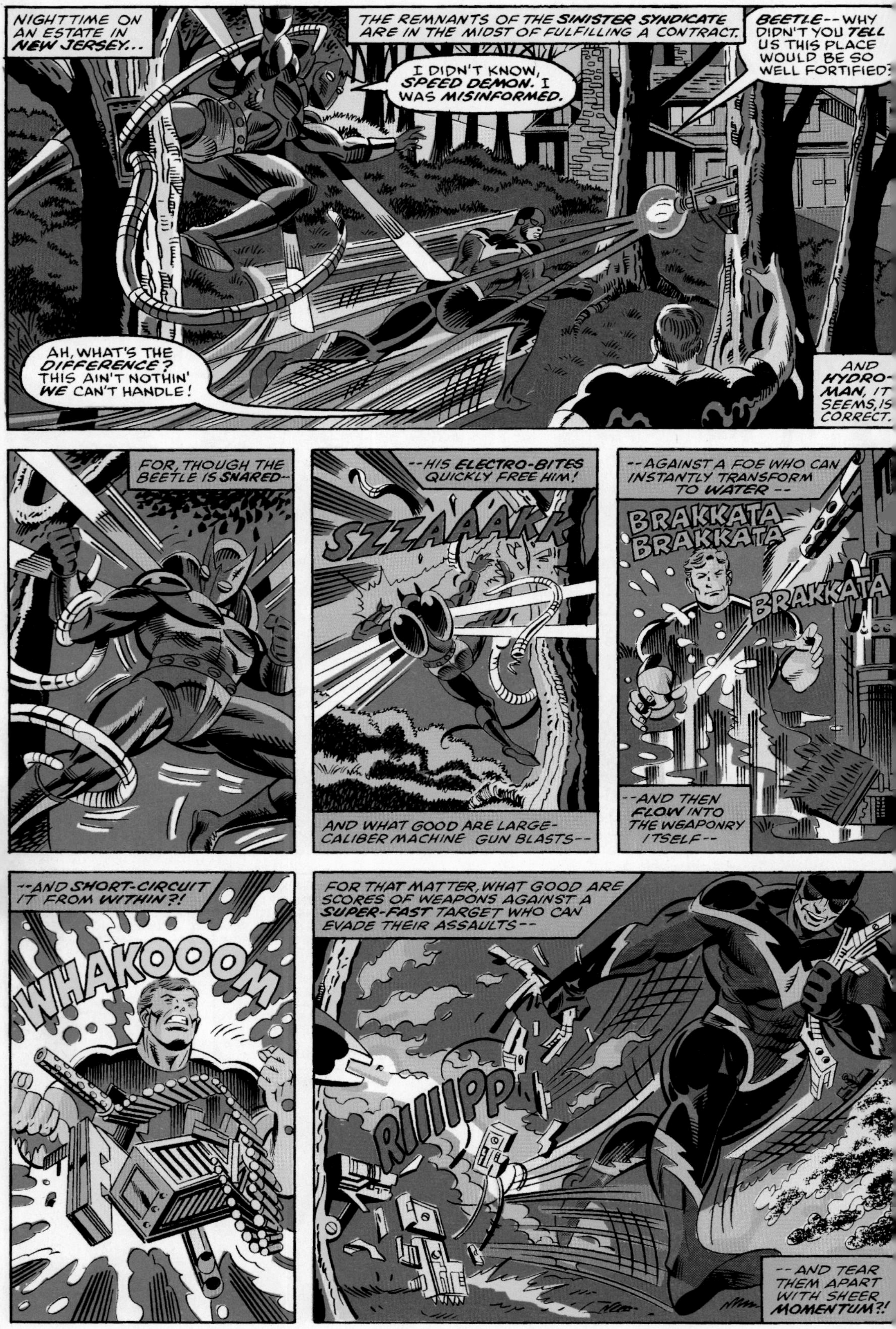
NIGHTTIME ON AN ESTATE IN NEW JERSEY...
THE REMNANTS OF THE SINISTER SYNDICATE ARE IN THE MIDST OF FULFILLING A CONTRACT.
BEETLE--WHY DIDN'T YOU TELL US THIS PLACE WOULD BE SO WELL FORTIFIED?
I DIDN'T KNOW, SPEED DEMON. I WAS MISINFORMED.
AH, WHAT'S THE DIFFERENCE? THIS AIN'T NOTHIN' WE CAN'T HANDLE!
AND HYDRO-MAN, IT SEEMS, IS CORRECT.
FOR, THOUGH THE BEETLE IS SNARED--
--HIS ELECTRO-BITES QUICKLY FREE HIM!
SZZAAAKK
AND WHAT GOOD ARE LARGE-CALIBER MACHINE GUN BLASTS--
--AGAINST A FOE WHO CAN INSTANTLY TRANSFORM TO WATER--
BRAKKATA BRAKKATA
BRAKKATA
--AND THEN FLOW INTO THE WEAPONRY ITSELF--
--AND SHORT-CIRCUIT IT FROM WITHIN?!
WHAKOOOM
FOR THAT MATTER, WHAT GOOD ARE SCORES OF WEAPONS AGAINST A SUPER-FAST TARGET WHO CAN EVADE THEIR ASSAULTS--
RIIIIPP
--AND TEAR THEM APART WITH SHEER MOMENTUM?!

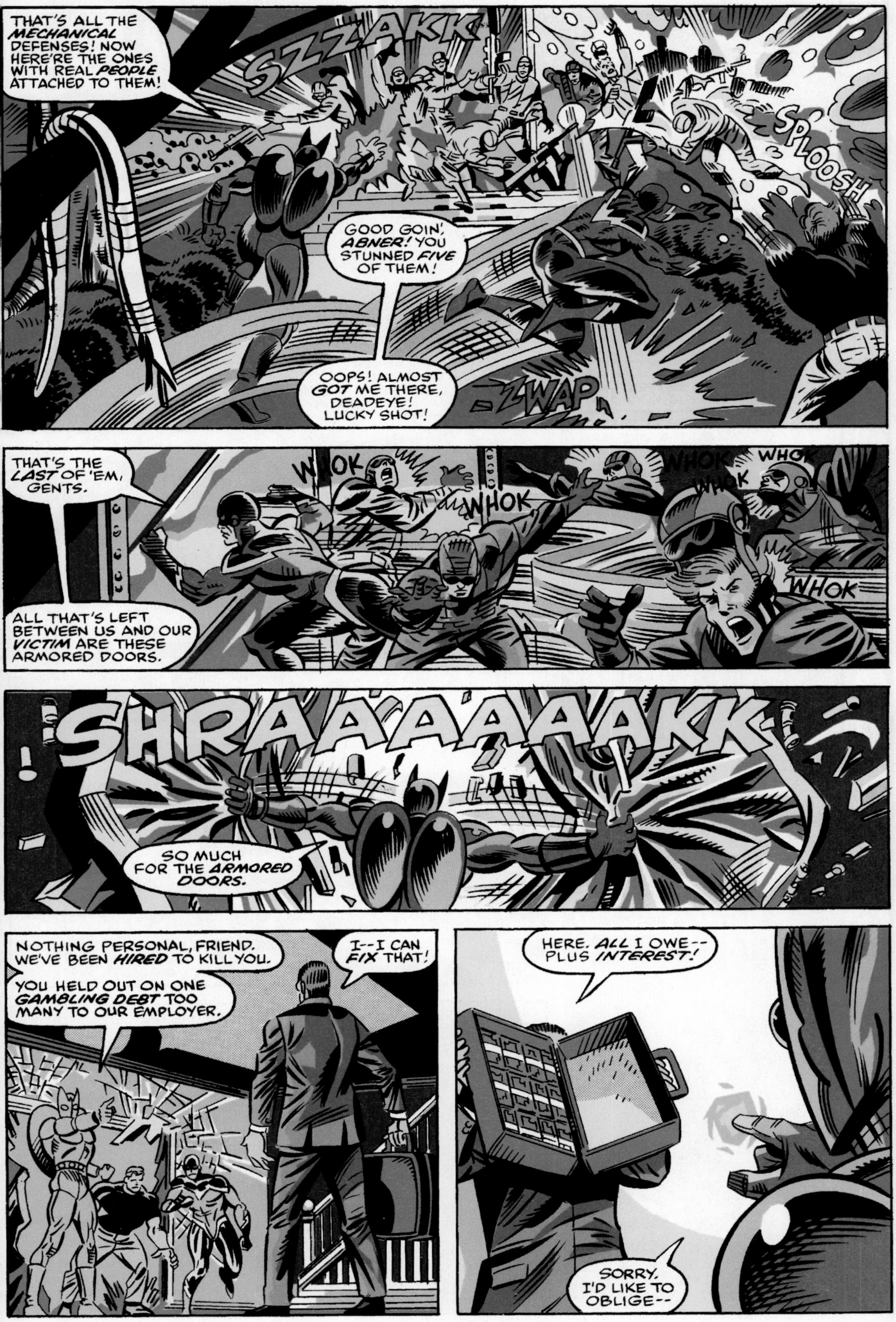
THAT'S ALL THE MECHANICAL DEFENSES! NOW HERE'RE THE ONES WITH REAL PEOPLE ATTACHED TO THEM!
SZZZAKK
SPLOOSH
GOOD GOIN', ABNER! YOU STUNNED FIVE OF THEM!
OOPS! ALMOST GOT ME THERE, DEADEYE! LUCKY SHOT!
ZWAP
THAT'S THE LAST OF 'EM, GENTS.
WHOK
WHOK
WHOK
WHOK
WHOK
WHOK
ALL THAT'S LEFT BETWEEN US AND OUR VICTIM ARE THESE ARMORED DOORS.
SHRAAAAAAKK
SO MUCH FOR THE ARMORED DOORS.
NOTHING PERSONAL, FRIEND. WE'VE BEEN HIRED TO KILL YOU.
YOU HELD OUT ON ONE GAMBLING DEBT TOO MANY TO OUR EMPLOYER.
I--I CAN FIX THAT!
HERE. ALL I OWE-- PLUS INTEREST!
SORRY. I'D LIKE TO OBLIGE--

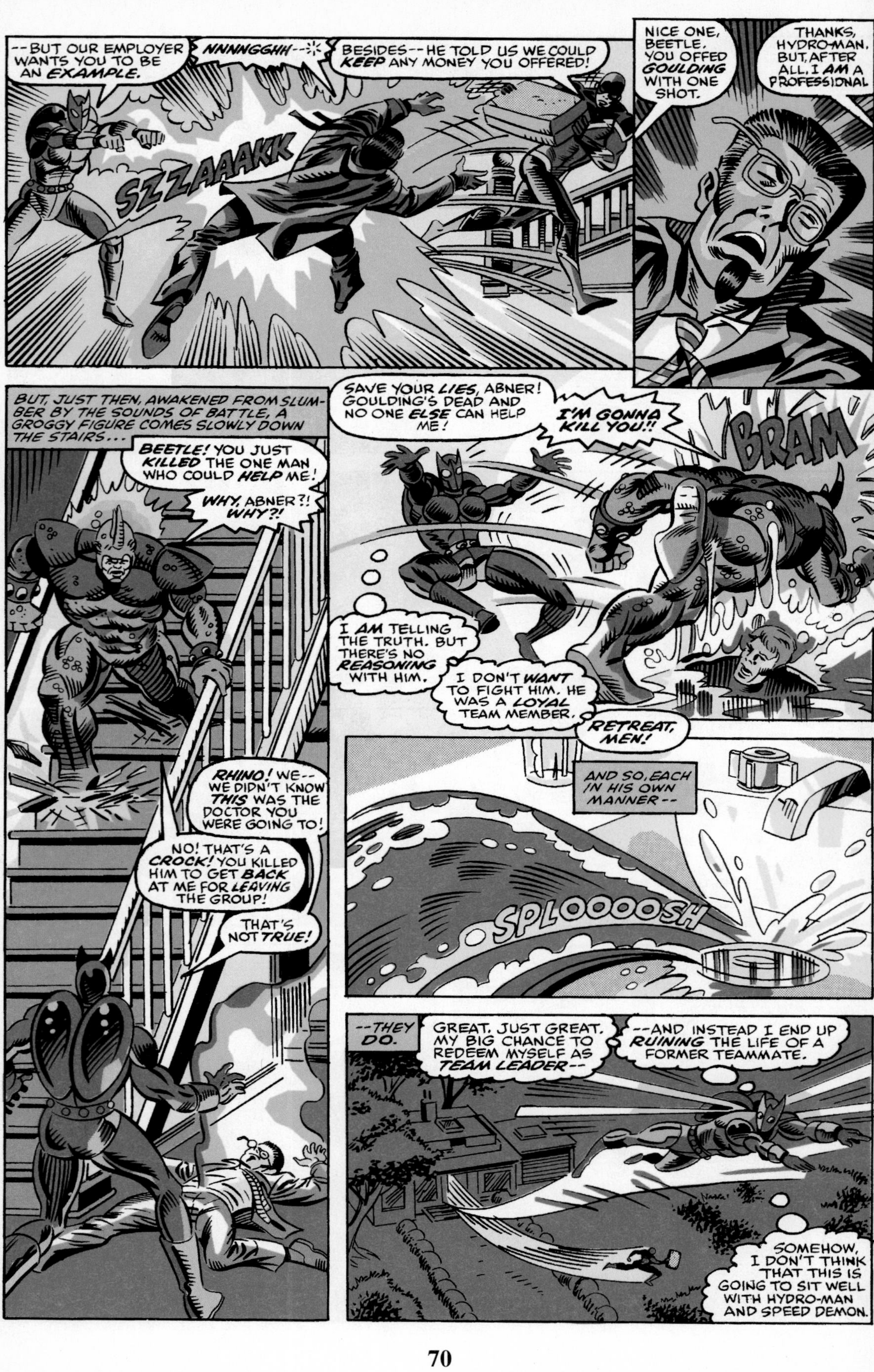
--BUT OUR EMPLOYER WANTS YOU TO BE AN EXAMPLE.
NNNNGGHH--
BESIDES--HE TOLD US WE COULD KEEP ANY MONEY YOU OFFERED!
SZZAAAKK
NICE ONE, BEETLE. YOU OFFED GOULDING WITH ONE SHOT.
THANKS, HYDRO-MAN. BUT, AFTER ALL, I AM A PROFESSIONAL
BUT, JUST THEN, AWAKENED FROM SLUMBER BY THE SOUNDS OF BATTLE, A GROGGY FIGURE COMES SLOWLY DOWN THE STAIRS...
BEETLE! YOU JUST KILLED THE ONE MAN WHO COULD HELP ME!
WHY, ABNER?! WHY?!
RHINO! WE--WE DIDN'T KNOW THIS WAS THE DOCTOR YOU WERE GOING TO!
NO! THAT'S A CROCK! YOU KILLED HIM TO GET BACK AT ME FOR LEAVING THE GROUP!
THAT'S NOT TRUE!
SAVE YOUR LIES, ABNER! GOULDING'S DEAD AND NO ONE ELSE CAN HELP ME!
I'M GONNA KILL YOU!!
BRAM
I AM TELLING THE TRUTH. BUT THERE'S NO REASONING WITH HIM.
I DON'T WANT TO FIGHT HIM. HE WAS A LOYAL TEAM MEMBER.
RETREAT, MEN!
AND SO, EACH IN HIS OWN MANNER--
SPLOOOOOSH
--THEY DO.
GREAT. JUST GREAT. MY BIG CHANCE TO REDEEM MYSELF AS TEAM LEADER--
--AND INSTEAD I END UP RUINING THE LIFE OF A FORMER TEAMMATE.
SOMEHOW, I DON'T THINK THAT THIS IS GOING TO SIT WELL WITH HYDRO-MAN AND SPEED DEMON.

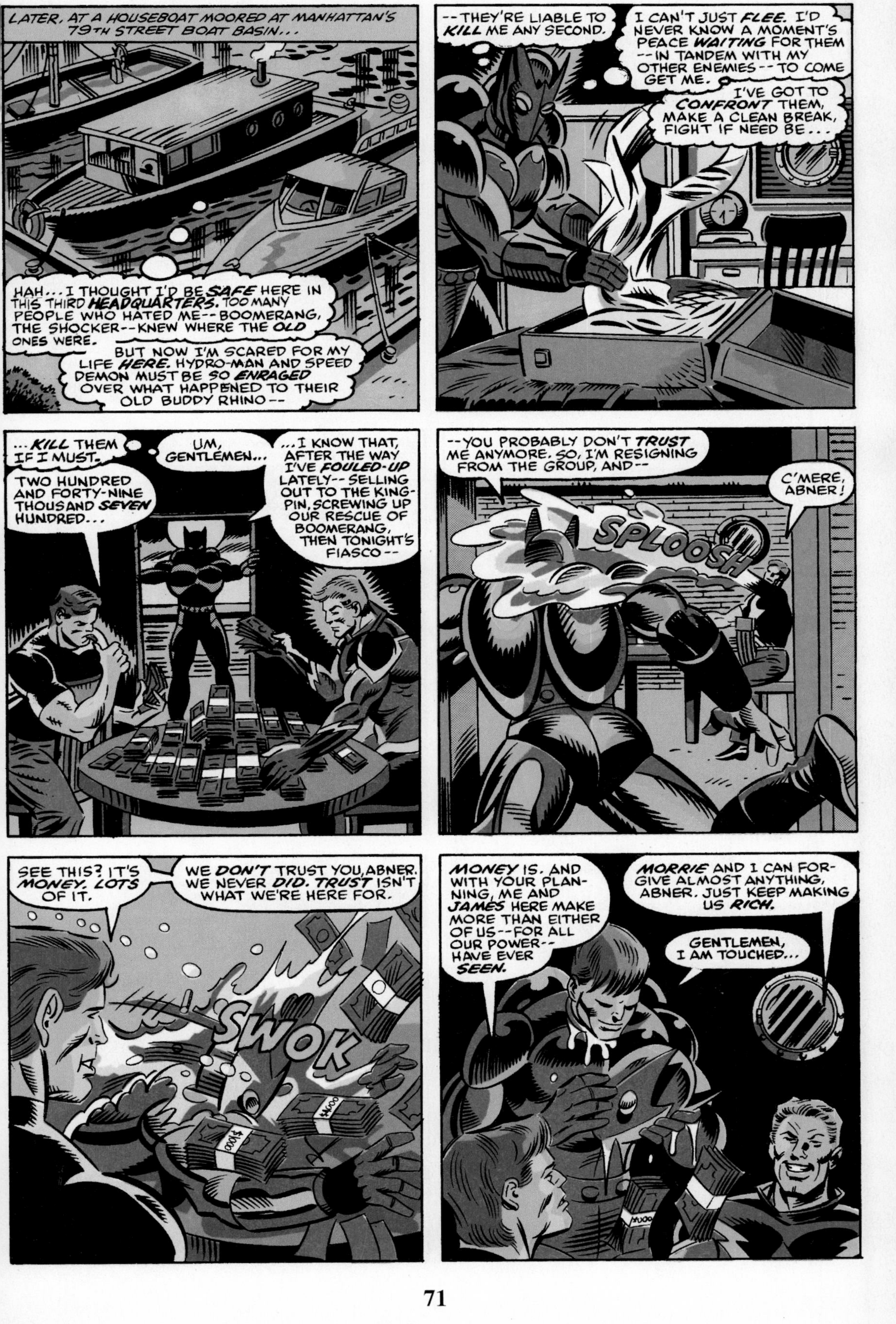
LATER, AT A HOUSEBOAT MOORED AT MANHATTAN'S 79TH STREET BOAT BASIN...
HAH... I THOUGHT I'D BE SAFE HERE IN THIS THIRD HEADQUARTERS. TOO MANY PEOPLE WHO HATED ME--BOOMERANG, THE SHOCKER--KNEW WHERE THE OLD ONES WERE.
BUT NOW I'M SCARED FOR MY LIFE HERE. HYDRO-MAN AND SPEED DEMON MUST BE SO ENRAGED OVER WHAT HAPPENED TO THEIR OLD BUDDY RHINO--
--THEY'RE LIABLE TO KILL ME ANY SECOND.
I CAN'T JUST FLEE. I'D NEVER KNOW A MOMENT'S PEACE WAITING FOR THEM --IN TANDEM WITH MY OTHER ENEMIES--TO COME GET ME.
I'VE GOT TO CONFRONT THEM, MAKE A CLEAN BREAK, FIGHT IF NEED BE...
...KILL THEM IF I MUST.
TWO HUNDRED AND FORTY-NINE THOUSAND SEVEN HUNDRED...
UM, GENTLEMEN...
...I KNOW THAT, AFTER THE WAY I'VE FOULED-UP LATELY--SELLING OUT TO THE KING-PIN, SCREWING UP OUR RESCUE OF BOOMERANG, THEN TONIGHT'S FIASCO--
--YOU PROBABLY DON'T TRUST ME ANYMORE. SO, I'M RESIGNING FROM THE GROUP, AND--
C'MERE, ABNER!
SPLOOSH
SEE THIS? IT'S MONEY. LOTS OF IT.
WE DON'T TRUST YOU, ABNER. WE NEVER DID. TRUST ISN'T WHAT WE'RE HERE FOR.
SWOK
MONEY IS. AND WITH YOUR PLANNING, ME AND JAMES HERE MAKE MORE THAN EITHER OF US--FOR ALL OUR POWER--HAVE EVER SEEN.
MORRIE AND I CAN FORGIVE ALMOST ANYTHING, ABNER. JUST KEEP MAKING US RICH.
GENTLEMEN, I AM TOUCHED...

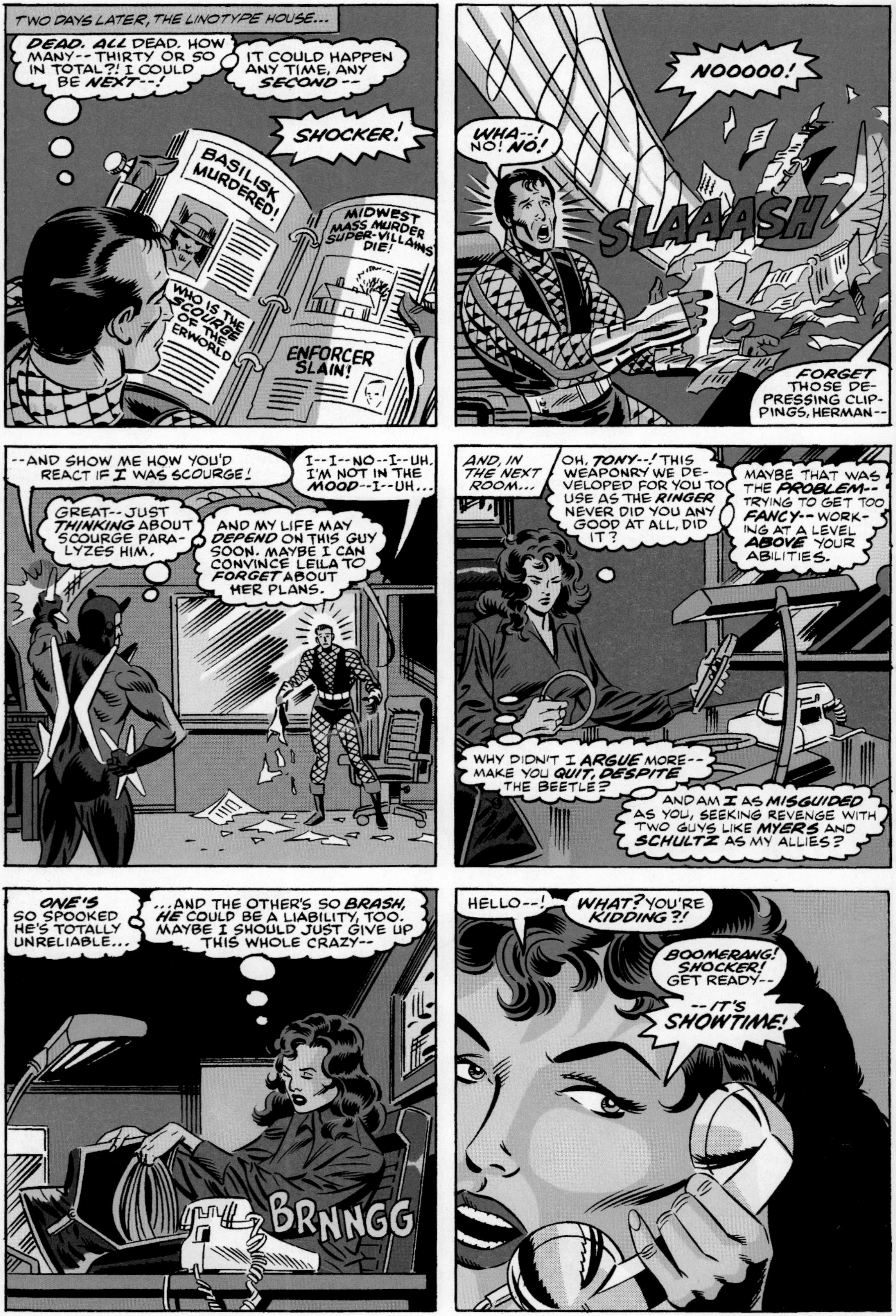
TWO DAYS LATER, THE LINOTYPE HOUSE...
DEAD. ALL DEAD. HOW MANY--THIRTY OR SO IN TOTAL?! I COULD BE NEXT--!
IT COULD HAPPEN ANY TIME, ANY SECOND--
SHOCKER!
BASILISK MURDERED!
MIDWEST MASS MURDER SUPER-VILLAINS DIE!
WHO IS THE SCOURGE OF THE ERWORLD
ENFORCER SLAIN!
NOOOOO!
WHA--! NO! NO!
SLAAASH
FORGET THOSE DEPRESSING CLIPPINGS, HERMAN--
--AND SHOW ME HOW YOU'D REACT IF I WAS SCOURGE!
I--I--NO--I--UH. I'M NOT IN THE MOOD--I--UH...
GREAT--JUST THINKING ABOUT SCOURGE PARALYZES HIM.
AND MY LIFE MAY DEPEND ON THIS GUY SOON. MAYBE I CAN CONVINCE LEILA TO FORGET ABOUT HER PLANS.
AND, IN THE NEXT ROOM...
OH, TONY--! THIS WEAPONRY WE DEVELOPED FOR YOU TO USE AS THE RINGER NEVER DID YOU ANY GOOD AT ALL, DID IT?
MAYBE THAT WAS THE PROBLEM--TRYING TO GET TOO FANCY--WORKING AT A LEVEL ABOVE YOUR ABILITIES.
WHY DIDN'T I ARGUE MORE--MAKE YOU QUIT, DESPITE THE BEETLE?
AND AM I AS MISGUIDED AS YOU, SEEKING REVENGE WITH TWO GUYS LIKE MYERS AND SCHULTZ AS MY ALLIES?
ONE'S SO SPOOKED HE'S TOTALLY UNRELIABLE...
...AND THE OTHER'S SO BRASH, HE COULD BE A LIABILITY, TOO. MAYBE I SHOULD JUST GIVE UP THIS WHOLE CRAZY--
BRNNGG
HELLO--!
WHAT? YOU'RE KIDDING?!
BOOMERANG! SHOCKER! GET READY--
--IT'S SHOWTIME!

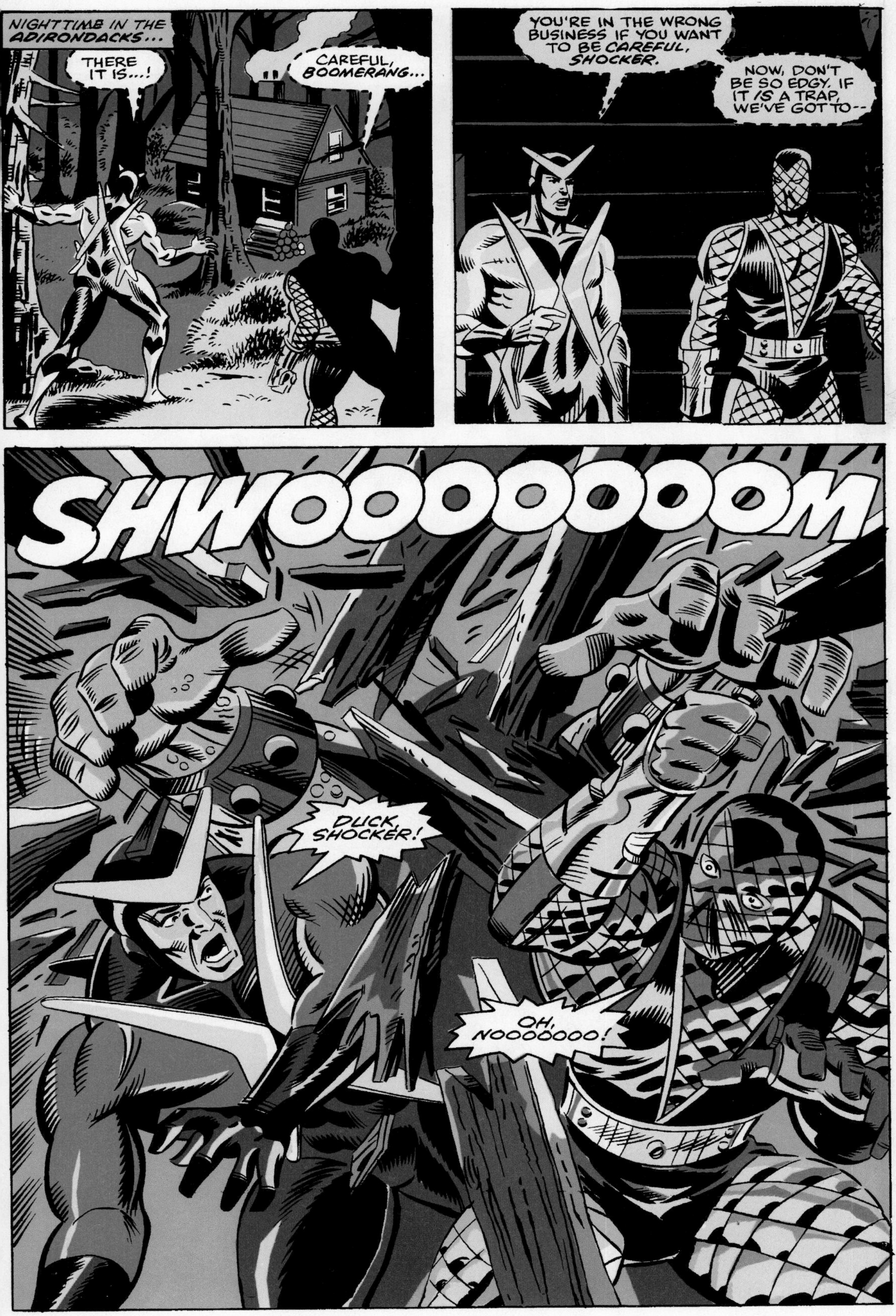
NIGHTTIME IN THE ADIRONDACKS...
THERE IT IS...!
CAREFUL, BOOMERANG...
YOU'RE IN THE WRONG BUSINESS IF YOU WANT TO BE CAREFUL, SHOCKER.
NOW, DON'T BE SO EDGY. IF IT IS A TRAP, WE'VE GOT TO--
SHWOOOOOOOOM
DUCK, SHOCKER!
OH, NOOOOOOO!

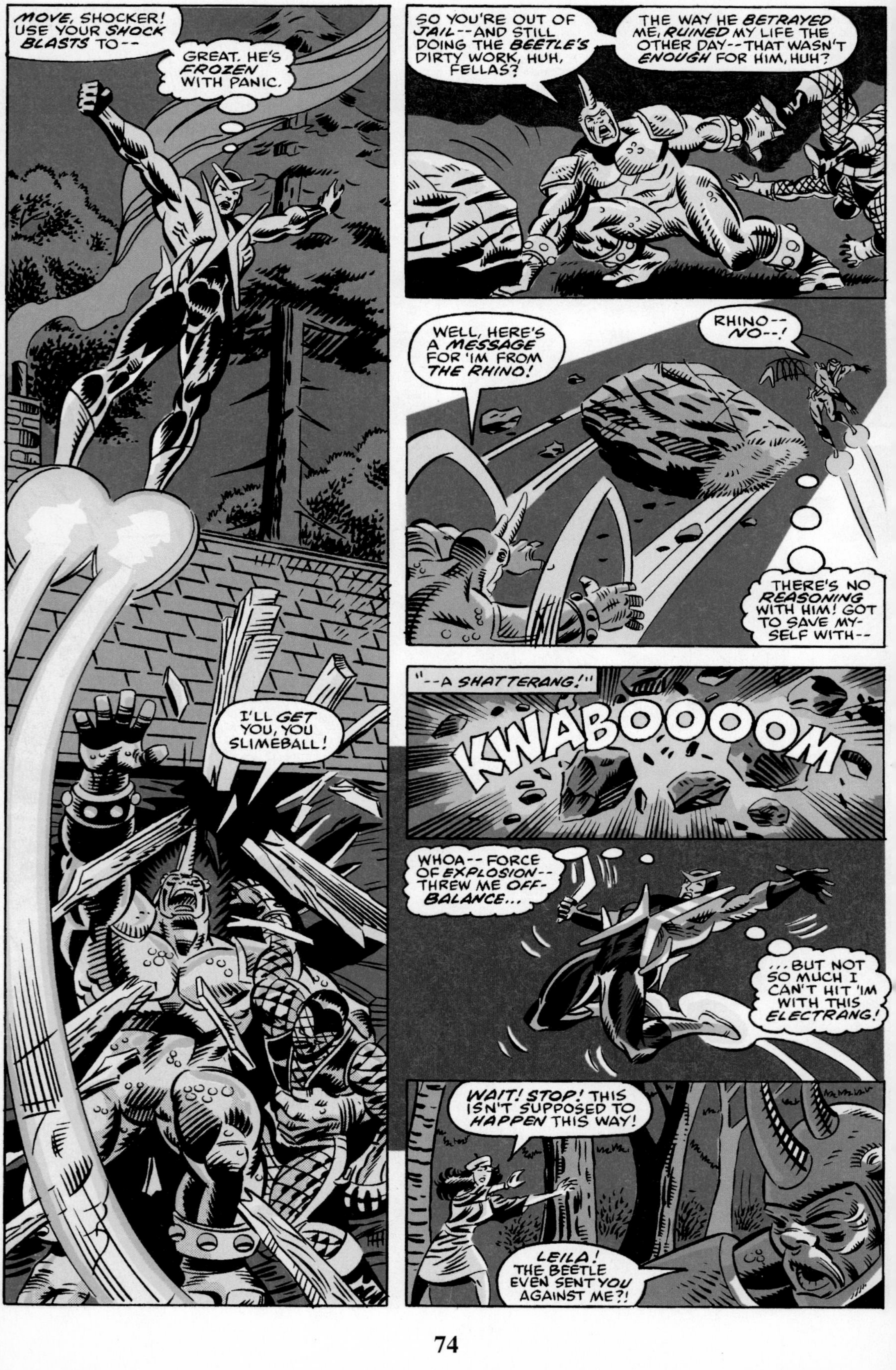
MOVE, SHOCKER! USE YOUR SHOCK BLASTS TO--
GREAT. HE'S FROZEN WITH PANIC.
I'LL GET YOU, YOU SLIMEBALL!
SO YOU'RE OUT OF JAIL--AND STILL DOING THE BEETLE'S DIRTY WORK, HUH, FELLAS?
THE WAY HE BETRAYED ME, RUINED MY LIFE THE OTHER DAY--THAT WASN'T ENOUGH FOR HIM, HUH?
WELL, HERE'S A MESSAGE FOR 'IM FROM THE RHINO!
RHINO-- NO--!
THERE'S NO REASONING WITH HIM! GOT TO SAVE MY-SELF WITH--
"--A SHATTERANG!"
KWABOOOOOM
WHOA--FORCE OF EXPLOSION--THREW ME OFF-BALANCE...
...BUT NOT SO MUCH I CAN'T HIT 'IM WITH THIS ELECTRANG!
WAIT! STOP! THIS ISN'T SUPPOSED TO HAPPEN THIS WAY!
LEILA! THE BEETLE EVEN SENT YOU AGAINST ME?!

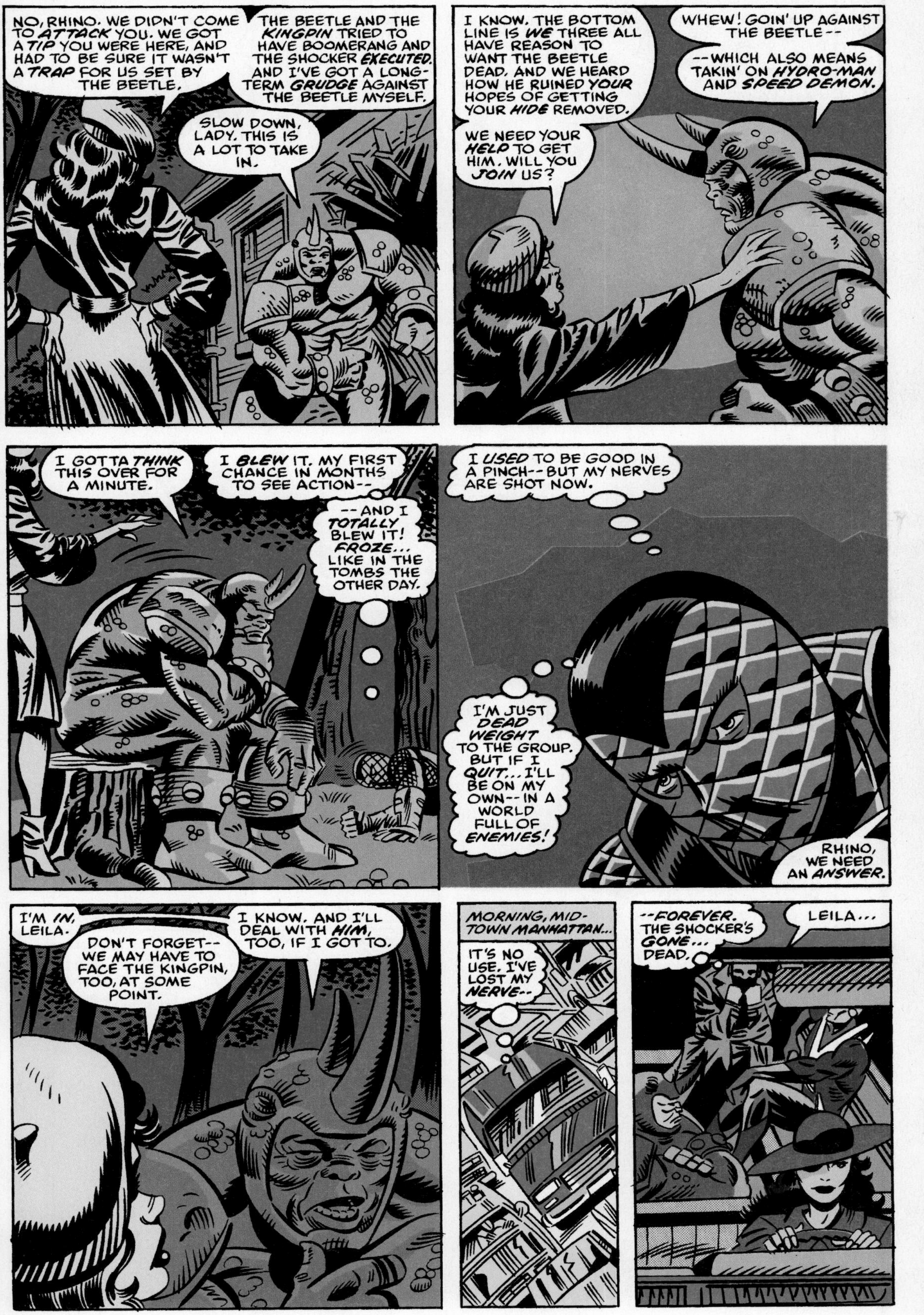

NO, RHINO. WE DIDN'T COME TO ATTACK YOU. WE GOT A TIP YOU WERE HERE, AND HAD TO BE SURE IT WASN'T A TRAP FOR US SET BY THE BEETLE.
THE BEETLE AND THE KINGPIN TRIED TO HAVE BOOMERANG AND THE SHOCKER EXECUTED. AND I'VE GOT A LONG-TERM GRUDGE AGAINST THE BEETLE MYSELF.
SLOW DOWN, LADY. THIS IS A LOT TO TAKE IN.
I KNOW. THE BOTTOM LINE IS WE THREE ALL HAVE REASON TO WANT THE BEETLE DEAD. AND WE HEARD HOW HE RUINED YOUR HOPES OF GETTING YOUR HIDE REMOVED.
WE NEED YOUR HELP TO GET HIM. WILL YOU JOIN US?
WHEW! GOIN' UP AGAINST THE BEETLE--
--WHICH ALSO MEANS TAKIN' ON HYDRO-MAN AND SPEED DEMON.
I GOTTA THINK THIS OVER FOR A MINUTE.
I BLEW IT. MY FIRST CHANCE IN MONTHS TO SEE ACTION--
--AND I TOTALLY BLEW IT! FROZE... LIKE IN THE TOMBS THE OTHER DAY.
I USED TO BE GOOD IN A PINCH--BUT MY NERVES ARE SHOT NOW.
I'M JUST DEAD WEIGHT TO THE GROUP. BUT IF I QUIT... I'LL BE ON MY OWN--IN A WORLD FULL OF ENEMIES!
RHINO, WE NEED AN ANSWER.
I'M IN, LEILA.
DON'T FORGET--WE MAY HAVE TO FACE THE KINGPIN, TOO, AT SOME POINT.
I KNOW. AND I'LL DEAL WITH HIM, TOO, IF I GOT TO.
MORNING, MID-TOWN MANHATTAN...
IT'S NO USE. I'VE LOST MY NERVE--
--FOREVER. THE SHOCKER'S GONE... DEAD.
LEILA...

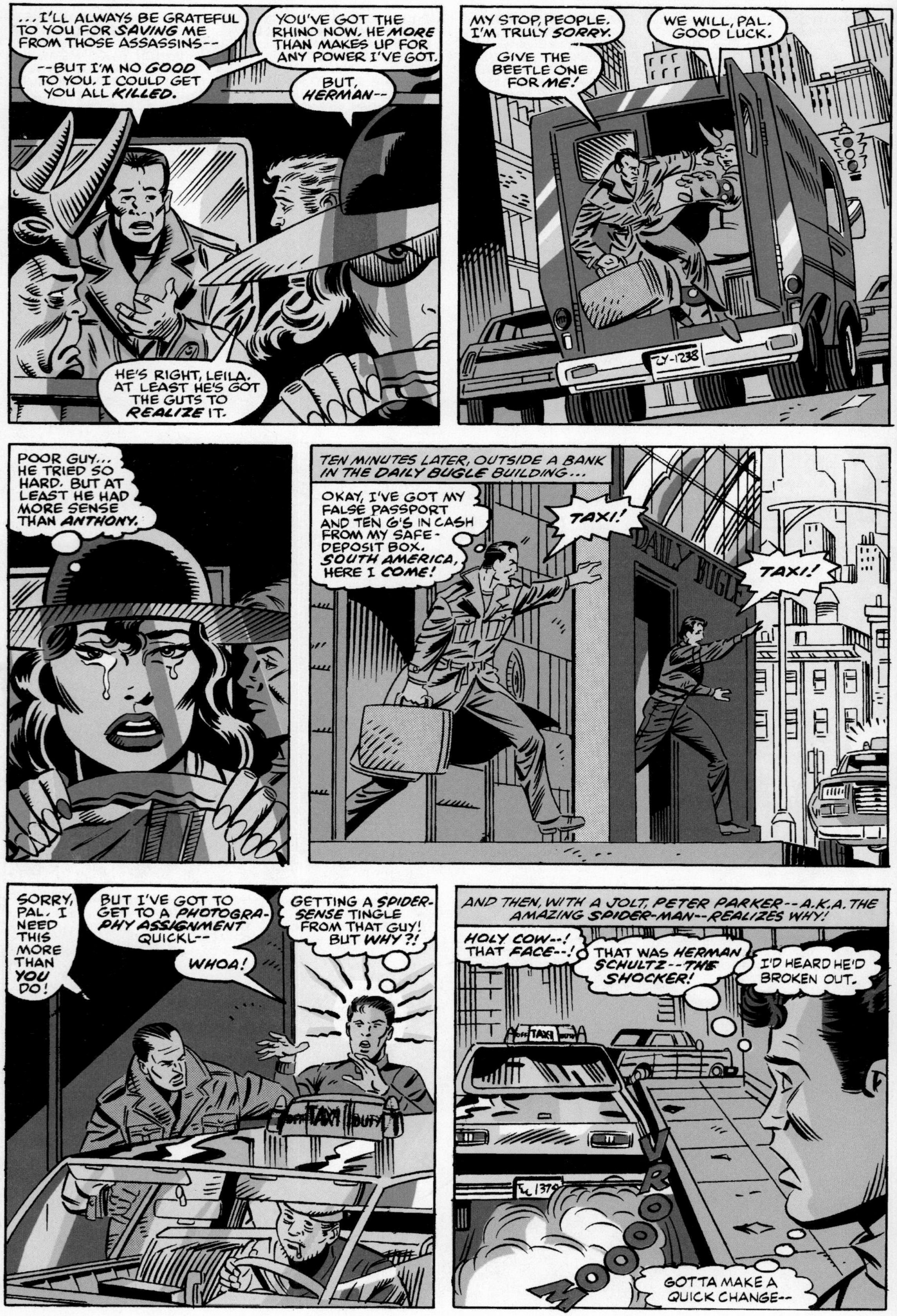

...I'LL ALWAYS BE GRATEFUL TO YOU FOR SAVING ME FROM THOSE ASSASSINS--
--BUT I'M NO GOOD TO YOU. I COULD GET YOU ALL KILLED.
YOU'VE GOT THE RHINO NOW. HE MORE THAN MAKES UP FOR ANY POWER I'VE GOT.
BUT, HERMAN--
HE'S RIGHT, LEILA. AT LEAST HE'S GOT THE GUTS TO REALIZE IT.
MY STOP, PEOPLE. I'M TRULY SORRY.
GIVE THE BEETLE ONE FOR ME!
WE WILL, PAL. GOOD LUCK.
POOR GUY... HE TRIED SO HARD. BUT AT LEAST HE HAD MORE SENSE THAN ANTHONY.
TEN MINUTES LATER, OUTSIDE A BANK IN THE DAILY BUGLE BUILDING...
OKAY, I'VE GOT MY FALSE PASSPORT AND TEN G'S IN CASH FROM MY SAFE-DEPOSIT BOX. SOUTH AMERICA, HERE I COME!
TAXI!
DAILY BUGLE
TAXI!
SORRY, PAL. I NEED THIS MORE THAN YOU DO!
BUT I'VE GOT TO GET TO A PHOTOGRAPHY ASSIGNMENT QUICKL--
WHOA!
GETTING A SPIDER-SENSE TINGLE FROM THAT GUY! BUT WHY?!
AND THEN, WITH A JOLT, PETER PARKER--A.K.A. THE AMAZING SPIDER-MAN--REALIZES WHY!
HOLY COW--! THAT FACE--!
THAT WAS HERMAN SCHULTZ--THE SHOCKER!
I'D HEARD HE'D BROKEN OUT.
VROOOOOM
GOTTA MAKE A QUICK CHANGE--

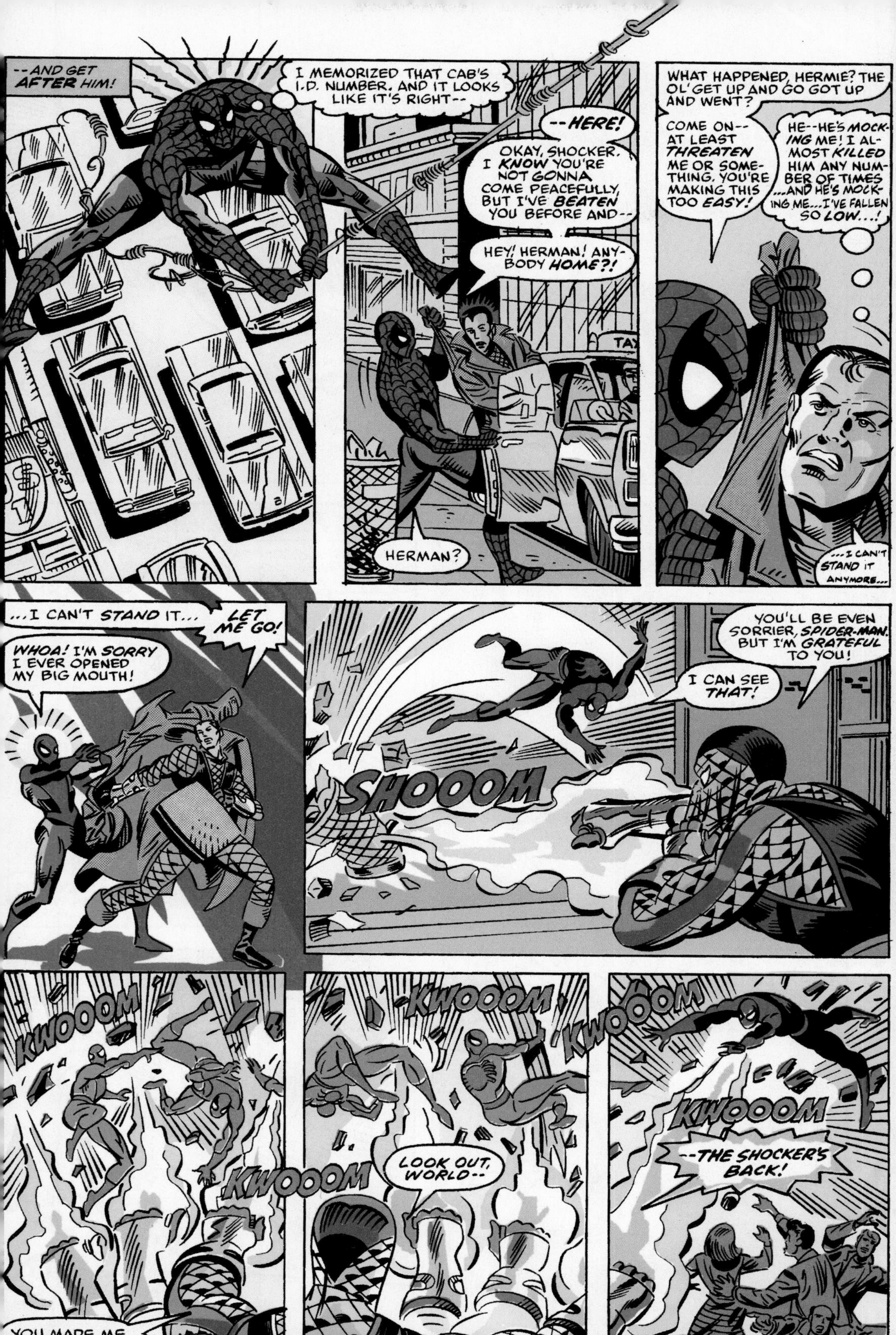

--AND GET AFTER HIM!
I MEMORIZED THAT CAB'S I.D. NUMBER. AND IT LOOKS LIKE IT'S RIGHT--
--HERE!
OKAY, SHOCKER. I KNOW YOU'RE NOT GONNA COME PEACEFULLY, BUT I'VE BEATEN YOU BEFORE AND--
HEY! HERMAN! ANYBODY HOME?!
HERMAN?
WHAT HAPPENED, HERMIE? THE OL' GET UP AND GO GOT UP AND WENT?
COME ON--AT LEAST THREATEN ME OR SOMETHING. YOU'RE MAKING THIS TOO EASY!
HE--HE'S MOCKING ME! I ALMOST KILLED HIM ANY NUMBER OF TIMES ...AND HE'S MOCKING ME...I'VE FALLEN SO LOW...!
...I CAN'T STAND IT ANYMORE...
...I CAN'T STAND IT...
LET ME GO!
WHOA! I'M SORRY I EVER OPENED MY BIG MOUTH!
SHOOOM
I CAN SEE THAT!
YOU'LL BE EVEN SORRIER, SPIDER-MAN. BUT I'M GRATEFUL TO YOU!
KWOOOM
KWOOOM
YOU MADE ME ANGRY ENOUGH TO FIGHT BACK!
KWOOOM
LOOK OUT, WORLD--
KWOOOM
KWOOOM
--THE SHOCKER'S BACK!

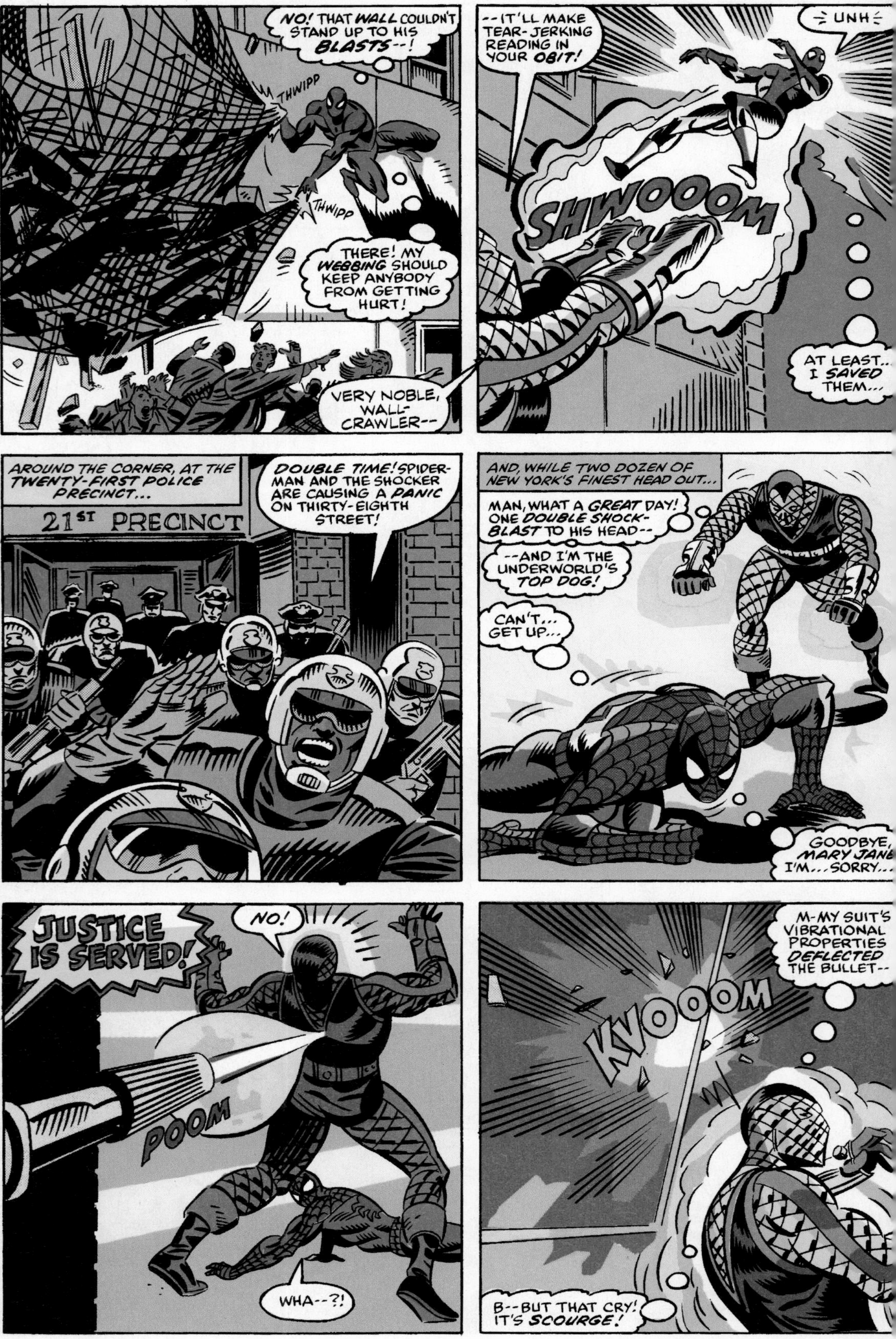

NO! THAT WALL COULDN'T STAND UP TO HIS BLASTS--!
THWIPP
THWIPP
THERE! MY WEBBING SHOULD KEEP ANYBODY FROM GETTING HURT!
VERY NOBLE, WALL-CRAWLER--
--IT'LL MAKE TEAR-JERKING READING IN YOUR OBIT!
UNH
SHWOOOM
AT LEAST... I SAVED THEM...
AROUND THE CORNER, AT THE TWENTY-FIRST POLICE PRECINCT...
DOUBLE TIME! SPIDER-MAN AND THE SHOCKER ARE CAUSING A PANIC ON THIRTY-EIGHTH STREET!
21ST PRECINCT
AND, WHILE TWO DOZEN OF NEW YORK'S FINEST HEAD OUT...
MAN, WHAT A GREAT DAY! ONE DOUBLE SHOCK-BLAST TO HIS HEAD--
--AND I'M THE UNDERWORLD'S TOP DOG!
CAN'T... GET UP...
GOODBYE, MARY JANE I'M... SORRY...
JUSTICE IS SERVED!
NO!
POOM
WHA--?!
M-MY SUIT'S VIBRATIONAL PROPERTIES DEFLECTED THE BULLET--
KVOOOM
B--BUT THAT CRY! IT'S SCOURGE!

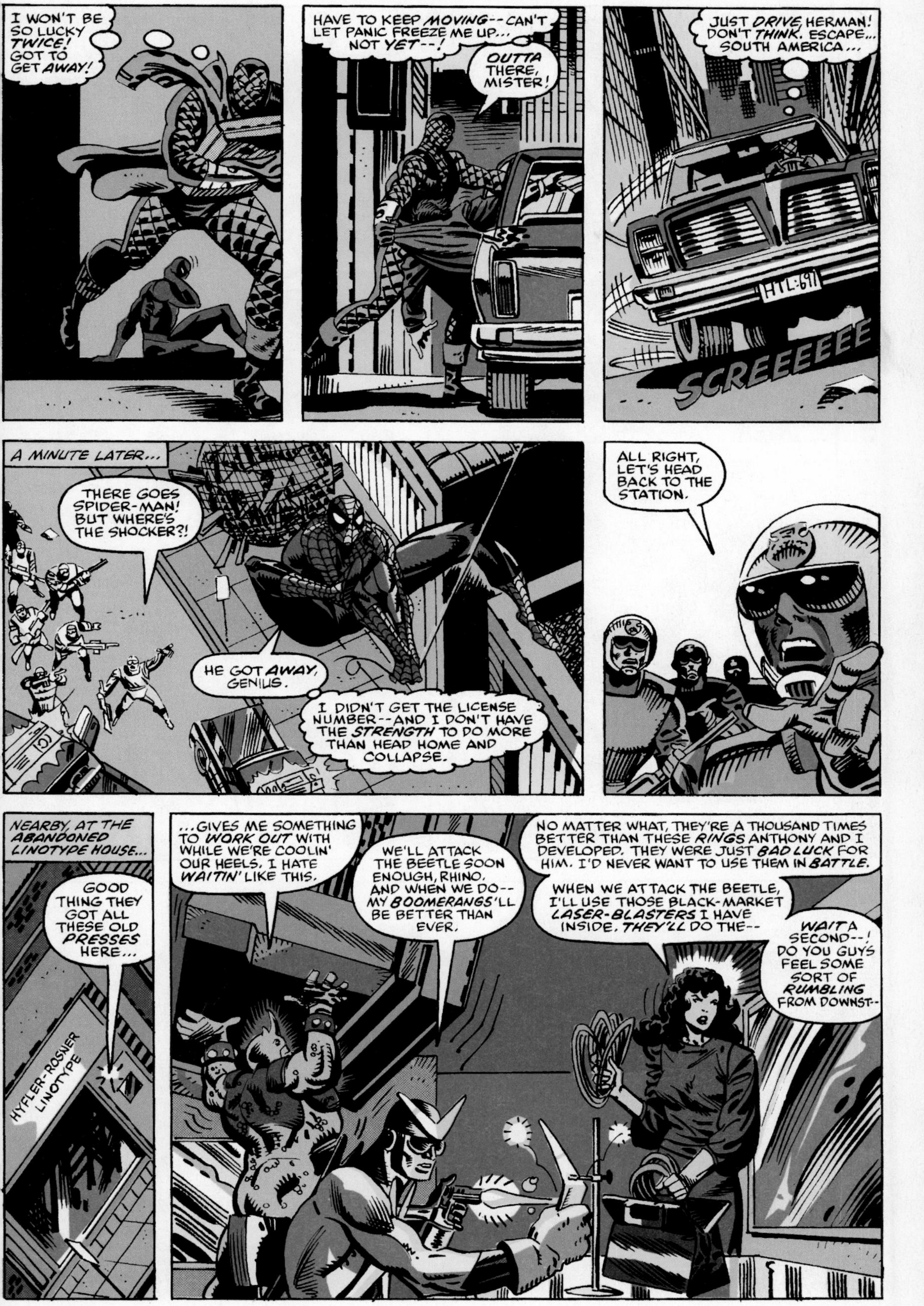

I WON'T BE SO LUCKY TWICE! GOT TO GET AWAY!
HAVE TO KEEP MOVING--CAN'T LET PANIC FREEZE ME UP... NOT YET--!
OUTTA THERE, MISTER!
JUST DRIVE, HERMAN! DON'T THINK. ESCAPE... SOUTH AMERICA...
HTL-691
SCREEEEEEE
A MINUTE LATER...
THERE GOES SPIDER-MAN! BUT WHERE'S THE SHOCKER?!
HE GOT AWAY, GENIUS.
I DIDN'T GET THE LICENSE NUMBER--AND I DON'T HAVE THE STRENGTH TO DO MORE THAN HEAD HOME AND COLLAPSE.
ALL RIGHT, LET'S HEAD BACK TO THE STATION.
NEARBY, AT THE ABANDONED LINOTYPE HOUSE...
GOOD THING THEY GOT ALL THESE OLD PRESSES HERE...
HYFLER-ROSNER LINOTYPE
...GIVES ME SOMETHING TO WORK OUT WITH WHILE WE'RE COOLIN' OUR HEELS. I HATE WAITIN' LIKE THIS.
WE'LL ATTACK THE BEETLE SOON ENOUGH, RHINO. AND WHEN WE DO--MY BOOMERANGS'LL BE BETTER THAN EVER.
NO MATTER WHAT, THEY'RE A THOUSAND TIMES BETTER THAN THESE RINGS ANTHONY AND I DEVELOPED. THEY WERE JUST BAD LUCK FOR HIM. I'D NEVER WANT TO USE THEM IN BATTLE.
WHEN WE ATTACK THE BEETLE, I'LL USE THOSE BLACK-MARKET LASER-BLASTERS I HAVE INSIDE. THEY'LL DO THE--
WAIT A SECOND--! DO YOU GUYS FEEL SOME SORT OF RUMBLING FROM DOWNST-

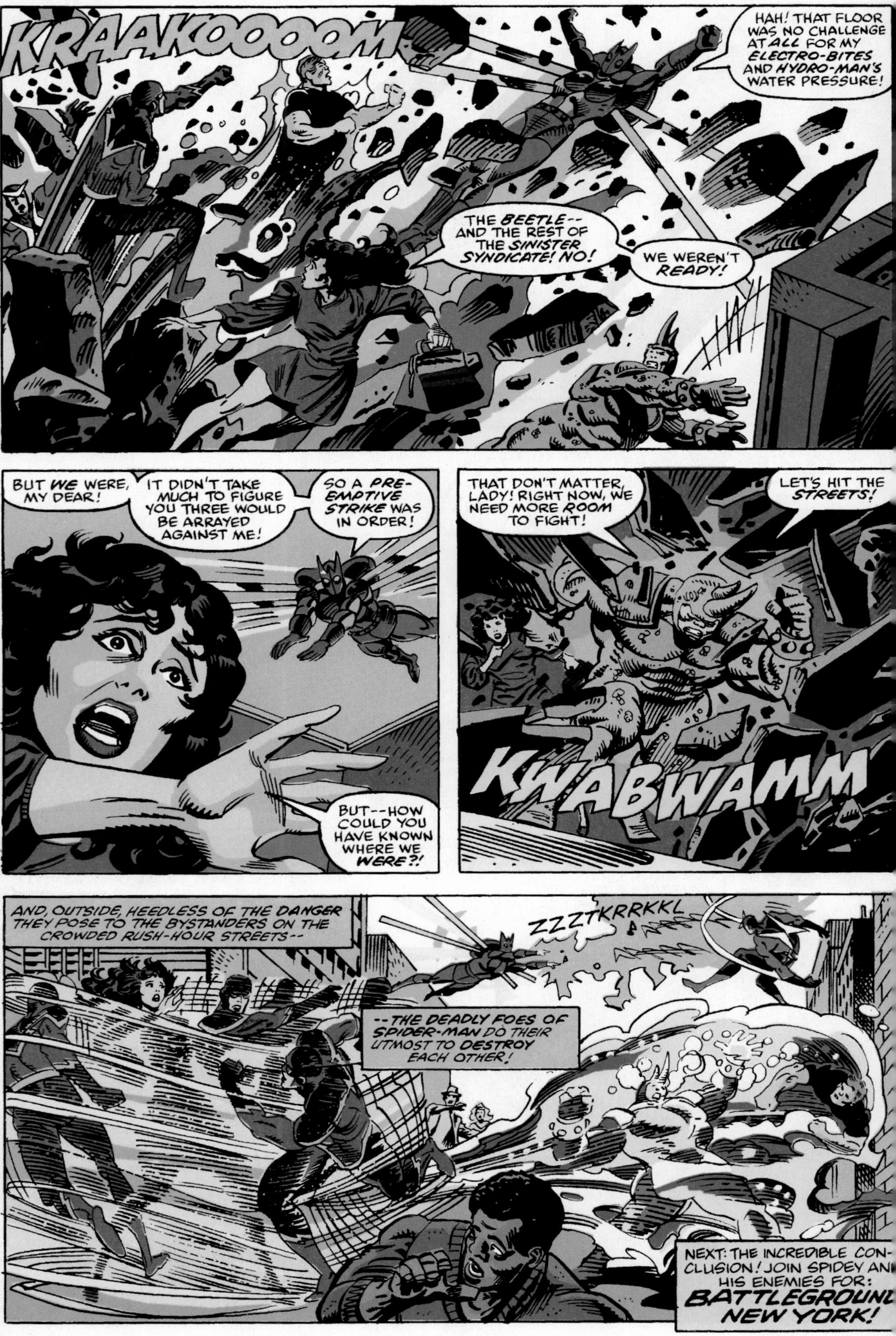
KRAAKOOOOM
HAH! THAT FLOOR WAS NO CHALLENGE AT ALL FOR MY ELECTRO-BITES AND HYDRO-MAN'S WATER PRESSURE!
THE BEETLE-- AND THE REST OF THE SINISTER SYNDICATE! NO!
WE WEREN'T READY!
BUT WE WERE, MY DEAR!
IT DIDN'T TAKE MUCH TO FIGURE YOU THREE WOULD BE ARRAYED AGAINST ME!
SO A PRE-EMPTIVE STRIKE WAS IN ORDER!
BUT--HOW COULD YOU HAVE KNOWN WHERE WE WERE?!
THAT DON'T MATTER, LADY! RIGHT NOW, WE NEED MORE ROOM TO FIGHT!
LET'S HIT THE STREETS!
KWABWAMM
AND, OUTSIDE, HEEDLESS OF THE DANGER THEY POSE TO THE BYSTANDERS ON THE CROWDED RUSH-HOUR STREETS--
ZZZTKRRKKL
--THE DEADLY FOES OF SPIDER-MAN DO THEIR UTMOST TO DESTROY EACH OTHER!
NEXT: THE INCREDIBLE CONCLUSION! JOIN SPIDEY AN HIS ENEMIES FOR: BATTLEGROUNI NEW YORK!

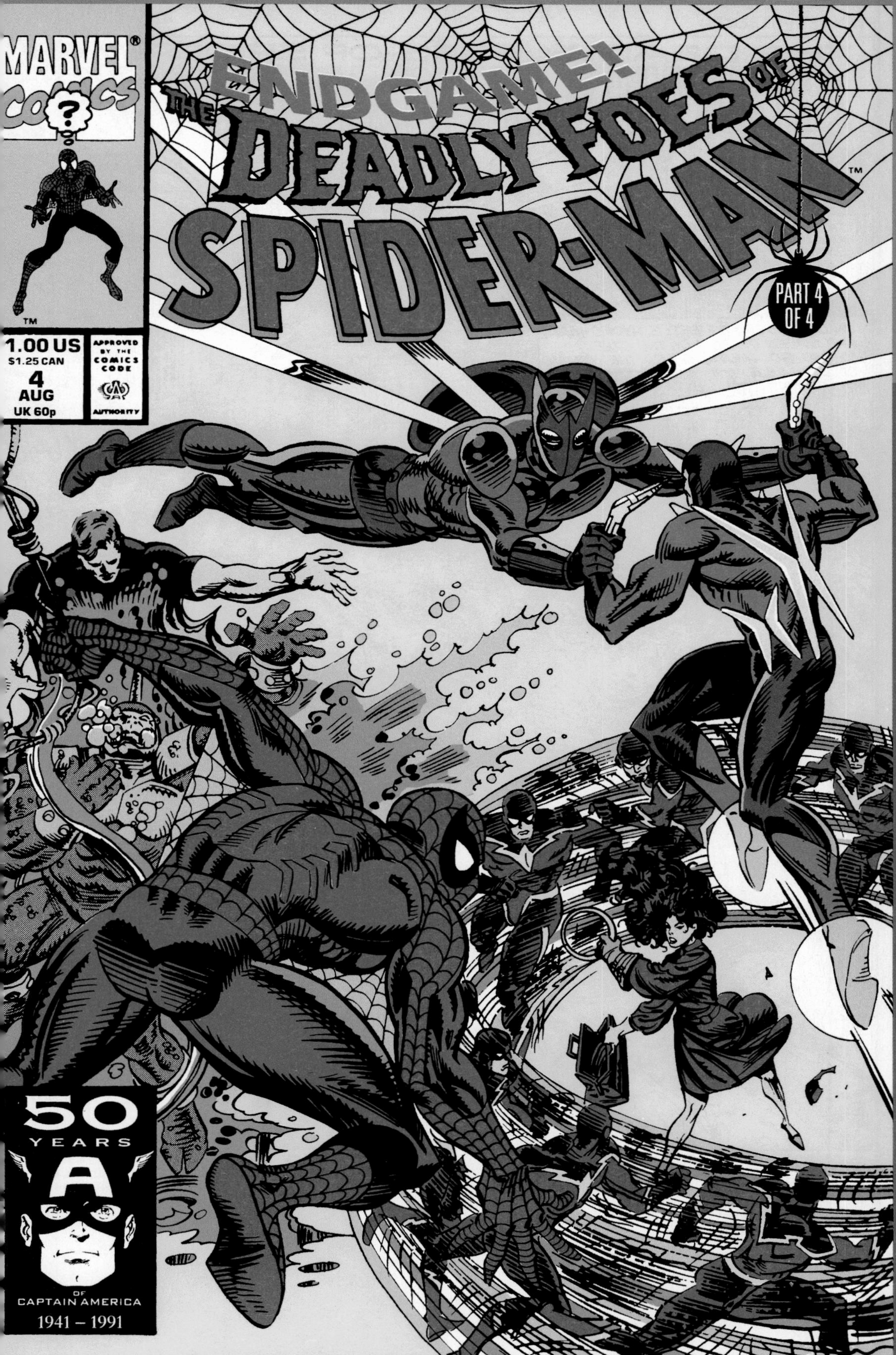

MARVEL® COMICS
TM
1.00 US
$1.25 CAN
4
AUG
UK 60p
APPROVED BY THE COMICS CODE AUTHORITY
ENDGAME!
THE DEADLY FOES OF SPIDER-MAN™
PART 4 OF 4
50 YEARS
A
OF CAPTAIN AMERICA
1941 – 1991

STAN LEE PRESENTS:

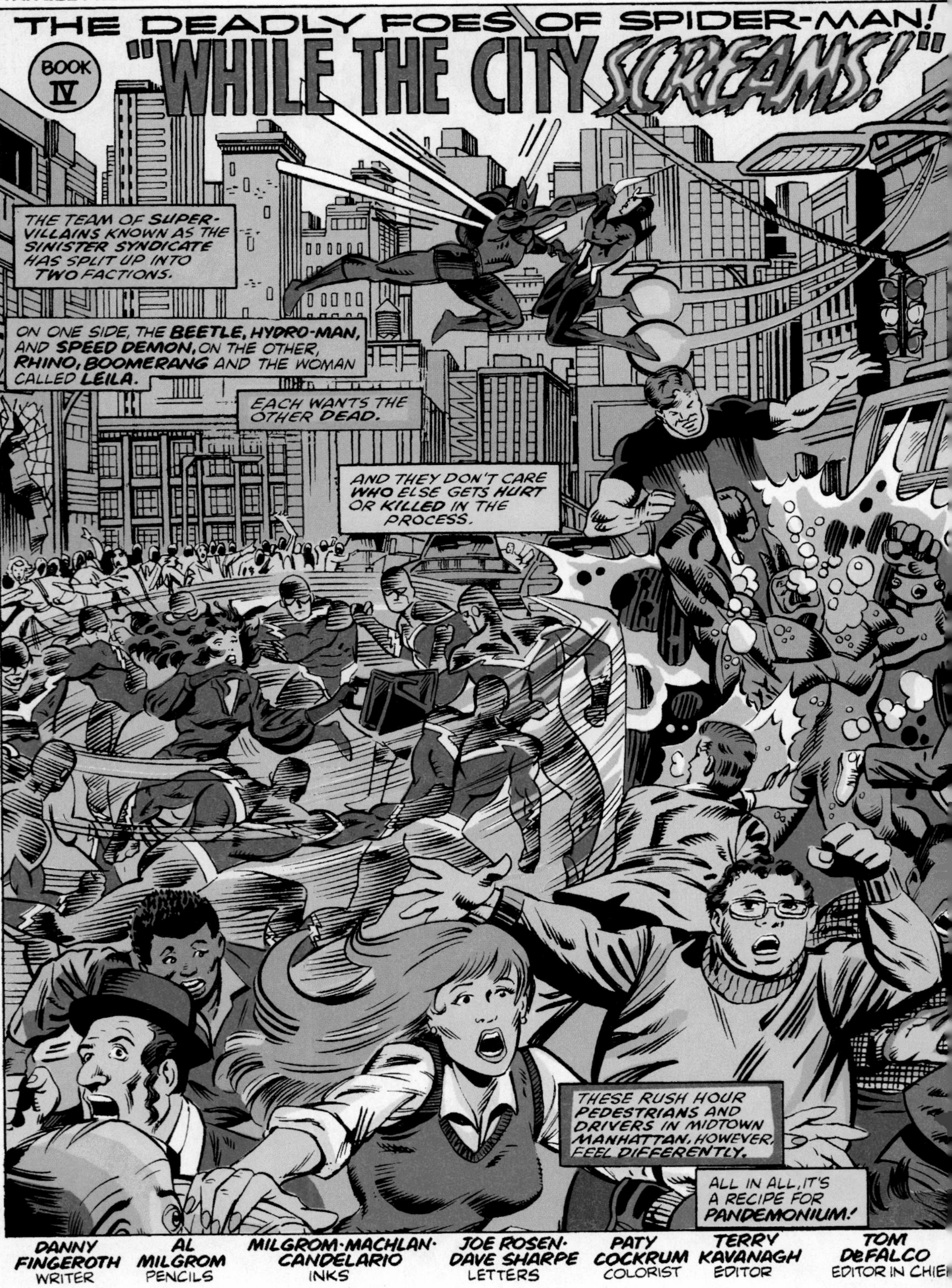

THE DEADLY FOES OF SPIDER-MAN!
BOOK IV
"WHILE THE CITY SCREAMS!"
THE TEAM OF SUPER-VILLAINS KNOWN AS THE SINISTER SYNDICATE HAS SPLIT UP INTO TWO FACTIONS.
ON ONE SIDE, THE BEETLE, HYDRO-MAN, AND SPEED DEMON, ON THE OTHER, RHINO, BOOMERANG AND THE WOMAN CALLED LEILA.
EACH WANTS THE OTHER DEAD.
AND THEY DON'T CARE WHO ELSE GETS HURT OR KILLED IN THE PROCESS.
THESE RUSH HOUR PEDESTRIANS AND DRIVERS IN MIDTOWN MANHATTAN, HOWEVER, FEEL DIFFERENTLY.
ALL IN ALL, IT'S A RECIPE FOR PANDEMONIUM!

DANNY FINGEROTH WRITER · AL MILGROM PENCILS · MILGROM-MACHLAN-CANDELARIO INKS · JOE ROSEN-DAVE SHARPE LETTERS · PATY COCKRUM COLORIST · TERRY KAVANAGH EDITOR · TOM DeFALCO EDITOR IN CHIEF

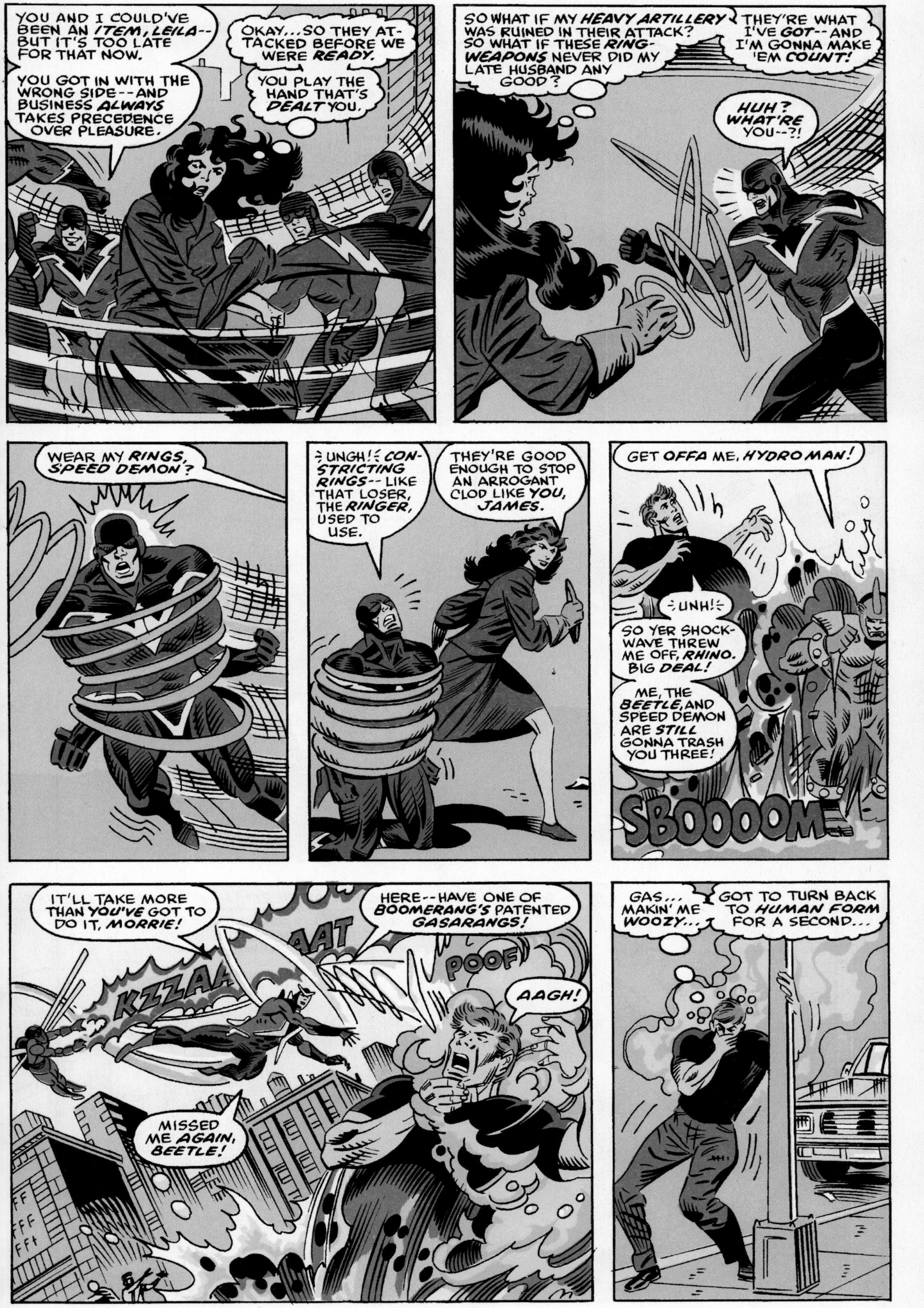
YOU AND I COULD'VE BEEN AN ITEM, LEILA-- BUT IT'S TOO LATE FOR THAT NOW.
YOU GOT IN WITH THE WRONG SIDE--AND BUSINESS ALWAYS TAKES PRECEDENCE OVER PLEASURE.
OKAY...SO THEY ATTACKED BEFORE WE WERE READY.
YOU PLAY THE HAND THAT'S DEALT YOU.
SO WHAT IF MY HEAVY ARTILLERY WAS RUINED IN THEIR ATTACK? SO WHAT IF THESE RING-WEAPONS NEVER DID MY LATE HUSBAND ANY GOOD?
THEY'RE WHAT I'VE GOT--AND I'M GONNA MAKE 'EM COUNT!
HUH? WHAT'RE YOU--?!
WEAR MY RINGS, SPEED DEMON?
UNGH! CONSTRICTING RINGS--LIKE THAT LOSER, THE RINGER, USED TO USE.
THEY'RE GOOD ENOUGH TO STOP AN ARROGANT CLOD LIKE YOU, JAMES.
GET OFFA ME, HYDRO MAN!
UNH!
SO YER SHOCKWAVE THREW ME OFF, RHINO. BIG DEAL!
ME, THE BEETLE, AND SPEED DEMON ARE STILL GONNA TRASH YOU THREE!
SBOOOOM
IT'LL TAKE MORE THAN YOU'VE GOT TO DO IT, MORRIE!
HERE--HAVE ONE OF BOOMERANG'S PATENTED GASARANGS!
KZZAA
AAT
POOF
AAGH!
MISSED ME AGAIN, BEETLE!
GAS... MAKIN' ME WOOZY...
GOT TO TURN BACK TO HUMAN FORM FOR A SECOND...

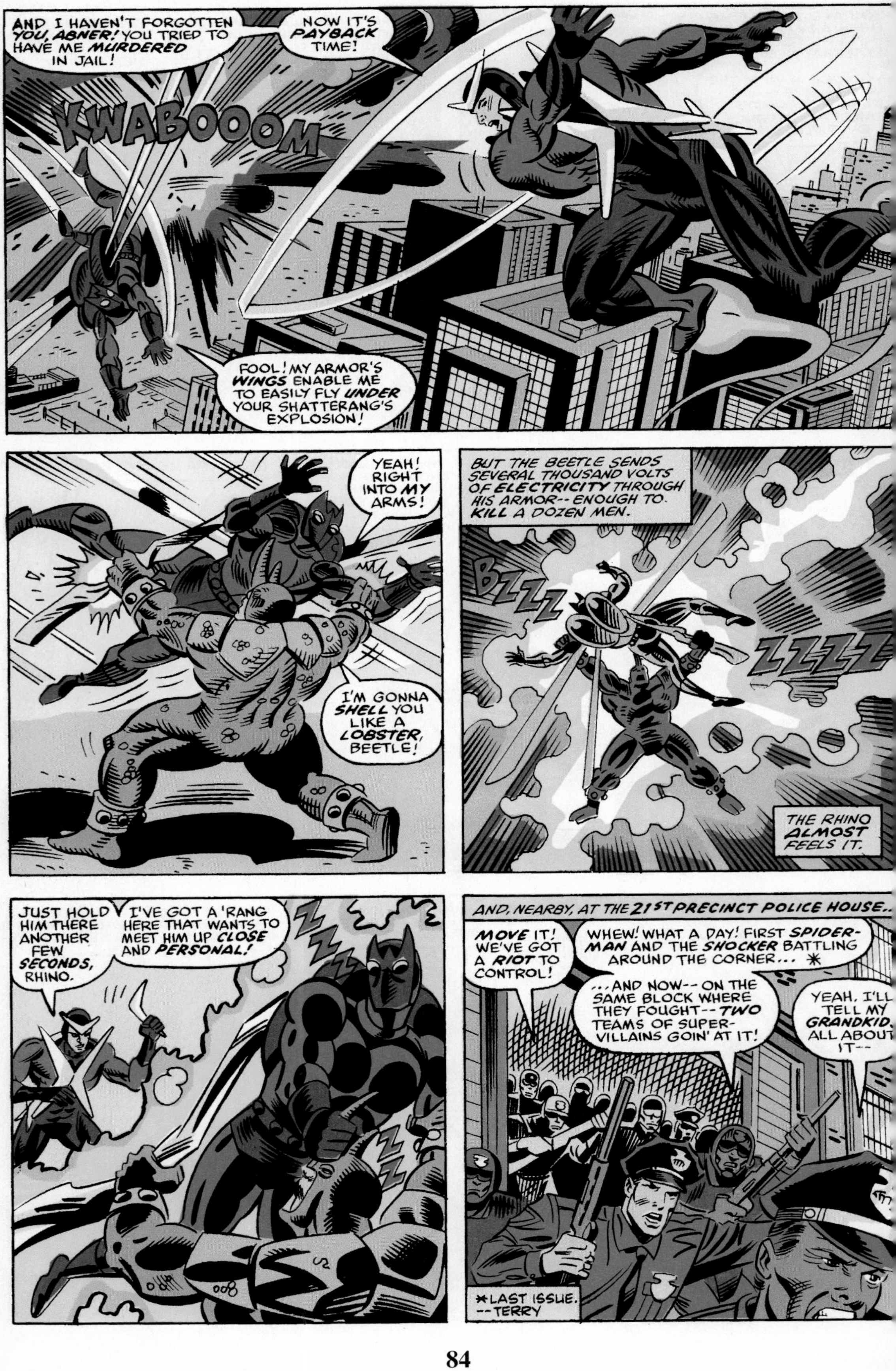
AND I HAVEN'T FORGOTTEN YOU, ABNER! YOU TRIED TO HAVE ME MURDERED IN JAIL!
NOW IT'S PAYBACK TIME!
KWABOOOM
FOOL! MY ARMOR'S WINGS ENABLE ME TO EASILY FLY UNDER YOUR SHATTERANG'S EXPLOSION!
YEAH! RIGHT INTO MY ARMS!
I'M GONNA SHELL YOU LIKE A LOBSTER, BEETLE!
BUT THE BEETLE SENDS SEVERAL THOUSAND VOLTS OF ELECTRICITY THROUGH HIS ARMOR-- ENOUGH TO KILL A DOZEN MEN.
BZZZ
ZZZZ
THE RHINO ALMOST FEELS IT.
JUST HOLD HIM THERE ANOTHER FEW SECONDS, RHINO.
I'VE GOT A 'RANG HERE THAT WANTS TO MEET HIM UP CLOSE AND PERSONAL!
AND, NEARBY, AT THE 21ST PRECINCT POLICE HOUSE...
MOVE IT! WE'VE GOT A RIOT TO CONTROL!
WHEW! WHAT A DAY! FIRST SPIDER-MAN AND THE SHOCKER BATTLING AROUND THE CORNER... *
...AND NOW-- ON THE SAME BLOCK WHERE THEY FOUGHT-- TWO TEAMS OF SUPER-VILLAINS GOIN' AT IT!
YEAH. I'LL TELL MY GRANDKIDS ALL ABOUT IT--
*LAST ISSUE. --TERRY

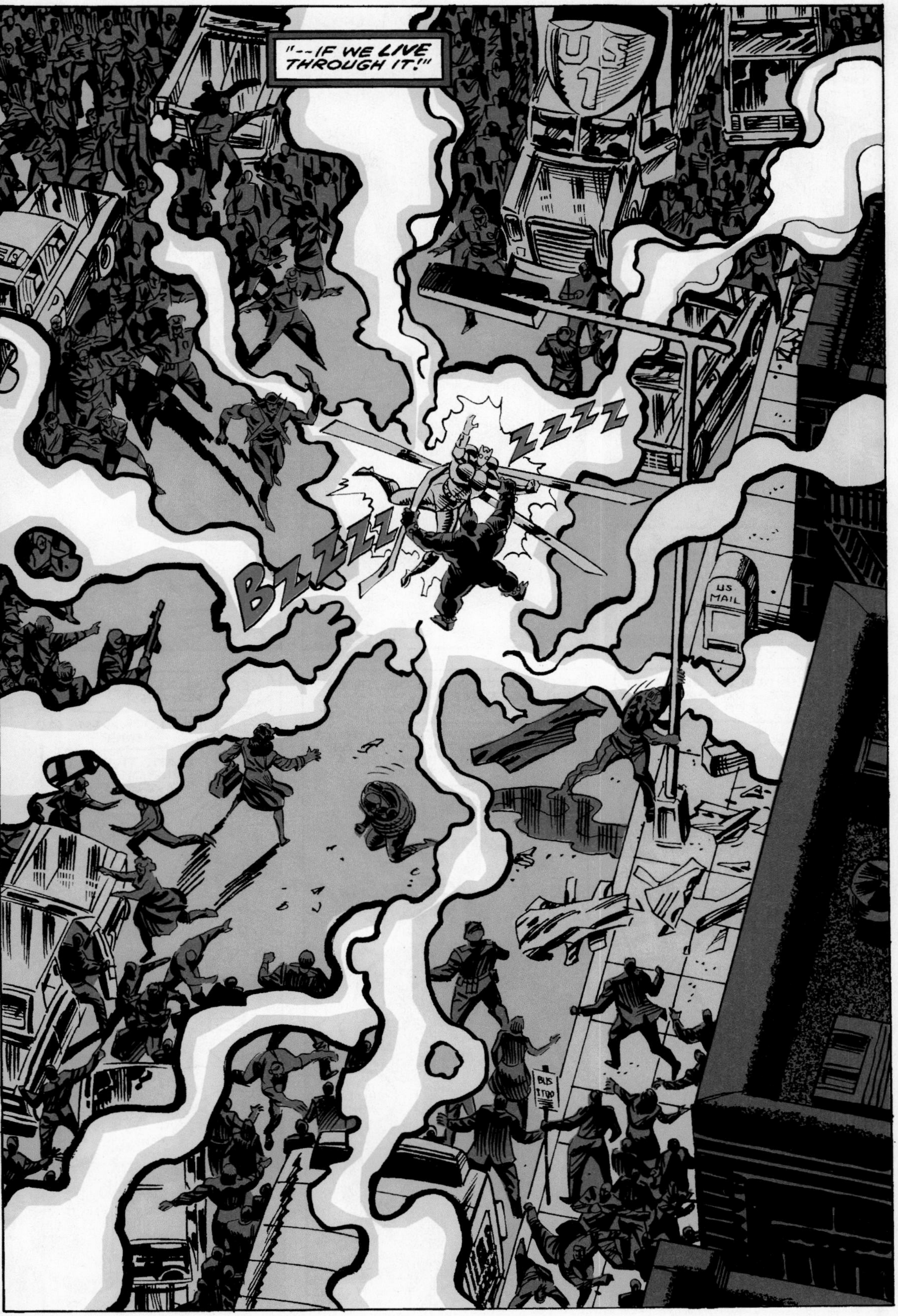
"--IF WE LIVE THROUGH IT!"
ZZZZ
BZZZZZ
US MAIL
BUS STOP

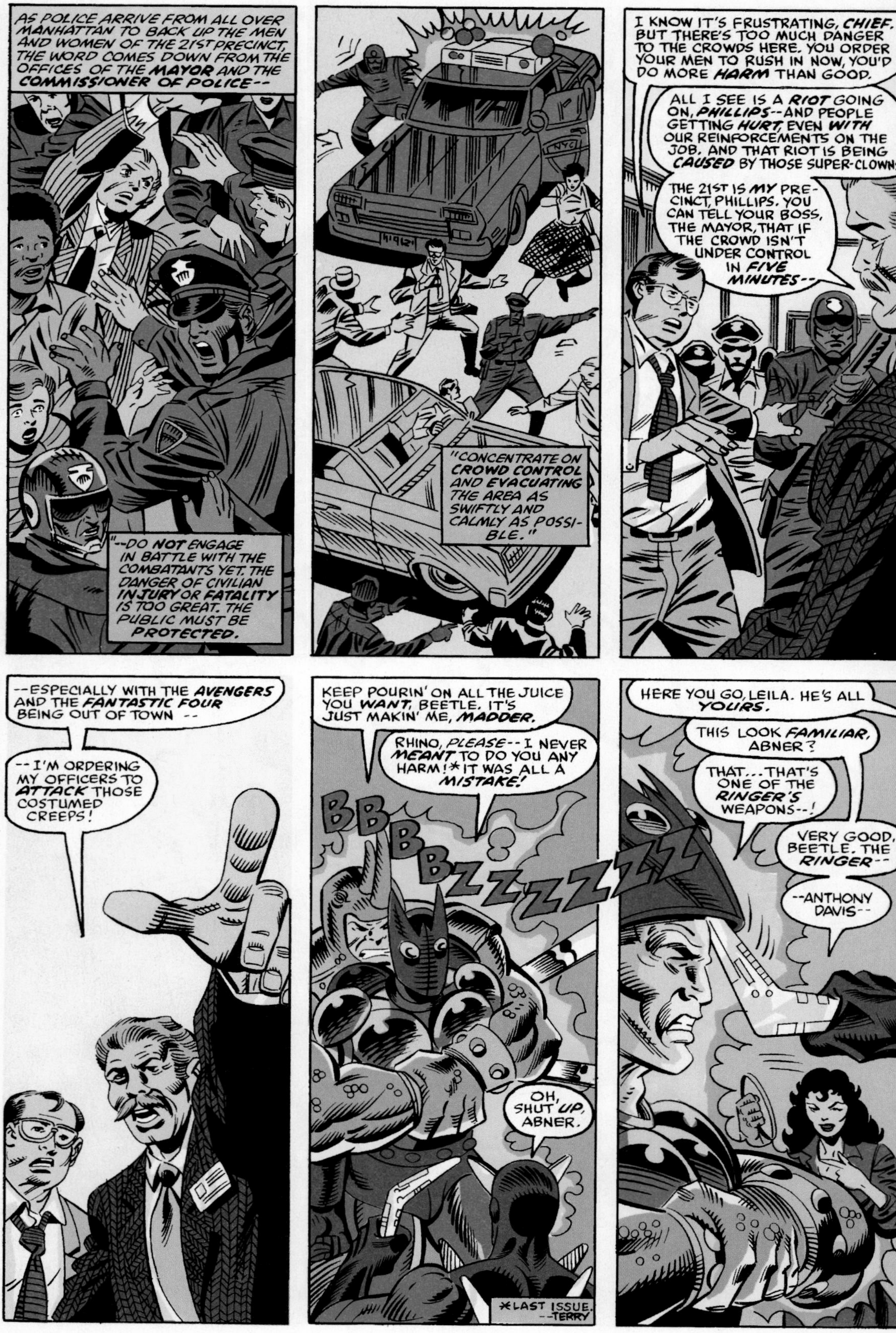
AS POLICE ARRIVE FROM ALL OVER MANHATTAN TO BACK UP THE MEN AND WOMEN OF THE 21ST PRECINCT, THE WORD COMES DOWN FROM THE OFFICES OF THE MAYOR AND THE COMMISSIONER OF POLICE--
"--DO NOT ENGAGE IN BATTLE WITH THE COMBATANTS YET. THE DANGER OF CIVILIAN INJURY OR FATALITY IS TOO GREAT. THE PUBLIC MUST BE PROTECTED.
"CONCENTRATE ON CROWD CONTROL AND EVACUATING THE AREA AS SWIFTLY AND CALMLY AS POSSIBLE."
I KNOW IT'S FRUSTRATING, CHIEF. BUT THERE'S TOO MUCH DANGER TO THE CROWDS HERE. YOU ORDER YOUR MEN TO RUSH IN NOW, YOU'D DO MORE HARM THAN GOOD.
ALL I SEE IS A RIOT GOING ON, PHILLIPS--AND PEOPLE GETTING HURT, EVEN WITH OUR REINFORCEMENTS ON THE JOB. AND THAT RIOT IS BEING CAUSED BY THOSE SUPER-CLOWNS.
THE 21ST IS MY PRECINCT, PHILLIPS. YOU CAN TELL YOUR BOSS, THE MAYOR, THAT IF THE CROWD ISN'T UNDER CONTROL IN FIVE MINUTES--
--ESPECIALLY WITH THE AVENGERS AND THE FANTASTIC FOUR BEING OUT OF TOWN --
--I'M ORDERING MY OFFICERS TO ATTACK THOSE COSTUMED CREEPS!
KEEP POURIN' ON ALL THE JUICE YOU WANT, BEETLE. IT'S JUST MAKIN' ME, MADDER.
RHINO, PLEASE--I NEVER MEANT TO DO YOU ANY HARM!* IT WAS ALL A MISTAKE!
BBBBZZZZZZZ
OH, SHUT UP, ABNER.
*LAST ISSUE. --TERRY
HERE YOU GO, LEILA. HE'S ALL YOURS.
THIS LOOK FAMILIAR, ABNER?
THAT...THAT'S ONE OF THE RINGER'S WEAPONS--!
VERY GOOD, BEETLE. THE RINGER--
--ANTHONY DAVIS--

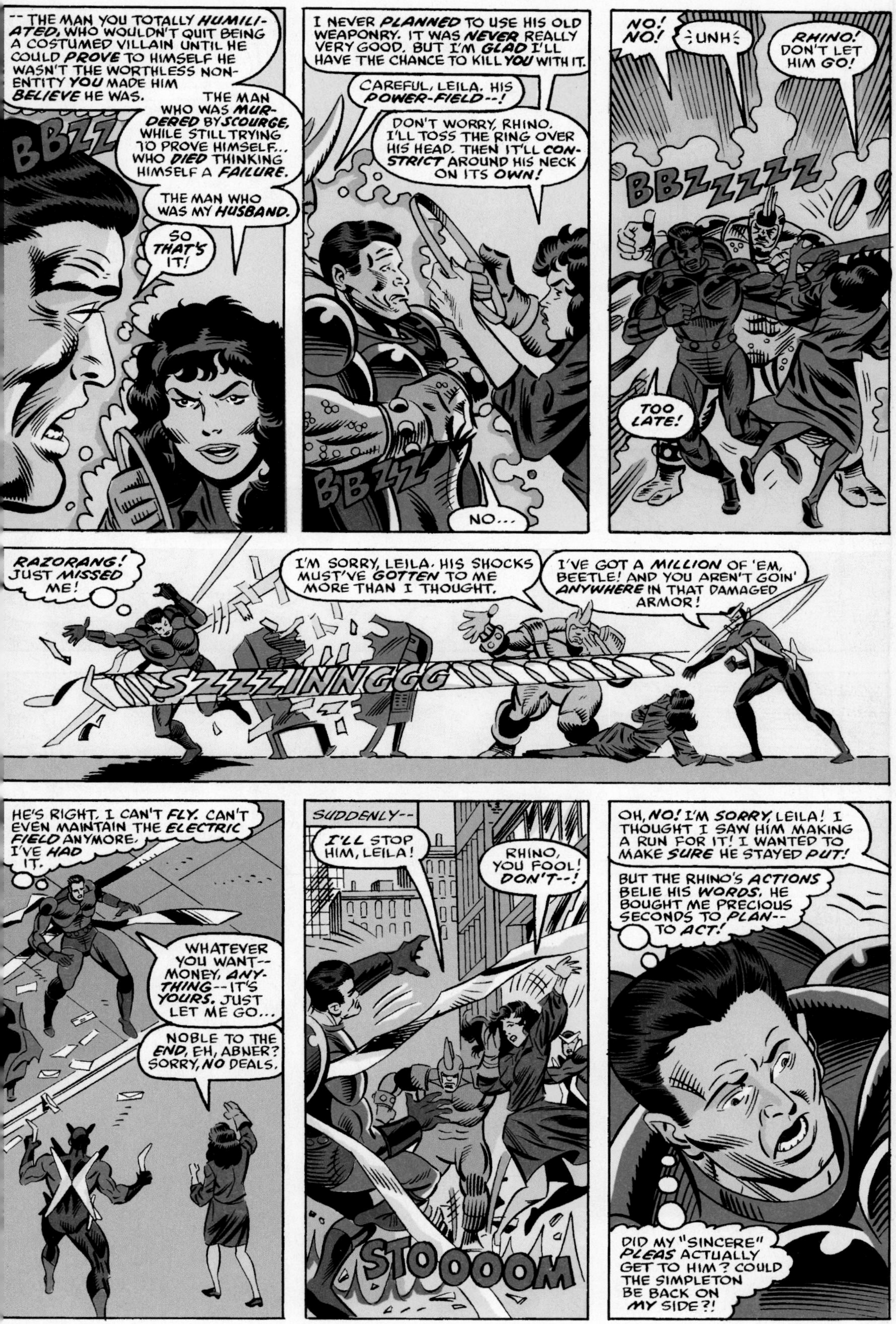
-- THE MAN YOU TOTALLY HUMILIATED, WHO WOULDN'T QUIT BEING A COSTUMED VILLAIN UNTIL HE COULD PROVE TO HIMSELF HE WASN'T THE WORTHLESS NON-ENTITY YOU MADE HIM BELIEVE HE WAS.
THE MAN WHO WAS MURDERED BY SCOURGE, WHILE STILL TRYING TO PROVE HIMSELF... WHO DIED THINKING HIMSELF A FAILURE.
THE MAN WHO WAS MY HUSBAND.
BBZZZ
SO THAT'S IT!
I NEVER PLANNED TO USE HIS OLD WEAPONRY. IT WAS NEVER REALLY VERY GOOD. BUT I'M GLAD I'LL HAVE THE CHANCE TO KILL YOU WITH IT.
CAREFUL, LEILA. HIS POWER-FIELD--!
DON'T WORRY, RHINO. I'LL TOSS THE RING OVER HIS HEAD. THEN IT'LL CONSTRICT AROUND HIS NECK ON ITS OWN!
BBZZZ
NO...
NO! NO!
UNH
RHINO! DON'T LET HIM GO!
BBZZZZZZ
TOO LATE!
RAZORANG! JUST MISSED ME!
I'M SORRY, LEILA. HIS SHOCKS MUST'VE GOTTEN TO ME MORE THAN I THOUGHT.
I'VE GOT A MILLION OF 'EM, BEETLE! AND YOU AREN'T GOIN' ANYWHERE IN THAT DAMAGED ARMOR!
SZZZZINNGGG
HE'S RIGHT. I CAN'T FLY. CAN'T EVEN MAINTAIN THE ELECTRIC FIELD ANYMORE. I'VE HAD IT.
WHATEVER YOU WANT-- MONEY, ANYTHING--IT'S YOURS. JUST LET ME GO...
NOBLE TO THE END, EH, ABNER? SORRY, NO DEALS.
SUDDENLY--
I'LL STOP HIM, LEILA!
RHINO, YOU FOOL! DON'T--!
STOOOOOM
OH, NO! I'M SORRY, LEILA! I THOUGHT I SAW HIM MAKING A RUN FOR IT! I WANTED TO MAKE SURE HE STAYED PUT!
BUT THE RHINO'S ACTIONS BELIE HIS WORDS. HE BOUGHT ME PRECIOUS SECONDS TO PLAN-- TO ACT!
DID MY "SINCERE" PLEAS ACTUALLY GET TO HIM? COULD THE SIMPLETON BE BACK ON MY SIDE?!

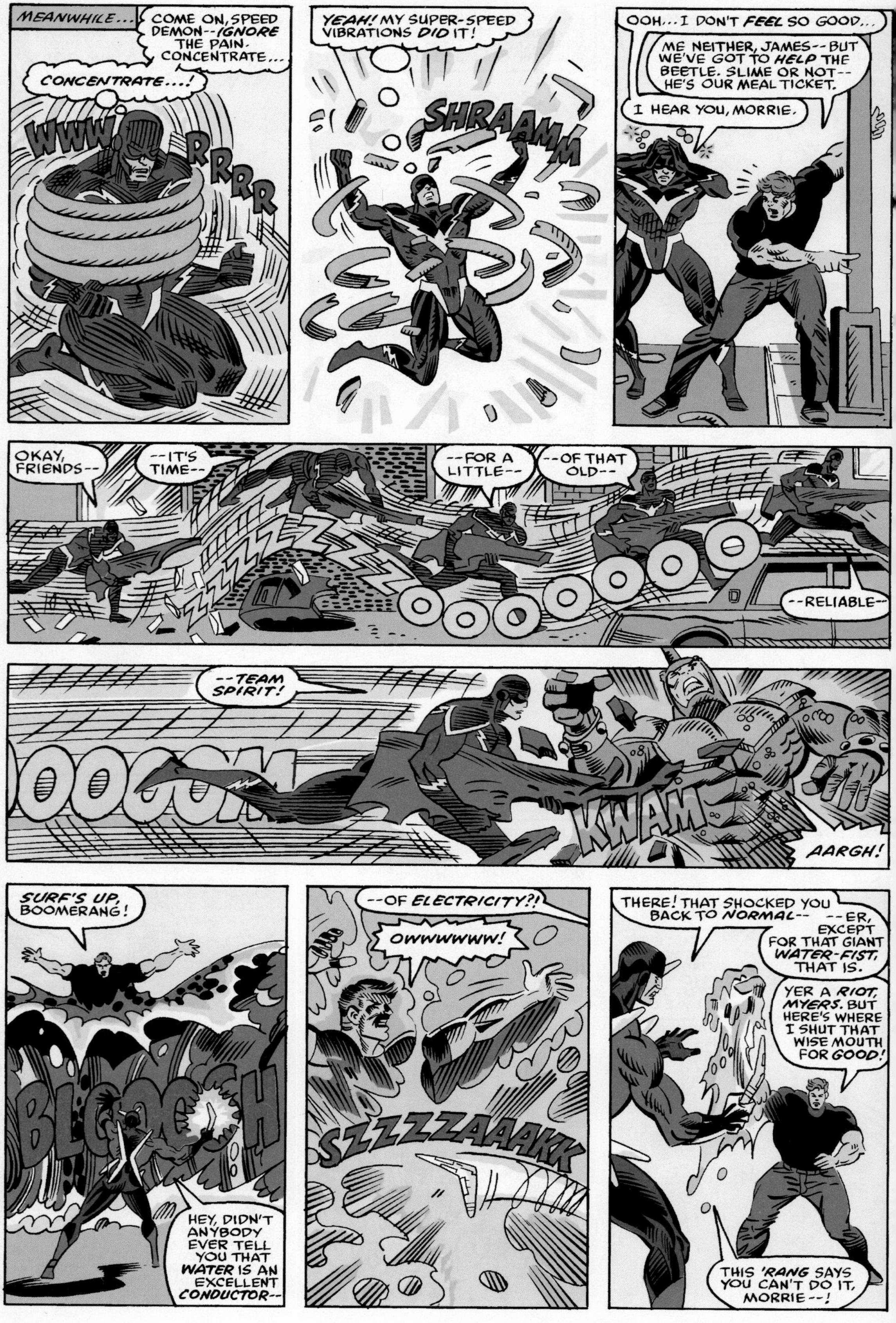
MEANWHILE...
COME ON, SPEED DEMON--IGNORE THE PAIN. CONCENTRATE...
CONCENTRATE...!
WWWRRRRR
YEAH! MY SUPER-SPEED VIBRATIONS DID IT!
SHRAAMM
OOH... I DON'T FEEL SO GOOD...
ME NEITHER, JAMES--BUT WE'VE GOT TO HELP THE BEETLE. SLIME OR NOT--HE'S OUR MEAL TICKET.
I HEAR YOU, MORRIE.
OKAY, FRIENDS--
--IT'S TIME--
--FOR A LITTLE--
--OF THAT OLD--
--RELIABLE--
--TEAM SPIRIT!
KWAM
AARGH!
SURF'S UP, BOOMERANG!
BLOOOSH
HEY, DIDN'T ANYBODY EVER TELL YOU THAT WATER IS AN EXCELLENT CONDUCTOR--
--OF ELECTRICITY?!
OWWWWWW!
SZZZZZAAAKK
THERE! THAT SHOCKED YOU BACK TO NORMAL--
--ER, EXCEPT FOR THAT GIANT WATER-FIST, THAT IS.
YER A RIOT, MYERS. BUT HERE'S WHERE I SHUT THAT WISE MOUTH FOR GOOD!
THIS 'RANG SAYS YOU CAN'T DO IT, MORRIE--!

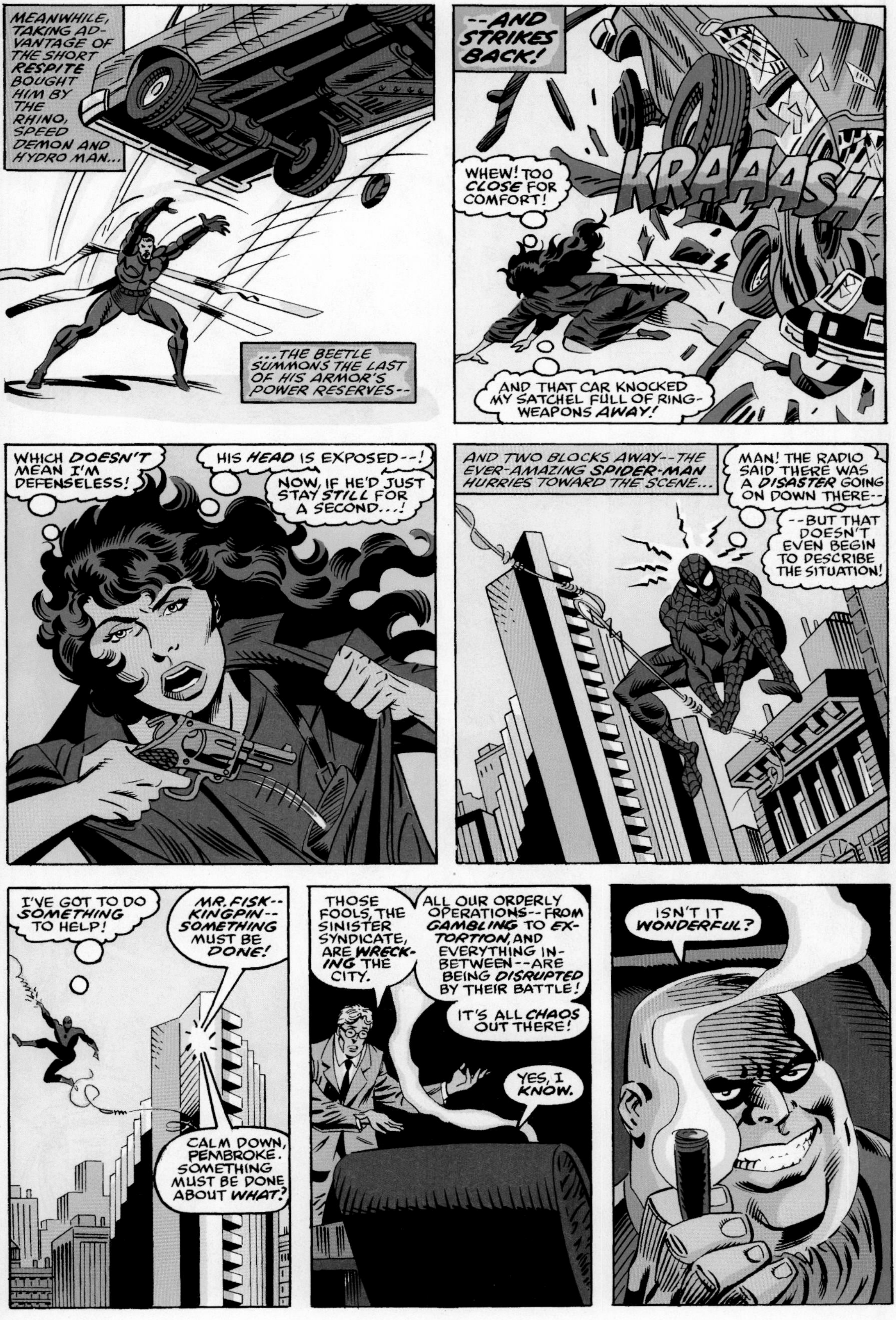
MEANWHILE, TAKING ADVANTAGE OF THE SHORT RESPITE BOUGHT HIM BY THE RHINO, SPEED DEMON AND HYDRO MAN...
...THE BEETLE SUMMONS THE LAST OF HIS ARMOR'S POWER RESERVES--
--AND STRIKES BACK!
KRAAASH!
WHEW! TOO CLOSE FOR COMFORT!
AND THAT CAR KNOCKED MY SATCHEL FULL OF RING-WEAPONS AWAY!
WHICH DOESN'T MEAN I'M DEFENSELESS!
HIS HEAD IS EXPOSED--!
NOW, IF HE'D JUST STAY STILL FOR A SECOND...!
AND TWO BLOCKS AWAY--THE EVER-AMAZING SPIDER-MAN HURRIES TOWARD THE SCENE...
MAN! THE RADIO SAID THERE WAS A DISASTER GOING ON DOWN THERE--
--BUT THAT DOESN'T EVEN BEGIN TO DESCRIBE THE SITUATION!
I'VE GOT TO DO SOMETHING TO HELP!
MR. FISK--KINGPIN--SOMETHING MUST BE DONE!
CALM DOWN, PEMBROKE. SOMETHING MUST BE DONE ABOUT WHAT?
THOSE FOOLS, THE SINISTER SYNDICATE, ARE WRECKING THE CITY.
ALL OUR ORDERLY OPERATIONS--FROM GAMBLING TO EXTORTION, AND EVERYTHING IN-BETWEEN--ARE BEING DISRUPTED BY THEIR BATTLE!
IT'S ALL CHAOS OUT THERE!
YES, I KNOW.
ISN'T IT WONDERFUL?

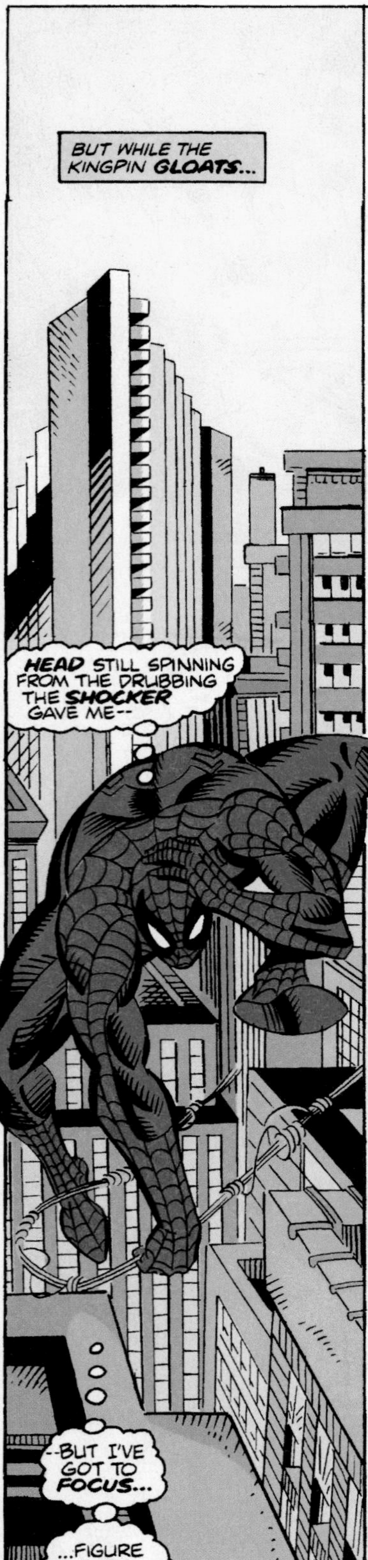
BUT WHILE THE KINGPIN GLOATS...
HEAD STILL SPINNING FROM THE DRUBBING THE SHOCKER GAVE ME--
--BUT I'VE GOT TO FOCUS...
...FIGURE OUT A STRATEGY.

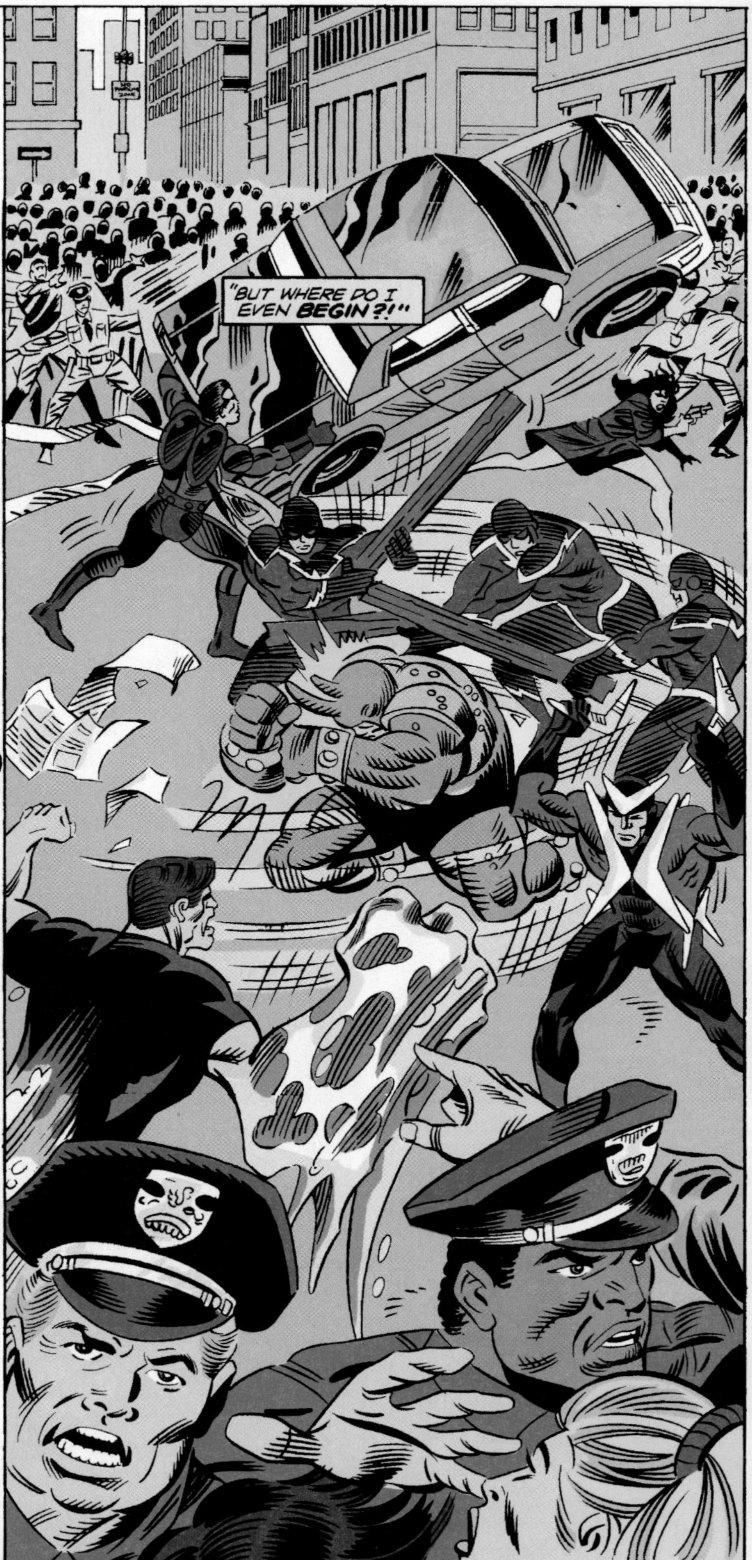
"BUT WHERE DO I EVEN BEGIN?!"

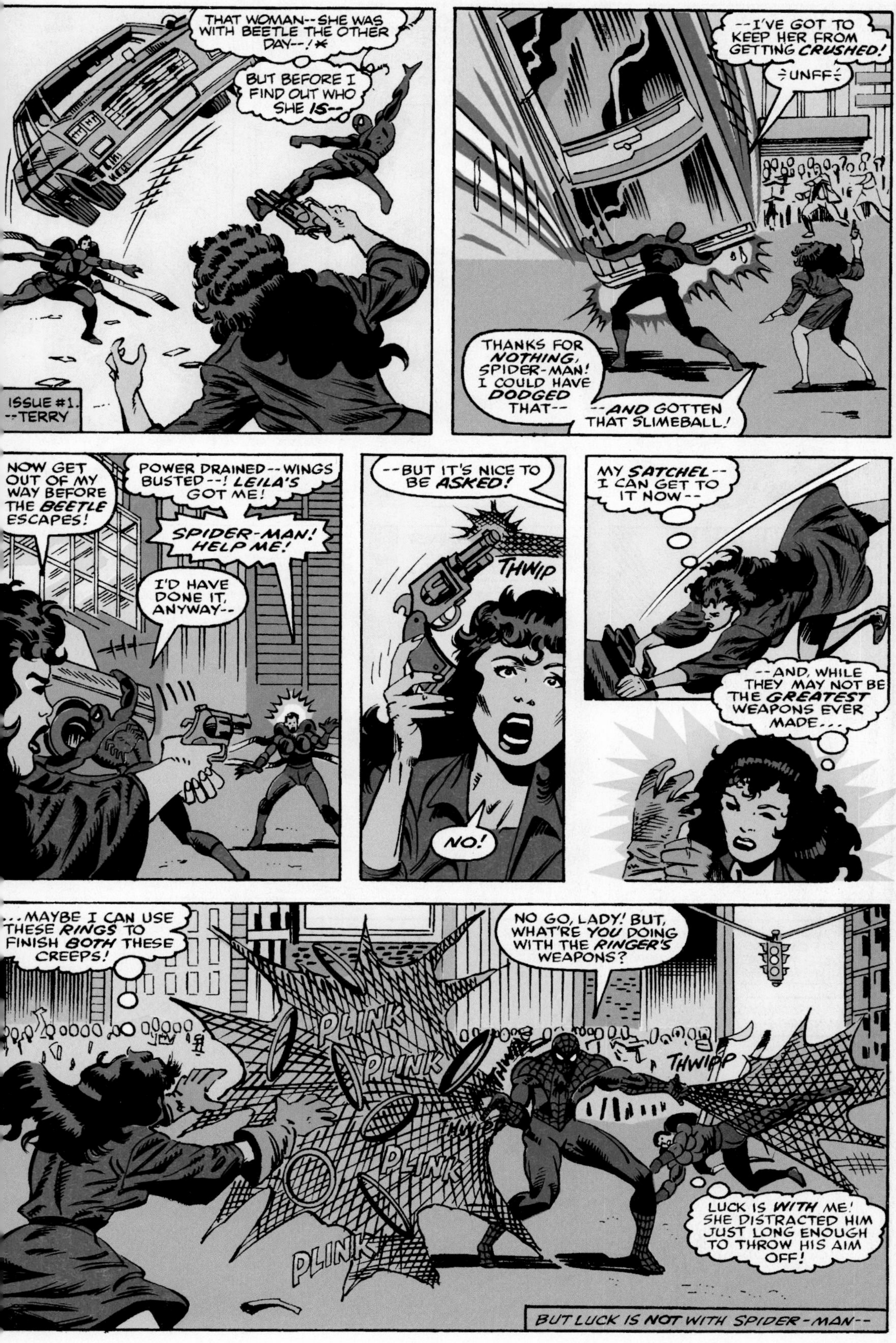
THAT WOMAN--SHE WAS WITH BEETLE THE OTHER DAY--!*
BUT BEFORE I FIND OUT WHO SHE IS--
*ISSUE #1. --TERRY
--I'VE GOT TO KEEP HER FROM GETTING CRUSHED!
UNFF
THANKS FOR NOTHING, SPIDER-MAN! I COULD HAVE DODGED THAT--
--AND GOTTEN THAT SLIMEBALL!
NOW GET OUT OF MY WAY BEFORE THE BEETLE ESCAPES!
POWER DRAINED--WINGS BUSTED--! LEILA'S GOT ME!
SPIDER-MAN! HELP ME!
I'D HAVE DONE IT, ANYWAY--
--BUT IT'S NICE TO BE ASKED!
THWIP
NO!
MY SATCHEL-- I CAN GET TO IT NOW--
--AND, WHILE THEY MAY NOT BE THE GREATEST WEAPONS EVER MADE...
...MAYBE I CAN USE THESE RINGS TO FINISH BOTH THESE CREEPS!
NO GO, LADY! BUT, WHAT'RE YOU DOING WITH THE RINGER'S WEAPONS?
PLINK
PLINK
PLINK
PLINK
THWIPP
LUCK IS WITH ME! SHE DISTRACTED HIM JUST LONG ENOUGH TO THROW HIS AIM OFF!
BUT LUCK IS NOT WITH SPIDER-MAN--

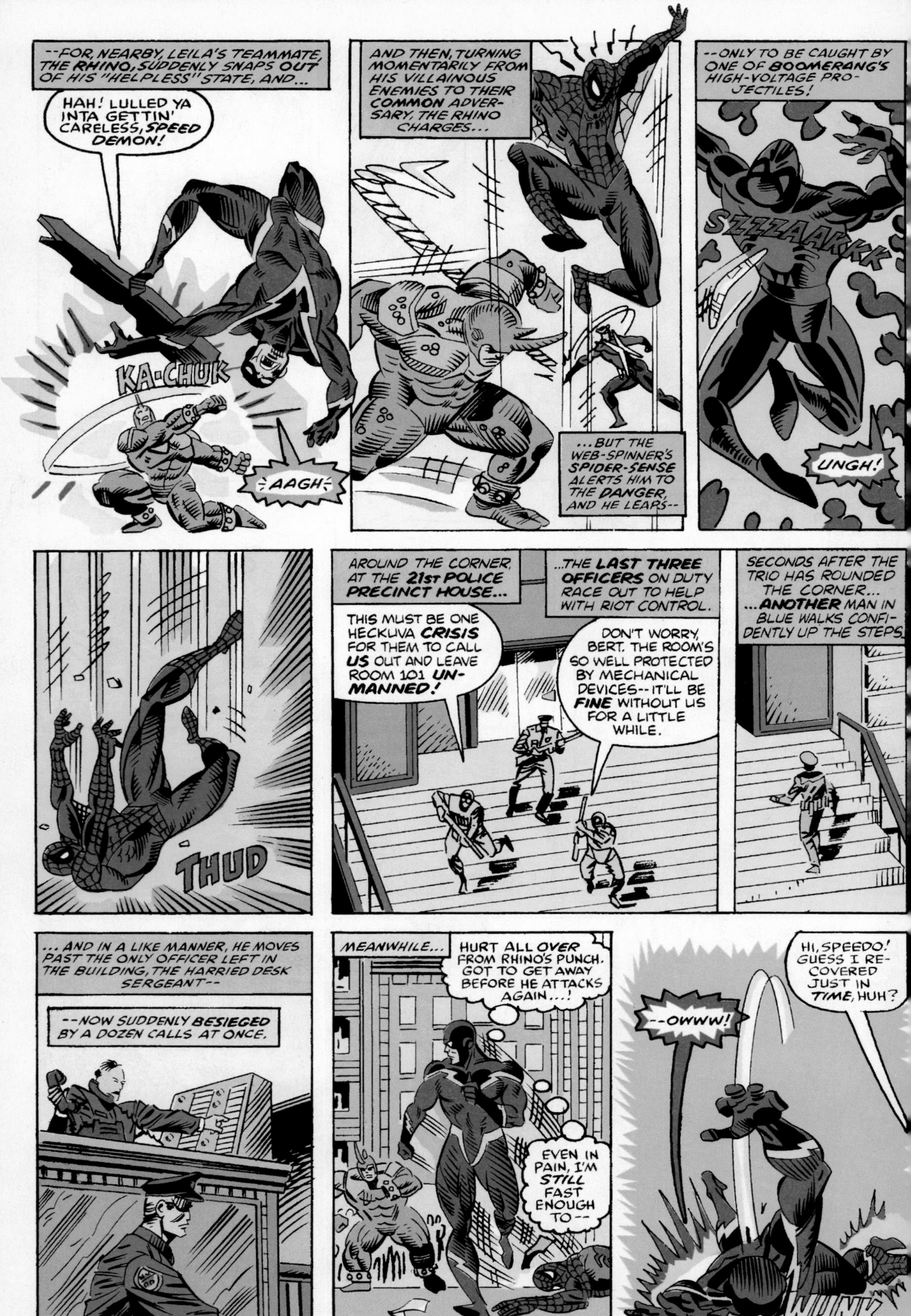
--FOR, NEARBY, LEILA'S TEAMMATE, THE RHINO, SUDDENLY SNAPS OUT OF HIS "HELPLESS" STATE, AND...
HAH! LULLED YA INTA GETTIN' CARELESS, SPEED DEMON!
KA-CHUK
AAGH
AND THEN, TURNING MOMENTARILY FROM HIS VILLAINOUS ENEMIES TO THEIR COMMON ADVERSARY, THE RHINO CHARGES...
...BUT THE WEB-SPINNER'S SPIDER-SENSE ALERTS HIM TO THE DANGER, AND HE LEAPS--
--ONLY TO BE CAUGHT BY ONE OF BOOMERANG'S HIGH-VOLTAGE PROJECTILES!
SZZZAARKKK
UNGH!
THUD
AROUND THE CORNER, AT THE 21st POLICE PRECINCT HOUSE...
...THE LAST THREE OFFICERS ON DUTY RACE OUT TO HELP WITH RIOT CONTROL.
THIS MUST BE ONE HECKUVA CRISIS FOR THEM TO CALL US OUT AND LEAVE ROOM 101 UNMANNED!
DON'T WORRY, BERT. THE ROOM'S SO WELL PROTECTED BY MECHANICAL DEVICES--IT'LL BE FINE WITHOUT US FOR A LITTLE WHILE.
SECONDS AFTER THE TRIO HAS ROUNDED THE CORNER... ...ANOTHER MAN IN BLUE WALKS CONFIDENTLY UP THE STEPS.
...AND IN A LIKE MANNER, HE MOVES PAST THE ONLY OFFICER LEFT IN THE BUILDING, THE HARRIED DESK SERGEANT--
--NOW SUDDENLY BESIEGED BY A DOZEN CALLS AT ONCE.
MEANWHILE...
HURT ALL OVER FROM RHINO'S PUNCH. GOT TO GET AWAY BEFORE HE ATTACKS AGAIN...!
EVEN IN PAIN, I'M STILL FAST ENOUGH TO--
--OWWW!
HI, SPEEDO! GUESS I RECOVERED JUST IN TIME, HUH?
WUNK

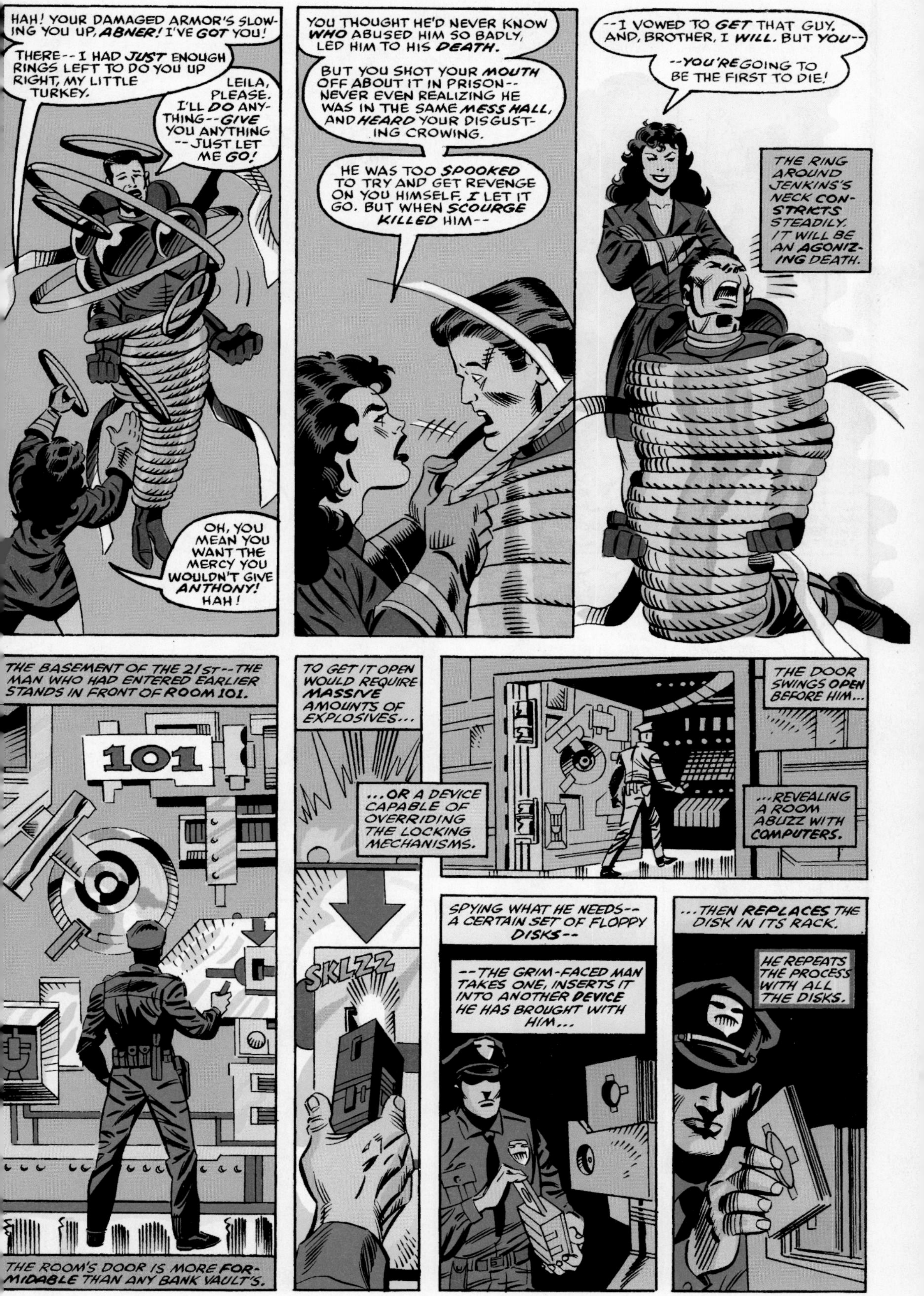
HAH! YOUR DAMAGED ARMOR'S SLOWING YOU UP, ABNER! I'VE GOT YOU!
THERE--I HAD JUST ENOUGH RINGS LEFT TO DO YOU UP RIGHT, MY LITTLE TURKEY.
LEILA, PLEASE. I'LL DO ANYTHING--GIVE YOU ANYTHING --JUST LET ME GO!
OH, YOU MEAN YOU WANT THE MERCY YOU WOULDN'T GIVE ANTHONY! HAH!
YOU THOUGHT HE'D NEVER KNOW WHO ABUSED HIM SO BADLY, LED HIM TO HIS DEATH.
BUT YOU SHOT YOUR MOUTH OFF ABOUT IT IN PRISON--NEVER EVEN REALIZING HE WAS IN THE SAME MESS HALL, AND HEARD YOUR DISGUSTING CROWING.
HE WAS TOO SPOOKED TO TRY AND GET REVENGE ON YOU HIMSELF. I LET IT GO. BUT WHEN SCOURGE KILLED HIM--
--I VOWED TO GET THAT GUY. AND, BROTHER, I WILL. BUT YOU--
--YOU'RE GOING TO BE THE FIRST TO DIE!
THE RING AROUND JENKINS'S NECK CONSTRICTS STEADILY. IT WILL BE AN AGONIZING DEATH.
THE BASEMENT OF THE 21ST--THE MAN WHO HAD ENTERED EARLIER STANDS IN FRONT OF ROOM 101.
101
THE ROOM'S DOOR IS MORE FORMIDABLE THAN ANY BANK VAULT'S.
TO GET IT OPEN WOULD REQUIRE MASSIVE AMOUNTS OF EXPLOSIVES...
...OR A DEVICE CAPABLE OF OVERRIDING THE LOCKING MECHANISMS.
SKLZZ
THE DOOR SWINGS OPEN BEFORE HIM...
...REVEALING A ROOM ABUZZ WITH COMPUTERS.
SPYING WHAT HE NEEDS--A CERTAIN SET OF FLOPPY DISKS--
--THE GRIM-FACED MAN TAKES ONE, INSERTS IT INTO ANOTHER DEVICE HE HAS BROUGHT WITH HIM...
...THEN REPLACES THE DISK IN ITS RACK.
HE REPEATS THE PROCESS WITH ALL THE DISKS.

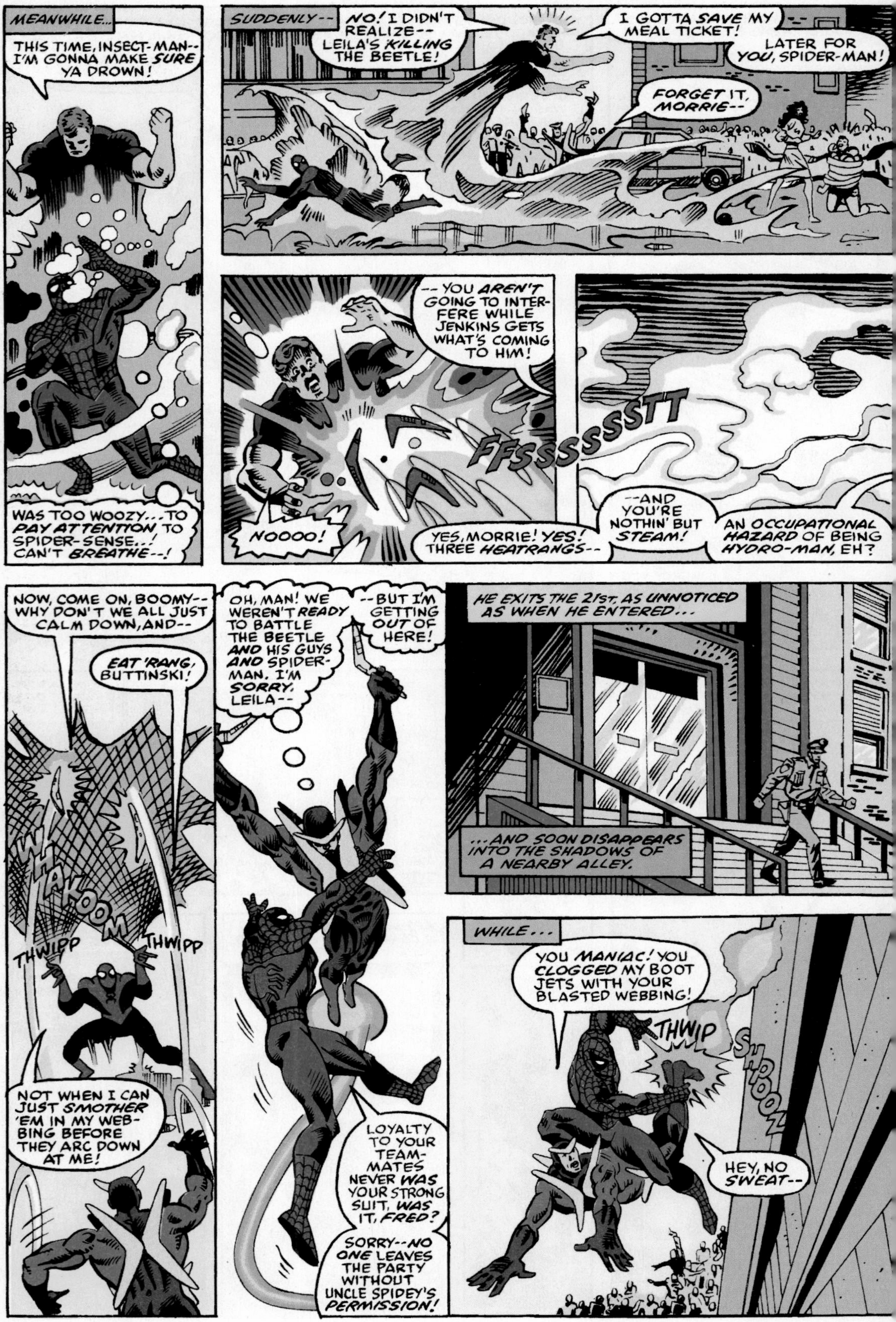
MEANWHILE...
THIS TIME, INSECT-MAN-- I'M GONNA MAKE SURE YA DROWN!
WAS TOO WOOZY... TO PAY ATTENTION TO SPIDER-SENSE..! CAN'T BREATHE--!
SUDDENLY--
NO! I DIDN'T REALIZE-- LEILA'S KILLING THE BEETLE!
I GOTTA SAVE MY MEAL TICKET!
LATER FOR YOU, SPIDER-MAN!
FORGET IT, MORRIE--
--YOU AREN'T GOING TO INTERFERE WHILE JENKINS GETS WHAT'S COMING TO HIM!
NOOOO!
FFSSSSSSTT
YES, MORRIE! YES! THREE HEATRANGS--
--AND YOU'RE NOTHIN' BUT STEAM!
AN OCCUPATIONAL HAZARD OF BEING HYDRO-MAN, EH?
NOW, COME ON, BOOMY-- WHY DON'T WE ALL JUST CALM DOWN, AND--
EAT 'RANG, BUTTINSKI!
WHAKOOM
THWIPP
THWIPP
NOT WHEN I CAN JUST SMOTHER 'EM IN MY WEBBING BEFORE THEY ARC DOWN AT ME!
OH, MAN! WE WEREN'T READY TO BATTLE THE BEETLE AND HIS GUYS AND SPIDER-MAN. I'M SORRY, LEILA--
--BUT I'M GETTING OUT OF HERE!
LOYALTY TO YOUR TEAMMATES NEVER WAS YOUR STRONG SUIT, WAS IT, FRED?
SORRY--NO ONE LEAVES THE PARTY WITHOUT UNCLE SPIDEY'S PERMISSION!
HE EXITS THE 21ST, AS UNNOTICED AS WHEN HE ENTERED...
...AND SOON DISAPPEARS INTO THE SHADOWS OF A NEARBY ALLEY.
WHILE...
YOU MANIAC! YOU CLOGGED MY BOOT JETS WITH YOUR BLASTED WEBBING!
THWIP
SHOOOM
HEY, NO SWEAT--

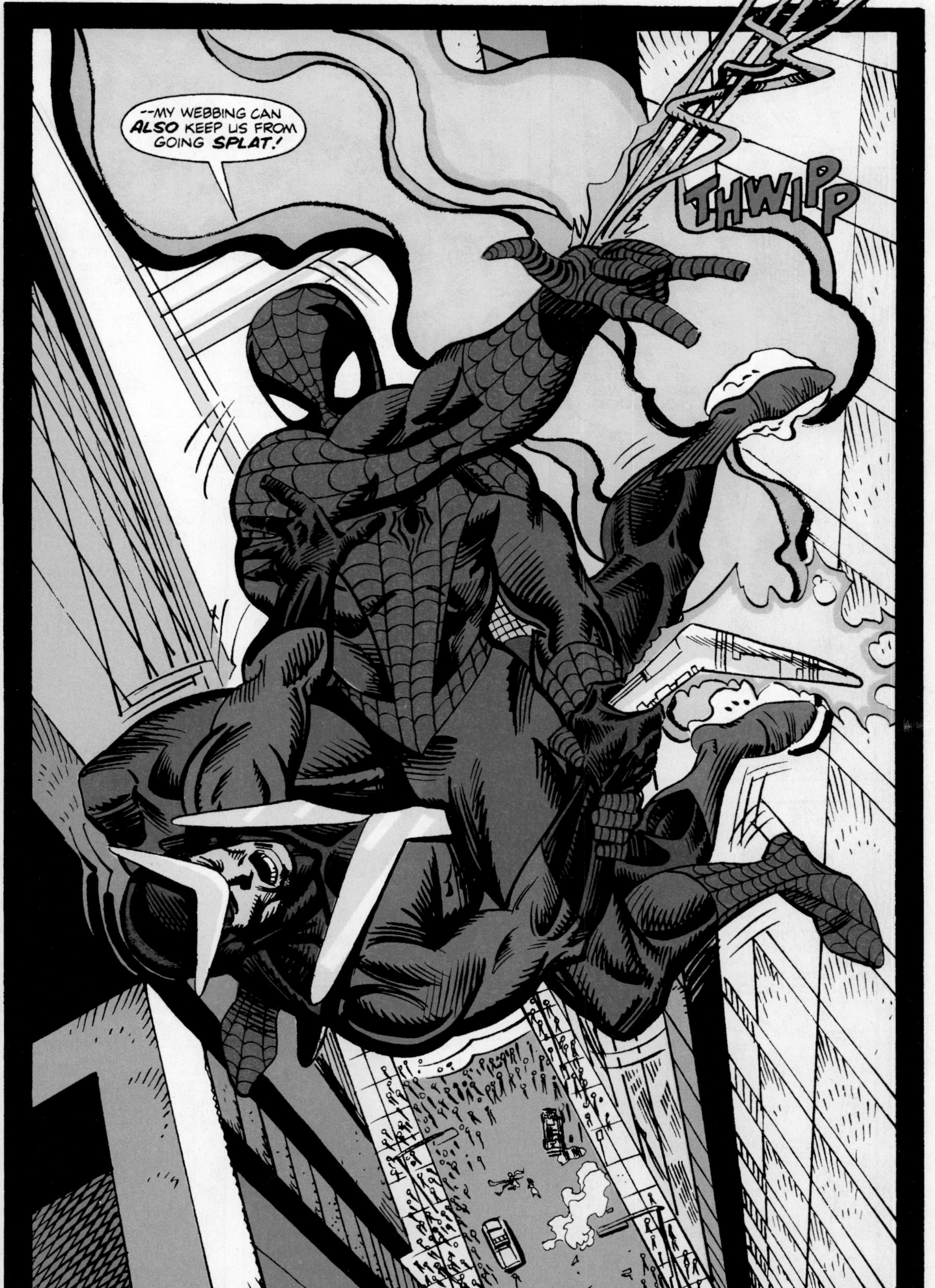
--MY WEBBING CAN ALSO KEEP US FROM GOING SPLAT!
THWIPP

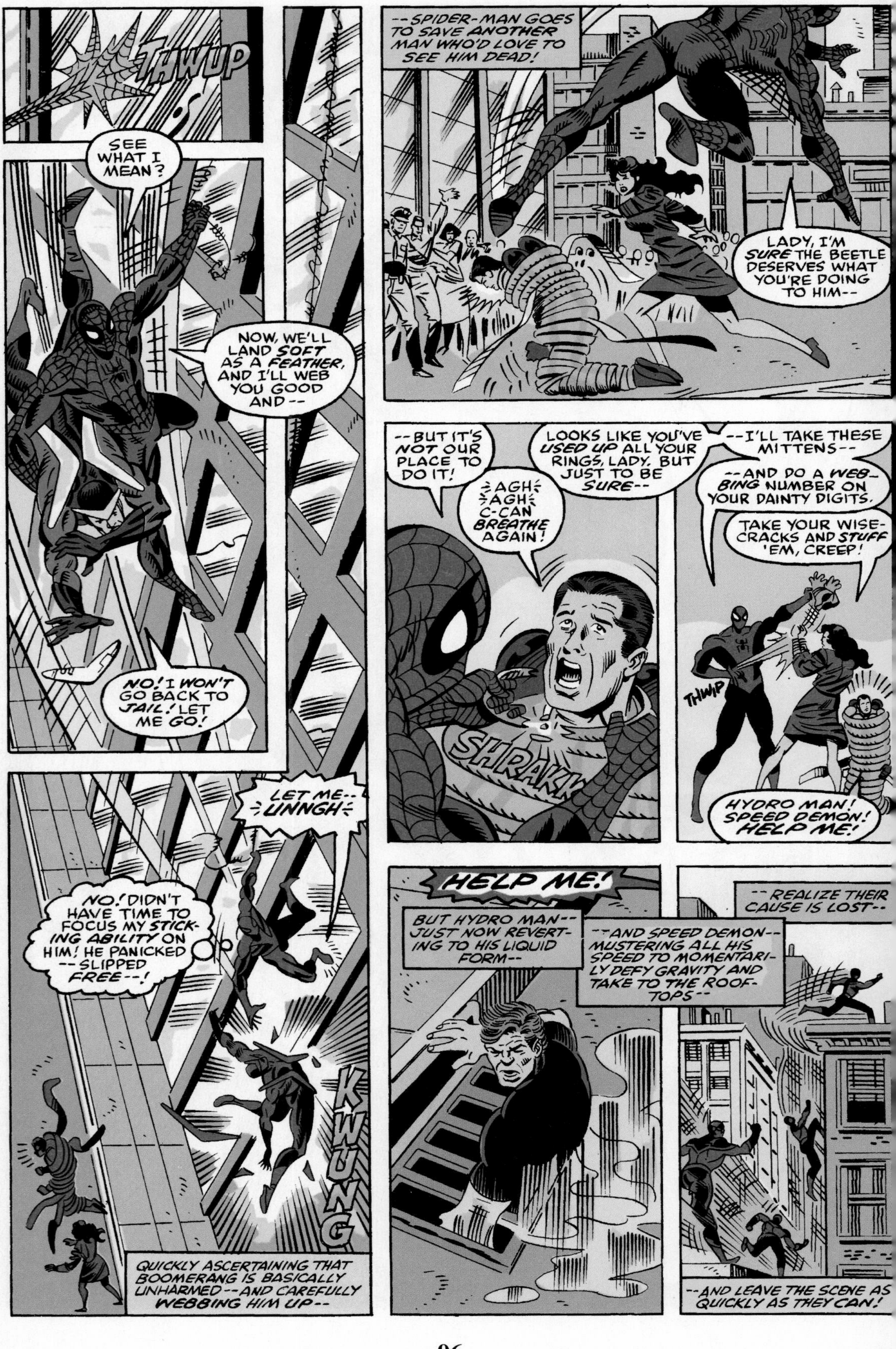
THWUP
SEE WHAT I MEAN?
NOW, WE'LL LAND SOFT AS A FEATHER, AND I'LL WEB YOU GOOD AND--
NO! I WON'T GO BACK TO JAIL! LET ME GO!
--SPIDER-MAN GOES TO SAVE ANOTHER MAN WHO'D LOVE TO SEE HIM DEAD!
LADY, I'M SURE THE BEETLE DESERVES WHAT YOU'RE DOING TO HIM--
LET ME-- UNNGH
NO! DIDN'T HAVE TIME TO FOCUS MY STICKING ABILITY ON HIM! HE PANICKED --SLIPPED FREE--!
KWUNG
QUICKLY ASCERTAINING THAT BOOMERANG IS BASICALLY UNHARMED--AND CAREFULLY WEBBING HIM UP--
--BUT IT'S NOT OUR PLACE TO DO IT!
LOOKS LIKE YOU'VE USED UP ALL YOUR RINGS, LADY. BUT JUST TO BE SURE--
AGH AGH C-CAN BREATHE AGAIN!
SHRAKK
--I'LL TAKE THESE MITTENS--
--AND DO A WEBBING NUMBER ON YOUR DAINTY DIGITS.
TAKE YOUR WISECRACKS AND STUFF 'EM, CREEP!
THWIP
HYDRO MAN! SPEED DEMON! HELP ME!
HELP ME!
BUT HYDRO MAN--JUST NOW REVERTING TO HIS LIQUID FORM--
--AND SPEED DEMON--MUSTERING ALL HIS SPEED TO MOMENTARILY DEFY GRAVITY AND TAKE TO THE ROOFTOPS--
--REALIZE THEIR CAUSE IS LOST--
--AND LEAVE THE SCENE AS QUICKLY AS THEY CAN!

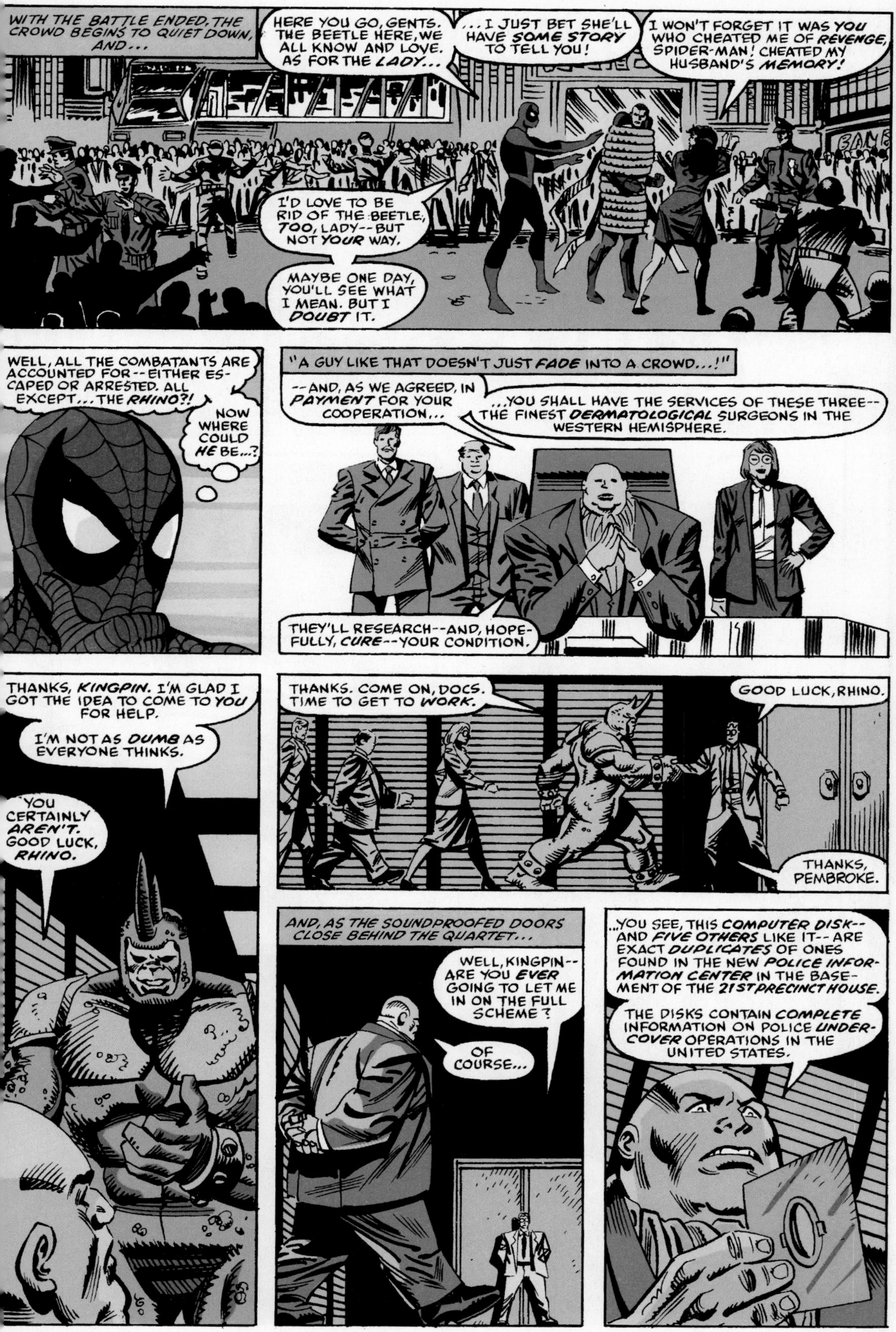
WITH THE BATTLE ENDED, THE CROWD BEGINS TO QUIET DOWN, AND...
HERE YOU GO, GENTS. THE BEETLE HERE, WE ALL KNOW AND LOVE. AS FOR THE LADY...
...I JUST BET SHE'LL HAVE SOME STORY TO TELL YOU!
I WON'T FORGET IT WAS YOU WHO CHEATED ME OF REVENGE, SPIDER-MAN! CHEATED MY HUSBAND'S MEMORY!
I'D LOVE TO BE RID OF THE BEETLE, TOO, LADY--BUT NOT YOUR WAY.
MAYBE ONE DAY, YOU'LL SEE WHAT I MEAN. BUT I DOUBT IT.
WELL, ALL THE COMBATANTS ARE ACCOUNTED FOR--EITHER ESCAPED OR ARRESTED. ALL EXCEPT... THE RHINO?!
NOW WHERE COULD HE BE...?
"A GUY LIKE THAT DOESN'T JUST FADE INTO A CROWD...!"
--AND, AS WE AGREED, IN PAYMENT FOR YOUR COOPERATION...
...YOU SHALL HAVE THE SERVICES OF THESE THREE--THE FINEST DERMATOLOGICAL SURGEONS IN THE WESTERN HEMISPHERE.
THEY'LL RESEARCH--AND, HOPEFULLY, CURE--YOUR CONDITION.
THANKS, KINGPIN. I'M GLAD I GOT THE IDEA TO COME TO YOU FOR HELP.
I'M NOT AS DUMB AS EVERYONE THINKS.
YOU CERTAINLY AREN'T. GOOD LUCK, RHINO.
THANKS. COME ON, DOCS. TIME TO GET TO WORK.
GOOD LUCK, RHINO.
THANKS, PEMBROKE.
AND, AS THE SOUNDPROOFED DOORS CLOSE BEHIND THE QUARTET...
WELL, KINGPIN--ARE YOU EVER GOING TO LET ME IN ON THE FULL SCHEME?
OF COURSE...
...YOU SEE, THIS COMPUTER DISK--AND FIVE OTHERS LIKE IT--ARE EXACT DUPLICATES OF ONES FOUND IN THE NEW POLICE INFORMATION CENTER IN THE BASEMENT OF THE 21ST PRECINCT HOUSE.
THE DISKS CONTAIN COMPLETE INFORMATION ON POLICE UNDERCOVER OPERATIONS IN THE UNITED STATES.

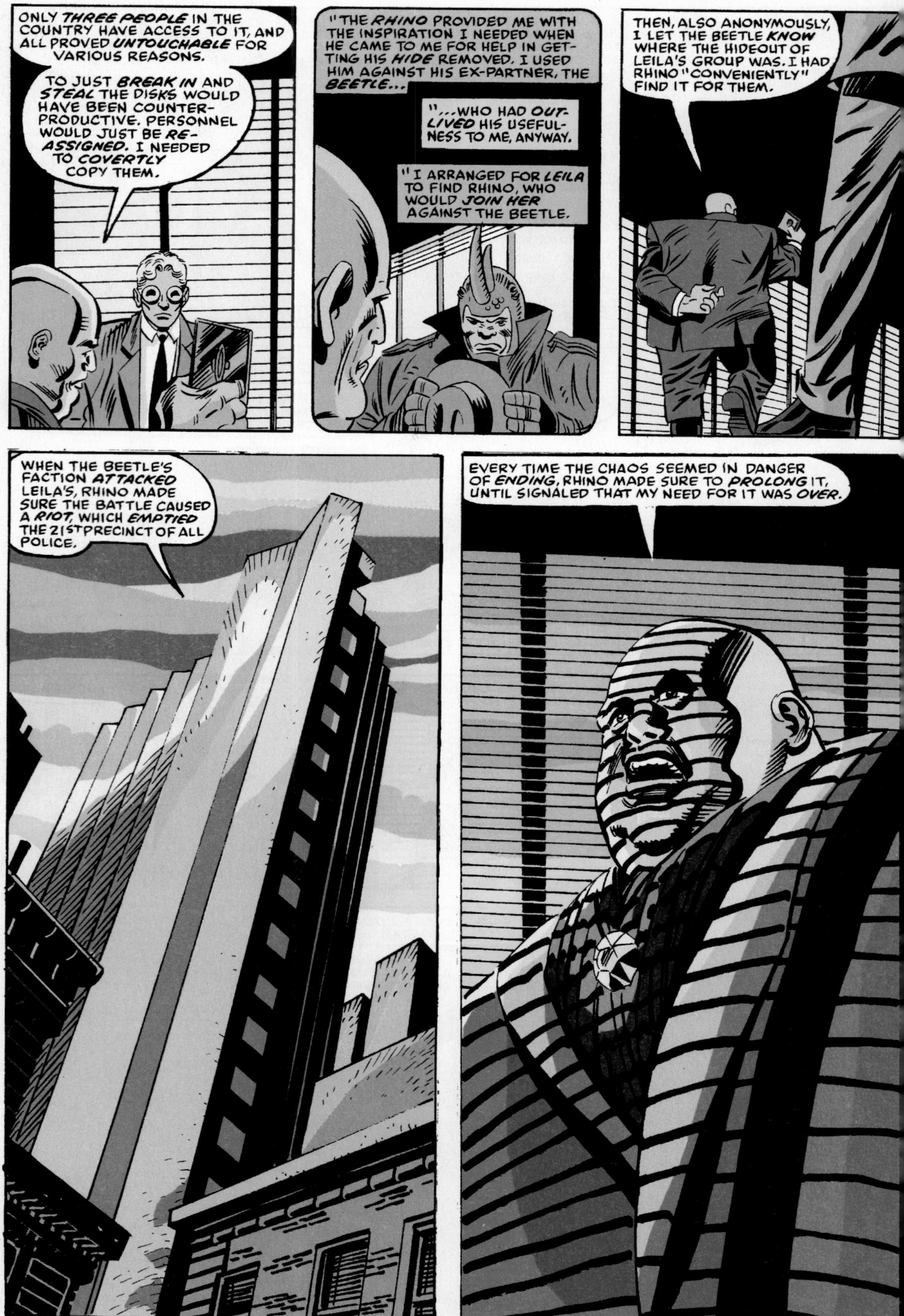
ONLY THREE PEOPLE IN THE COUNTRY HAVE ACCESS TO IT, AND ALL PROVED UNTOUCHABLE FOR VARIOUS REASONS.
TO JUST BREAK IN AND STEAL THE DISKS WOULD HAVE BEEN COUNTER-PRODUCTIVE. PERSONNEL WOULD JUST BE RE-ASSIGNED. I NEEDED TO COVERTLY COPY THEM.
"THE RHINO PROVIDED ME WITH THE INSPIRATION I NEEDED WHEN HE CAME TO ME FOR HELP IN GETTING HIS HIDE REMOVED. I USED HIM AGAINST HIS EX-PARTNER, THE BEETLE...
"...WHO HAD OUTLIVED HIS USEFULNESS TO ME, ANYWAY.
"I ARRANGED FOR LEILA TO FIND RHINO, WHO WOULD JOIN HER AGAINST THE BEETLE.
THEN, ALSO ANONYMOUSLY, I LET THE BEETLE KNOW WHERE THE HIDEOUT OF LEILA'S GROUP WAS. I HAD RHINO "CONVENIENTLY" FIND IT FOR THEM.
WHEN THE BEETLE'S FACTION ATTACKED LEILA'S, RHINO MADE SURE THE BATTLE CAUSED A RIOT, WHICH EMPTIED THE 21ST PRECINCT OF ALL POLICE.
EVERY TIME THE CHAOS SEEMED IN DANGER OF ENDING, RHINO MADE SURE TO PROLONG IT, UNTIL SIGNALED THAT MY NEED FOR IT WAS OVER.

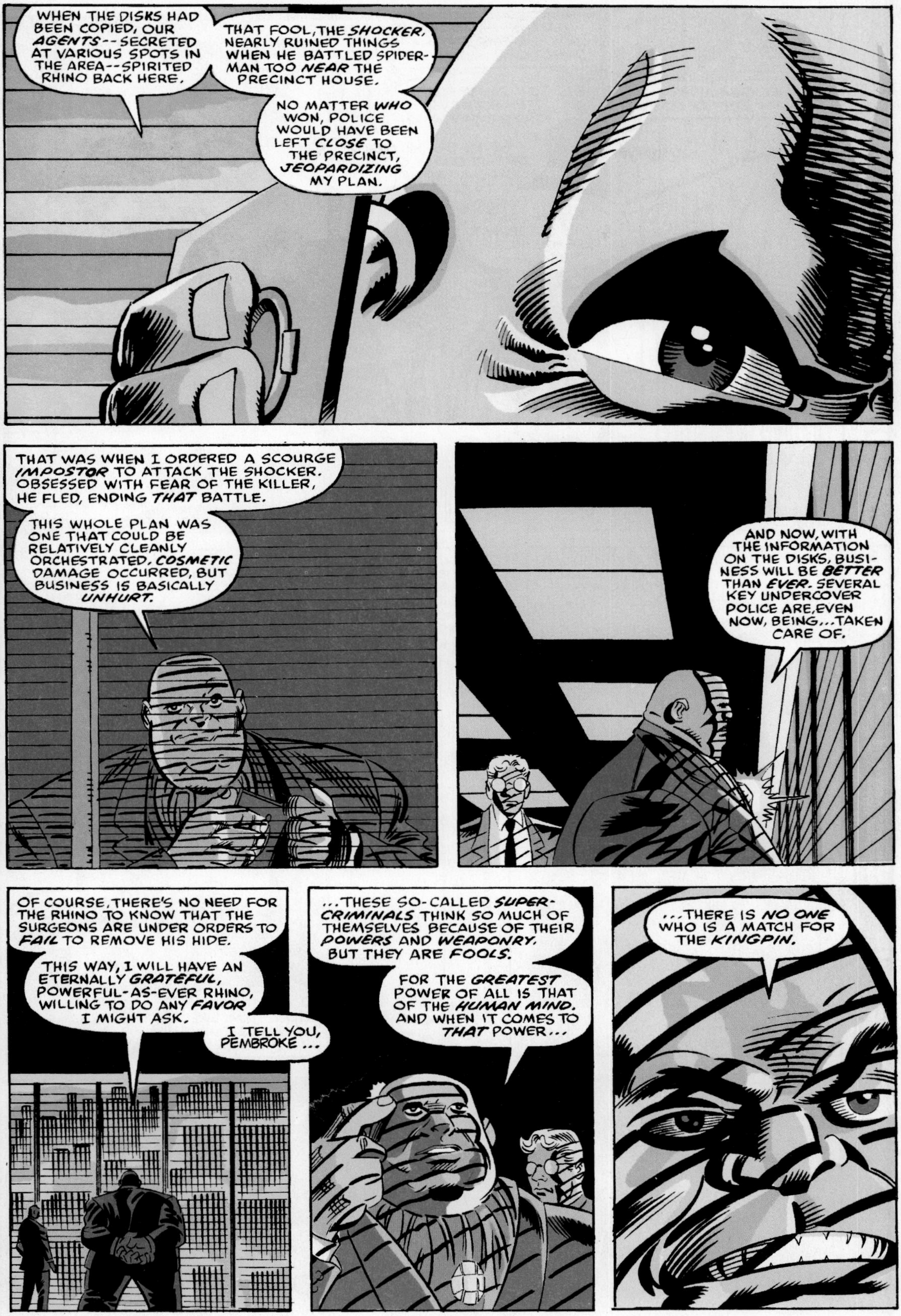
WHEN THE DISKS HAD BEEN COPIED, OUR AGENTS--SECRETED AT VARIOUS SPOTS IN THE AREA--SPIRITED RHINO BACK HERE.
THAT FOOL, THE SHOCKER, NEARLY RUINED THINGS WHEN HE BATTLED SPIDER-MAN TOO NEAR THE PRECINCT HOUSE.
NO MATTER WHO WON, POLICE WOULD HAVE BEEN LEFT CLOSE TO THE PRECINCT, JEOPARDIZING MY PLAN.
THAT WAS WHEN I ORDERED A SCOURGE IMPOSTOR TO ATTACK THE SHOCKER. OBSESSED WITH FEAR OF THE KILLER, HE FLED, ENDING THAT BATTLE.
THIS WHOLE PLAN WAS ONE THAT COULD BE RELATIVELY CLEANLY ORCHESTRATED. COSMETIC DAMAGE OCCURRED, BUT BUSINESS IS BASICALLY UNHURT.
AND NOW, WITH THE INFORMATION ON THE DISKS, BUSINESS WILL BE BETTER THAN EVER. SEVERAL KEY UNDERCOVER POLICE ARE, EVEN NOW, BEING...TAKEN CARE OF.
OF COURSE, THERE'S NO NEED FOR THE RHINO TO KNOW THAT THE SURGEONS ARE UNDER ORDERS TO FAIL TO REMOVE HIS HIDE.
THIS WAY, I WILL HAVE AN ETERNALLY GRATEFUL, POWERFUL-AS-EVER RHINO, WILLING TO DO ANY FAVOR I MIGHT ASK.
I TELL YOU, PEMBROKE...
...THESE SO-CALLED SUPER-CRIMINALS THINK SO MUCH OF THEMSELVES BECAUSE OF THEIR POWERS AND WEAPONRY. BUT THEY ARE FOOLS.
FOR THE GREATEST POWER OF ALL IS THAT OF THE HUMAN MIND. AND WHEN IT COMES TO THAT POWER...
...THERE IS NO ONE WHO IS A MATCH FOR THE KINGPIN.

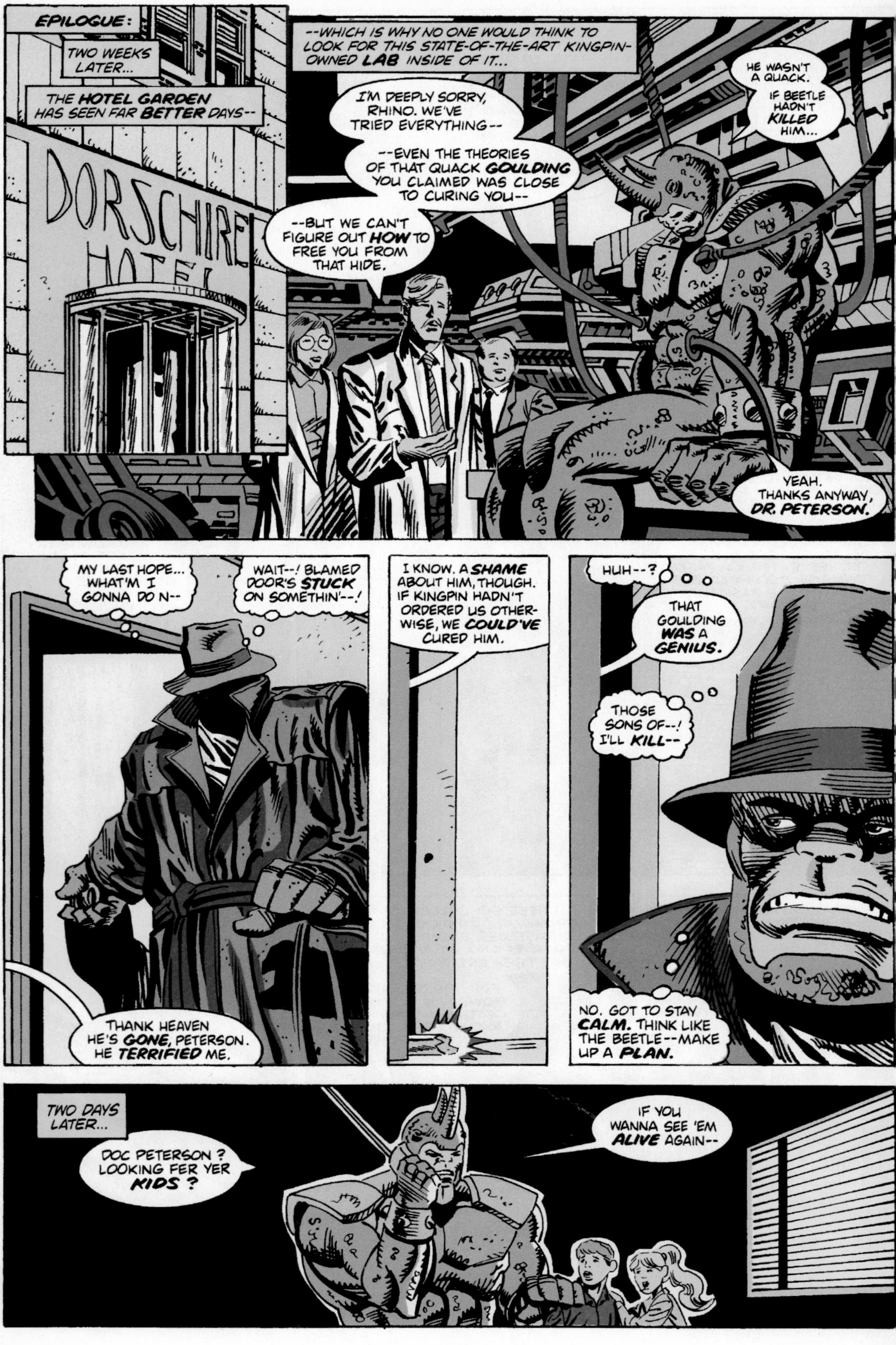
EPILOGUE:
TWO WEEKS LATER...
THE HOTEL GARDEN HAS SEEN FAR BETTER DAYS--
DORSCHIRE HOTEL
--WHICH IS WHY NO ONE WOULD THINK TO LOOK FOR THIS STATE-OF-THE-ART KINGPIN-OWNED LAB INSIDE OF IT...
I'M DEEPLY SORRY, RHINO. WE'VE TRIED EVERYTHING--
--EVEN THE THEORIES OF THAT QUACK GOULDING YOU CLAIMED WAS CLOSE TO CURING YOU--
--BUT WE CAN'T FIGURE OUT HOW TO FREE YOU FROM THAT HIDE.
HE WASN'T A QUACK.
IF BEETLE HADN'T KILLED HIM...
YEAH. THANKS ANYWAY, DR. PETERSON.
MY LAST HOPE... WHAT'M I GONNA DO N--
WAIT--! BLAMED DOOR'S STUCK ON SOMETHIN'--!
THANK HEAVEN HE'S GONE, PETERSON. HE TERRIFIED ME.
I KNOW. A SHAME ABOUT HIM, THOUGH. IF KINGPIN HADN'T ORDERED US OTHERWISE, WE COULD'VE CURED HIM.
HUH--?
THAT GOULDING WAS A GENIUS.
THOSE SONS OF--! I'LL KILL--
NO. GOT TO STAY CALM. THINK LIKE THE BEETLE--MAKE UP A PLAN.
TWO DAYS LATER...
DOC PETERSON? LOOKING FER YER KIDS?
IF YOU WANNA SEE 'EM ALIVE AGAIN--

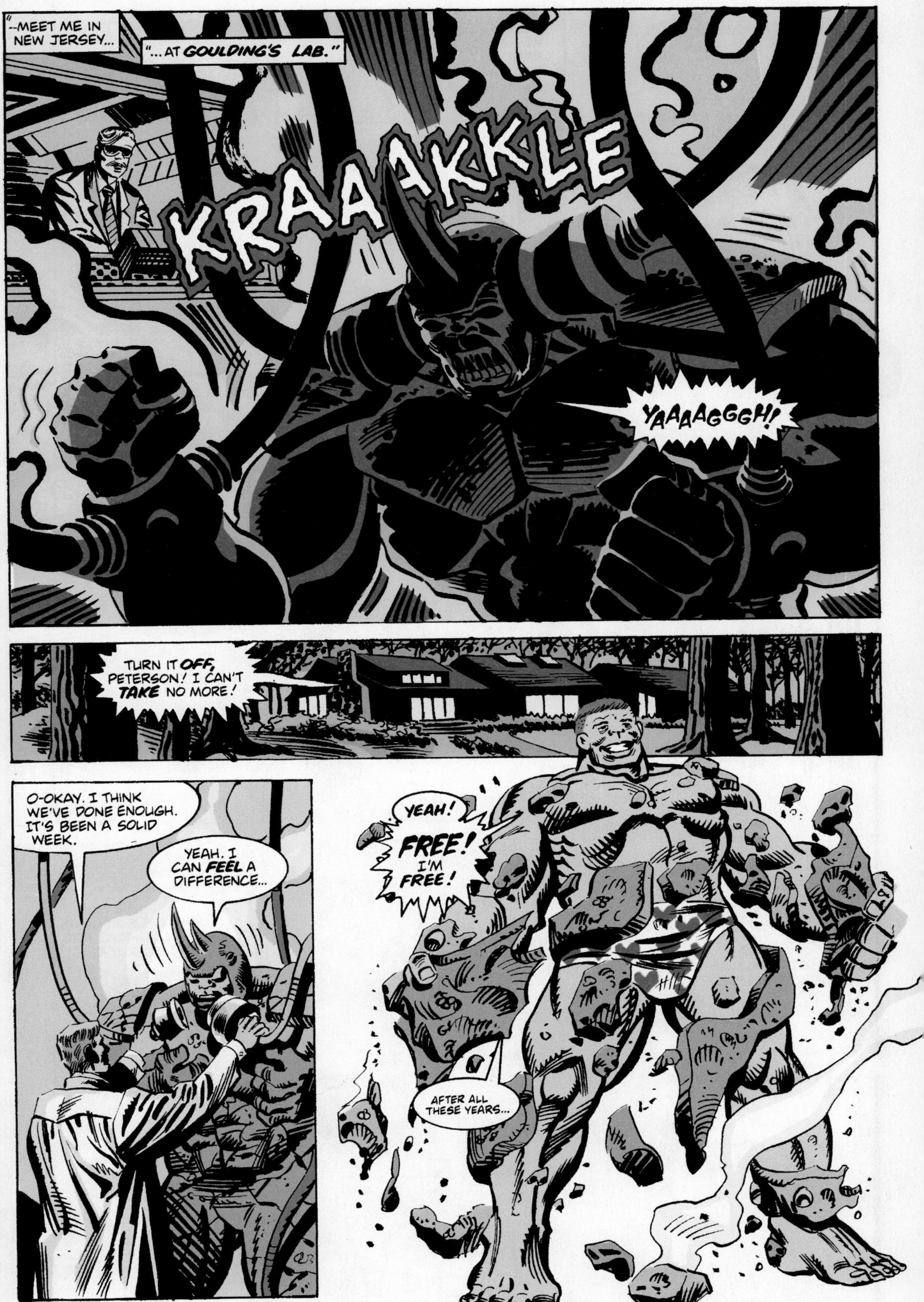
"--MEET ME IN NEW JERSEY...
"...AT GOULDING'S LAB."
KRAAAKKLE
YAAAAGGGH!
TURN IT OFF, PETERSON! I CAN'T TAKE NO MORE!
O-OKAY. I THINK WE'VE DONE ENOUGH. IT'S BEEN A SOLID WEEK.
YEAH. I CAN FEEL A DIFFERENCE...
YEAH! FREE! I'M FREE!
AFTER ALL THESE YEARS...

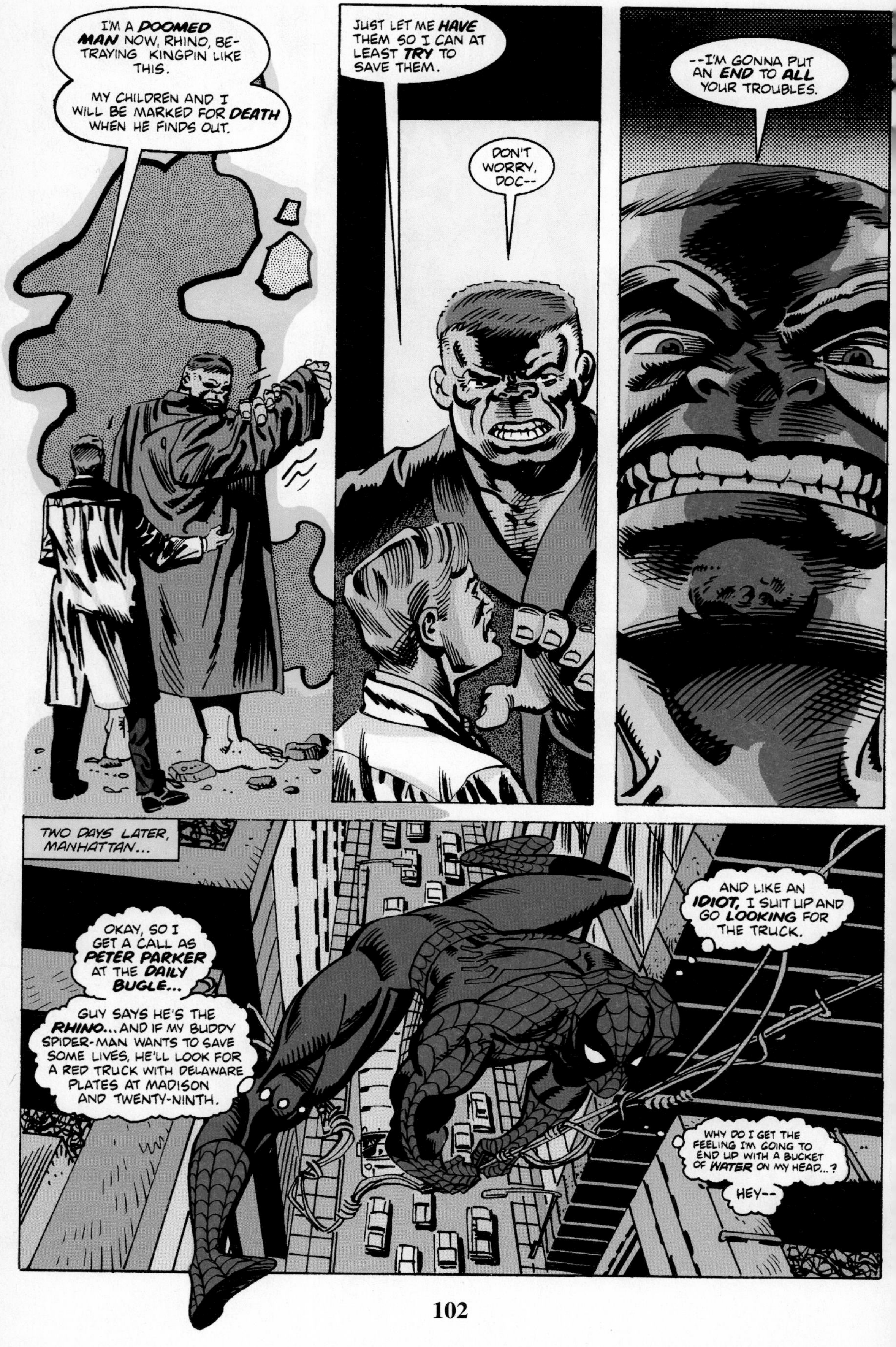
I'M A DOOMED MAN NOW, RHINO, BE-TRAYING KINGPIN LIKE THIS.
MY CHILDREN AND I WILL BE MARKED FOR DEATH WHEN HE FINDS OUT.
JUST LET ME HAVE THEM SO I CAN AT LEAST TRY TO SAVE THEM.
DON'T WORRY, DOC--
--I'M GONNA PUT AN END TO ALL YOUR TROUBLES.
TWO DAYS LATER, MANHATTAN...
OKAY, SO I GET A CALL AS PETER PARKER AT THE DAILY BUGLE...
GUY SAYS HE'S THE RHINO... AND IF MY BUDDY SPIDER-MAN WANTS TO SAVE SOME LIVES, HE'LL LOOK FOR A RED TRUCK WITH DELAWARE PLATES AT MADISON AND TWENTY-NINTH.
AND LIKE AN IDIOT, I SUIT UP AND GO LOOKING FOR THE TRUCK.
WHY DO I GET THE FEELING I'M GOING TO END UP WITH A BUCKET OF WATER ON MY HEAD...?
HEY--

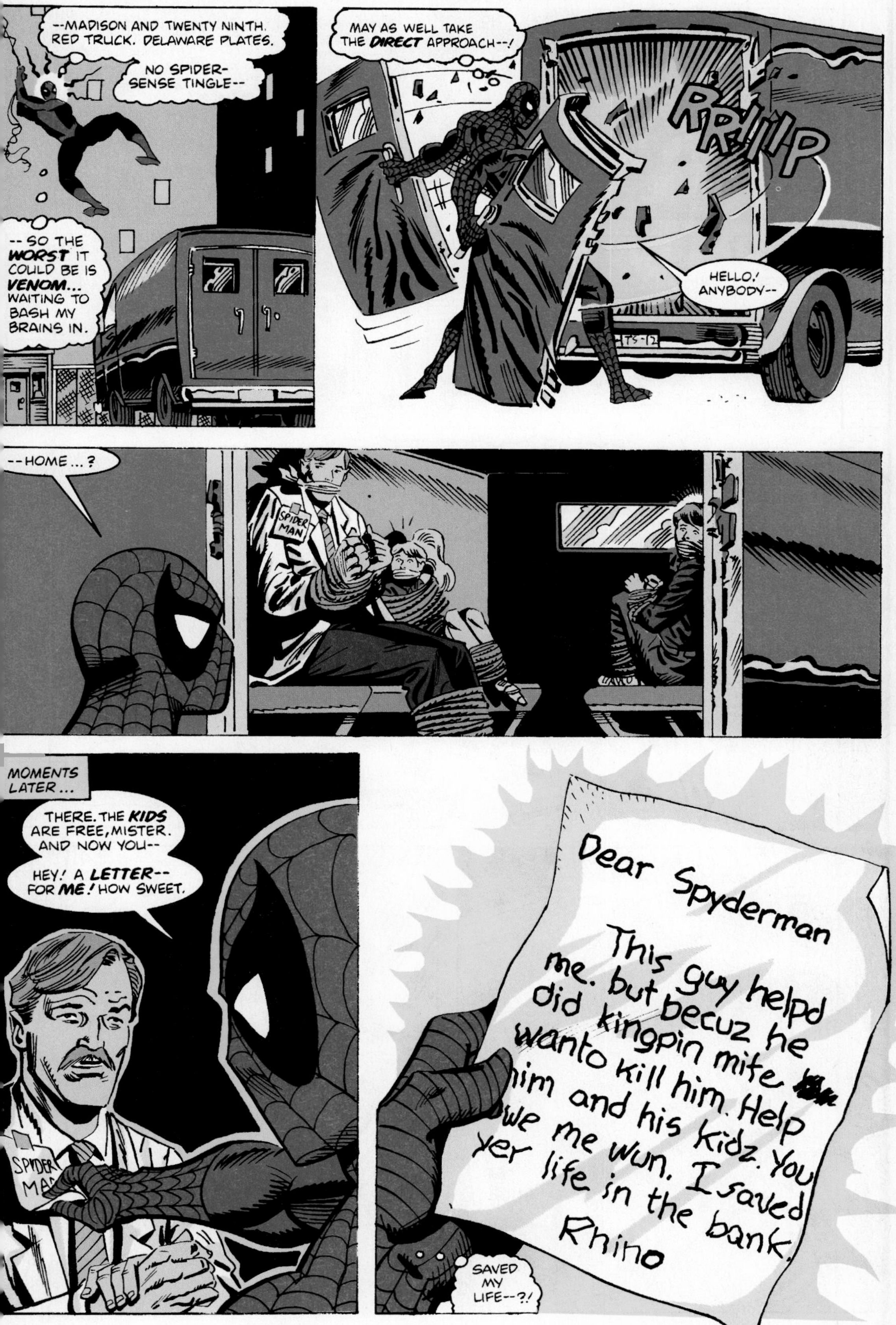
--MADISON AND TWENTY NINTH. RED TRUCK. DELAWARE PLATES.
NO SPIDER-SENSE TINGLE--
--SO THE WORST IT COULD BE IS VENOM... WAITING TO BASH MY BRAINS IN.
MAY AS WELL TAKE THE DIRECT APPROACH--!
RRIIIP
HELLO! ANYBODY--
--HOME...?
SPIDER MAN
MOMENTS LATER...
THERE. THE KIDS ARE FREE, MISTER. AND NOW YOU--
HEY! A LETTER-- FOR ME! HOW SWEET.
Dear Spyderman
This guy helpd me. but becuz he did kingpin mite wanto kill him. Help him and his kidz. You owe me wun. I saved yer life in the bank.
Rhino
SAVED MY LIFE--?!

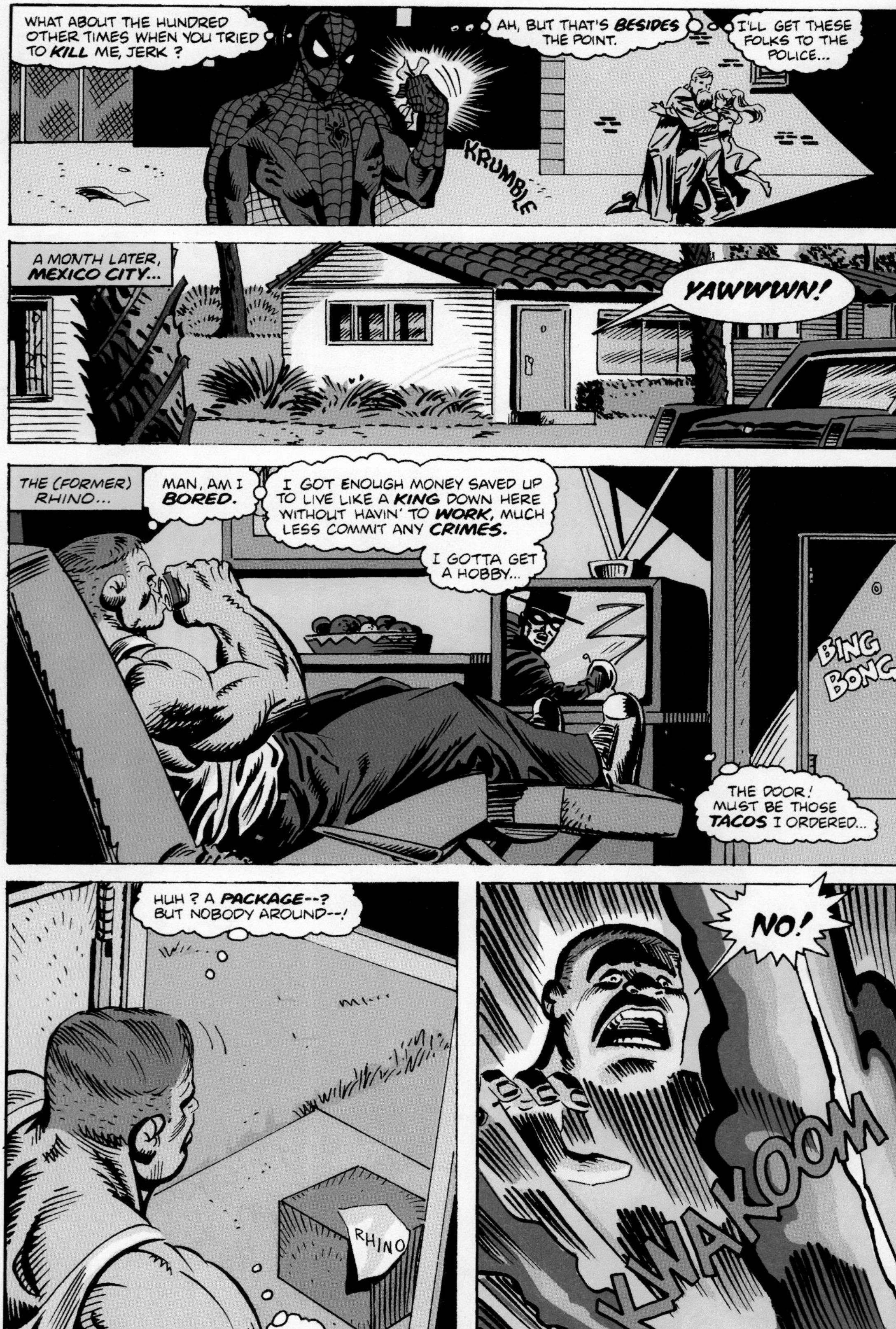
WHAT ABOUT THE HUNDRED OTHER TIMES WHEN YOU TRIED TO KILL ME, JERK ?
AH, BUT THAT'S BESIDES THE POINT.
I'LL GET THESE FOLKS TO THE POLICE...
KRUMBLE
A MONTH LATER, MEXICO CITY...
YAWWWN!
THE (FORMER) RHINO...
MAN, AM I BORED.
I GOT ENOUGH MONEY SAVED UP TO LIVE LIKE A KING DOWN HERE WITHOUT HAVIN' TO WORK, MUCH LESS COMMIT ANY CRIMES.
I GOTTA GET A HOBBY...
BING BONG
THE DOOR! MUST BE THOSE TACOS I ORDERED...
HUH ? A PACKAGE--? BUT NOBODY AROUND--!
RHINO
OH, NO--
NO!
KWAKOOM

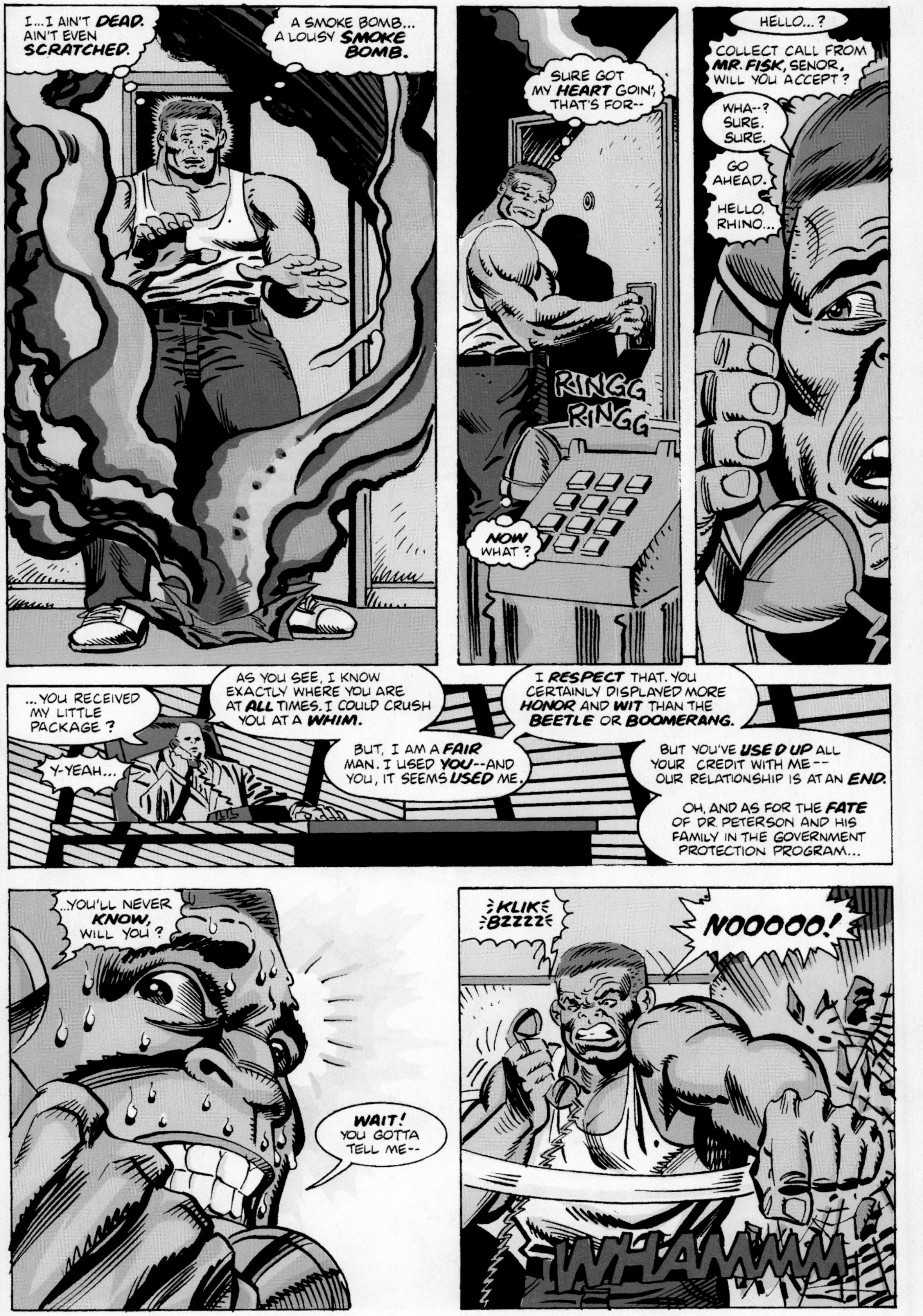
I...I AIN'T DEAD. AIN'T EVEN SCRATCHED.
A SMOKE BOMB... A LOUSY SMOKE BOMB.
SURE GOT MY HEART GOIN', THAT'S FOR--
RINGG RINGG
NOW WHAT?
HELLO...?
COLLECT CALL FROM MR. FISK, SENOR. WILL YOU ACCEPT?
WHA--? SURE. SURE.
GO AHEAD.
HELLO, RHINO...
...YOU RECEIVED MY LITTLE PACKAGE?
Y-YEAH...
AS YOU SEE, I KNOW EXACTLY WHERE YOU ARE AT ALL TIMES. I COULD CRUSH YOU AT A WHIM.
BUT, I AM A FAIR MAN. I USED YOU--AND YOU, IT SEEMS USED ME.
I RESPECT THAT. YOU CERTAINLY DISPLAYED MORE HONOR AND WIT THAN THE BEETLE OR BOOMERANG.
BUT YOU'VE USED UP ALL YOUR CREDIT WITH ME-- OUR RELATIONSHIP IS AT AN END.
OH, AND AS FOR THE FATE OF DR. PETERSON AND HIS FAMILY IN THE GOVERNMENT PROTECTION PROGRAM...
...YOU'LL NEVER KNOW, WILL YOU?
WAIT! YOU GOTTA TELL ME--
KLIK BZZZZ
NOOOOO!
WHAMMM

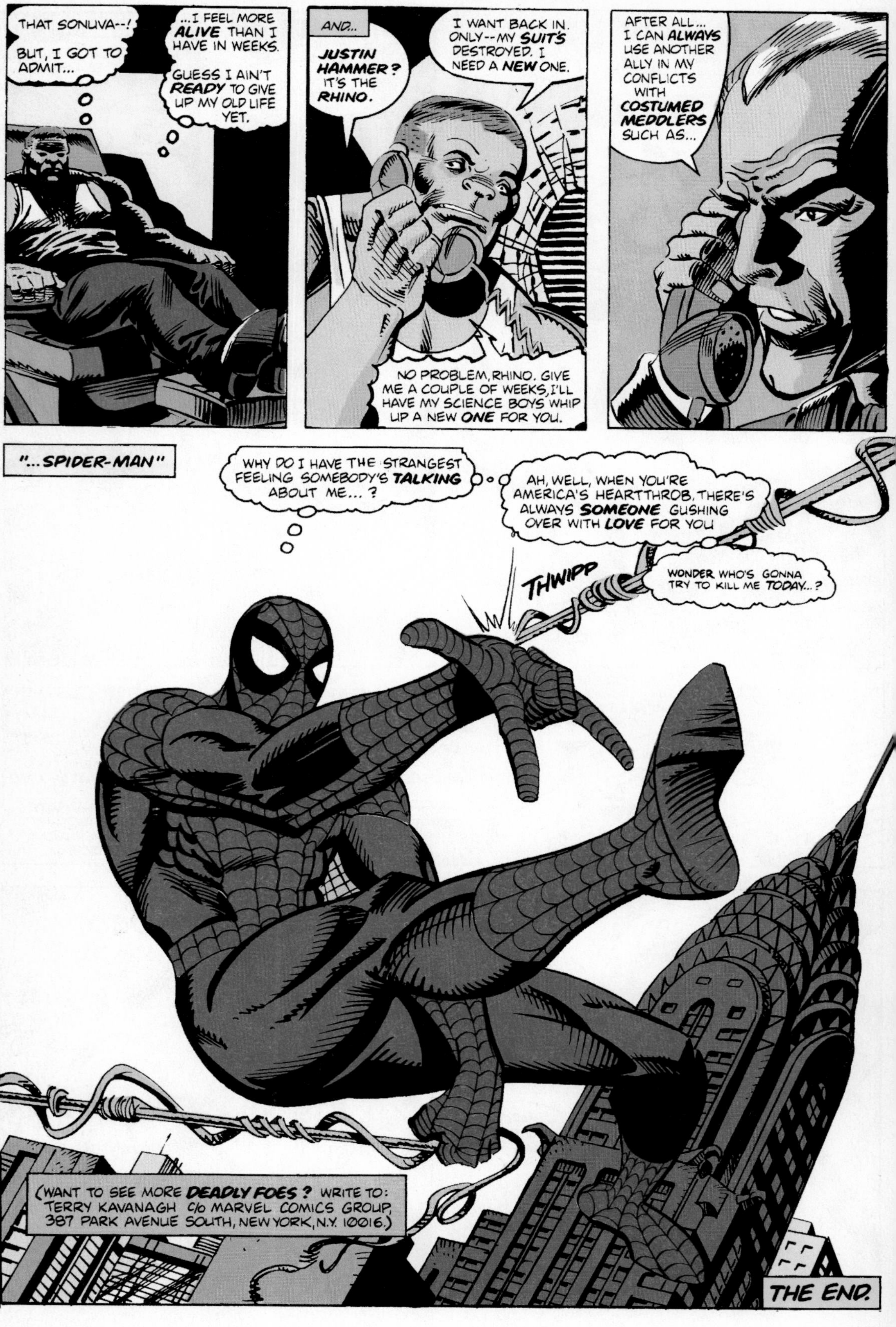
THAT SONUVA--!
BUT, I GOT TO ADMIT...
...I FEEL MORE ALIVE THAN I HAVE IN WEEKS.
GUESS I AIN'T READY TO GIVE UP MY OLD LIFE YET.
AND...
JUSTIN HAMMER? IT'S THE RHINO.
I WANT BACK IN. ONLY--MY SUIT'S DESTROYED. I NEED A NEW ONE.
NO PROBLEM, RHINO. GIVE ME A COUPLE OF WEEKS, I'LL HAVE MY SCIENCE BOYS WHIP UP A NEW ONE FOR YOU.
AFTER ALL... I CAN ALWAYS USE ANOTHER ALLY IN MY CONFLICTS WITH COSTUMED MEDDLERS SUCH AS...
"...SPIDER-MAN"
WHY DO I HAVE THE STRANGEST FEELING SOMEBODY'S TALKING ABOUT ME... ?
AH, WELL, WHEN YOU'RE AMERICA'S HEARTTHROB, THERE'S ALWAYS SOMEONE GUSHING OVER WITH LOVE FOR YOU
THWIPP
WONDER WHO'S GONNA TRY TO KILL ME TODAY...?
(WANT TO SEE MORE DEADLY FOES? WRITE TO: TERRY KAVANAGH C/O MARVEL COMICS GROUP, 387 PARK AVENUE SOUTH, NEW YORK, N.Y. 10016.)
THE END.

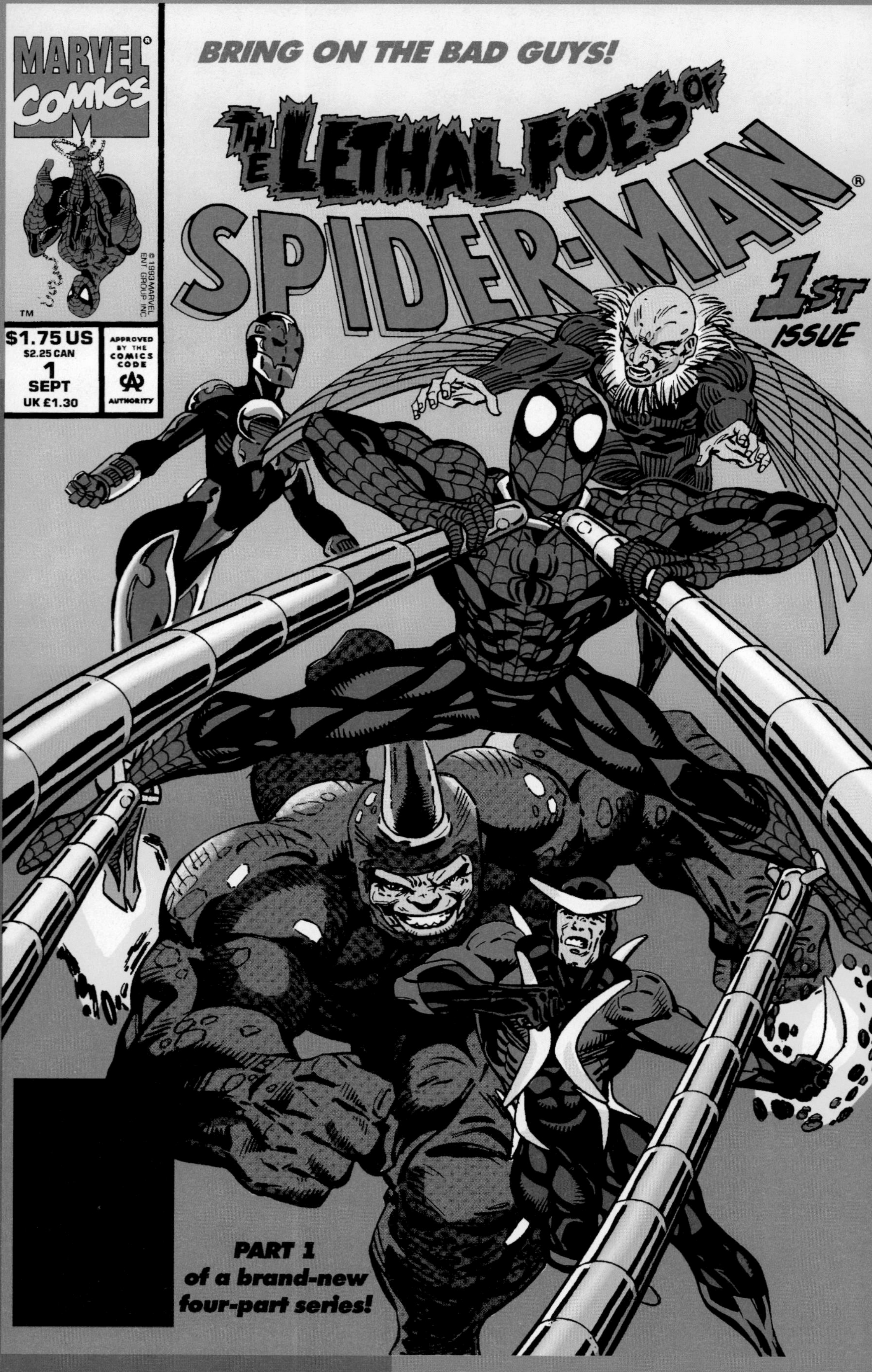
MARVEL COMICS
BRING ON THE BAD GUYS!
THE LETHAL FOES OF SPIDER-MAN
1ST ISSUE
© 1993 MARVEL ENT GROUP INC.
TM
$1.75 US
$2.25 CAN
1
SEPT
UK £1.30
APPROVED BY THE COMICS CODE AUTHORITY
PART 1
of a brand-new
four-part series!

UNITED IN NOTHING BUT THEIR *HATRED* FOR ONE MAN AND THEIR THIRST FOR *POWER*, MURDEROUS INDIVIDUALS BAND TOGETHER TO FURTHER THEIR TWISTED GOALS. AND THEY WILL LET *NOTHING* STAND IN THEIR WAY!

STAN LEE PRESENTS... THE LETHAL FOES OF SPIDER-MAN!

CHAPTER ONE: DEADLY REUNION

DANNY FINGEROTH WRITER / SCOTT McDANIEL PENCILER / BRAD VANCATA INKER / DAVE SAMPSON COLORIST / DIANA ALBERS LETTERER / ROB TOKAR EDITOR / TOM DeFALCO EDITOR IN CHIEF

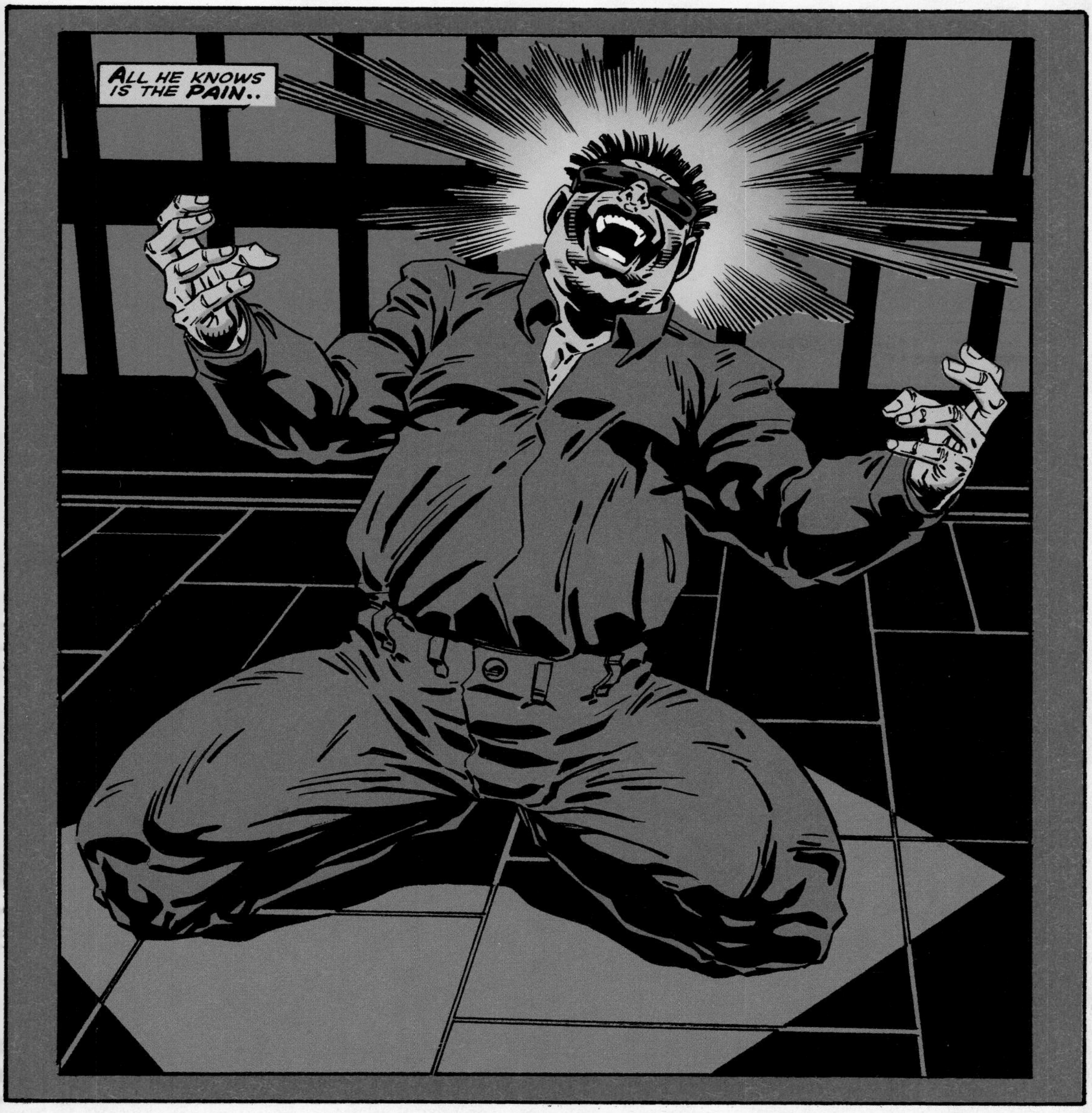
ALL HE KNOWS IS THE PAIN..

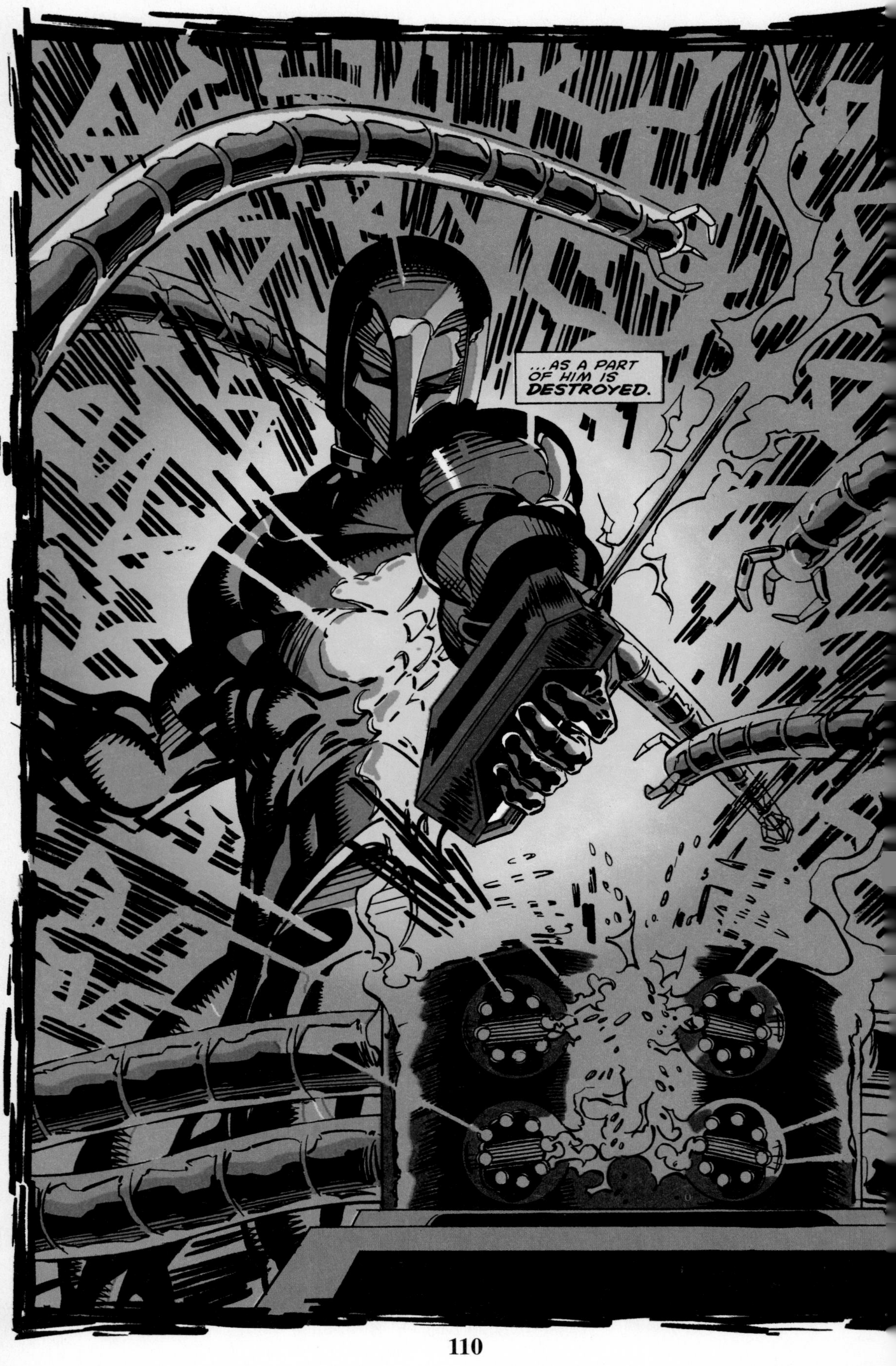
...AS A PART OF HIM IS DESTROYED.

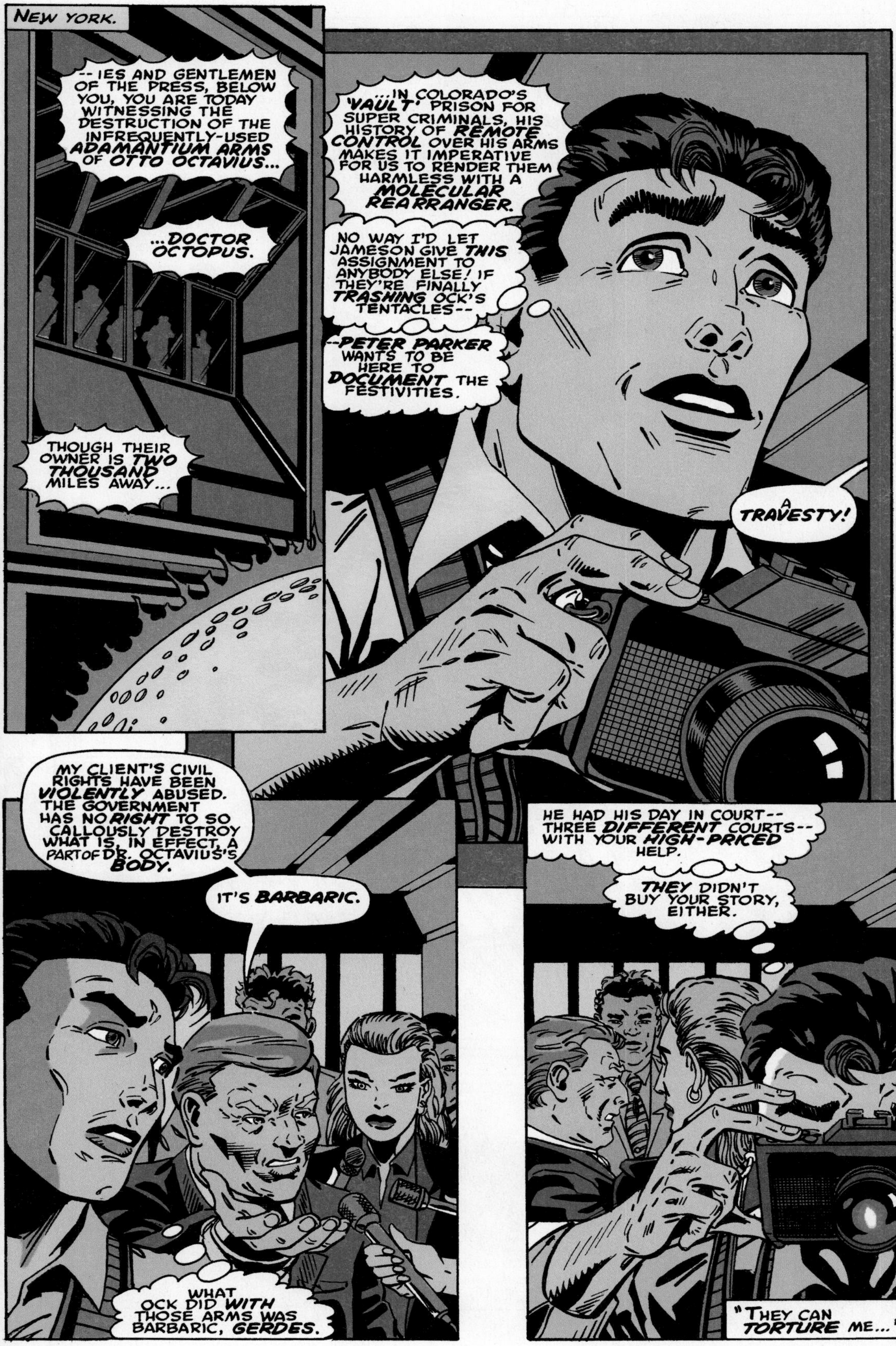

NEW YORK.
-- IES AND GENTLEMEN OF THE PRESS, BELOW YOU, YOU ARE TODAY WITNESSING THE DESTRUCTION OF THE INFREQUENTLY-USED ADAMANTIUM ARMS OF OTTO OCTAVIUS...
...DOCTOR OCTOPUS.
THOUGH THEIR OWNER IS TWO THOUSAND MILES AWAY...
...IN COLORADO'S 'VAULT' PRISON FOR SUPER CRIMINALS, HIS HISTORY OF REMOTE CONTROL OVER HIS ARMS MAKES IT IMPERATIVE FOR US TO RENDER THEM HARMLESS WITH A MOLECULAR REARRANGER.
NO WAY I'D LET JAMESON GIVE THIS ASSIGNMENT TO ANYBODY ELSE! IF THEY'RE FINALLY TRASHING OCK'S TENTACLES--
--PETER PARKER WANTS TO BE HERE TO DOCUMENT THE FESTIVITIES.
A TRAVESTY!
MY CLIENT'S CIVIL RIGHTS HAVE BEEN VIOLENTLY ABUSED. THE GOVERNMENT HAS NO RIGHT TO SO CALLOUSLY DESTROY WHAT IS, IN EFFECT, A PART OF DR. OCTAVIUS'S BODY.
IT'S BARBARIC.
WHAT OCK DID WITH THOSE ARMS WAS BARBARIC, GERDES.
HE HAD HIS DAY IN COURT-- THREE DIFFERENT COURTS-- WITH YOUR HIGH-PRICED HELP.
THEY DIDN'T BUY YOUR STORY, EITHER.
"THEY CAN TORTURE ME..."

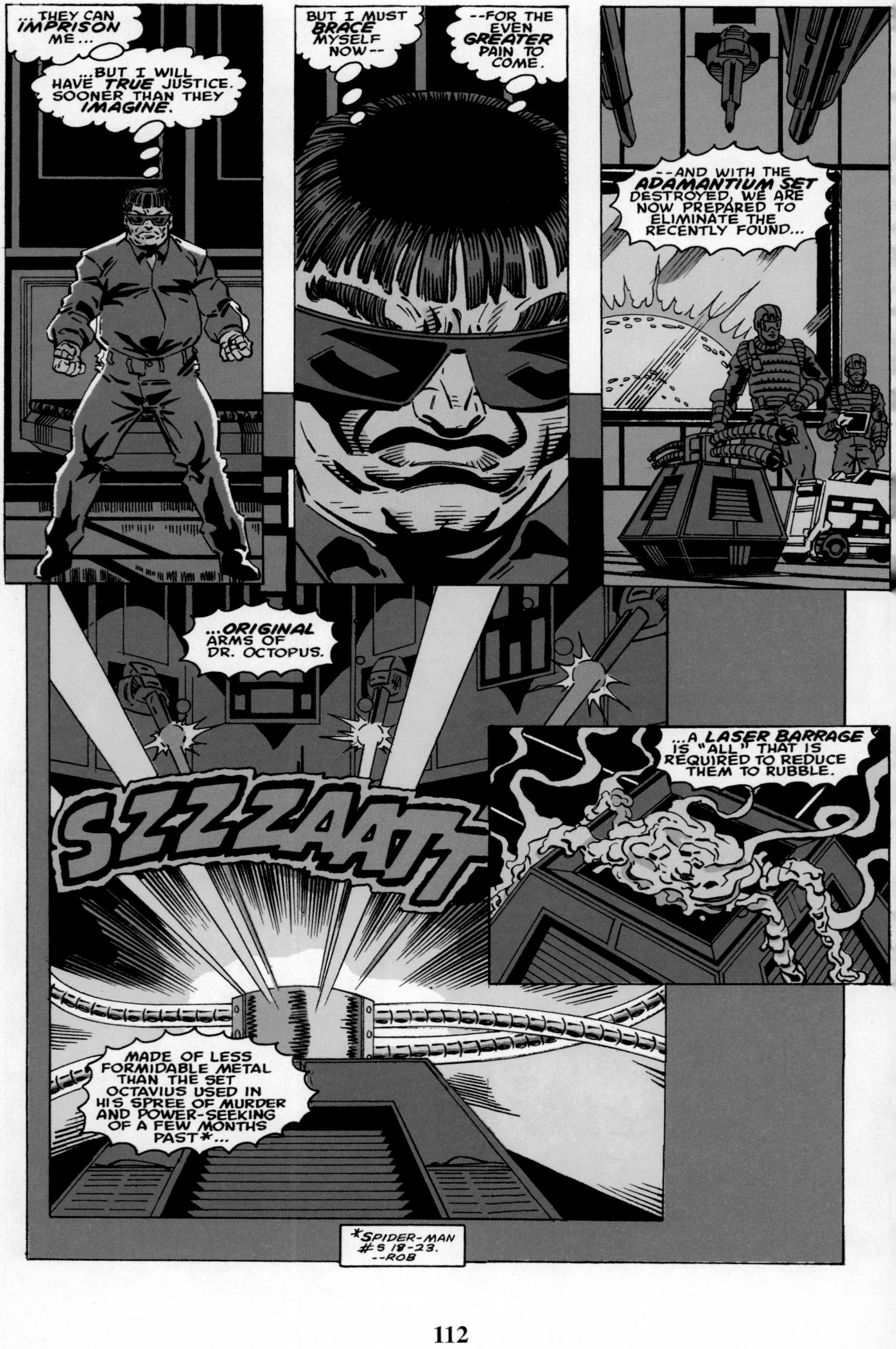
...THEY CAN IMPRISON ME...
...BUT I WILL HAVE TRUE JUSTICE. SOONER THAN THEY IMAGINE.
BUT I MUST BRACE MYSELF NOW--
--FOR THE EVEN GREATER PAIN TO COME.
--AND WITH THE ADAMANTIUM SET DESTROYED, WE ARE NOW PREPARED TO ELIMINATE THE RECENTLY FOUND...
...ORIGINAL ARMS OF DR. OCTOPUS.
SZZZAAATT
MADE OF LESS FORMIDABLE METAL THAN THE SET OCTAVIUS USED IN HIS SPREE OF MURDER AND POWER-SEEKING OF A FEW MONTHS PAST*...
...A LASER BARRAGE IS "ALL" THAT IS REQUIRED TO REDUCE THEM TO RUBBLE.
*SPIDER-MAN #S 18-23. --ROB

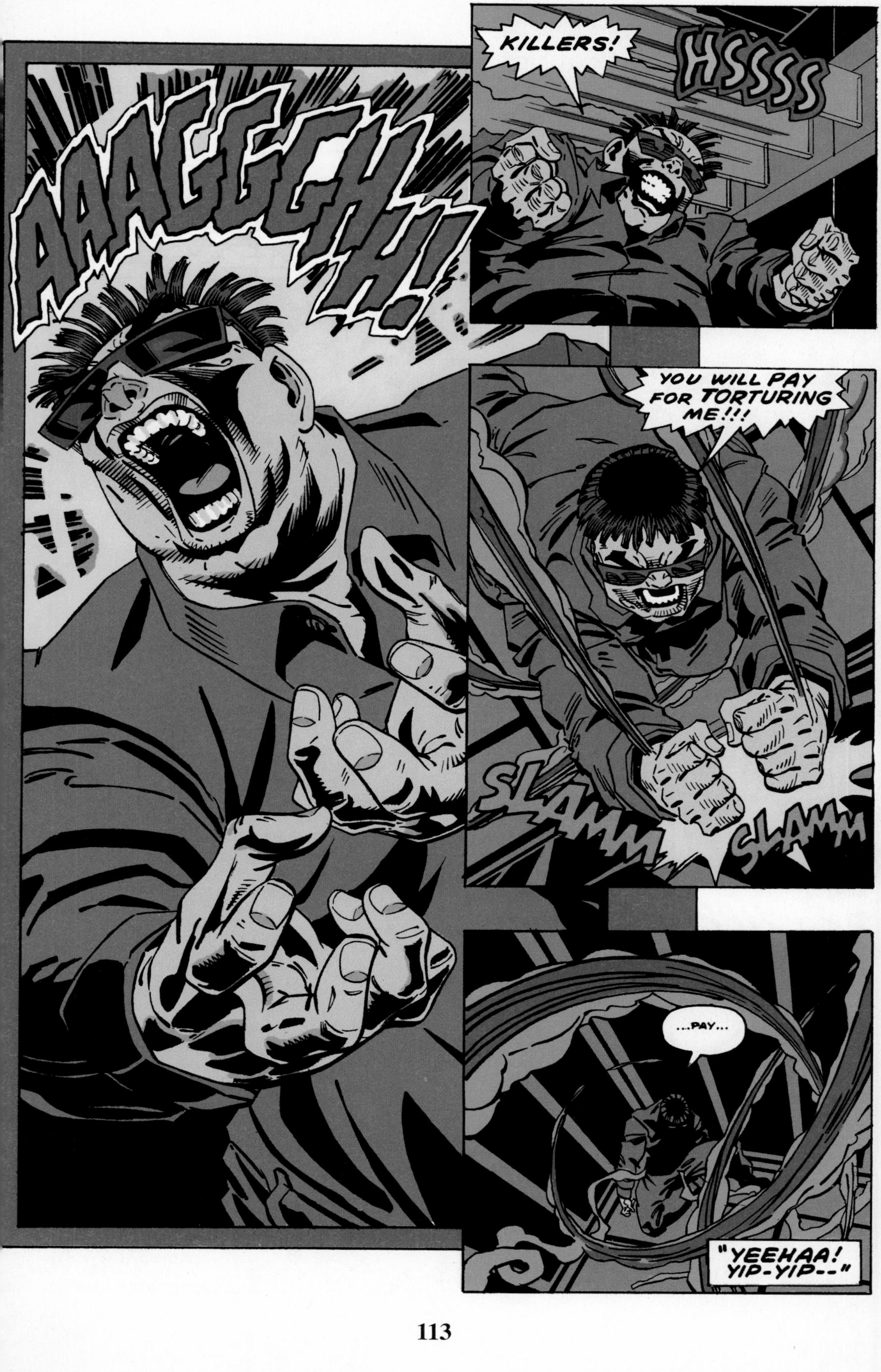
AAAGGGHH!
KILLERS!
HSSSS
YOU WILL PAY FOR TORTURING ME!!!
SLAMM
SLAMM
...PAY...
"YEEHAA! YIP-YIP--"

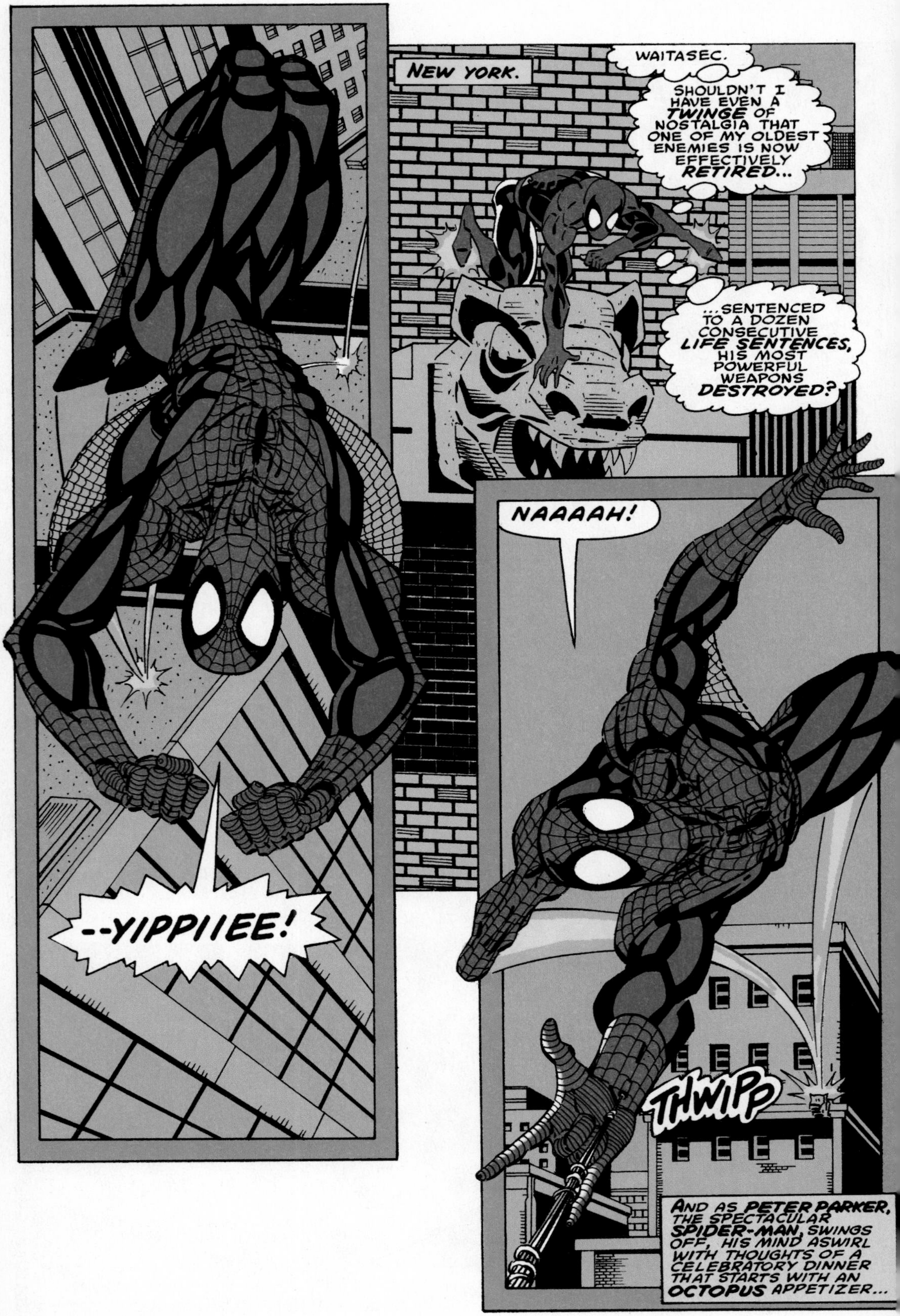

NEW YORK.
WAITASEC.
SHOULDN'T I HAVE EVEN A TWINGE OF NOSTALGIA THAT ONE OF MY OLDEST ENEMIES IS NOW EFFECTIVELY RETIRED...
...SENTENCED TO A DOZEN CONSECUTIVE LIFE SENTENCES, HIS MOST POWERFUL WEAPONS DESTROYED?
NAAAAH!
--YIPPIIEE!
THWIPP
AND AS PETER PARKER, THE SPECTACULAR SPIDER-MAN, SWINGS OFF, HIS MIND ASWIRL WITH THOUGHTS OF A CELEBRATORY DINNER THAT STARTS WITH AN OCTOPUS APPETIZER...

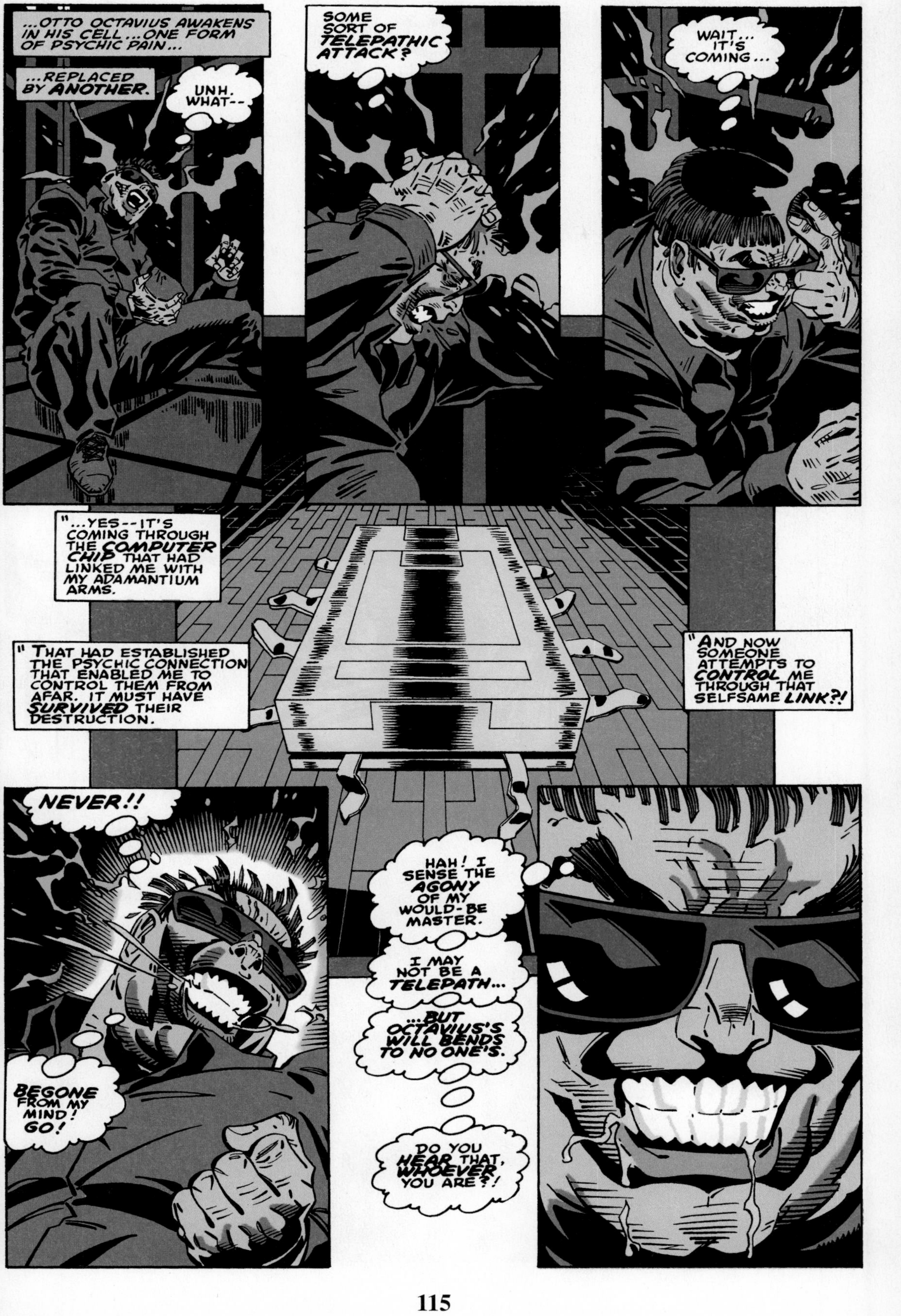

...OTTO OCTAVIUS AWAKENS IN HIS CELL...ONE FORM OF PSYCHIC PAIN...
...REPLACED BY ANOTHER.
UNH. WHAT--
SOME SORT OF TELEPATHIC ATTACK?
WAIT... IT'S COMING...
"...YES--IT'S COMING THROUGH THE COMPUTER CHIP THAT HAD LINKED ME WITH MY ADAMANTIUM ARMS.
" THAT HAD ESTABLISHED THE PSYCHIC CONNECTION THAT ENABLED ME TO CONTROL THEM FROM AFAR. IT MUST HAVE SURVIVED THEIR DESTRUCTION.
"AND NOW SOMEONE ATTEMPTS TO CONTROL ME THROUGH THAT SELFSAME LINK?!
NEVER!!
BEGONE FROM MY MIND! GO!
HAH! I SENSE THE AGONY OF MY WOULD-BE MASTER.
I MAY NOT BE A TELEPATH...
...BUT OCTAVIUS'S WILL BENDS TO NO ONE'S.
DO YOU HEAR THAT, WHOEVER YOU ARE?!

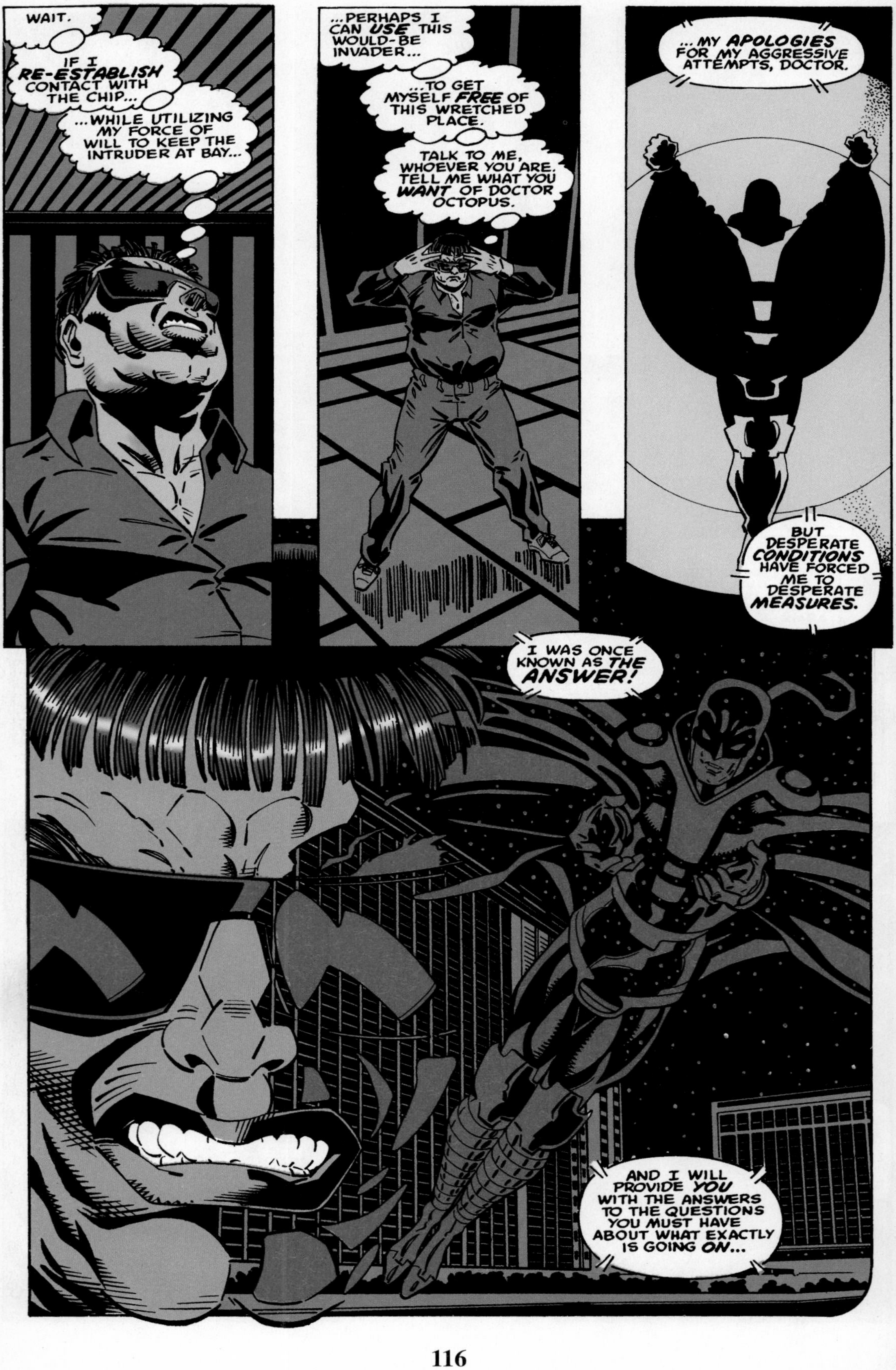
WAIT.
IF I RE-ESTABLISH CONTACT WITH THE CHIP...
...WHILE UTILIZING MY FORCE OF WILL TO KEEP THE INTRUDER AT BAY...
...PERHAPS I CAN USE THIS WOULD-BE INVADER...
...TO GET MYSELF FREE OF THIS WRETCHED PLACE.
TALK TO ME, WHOEVER YOU ARE. TELL ME WHAT YOU WANT OF DOCTOR OCTOPUS.
...MY APOLOGIES FOR MY AGGRESSIVE ATTEMPTS, DOCTOR.
BUT DESPERATE CONDITIONS HAVE FORCED ME TO DESPERATE MEASURES.
I WAS ONCE KNOWN AS THE ANSWER!
AND I WILL PROVIDE YOU WITH THE ANSWERS TO THE QUESTIONS YOU MUST HAVE ABOUT WHAT EXACTLY IS GOING ON...

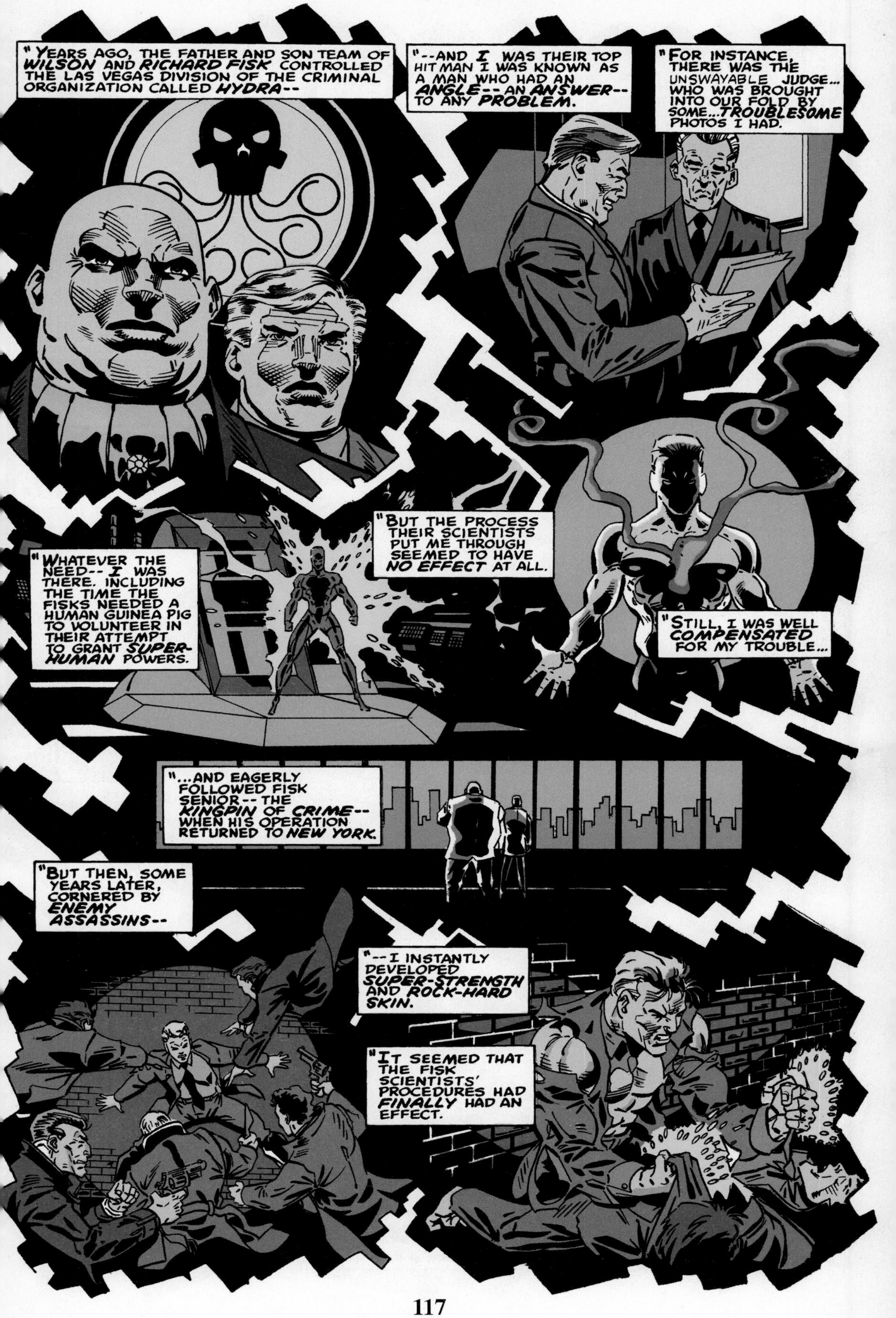
"YEARS AGO, THE FATHER AND SON TEAM OF WILSON AND RICHARD FISK CONTROLLED THE LAS VEGAS DIVISION OF THE CRIMINAL ORGANIZATION CALLED HYDRA--
"--AND I WAS THEIR TOP HIT MAN. I WAS KNOWN AS A MAN WHO HAD AN ANGLE-- AN ANSWER-- TO ANY PROBLEM.
"FOR INSTANCE, THERE WAS THE UNSWAYABLE JUDGE... WHO WAS BROUGHT INTO OUR FOLD BY SOME... TROUBLESOME PHOTOS I HAD.
"WHATEVER THE NEED-- I WAS THERE. INCLUDING THE TIME THE FISKS NEEDED A HUMAN GUINEA PIG TO VOLUNTEER IN THEIR ATTEMPT TO GRANT SUPER-HUMAN POWERS.
"BUT THE PROCESS THEIR SCIENTISTS PUT ME THROUGH SEEMED TO HAVE NO EFFECT AT ALL.
"STILL, I WAS WELL COMPENSATED FOR MY TROUBLE...
"...AND EAGERLY FOLLOWED FISK SENIOR-- THE KINGPIN OF CRIME-- WHEN HIS OPERATION RETURNED TO NEW YORK.
"BUT THEN, SOME YEARS LATER, CORNERED BY ENEMY ASSASSINS--
"--I INSTANTLY DEVELOPED SUPER-STRENGTH AND ROCK-HARD SKIN.
"IT SEEMED THAT THE FISK SCIENTISTS' PROCEDURES HAD FINALLY HAD AN EFFECT.

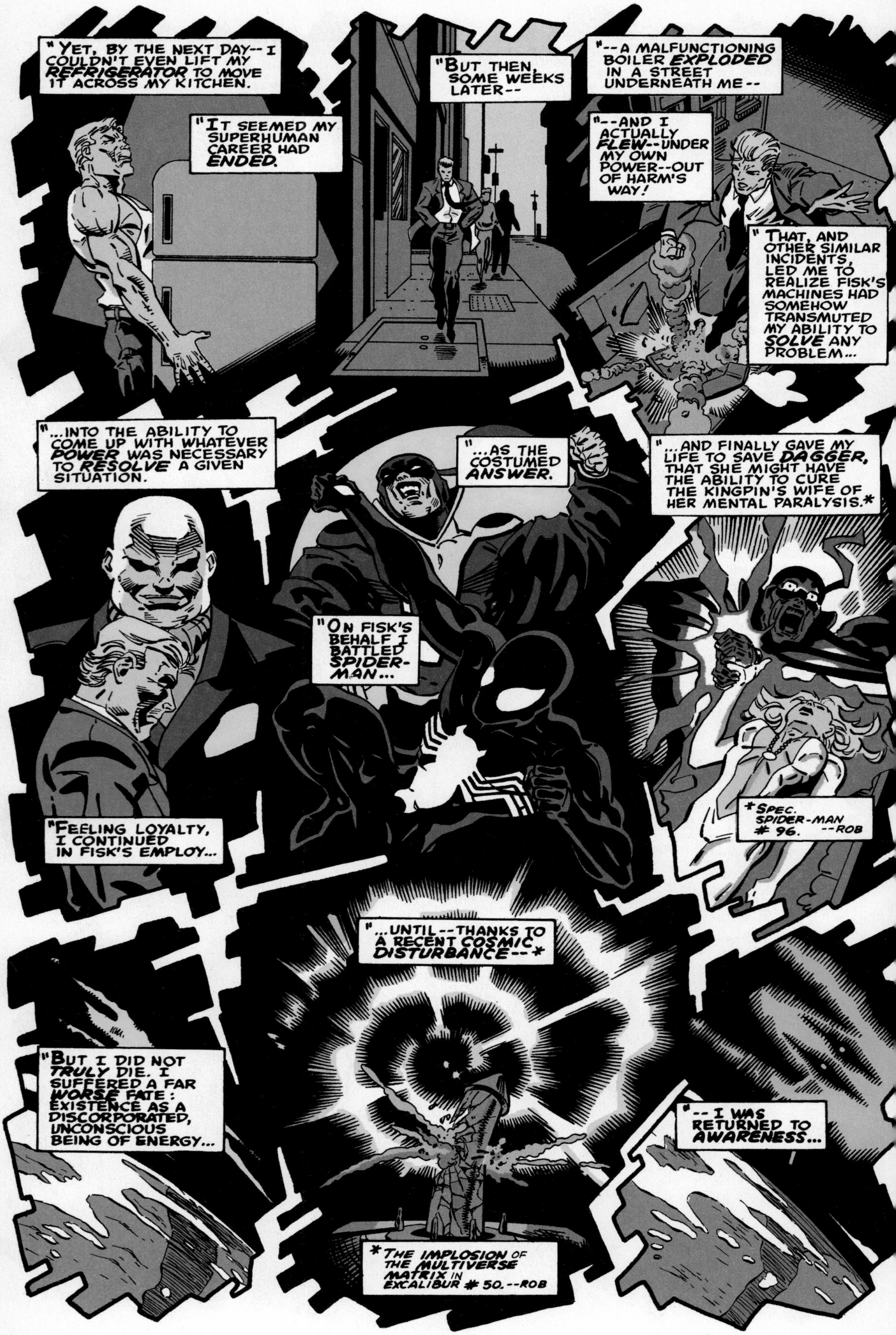
"YET, BY THE NEXT DAY-- I COULDN'T EVEN LIFT MY REFRIGERATOR TO MOVE IT ACROSS MY KITCHEN.
"IT SEEMED MY SUPERHUMAN CAREER HAD ENDED.
"BUT THEN, SOME WEEKS LATER--
"--A MALFUNCTIONING BOILER EXPLODED IN A STREET UNDERNEATH ME--
"--AND I ACTUALLY FLEW--UNDER MY OWN POWER--OUT OF HARM'S WAY!
"THAT, AND OTHER SIMILAR INCIDENTS, LED ME TO REALIZE FISK'S MACHINES HAD SOMEHOW TRANSMUTED MY ABILITY TO SOLVE ANY PROBLEM...
"...INTO THE ABILITY TO COME UP WITH WHATEVER POWER WAS NECESSARY TO RESOLVE A GIVEN SITUATION.
"FEELING LOYALTY, I CONTINUED IN FISK'S EMPLOY...
"...AS THE COSTUMED ANSWER.
"ON FISK'S BEHALF I BATTLED SPIDER-MAN...
"...AND FINALLY GAVE MY LIFE TO SAVE DAGGER, THAT SHE MIGHT HAVE THE ABILITY TO CURE THE KINGPIN'S WIFE OF HER MENTAL PARALYSIS.*
*SPEC. SPIDER-MAN # 96. --ROB
"BUT I DID NOT TRULY DIE. I SUFFERED A FAR WORSE FATE: EXISTENCE AS A DISCORPORATED, UNCONSCIOUS BEING OF ENERGY...
"...UNTIL--THANKS TO A RECENT COSMIC DISTURBANCE--*
"--I WAS RETURNED TO AWARENESS...
*THE IMPLOSION OF THE MULTIVERSE MATRIX IN EXCALIBUR # 50.--ROB

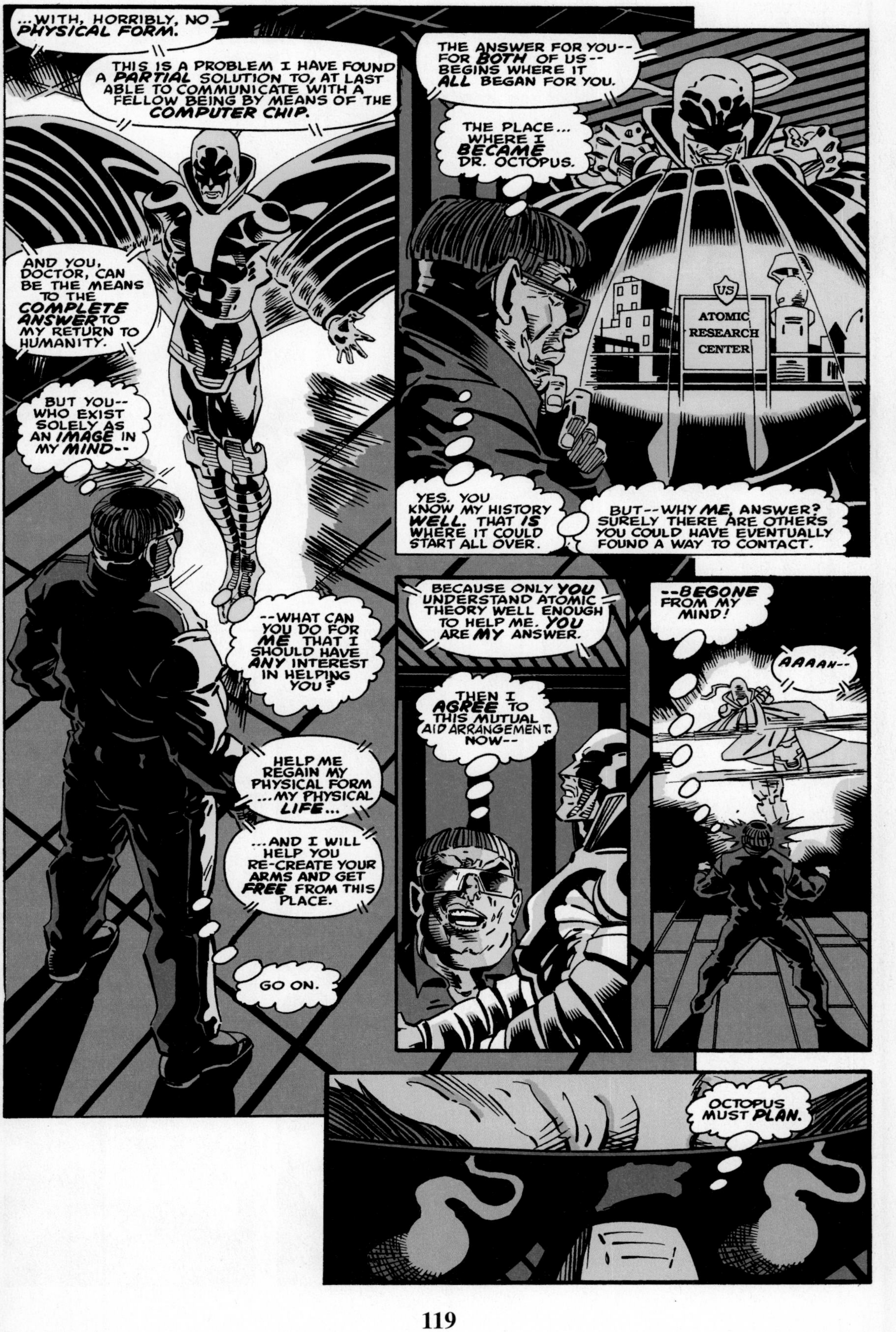
...WITH, HORRIBLY, NO PHYSICAL FORM.
THIS IS A PROBLEM I HAVE FOUND A PARTIAL SOLUTION TO, AT LAST ABLE TO COMMUNICATE WITH A FELLOW BEING BY MEANS OF THE COMPUTER CHIP.
AND YOU, DOCTOR, CAN BE THE MEANS TO THE COMPLETE ANSWER TO MY RETURN TO HUMANITY.
BUT YOU-- WHO EXIST SOLELY AS AN IMAGE IN MY MIND--
--WHAT CAN YOU DO FOR ME THAT I SHOULD HAVE ANY INTEREST IN HELPING YOU?
HELP ME REGAIN MY PHYSICAL FORM ...MY PHYSICAL LIFE...
...AND I WILL HELP YOU RE-CREATE YOUR ARMS AND GET FREE FROM THIS PLACE.
GO ON.
THE ANSWER FOR YOU-- FOR BOTH OF US-- BEGINS WHERE IT ALL BEGAN FOR YOU.
THE PLACE... WHERE I BECAME DR. OCTOPUS.
US
ATOMIC RESEARCH CENTER
YES. YOU KNOW MY HISTORY WELL. THAT IS WHERE IT COULD START ALL OVER.
BUT--WHY ME, ANSWER? SURELY THERE ARE OTHERS YOU COULD HAVE EVENTUALLY FOUND A WAY TO CONTACT.
BECAUSE ONLY YOU UNDERSTAND ATOMIC THEORY WELL ENOUGH TO HELP ME. YOU ARE MY ANSWER.
THEN I AGREE TO THIS MUTUAL AID ARRANGEMENT. NOW--
--BEGONE FROM MY MIND!
AAAAH--
OCTOPUS MUST PLAN.

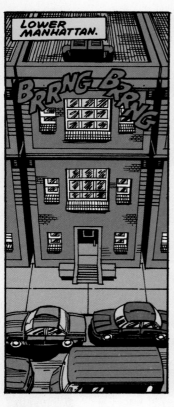

LOWER MANHATTAN.

BRRNG BRRNG

HELLO. YES, THIS IS *HARGROVE*.

MICHAEL WHO? *GERDES*? *HIS* LAWYER...?!

WH-WHAT DO YOU WANT... AFTER ALL THIS *TIME*...?

YES. OF COURSE.

I'M DOOMED.

RYKER'S ISLAND PRISON.

WELL, THIS IS THE BIG DAY, *LEILA*.

YUP. GLAD TO BE LEAVING *THIS* PLACE BEHIND.

YOU WERE LEGIT *BEFORE* ALL THAT CRAZINESS.

YOU CAN BE LEGIT *AGAIN*.

DON'T WORRY, MAGGIE...

YOU'LL NEVER SEE *ME* IN THIS PLACE AGAIN.

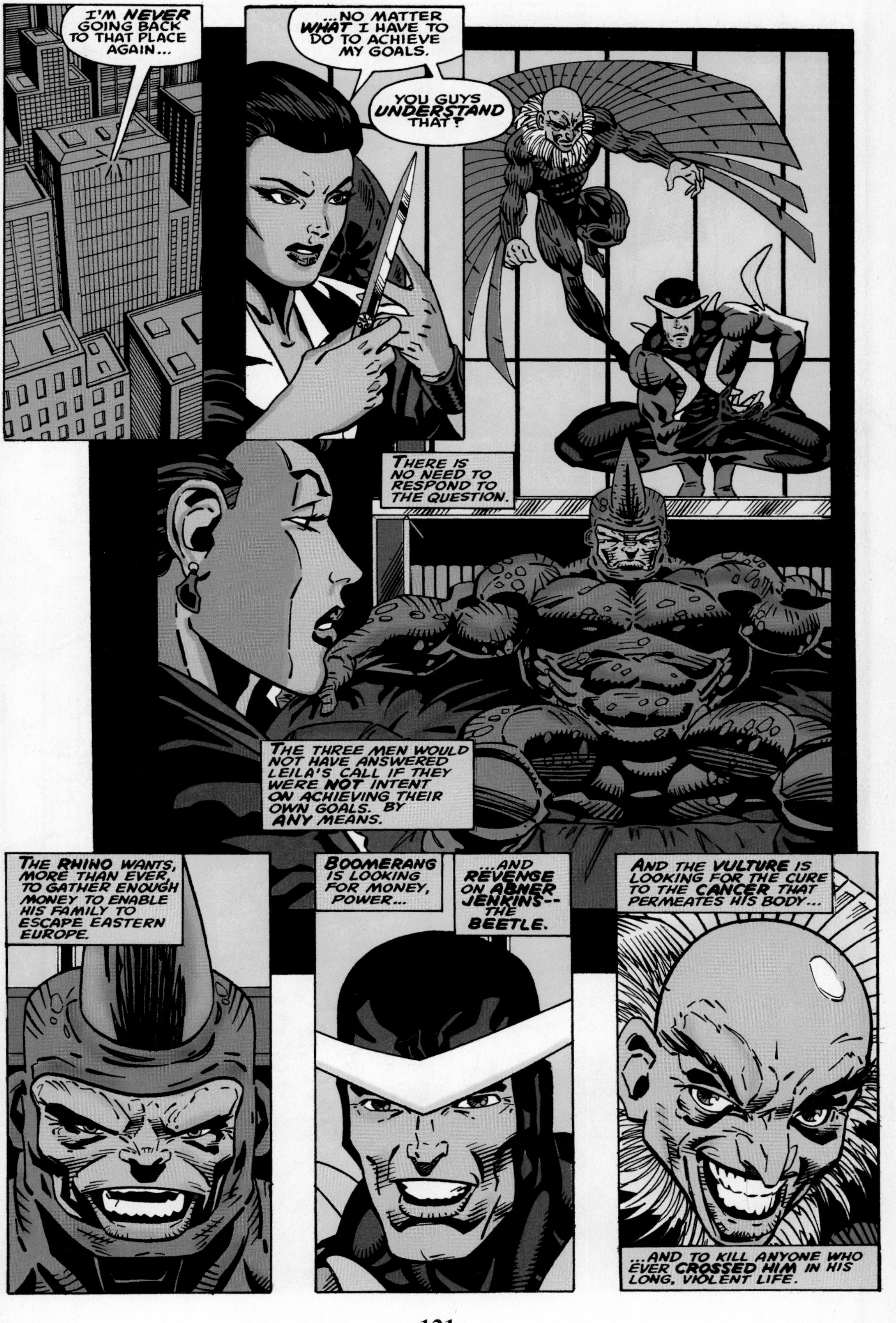
I'M NEVER GOING BACK TO THAT PLACE AGAIN...
...NO MATTER WHAT I HAVE TO DO TO ACHIEVE MY GOALS.
YOU GUYS UNDERSTAND THAT?
THERE IS NO NEED TO RESPOND TO THE QUESTION.
THE THREE MEN WOULD NOT HAVE ANSWERED LEILA'S CALL IF THEY WERE NOT INTENT ON ACHIEVING THEIR OWN GOALS. BY ANY MEANS.
THE RHINO WANTS, MORE THAN EVER, TO GATHER ENOUGH MONEY TO ENABLE HIS FAMILY TO ESCAPE EASTERN EUROPE.
BOOMERANG IS LOOKING FOR MONEY, POWER...
...AND REVENGE ON ABNER JENKINS-- THE BEETLE.
AND THE VULTURE IS LOOKING FOR THE CURE TO THE CANCER THAT PERMEATES HIS BODY...
...AND TO KILL ANYONE WHO EVER CROSSED HIM IN HIS LONG, VIOLENT LIFE.

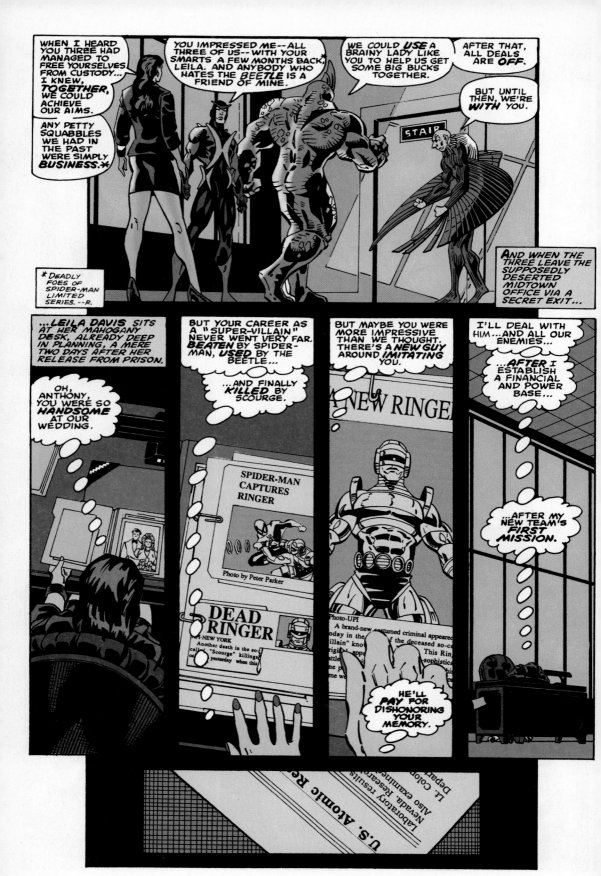

WHEN I HEARD YOU THREE HAD MANAGED TO FREE YOURSELVES FROM CUSTODY... I KNEW, *TOGETHER,* WE COULD ACHIEVE OUR AIMS. ANY PETTY SQUABBLES WE HAD IN THE PAST WERE SIMPLY *BUSINESS.**

YOU IMPRESSED ME--ALL THREE OF US--WITH YOUR SMARTS A FEW MONTHS BACK, LEILA. AND ANYBODY WHO HATES THE *BEETLE* IS A FRIEND OF MINE.

WE COULD *USE* A BRAINY LADY LIKE YOU TO HELP US GET SOME BIG BUCKS TOGETHER.

AFTER THAT, ALL DEALS ARE *OFF.*

BUT UNTIL THEN, WE'RE *WITH* YOU.

* DEADLY FOES OF SPIDER-MAN LIMITED SERIES. --R.

AND WHEN THE THREE LEAVE THE SUPPOSEDLY DESERTED MIDTOWN OFFICE VIA A SECRET EXIT...

...*LEILA DAVIS* SITS AT HER MAHOGANY DESK, ALREADY DEEP IN PLANNING, A MERE TWO DAYS AFTER HER RELEASE FROM PRISON.

OH, ANTHONY, YOU WERE SO *HANDSOME* AT OUR WEDDING.

BUT YOUR CAREER AS A "SUPER-VILLAIN" NEVER WENT VERY FAR. *BEATEN* BY SPIDER-MAN, *USED* BY THE BEETLE...

...AND FINALLY *KILLED* BY SCOURGE.

SPIDER-MAN CAPTURES RINGER

Photo by Peter Parker

DEAD RINGER

-NEW YORK

Another death in the so-called "Scourge" killings oc... yesterday when this

BUT MAYBE YOU WERE MORE IMPRESSIVE THAN WE THOUGHT. THERE'S A *NEW GUY* AROUND *IMITATING* YOU.

A NEW RINGER

Photo-UPI

A brand-new costumed criminal appeared today in the ... of the deceased so-ca... villain" kno... ...rigi... app... This Rin... ...attle... ...sophistica... ...ne p... ...me we...

HE'LL *PAY* FOR DISHONORING YOUR MEMORY.

I'LL DEAL WITH HIM...AND ALL OUR ENEMIES...

...*AFTER* I ESTABLISH A FINANCIAL AND POWER BASE...

...AFTER MY NEW TEAM'S *FIRST* MISSION.

U.S. Atomic Re...

...avoratory results
...Nevada. Research...
...also examine...
Lt. Colo...
Depart...

122

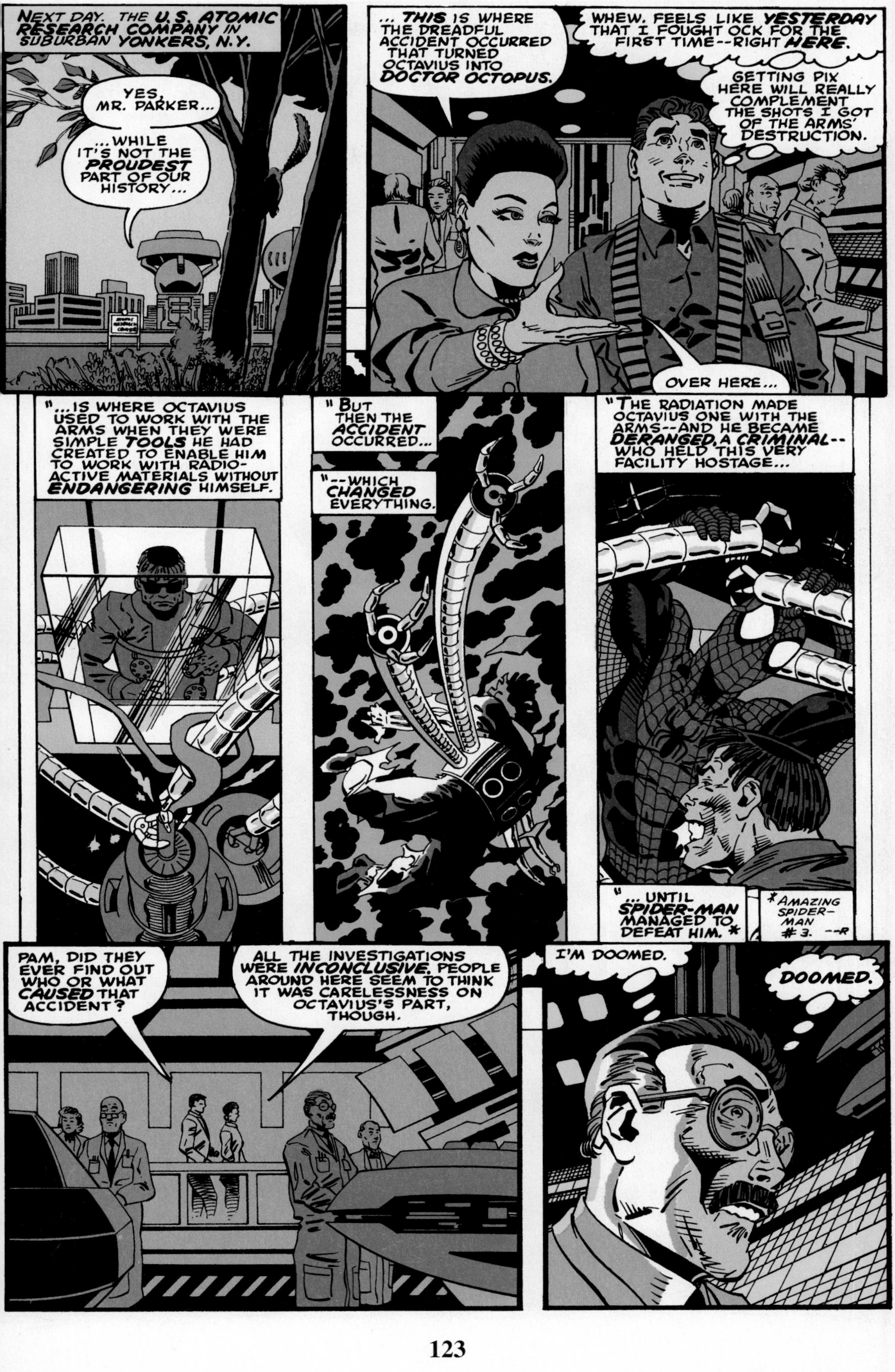
NEXT DAY. THE U.S. ATOMIC RESEARCH COMPANY IN SUBURBAN YONKERS, N.Y.
YES, MR. PARKER...
...WHILE IT'S NOT THE PROUDEST PART OF OUR HISTORY...
...THIS IS WHERE THE DREADFUL ACCIDENT OCCURRED THAT TURNED OCTAVIUS INTO DOCTOR OCTOPUS.
WHEW. FEELS LIKE YESTERDAY THAT I FOUGHT OCK FOR THE FIRST TIME--RIGHT HERE.
GETTING PIX HERE WILL REALLY COMPLEMENT THE SHOTS I GOT OF THE ARMS' DESTRUCTION.
OVER HERE...
"...IS WHERE OCTAVIUS USED TO WORK WITH THE ARMS WHEN THEY WERE SIMPLE TOOLS HE HAD CREATED TO ENABLE HIM TO WORK WITH RADIO-ACTIVE MATERIALS WITHOUT ENDANGERING HIMSELF.
"BUT THEN THE ACCIDENT OCCURRED...
"--WHICH CHANGED EVERYTHING.
"THE RADIATION MADE OCTAVIUS ONE WITH THE ARMS--AND HE BECAME DERANGED, A CRIMINAL--WHO HELD THIS VERY FACILITY HOSTAGE...
"...UNTIL SPIDER-MAN MANAGED TO DEFEAT HIM.*
*AMAZING SPIDER-MAN #3. --R
PAM, DID THEY EVER FIND OUT WHO OR WHAT CAUSED THAT ACCIDENT?
ALL THE INVESTIGATIONS WERE INCONCLUSIVE. PEOPLE AROUND HERE SEEM TO THINK IT WAS CARELESSNESS ON OCTAVIUS'S PART, THOUGH.
I'M DOOMED.
DOOMED.

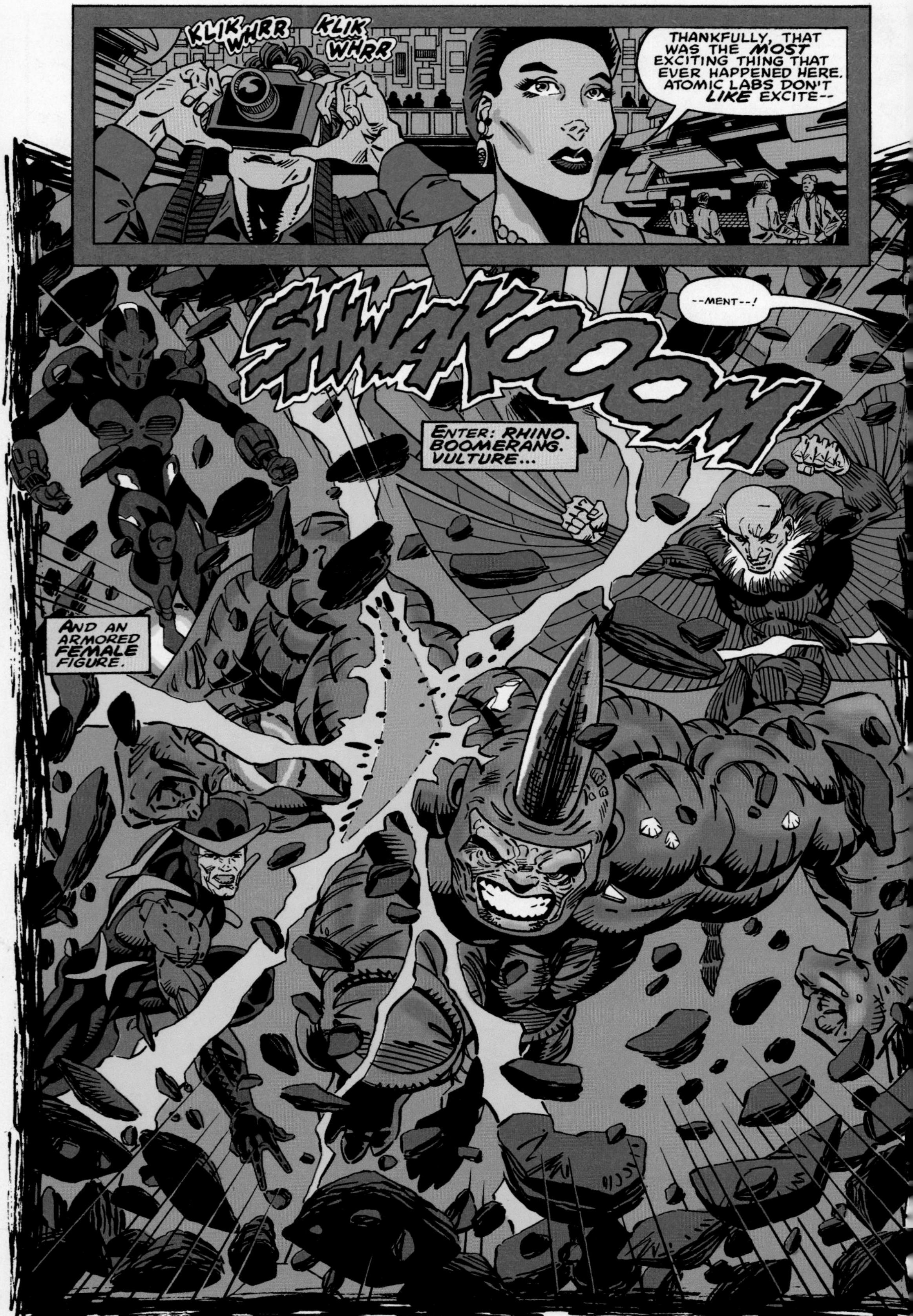
KLIK WHRR KLIK WHRR
THANKFULLY, THAT WAS THE MOST EXCITING THING THAT EVER HAPPENED HERE. ATOMIC LABS DON'T LIKE EXCITE--
SHWAKOOOM
--MENT--!
ENTER: RHINO. BOOMERANG. VULTURE...
AND AN ARMORED FEMALE FIGURE.

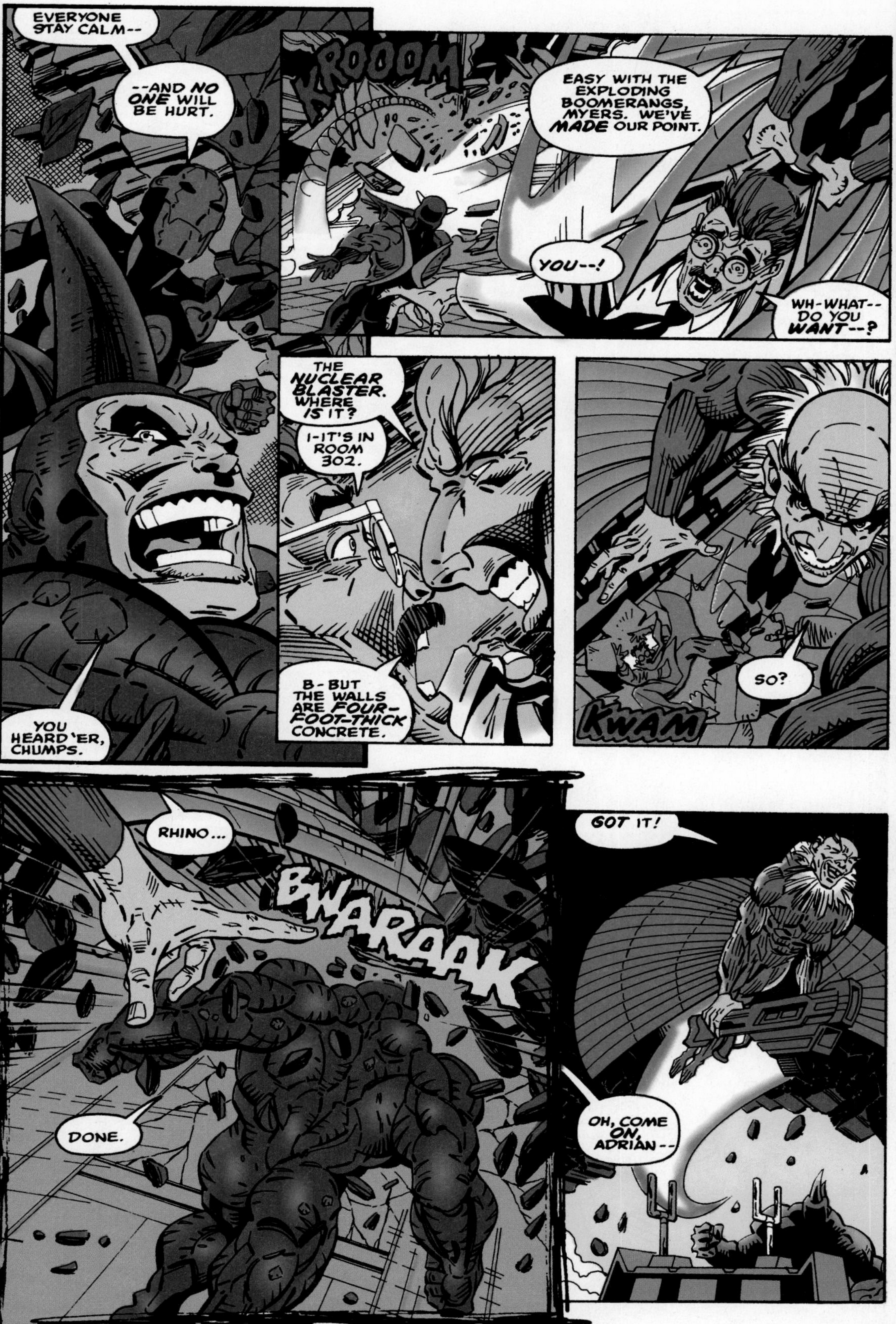
EVERYONE STAY CALM--
--AND NO ONE WILL BE HURT.
KROOOM
EASY WITH THE EXPLODING BOOMERANGS, MYERS. WE'VE MADE OUR POINT.
YOU--!
WH-WHAT--DO YOU WANT--?
THE NUCLEAR BLASTER. WHERE IS IT?
I-IT'S IN ROOM 302.
B-BUT THE WALLS ARE FOUR-FOOT-THICK CONCRETE.
YOU HEARD 'ER, CHUMPS.
SO?
KWAM
RHINO...
BWARAAAK
DONE.
GOT IT!
OH, COME ON, ADRIAN--

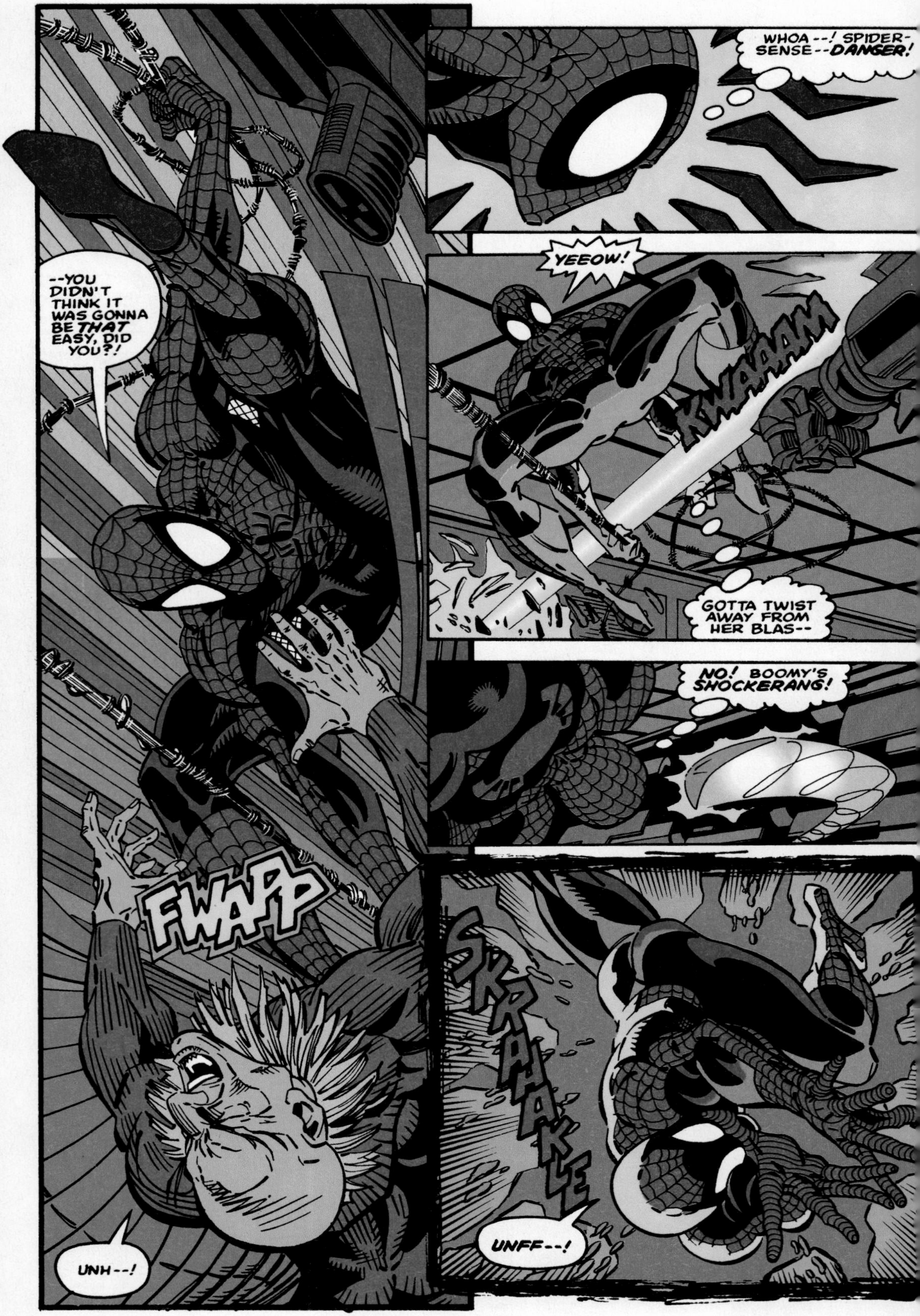

--YOU DIDN'T THINK IT WAS GONNA BE THAT EASY, DID YOU?!
WHOA--! SPIDER-SENSE--DANGER!
YEEOW!
KWAAAM
GOTTA TWIST AWAY FROM HER BLAS--
NO! BOOMY'S SHOCKERANG!
FWAPP
SKRAAAKLE
UNH--!
UNFF--!

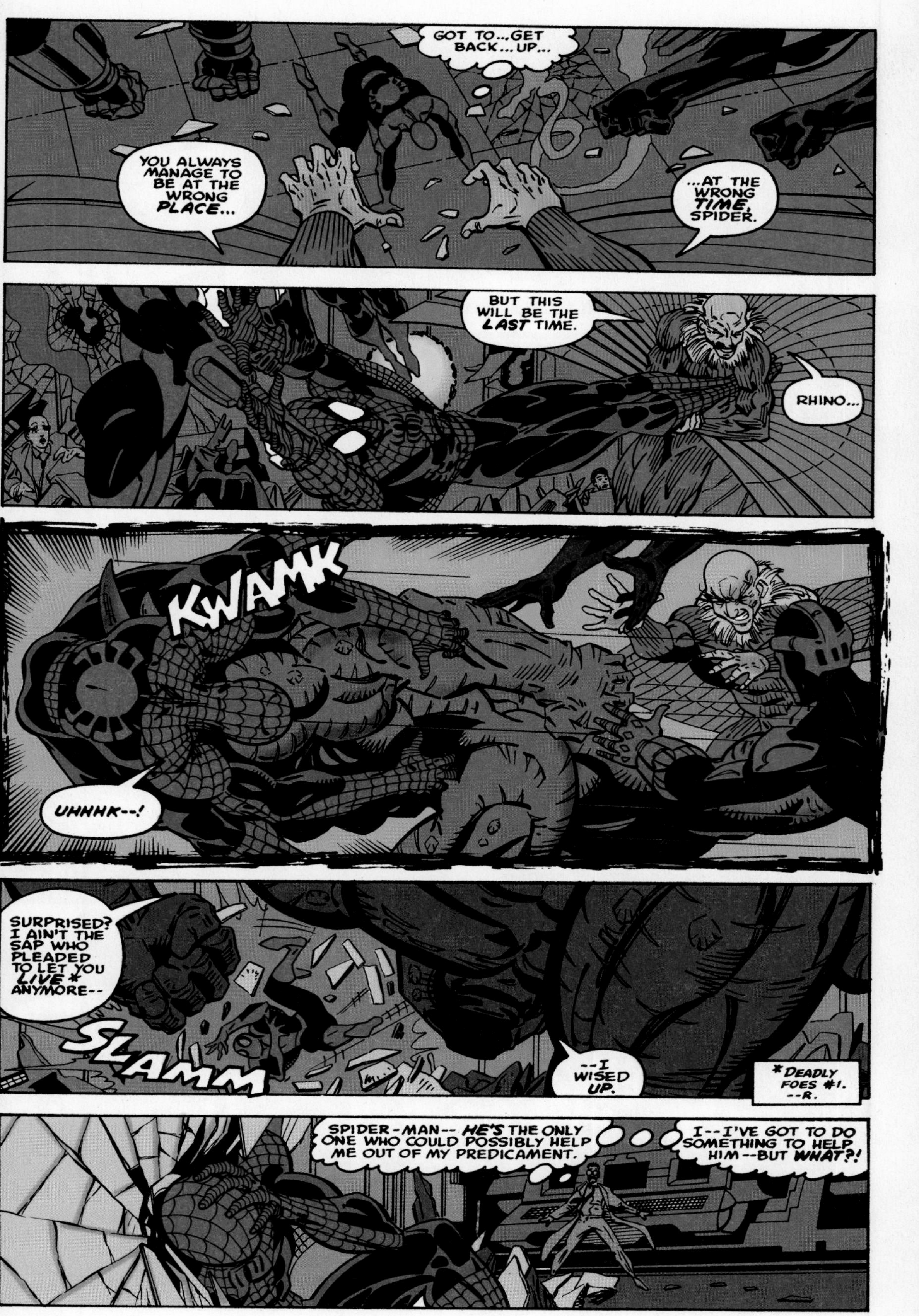
GOT TO...GET BACK...UP...
YOU ALWAYS MANAGE TO BE AT THE WRONG PLACE...
...AT THE WRONG TIME, SPIDER.
BUT THIS WILL BE THE LAST TIME.
RHINO...
KWAMK
UHHHK--!
SURPRISED? I AIN'T THE SAP WHO PLEADED TO LET YOU LIVE* ANYMORE--
SLAMM
--I WISED UP.
*DEADLY FOES #1. --R.
SPIDER-MAN-- HE'S THE ONLY ONE WHO COULD POSSIBLY HELP ME OUT OF MY PREDICAMENT.
I--I'VE GOT TO DO SOMETHING TO HELP HIM--BUT WHAT?!

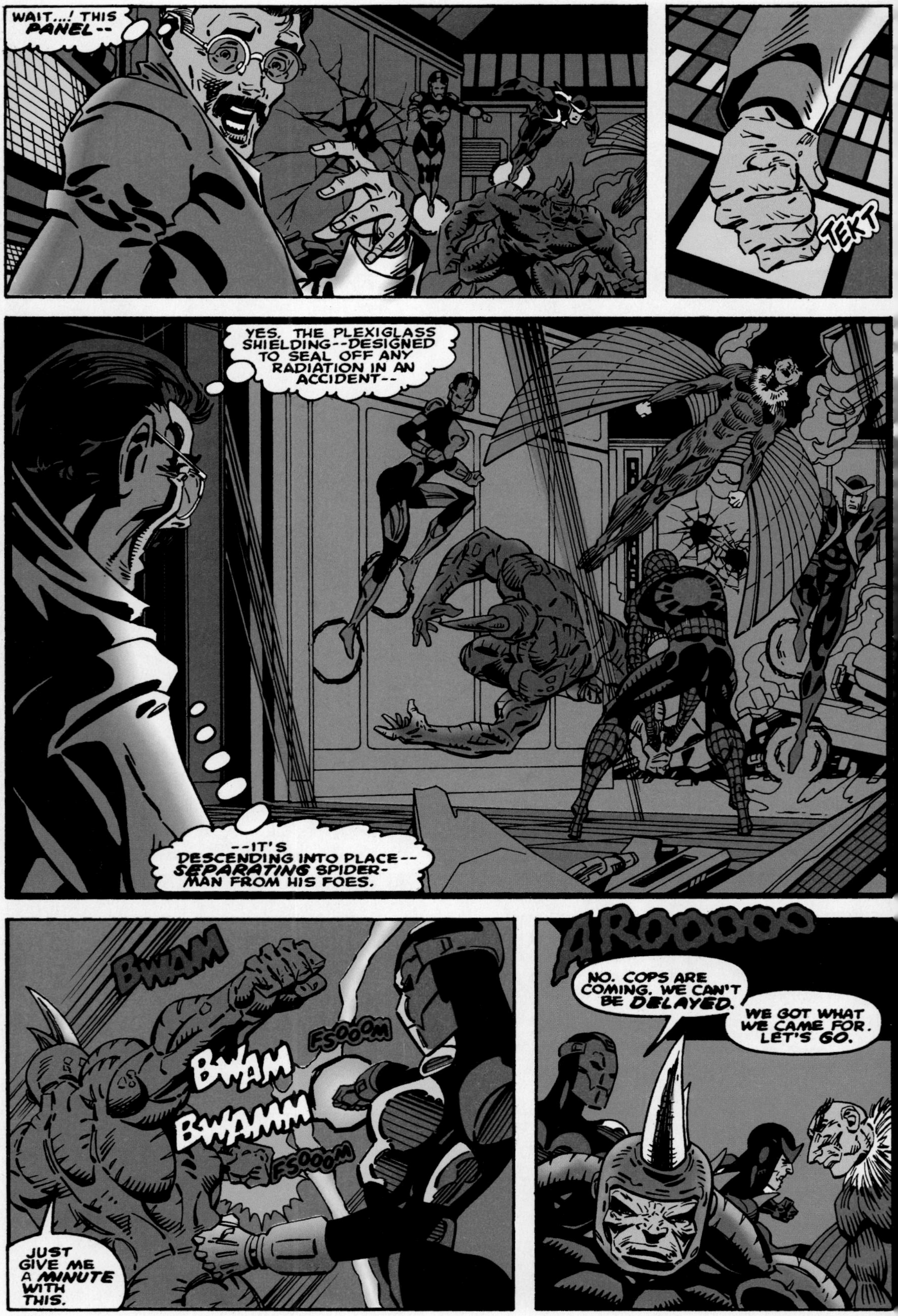
WAIT...! THIS PANEL--
TEKT
YES. THE PLEXIGLASS SHIELDING--DESIGNED TO SEAL OFF ANY RADIATION IN AN ACCIDENT--
--IT'S DESCENDING INTO PLACE--SEPARATING SPIDER-MAN FROM HIS FOES.
BWAM
BWAM
FSOOOM
BWAMM
FSOOOM
JUST GIVE ME A MINUTE WITH THIS.
AROOOOO
NO. COPS ARE COMING. WE CAN'T BE DELAYED.
WE GOT WHAT WE CAME FOR. LET'S GO.

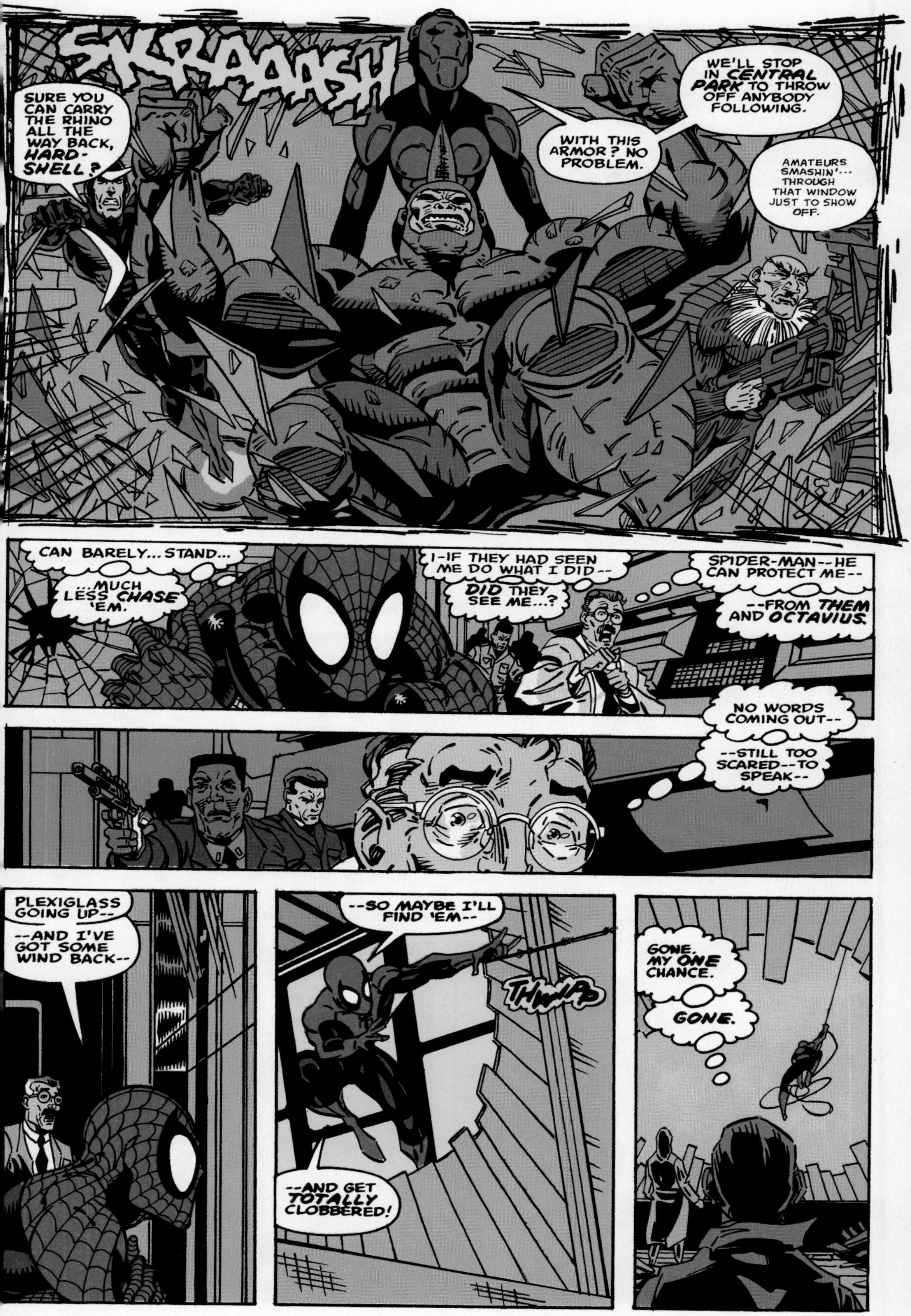
SKRAAASH
SURE YOU CAN CARRY THE RHINO ALL THE WAY BACK, HARD-SHELL?
WITH THIS ARMOR? NO PROBLEM.
WE'LL STOP IN CENTRAL PARK TO THROW OFF ANYBODY FOLLOWING.
AMATEURS SMASHIN'... THROUGH THAT WINDOW JUST TO SHOW OFF.
CAN BARELY... STAND...
...MUCH LESS CHASE 'EM.
I-IF THEY HAD SEEN ME DO WHAT I DID--
DID THEY SEE ME...?
SPIDER-MAN--HE CAN PROTECT ME--
--FROM THEM AND OCTAVIUS.
NO WORDS COMING OUT--
--STILL TOO SCARED--TO SPEAK--
PLEXIGLASS GOING UP--
--AND I'VE GOT SOME WIND BACK--
--SO MAYBE I'LL FIND 'EM--
THWIPP
--AND GET TOTALLY CLOBBERED!
GONE. MY ONE CHANCE.
GONE.

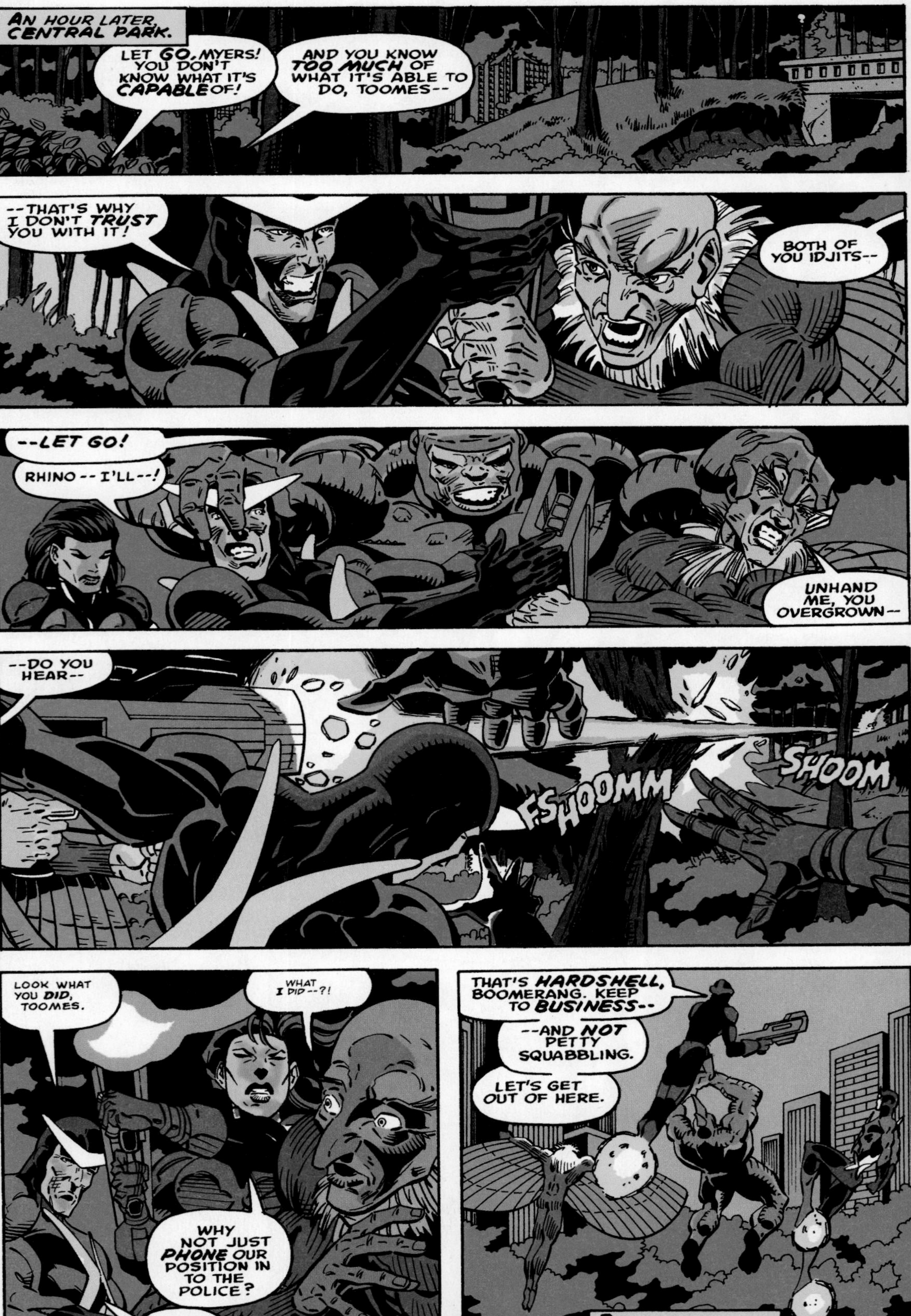
AN HOUR LATER, CENTRAL PARK.
LET GO, MYERS! YOU DON'T KNOW WHAT IT'S CAPABLE OF!
AND YOU KNOW TOO MUCH OF WHAT IT'S ABLE TO DO, TOOMES--
--THAT'S WHY I DON'T TRUST YOU WITH IT!
BOTH OF YOU IDJITS--
--LET GO!
RHINO -- I'LL --!
UNHAND ME, YOU OVERGROWN--
--DO YOU HEAR--
FSHOOMM
SHOOM
LOOK WHAT YOU DID, TOOMES.
WHAT I DID --?!
WHY NOT JUST PHONE OUR POSITION IN TO THE POLICE?
SORRY, LEILA.
THAT'S HARDSHELL, BOOMERANG. KEEP TO BUSINESS--
--AND NOT PETTY SQUABBLING.
LET'S GET OUT OF HERE.
BUT AS LEILA AND COMPANY DEPART...

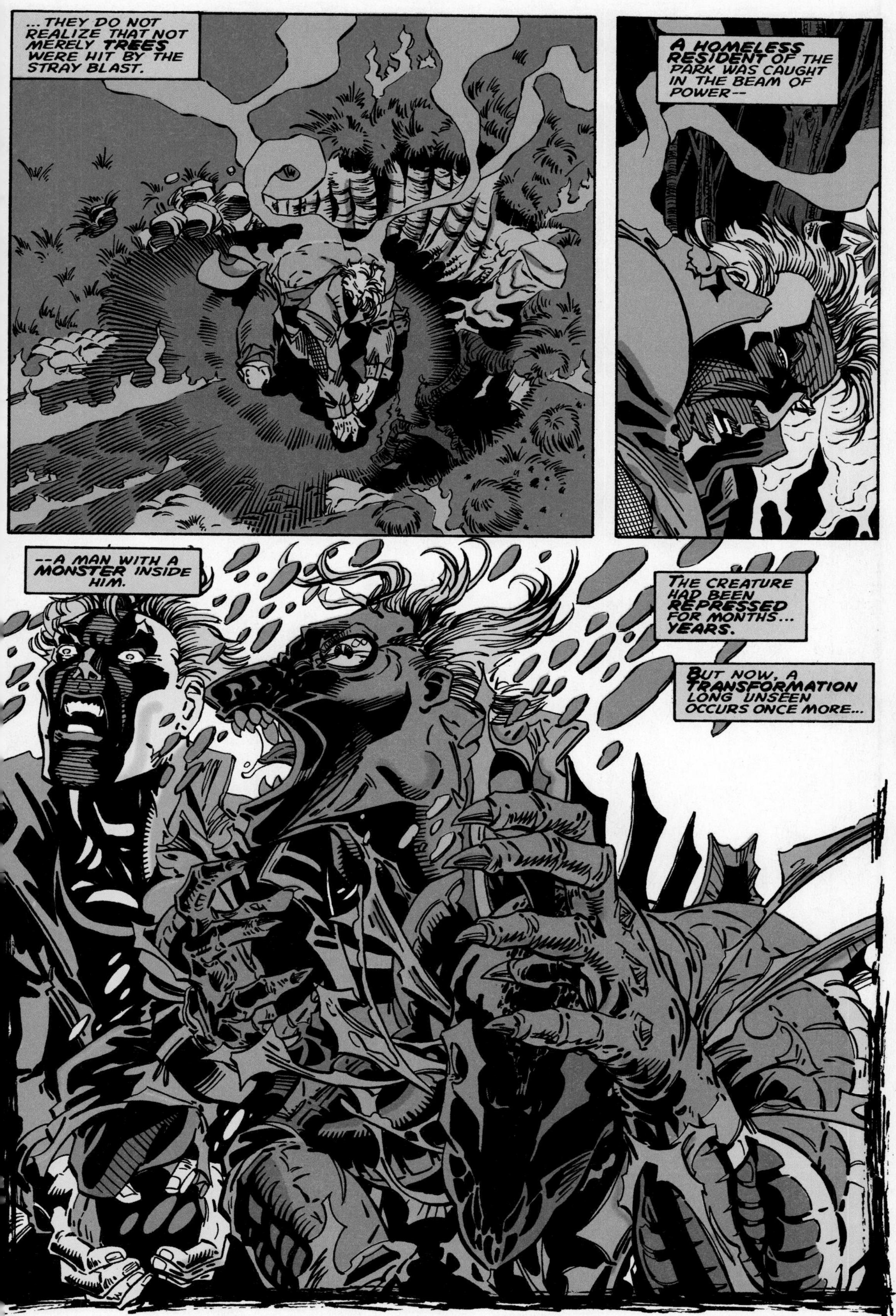
...THEY DO NOT REALIZE THAT NOT MERELY TREES WERE HIT BY THE STRAY BLAST.
A HOMELESS RESIDENT OF THE PARK WAS CAUGHT IN THE BEAM OF POWER--
--A MAN WITH A MONSTER INSIDE HIM.
THE CREATURE HAD BEEN REPRESSED FOR MONTHS... YEARS.
BUT NOW, A TRANSFORMATION LONG UNSEEN OCCURS ONCE MORE...

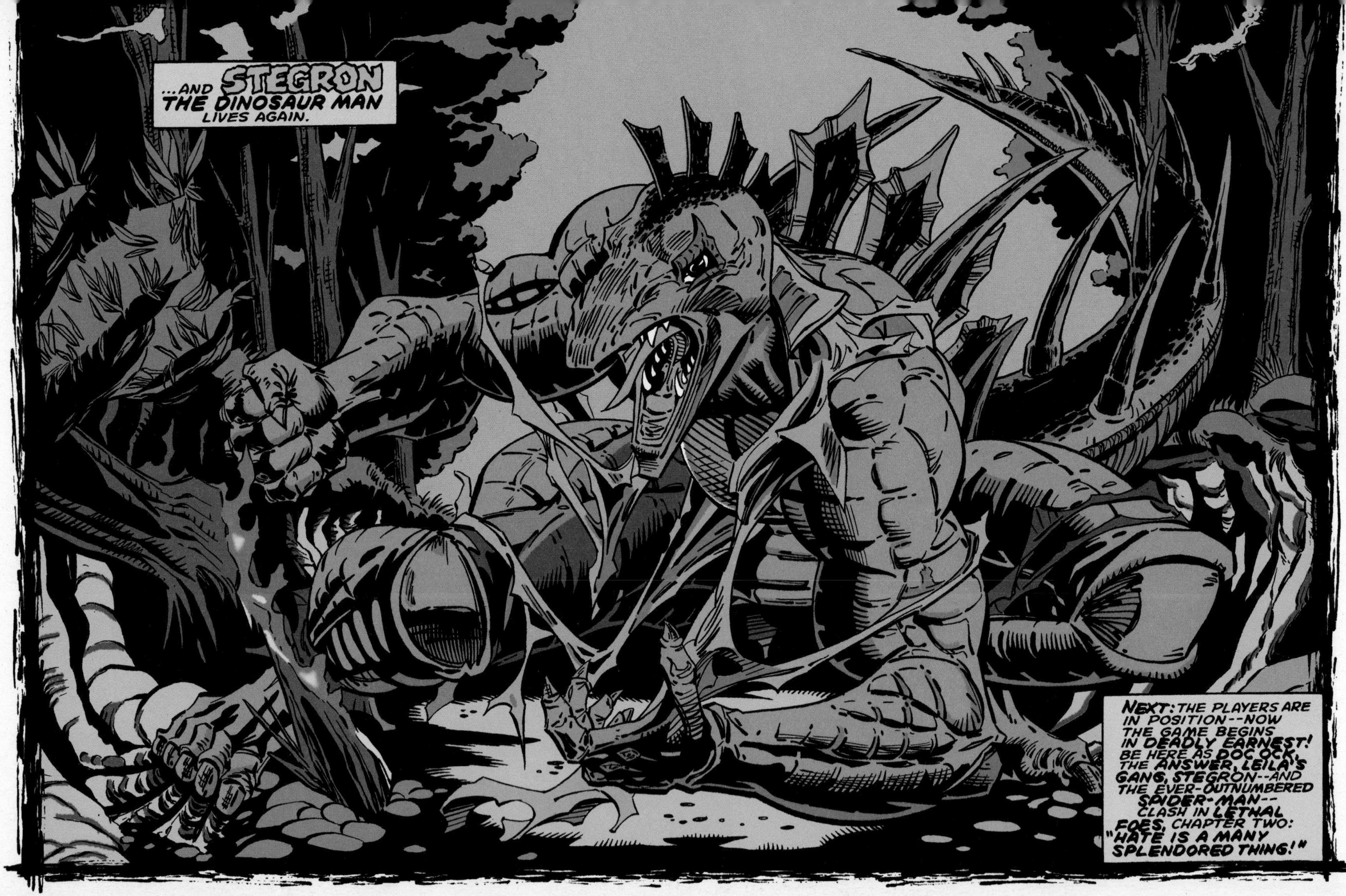
...AND STEGRON THE DINOSAUR MAN LIVES AGAIN.
NEXT: THE PLAYERS ARE IN POSITION--NOW THE GAME BEGINS IN DEADLY EARNEST! BE HERE AS DOC OCK, THE ANSWER, LEILA'S GANG, STEGRON--AND THE EVER-OUTNUMBERED SPIDER-MAN--CLASH IN LETHAL FOES, CHAPTER TWO: "HATE IS A MANY SPLENDORED THING!"

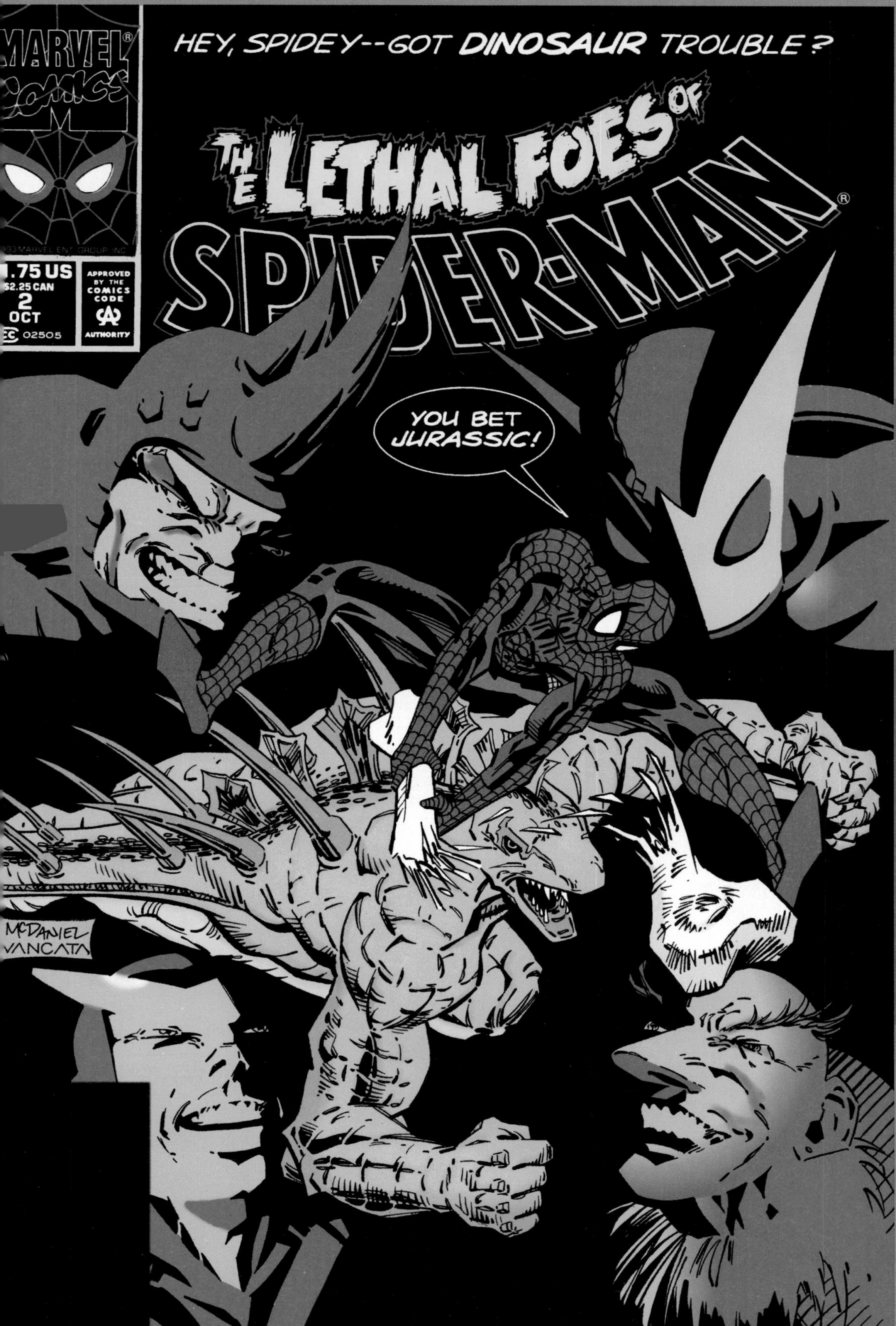
MARVEL COMICS
HEY, SPIDEY--GOT DINOSAUR TROUBLE?
THE LETHAL FOES OF SPIDER-MAN
1.75 US
$2.25 CAN
2
OCT
APPROVED BY THE COMICS CODE AUTHORITY
02505
YOU BET JURASSIC!
McDANIEL
VANCATA

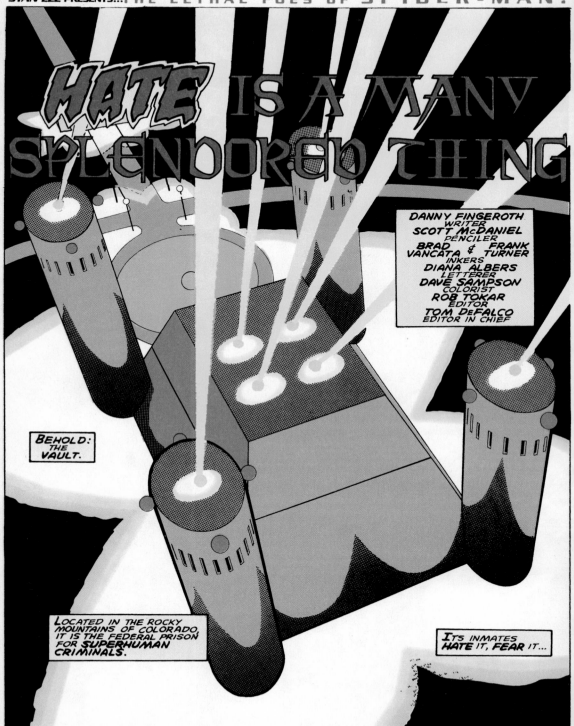

UNITED IN NOTHING BUT THEIR *HATRED* FOR ONE MAN AND THEIR THIRST FOR *POWER*, MURDEROUS INDIVIDUALS BAND TOGETHER TO FURTHER THEIR TWISTED GOALS. AND THEY WILL LET *NOTHING* STAND IN THEIR WAY!

STAN LEE PRESENTS... THE LETHAL FOES OF *SPIDER-MAN!*

HATE IS A MANY SPLENDORED THING

DANNY FINGEROTH
WRITER
SCOTT McDANIEL
PENCILER
BRAD & FRANK
VANCATA & TURNER
INKERS
DIANA ALBERS
LETTERER
DAVE SAMPSON
COLORIST
ROB TOKAR
EDITOR
TOM DeFALCO
EDITOR IN CHIEF

BEHOLD: THE VAULT.

LOCATED IN THE ROCKY MOUNTAINS OF COLORADO, IT IS THE FEDERAL PRISON FOR *SUPERHUMAN* CRIMINALS.

ITS INMATES *HATE* IT, FEAR IT...

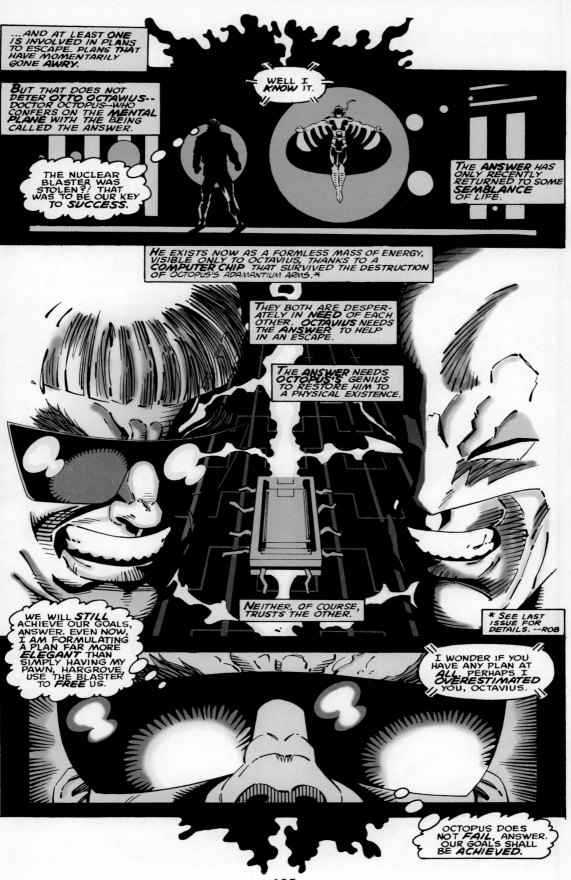

...AND AT LEAST ONE IS INVOLVED IN PLANS TO ESCAPE. PLANS THAT HAVE MOMENTARILY GONE AWRY.

BUT THAT DOES NOT DETER OTTO OCTAVIUS--DOCTOR OCTOPUS--WHO CONFERS ON THE MENTAL PLANE WITH THE BEING CALLED THE ANSWER.

WELL I KNOW IT.

THE NUCLEAR BLASTER WAS STOLEN?! THAT WAS TO BE OUR KEY TO SUCCESS.

THE ANSWER HAS ONLY RECENTLY RETURNED TO SOME SEMBLANCE OF LIFE.

HE EXISTS NOW AS A FORMLESS MASS OF ENERGY, VISIBLE ONLY TO OCTAVIUS, THANKS TO A COMPUTER CHIP THAT SURVIVED THE DESTRUCTION OF OCTOPUS'S ADAMANTIUM ARMS.*

THEY BOTH ARE DESPERATELY IN NEED OF EACH OTHER. OCTAVIUS NEEDS THE ANSWER TO HELP IN AN ESCAPE.

THE ANSWER NEEDS OCTOPUS'S GENIUS TO RESTORE HIM TO A PHYSICAL EXISTENCE.

NEITHER, OF COURSE, TRUSTS THE OTHER.

* SEE LAST ISSUE FOR DETAILS. --ROB

WE WILL STILL ACHIEVE OUR GOALS, ANSWER. EVEN NOW, I AM FORMULATING A PLAN FAR MORE ELEGANT THAN SIMPLY HAVING MY PAWN, HARGROVE, USE THE BLASTER TO FREE US.

I WONDER IF YOU HAVE ANY PLAN AT ALL. PERHAPS I OVERESTIMATED YOU, OCTAVIUS.

OCTOPUS DOES NOT FAIL, ANSWER. OUR GOALS SHALL BE ACHIEVED.

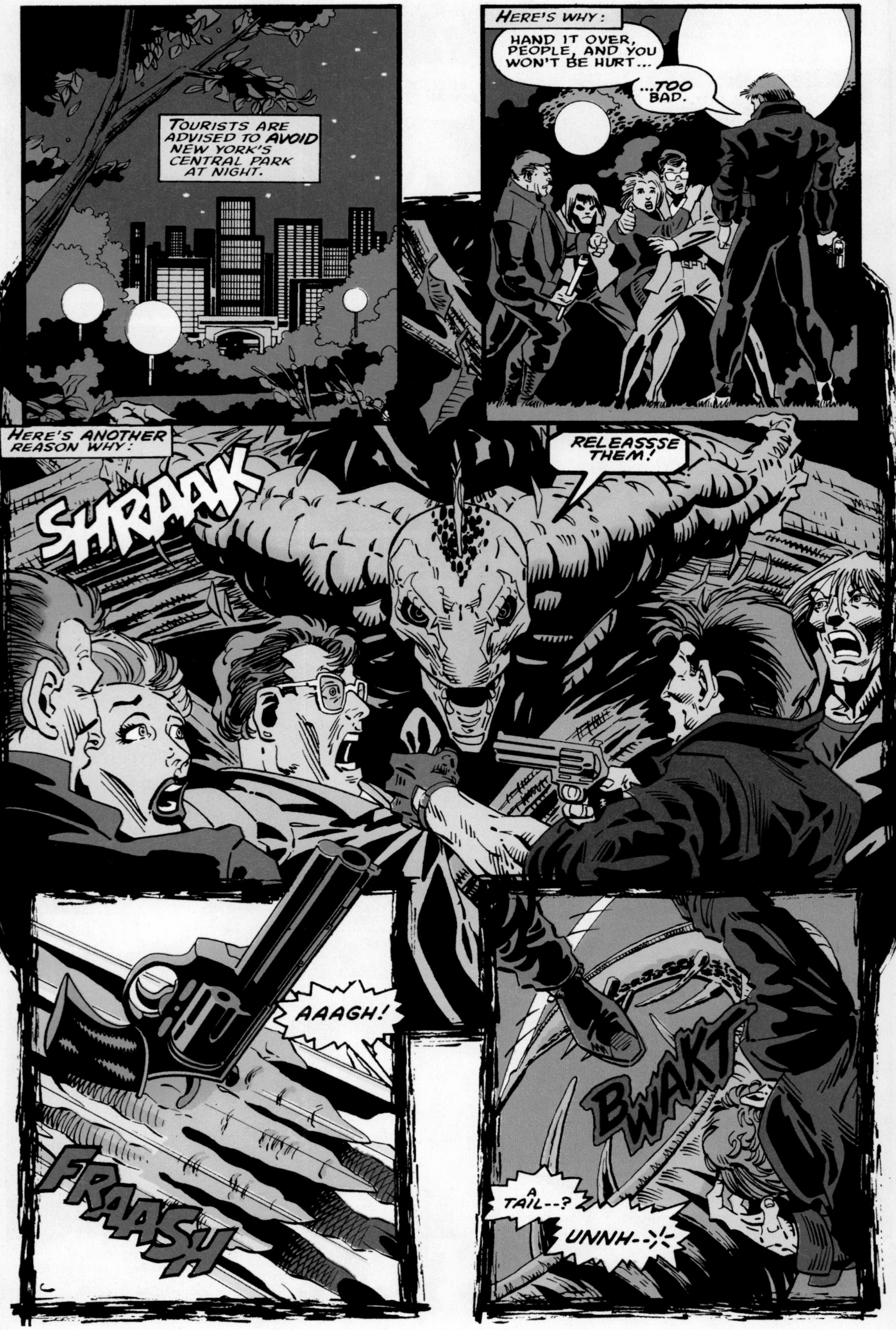
TOURISTS ARE ADVISED TO AVOID NEW YORK'S CENTRAL PARK AT NIGHT.
HERE'S WHY:
HAND IT OVER, PEOPLE, AND YOU WON'T BE HURT...
...TOO BAD.
HERE'S ANOTHER REASON WHY:
SHRAAAK
RELEASSSE THEM!
AAAGH!
FRAASH
BWAKT
A TAIL--?
UNNH--!

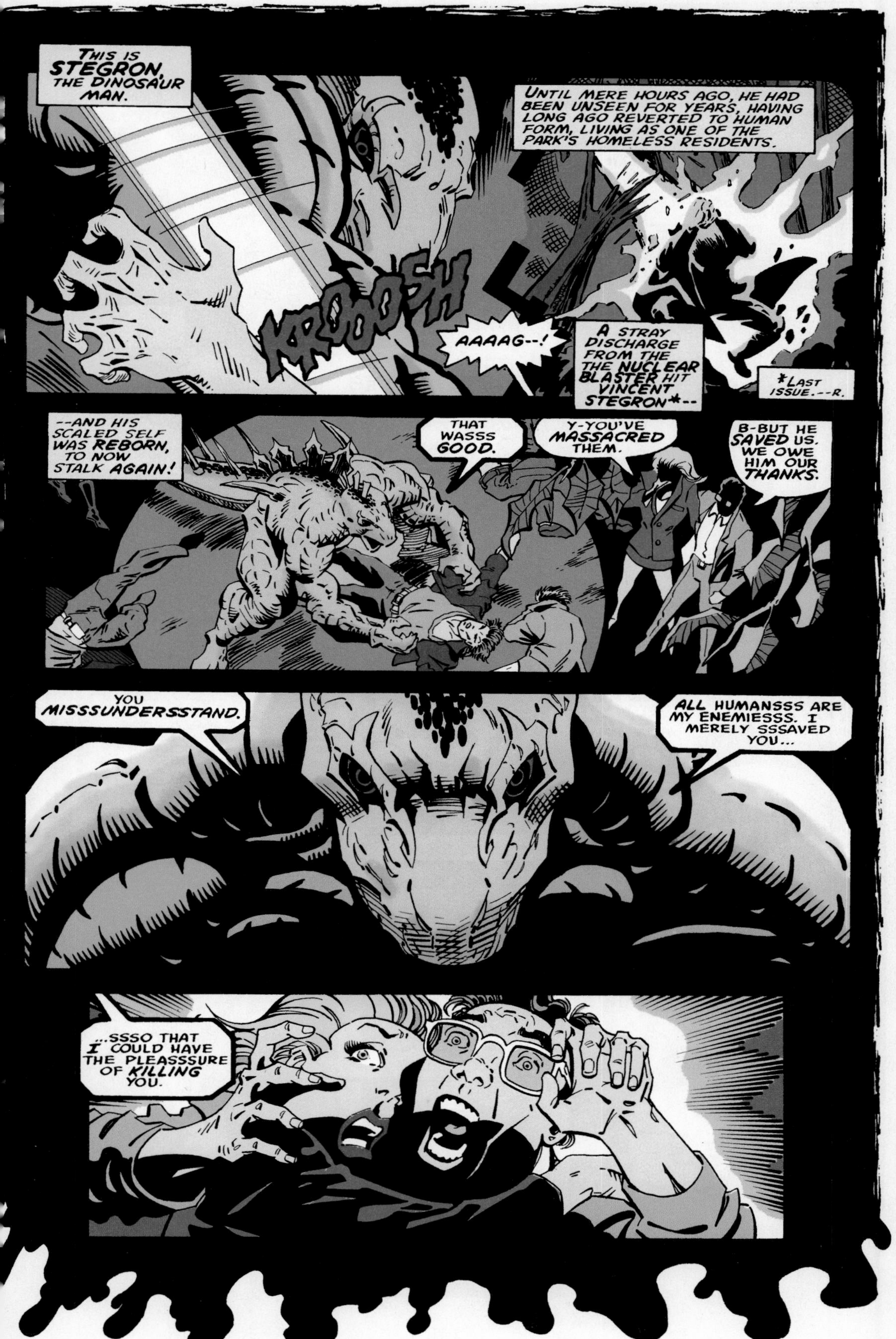

THIS IS STEGRON, THE DINOSAUR MAN.
UNTIL MERE HOURS AGO, HE HAD BEEN UNSEEN FOR YEARS, HAVING LONG AGO REVERTED TO HUMAN FORM, LIVING AS ONE OF THE PARK'S HOMELESS RESIDENTS.
KROOOSH
AAAAG--!
A STRAY DISCHARGE FROM THE THE NUCLEAR BLASTER HIT VINCENT STEGRON*--
*LAST ISSUE.--R.
--AND HIS SCALED SELF WAS REBORN, TO NOW STALK AGAIN!
THAT WASSS GOOD.
Y-YOU'VE MASSACRED THEM.
B-BUT HE SAVED US. WE OWE HIM OUR THANKS.
YOU MISSSUNDERSSTAND.
ALL HUMANSSS ARE MY ENEMIESSS. I MERELY SSSAVED YOU...
...SSSO THAT I COULD HAVE THE PLEASSSURE OF KILLING YOU.

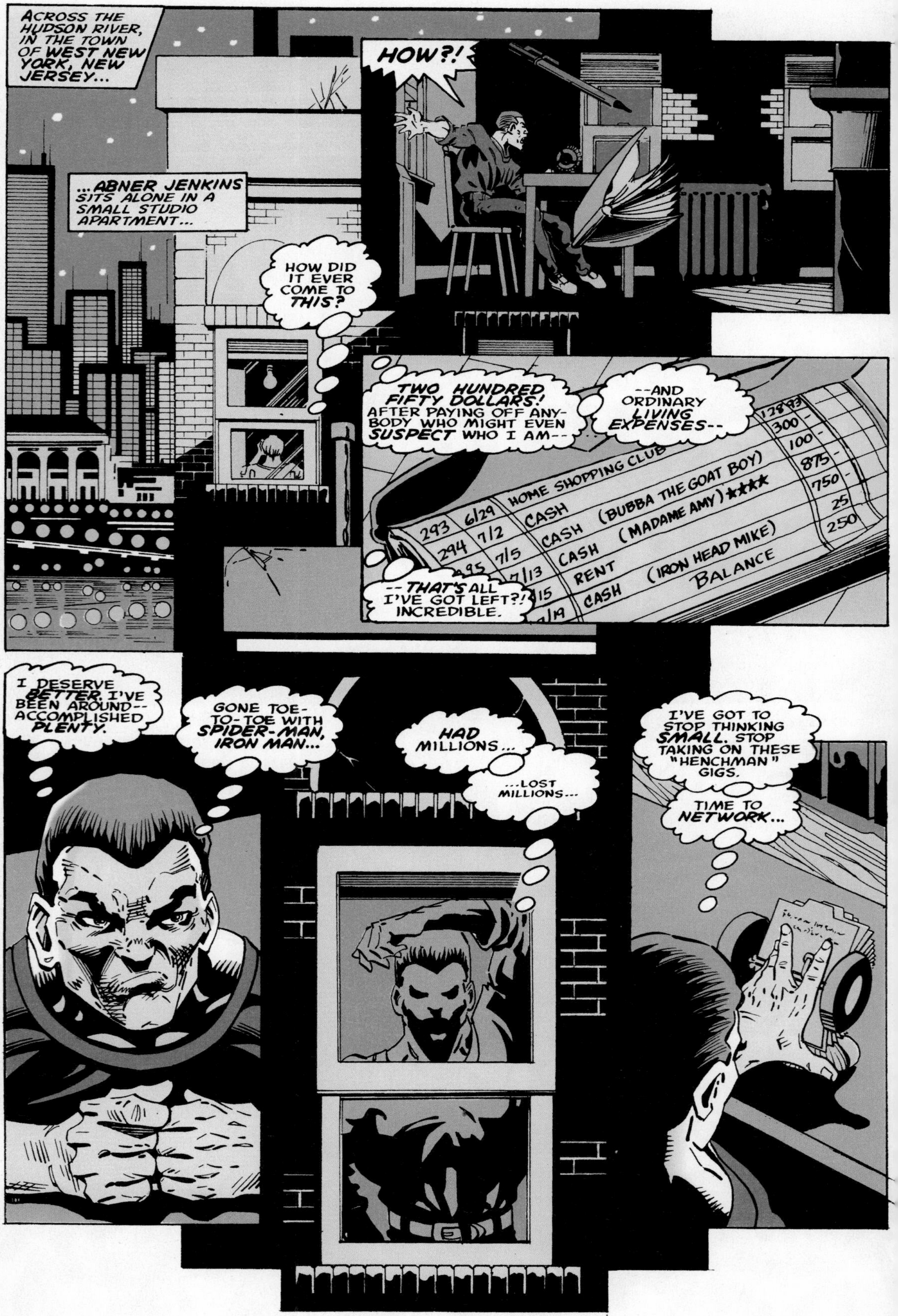

ACROSS THE HUDSON RIVER, IN THE TOWN OF WEST NEW YORK, NEW JERSEY...
HOW?!
...ABNER JENKINS SITS ALONE IN A SMALL STUDIO APARTMENT...
HOW DID IT EVER COME TO THIS?
TWO HUNDRED FIFTY DOLLARS! AFTER PAYING OFF ANYBODY WHO MIGHT EVEN SUSPECT WHO I AM--
--AND ORDINARY LIVING EXPENSES--
HOME SHOPPING CLUB
293 6/29 CASH (BUBBA THE GOAT BOY)
294 7/2 CASH (MADAME AMY)★★★★
7/5 CASH
7/13 RENT
CASH (IRON HEAD MIKE)
BALANCE
128 93
300
100
875
750
25
250
--THAT'S ALL I'VE GOT LEFT?! INCREDIBLE.
I DESERVE BETTER. I'VE BEEN AROUND-- ACCOMPLISHED PLENTY.
GONE TOE-TO-TOE WITH SPIDER-MAN, IRON MAN...
HAD MILLIONS...
...LOST MILLIONS...
I'VE GOT TO STOP THINKING SMALL. STOP TAKING ON THESE "HENCHMAN" GIGS.
TIME TO NETWORK...

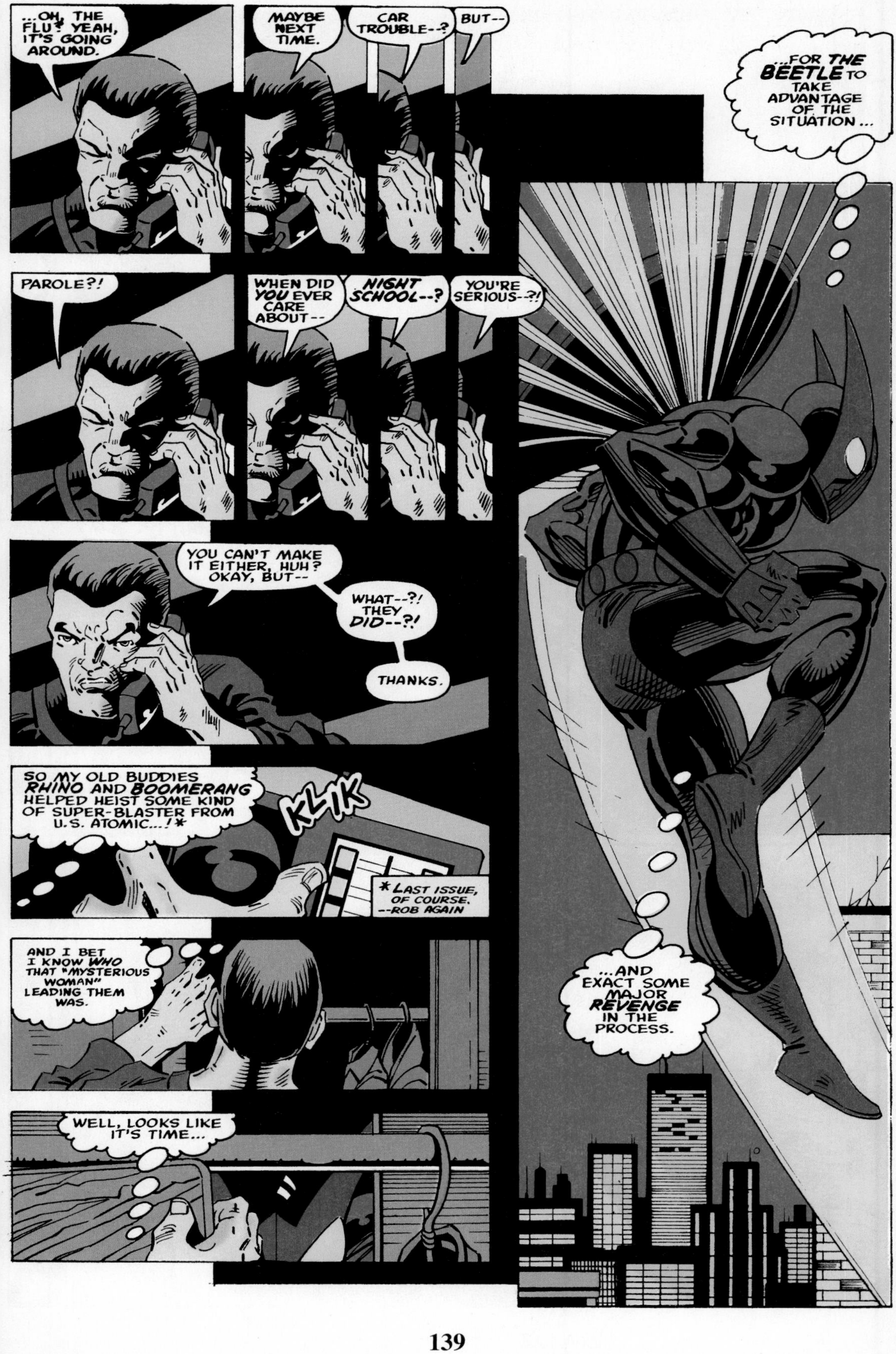
...OH, THE FLU? YEAH, IT'S GOING AROUND.
MAYBE NEXT TIME.
CAR TROUBLE--?
BUT--
...FOR THE BEETLE TO TAKE ADVANTAGE OF THE SITUATION...
PAROLE?!
WHEN DID YOU EVER CARE ABOUT--
NIGHT SCHOOL--?
YOU'RE SERIOUS--?!
YOU CAN'T MAKE IT EITHER, HUH? OKAY, BUT--
WHAT--?! THEY DID--?!
THANKS.
SO MY OLD BUDDIES RHINO AND BOOMERANG HELPED HEIST SOME KIND OF SUPER-BLASTER FROM U.S. ATOMIC...!*
KLIK
*LAST ISSUE, OF COURSE. --ROB AGAIN
AND I BET I KNOW WHO THAT "MYSTERIOUS WOMAN" LEADING THEM WAS.
WELL, LOOKS LIKE IT'S TIME...
...AND EXACT SOME MAJOR REVENGE IN THE PROCESS.

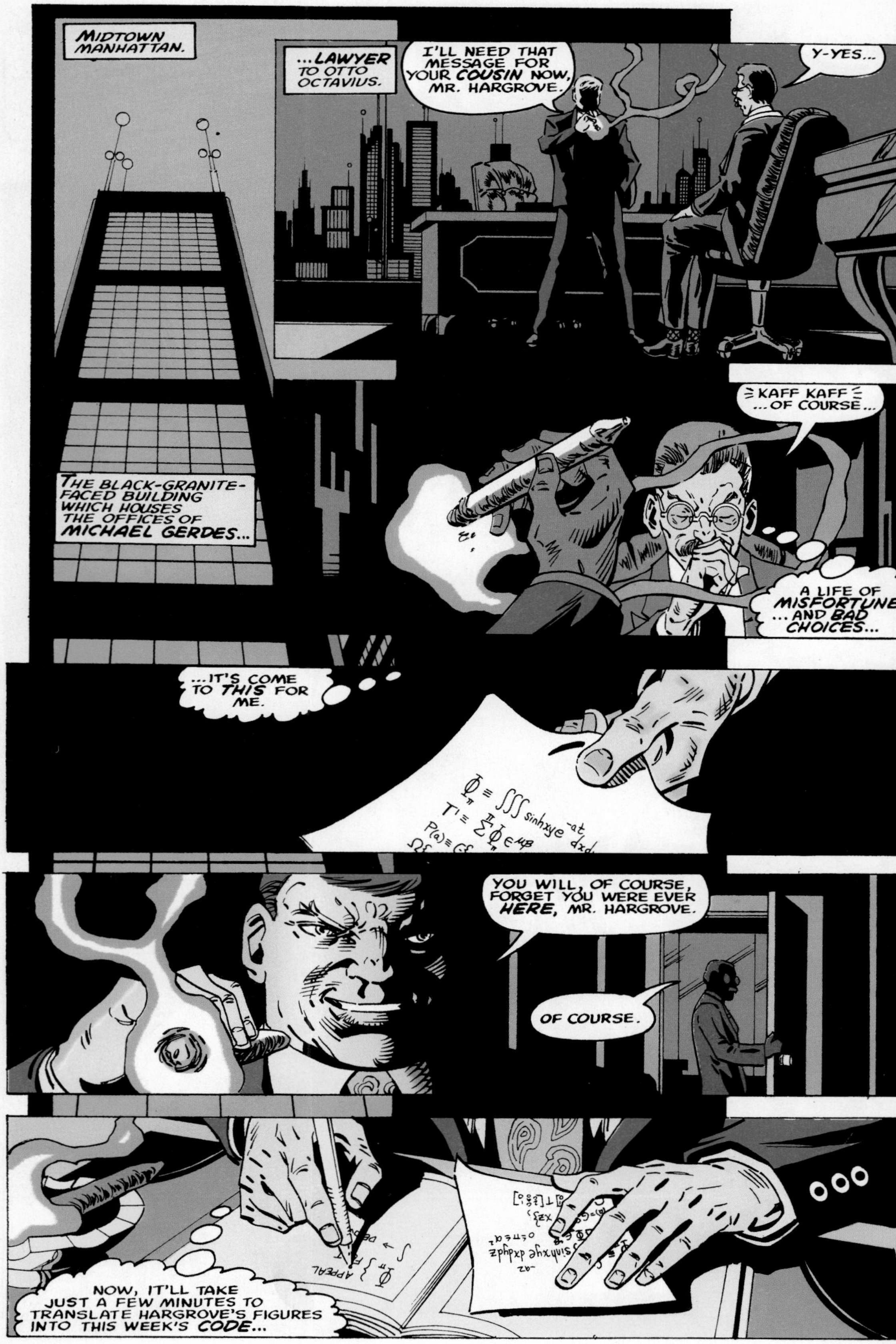
MIDTOWN MANHATTAN.
THE BLACK-GRANITE-FACED BUILDING WHICH HOUSES THE OFFICES OF MICHAEL GERDES...
...LAWYER TO OTTO OCTAVIUS.
I'LL NEED THAT MESSAGE FOR YOUR COUSIN NOW, MR. HARGROVE.
Y-YES...
KAFF KAFF ...OF COURSE...
A LIFE OF MISFORTUNE ...AND BAD CHOICES...
...IT'S COME TO THIS FOR ME.
YOU WILL, OF COURSE, FORGET YOU WERE EVER HERE, MR. HARGROVE.
OF COURSE.
NOW, IT'LL TAKE JUST A FEW MINUTES TO TRANSLATE HARGROVE'S FIGURES INTO THIS WEEK'S CODE...

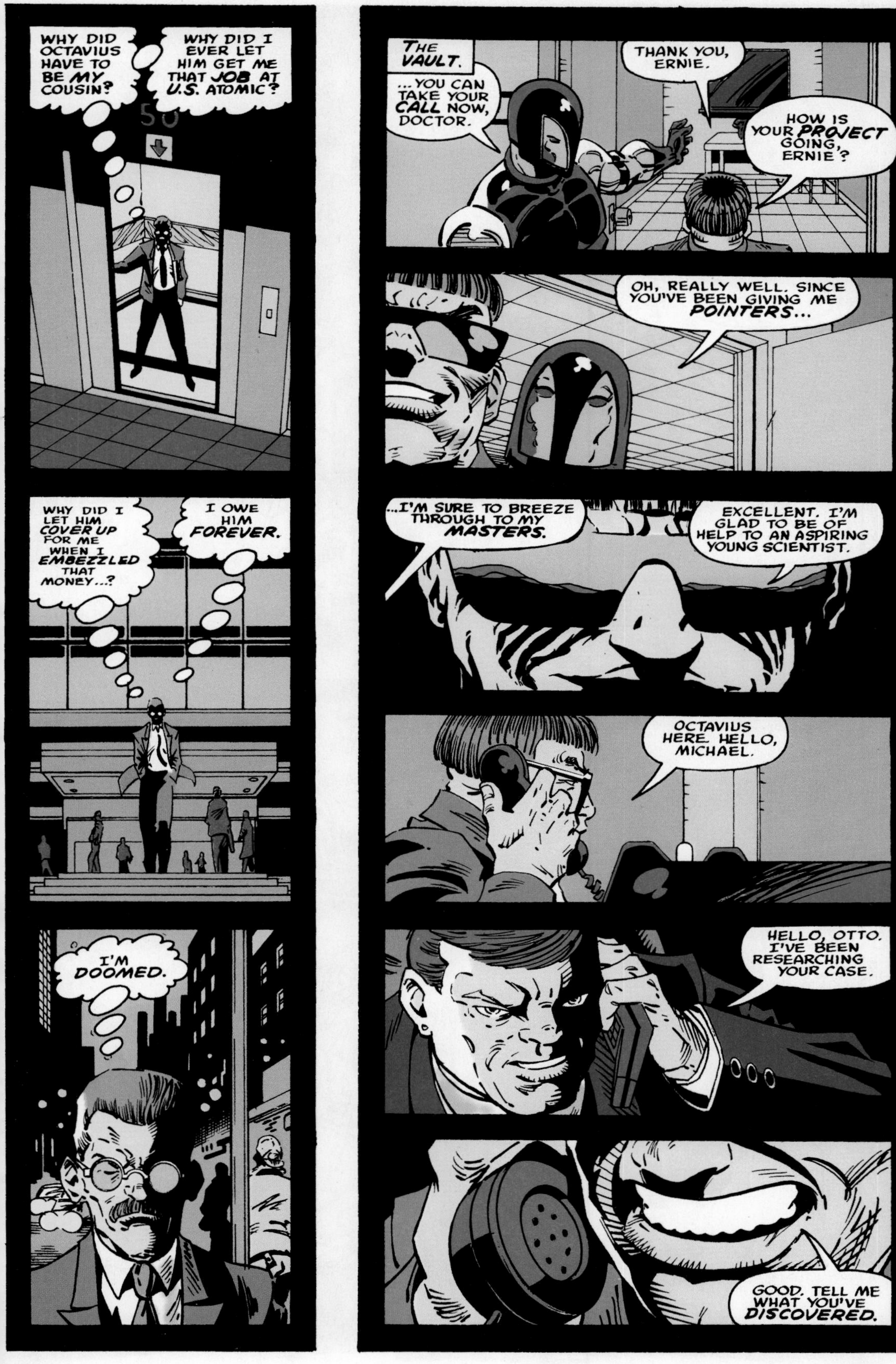
WHY DID OCTAVIUS HAVE TO BE MY COUSIN?
WHY DID I EVER LET HIM GET ME THAT JOB AT U.S. ATOMIC?
50
WHY DID I LET HIM COVER UP FOR ME WHEN I EMBEZZLED THAT MONEY...?
I OWE HIM FOREVER.
I'M DOOMED.
THE VAULT.
...YOU CAN TAKE YOUR CALL NOW, DOCTOR.
THANK YOU, ERNIE.
HOW IS YOUR PROJECT GOING, ERNIE?
OH, REALLY WELL. SINCE YOU'VE BEEN GIVING ME POINTERS...
...I'M SURE TO BREEZE THROUGH TO MY MASTERS.
EXCELLENT. I'M GLAD TO BE OF HELP TO AN ASPIRING YOUNG SCIENTIST.
OCTAVIUS HERE. HELLO, MICHAEL.
HELLO, OTTO. I'VE BEEN RESEARCHING YOUR CASE.
GOOD. TELL ME WHAT YOU'VE DISCOVERED.

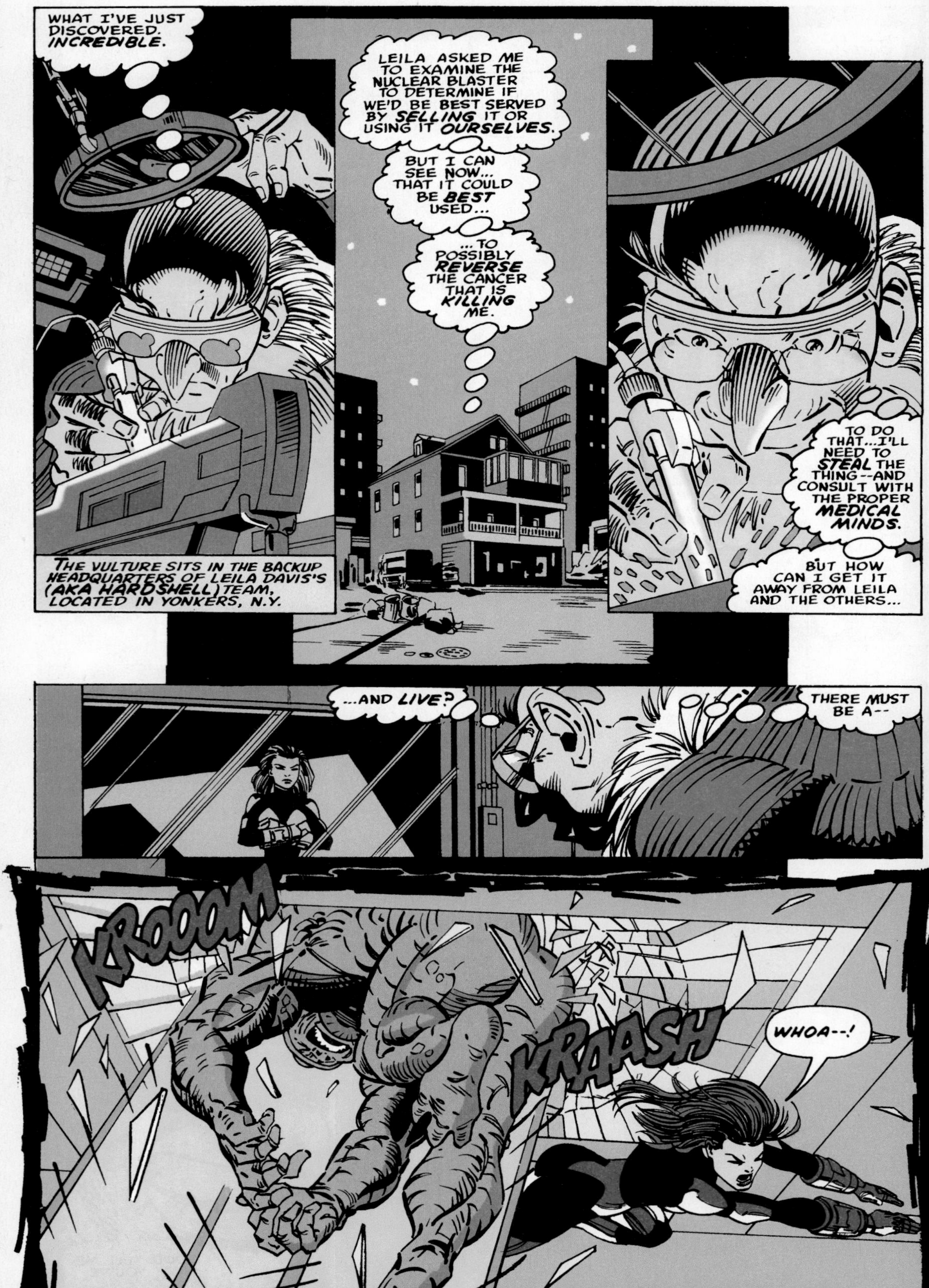
WHAT I'VE JUST DISCOVERED. INCREDIBLE.
THE VULTURE SITS IN THE BACKUP HEADQUARTERS OF LEILA DAVIS'S (AKA HARDSHELL) TEAM, LOCATED IN YONKERS, N.Y.
LEILA ASKED ME TO EXAMINE THE NUCLEAR BLASTER TO DETERMINE IF WE'D BE BEST SERVED BY SELLING IT OR USING IT OURSELVES.
BUT I CAN SEE NOW... THAT IT COULD BE BEST USED...
...TO POSSIBLY REVERSE THE CANCER THAT IS KILLING ME.
TO DO THAT...I'LL NEED TO STEAL THE THING--AND CONSULT WITH THE PROPER MEDICAL MINDS.
BUT HOW CAN I GET IT AWAY FROM LEILA AND THE OTHERS...
...AND LIVE?
THERE MUST BE A--
KROOOM
KRAASH
WHOA--!

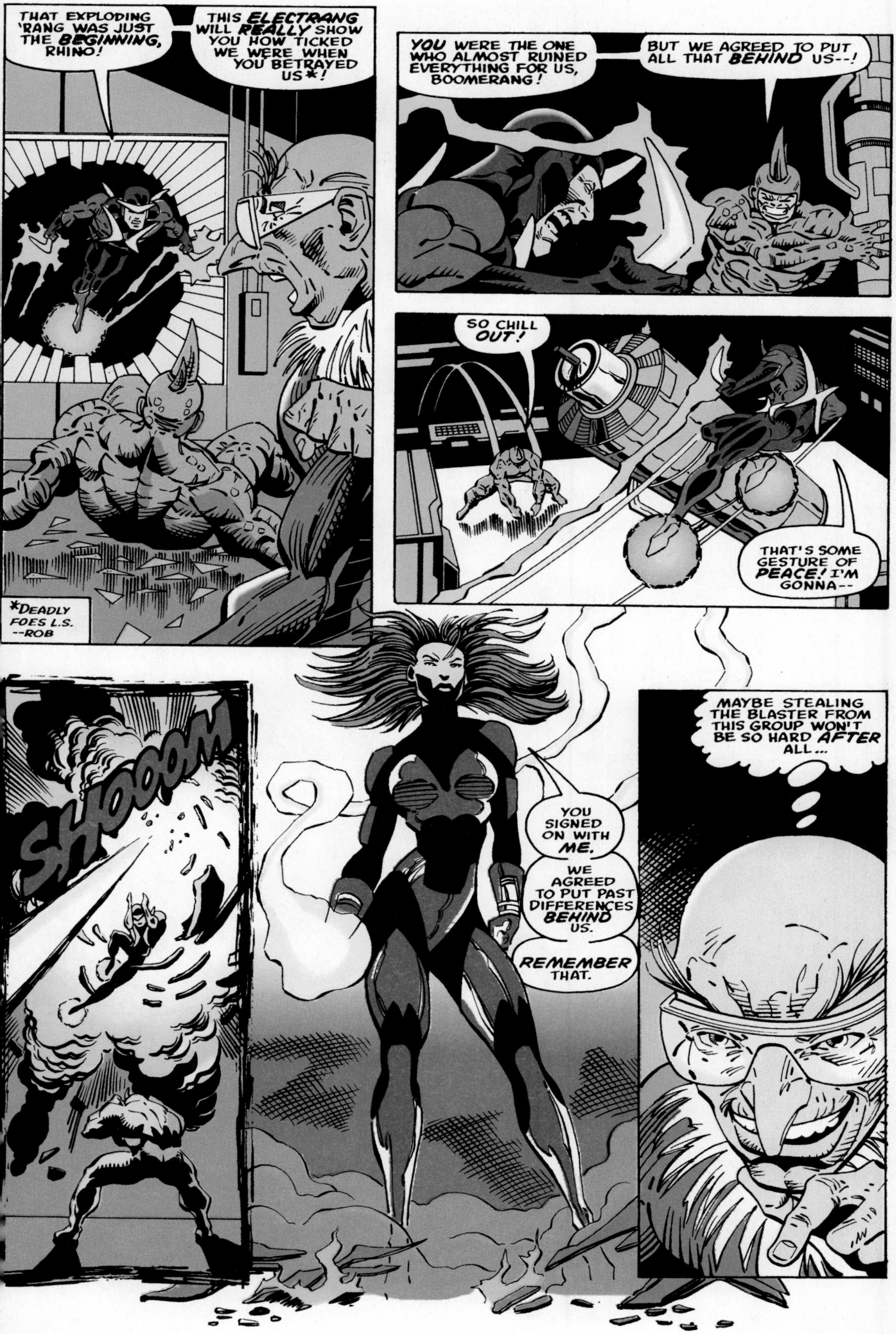

THAT EXPLODING 'RANG WAS JUST THE BEGINNING, RHINO!
THIS ELECTRANG WILL REALLY SHOW YOU HOW TICKED WE WERE WHEN YOU BETRAYED US*!
*DEADLY FOES L.S. --ROB
YOU WERE THE ONE WHO ALMOST RUINED EVERYTHING FOR US, BOOMERANG!
BUT WE AGREED TO PUT ALL THAT BEHIND US--!
SO CHILL OUT!
THAT'S SOME GESTURE OF PEACE! I'M GONNA--
SHOOOM
YOU SIGNED ON WITH ME.
WE AGREED TO PUT PAST DIFFERENCES BEHIND US.
REMEMBER THAT.
MAYBE STEALING THE BLASTER FROM THIS GROUP WON'T BE SO HARD AFTER ALL...

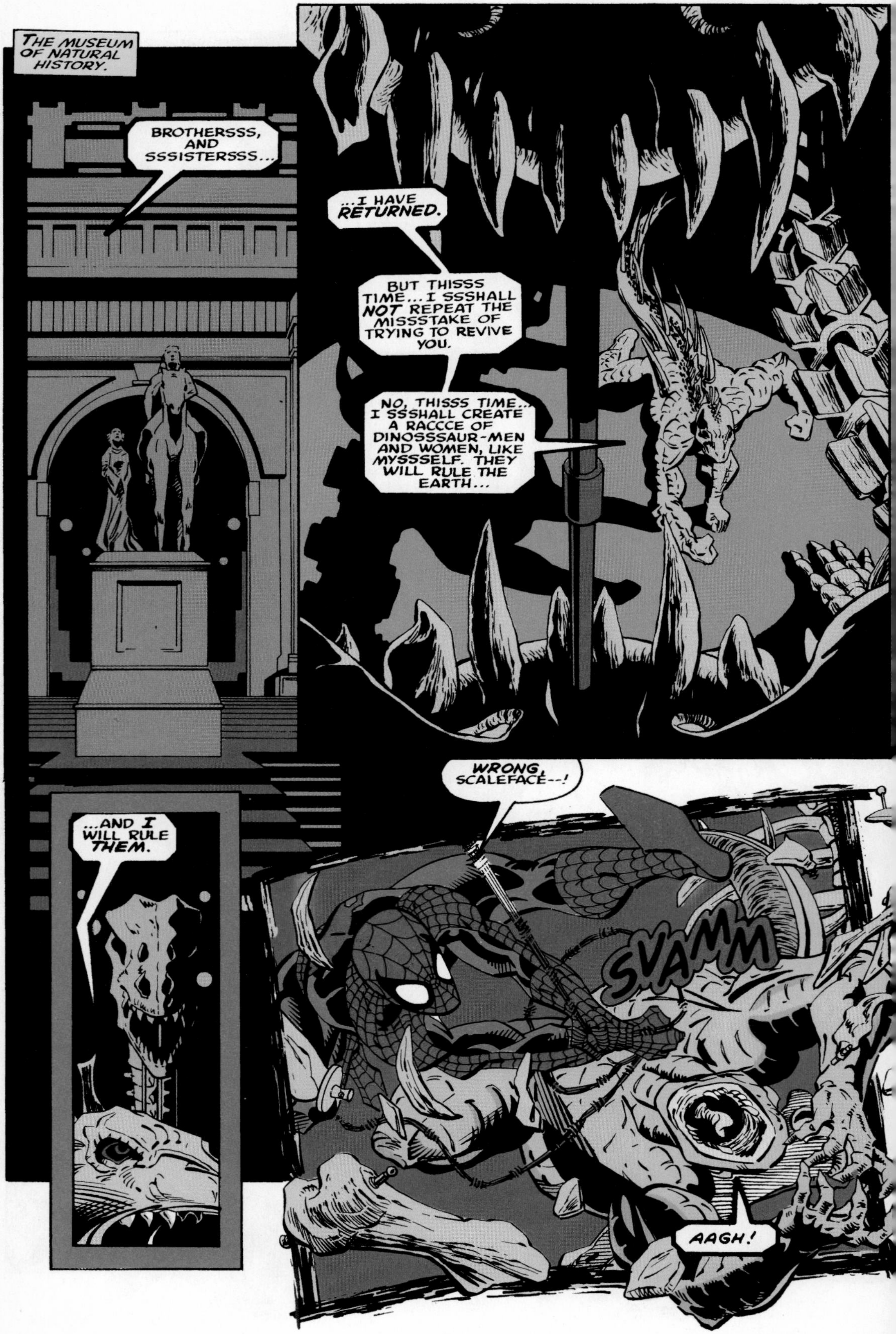
THE MUSEUM OF NATURAL HISTORY.
BROTHERSSS, AND SSSISTERSSS...
...I HAVE RETURNED.
BUT THISSS TIME... I SSSHALL NOT REPEAT THE MISSSTAKE OF TRYING TO REVIVE YOU.
NO, THISSS TIME... I SSSHALL CREATE A RACCCE OF DINOSSSAUR-MEN AND WOMEN, LIKE MYSSSELF. THEY WILL RULE THE EARTH...
...AND I WILL RULE THEM.
WRONG, SCALEFACE--!
SVAMM
AAGH!

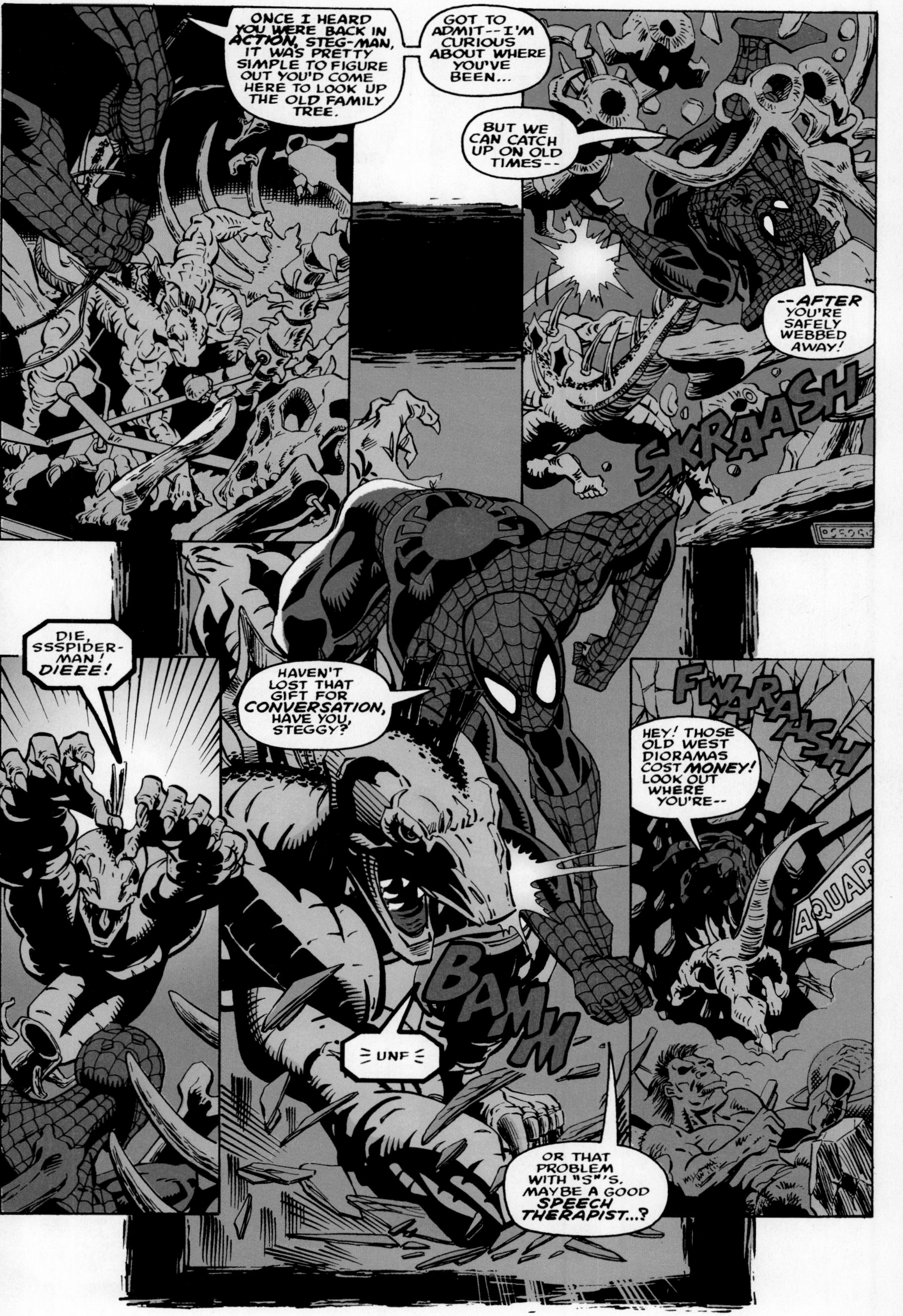
ONCE I HEARD YOU WERE BACK IN ACTION, STEG-MAN, IT WAS PRETTY SIMPLE TO FIGURE OUT YOU'D COME HERE TO LOOK UP THE OLD FAMILY TREE.
GOT TO ADMIT--I'M CURIOUS ABOUT WHERE YOU'VE BEEN...
BUT WE CAN CATCH UP ON OLD TIMES--
--AFTER YOU'RE SAFELY WEBBED AWAY!
SKRAASH
DIE, SSSPIDER-MAN! DIEEE!
HAVEN'T LOST THAT GIFT FOR CONVERSATION, HAVE YOU, STEGGY?
BAMM
UNF
OR THAT PROBLEM WITH "S"'S. MAYBE A GOOD SPEECH THERAPIST...?
FWARAASH
HEY! THOSE OLD WEST DIORAMAS COST MONEY! LOOK OUT WHERE YOU'RE--
AQUAR

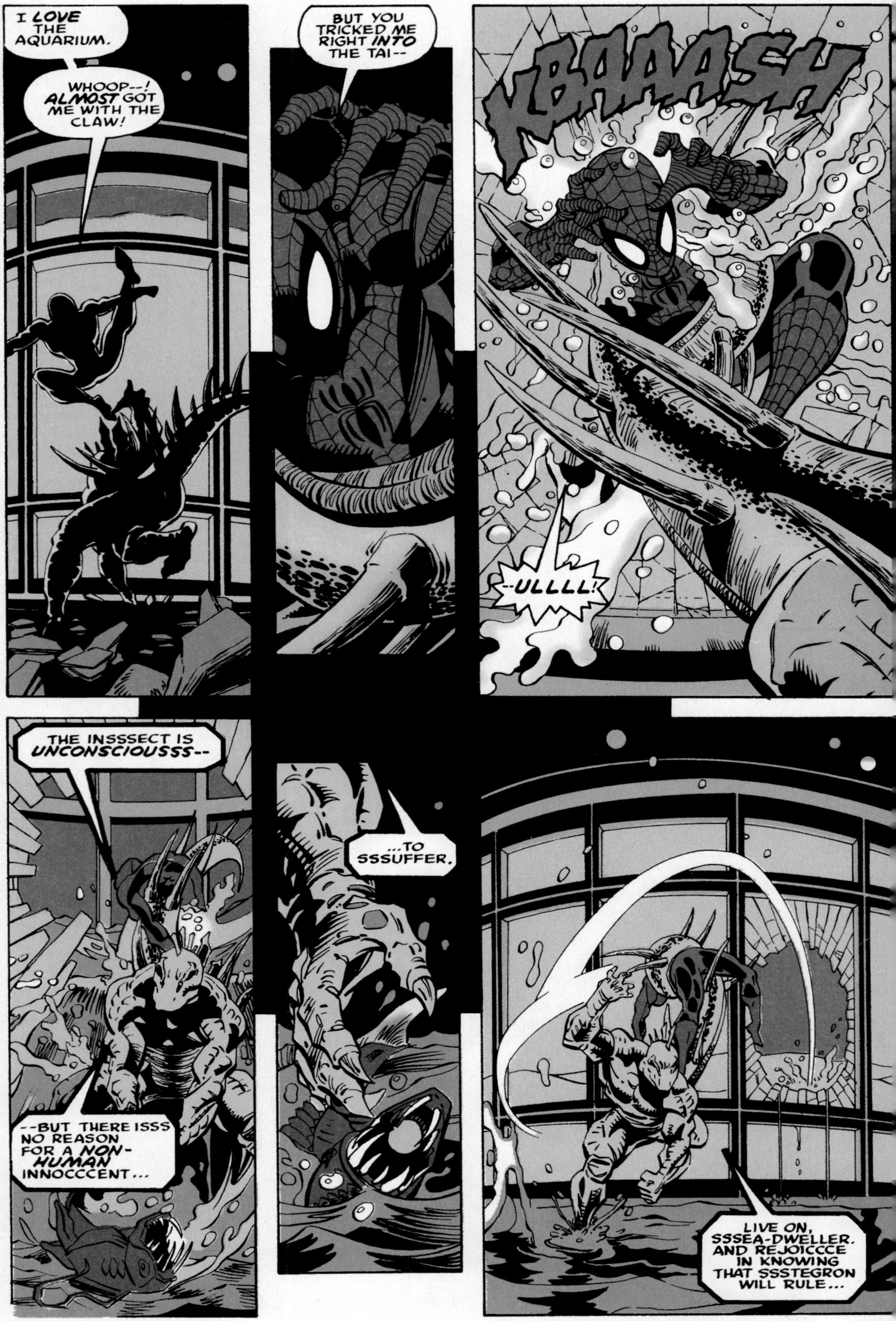
I LOVE THE AQUARIUM.
WHOOP--! ALMOST GOT ME WITH THE CLAW!
BUT YOU TRICKED ME RIGHT INTO THE TAI--
KBAAASH
--ULLLL!
THE INSSSECT IS UNCONSCIOUSSS--
--BUT THERE ISSS NO REASON FOR A NON-HUMAN INNOCCCENT...
...TO SSSUFFER.
LIVE ON, SSSEA-DWELLER. AND REJOICCCE IN KNOWING THAT SSSTEGRON WILL RULE...

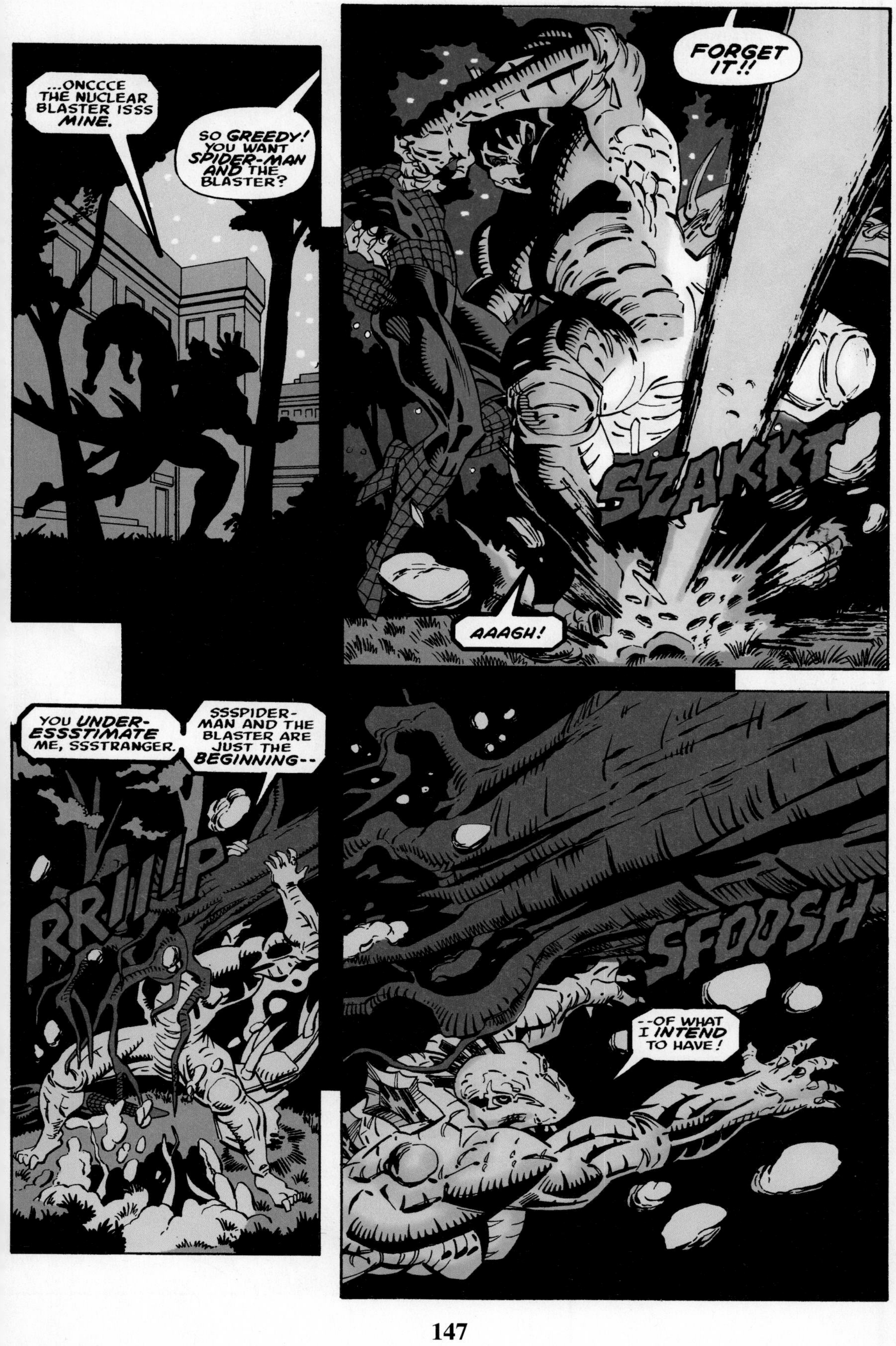
...ONCCCE THE NUCLEAR BLASTER ISSS MINE.
SO GREEDY! YOU WANT SPIDER-MAN AND THE BLASTER?
FORGET IT!!
SZAKKT
AAAGH!
YOU UNDER-ESSSTIMATE ME, SSSTRANGER.
SSSPIDER-MAN AND THE BLASTER ARE JUST THE BEGINNING--
RRIIIP
SFOOSH
--OF WHAT I INTEND TO HAVE!

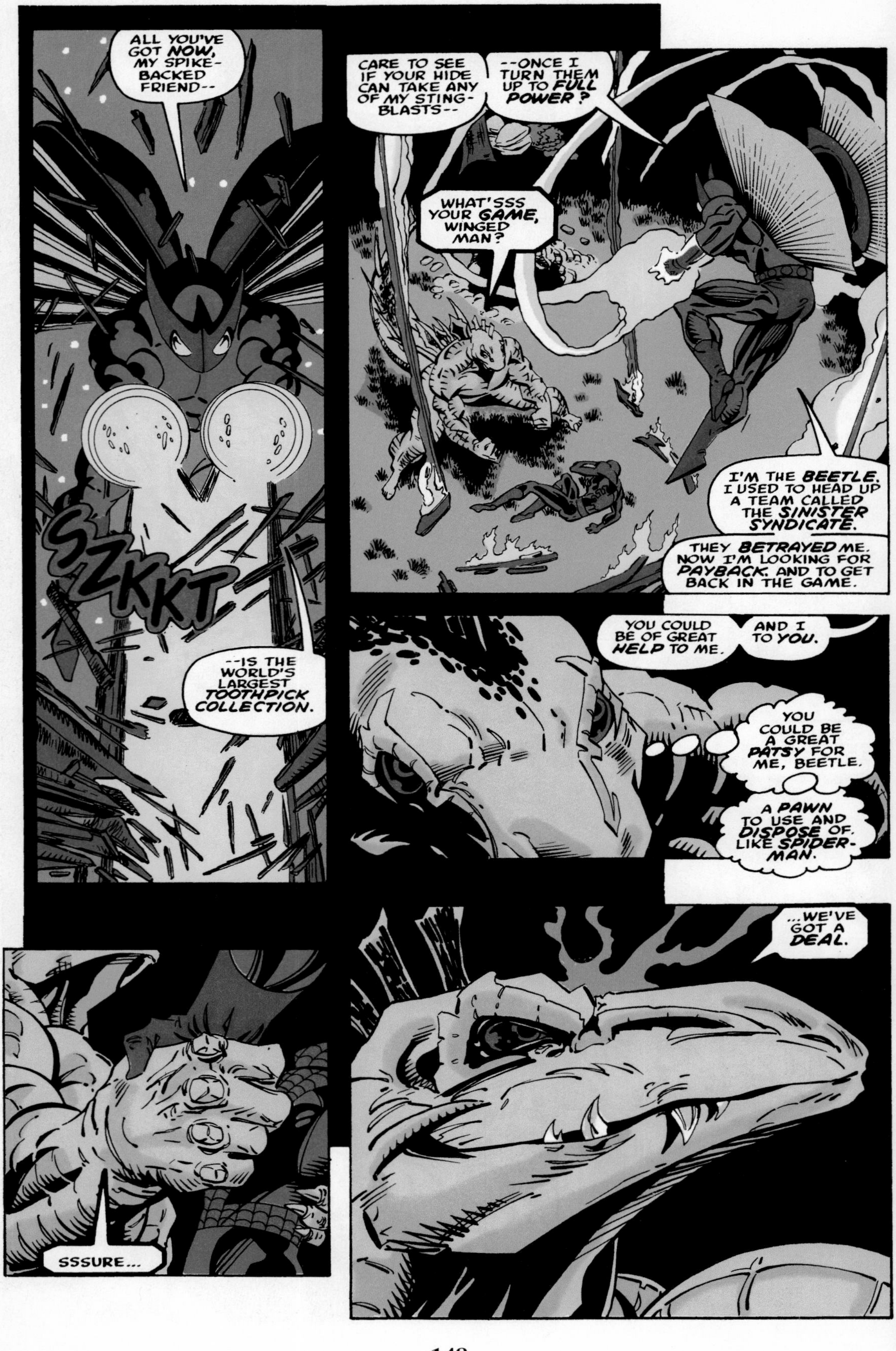
ALL YOU'VE GOT NOW, MY SPIKE-BACKED FRIEND--
SZKKT
--IS THE WORLD'S LARGEST TOOTHPICK COLLECTION.
CARE TO SEE IF YOUR HIDE CAN TAKE ANY OF MY STING-BLASTS--
--ONCE I TURN THEM UP TO FULL POWER?
WHAT'SSS YOUR GAME, WINGED MAN?
I'M THE BEETLE. I USED TO HEAD UP A TEAM CALLED THE SINISTER SYNDICATE.
THEY BETRAYED ME. NOW I'M LOOKING FOR PAYBACK, AND TO GET BACK IN THE GAME.
YOU COULD BE OF GREAT HELP TO ME.
AND I TO YOU.
YOU COULD BE A GREAT PATSY FOR ME, BEETLE.
A PAWN TO USE AND DISPOSE OF. LIKE SPIDER-MAN.
SSSURE...
...WE'VE GOT A DEAL.

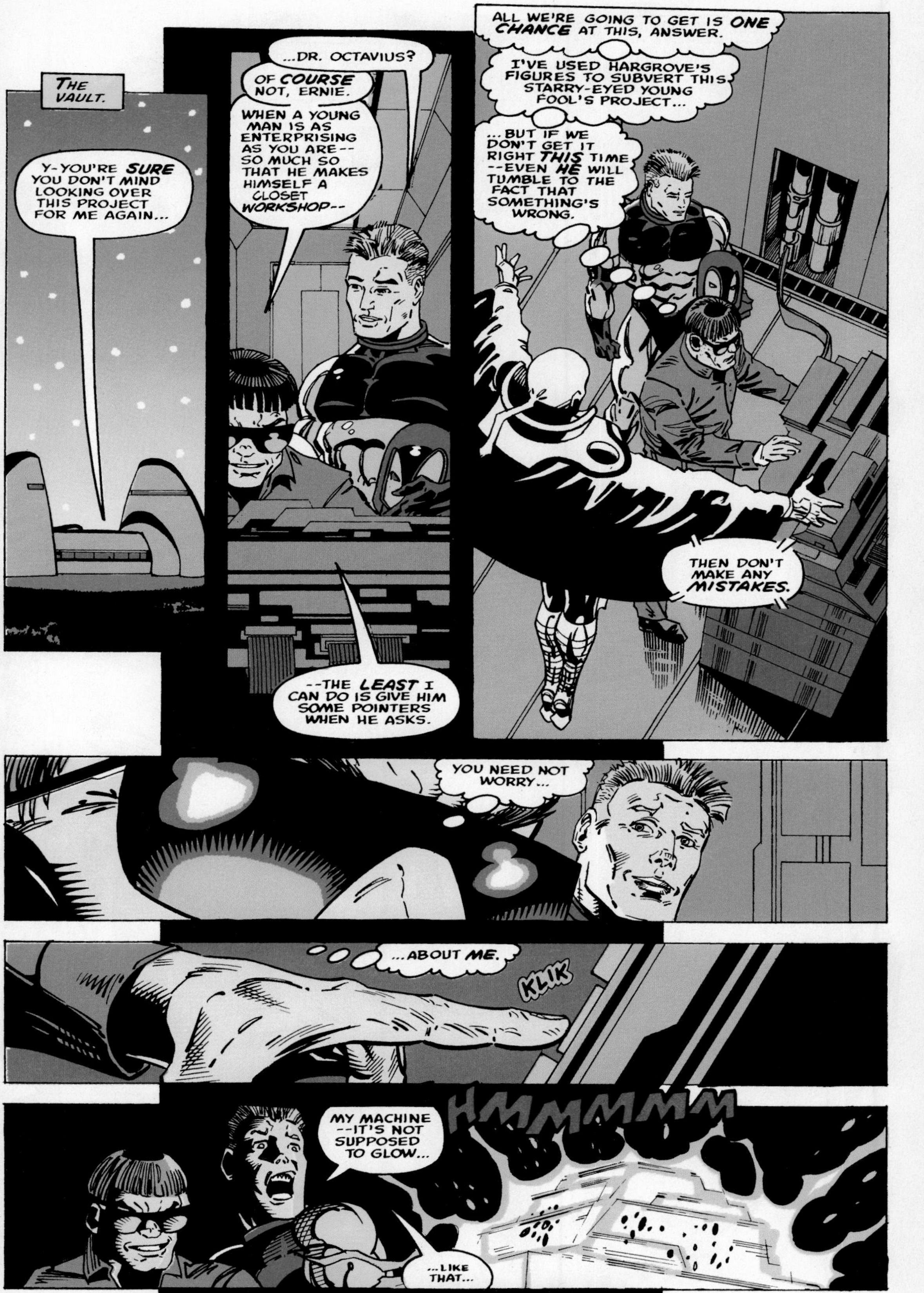

THE VAULT.
Y-YOU'RE SURE YOU DON'T MIND LOOKING OVER THIS PROJECT FOR ME AGAIN...
...DR. OCTAVIUS?
OF COURSE NOT, ERNIE.
WHEN A YOUNG MAN IS AS ENTERPRISING AS YOU ARE-- SO MUCH SO THAT HE MAKES HIMSELF A CLOSET WORKSHOP--
--THE LEAST I CAN DO IS GIVE HIM SOME POINTERS WHEN HE ASKS.
ALL WE'RE GOING TO GET IS ONE CHANCE AT THIS, ANSWER.
I'VE USED HARGROVE'S FIGURES TO SUBVERT THIS STARRY-EYED YOUNG FOOL'S PROJECT...
...BUT IF WE DON'T GET IT RIGHT THIS TIME --EVEN HE WILL TUMBLE TO THE FACT THAT SOMETHING'S WRONG.
THEN DON'T MAKE ANY MISTAKES.
YOU NEED NOT WORRY...
...ABOUT ME.
KLIK
MY MACHINE --IT'S NOT SUPPOSED TO GLOW...
HMMMMM
...LIKE THAT...

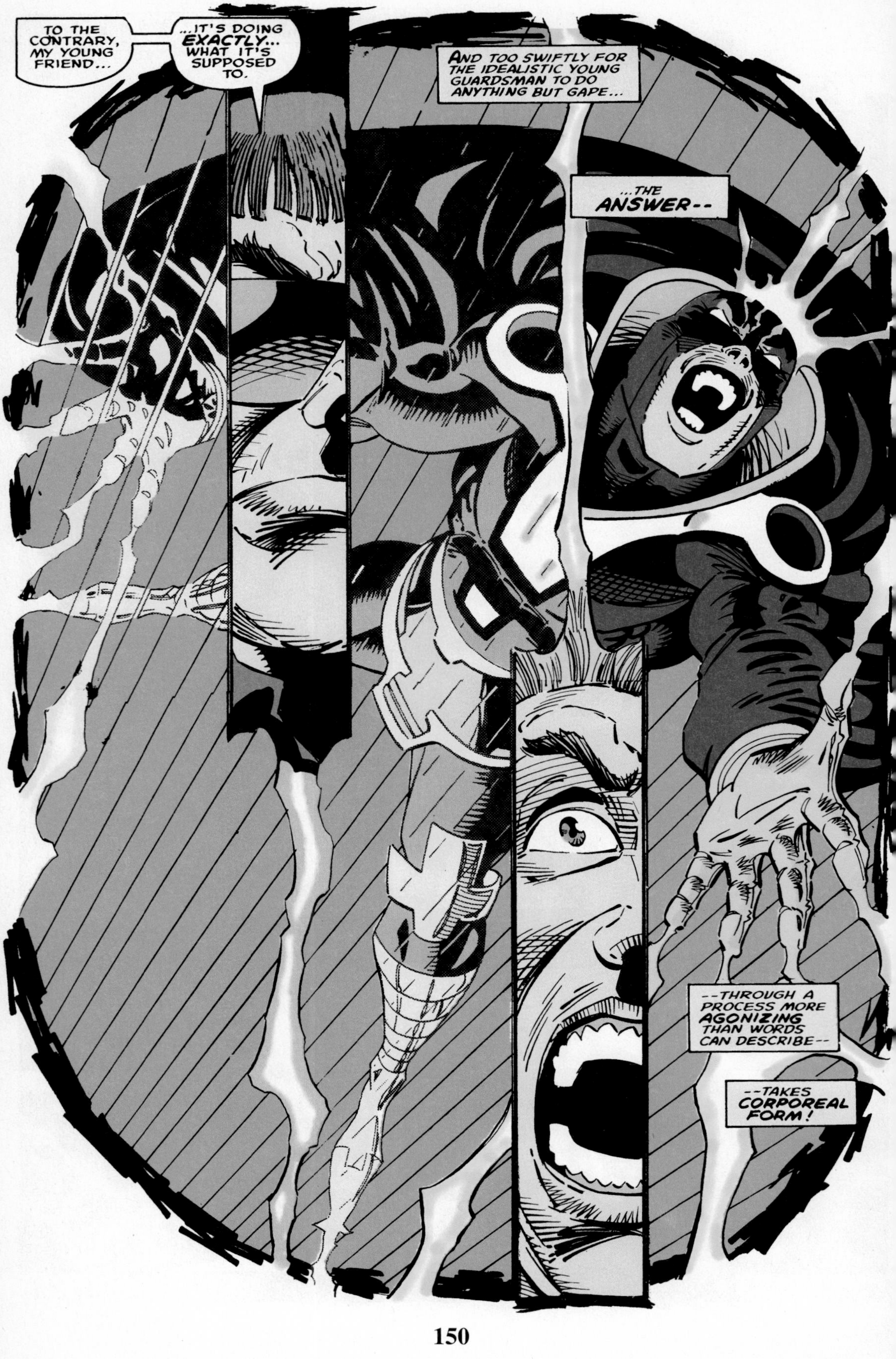
TO THE CONTRARY, MY YOUNG FRIEND...
...IT'S DOING EXACTLY... WHAT IT'S SUPPOSED TO.
AND TOO SWIFTLY FOR THE IDEALISTIC YOUNG GUARDSMAN TO DO ANYTHING BUT GAPE...
...THE ANSWER--
--THROUGH A PROCESS MORE AGONIZING THAN WORDS CAN DESCRIBE--
--TAKES CORPOREAL FORM!

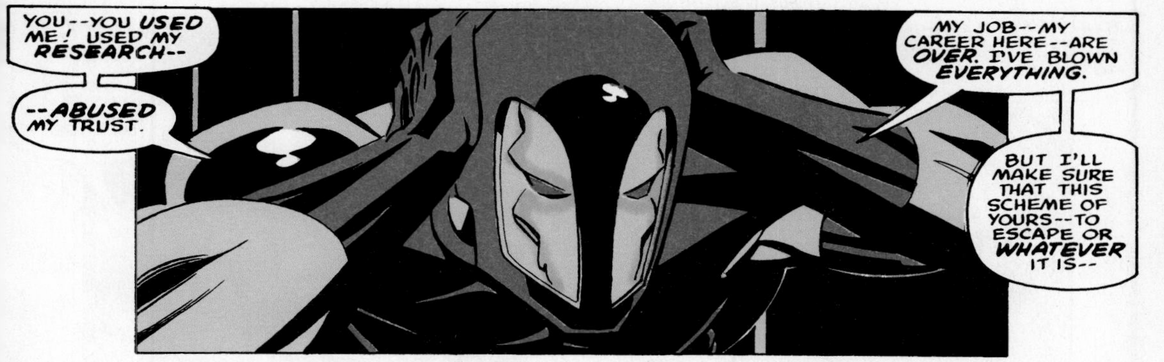

YOU--YOU USED ME! USED MY RESEARCH--
--ABUSED MY TRUST.
MY JOB--MY CAREER HERE--ARE OVER. I'VE BLOWN EVERYTHING.
BUT I'LL MAKE SURE THAT THIS SCHEME OF YOURS--TO ESCAPE OR WHATEVER IT IS--

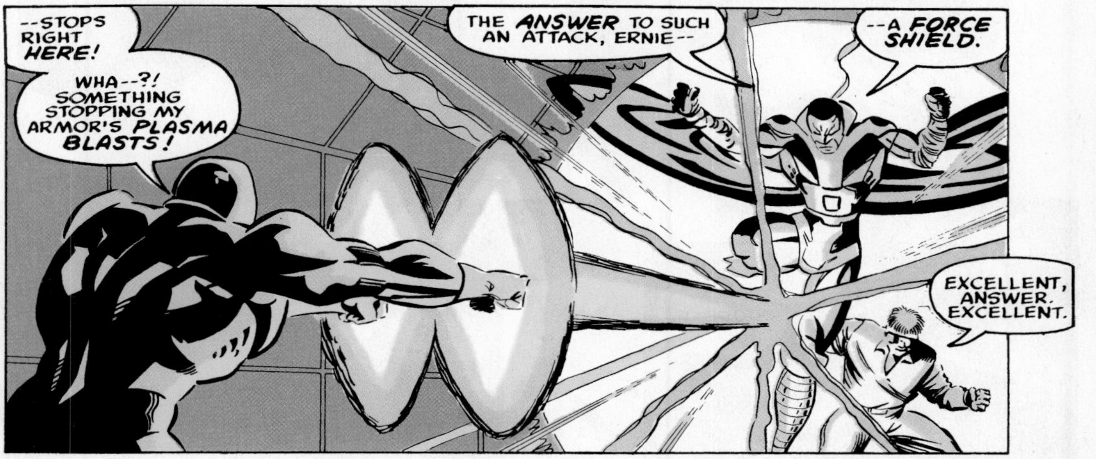

--STOPS RIGHT HERE!
WHA--?! SOMETHING STOPPING MY ARMOR'S PLASMA BLASTS!
THE ANSWER TO SUCH AN ATTACK, ERNIE--
--A FORCE SHIELD.
EXCELLENT, ANSWER. EXCELLENT.

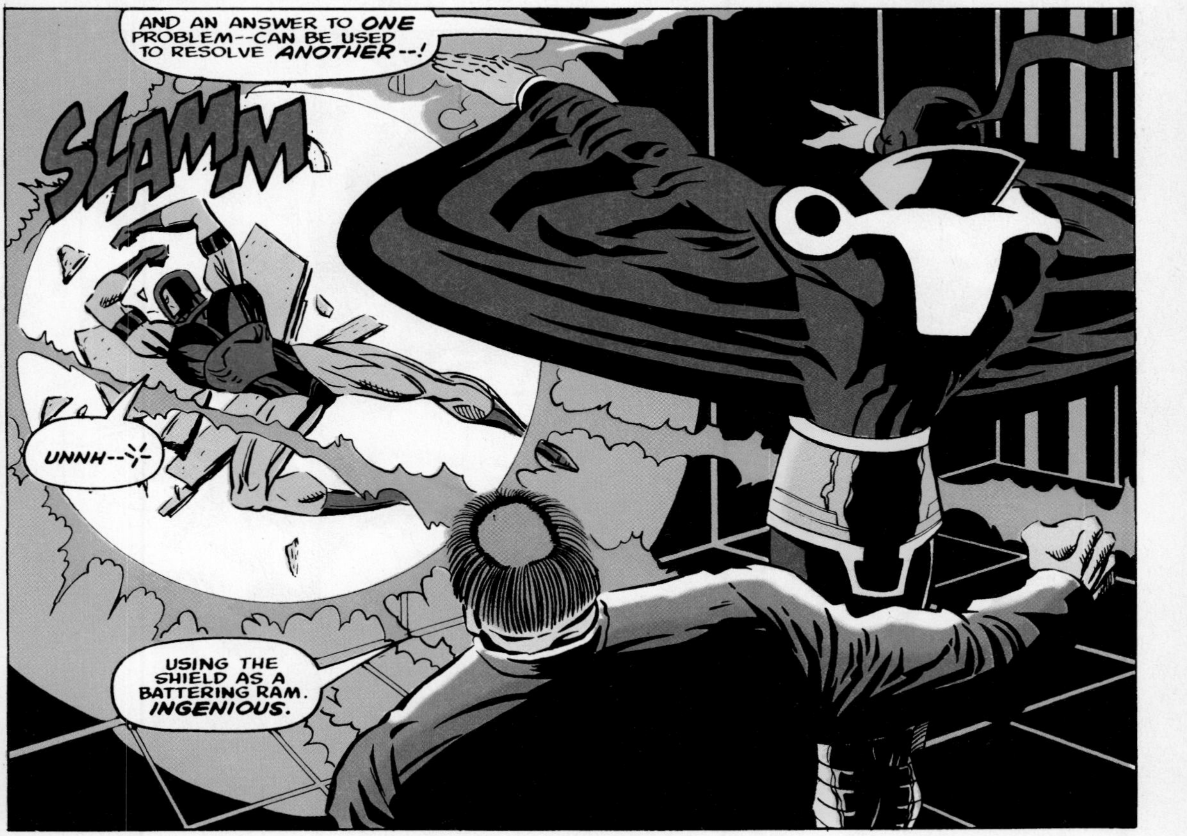

AND AN ANSWER TO ONE PROBLEM--CAN BE USED TO RESOLVE ANOTHER--!
SLAMM
UNNH--!
USING THE SHIELD AS A BATTERING RAM. INGENIOUS.

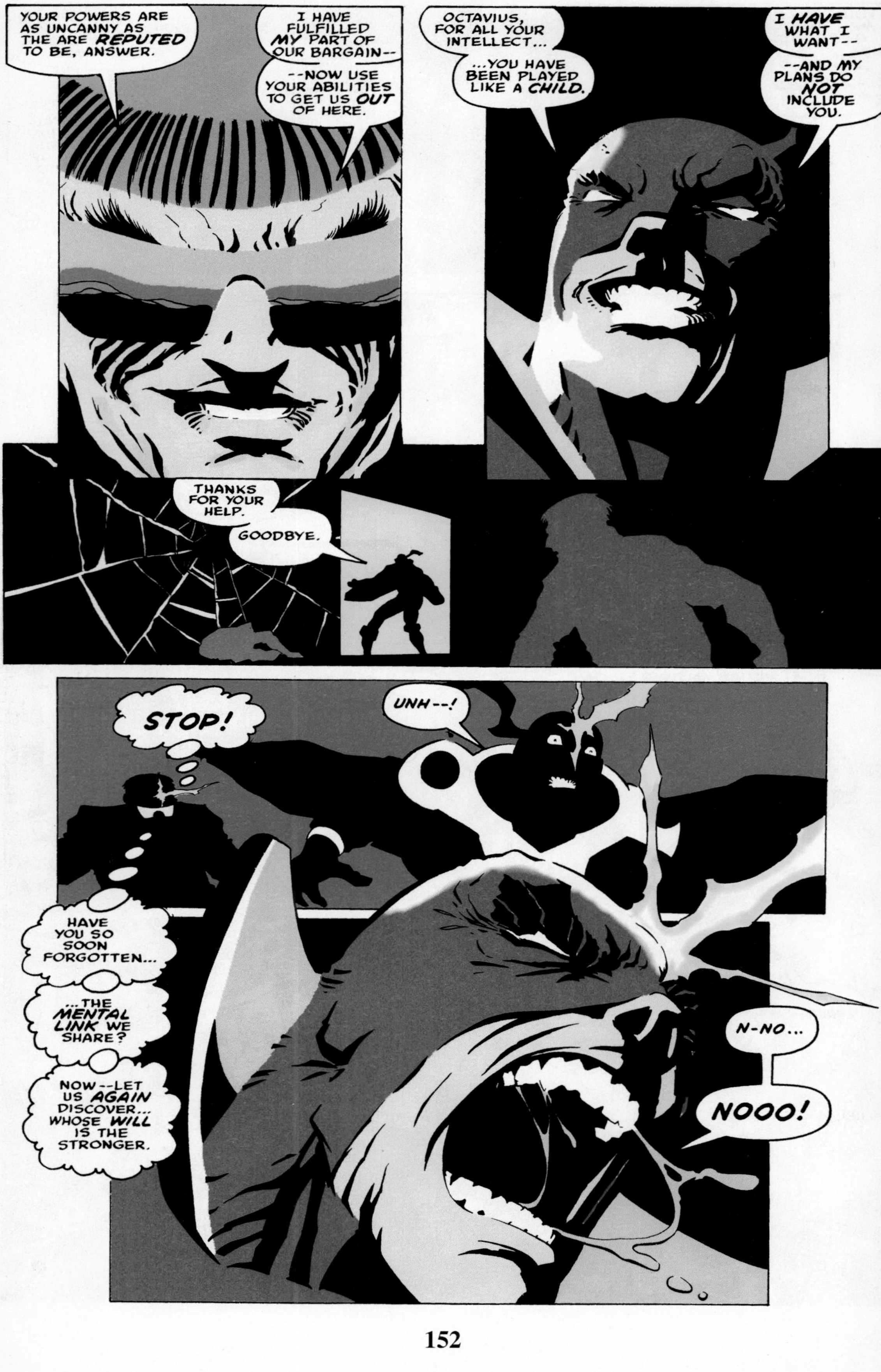
YOUR POWERS ARE AS UNCANNY AS THE ARE REPUTED TO BE, ANSWER.
I HAVE FULFILLED MY PART OF OUR BARGAIN--
--NOW USE YOUR ABILITIES TO GET US OUT OF HERE.
OCTAVIUS, FOR ALL YOUR INTELLECT...
...YOU HAVE BEEN PLAYED LIKE A CHILD.
I HAVE WHAT I WANT--
--AND MY PLANS DO NOT INCLUDE YOU.
THANKS FOR YOUR HELP.
GOODBYE.
STOP!
UNH--!
HAVE YOU SO SOON FORGOTTEN...
...THE MENTAL LINK WE SHARE?
NOW--LET US AGAIN DISCOVER... WHOSE WILL IS THE STRONGER.
N-NO...
NOOO!

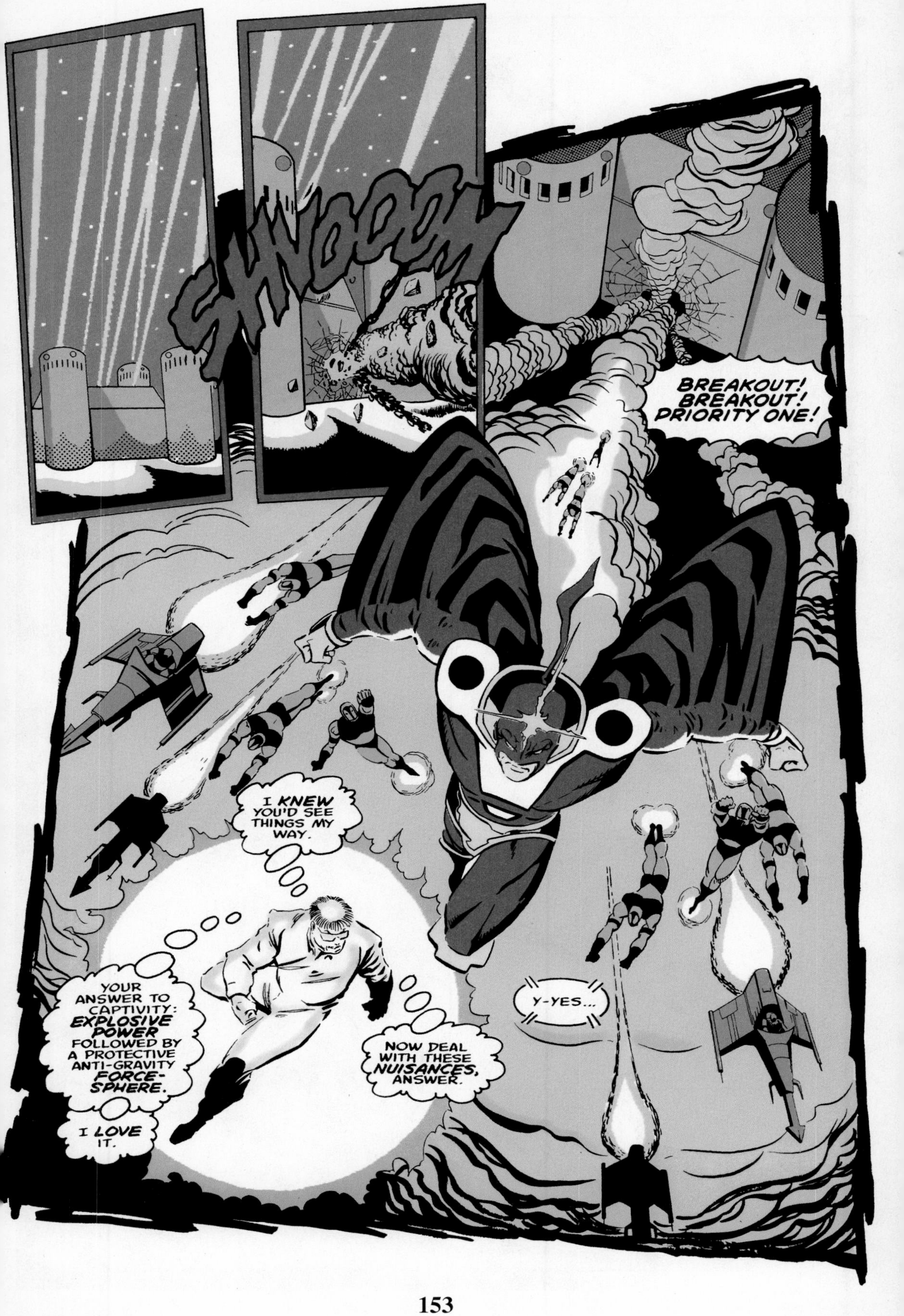
SHOOOM
BREAKOUT! BREAKOUT! PRIORITY ONE!
I KNEW YOU'D SEE THINGS MY WAY.
YOUR ANSWER TO CAPTIVITY: EXPLOSIVE POWER FOLLOWED BY A PROTECTIVE ANTI-GRAVITY FORCE-SPHERE.
I LOVE IT.
NOW DEAL WITH THESE NUISANCES, ANSWER.
Y-YES...

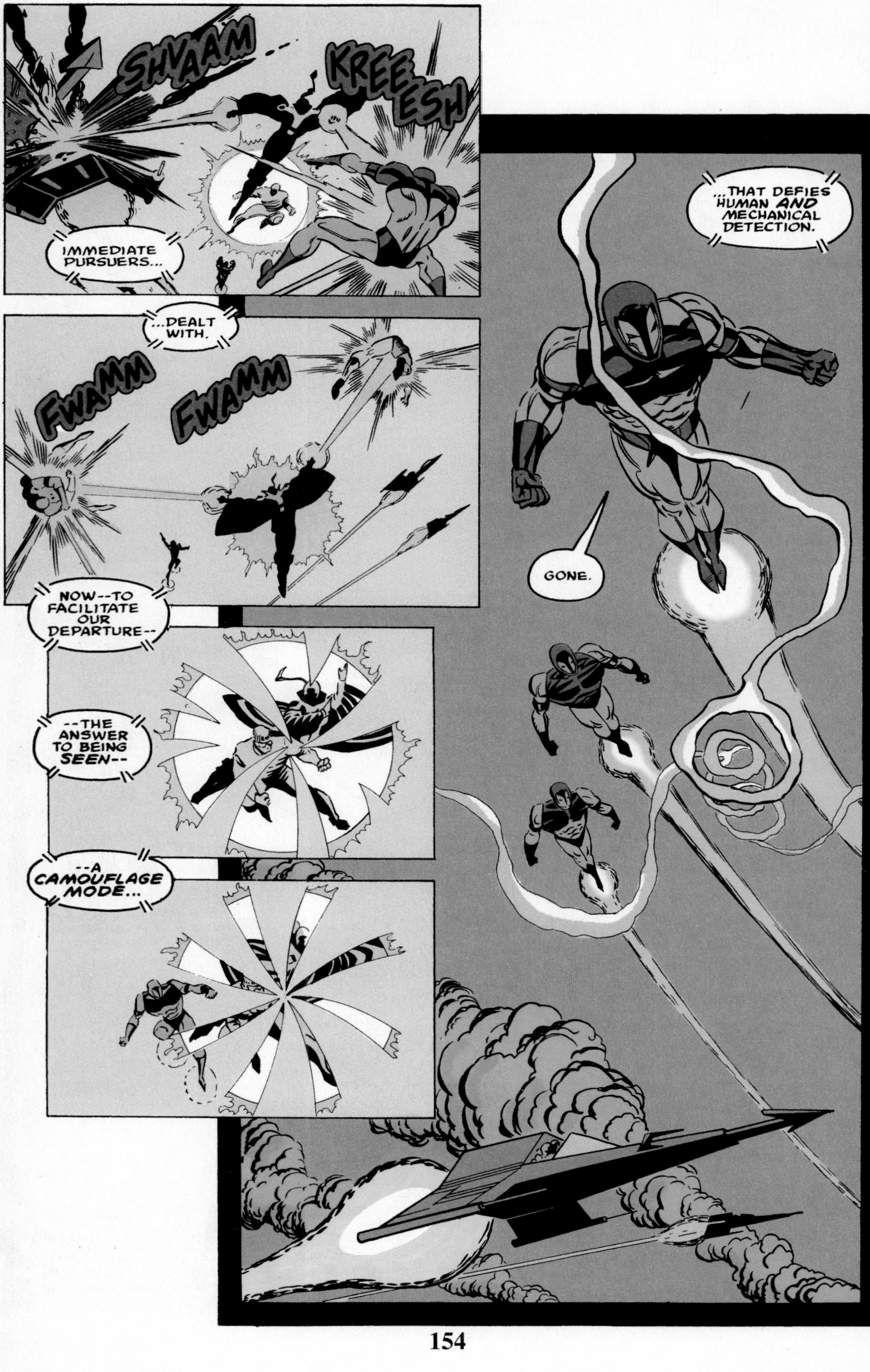
SHVAAM
KREEESH
IMMEDIATE PURSUERS...
...DEALT WITH.
FWAMM
FWAMM
NOW--TO FACILITATE OUR DEPARTURE--
--THE ANSWER TO BEING SEEN--
--A CAMOUFLAGE MODE...
...THAT DEFIES HUMAN AND MECHANICAL DETECTION.
GONE.

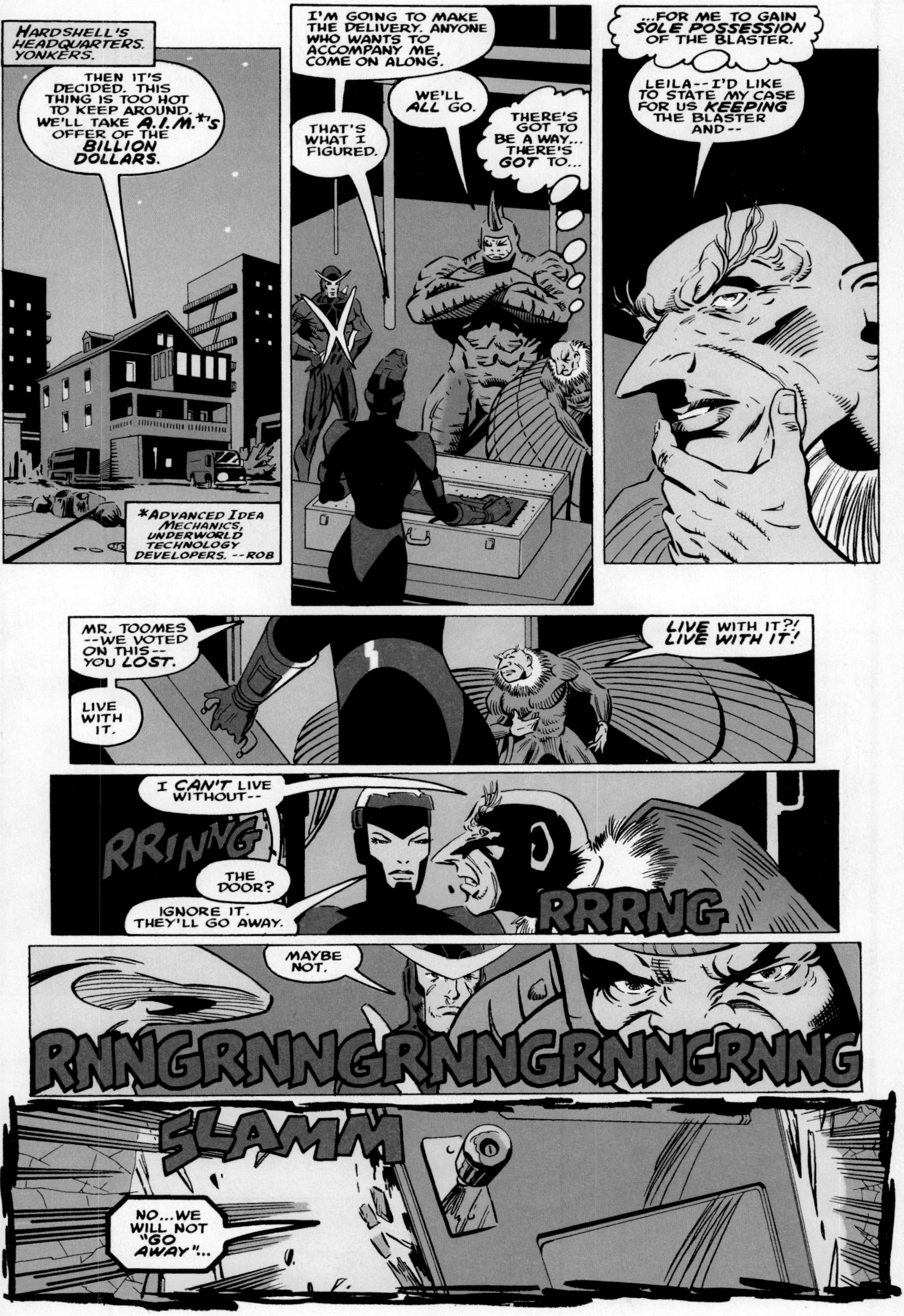
HARDSHELL'S HEADQUARTERS. YONKERS.
THEN IT'S DECIDED. THIS THING IS TOO HOT TO KEEP AROUND. WE'LL TAKE A.I.M.*'S OFFER OF THE BILLION DOLLARS.
*ADVANCED IDEA MECHANICS, UNDERWORLD TECHNOLOGY DEVELOPERS. --ROB
I'M GOING TO MAKE THE DELIVERY. ANYONE WHO WANTS TO ACCOMPANY ME, COME ON ALONG.
THAT'S WHAT I FIGURED.
WE'LL ALL GO.
THERE'S GOT TO BE A WAY... THERE'S GOT TO...
...FOR ME TO GAIN SOLE POSSESSION OF THE BLASTER.
LEILA--I'D LIKE TO STATE MY CASE FOR US KEEPING THE BLASTER AND--
MR. TOOMES --WE VOTED ON THIS-- YOU LOST.
LIVE WITH IT.
LIVE WITH IT?! LIVE WITH IT!
I CAN'T LIVE WITHOUT--
RRINNG
THE DOOR?
IGNORE IT. THEY'LL GO AWAY.
RRRNG
MAYBE NOT.
RNNGRNNGRNNGRNNGRNNG
SLAMM
NO...WE WILL NOT "GO AWAY"...

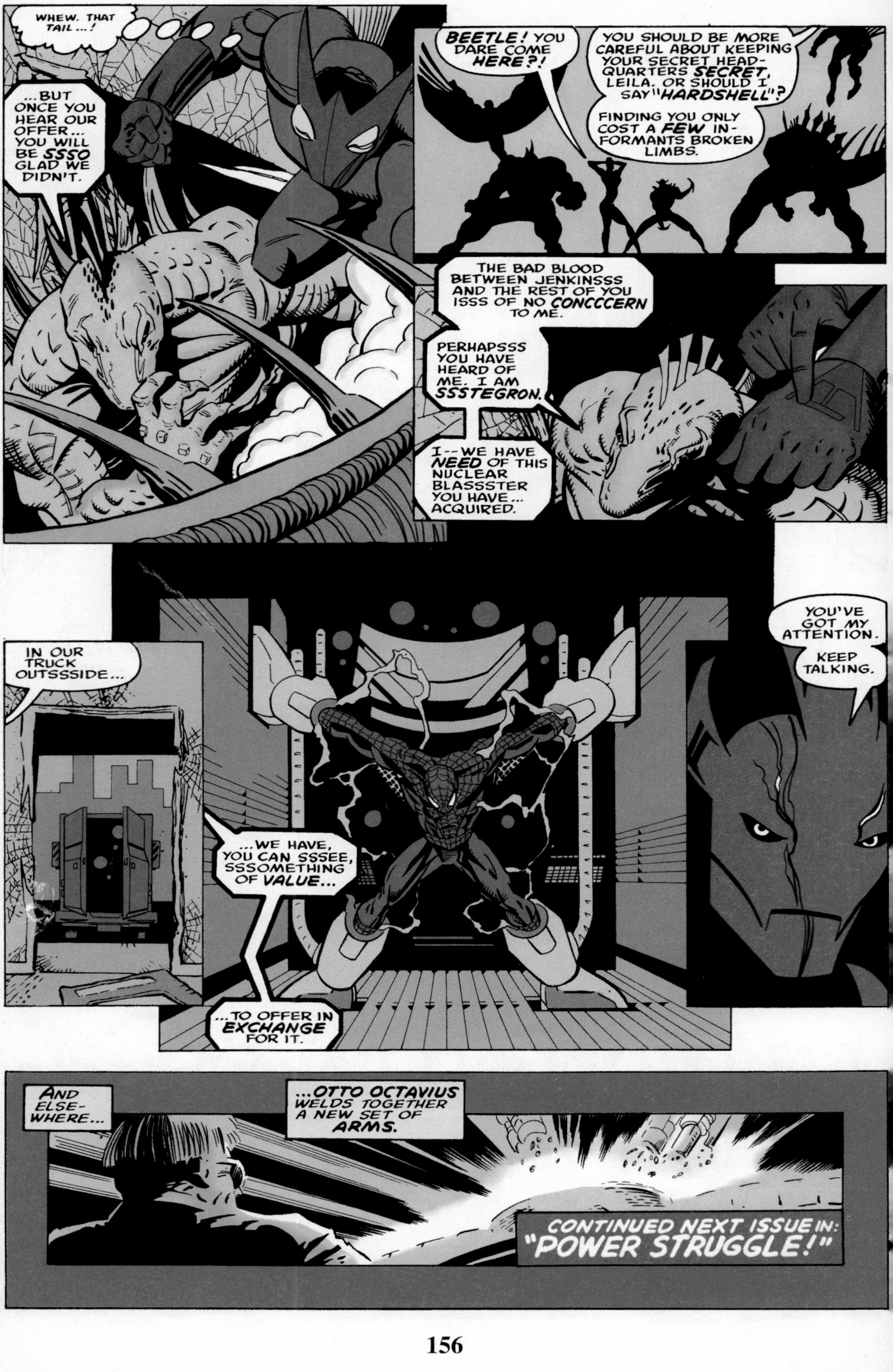
WHEW. THAT TAIL...!
...BUT ONCE YOU HEAR OUR OFFER... YOU WILL BE SSSO GLAD WE DIDN'T.
BEETLE! YOU DARE COME HERE?!
YOU SHOULD BE MORE CAREFUL ABOUT KEEPING YOUR SECRET HEAD-QUARTERS SECRET, LEILA. OR SHOULD I SAY "HARDSHELL"?
FINDING YOU ONLY COST A FEW IN-FORMANTS BROKEN LIMBS.
THE BAD BLOOD BETWEEN JENKINSSS AND THE REST OF YOU ISSS OF NO CONCCCERN TO ME.
PERHAPSSS YOU HAVE HEARD OF ME. I AM SSSTEGRON.
I--WE HAVE NEED OF THIS NUCLEAR BLASSSTER YOU HAVE... ACQUIRED.
IN OUR TRUCK OUTSSSIDE...
...WE HAVE, YOU CAN SSSEE, SSSOMETHING OF VALUE...
...TO OFFER IN EXCHANGE FOR IT.
YOU'VE GOT MY ATTENTION.
KEEP TALKING.
AND ELSE-WHERE...
...OTTO OCTAVIUS WELDS TOGETHER A NEW SET OF ARMS.
CONTINUED NEXT ISSUE IN: "POWER STRUGGLE!"

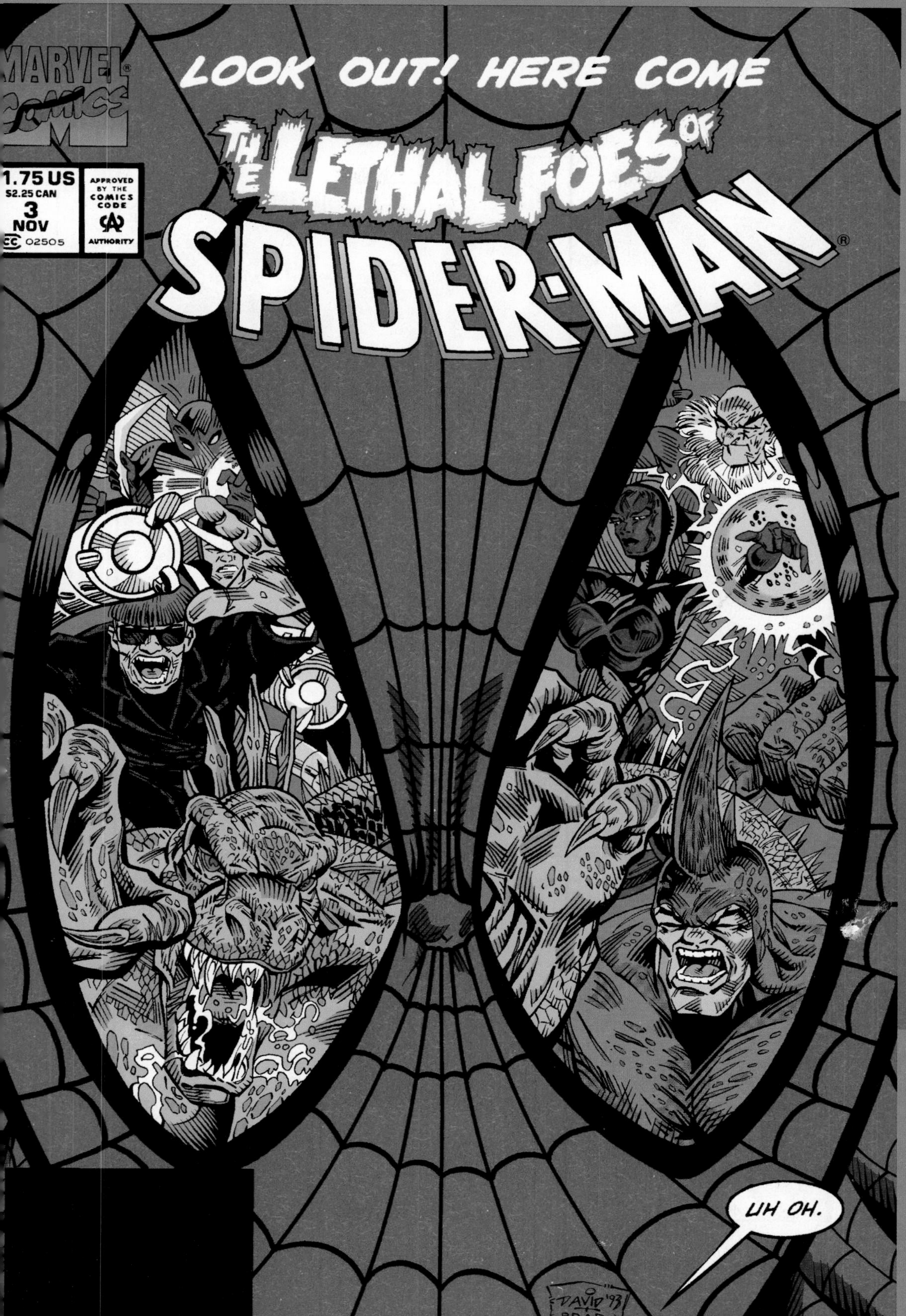
MARVEL COMICS
1.75 US
$2.25 CAN
3
NOV
APPROVED BY THE COMICS CODE AUTHORITY
LOOK OUT! HERE COME
THE LETHAL FOES OF
SPIDER-MAN
UH OH.
DAVID '93
BRAD

UNITED IN NOTHING BUT THEIR *HATRED* FOR ONE MAN AND THEIR THIRST FOR *POWER*, MURDEROUS INDIVIDUALS BAND TOGETHER TO FURTHER THEIR TWISTED GOALS. AND THEY WILL LET *NOTHING* STAND IN THEIR WAY!

STAN LEE PRESENTS... THE LETHAL FOES OF SPIDER-MAN!

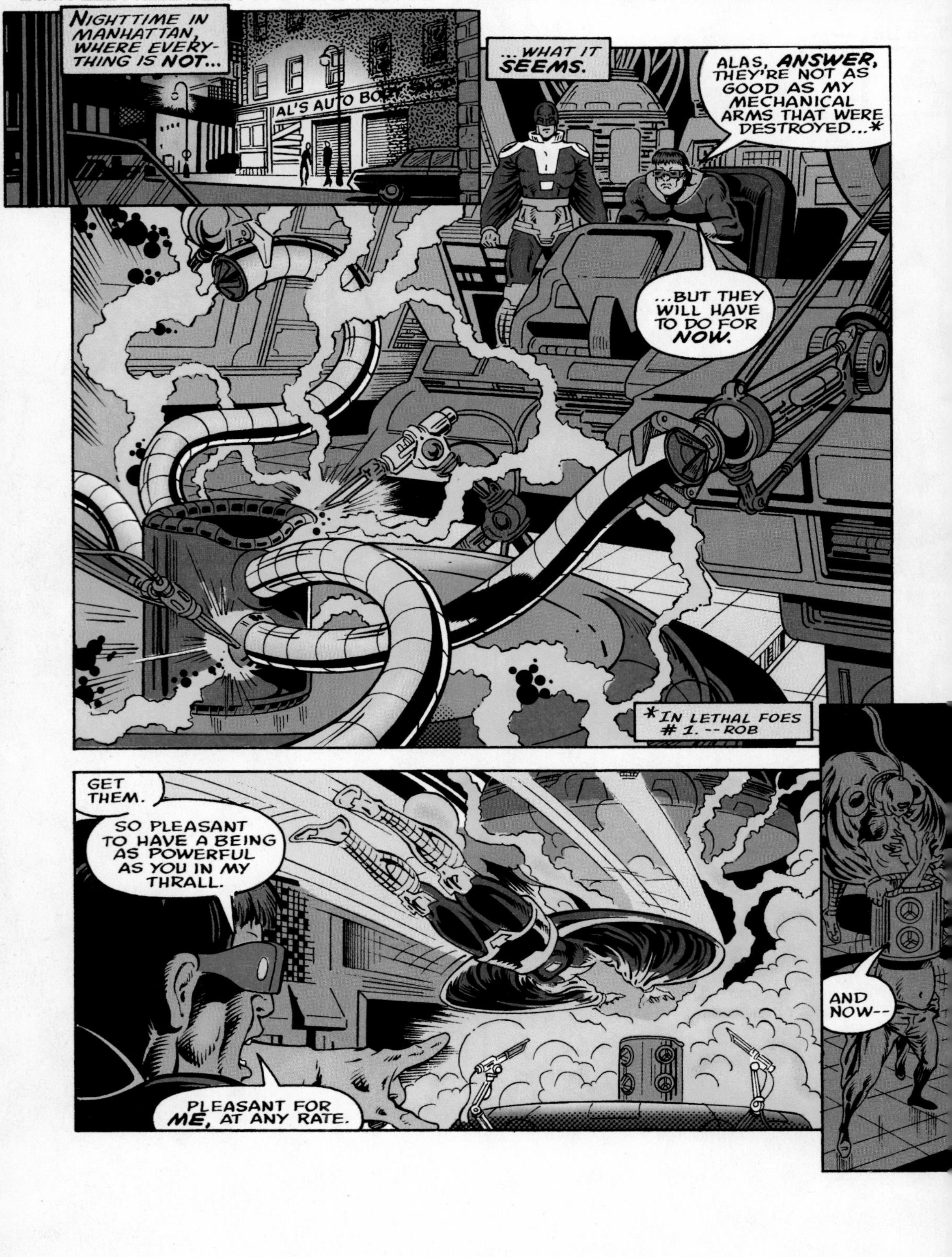
NIGHTTIME IN MANHATTAN, WHERE EVERYTHING IS NOT...
AL'S AUTO BODY SHOP
...WHAT IT SEEMS.
ALAS, ANSWER, THEY'RE NOT AS GOOD AS MY MECHANICAL ARMS THAT WERE DESTROYED...*
...BUT THEY WILL HAVE TO DO FOR NOW.
*IN LETHAL FOES # 1. --ROB
GET THEM.
SO PLEASANT TO HAVE A BEING AS POWERFUL AS YOU IN MY THRALL.
PLEASANT FOR ME, AT ANY RATE.
AND NOW--

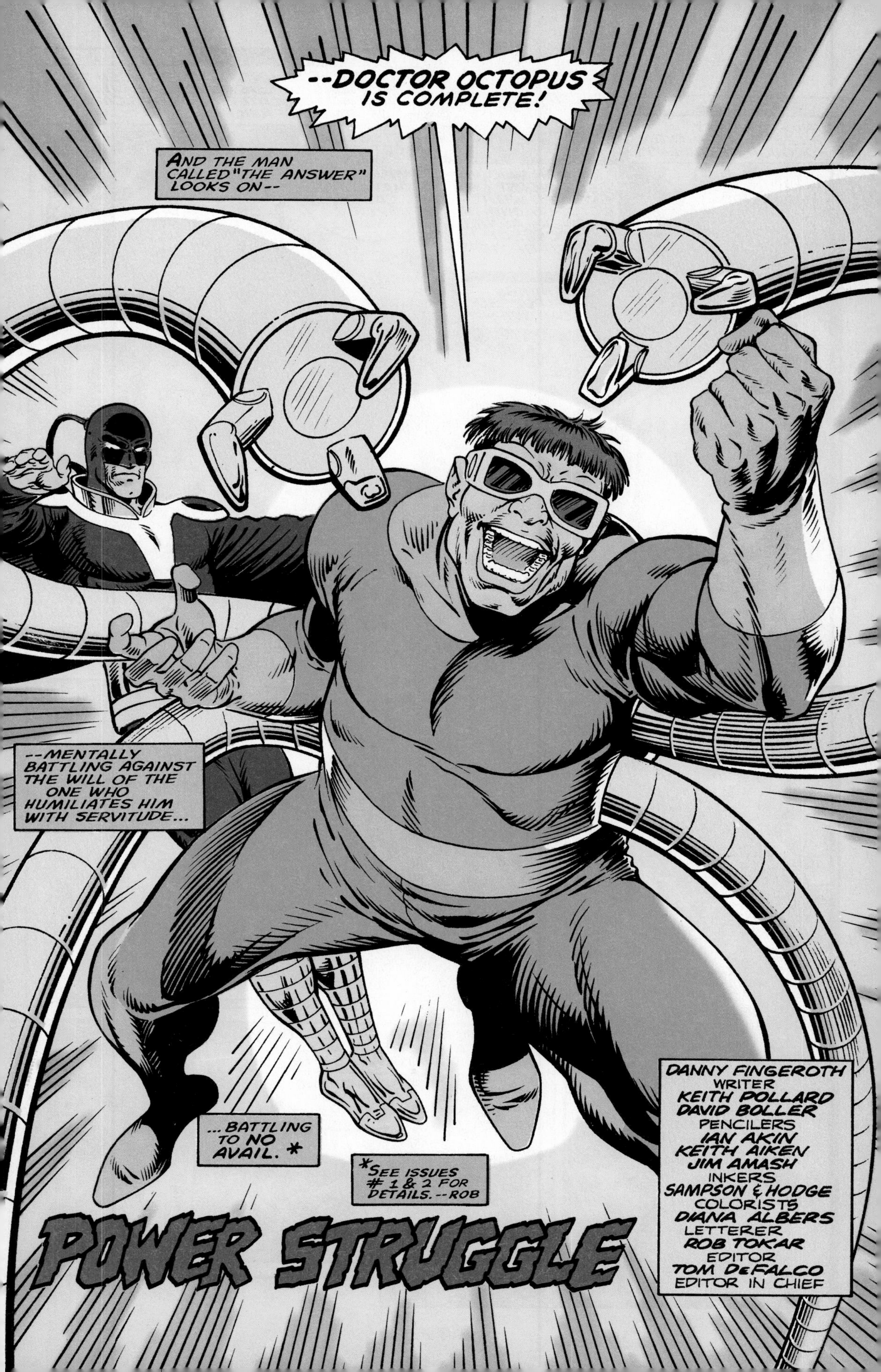
--DOCTOR OCTOPUS IS COMPLETE!
AND THE MAN CALLED "THE ANSWER" LOOKS ON--
--MENTALLY BATTLING AGAINST THE WILL OF THE ONE WHO HUMILIATES HIM WITH SERVITUDE...
...BATTLING TO NO AVAIL. *
*SEE ISSUES #1 & 2 FOR DETAILS.--ROB
POWER STRUGGLE
DANNY FINGEROTH WRITER
KEITH POLLARD DAVID BOLLER PENCILERS
IAN AKIN KEITH AIKEN JIM AMASH INKERS
SAMPSON & HODGE COLORISTS
DIANA ALBERS LETTERER
ROB TOKAR EDITOR
TOM DeFALCO EDITOR IN CHIEF

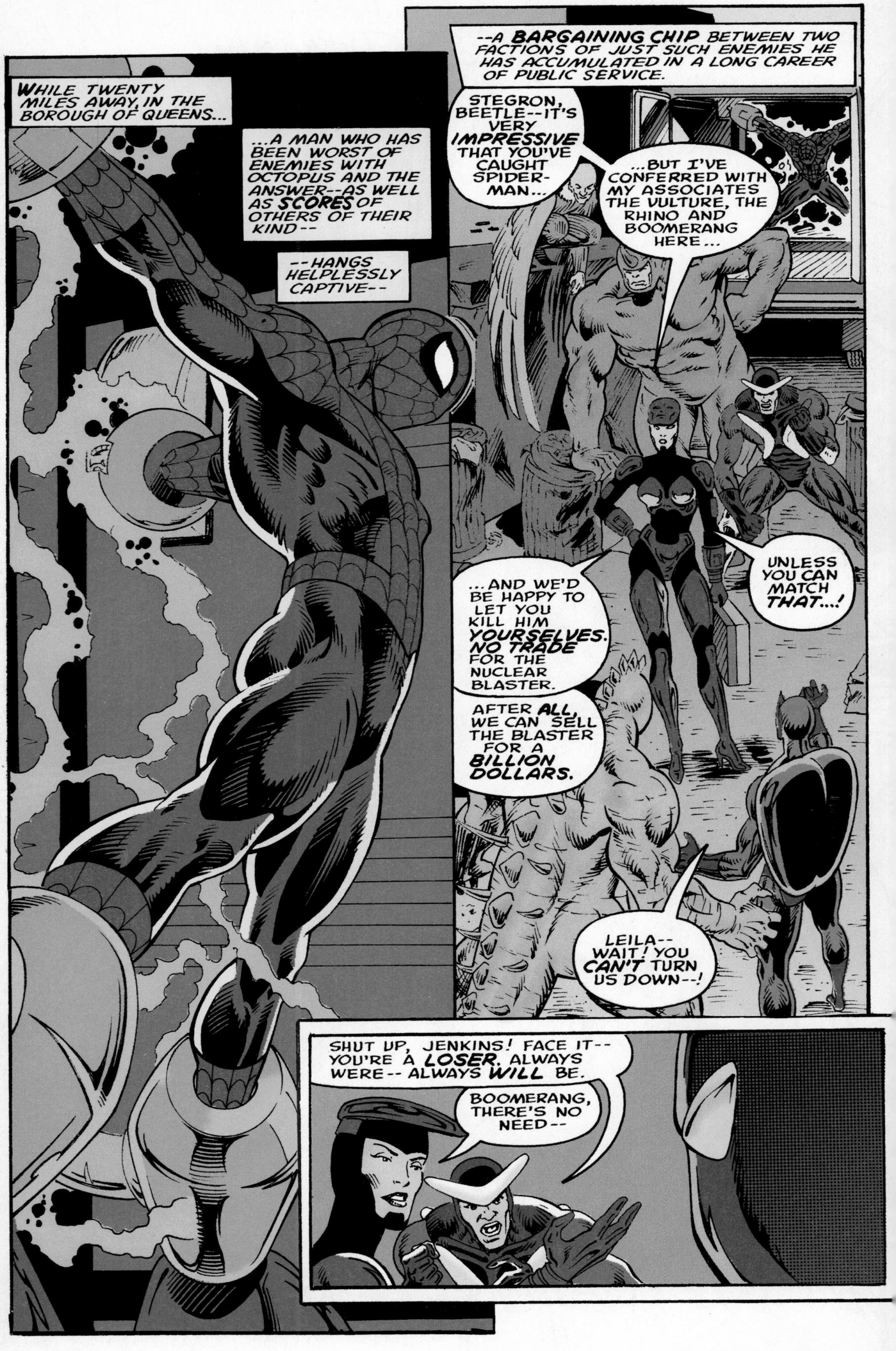
WHILE TWENTY MILES AWAY, IN THE BOROUGH OF QUEENS...
...A MAN WHO HAS BEEN WORST OF ENEMIES WITH OCTOPUS AND THE ANSWER--AS WELL AS SCORES OF OTHERS OF THEIR KIND--
--HANGS HELPLESSLY CAPTIVE--
--A BARGAINING CHIP BETWEEN TWO FACTIONS OF JUST SUCH ENEMIES HE HAS ACCUMULATED IN A LONG CAREER OF PUBLIC SERVICE.
STEGRON, BEETLE--IT'S VERY IMPRESSIVE THAT YOU'VE CAUGHT SPIDER-MAN...
...BUT I'VE CONFERRED WITH MY ASSOCIATES THE VULTURE, THE RHINO AND BOOMERANG HERE...
...AND WE'D BE HAPPY TO LET YOU KILL HIM YOURSELVES. NO TRADE FOR THE NUCLEAR BLASTER.
AFTER ALL, WE CAN SELL THE BLASTER FOR A BILLION DOLLARS.
UNLESS YOU CAN MATCH THAT...!
LEILA--WAIT! YOU CAN'T TURN US DOWN--!
SHUT UP, JENKINS! FACE IT--YOU'RE A LOSER. ALWAYS WERE--ALWAYS WILL BE.
BOOMERANG, THERE'S NO NEED--

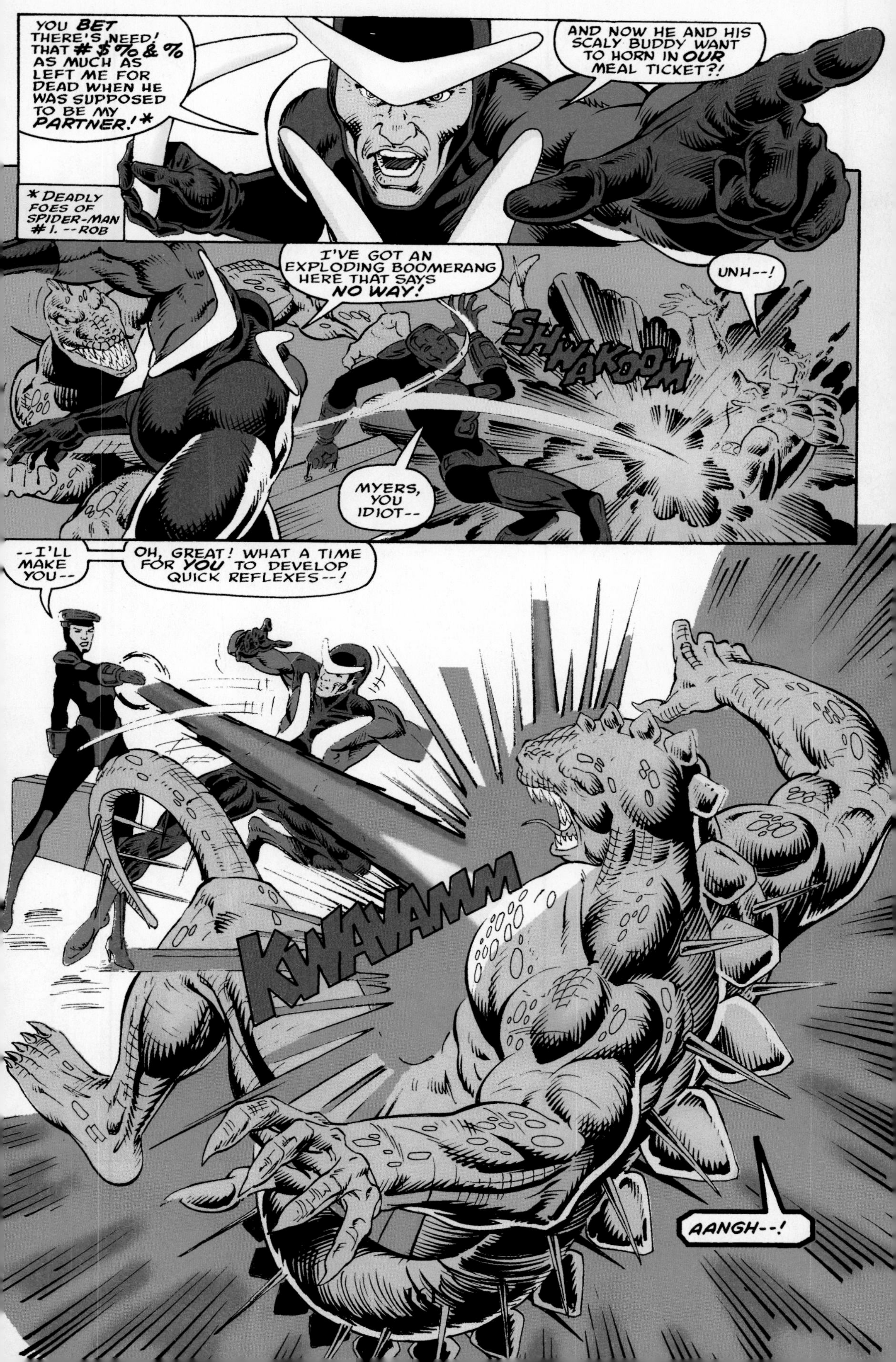

YOU BET THERE'S NEED! THAT #$%&% AS MUCH AS LEFT ME FOR DEAD WHEN HE WAS SUPPOSED TO BE MY PARTNER!*
AND NOW HE AND HIS SCALY BUDDY WANT TO HORN IN OUR MEAL TICKET?!
* DEADLY FOES OF SPIDER-MAN #1. --ROB
I'VE GOT AN EXPLODING BOOMERANG HERE THAT SAYS NO WAY!
UNH--!
SHWAKOOM
MYERS, YOU IDIOT--
--I'LL MAKE YOU--
OH, GREAT! WHAT A TIME FOR YOU TO DEVELOP QUICK REFLEXES--!
KWAVAMM
AANGH--!

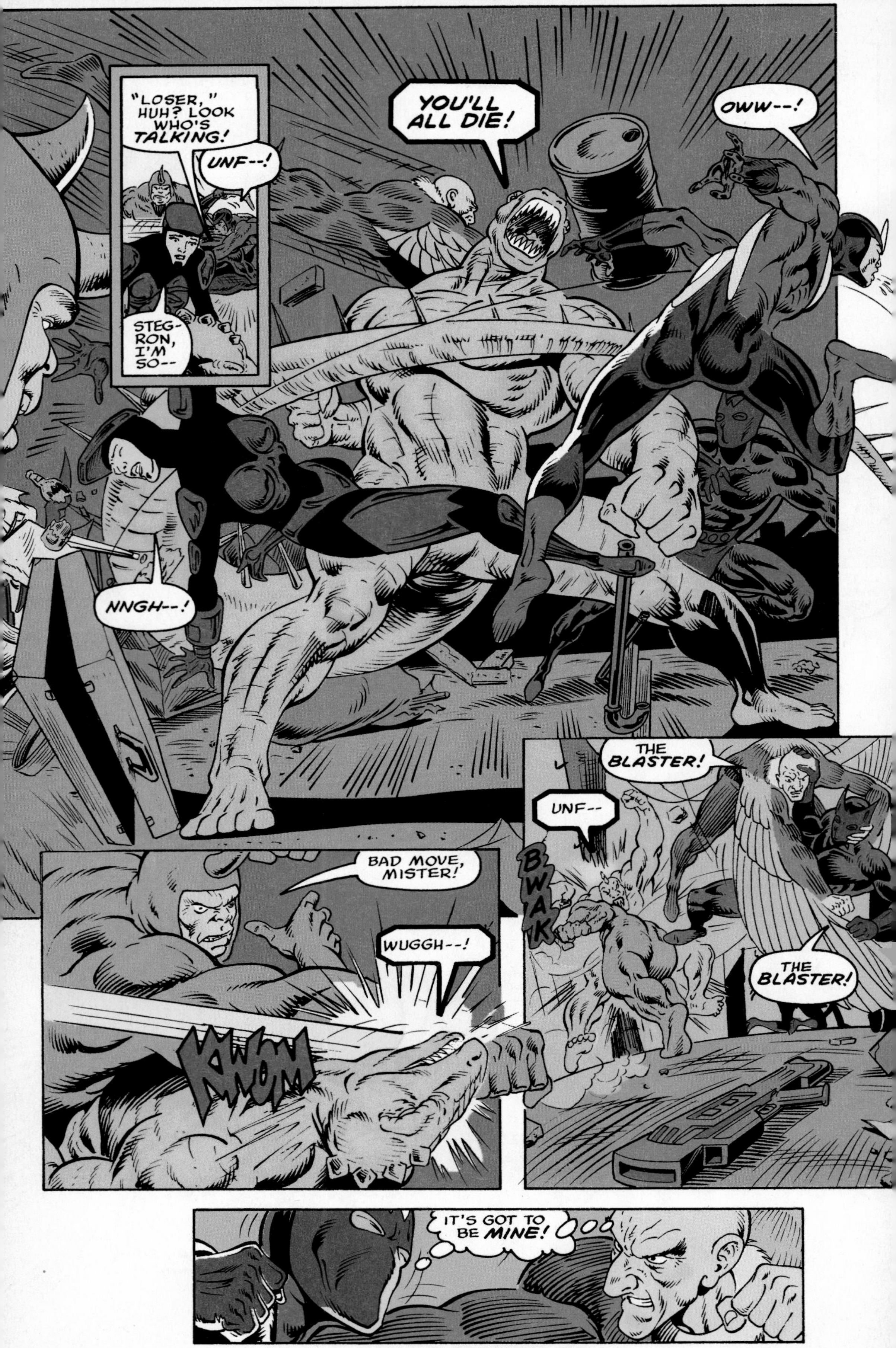
"LOSER," HUH? LOOK WHO'S TALKING!
UNF--!
STEG-RON, I'M SO--
YOU'LL ALL DIE!
OWW--!
NNGH--!
BAD MOVE, MISTER!
WUGGH--!
KWOM
THE BLASTER!
UNF--
BWAK
THE BLASTER!
IT'S GOT TO BE MINE!

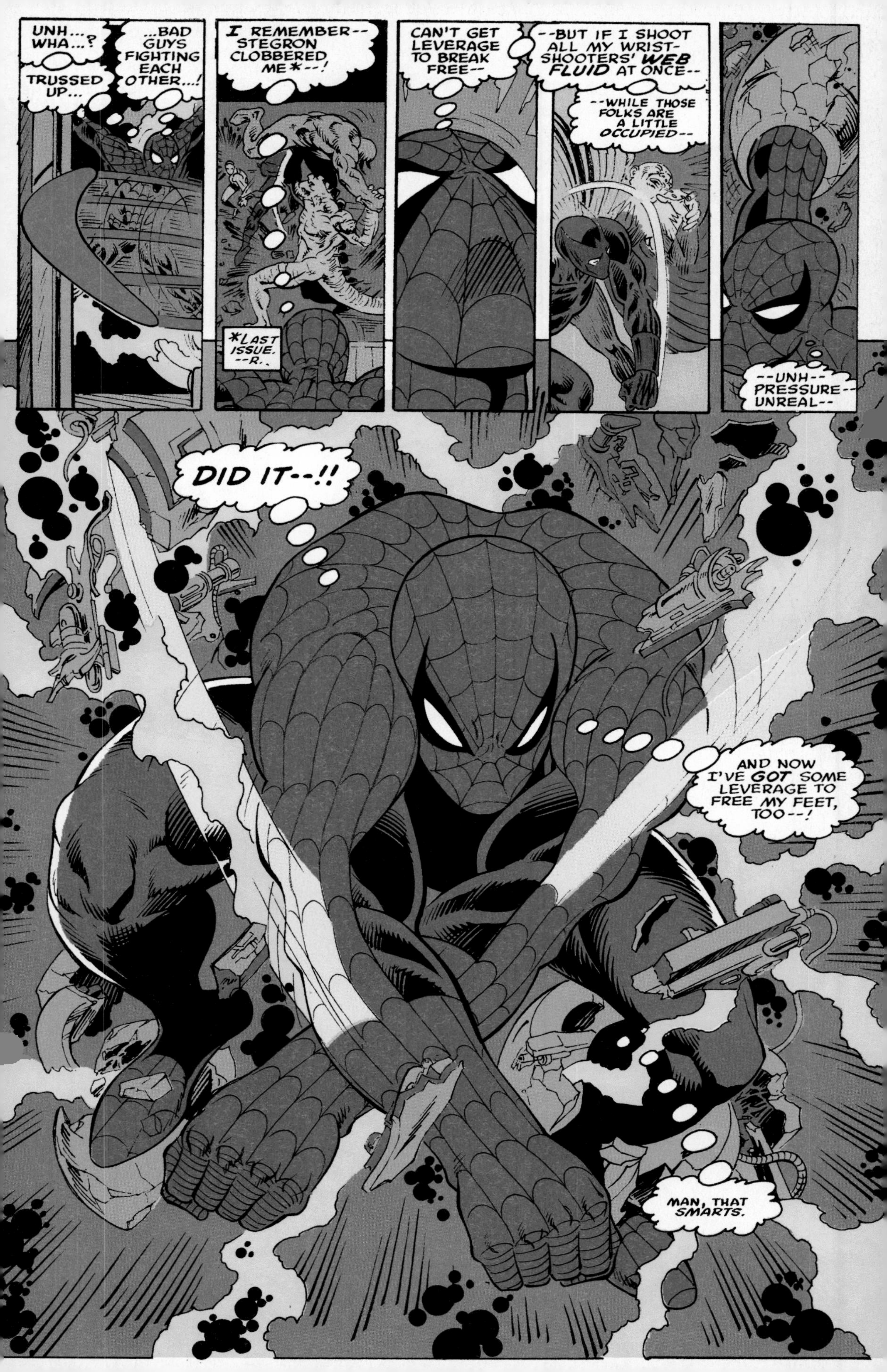

UNH... WHA...?
TRUSSED UP...
...BAD GUYS FIGHTING EACH OTHER...!
I REMEMBER-- STEGRON CLOBBERED ME*--!
*LAST ISSUE. --R.
CAN'T GET LEVERAGE TO BREAK FREE--
--BUT IF I SHOOT ALL MY WRIST-SHOOTERS' WEB FLUID AT ONCE--
--WHILE THOSE FOLKS ARE A LITTLE OCCUPIED--
--UNH--PRESSURE--UNREAL--
DID IT--!!
AND NOW I'VE GOT SOME LEVERAGE TO FREE MY FEET, TOO--!
MAN, THAT SMARTS.

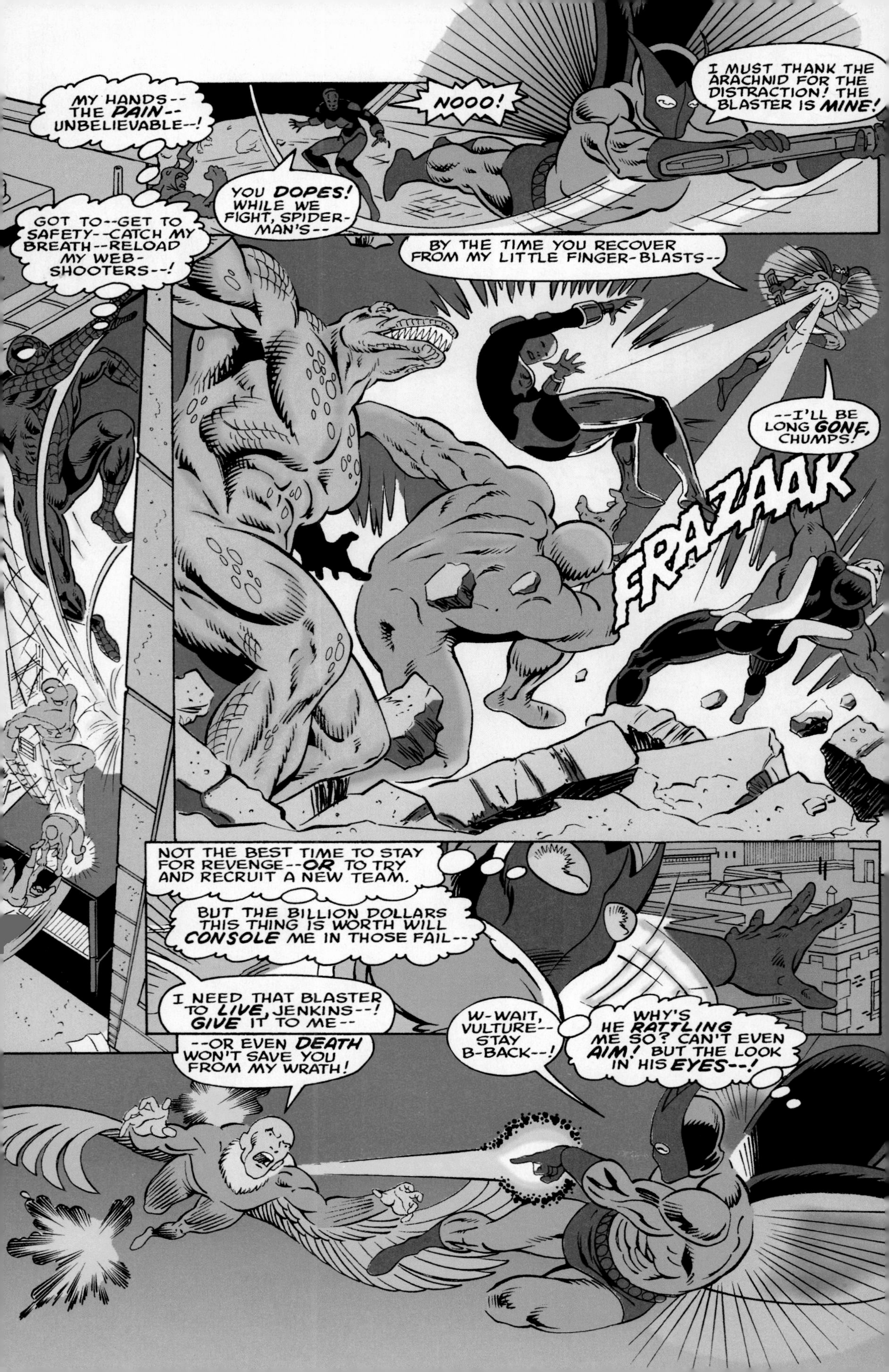
MY HANDS-- THE PAIN-- UNBELIEVABLE--!
NOOO!
I MUST THANK THE ARACHNID FOR THE DISTRACTION! THE BLASTER IS MINE!
YOU DOPES! WHILE WE FIGHT, SPIDER-MAN'S--
GOT TO--GET TO SAFETY--CATCH MY BREATH--RELOAD MY WEB-SHOOTERS--!
BY THE TIME YOU RECOVER FROM MY LITTLE FINGER-BLASTS--
--I'LL BE LONG GONE, CHUMPS!
FRAZAAK
NOT THE BEST TIME TO STAY FOR REVENGE--OR TO TRY AND RECRUIT A NEW TEAM.
BUT THE BILLION DOLLARS THIS THING IS WORTH WILL CONSOLE ME IN THOSE FAIL--
I NEED THAT BLASTER TO LIVE, JENKINS--! GIVE IT TO ME--
--OR EVEN DEATH WON'T SAVE YOU FROM MY WRATH!
W-WAIT, VULTURE-- STAY B-BACK--!
WHY'S HE RATTLING ME SO? CAN'T EVEN AIM! BUT THE LOOK IN HIS EYES--!

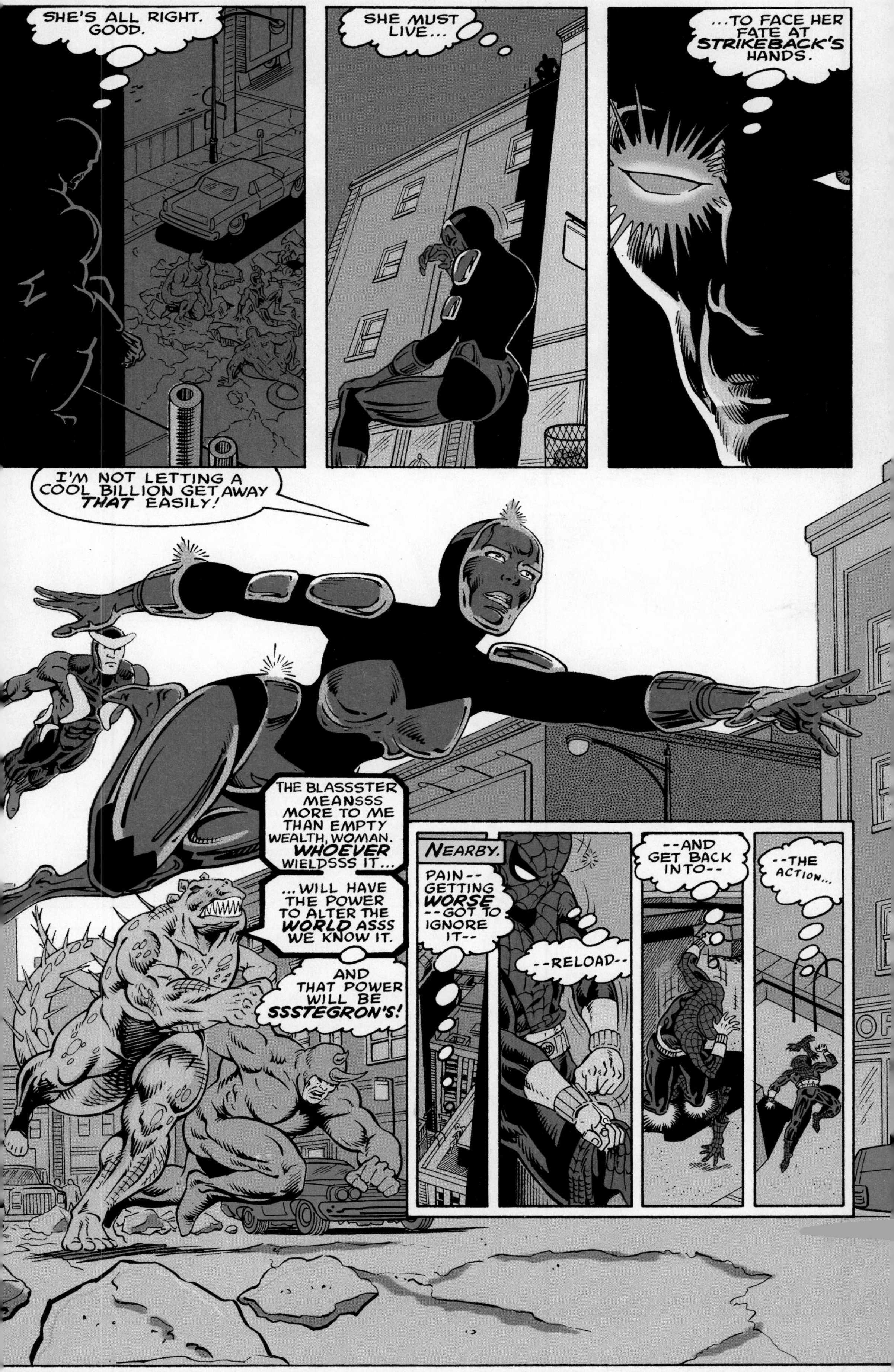
SHE'S ALL RIGHT. GOOD.
SHE MUST LIVE...
...TO FACE HER FATE AT STRIKEBACK'S HANDS.
I'M NOT LETTING A COOL BILLION GET AWAY THAT EASILY!
THE BLASSSTER MEANSSS MORE TO ME THAN EMPTY WEALTH, WOMAN. WHOEVER WIELDSSS IT...
...WILL HAVE THE POWER TO ALTER THE WORLD ASSS WE KNOW IT.
AND THAT POWER WILL BE SSSTEGRON'S!
NEARBY.
PAIN--GETTING WORSE--GOT TO IGNORE IT--
--RELOAD--
--AND GET BACK INTO--
--THE ACTION...

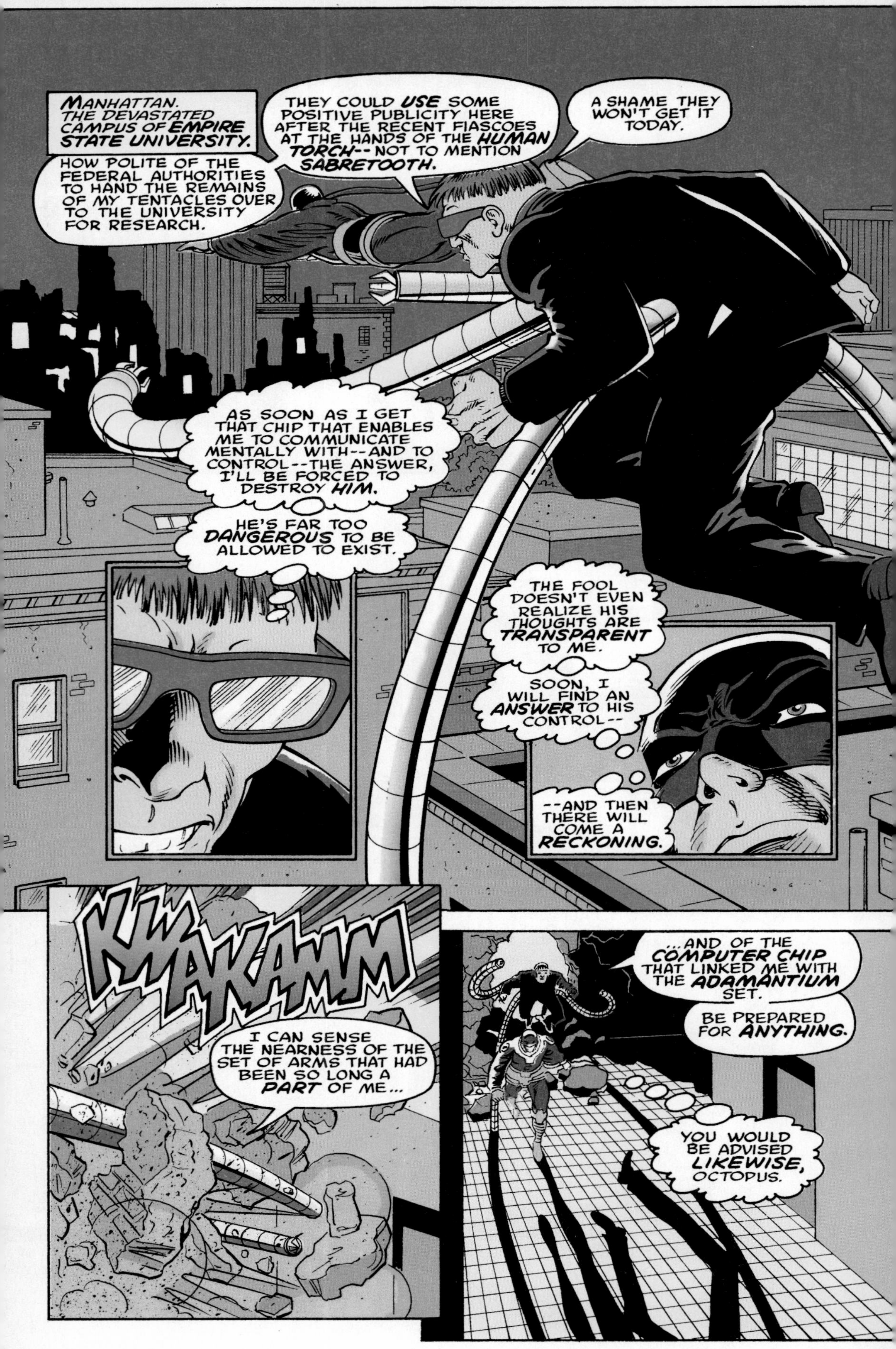
MANHATTAN. THE DEVASTATED CAMPUS OF EMPIRE STATE UNIVERSITY.
HOW POLITE OF THE FEDERAL AUTHORITIES TO HAND THE REMAINS OF MY TENTACLES OVER TO THE UNIVERSITY FOR RESEARCH.
THEY COULD USE SOME POSITIVE PUBLICITY HERE AFTER THE RECENT FIASCOES AT THE HANDS OF THE HUMAN TORCH--NOT TO MENTION SABRETOOTH.
A SHAME THEY WON'T GET IT TODAY.
AS SOON AS I GET THAT CHIP THAT ENABLES ME TO COMMUNICATE MENTALLY WITH--AND TO CONTROL--THE ANSWER, I'LL BE FORCED TO DESTROY HIM.
HE'S FAR TOO DANGEROUS TO BE ALLOWED TO EXIST.
THE FOOL DOESN'T EVEN REALIZE HIS THOUGHTS ARE TRANSPARENT TO ME.
SOON, I WILL FIND AN ANSWER TO HIS CONTROL--
--AND THEN THERE WILL COME A RECKONING.
KWAKAMM
I CAN SENSE THE NEARNESS OF THE SET OF ARMS THAT HAD BEEN SO LONG A PART OF ME...
...AND OF THE COMPUTER CHIP THAT LINKED ME WITH THE ADAMANTIUM SET.
BE PREPARED FOR ANYTHING.
YOU WOULD BE ADVISED LIKEWISE, OCTOPUS.

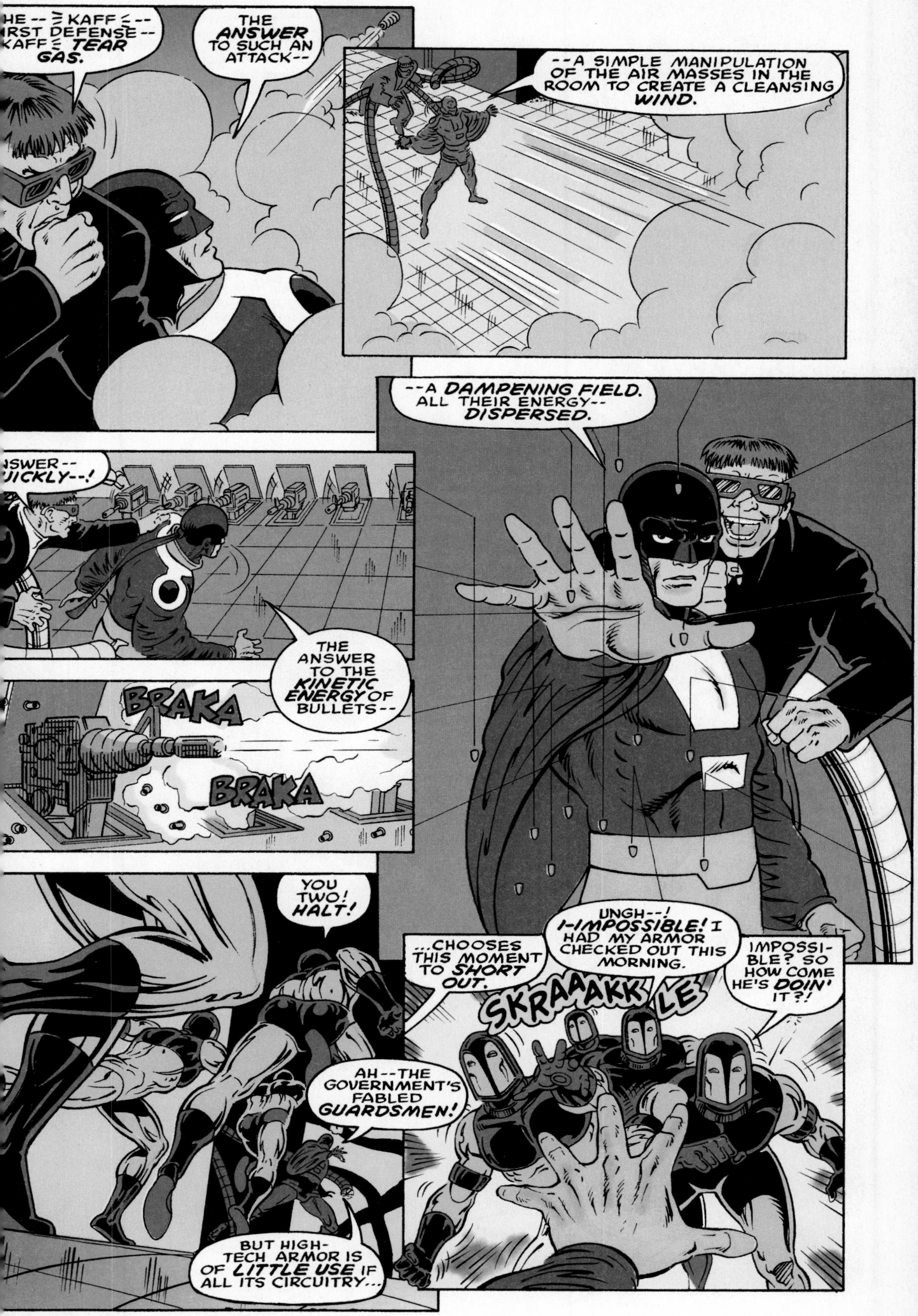

HE -- KAFF -- IRST DEFENSE -- KAFF TEAR GAS.
THE ANSWER TO SUCH AN ATTACK--
--A SIMPLE MANIPULATION OF THE AIR MASSES IN THE ROOM TO CREATE A CLEANSING WIND.
NSWER -- UICKLY--!
THE ANSWER TO THE KINETIC ENERGY OF BULLETS--
BRAKA
BRAKA
--A DAMPENING FIELD. ALL THEIR ENERGY-- DISPERSED.
YOU TWO! HALT!
AH--THE GOVERNMENT'S FABLED GUARDSMEN!
BUT HIGH-TECH ARMOR IS OF LITTLE USE IF ALL ITS CIRCUITRY...
...CHOOSES THIS MOMENT TO SHORT OUT.
UNGH--! I-IMPOSSIBLE! I HAD MY ARMOR CHECKED OUT THIS MORNING.
IMPOSSI-BLE? SO HOW COME HE'S DOIN' IT?!
SKRAAAKKLE

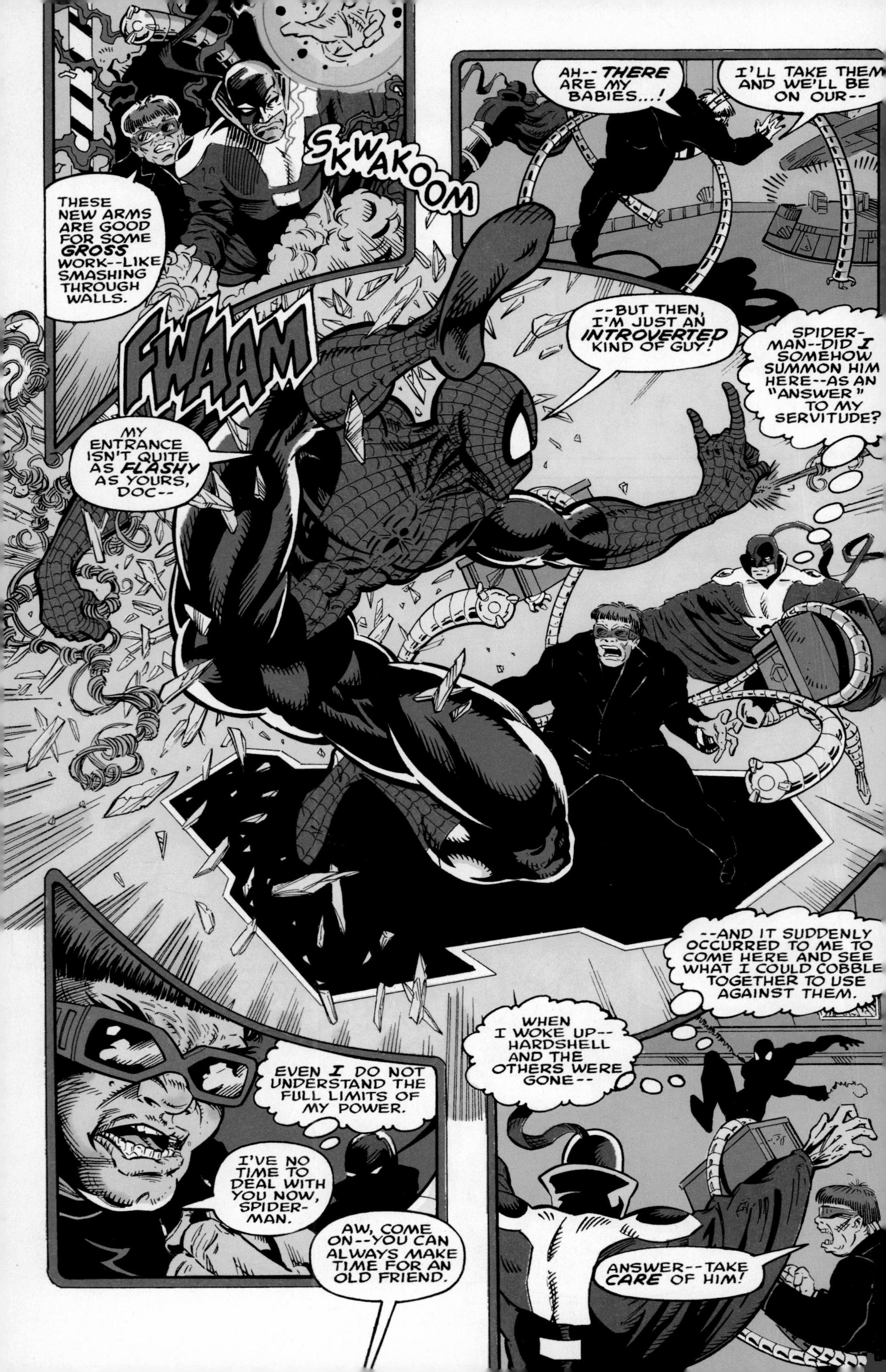
SKWAKOOM
THESE NEW ARMS ARE GOOD FOR SOME GROSS WORK--LIKE SMASHING THROUGH WALLS.
AH-- THERE ARE MY BABIES...!
I'LL TAKE THEM AND WE'LL BE ON OUR--
FWAAM
MY ENTRANCE ISN'T QUITE AS FLASHY AS YOURS, DOC--
--BUT THEN, I'M JUST AN INTROVERTED KIND OF GUY!
SPIDER-MAN--DID I SOMEHOW SUMMON HIM HERE--AS AN "ANSWER" TO MY SERVITUDE?
--AND IT SUDDENLY OCCURRED TO ME TO COME HERE AND SEE WHAT I COULD COBBLE TOGETHER TO USE AGAINST THEM.
WHEN I WOKE UP-- HARDSHELL AND THE OTHERS WERE GONE--
EVEN I DO NOT UNDERSTAND THE FULL LIMITS OF MY POWER.
I'VE NO TIME TO DEAL WITH YOU NOW, SPIDER-MAN.
AW, COME ON--YOU CAN ALWAYS MAKE TIME FOR AN OLD FRIEND.
ANSWER--TAKE CARE OF HIM!

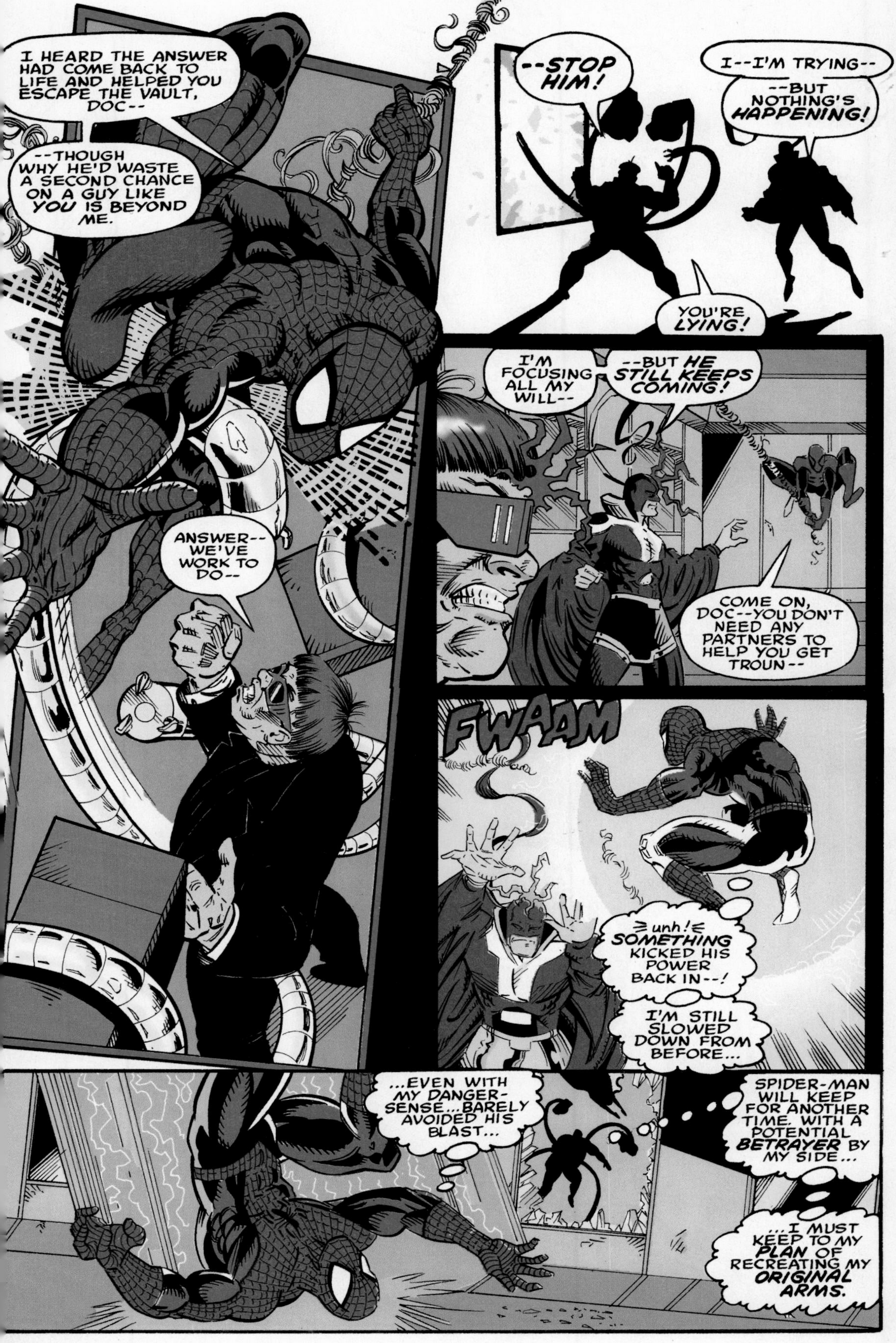

I HEARD THE ANSWER HAD COME BACK TO LIFE AND HELPED YOU ESCAPE THE VAULT, DOC--
--THOUGH WHY HE'D WASTE A SECOND CHANCE ON A GUY LIKE YOU IS BEYOND ME.
ANSWER-- WE'VE WORK TO DO--
--STOP HIM!
I--I'M TRYING--
--BUT NOTHING'S HAPPENING!
YOU'RE LYING!
I'M FOCUSING ALL MY WILL--
--BUT HE STILL KEEPS COMING!
COME ON, DOC--YOU DON'T NEED ANY PARTNERS TO HELP YOU GET TROUN--
FWAAM
unh! SOMETHING KICKED HIS POWER BACK IN--!
I'M STILL SLOWED DOWN FROM BEFORE...
...EVEN WITH MY DANGER-SENSE...BARELY AVOIDED HIS BLAST...
SPIDER-MAN WILL KEEP FOR ANOTHER TIME. WITH A POTENTIAL BETRAYER BY MY SIDE...
...I MUST KEEP TO MY PLAN OF RECREATING MY ORIGINAL ARMS.

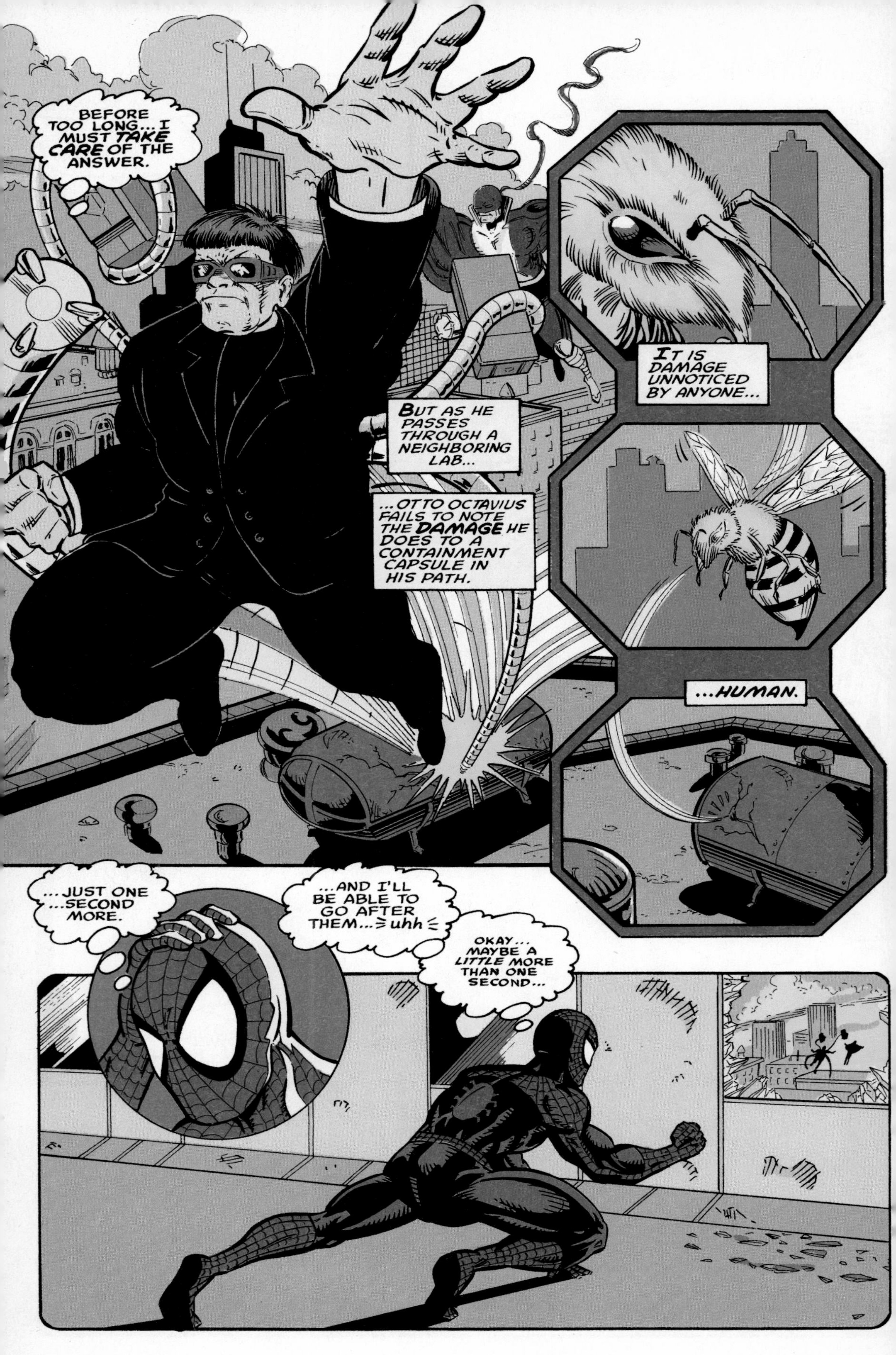
BEFORE TOO LONG... I MUST TAKE CARE OF THE ANSWER.
BUT AS HE PASSES THROUGH A NEIGHBORING LAB...
...OTTO OCTAVIUS FAILS TO NOTE THE DAMAGE HE DOES TO A CONTAINMENT CAPSULE IN HIS PATH.
IT IS DAMAGE UNNOTICED BY ANYONE...
...HUMAN.
...JUST ONE ...SECOND MORE.
...AND I'LL BE ABLE TO GO AFTER THEM... uhh
OKAY... MAYBE A LITTLE MORE THAN ONE SECOND...

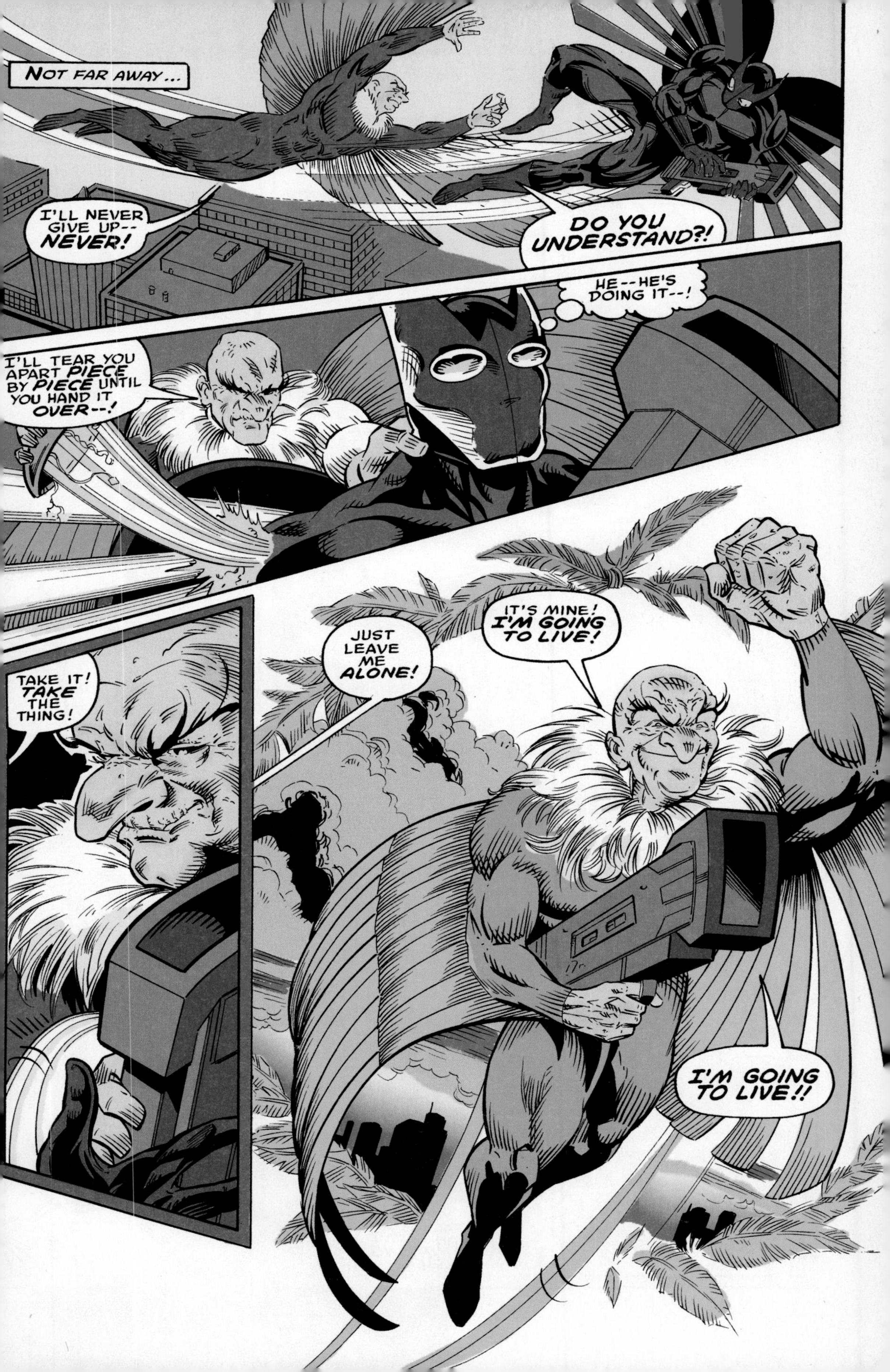
NOT FAR AWAY...
I'LL NEVER GIVE UP-- NEVER!
DO YOU UNDERSTAND?!
HE--HE'S DOING IT--!
I'LL TEAR YOU APART PIECE BY PIECE UNTIL YOU HAND IT OVER--!
TAKE IT! TAKE THE THING!
JUST LEAVE ME ALONE!
IT'S MINE! I'M GOING TO LIVE!
I'M GOING TO LIVE!!

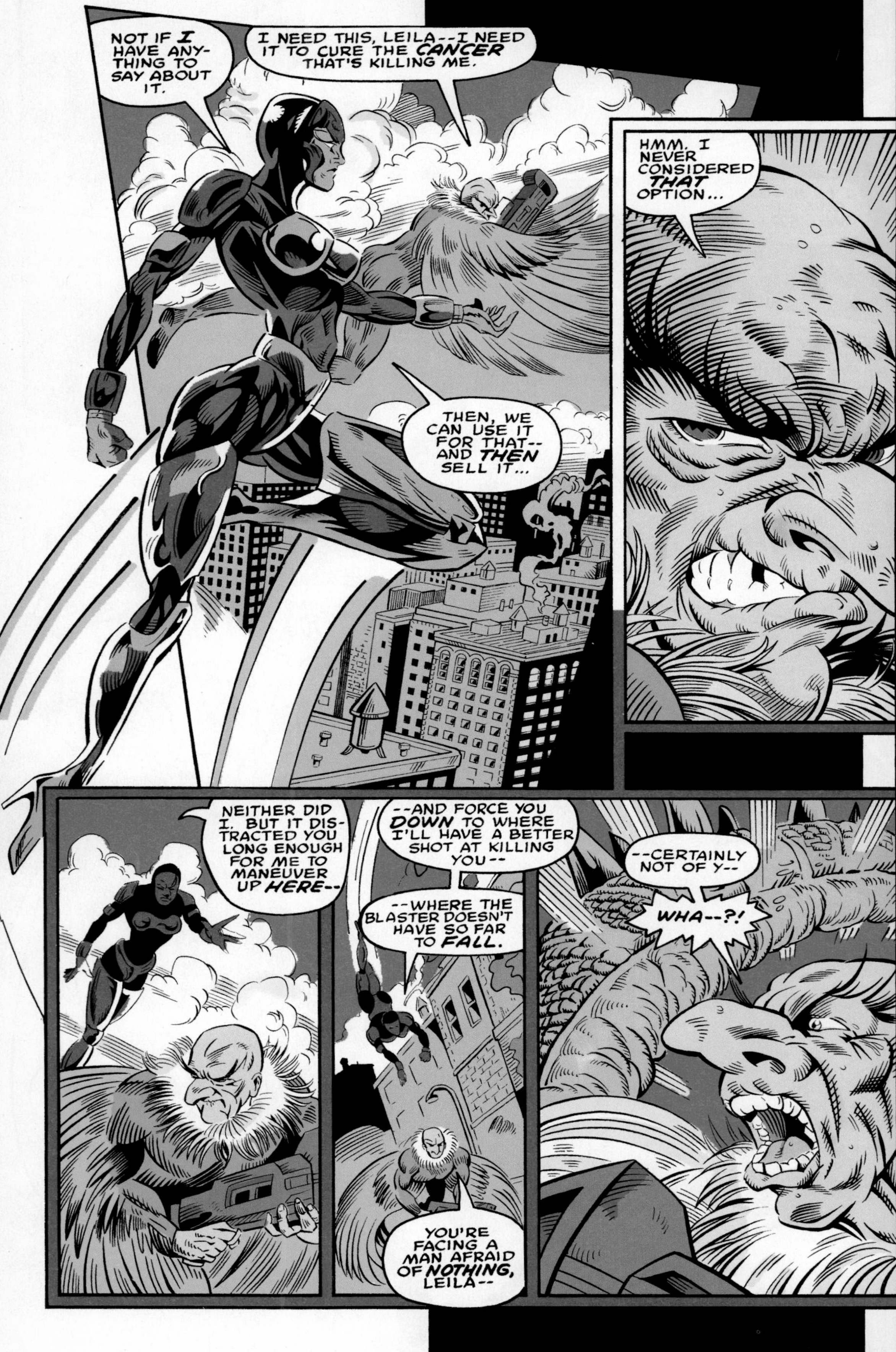

NOT IF *I* HAVE ANYTHING TO SAY ABOUT IT.
I NEED THIS, LEILA--I NEED IT TO CURE THE *CANCER* THAT'S KILLING ME.
THEN, WE CAN USE IT FOR THAT--AND *THEN* SELL IT...
HMM. I NEVER CONSIDERED *THAT* OPTION...
NEITHER DID I. BUT IT DISTRACTED YOU LONG ENOUGH FOR ME TO MANEUVER UP *HERE*--
--AND FORCE YOU *DOWN* TO WHERE I'LL HAVE A BETTER SHOT AT KILLING YOU--
--WHERE THE BLASTER DOESN'T HAVE SO FAR TO *FALL*.
YOU'RE FACING A MAN AFRAID OF *NOTHING*, LEILA--
--CERTAINLY NOT OF Y--
WHA--?!

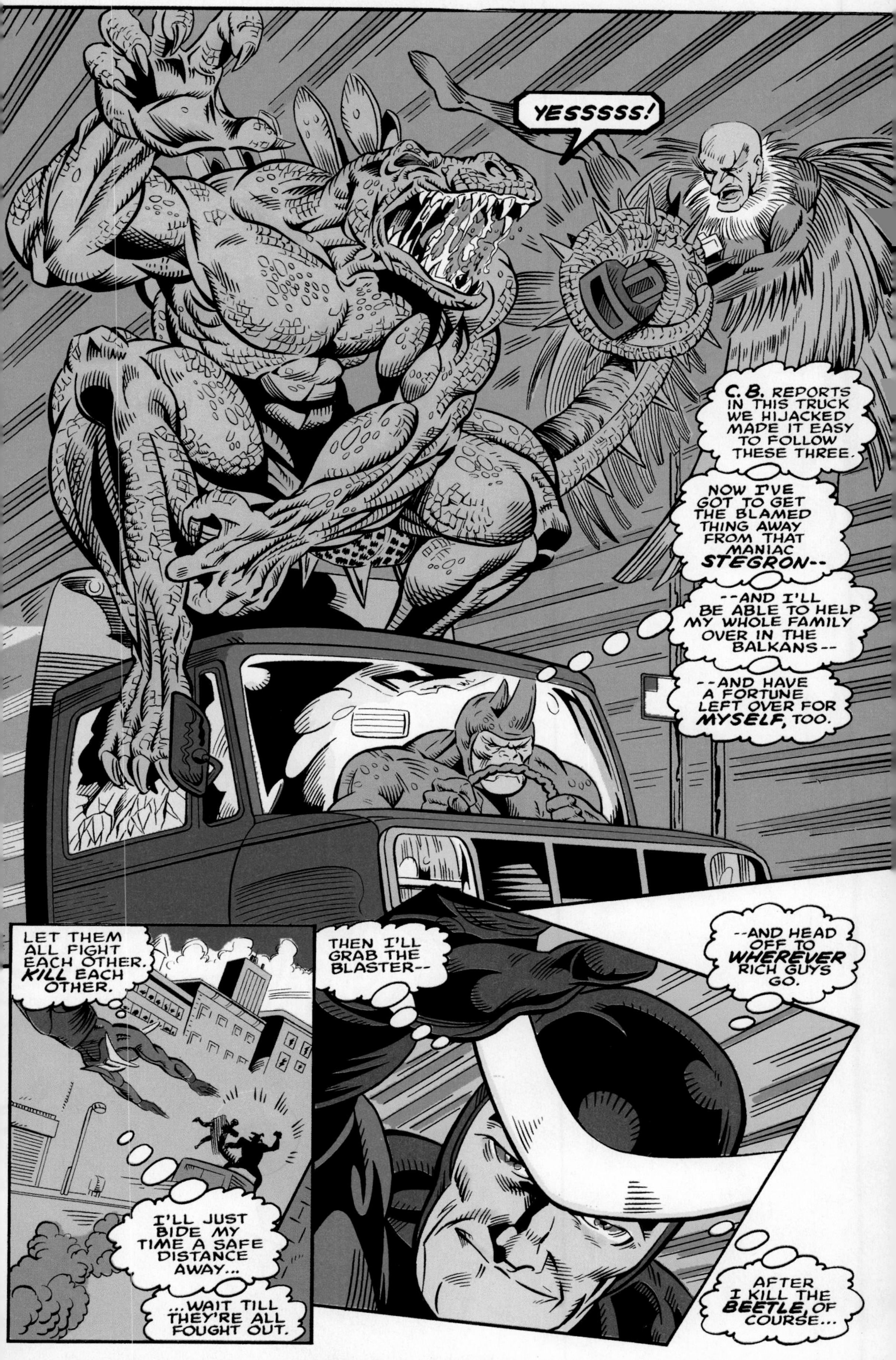
YESSSSS!
C.B. REPORTS IN THIS TRUCK WE HIJACKED MADE IT EASY TO FOLLOW THESE THREE.
NOW I'VE GOT TO GET THE BLAMED THING AWAY FROM THAT MANIAC STEGRON--
--AND I'LL BE ABLE TO HELP MY WHOLE FAMILY OVER IN THE BALKANS--
--AND HAVE A FORTUNE LEFT OVER FOR MYSELF, TOO.
LET THEM ALL FIGHT EACH OTHER. KILL EACH OTHER.
I'LL JUST BIDE MY TIME A SAFE DISTANCE AWAY...
...WAIT TILL THEY'RE ALL FOUGHT OUT.
THEN I'LL GRAB THE BLASTER--
--AND HEAD OFF TO WHEREVER RICH GUYS GO.
AFTER I KILL THE BEETLE, OF COURSE...

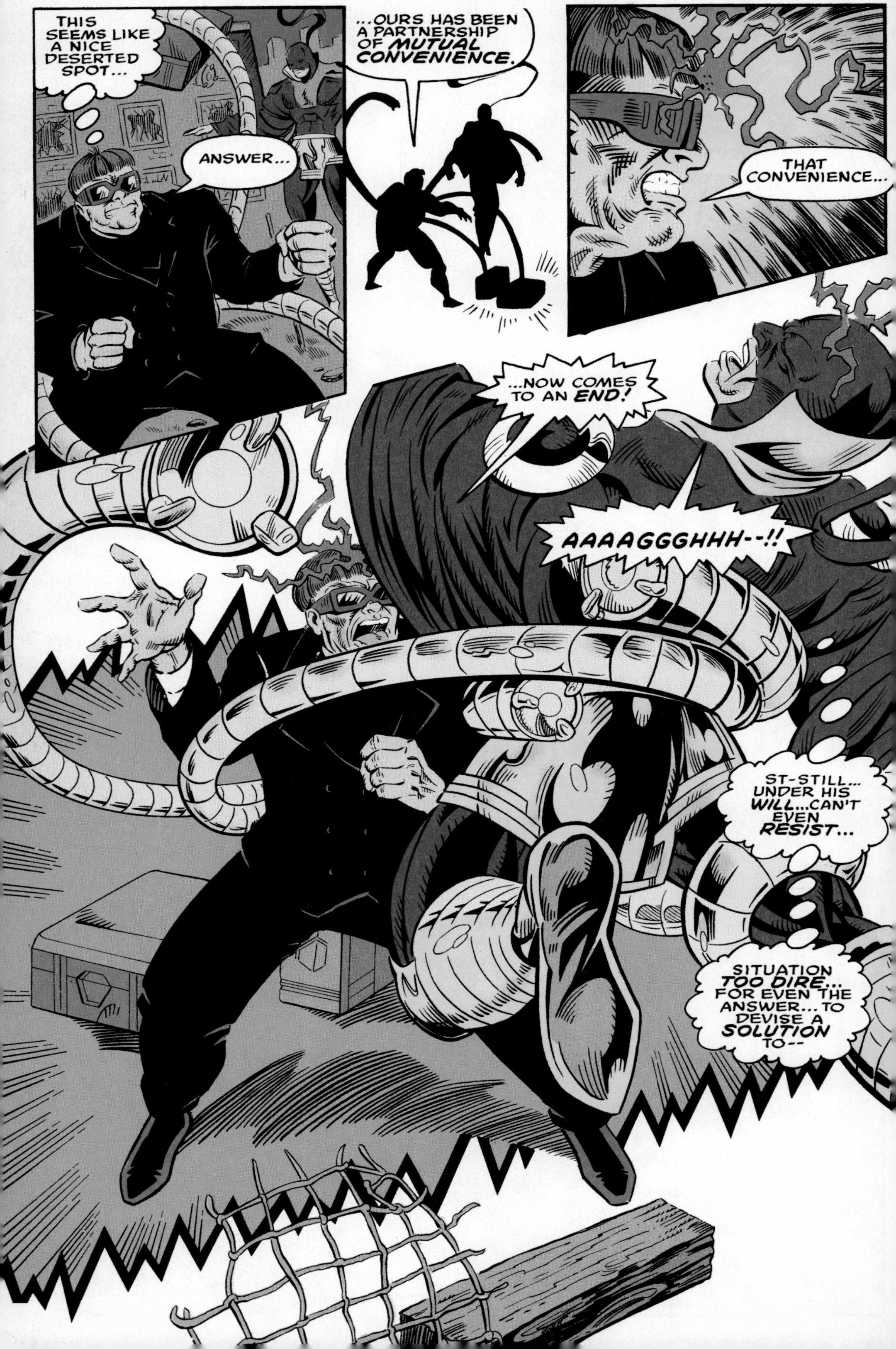
THIS SEEMS LIKE A NICE DESERTED SPOT...
ANSWER...
...OURS HAS BEEN A PARTNERSHIP OF MUTUAL CONVENIENCE.
THAT CONVENIENCE...
...NOW COMES TO AN END!
AAAAGGGHHH--!!
ST-STILL... UNDER HIS WILL...CAN'T EVEN RESIST...
SITUATION TOO DIRE... FOR EVEN THE ANSWER... TO DEVISE A SOLUTION TO--

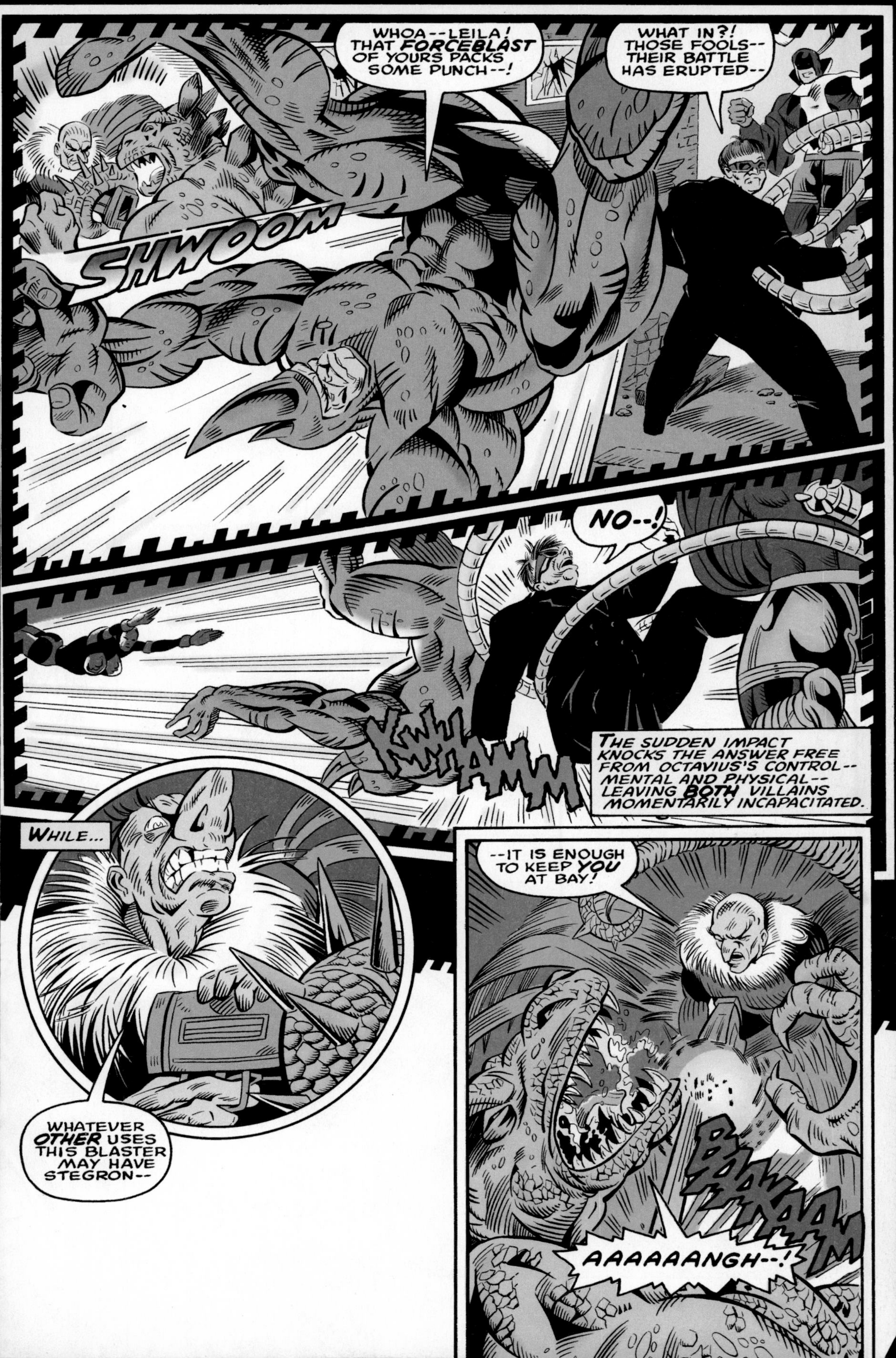
WHOA--LEILA! THAT FORCEBLAST OF YOURS PACKS SOME PUNCH--!
WHAT IN?! THOSE FOOLS-- THEIR BATTLE HAS ERUPTED--
SHWOOM
NO--!
KWHAMM
THE SUDDEN IMPACT KNOCKS THE ANSWER FREE FROM OCTAVIUS'S CONTROL-- MENTAL AND PHYSICAL-- LEAVING BOTH VILLAINS MOMENTARILY INCAPACITATED.
WHILE...
WHATEVER OTHER USES THIS BLASTER MAY HAVE STEGRON--
--IT IS ENOUGH TO KEEP YOU AT BAY!
BRAKAAM
AAAAAANGH--!

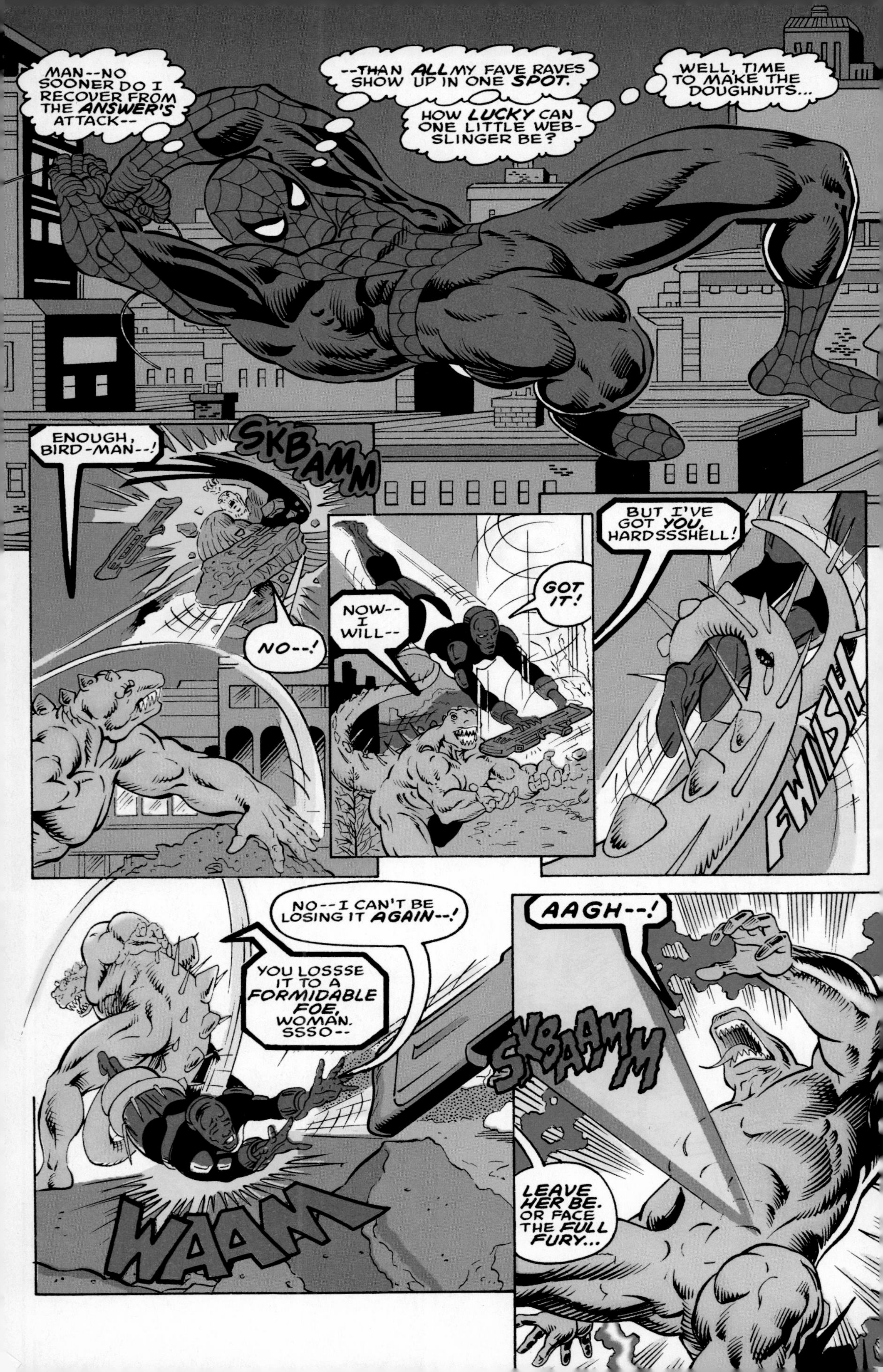
MAN--NO SOONER DO I RECOVER FROM THE ANSWER'S ATTACK--
--THAN ALL MY FAVE RAVES SHOW UP IN ONE SPOT.
HOW LUCKY CAN ONE LITTLE WEB-SLINGER BE?
WELL, TIME TO MAKE THE DOUGHNUTS...
ENOUGH, BIRD-MAN--!
SKBAMM
NO--!
NOW--I WILL--
GOT IT!
BUT I'VE GOT YOU, HARDSSSHELL!
FWISH
NO--I CAN'T BE LOSING IT AGAIN--!
YOU LOSSSE IT TO A FORMIDABLE FOE, WOMAN. SSSO--
WAAM
AAGH--!
SKBAAMM
LEAVE HER BE. OR FACE THE FULL FURY...

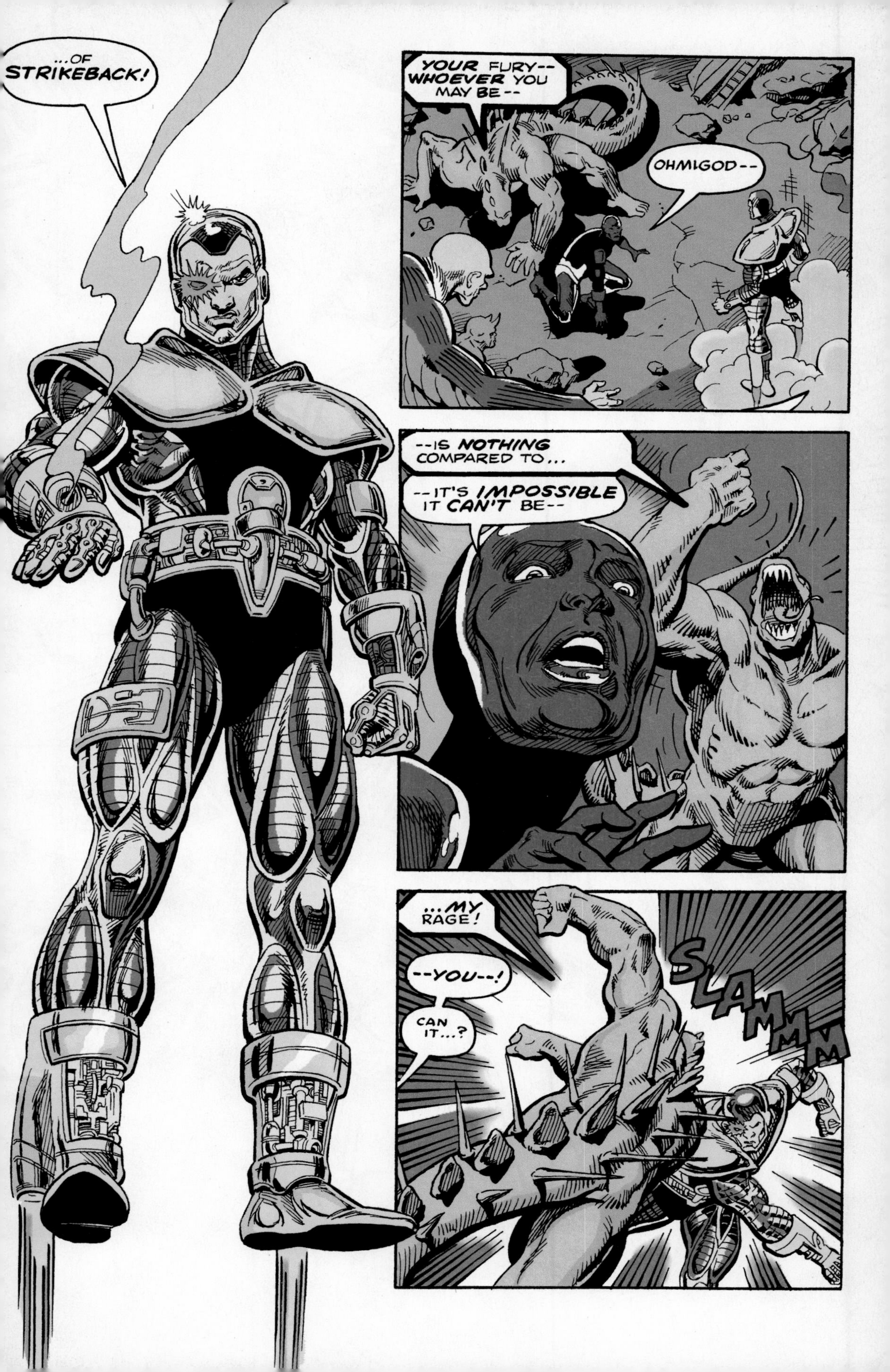
...OF STRIKEBACK!
YOUR FURY--
WHOEVER YOU MAY BE--
OHMIGOD--
--IS NOTHING COMPARED TO...
--IT'S IMPOSSIBLE
IT CAN'T BE--
...MY RAGE!
--YOU--!
CAN IT...?
SLAMMMM

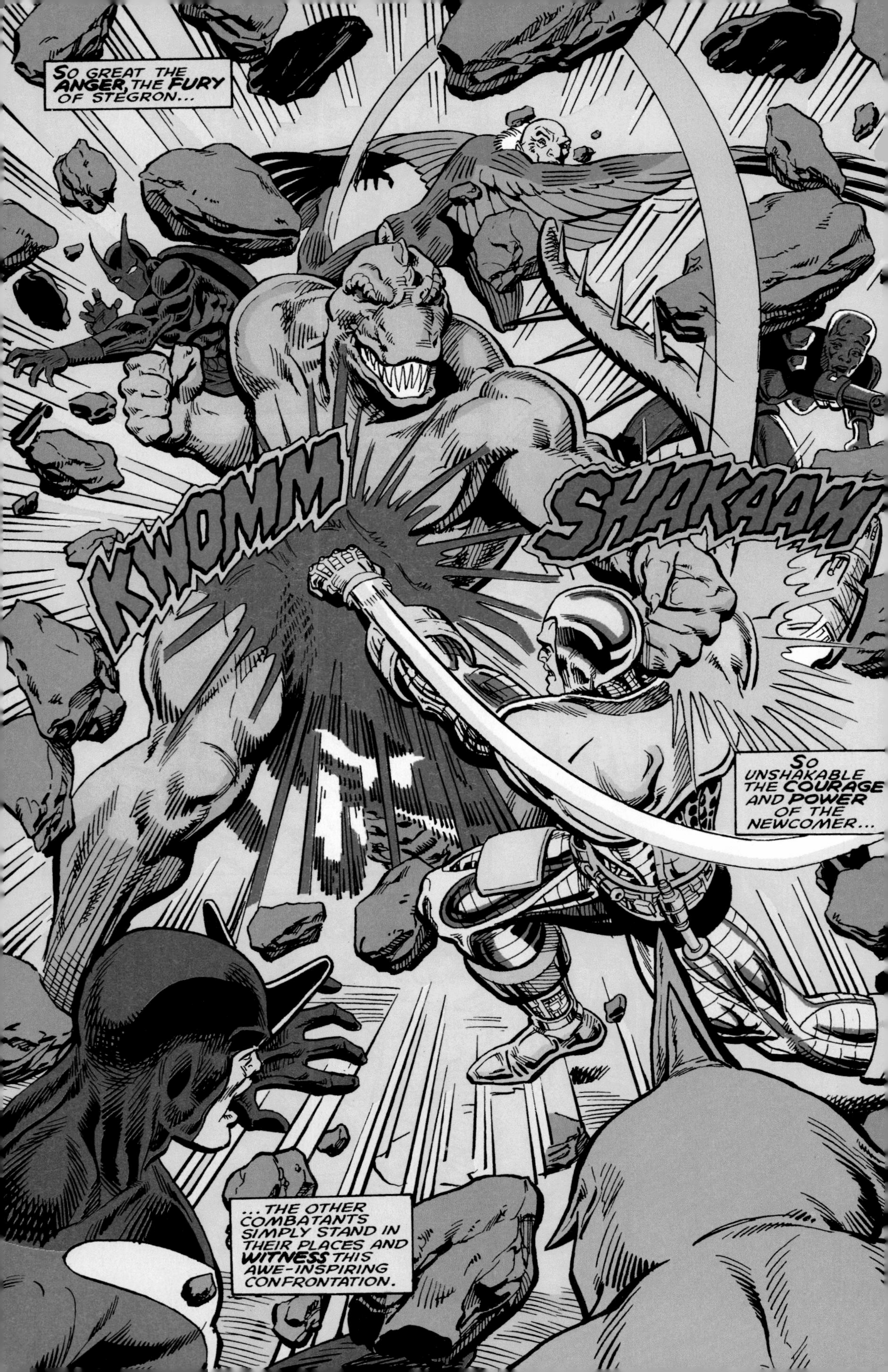
SO GREAT THE ANGER, THE FURY OF STEGRON...
KWOMM
SHAKAAM
SO UNSHAKABLE THE COURAGE AND POWER OF THE NEWCOMER...
...THE OTHER COMBATANTS SIMPLY STAND IN THEIR PLACES AND WITNESS THIS AWE-INSPIRING CONFRONTATION.

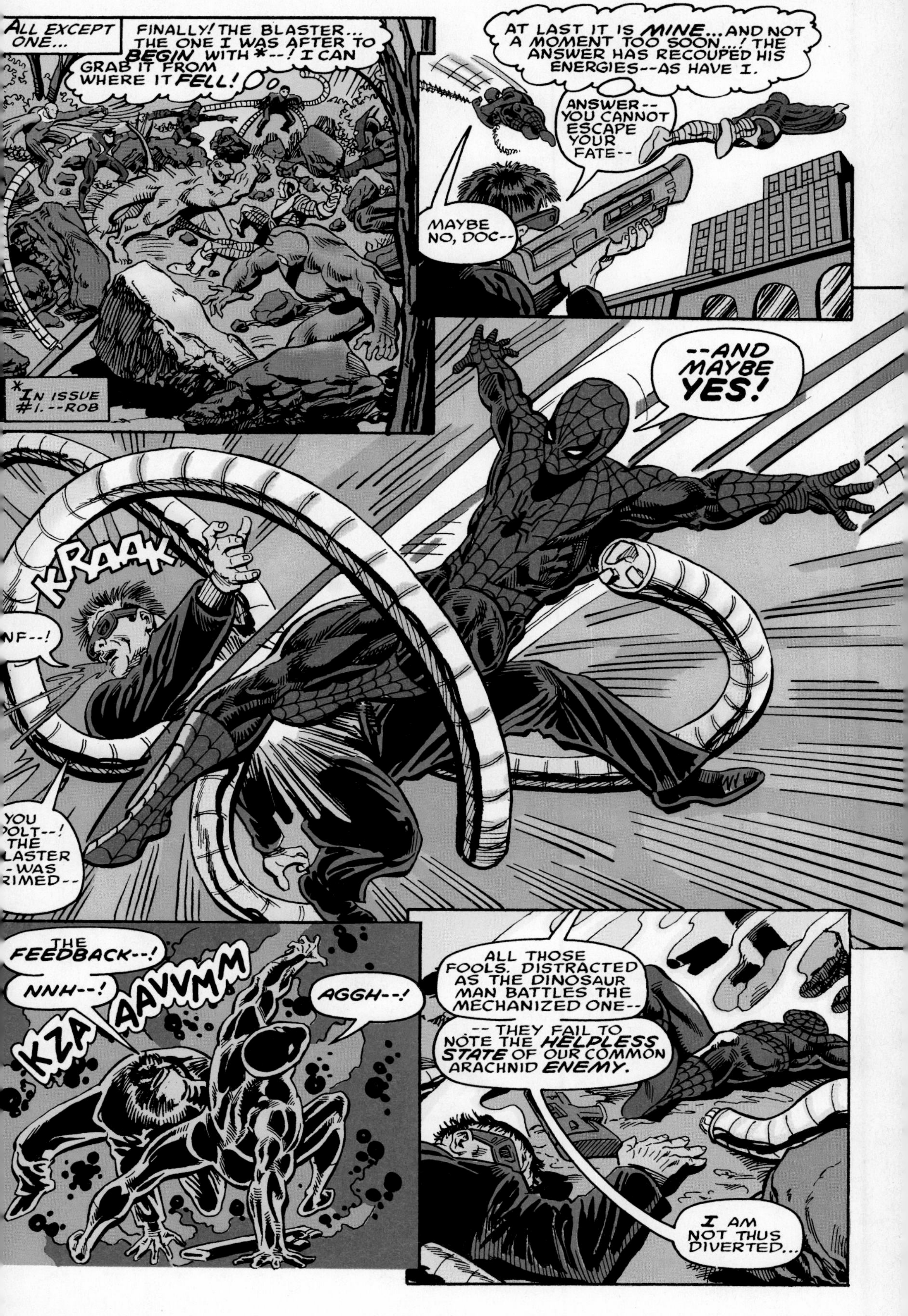
ALL EXCEPT ONE...
FINALLY! THE BLASTER... THE ONE I WAS AFTER TO BEGIN WITH*--! I CAN GRAB IT FROM WHERE IT FELL!
*IN ISSUE #1. --ROB
AT LAST IT IS MINE...AND NOT A MOMENT TOO SOON...! THE ANSWER HAS RECOUPED HIS ENERGIES--AS HAVE I.
ANSWER-- YOU CANNOT ESCAPE YOUR FATE--
MAYBE NO, DOC--
--AND MAYBE YES!
KRAAK
NF--!
YOU OLT--! THE LASTER -WAS RIMED--
THE FEEDBACK--!
NNH--!
KZA AAVVMM
AGGH--!
ALL THOSE FOOLS. DISTRACTED AS THE DINOSAUR MAN BATTLES THE MECHANIZED ONE--
--THEY FAIL TO NOTE THE HELPLESS STATE OF OUR COMMON ARACHNID ENEMY.
I AM NOT THUS DIVERTED...

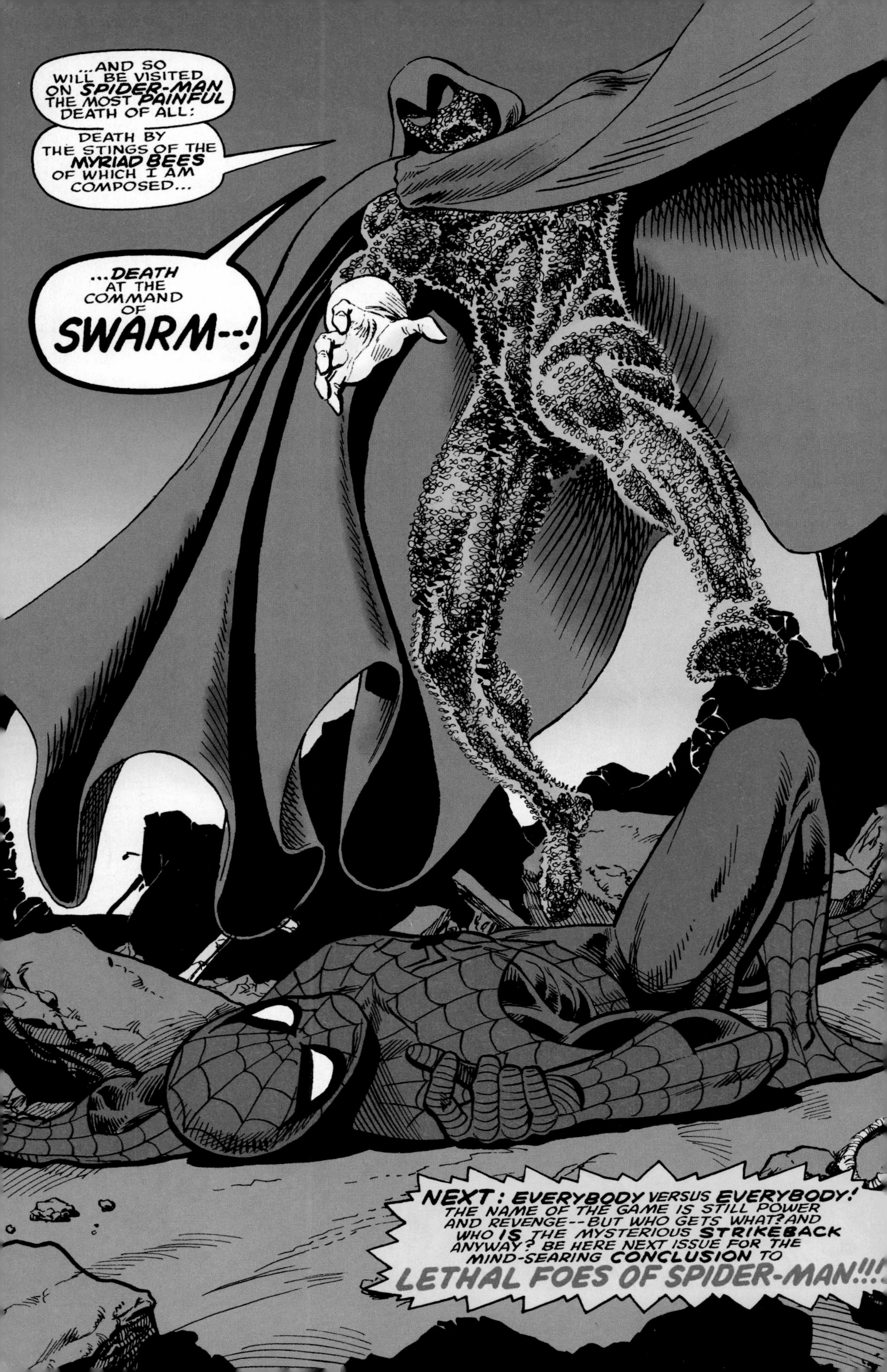
...AND SO WILL BE VISITED ON SPIDER-MAN THE MOST PAINFUL DEATH OF ALL:
DEATH BY THE STINGS OF THE MYRIAD BEES OF WHICH I AM COMPOSED...
...DEATH AT THE COMMAND OF SWARM--!
NEXT: EVERYBODY VERSUS EVERYBODY! THE NAME OF THE GAME IS STILL POWER AND REVENGE--BUT WHO GETS WHAT? AND WHO IS THE MYSTERIOUS STRIKEBACK ANYWAY? BE HERE NEXT ISSUE FOR THE MIND-SEARING CONCLUSION TO
LETHAL FOES OF SPIDER-MAN!!!

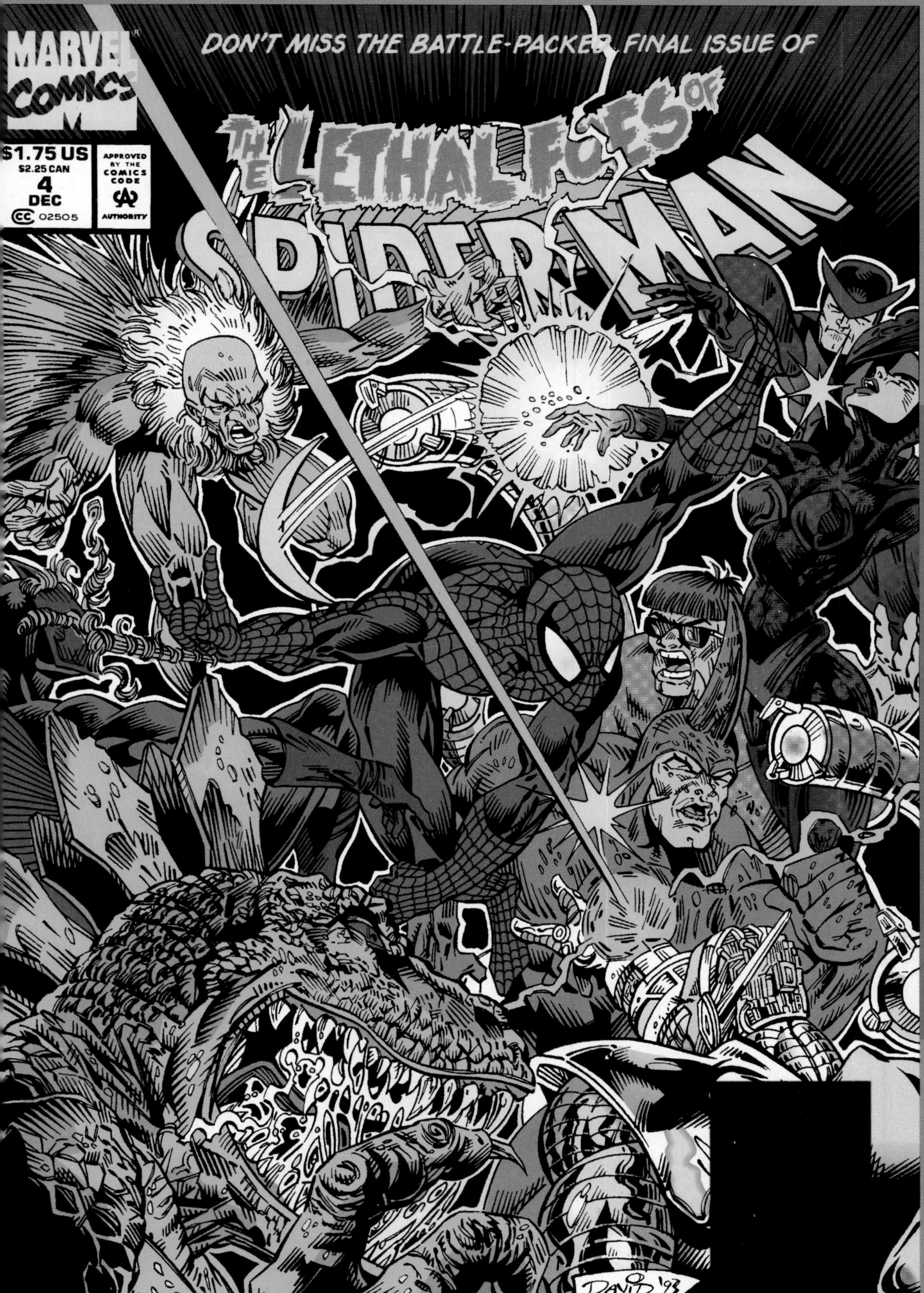
MARVEL COMICS
DON'T MISS THE BATTLE-PACKED FINAL ISSUE OF
THE LETHAL FOES OF SPIDER-MAN
$1.75 US
$2.25 CAN
4
DEC
CC 02505
APPROVED BY THE COMICS CODE AUTHORITY
DAVID '93
BRAD

UNITED IN NOTHING BUT THEIR *HATRED* FOR ONE MAN AND THEIR THIRST FOR *POWER*, MURDEROUS INDIVIDUALS BAND TOGETHER TO FURTHER THEIR TWISTED GOALS. AND THEY WILL LET *NOTHING* STAND IN THEIR WAY!

***STAN LEE* PRESENTS...THE LETHAL FOES OF SPIDER-MAN!**

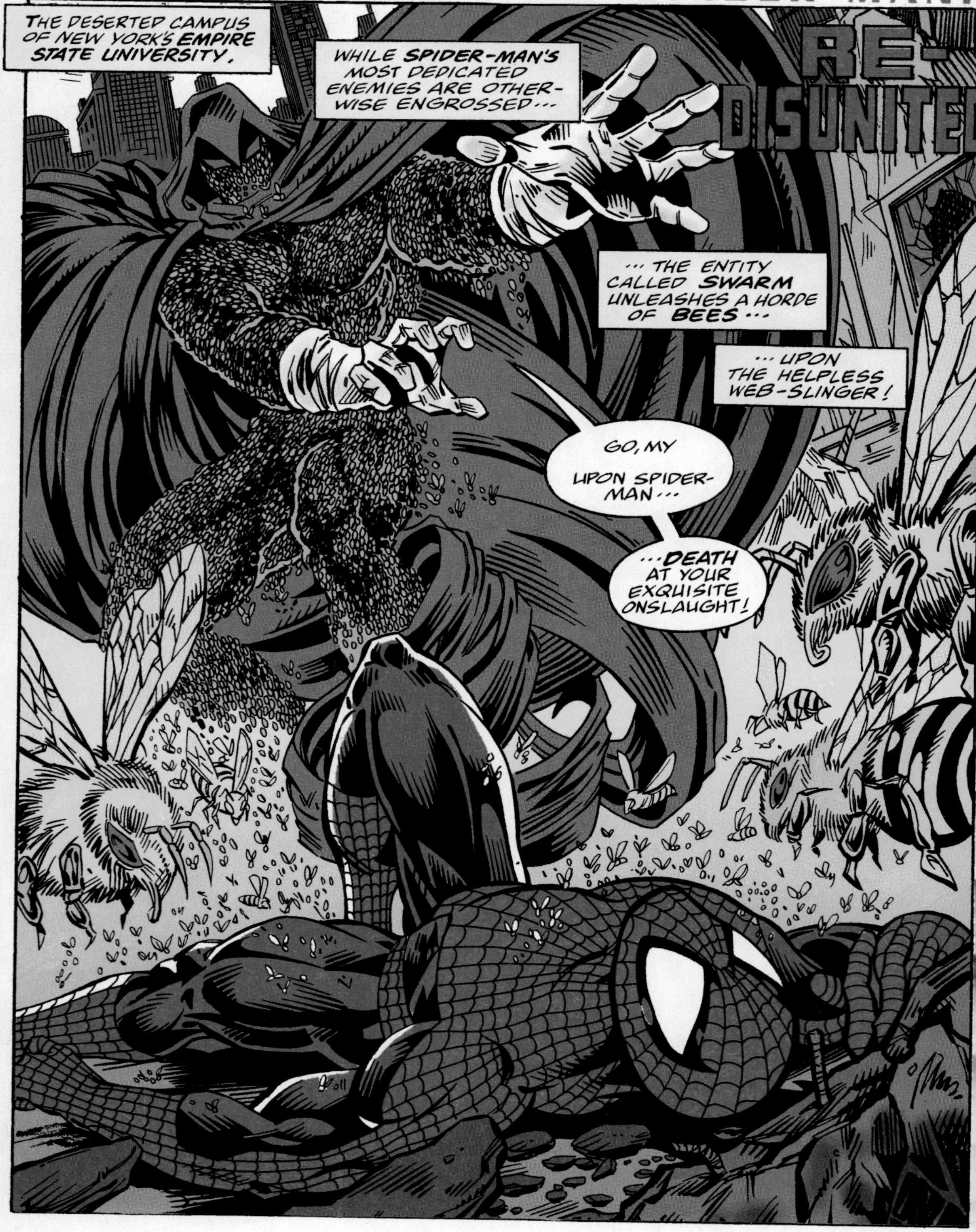
RE-DISUNITED
THE DESERTED CAMPUS OF NEW YORK'S EMPIRE STATE UNIVERSITY.
WHILE SPIDER-MAN'S MOST DEDICATED ENEMIES ARE OTHERWISE ENGROSSED...
...THE ENTITY CALLED SWARM UNLEASHES A HORDE OF BEES...
...UPON THE HELPLESS WEB-SLINGER!
GO, MY
UPON SPIDER-MAN...
...DEATH AT YOUR EXQUISITE ONSLAUGHT!

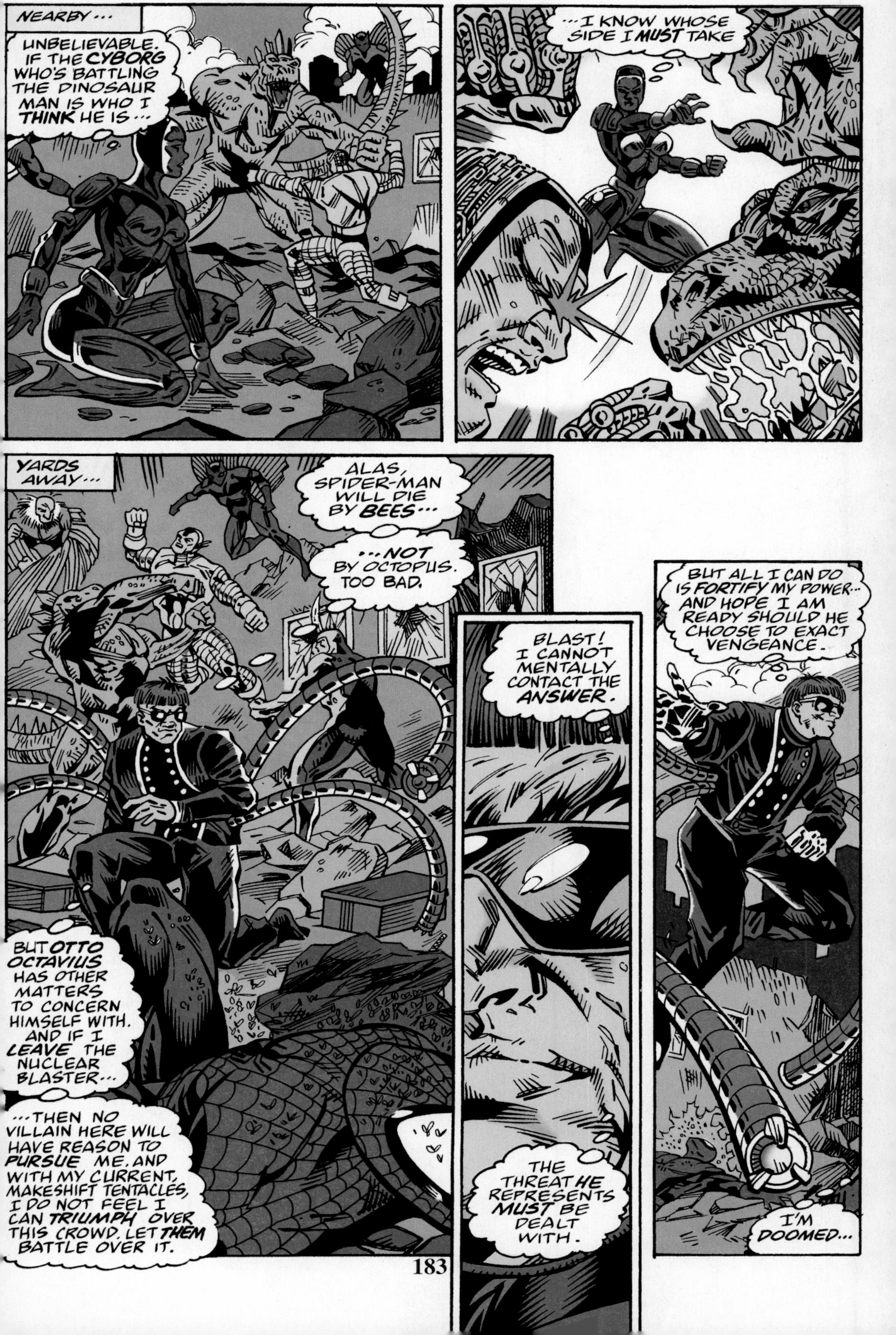

NEARBY...
UNBELIEVABLE. IF THE CYBORG WHO'S BATTLING THE DINOSAUR MAN IS WHO I THINK HE IS...
...I KNOW WHOSE SIDE I MUST TAKE
YARDS AWAY...
ALAS, SPIDER-MAN WILL DIE BY BEES...
...NOT BY OCTOPUS. TOO BAD.
BUT OTTO OCTAVIUS HAS OTHER MATTERS TO CONCERN HIMSELF WITH. AND IF I LEAVE THE NUCLEAR BLASTER...
...THEN NO VILLAIN HERE WILL HAVE REASON TO PURSUE ME. AND WITH MY CURRENT, MAKESHIFT TENTACLES, I DO NOT FEEL I CAN TRIUMPH OVER THIS CROWD. LET THEM BATTLE OVER IT.
BLAST! I CANNOT MENTALLY CONTACT THE ANSWER.
THE THREAT HE REPRESENTS MUST BE DEALT WITH.
BUT ALL I CAN DO IS FORTIFY MY POWER... AND HOPE I AM READY SHOULD HE CHOOSE TO EXACT VENGEANCE.
I'M DOOMED...

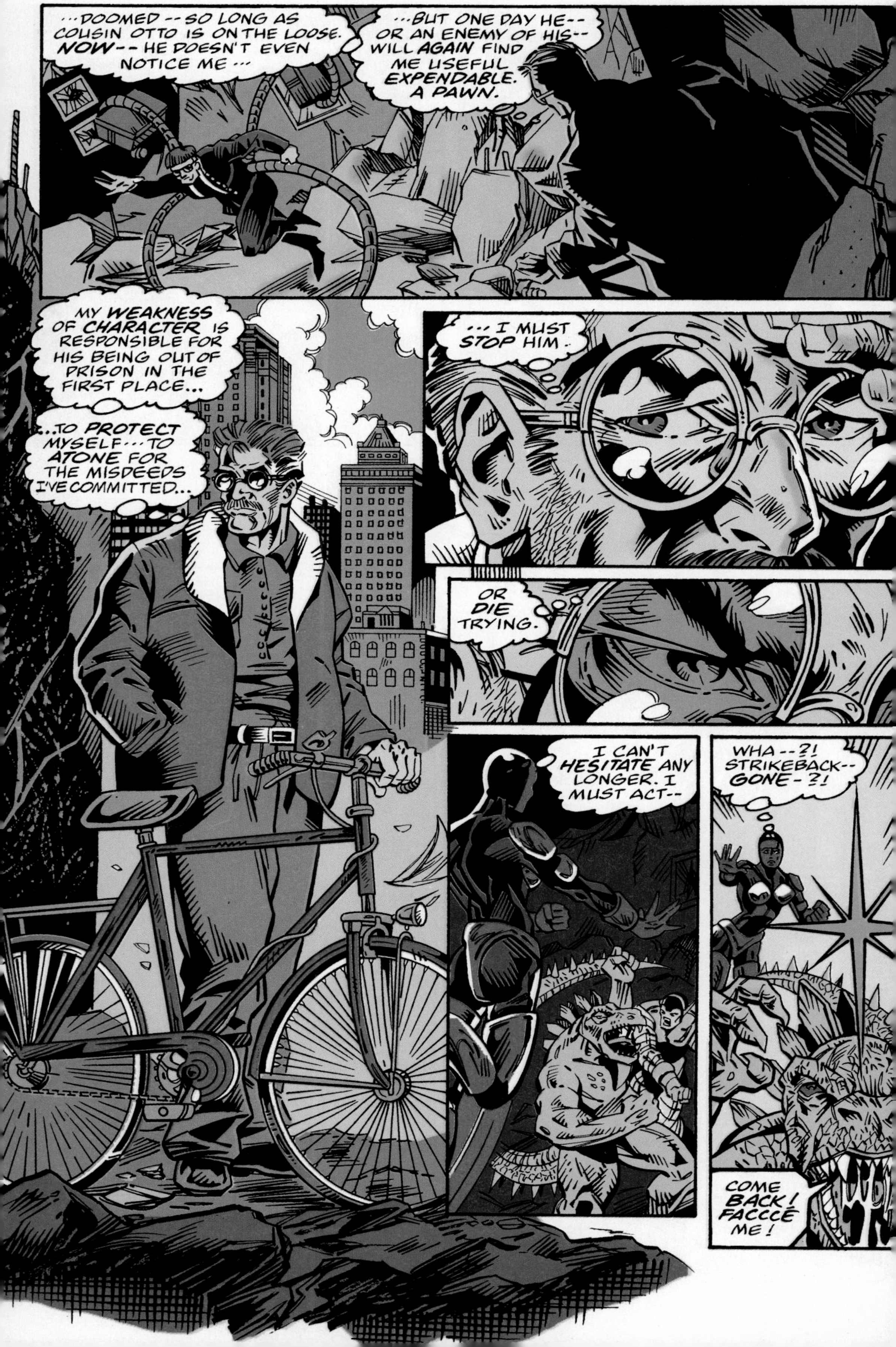
...DOOMED -- SO LONG AS COUSIN OTTO IS ON THE LOOSE. NOW -- HE DOESN'T EVEN NOTICE ME...
...BUT ONE DAY HE -- OR AN ENEMY OF HIS -- WILL AGAIN FIND ME USEFUL EXPENDABLE. A PAWN.
MY WEAKNESS OF CHARACTER IS RESPONSIBLE FOR HIS BEING OUT OF PRISON IN THE FIRST PLACE...
...TO PROTECT MYSELF... TO ATONE FOR THE MISDEEDS I'VE COMMITTED...
...I MUST STOP HIM.
OR DIE TRYING.
I CAN'T HESITATE ANY LONGER. I MUST ACT--
WHA--?! STRIKEBACK-- GONE--?!
COME BACK! FACCCE ME!

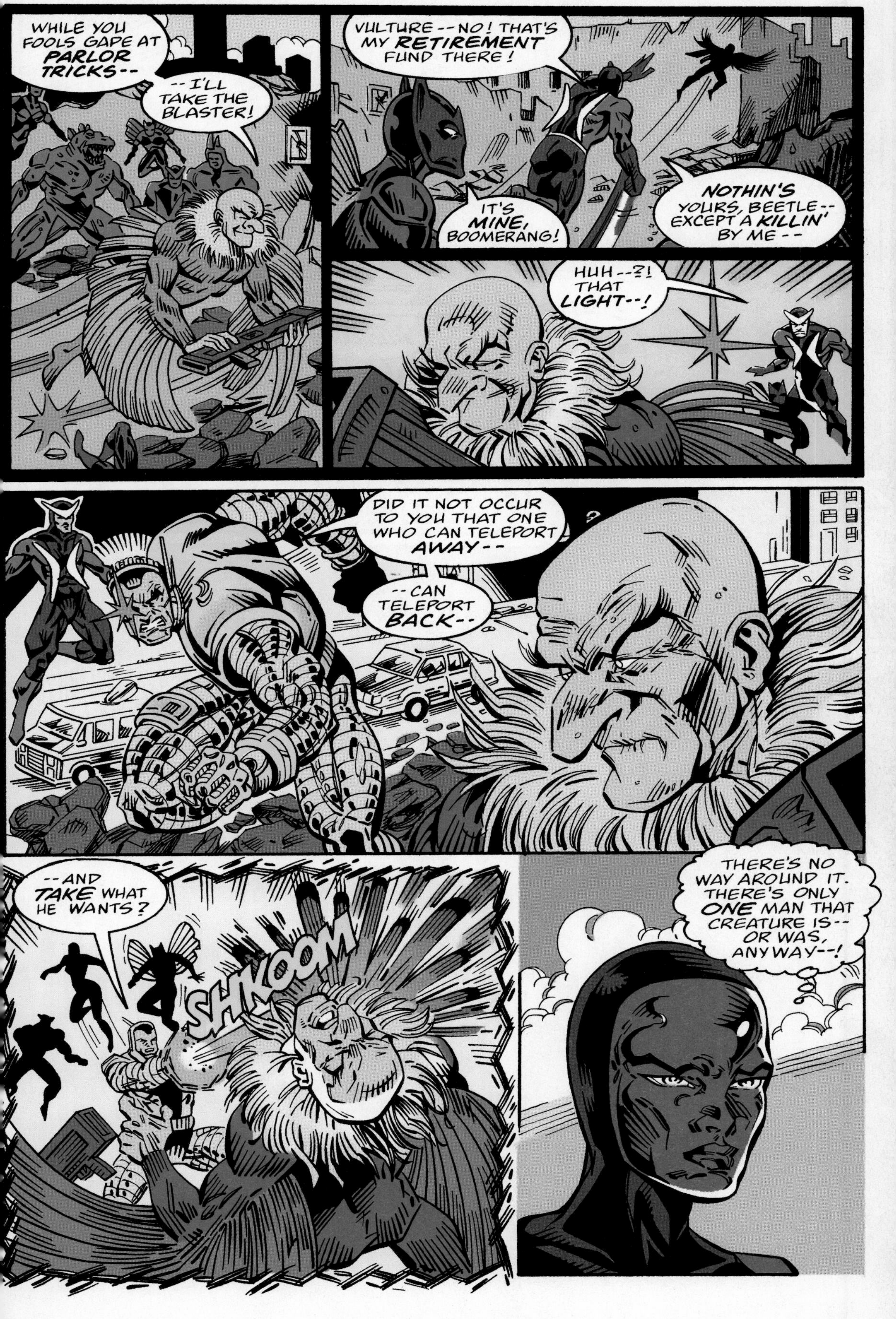
WHILE YOU FOOLS GAPE AT PARLOR TRICKS--
--I'LL TAKE THE BLASTER!
VULTURE--NO! THAT'S MY RETIREMENT FUND THERE!
IT'S MINE, BOOMERANG!
NOTHIN'S YOURS, BEETLE--EXCEPT A KILLIN' BY ME--
HUH--?! THAT LIGHT--!
DID IT NOT OCCUR TO YOU THAT ONE WHO CAN TELEPORT AWAY--
--CAN TELEPORT BACK--
--AND TAKE WHAT HE WANTS?
SHHOOM
THERE'S NO WAY AROUND IT. THERE'S ONLY ONE MAN THAT CREATURE IS--OR WAS, ANYWAY--!

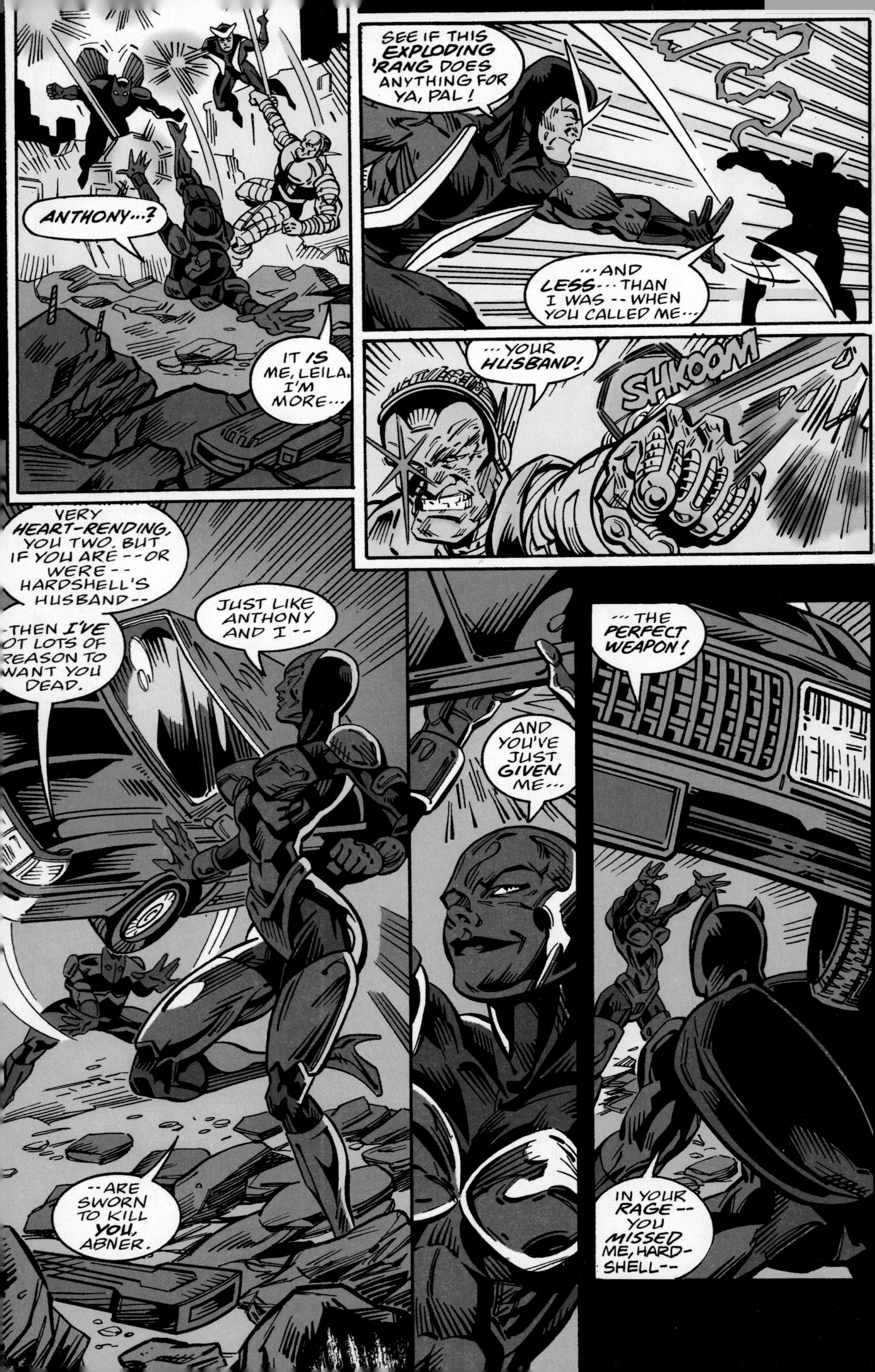
ANTHONY...?
IT IS ME, LEILA. I'M MORE...
SEE IF THIS EXPLODING 'RANG DOES ANYTHING FOR YA, PAL!
...AND LESS... THAN I WAS -- WHEN YOU CALLED ME...
...YOUR HUSBAND!
SHKOOM
VERY HEART-RENDING, YOU TWO. BUT IF YOU ARE -- OR WERE -- HARDSHELL'S HUSBAND --
-THEN I'VE OT LOTS OF REASON TO WANT YOU DEAD.
JUST LIKE ANTHONY AND I --
--ARE SWORN TO KILL YOU, ABNER.
AND YOU'VE JUST GIVEN ME...
...THE PERFECT WEAPON!
IN YOUR RAGE -- YOU MISSED ME, HARD-SHELL--

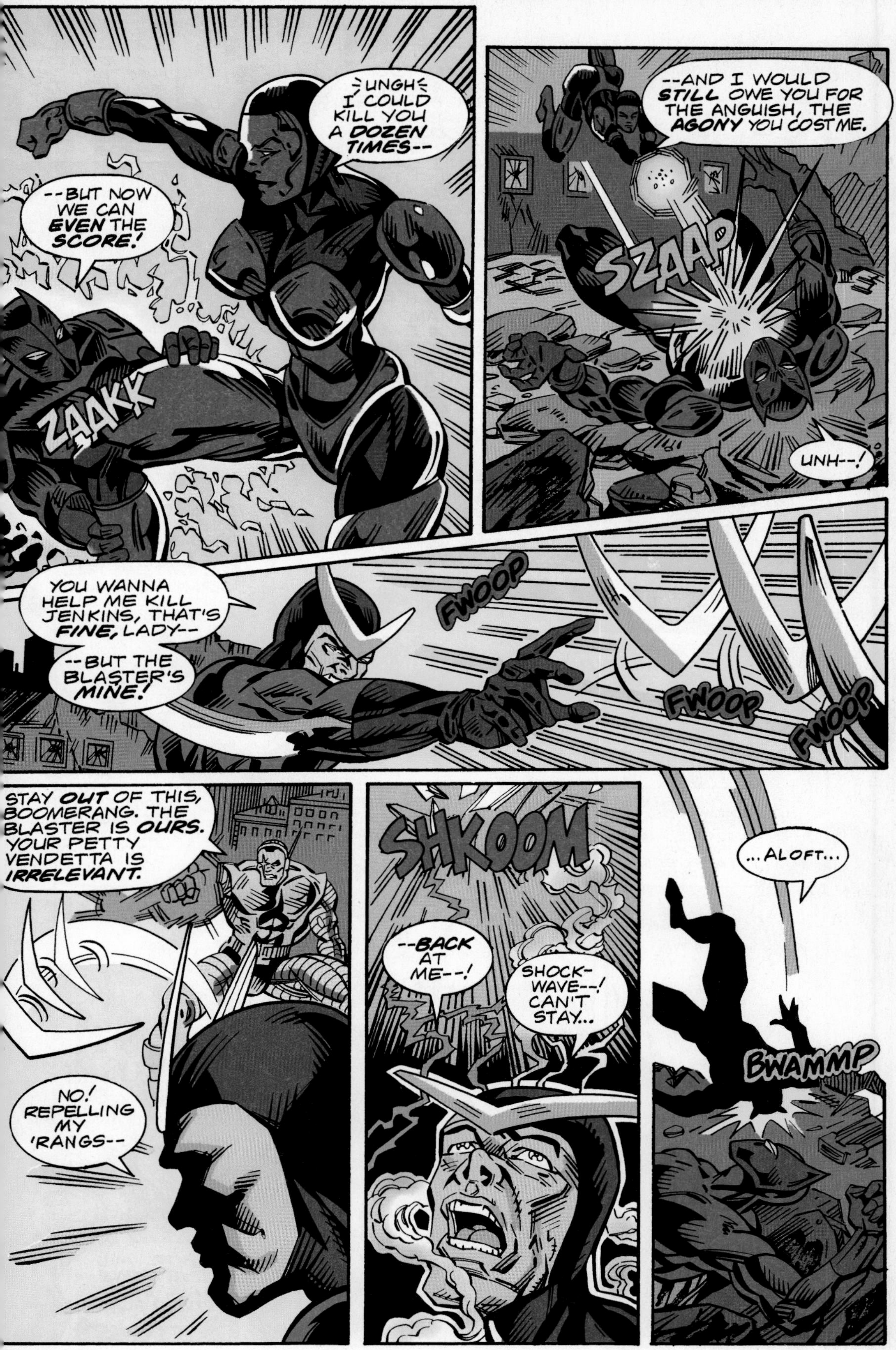
UNGH I COULD KILL YOU A DOZEN TIMES--
--BUT NOW WE CAN EVEN THE SCORE!
ZAAKK
--AND I WOULD STILL OWE YOU FOR THE ANGUISH, THE AGONY YOU COST ME.
SZAAP
UNH--!
YOU WANNA HELP ME KILL JENKINS, THAT'S FINE, LADY--
--BUT THE BLASTER'S MINE!
FWOOP
FWOOP
FWOOP
STAY OUT OF THIS, BOOMERANG. THE BLASTER IS OURS. YOUR PETTY VENDETTA IS IRRELEVANT.
NO! REPELLING MY 'RANGS--
SHKOOM
--BACK AT ME--!
SHOCK-WAVE--! CAN'T STAY...
...ALOFT...
BWAMMP

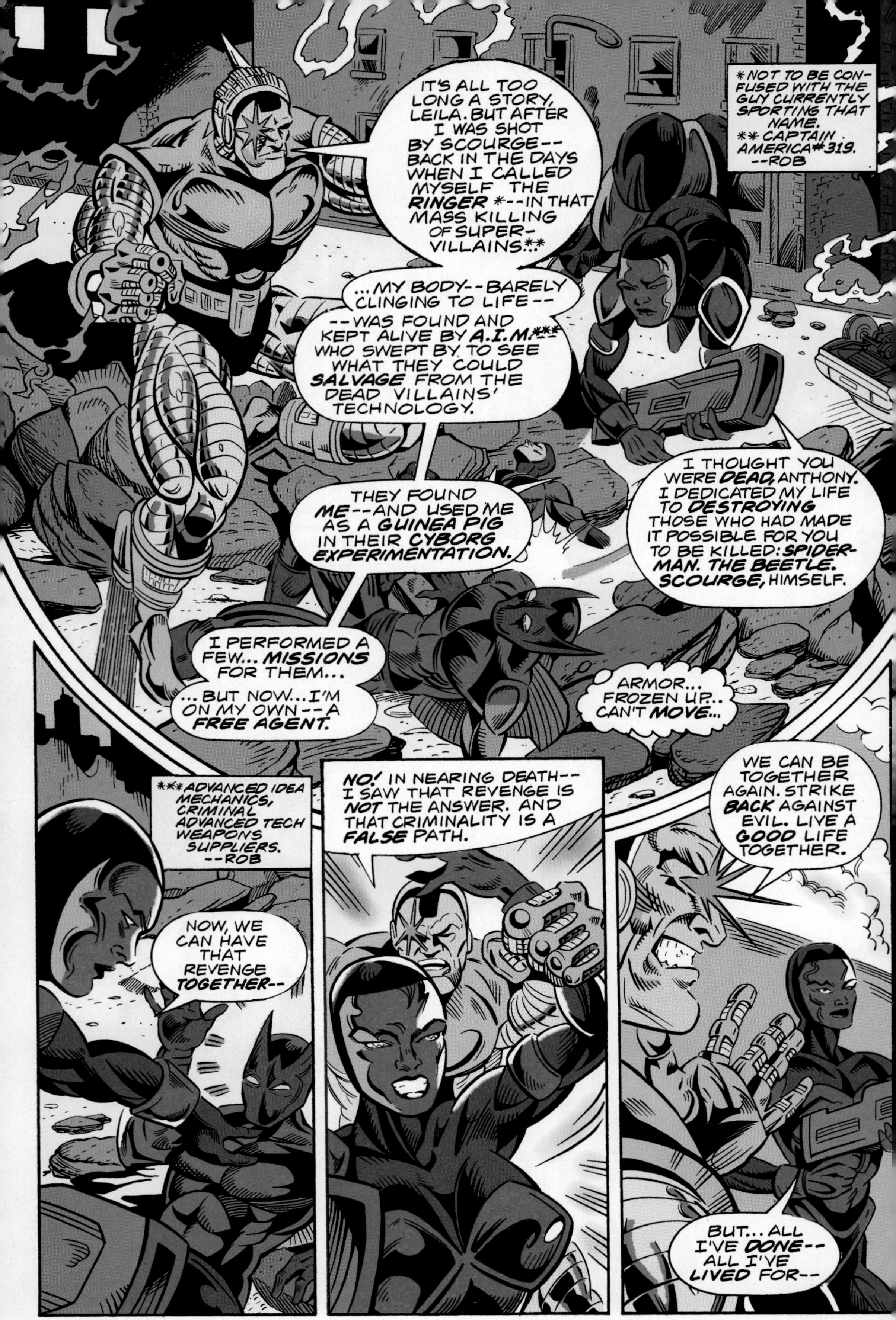
IT'S ALL TOO LONG A STORY, LEILA. BUT AFTER I WAS SHOT BY SCOURGE-- BACK IN THE DAYS WHEN I CALLED MYSELF THE RINGER *--IN THAT MASS KILLING OF SUPER-VILLAINS.**
*NOT TO BE CONFUSED WITH THE GUY CURRENTLY SPORTING THAT NAME. ** CAPTAIN AMERICA #319. --ROB
...MY BODY--BARELY CLINGING TO LIFE--
--WAS FOUND AND KEPT ALIVE BY A.I.M.*** WHO SWEPT BY TO SEE WHAT THEY COULD SALVAGE FROM THE DEAD VILLAINS' TECHNOLOGY.
THEY FOUND ME--AND USED ME AS A GUINEA PIG IN THEIR CYBORG EXPERIMENTATION.
I THOUGHT YOU WERE DEAD, ANTHONY. I DEDICATED MY LIFE TO DESTROYING THOSE WHO HAD MADE IT POSSIBLE FOR YOU TO BE KILLED: SPIDER-MAN. THE BEETLE. SCOURGE, HIMSELF.
I PERFORMED A FEW... MISSIONS FOR THEM...
...BUT NOW...I'M ON MY OWN--A FREE AGENT.
ARMOR... FROZEN UP... CAN'T MOVE...
***ADVANCED IDEA MECHANICS, CRIMINAL ADVANCED TECH WEAPONS SUPPLIERS. --ROB
NOW, WE CAN HAVE THAT REVENGE TOGETHER--
NO! IN NEARING DEATH-- I SAW THAT REVENGE IS NOT THE ANSWER. AND THAT CRIMINALITY IS A FALSE PATH.
WE CAN BE TOGETHER AGAIN. STRIKE BACK AGAINST EVIL. LIVE A GOOD LIFE TOGETHER.
BUT... ALL I'VE DONE-- ALL I'VE LIVED FOR--

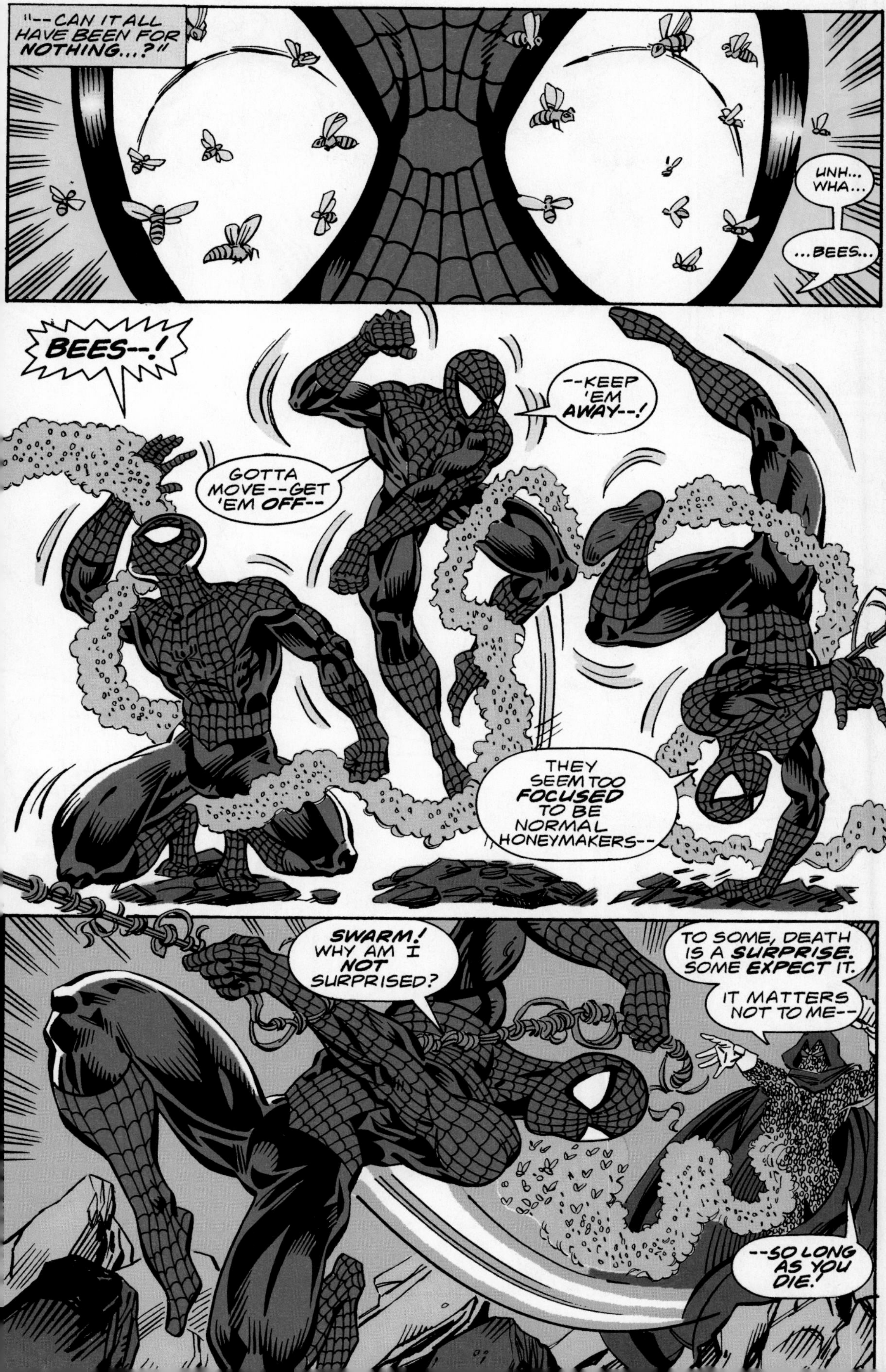
"--CAN IT ALL HAVE BEEN FOR NOTHING...?"
UNH... WHA...
...BEES...
BEES--!
--KEEP 'EM AWAY--!
GOTTA MOVE--GET 'EM OFF--
THEY SEEM TOO FOCUSED TO BE NORMAL HONEYMAKERS--
SWARM! WHY AM I NOT SURPRISED?
TO SOME, DEATH IS A SURPRISE. SOME EXPECT IT.
IT MATTERS NOT TO ME--
--SO LONG AS YOU DIE!

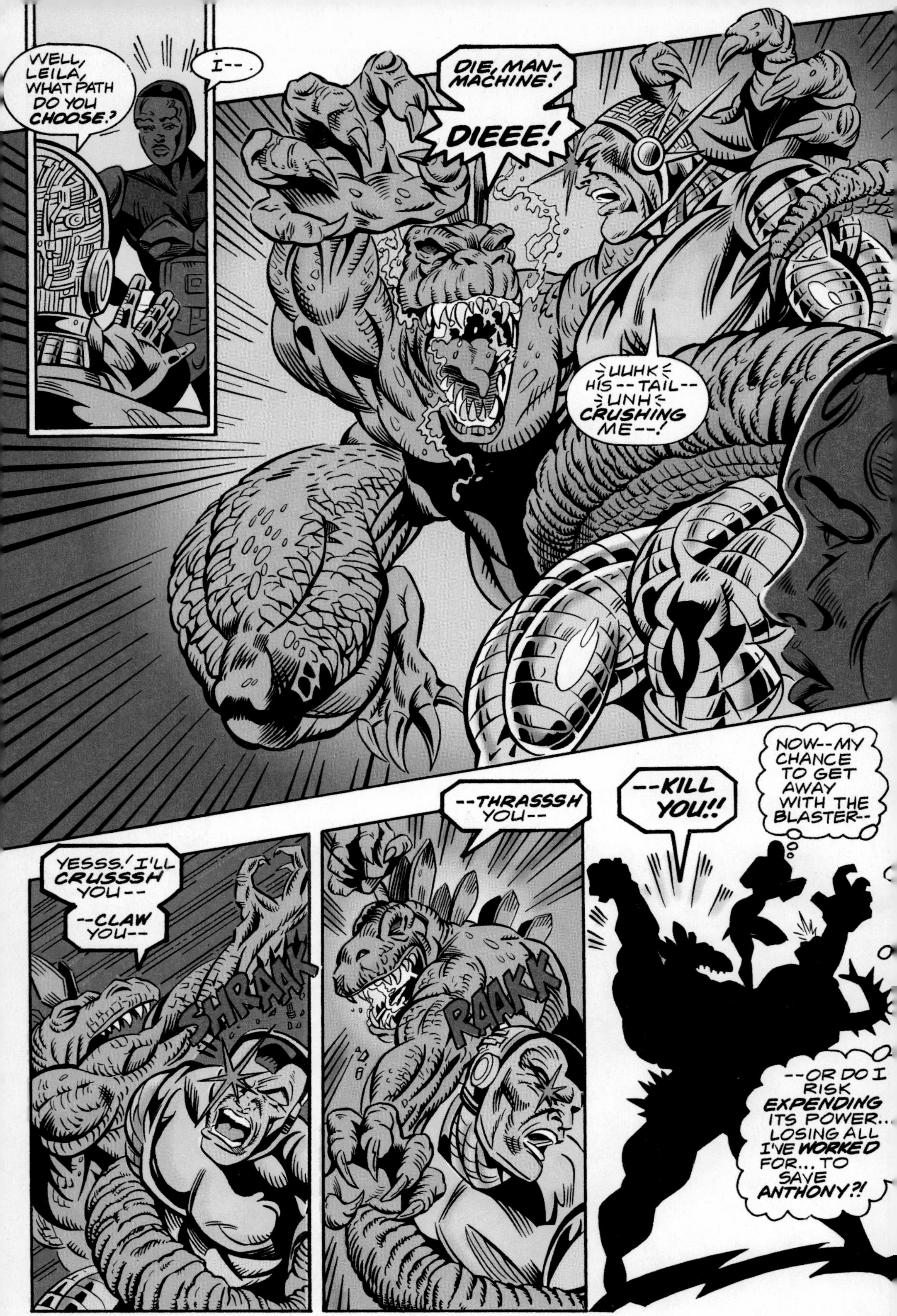
WELL, LEILA, WHAT PATH DO YOU CHOOSE?
I--.
DIE, MAN-MACHINE!
DIEEE!
UUHK HIS--TAIL-- UNH CRUSHING ME--!
YESSS! I'LL CRUSSSH YOU--
--CLAW YOU--
SHRAAK
--THRASSSH YOU--
RAAKK
--KILL YOU!!
NOW--MY CHANCE TO GET AWAY WITH THE BLASTER--
--OR DO I RISK EXPENDING ITS POWER... LOSING ALL I'VE WORKED FOR... TO SAVE ANTHONY?!

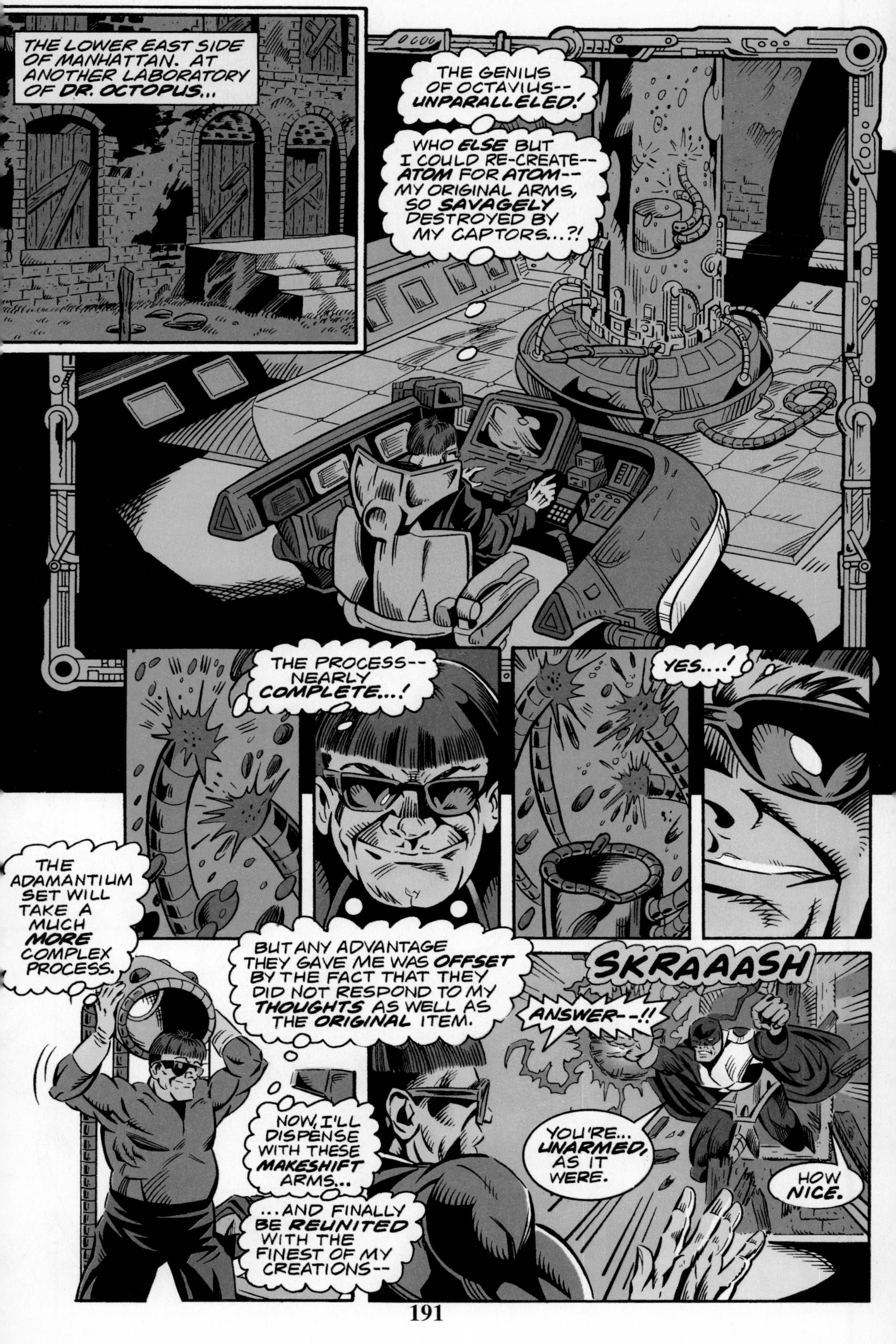
THE LOWER EAST SIDE OF MANHATTAN. AT ANOTHER LABORATORY OF DR. OCTOPUS...
THE GENIUS OF OCTAVIUS-- UNPARALLELED!
WHO ELSE BUT I COULD RE-CREATE-- ATOM FOR ATOM-- MY ORIGINAL ARMS, SO SAVAGELY DESTROYED BY MY CAPTORS...?!
THE PROCESS-- NEARLY COMPLETE...!
YES....!
THE ADAMANTIUM SET WILL TAKE A MUCH MORE COMPLEX PROCESS.
BUT ANY ADVANTAGE THEY GAVE ME WAS OFFSET BY THE FACT THAT THEY DID NOT RESPOND TO MY THOUGHTS AS WELL AS THE ORIGINAL ITEM.
NOW, I'LL DISPENSE WITH THESE MAKESHIFT ARMS...
...AND FINALLY BE REUNITED WITH THE FINEST OF MY CREATIONS--
SKRAAASH
ANSWER--!!
YOU'RE... UNARMED, AS IT WERE.
HOW NICE.

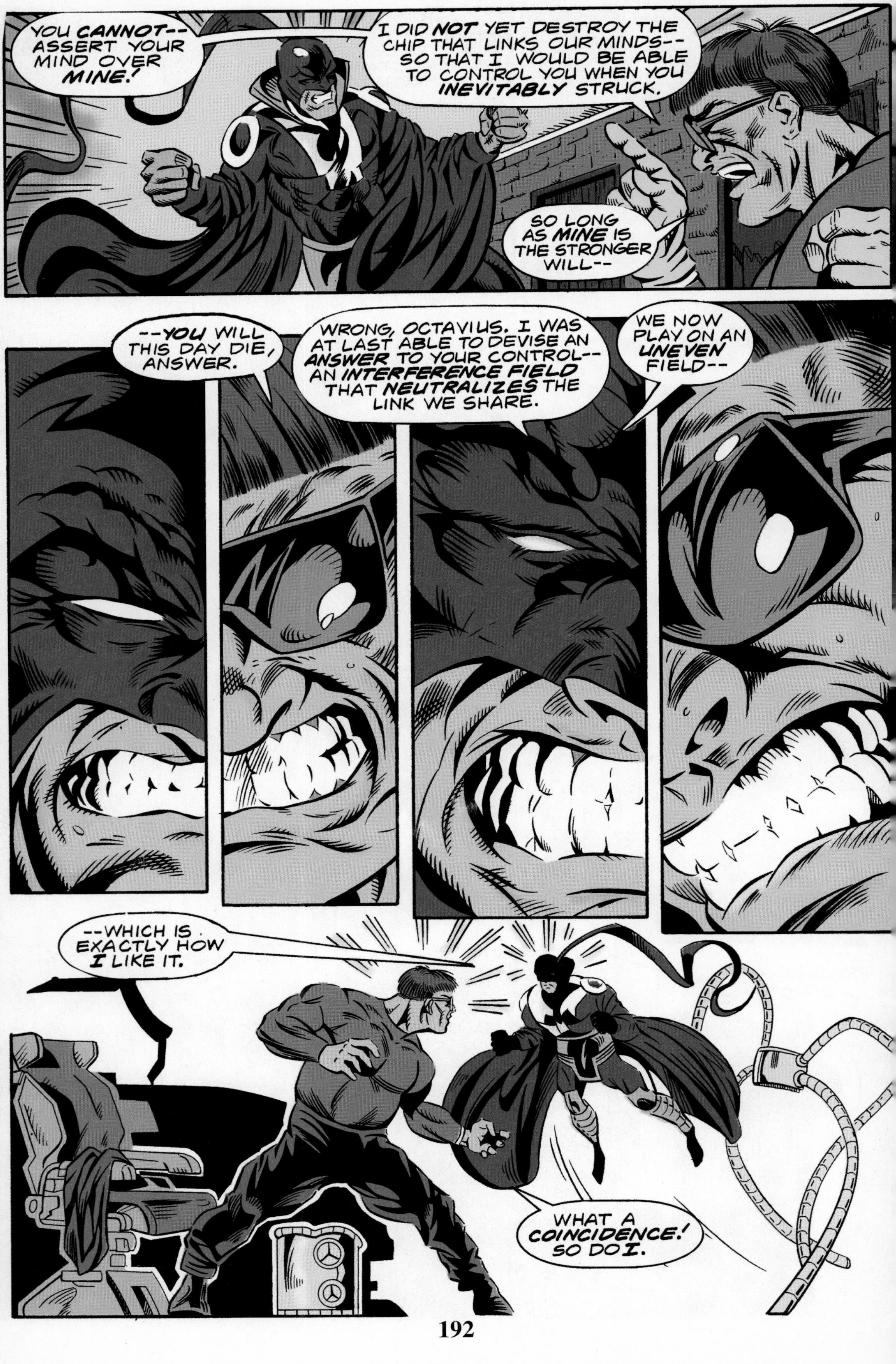
YOU CANNOT--ASSERT YOUR MIND OVER MINE!
I DID NOT YET DESTROY THE CHIP THAT LINKS OUR MINDS--SO THAT I WOULD BE ABLE TO CONTROL YOU WHEN YOU INEVITABLY STRUCK.
SO LONG AS MINE IS THE STRONGER WILL--
--YOU WILL THIS DAY DIE, ANSWER.
WRONG, OCTAVIUS. I WAS AT LAST ABLE TO DEVISE AN ANSWER TO YOUR CONTROL--AN INTERFERENCE FIELD THAT NEUTRALIZES THE LINK WE SHARE.
WE NOW PLAY ON AN UNEVEN FIELD--
--WHICH IS EXACTLY HOW I LIKE IT.
WHAT A COINCIDENCE! SO DO I.

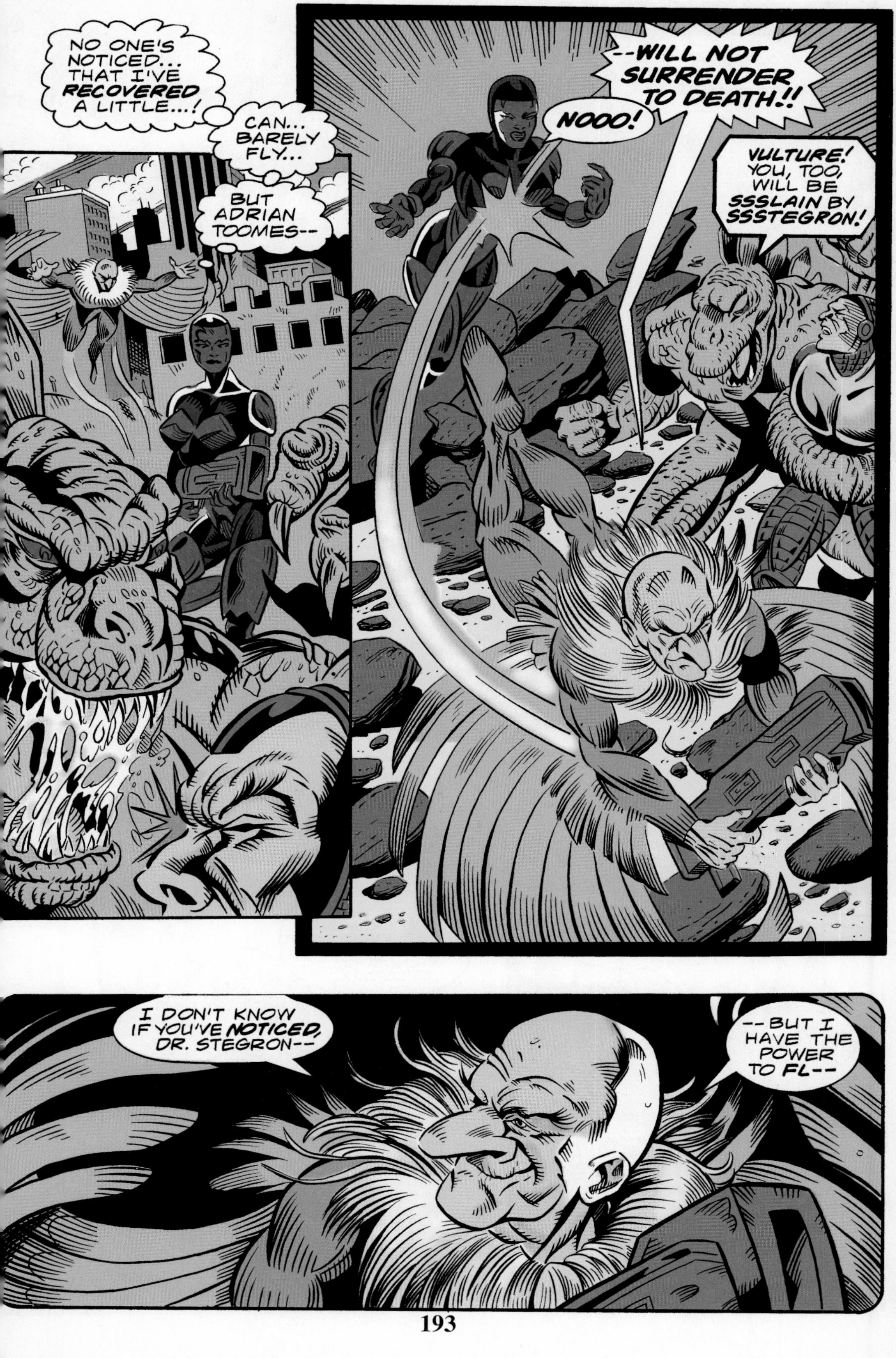
NO ONE'S NOTICED... THAT I'VE RECOVERED A LITTLE...!
CAN... BARELY FLY...
BUT ADRIAN TOOMES--
--WILL NOT SURRENDER TO DEATH!!
NOOO!
VULTURE! YOU, TOO, WILL BE SSSLAIN BY SSSTEGRON!
I DON'T KNOW IF YOU'VE NOTICED, DR. STEGRON--
--BUT I HAVE THE POWER TO FL--

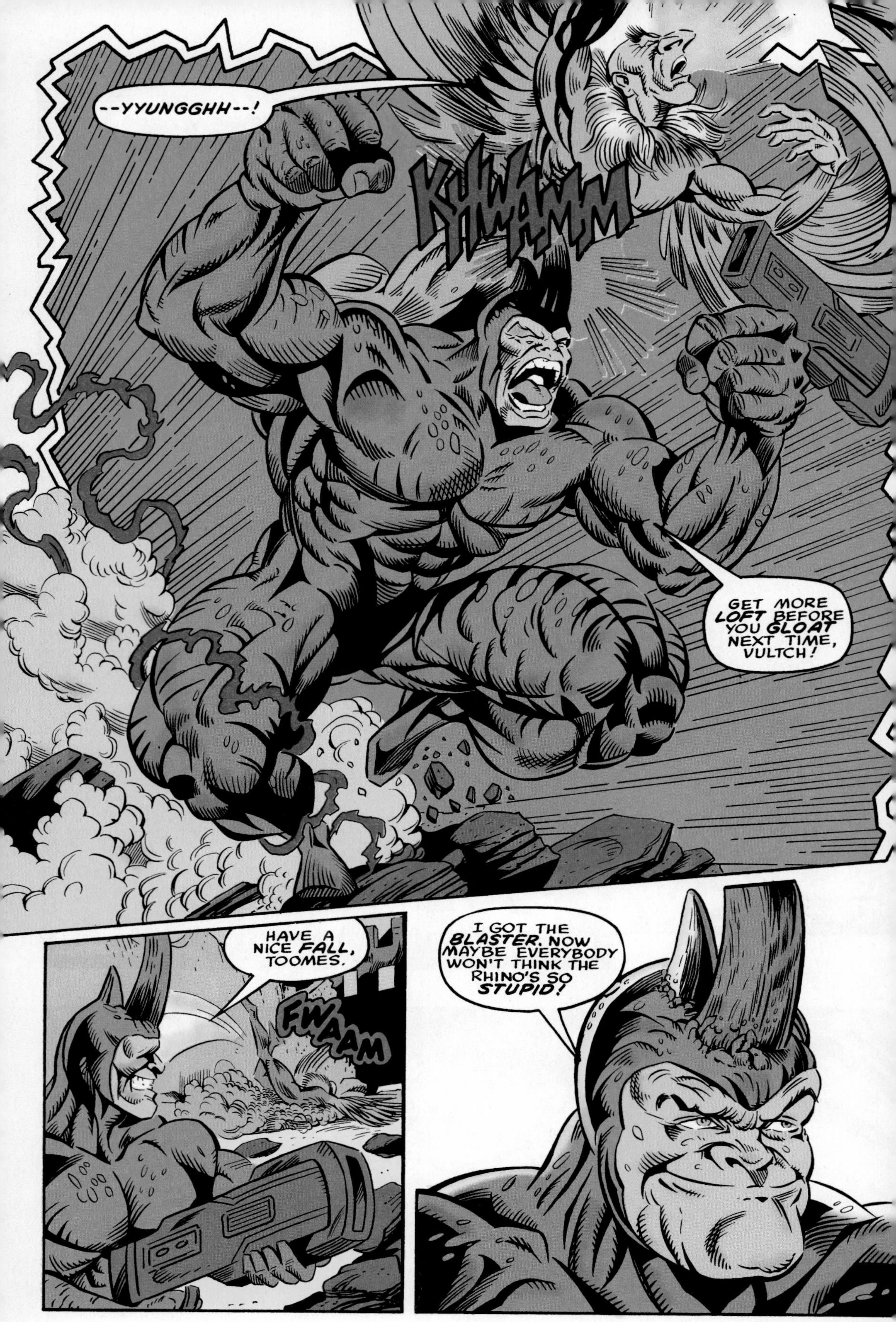
--YYUNGGHH--!
KHWAMM
GET MORE LOFT BEFORE YOU GLOAT NEXT TIME, VULTCH!
HAVE A NICE FALL, TOOMES.
FWAAM
I GOT THE BLASTER. NOW MAYBE EVERYBODY WON'T THINK THE RHINO'S SO STUPID!

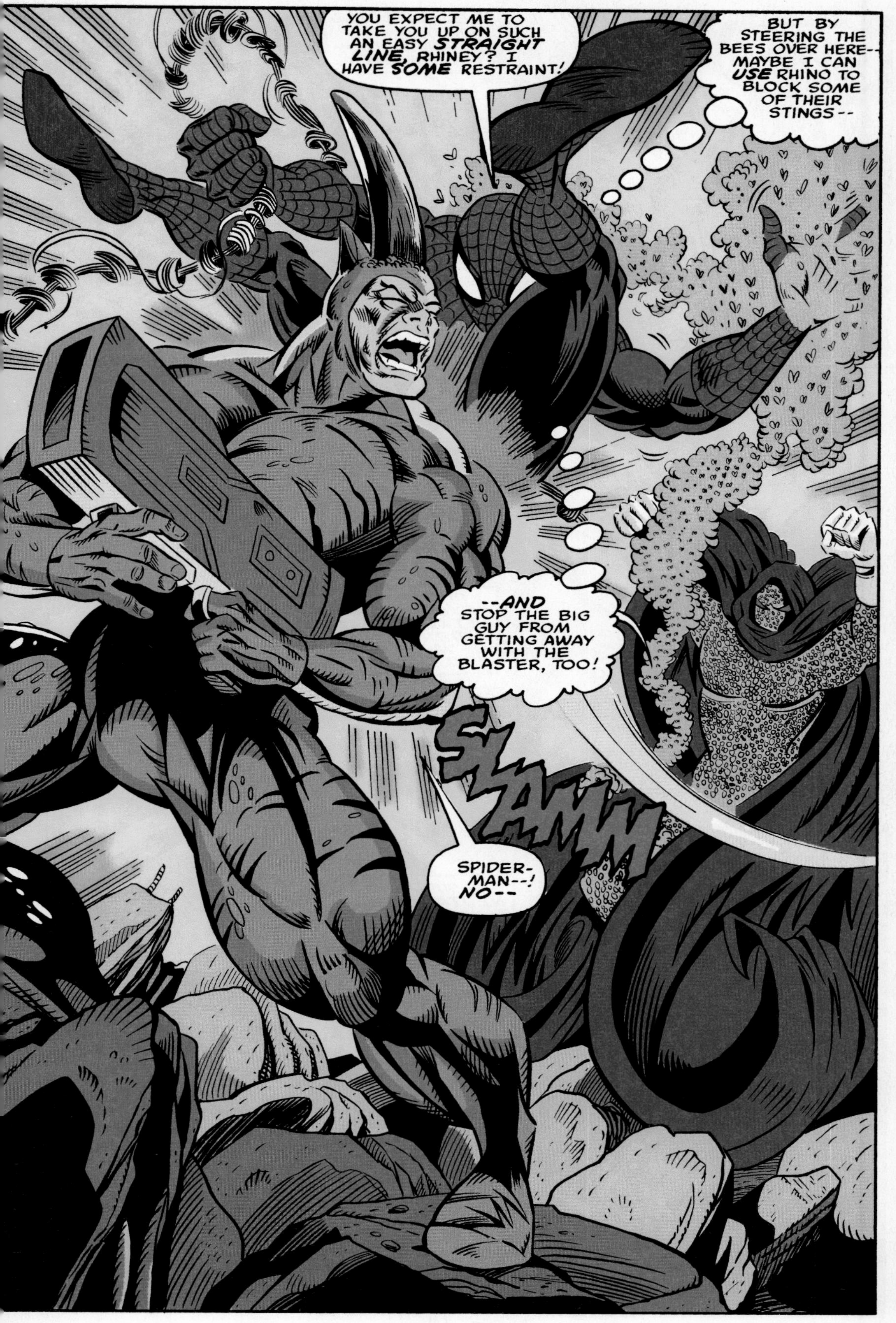
YOU EXPECT ME TO TAKE YOU UP ON SUCH AN EASY STRAIGHT LINE, RHINEY? I HAVE SOME RESTRAINT!
BUT BY STEERING THE BEES OVER HERE-- MAYBE I CAN USE RHINO TO BLOCK SOME OF THEIR STINGS--
--AND STOP THE BIG GUY FROM GETTING AWAY WITH THE BLASTER, TOO!
SLAMM
SPIDER-MAN--! NO--

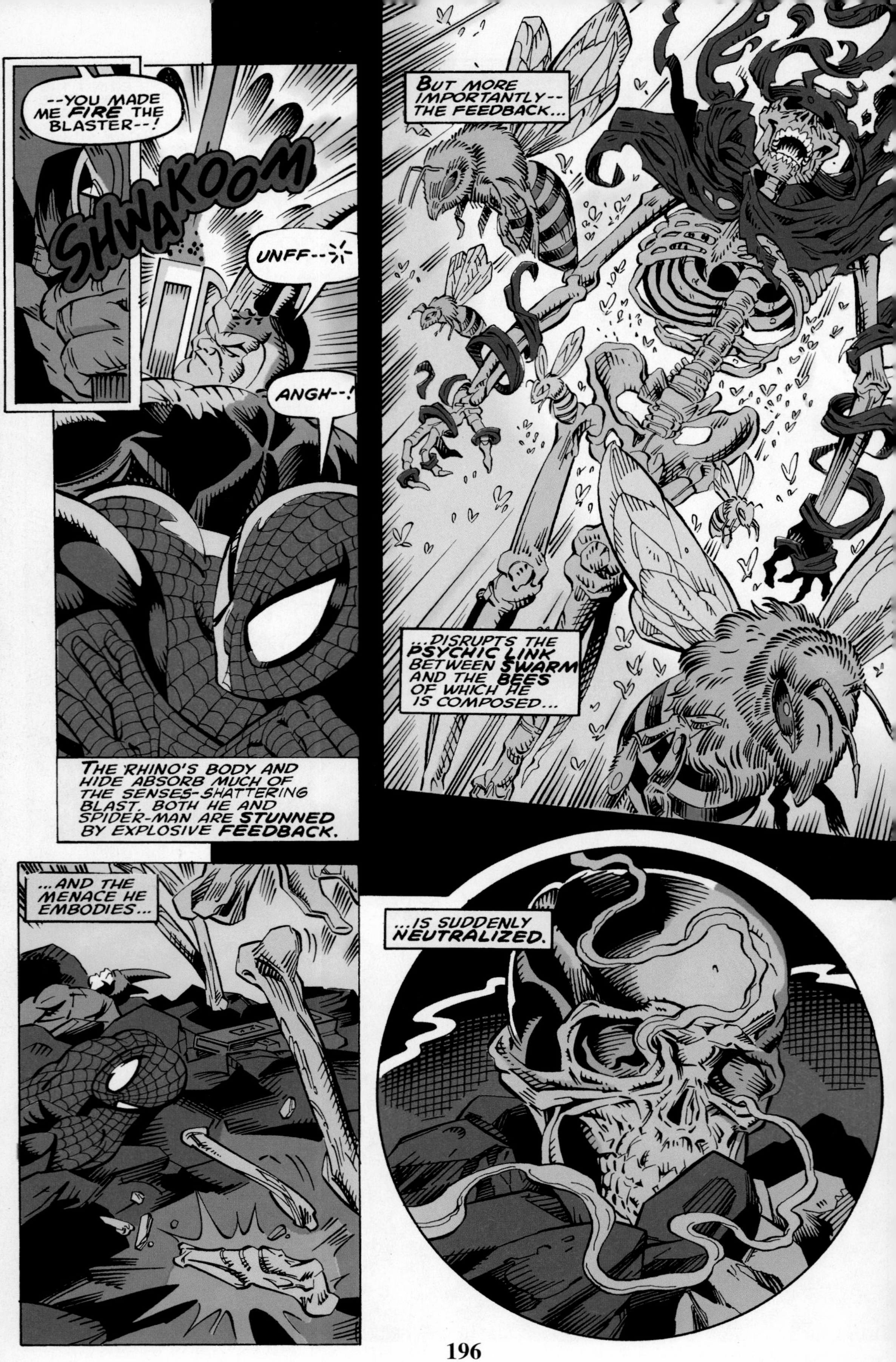
--YOU MADE ME FIRE THE BLASTER--!
SHWAKOOM
UNFF--
ANGH--!
THE RHINO'S BODY AND HIDE ABSORB MUCH OF THE SENSES-SHATTERING BLAST. BOTH HE AND SPIDER-MAN ARE STUNNED BY EXPLOSIVE FEEDBACK.
BUT MORE IMPORTANTLY--THE FEEDBACK...
...DISRUPTS THE PSYCHIC LINK BETWEEN SWARM AND THE BEES OF WHICH HE IS COMPOSED...
...AND THE MENACE HE EMBODIES...
...IS SUDDENLY NEUTRALIZED.

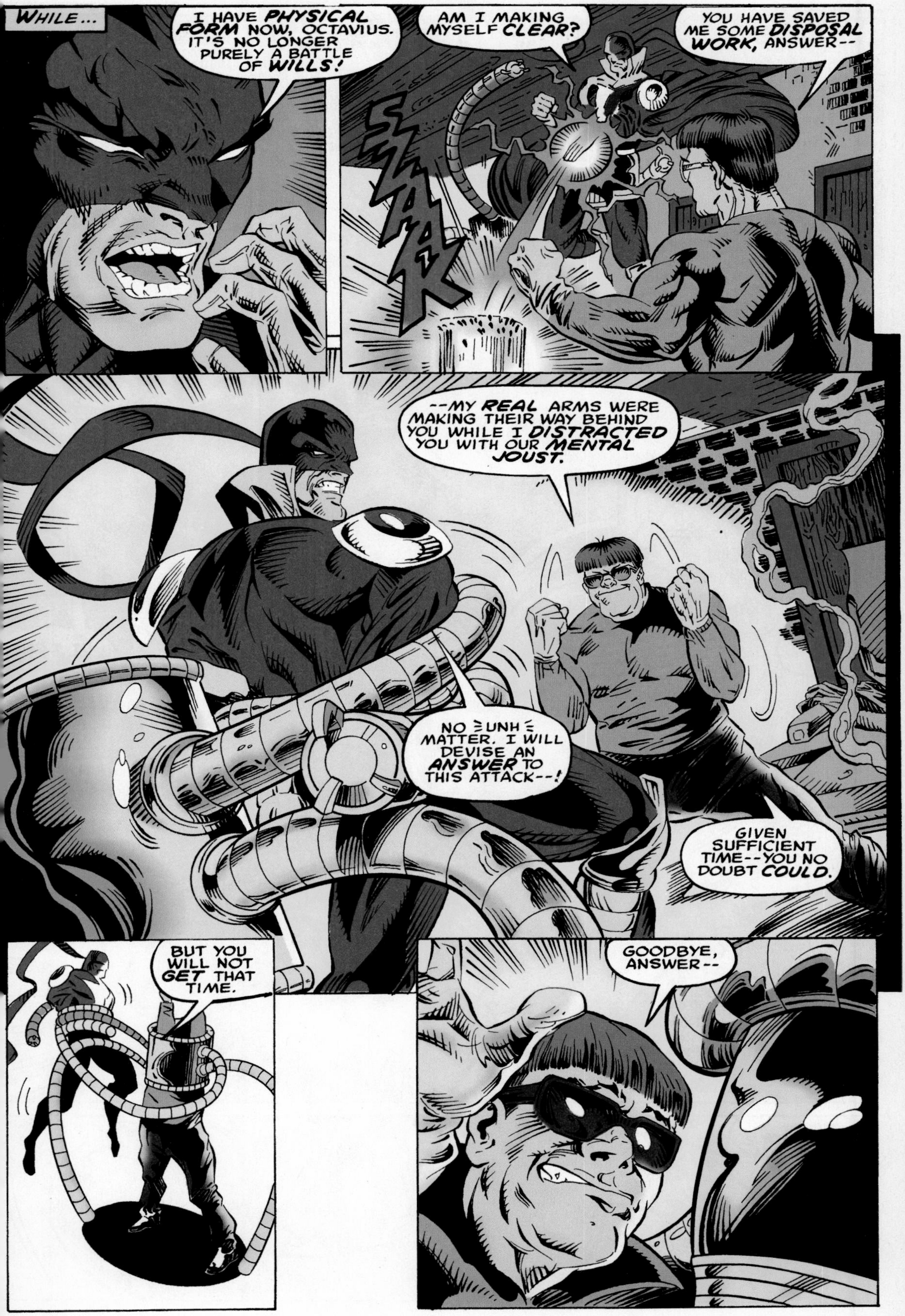
WHILE...
I HAVE PHYSICAL FORM NOW, OCTAVIUS. IT'S NO LONGER PURELY A BATTLE OF WILLS!
AM I MAKING MYSELF CLEAR?
SHAK
YOU HAVE SAVED ME SOME DISPOSAL WORK, ANSWER--
--MY REAL ARMS WERE MAKING THEIR WAY BEHIND YOU WHILE I DISTRACTED YOU WITH OUR MENTAL JOUST.
NO UNH MATTER. I WILL DEVISE AN ANSWER TO THIS ATTACK--!
GIVEN SUFFICIENT TIME--YOU NO DOUBT COULD.
BUT YOU WILL NOT GET THAT TIME.
GOODBYE, ANSWER--

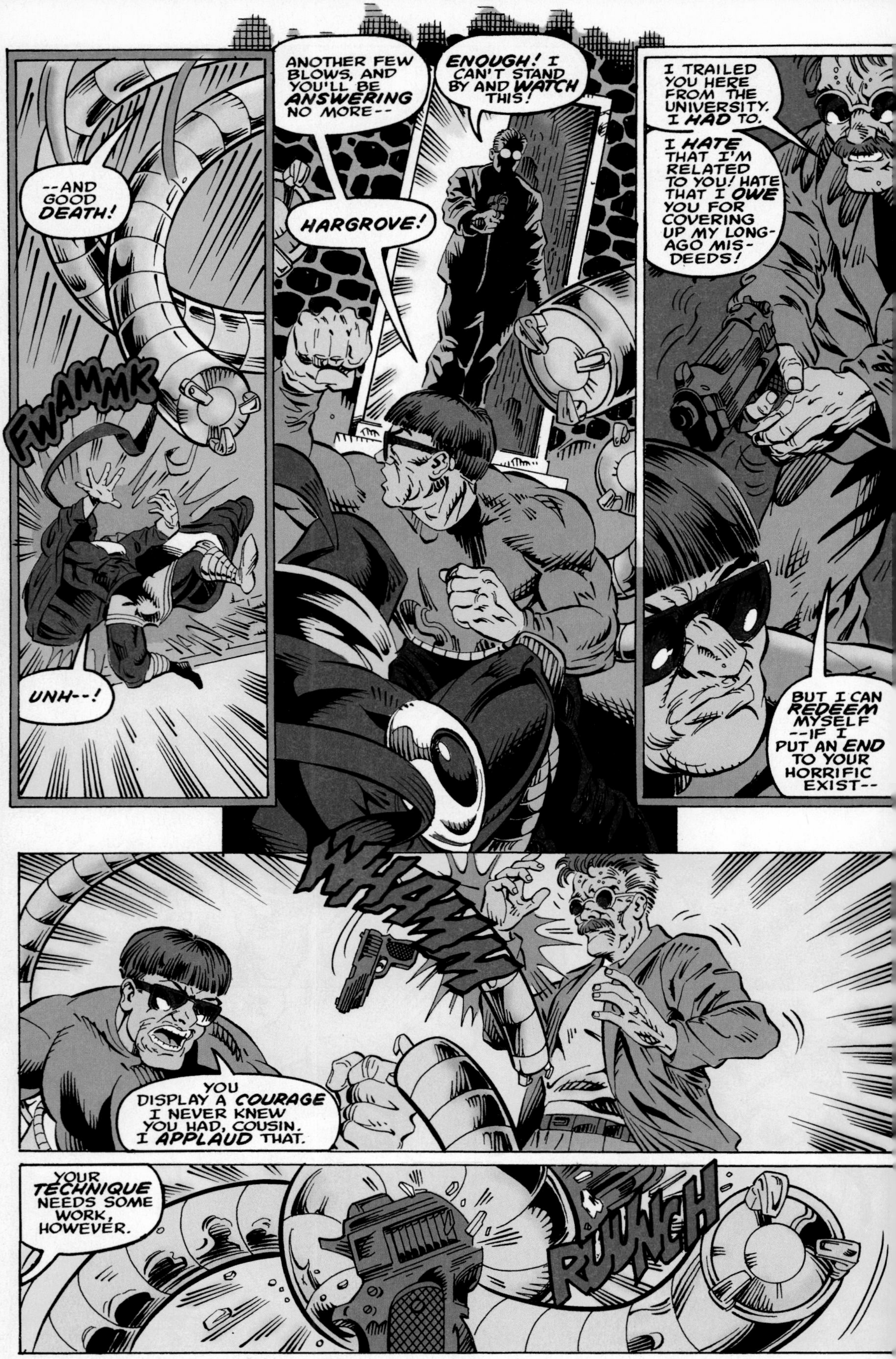
--AND GOOD DEATH!
FWAMMK
UNH--!
ANOTHER FEW BLOWS, AND YOU'LL BE ANSWERING NO MORE--
ENOUGH! I CAN'T STAND BY AND WATCH THIS!
HARGROVE!
I TRAILED YOU HERE FROM THE UNIVERSITY. I HAD TO.
I HATE THAT I'M RELATED TO YOU! HATE THAT I OWE YOU FOR COVERING UP MY LONG-AGO MIS-DEEDS!
BUT I CAN REDEEM MYSELF --IF I PUT AN END TO YOUR HORRIFIC EXIST--
WHAMM
YOU DISPLAY A COURAGE I NEVER KNEW YOU HAD, COUSIN. I APPLAUD THAT.
YOUR TECHNIQUE NEEDS SOME WORK, HOWEVER.
KRUNCH

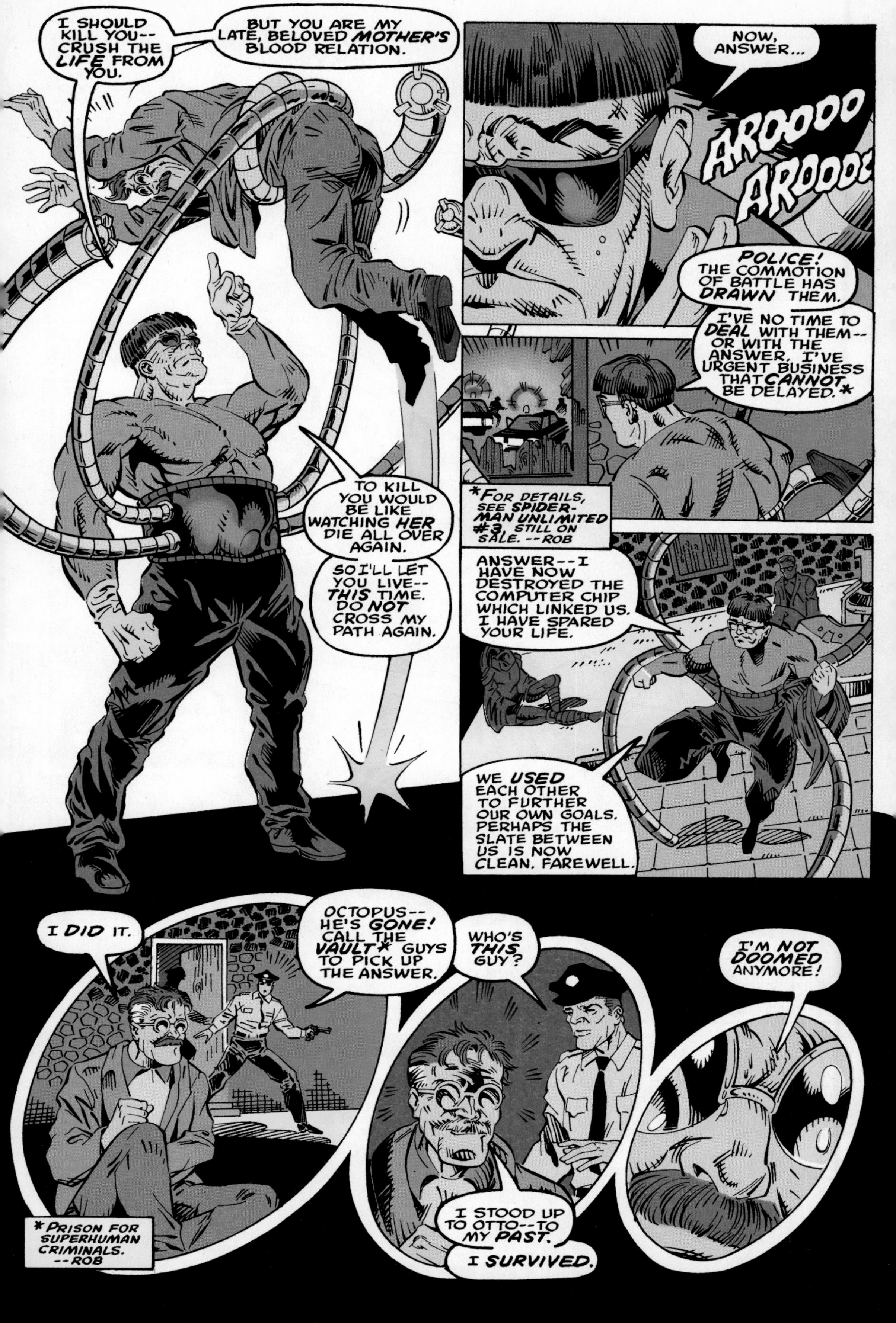

I SHOULD KILL YOU-- CRUSH THE LIFE FROM YOU.
BUT YOU ARE MY LATE, BELOVED MOTHER'S BLOOD RELATION.
TO KILL YOU WOULD BE LIKE WATCHING HER DIE ALL OVER AGAIN.
SO I'LL LET YOU LIVE-- THIS TIME. DO NOT CROSS MY PATH AGAIN.
NOW, ANSWER...
AROOOO AROOOO
POLICE! THE COMMOTION OF BATTLE HAS DRAWN THEM.
I'VE NO TIME TO DEAL WITH THEM-- OR WITH THE ANSWER. I'VE URGENT BUSINESS THAT CANNOT BE DELAYED.*
*FOR DETAILS, SEE SPIDER-MAN UNLIMITED #3, STILL ON SALE. --ROB
ANSWER--I HAVE NOW DESTROYED THE COMPUTER CHIP WHICH LINKED US. I HAVE SPARED YOUR LIFE.
WE USED EACH OTHER TO FURTHER OUR OWN GOALS. PERHAPS THE SLATE BETWEEN US IS NOW CLEAN. FAREWELL.
I DID IT.
OCTOPUS-- HE'S GONE! CALL THE VAULT* GUYS TO PICK UP THE ANSWER.
*PRISON FOR SUPERHUMAN CRIMINALS. --ROB
WHO'S THIS GUY?
I STOOD UP TO OTTO--TO MY PAST.
I SURVIVED.
I'M NOT DOOMED ANYMORE!

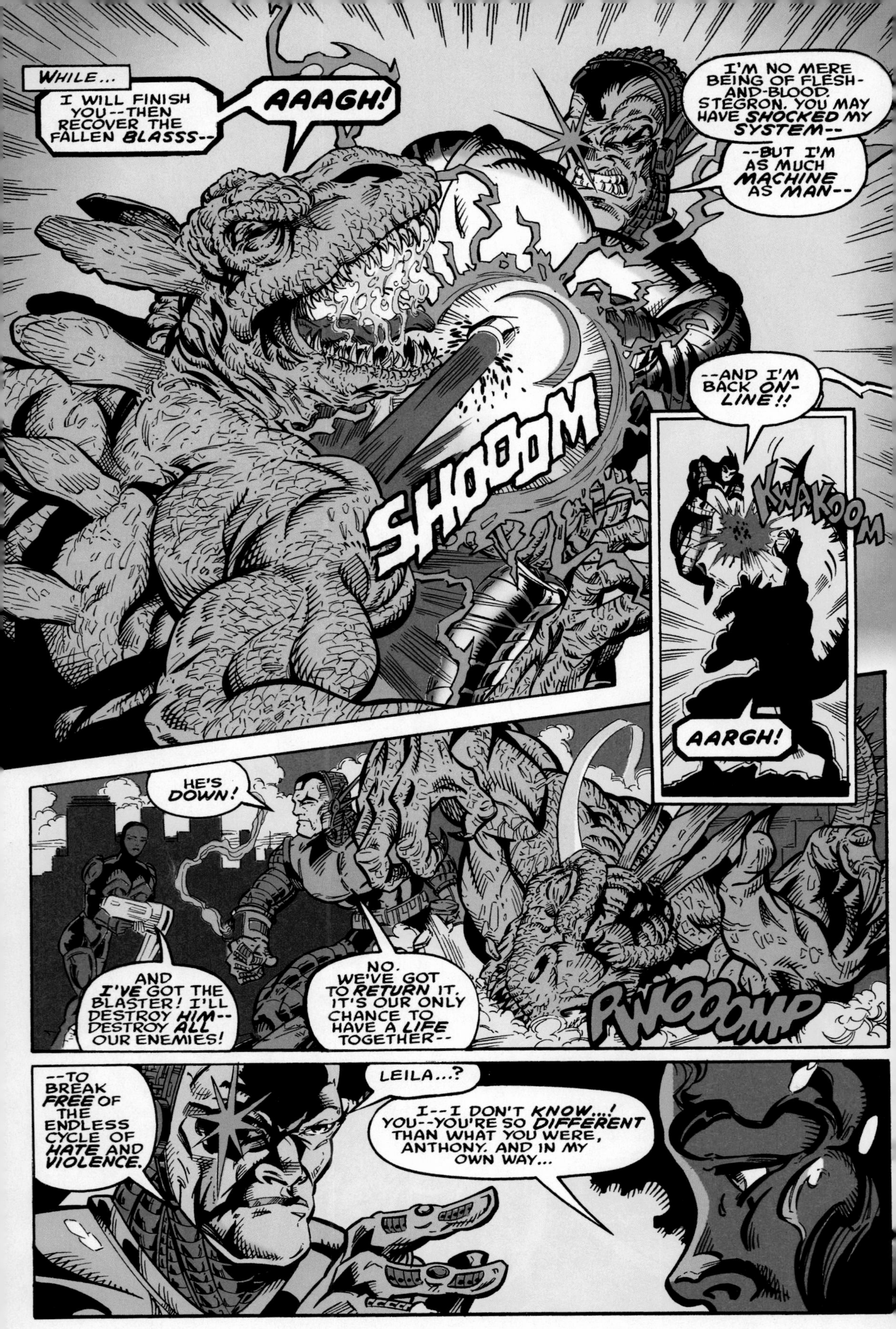

WHILE...
I WILL FINISH YOU--THEN RECOVER THE FALLEN BLASSS--
AAAGH!
I'M NO MERE BEING OF FLESH-AND-BLOOD, STEGRON. YOU MAY HAVE SHOCKED MY SYSTEM--
--BUT I'M AS MUCH MACHINE AS MAN--
SHOOOM
--AND I'M BACK ON-LINE!!
KWAKOOM
AARGH!
HE'S DOWN!
AND I'VE GOT THE BLASTER! I'LL DESTROY HIM--DESTROY ALL OUR ENEMIES!
NO. WE'VE GOT TO RETURN IT. IT'S OUR ONLY CHANCE TO HAVE A LIFE TOGETHER--
PWOOOOMP
--TO BREAK FREE OF THE ENDLESS CYCLE OF HATE AND VIOLENCE.
LEILA...?
I--I DON'T KNOW...! YOU--YOU'RE SO DIFFERENT THAN WHAT YOU WERE, ANTHONY. AND IN MY OWN WAY...

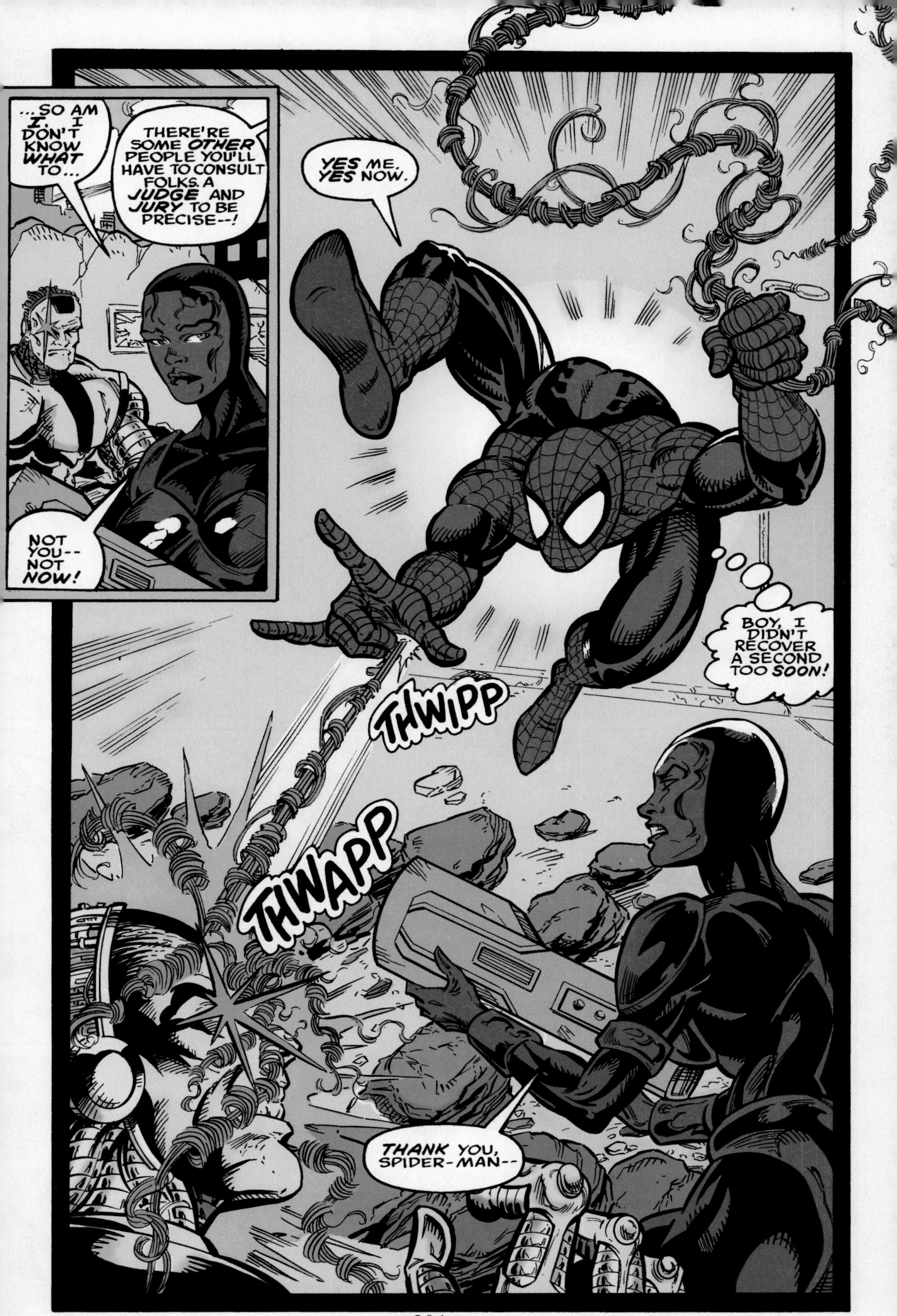
...SO AM *I*. I DON'T KNOW *WHAT* TO...
THERE'RE SOME *OTHER* PEOPLE YOU'LL HAVE TO CONSULT FOLKS. A *JUDGE* AND *JURY* TO BE PRECISE--!
NOT YOU-- NOT *NOW*!
YES ME. *YES* NOW.
BOY, I DIDN'T RECOVER A SECOND TOO *SOON*!
THWIPP
THWAPP
THANK YOU, SPIDER-MAN--

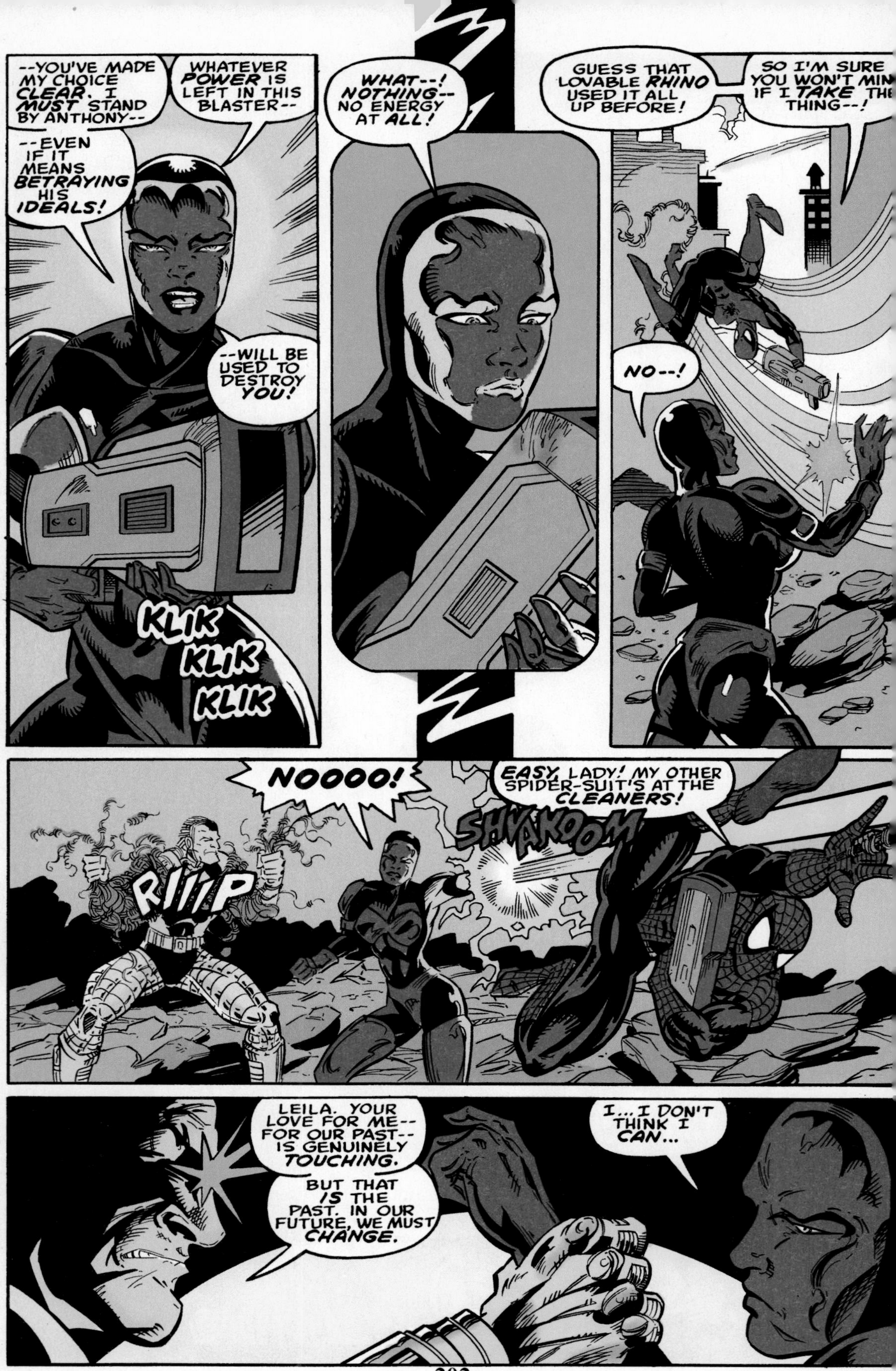
--YOU'VE MADE MY CHOICE CLEAR. I MUST STAND BY ANTHONY--
--EVEN IF IT MEANS BETRAYING HIS IDEALS!
WHATEVER POWER IS LEFT IN THIS BLASTER--
--WILL BE USED TO DESTROY YOU!
KLIK KLIK KLIK
WHAT--! NOTHING-- NO ENERGY AT ALL!
GUESS THAT LOVABLE RHINO USED IT ALL UP BEFORE!
SO I'M SURE YOU WON'T MIN IF I TAKE THE THING--!
NO--!
NOOOO!
EASY, LADY! MY OTHER SPIDER-SUIT'S AT THE CLEANERS!
SHVAKOOM
RIIIP
LEILA. YOUR LOVE FOR ME-- FOR OUR PAST-- IS GENUINELY TOUCHING.
BUT THAT IS THE PAST. IN OUR FUTURE, WE MUST CHANGE.
I... I DON'T THINK I CAN...

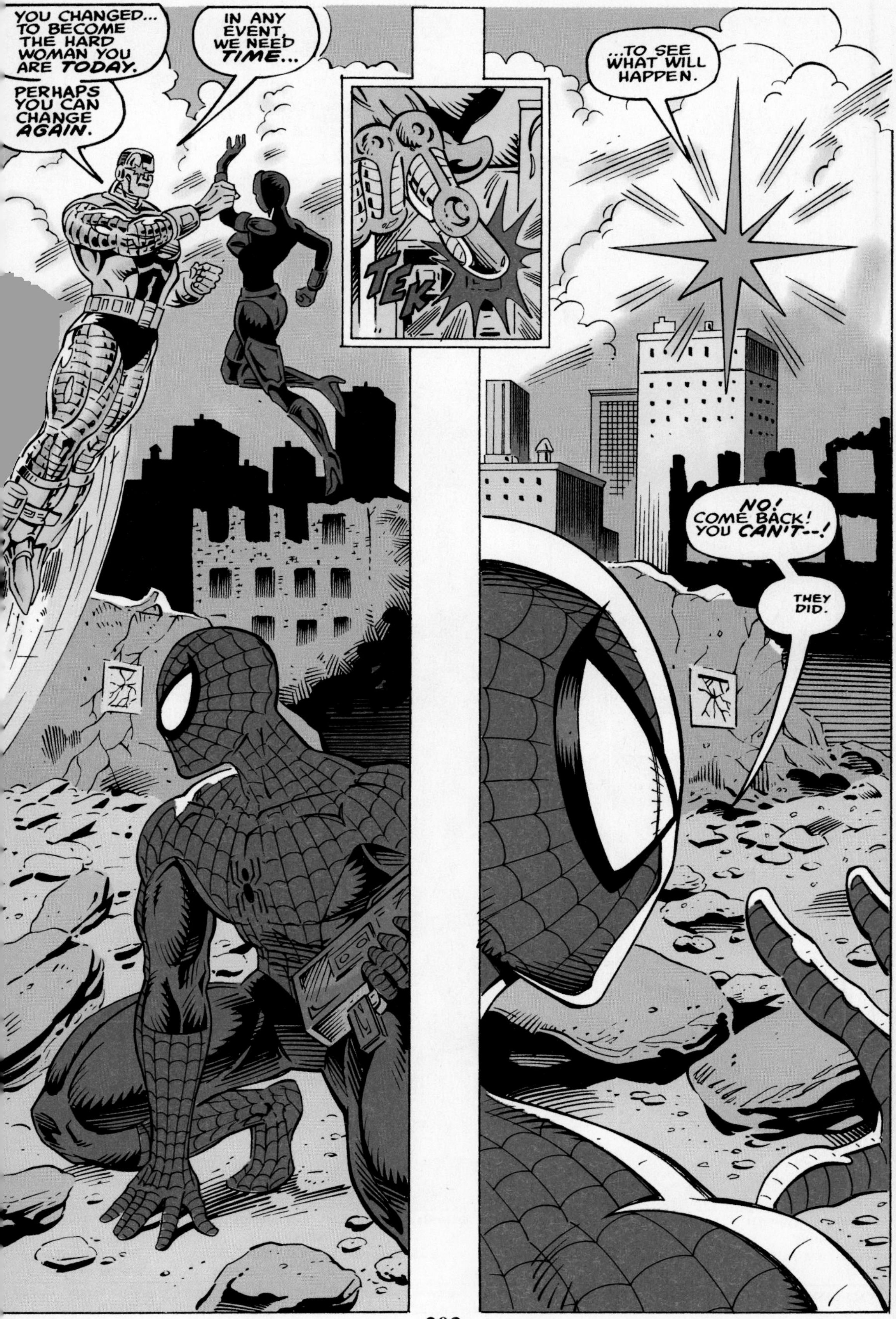
YOU CHANGED... TO BECOME THE HARD WOMAN YOU ARE TODAY.
PERHAPS YOU CAN CHANGE AGAIN.
IN ANY EVENT, WE NEED TIME...
TEK
...TO SEE WHAT WILL HAPPEN.
NO! COME BACK! YOU CAN'T--!
THEY DID.

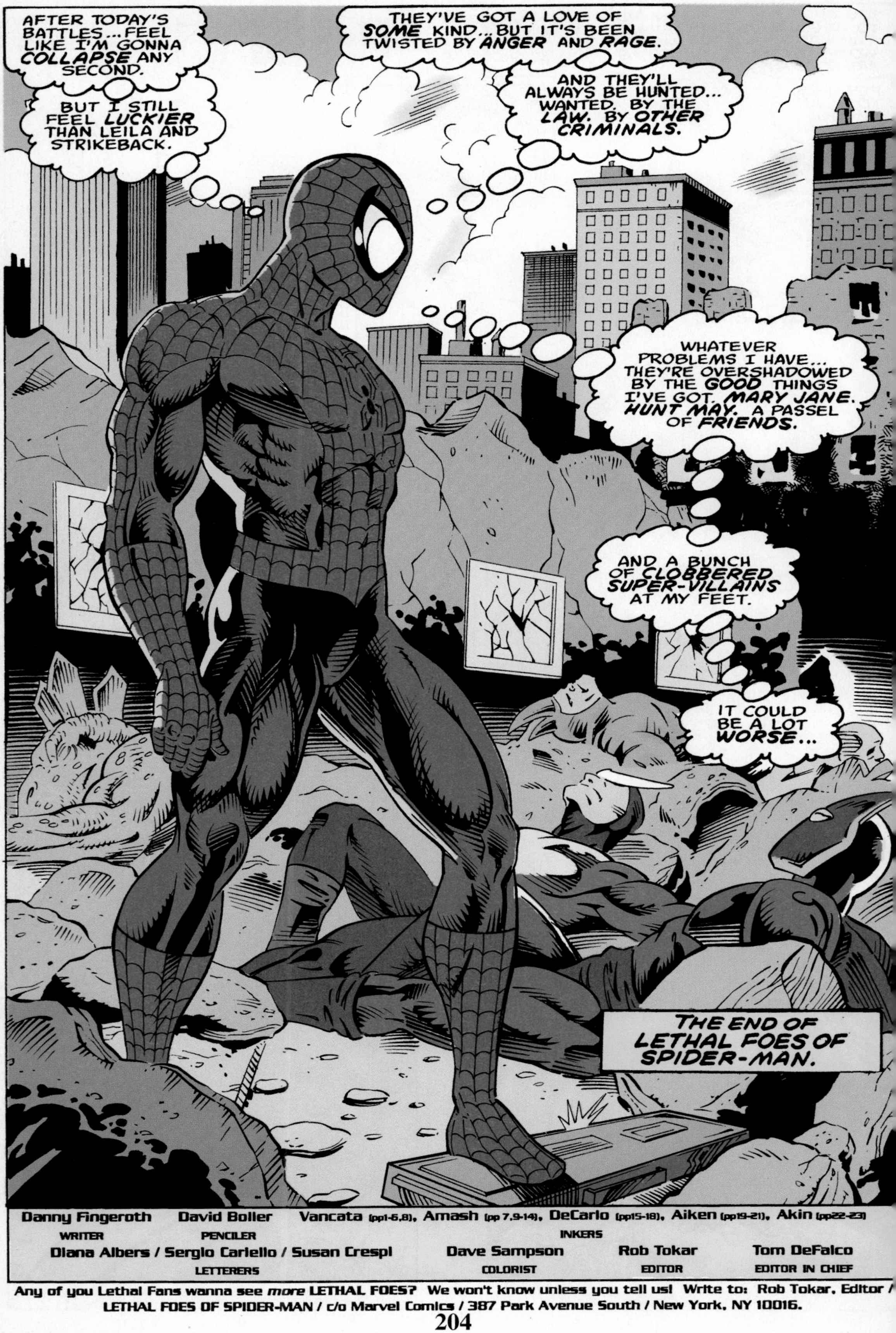
AFTER TODAY'S BATTLES...FEEL LIKE I'M GONNA COLLAPSE ANY SECOND.
BUT I STILL FEEL LUCKIER THAN LEILA AND STRIKEBACK.
THEY'VE GOT A LOVE OF SOME KIND...BUT IT'S BEEN TWISTED BY ANGER AND RAGE.
AND THEY'LL ALWAYS BE HUNTED... WANTED. BY THE LAW. BY OTHER CRIMINALS.
WHATEVER PROBLEMS I HAVE... THEY'RE OVERSHADOWED BY THE GOOD THINGS I'VE GOT. MARY JANE. AUNT MAY. A PASSEL OF FRIENDS.
AND A BUNCH OF CLOBBERED SUPER-VILLAINS AT MY FEET.
IT COULD BE A LOT WORSE...
THE END OF LETHAL FOES OF SPIDER-MAN.

Danny Fingeroth WRITER — David Boller PENCILER — Vancata (pp1-6,8), Amash (pp 7,9-14), DeCarlo (pp15-18), Aiken (pp19-21), Akin (pp22-23) INKERS

Diana Albers / Sergio Cariello / Susan Crespi LETTERERS — Dave Sampson COLORIST — Rob Tokar EDITOR — Tom DeFalco EDITOR IN CHIEF

Any of you Lethal Fans wanna see *more* LETHAL FOES? We won't know unless you tell us! Write to: Rob Tokar, Editor / LETHAL FOES OF SPIDER-MAN / c/o Marvel Comics / 387 Park Avenue South / New York, NY 10016.

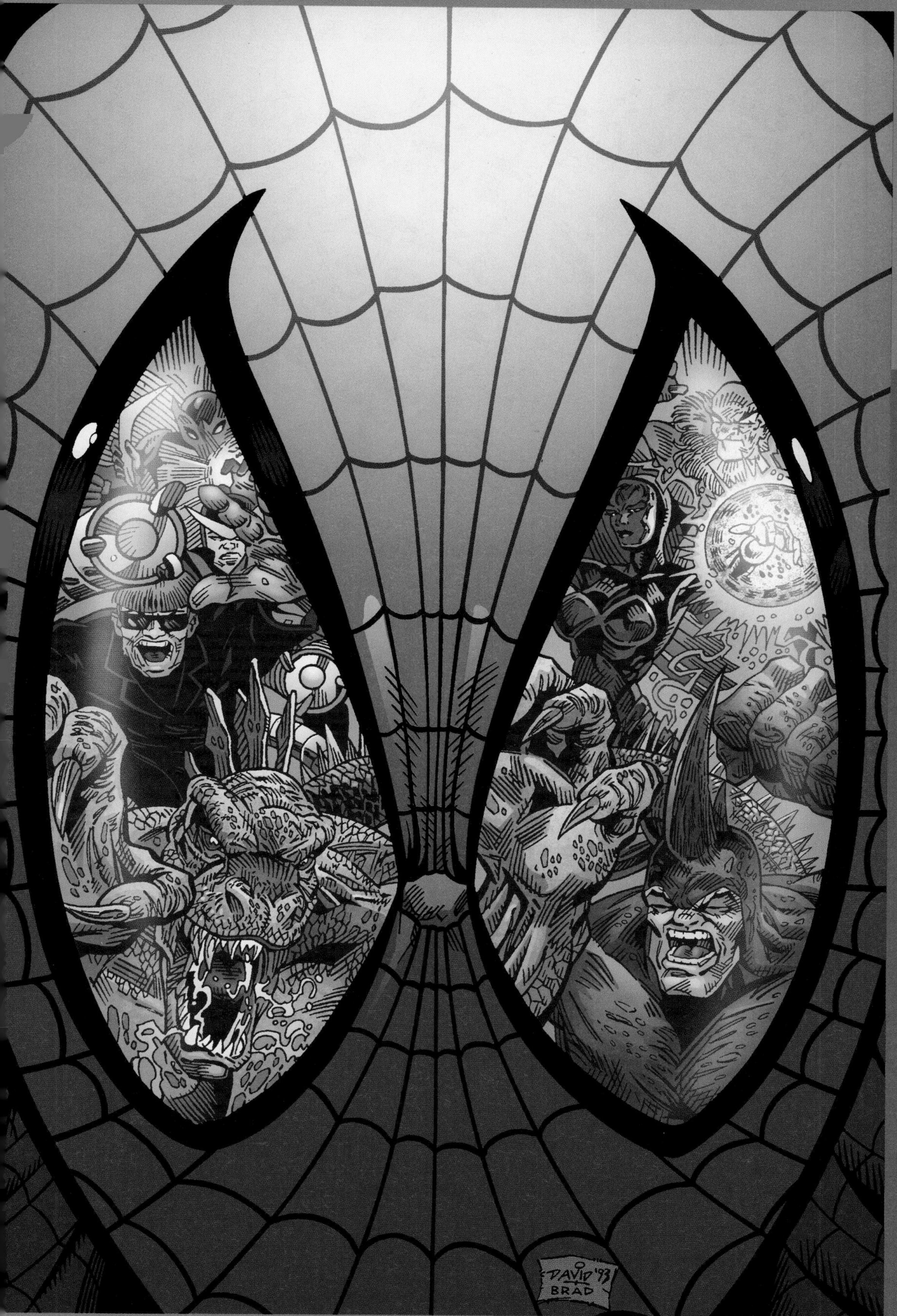
DAVID '93
BRAD

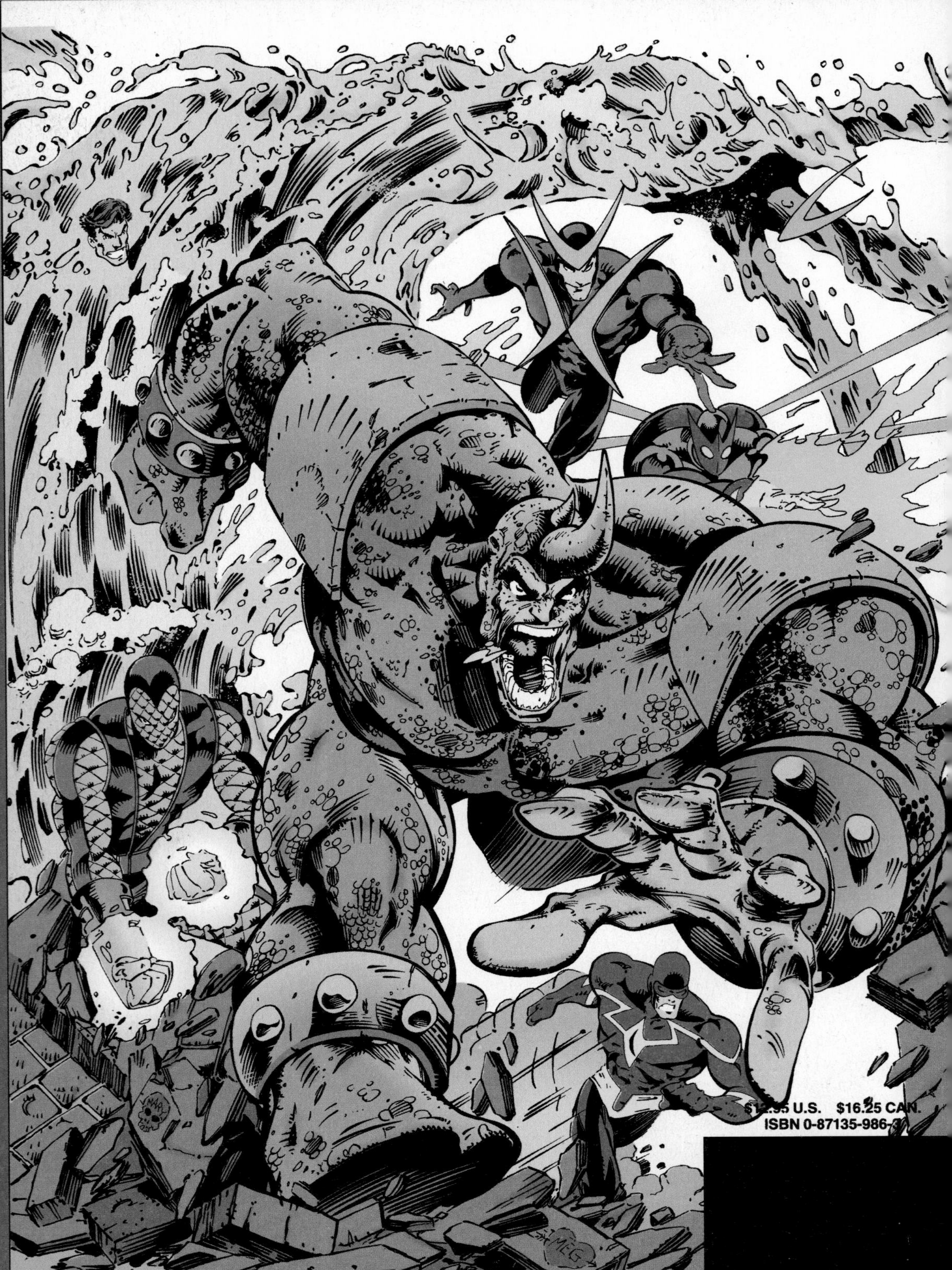
.95 U.S. $16.25 CAN.
ISBN 0-87135-986-

Deadly Foes of Spider-Man TPB (1993) cover by Joe Madureira & Harry Candelario

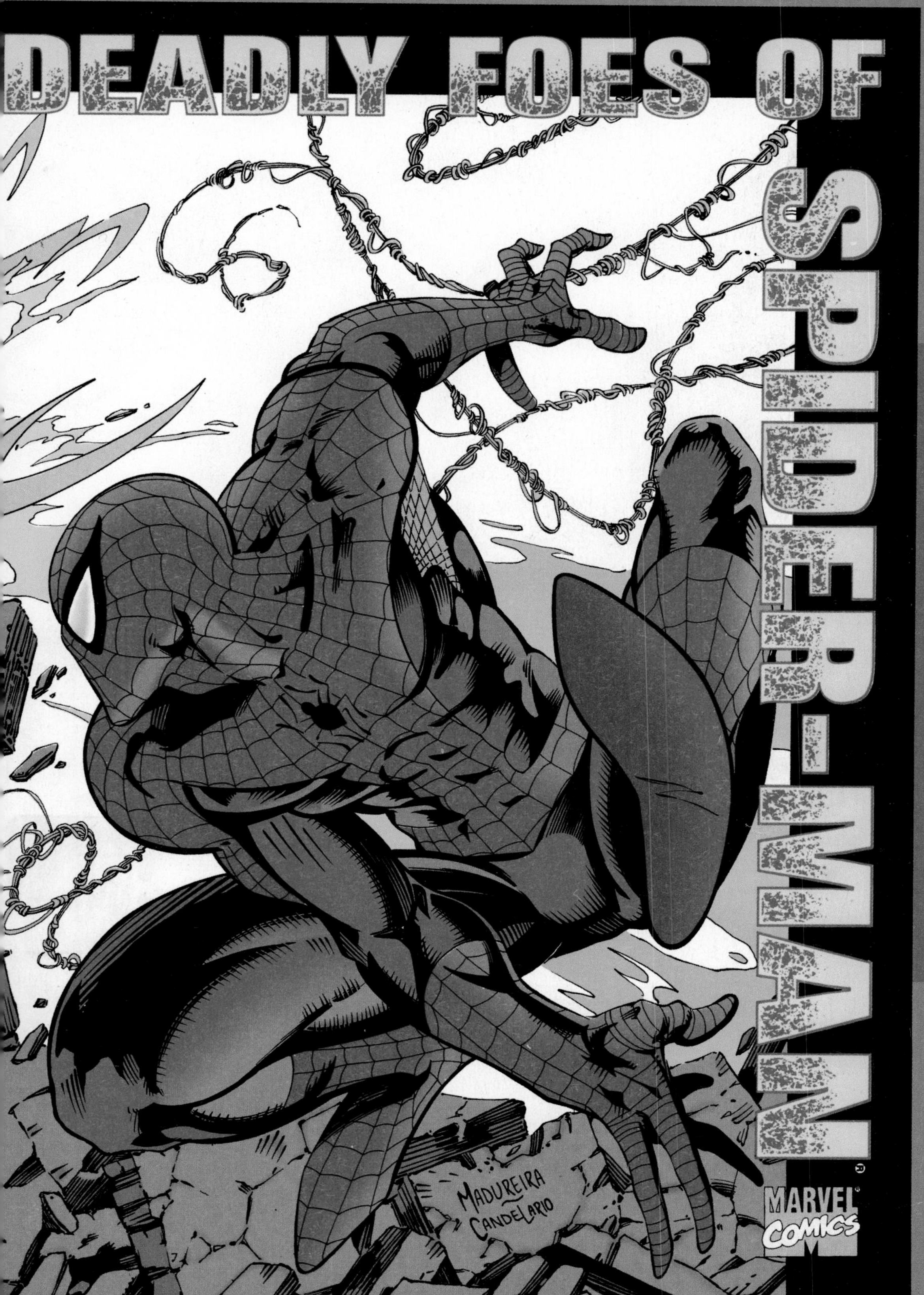
DEADLY FOES OF SPIDER-MAN
MADUREIRA
CANDELARIO
MARVEL COMICS

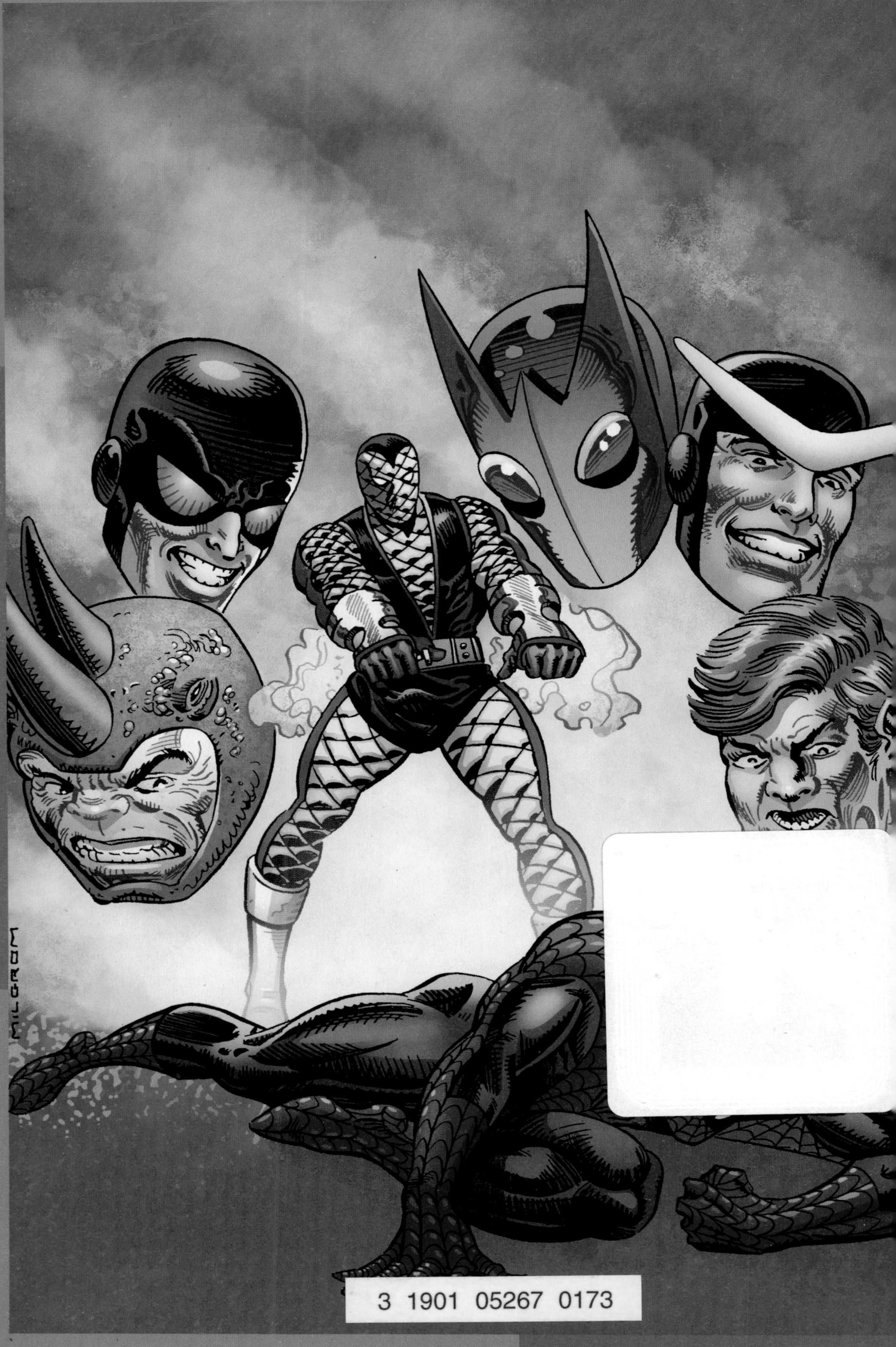
MILGROM